Free for All?

Lessons from the RAND Health Insurance Experiment

Joseph P. Newhouse
and
The Insurance Experiment Group

A RAND Study

HARVARD UNIVERSITY PRESS

Cambridge, Massachusetts
London, England

First Harvard University Press paperback edition, 1996

Library of Congress Cataloging-in-Publication Data

Newhouse, Joseph P.
  Free for all?: lessons from the RAND Health Insurance Experiment
  Joseph P. Newhouse and the Insurance Experiment Group
      p.   cm.
  Includes bibliographical references and index.
  ISBN 0-674-31846-3 (cloth)
  ISBN 0-674-31914-1 (pbk.)
  1. Medical care, Cost of—United States.   2. Medical care—United States—Utilization.
  3. Insurance, Health—Research—United States.   4. Insurance, Health—United States—
  Coinsurance.   5. Rand Health Insurance Experiment.   I. Title.
      [DNLM: 1. Insurance, Health—United States. 2. Delivery of Health Care—economics—
  United States 3. Health Status—United States.
  W275 AA1 H54f 1993]
  RA410.53.N52   1993
  368.3'82'00973—dc20
  DNLM/DLC
  for Library of Congress   93–1356
                                        CIP

Contents

Acknowledgments

The RAND Health Insurance Experiment, sometimes referred to as the RAND Health Insurance Study, remains one of the largest and longest-running social science research projects ever completed. I was the principal investigator for and director of the project and wrote this book, drawing on the contributions of the Insurance Experiment Group, whose members are listed facing the title page. These other authors, part of a multidisciplinary research team, played the following roles:

Rae Archibald was the deputy director of the project with responsibilities for field operations, including claims processing, fielding of surveys and screening examinations, and data processing.

Howard Bailit had primary responsibility for the analysis and interpretation of the dental health outcomes and quality of care, and assisted with studies of the use of dental services.

Robert Brook directed the team that developed the health status and quality of care measures and examined how they were charged by insurance plan and other policy variables.

Marie Brown was a leader of the project's administrative team that was responsible for financial and contract management, implementation of project design, data collection and processing, and supervision of subcontractors.

Allyson Ross Davies, a member of the analytical team focused on health status, had primary responsibility for experimental analyses of the effects of prepaid and fee-for-service arrangements on enrollees' attitudes toward their medical care and services. In addition, she participated in the measurement research that led to development of the adult health status and attitudinal measures.

Naihua Duan, a statistician, worked on analyzing the utilization data, developing the smearing retransformation and methods for testing specification.

George Goldberg worked with both analytical and operations teams. He provided overall medical supervision of the subcontractor for claims processing and coding; participated in the analysis of data from claim forms and other sources; served as medical liaison with organized professional groups (physicians, dentists, pharmacists) at each site; was the medical participant in coverage policy determinations for the insurance benefit package; had overall medical responsibility for on-site multiphasic screening examinations; supervised the abstraction of medical information from patients' records at the cooperating health maintenance organization (HMO); and served as general liaison with that HMO.

Emmett Keeler collaborated in developing the theory related to use by episode of illness and subsequently led the effort to implement that theory by dividing claims into episodes of treatment and analyzing the results. He also led the analysis of physiological health outcomes.

Arleen Leibowitz contrasted health care use by HMO enrollees with that of individuals using fee-for-service medical care, examined the effect of cost sharing on the demand for pediatric care, and analyzed how cost sharing affected expenditures for prescription and over-the-counter drugs.

Kathleen Lohr helped develop the health status assessment instruments and the overall strategy for measuring health at the beginning and end of the study, and edited a series of more than two dozen monographs on the conceptualization and measurement of health. She was also a principal in the design and conduct of analyses relating to quality of care. Finally, she headed the team that produced the analyses of the effect of plan on the use of diagnosis- and service-specific ambulatory services, including the effect on use of medically effective and ineffective services and differences in utilization rates by population subgroups.

Willard Manning had the chief responsibility for comparing use and expenditure across plans and the HMO groups.

Kent Marquis designed the data collection system for utilization and assessed its performance. He also monitored the survey work.

Susan Marquis designed and monitored numerous data collection forms and analyzed consumer knowledge, provider choice, and demand for insurance.

Carl Morris had responsibility for the statistical design of the Experiment. As part of this effort, he designed the Finite Selection Model.

Charles Phelps participated in the initial design and implementation phases of the Experiment, including experimental design, conceptualization of the episode-of-illness model, and its implementation through data collection instruments. He also directed the design and analysis of the demand-for-insurance portion of the study implemented through willingness-to-pay questions. He was active in the design of data collection systems and in the design and testing of forms leading to much of the economic data used throughout the analysis of the experimental data.

William Rogers was the lead statistician for the health outcome analysis and developed the statistical design of the utilization verification study.

Cathy Donald Sherbourne was the primary sociologist working on health status management and the analyses of life stress, social and role functioning, social support, and mental health status. She developed many of the self-report health measures for both children and adults and participated in the main analyses of general health outcomes.

Robert Valdez served as the primary analyst for the evaluation of child health outcomes both in the fee-for-service system and at the HMO.

John Ware designed, assessed, and analyzed the measures of self-reported physical, mental, and social health and general health perceptions, as well as the measures of patient satisfaction.

Kenneth Wells, a psychiatrist, had principal responsibility for analyzing the process and outcomes of mental health utilization.

This book draws liberally upon the journal articles, RAND reports, and analyses performed over the years using data from the Experiment. Although the data were not always complete when these analyses were done, it seems extremely unlikely that the results reported would materially change if the analyses were based on the complete data from the Experiment. For those wishing to round out the incomplete portions of the work reported here, sixty-seven public use file data tapes are available from the National Archives or from RAND, and publications describing their documentation are listed at the beginning of Appendix A. Potential users of the tapes should begin with Christine d'Arc Taylor and colleagues, *User's Guide to HIE Data*. This resource and the other RAND publications cited in the references are available at many libraries and can also be purchased from RAND, 1700 Main Street, Santa Monica, California 90406.

No project as large as the Health Insurance Experiment could have taken place without the assistance of a vast number of individuals. One in particular should be singled out. Larry Orr, the original project officer, was an intellectual force throughout the design and early analyses and was a bureaucratic force in ensuring that the project went forward. Without him the Experiment simply would not have existed.

My coauthors and I are also deeply indebted to many other people too numerous to enumerate here. The following, however, were particularly important. At RAND: Jan Acton, Carolyn André, Sjoerd Beck, Alicia Bell, Robert Bell, Bernadette Benjamin, Avi Black, Darlene Blake, Ellen Bloomfield, Joan Buchanan, Thomas Calabro, Patricia Camp, Nancy Campbell, Clairessa Cantrell, Maureen Carney, Lorraine Clasquin, William Dunn, Carol Edwards, Marvin Eisen, Bonnie Feldman, William Fowler, Betsy Foxman, Earl Gardner, Janet Hanley, Susan Holtby, Jeanne Hurley, Geraldine Jaimovitch, Shawn Johnston, Caren Kamberg, Robert Kane, Rosalie Kane, Joan Keesey, Kenneth Krug, Eanswythe Leicester, David Lyon, Joy McCully, Helene Mills, Bryant Mori, Mark Nelsen, Kevin O'Grady, Belinda Operskalski, Christine Peterson, Jane Peterson, Cordell Pierson, Suzanne Polich, David Reboussin, Donald Rice, Tom Rockwell, John Rolph, Marc Rosenthal, Randi Rubenstein, Bonnie Scott, Martin Seda, Martin Shapiro, Gustave Shubert, Albert Siu, Elizabeth Sloss, Lisa Smith, Vladimir Spolsky, Anita Stewart, David Stewart, Christine d'Arc Taylor, Laura Tosi, Sherry Trees, Kathy Van Riesen, Clarice Veit, Deborah Wesley, Albert Williams, Ann Williams, Beatrice Yormark, Robert Young, John Zielske, and Jack Zwanziger. At Mathematica Policy Research: Charles Berry, J. Alan Brewster, Phil Held, David Kershaw, and Cheri Marshall. At the National Opinion Research Center: Mary Kay Burek, Martin Frankel, James Murray, and Eve Weinberg. At Glen Slaughter and Associates: Marilyn Hecox, Lauren Lindstrom, Glen Slaughter, and Cliff Wingo. In the U.S. government: Henry Aaron, Stuart Altman, Martha Blaxall, Karen Davis, Harold Dupuy, Thomas Glennan, Edward Gramlich, Robert Helms, Martin Holmer, William Morrill, Paul O'Neill, John Palmer, Robert Rubin, James Schuttinga, and Caspar Weinberger. Others: Ronald Andersen, Kenneth Arrow, James Coleman, James Gaither, Irwin Garfinkel, William Klein, Robert Patrick, Alice Rivlin, Harold Watts, and Christopher Westover.

In addition, I am grateful to Marilyn Martino, who moved with me and a partially completed manuscript from Santa Monica to Cambridge, typed the final manuscript, and transferred the entire manuscript from one text processing system to another. Felicity Skidmore's initial editing tightened the writing and made the book much more readable.

Finally, we owe a special debt of thanks to the participants in this project. Without them there would be nothing to report.

Joseph P. Newhouse
Cambridge, Massachusetts

Free for All?

Part I

Introduction

Chapter 1

Background

Medical care financing has been on the political agenda of nations world-wide for more than a century (Starr 1982). Recently it has moved again to the forefront of the American political agenda, as it did in the 1960s and 1970s. The vast expansion of private health insurance in the 1940s and 1950s, together with enactment of Medicare and Medicaid in 1965, led to coverage of the great majority of Americans by some form of health insurance by the late 1960s. Nonetheless, many sought coverage of all Americans, and in the early 1970s an active debate began about the wisdom of adopting a national or universal health insurance plan.

The debate generated a range of proposals. One group, identified with Senator Edward Kennedy and organized labor, sought universal coverage of most medical services with no cost sharing (that is, no out-of-pocket payment at the time of use). The Nixon administration favored mandated insurance coverage through the place of employment, with some initial cost sharing allowed and coverage for those unemployed or not in the labor market through a residual public program. Senators Russell Long and Abraham Ribicoff advocated a plan that would cover extraordinarily large medical expenditures, so-called catastrophic insurance. Senator Jacob Javits simply wished to extend Medicare to the entire population.

The debate about these and other proposals continued through much of the 1970s. Initially it was rather ideological, influenced more by anecdote than by systematic analysis of potential effects. Indeed, at the beginning of the decade one informed observer testified before congressional hearings that he knew of no evidence that full insurance for medical services would affect demand (Fein 1971).

There was also debate, mostly within government, about possible changes in Medicaid. Whereas Medicare was widely hailed as a success,

Medicaid was seen as a costly program with few favorable effects. This impression would later be modified by more systematic analysis (Davis and Schoen 1978; Rogers, Blendon, and Moloney 1982), but in the early 1970s a question arose as to whether Medicaid should require cost sharing, which at that time it did not. Cost sharing appealed to many conservatives, who believed that patients sought (or physicians delivered) much "unnecessary" medical care when care was free. But many liberals saw cost sharing as a barrier, especially for the poor, to receiving "necessary" care. Both, of course, could be right—cost sharing might reduce both necessary and unnecessary care—in which case the overall appraisal might turn on cost sharing's ultimate effects on health and cost. These effects were unknown in the 1970s.

While this debate was taking place, the notion of conducting field experiments for policy purposes was gaining ground in the research community. In the mid-1960s the federal government, in what was seen as a major advance in social policymaking (Riecken and Boruch 1974; Rivlin 1974), began field experiments in income maintenance programs, sometimes referred to as negative income tax experiments. Although no income maintenance reform had passed Congress by 1970, there had been enough experience to indicate that such experiments could be useful—both in raising the level of the debate about the desirability of such a program, and in facilitating implementation should legislation ever be enacted.

The question naturally arose whether the government should attempt a similar approach to informing policy on medical care financing.

This political and policymaking milieu provided the setting and impetus for the RAND Health Insurance Study, initially supported by the Office of Economic Opportunity and subsequently by the Department of Health, Education and Welfare, now the Department of Health and Human Services. Its centerpiece was the Health Insurance Experiment, but it also included nonexperimental work (that is, work with existing data). The Experiment was a randomized field trial of alternative insurance plans. The nonexperimental work addressed certain topics not considered by the Experiment, such as financing, and attempted to obtain preliminary answers to questions that the Experiment's data would ultimately address. This book presents the results and implications of the Experiment; all of the Study's publications, both experimental and nonexperimental, are listed in Appendix A.[1]

Planning for the Experiment began in 1971, a pilot sample was enrolled in late 1973, and the regular sample began to enroll in late 1974. Participation of sample families ended in 1982. Some data collection and much analysis continued through the 1980s. Thus, whereas the political environment in which the Experiment began was concerned with expanding access to medical care and the possibility of national health insurance, the environment in which it ended was concerned with cost containment and contemplating increasing price competition in medical care. Advocates of increased price competition, pressed in the early 1980s about how to implement it, commonly cited the health maintenance organization (HMO), an entity widely regarded as a better method than traditional fee-for-service medicine to finance and deliver medical care. One reason for this enthusiasm was the reduced use of services observed at existing prepaid group practices, a particular type of HMO. Although advocates assumed that these reductions did not jeopardize health status or quality of care, there were numerous skeptics on that score. The Experiment also sought to address this aspect of the debate.

The debate on health insurance and health care reform has now revived. The objectives of the Experiment touch on many of the concerns being raised today, particularly about the best way to finance medical care:

1. Every insurance plan, public and private, must determine which services to cover. Although virtually all insurance plans cover inpatient services, in 1971 plans varied widely in coverage of outpatient physician services. Typically they provided little or no coverage of services such as dental care, prescription drugs, and mental health services. Coverage of these services has since increased and indeed is now mandated by some states. One goal of the Experiment was to ascertain how cost and health status were affected by inclusion of a variety of services in the benefits package.

2. A particular service does not have to be covered completely by an insurance plan. Patients may be required to pay something at the time of service. The principal objective of the Experiment was to ascertain the consequences of alternative cost-sharing levels for both cost and health outcomes.[2]

3. One critical issue, the effect of insurance plans on health outcomes, had not been addressed empirically when the Experiment began, in part because of the primitive nature of the techniques then available to measure health status. One of our objectives was to find better techniques for measuring health outcomes in a general population, and apply them to answer questions 1 and 2 above.

4. Although HMOs were widely believed to deliver care more cheaply than the fee-for-service sector, with little or no sacrifice in health status and

quality of care, this assumption was based on comparisons of the experiences of HMO enrollees with those of fee-for-service patients. Most of these comparisons addressed only utilization. Because health outcomes were seldom measured, skeptics wondered if HMO enrollees in fact had the same mix of health risks as people in the general population. Some argued that HMOs, with their generally modest cost sharing, tended to attract poorer health risks. Others argued that HMOs might attract healthier members because people with a chronic disease were more likely to have a well-established relationship with a physician and were therefore more likely to continue with their existing physician when offered the opportunity to join an HMO. (See Berki and Ashcraft 1980; Luft 1981; and Luft and Morrison 1991 for a review of this literature.) Thus, another objective was to find out how much, if any, of the observed reduction in use at an HMO was attributable to favorable selection of enrollees, and how much to fewer services delivered to a given group of enrollees. If the HMO was found to deliver fewer services to a given group, the further question would then be how this reduction affected health status and quality of care.

5. One argument against cost sharing was (and is) that it was unfair to the poor and the sick. Thus, cost sharing was often characterized as regressive or as a tax on the sick. To address this objection in part, Feldstein (1971, 1977) advocated income-related cost sharing. Although this proposal addressed the issue of regressivity, opponents objected that the complex task of implementing income-related cost sharing might make it an administrative monstrosity. Thus another goal of the Experiment was to obtain information on the difficulties of administering income-related cost sharing.

6. Because social experimentation was in its infancy when the Experiment began, another of our objectives was to improve the methods used to conduct social experiments.

7. Early nonexperimental work (Newhouse, Phelps, and Schwartz 1974) indicated that full coverage of ambulatory services (no cost sharing), if implemented universally, would stimulate such a large increase in demand that, in the short run, it would almost certainly call into play non-price rationing mechanisms. Exactly what these mechanisms might be, however, and who would receive what kind of care under them were not well understood. One study in Canada suggested that in such circumstances increases in waiting times to an appointment might be a principal mechanism for rationing care (Enterline et al. 1973).

   It had been clear from the outset that the Experiment would not cover a large enough sample to call such rationing mechanisms into play. Indeed, because some participants would receive reduced coverage under the Experiment, it was not obvious whether the net effect of the Experiment would be to increase or decrease community demand. Whatever the effect, the increment or decrement was sure to be small relative to overall community demand. We therefore decided to try to study the consequences of non-price rationing mechanisms by selecting our sites carefully, as described in Chapter 2.

Information about the results of this endeavor can improve both public and private decision making about the financing of medical care services. In the following chapters we try to quantify the benefits and costs of various combinations of covered services and cost sharing. Those choices will always be present, although the preferred answers may change as medical technology changes. Technology has already changed in the decade since the Experiment ended. But our results remain the best information available on this set of issues.

Chapter 2

The Design of the Experiment

The Experiment had the following major design features:

- Approximately 2,000 nonelderly families were assigned to insurance plans that varied the price of services to them.
- These families came from six areas of the country and participated for either three or five years. Enrollment began in Dayton, Ohio, in late 1974, and in 1976 and early 1977 in Seattle, Washington; Fitchburg and Leominster, Massachusetts; Franklin County, Massachusetts; Charleston, South Carolina; and Georgetown County, South Carolina.
- While they participated in the Experiment, the families used only an insurance plan administered by the Experiment.
- Additional families were enrolled in a staff model HMO, the Group Health Cooperative of Puget Sound, in Seattle.[1]

The Insurance Plans

We assigned Experiment participants to one of 14 fee-for-service insurance plans or to a prepaid group practice. The fee-for-service insurance plans varied along two principal dimensions: the coinsurance rate (the fraction of billed charges paid by the participant) and the maximum dollar expenditure (MDE), a cap on family out-of-pocket expenditures during a 12-month accounting period.

We used four coinsurance percentages — 0 (free care), 25, 50, and 95[2] — and three levels of MDE — 5, 10, or 15 percent of family income, up to a maximum of $1,000. In one exceptional plan we set the MDE at $150 per person or $450 per family. We combined these various coinsurance and MDE rates as follows:

- One plan with zero coinsurance (free care).

- Three plans with 25 percent coinsurance and MDEs of 5, 10, or 15 percent of family income or $1,000, whichever was less.[3]
- Three plans with 50 percent coinsurance and MDEs of 5, 10, or 15 percent of family income or $1,000, whichever was less.
- Three plans with 95 percent coinsurance and MDEs of 5, 10, or 15 percent of family income or $1,000, whichever was less. When contrasted with the Individual Deductible plan described below, these plans are sometimes called the Family Deductible plans, because if the coinsurance rate were raised from 95 to 100 percent, they would be exactly a family deductible.
- Three plans with 25 percent coinsurance for all services except outpatient mental health and dental, which were subject to 50 percent coinsurance; and MDEs of 5, 10, or 15 percent of family income or $1,000, whichever was less. These plans are sometimes referred to as the 25/50 plans.
- One plan with 95 percent coinsurance for outpatient services and 0 percent coinsurance (free care) for inpatient services and an MDE of $150 per person, subject to a maximum of $450 per family. This plan is called the Individual Deductible plan.

In general we paid providers their billed charges. In exceptional cases we questioned what we thought were excessive charges and sometimes negotiated a lower figure. Although we did not keep an exact count of the number of times this was done, renegotiation occurred in well under 1 percent of the cases. No prior authorizations were required except for relatively expensive dental services.[4]

At the HMO we studied two different groups. One was a random sample of those who had not previously been enrolled in the HMO but who agreed to enroll for the duration of the Experiment; this group is referred to as experimentals. The second was a random sample of those who had previously been enrolled in the HMO and who otherwise satisfied the eligibility restrictions that applied to the experimentals, as described below; this group is referred to as controls.

HMO experimentals faced no cost sharing and in general had the same plan of benefits as those on the Experiment's fee-for-service plan with zero coinsurance. HMO controls remained on whatever plan they already had; in general, they faced no cost sharing for either office visits or hospital use but did have minimal cost sharing for certain services.[5]

The rationale for these plan choices is covered in Appendix B.

Services Covered

In keeping with our objective of providing information on the consequences of covering a wide variety of services, the experimental plans covered almost all medical services: hospital, physician, and dental services; drugs; vision and hearing services; and medical supplies. We also covered services of allied health personnel, such as psychologists, psychiatric social workers, optometrists, podiatrists, physical therapists, occupational therapists, speech therapists, and chiropractors. Finally, we covered skilled nursing facilities and home health care services. The schedule of benefits is described in full in Appendix C.

Within this general coverage pattern there were a few variations. The most important for the analysis was that we treated dental and mental health services differently in the first year of the Experiment in Dayton, Ohio; this difference has a modest effect on the analysis. In that site and year dental services for adults (those 18 years of age and over) were covered only on the free plan (dental services for children were covered on all plans). In addition, in that year expenditure on outpatient mental health services did not count toward the MDE; thus such services were in effect not covered in the 100 percent coinsurance plans (which became the 95 percent coinsurance plans after the first year).

We did not cover orthodontia with fixed appliances or cosmetic surgery for preexisting conditions during the entire Experiment. Few existing insurance plans covered such services, and we thought it unlikely that future private or public health insurance plans would cover them either. Moreover, their "durable good" nature, combined with the lack of existing insurance, suggested that there could be an initial surge in demand under new coverage. If this took most of the Experiment to dissipate, we could not infer much about steady-state demand. Finally, because of our limited budget, the cost of covering these services would have compelled us to reduce our sample. For the same reasons, psychoanalysis, which can require three or four visits per week, was only partially covered, because we limited reimbursement for outpatient mental health visits to 52 per person per year.

Neither did we cover certain convenience items, including additional charges for a private hospital room (unless a private room was medically necessary or unless a semiprivate room was not available) and hospital charges for personal items such as telephone and television.

We covered all drugs that could be obtained only by prescription. We also covered some over-the-counter drugs for individuals with certain chronic conditions if such drugs were a reasonable treatment for such conditions.[6] Although services covered under workers' compensation, employer liability laws, or automobile accident insurance were not covered by the Experiment, participants were asked to file duplicate claims with the Experiment for services that fell in this category so that our data on medical care use would be complete. The rationale for our choices of covered services is described in Appendix B.

Eligibility

All age groups were eligible to participate in the Experiment except those who were or would become eligible for Medicare during the period of our study. We therefore excluded people age 62 or over at the time of enrollment or people under age 62 who were eligible for the Medicare program (because they had end-stage renal disease or had been out of the labor force for more than two years and had a medically certified disability).[7]

Those eligible for Medicare were excluded for three reasons:

1. At the time the Experiment began, there was little federal interest in changing the Medicare program for those eligible. Indeed, Medicare was so popular that Senator Javits' plan for national health insurance contemplated extending it to the entire population, as mentioned in Chapter 1. Thus, information about the effect of cost sharing was perceived to be of less value for the elderly than for the rest of the population.

2. It seemed possible that responses to variation in cost sharing would be different among the elderly, especially because of the greater prevalence among them of multiple chronic diseases. This potential difference suggested that the elderly would have to be analyzed as a separate group, and substantial oversampling would be required to yield enough observation points to support separate statistical analysis. The result would be to reduce our precision in analyses of the nonelderly.

3. When the Experiment was being designed, there was considerable doubt that it could be successfully implemented, and the elderly were thought to be an even more difficult population group to include than the nonelderly, for several reasons. First, it would often be more difficult to determine whether informed consent had been obtained. Second, transportation to a screening examination center would more often be a problem. And finally, lengthy periodic in-person interviews would be likely to exceed the tolerance of a high share of elderly individuals.

For all these reasons we decided at least to begin with the nonelderly, assuming that we could always include the elderly later if the Experiment got under way at all. The federal government was never interested in supporting the inclusion of the elderly, but we now have little doubt that we could have included that group in the Experiment, though at substantially greater cost.

Several small groups were also excluded, as described in Appendix B.

Oversampling of the Low-Income Population

Because one of our objectives was to ascertain whether low-income individuals responded differently to cost sharing from the average individual, we oversampled low-income individuals in all sites except Seattle, in order to be sure we had a large enough low-income sample for analysis. We followed one oversampling scheme in Dayton and a different one in the two Massachusetts and two South Carolina sites. These are described in Appendix B.

Participation Incentive

In order to derive unbiased estimates of how cost-sharing affected health status and service use, we had to ensure that all families we sought to enroll were equally likely to participate, whatever their previous insurance status and whatever experimental plan they were assigned to. Thus we had to guarantee that no one would become financially worse off as a result of participation in the Experiment. Accordingly, we developed a method of side payments called Participation Incentive (PI) payments. The PIs were calculated as the maximum loss risked by changing to the experimental plan from existing coverage, and were independent of health care use. (The PI is described fully in Clasquin and Brown 1977.)

To estimate whether the PIs themselves distorted health care utilization, we introduced a Super Participation Incentive (SPI) for a randomly chosen proportion of persons on the Family and Individual Deductible plans for their last participation year. This approach enabled us to measure any utilization changes attributable to the additional side payment.

The SPI is one example of a more general strategy we applied to measure "methods effects" or "Hawthorne effects"—that is, effects stemming from artificial elements introduced by the fact of an experiment rather than from the experimental "treatment" itself. These "subexperiments" are described fully in Newhouse et al. (1979) and described briefly later in this chapter.

Details of how we calculated the PIs and how we ensured that families did not use their previous plan are contained in Appendix B.

Some Quantitative Design Decisions

Appendix B describes how we chose the number of sites, the number of people on each plan and at each site, and how we allocated people to a plan. The key features of these decisions are as follows:

- The distribution of people's characteristics on each plan was essentially the same within each site. We developed the Finite Selection Model (FSM) to make the distribution more similar than would occur at random (on expectation). The FSM is one of the central methodological developments to come from the Experiment, but its description is not critical for understanding the results, and we have therefore relegated a description to Appendix B.
- We deliberately assigned fewer people to the 50 percent coinsurance plan in all sites and none in Seattle.
- The fact that the 25/50 plans were not used in Dayton resulted in an imbalance across the sites with the 50 percent plans and the 25/50 plans.
- We enrolled all eligible persons in a family.

Subexperiments to Detect Measurement Effects

The design of the Experiment incorporated a number of subexperiments to test for measurement effects, sometimes called methods, instrumentation, or Hawthorne effects. (These experiments are described in detail in Newhouse et al. 1979.) It is important to search for measurement effects because, if undetected, they may distort interpretation of the observed results.

Utilization Effect of the PI

The question arose whether the Participation Incentive (PI) payments would themselves distort utilization. According to economic theory, the PI should have had only an income effect. Given the magnitude of the payment and the estimated income elasticities for medical care (see Chapter 3), the effect of these payments on utilization should have been quantitatively negligible. Nonetheless, at the outset some feared that families would earmark these payments for health care expenditure, considering them as extra funds for health care. Because the payments were larger on the plans with cost sharing, such a response could cause the observed difference in use among the plans to underestimate the real response to cost sharing.

In order to measure response to the PI payment better, we introduced the Super Participation Incentive (SPI). For a randomly chosen 44 percent of the families on the Family and Individual Deductible plans in their next-to-last year of participation, we did not discount the PI to take account of the Completion Bonus (paid at the end), but instead paid the full amount—to a maximum of $250.[8] This created variation in the PI that was independent of income and left us better placed to estimate any effect the PI might have on utilization.

Utilization Effect of an Initial Physical Examination

A prime experimental objective was measurement of health status, a key aspect of which was the physiologic measures obtained in a screening examination. We could have conducted an examination only at the end of the Experiment. Our power calculations (that is, calculations of expected precision), however, showed that precision would be greatly enhanced by a baseline value for the physiologic measures because most such measures had high intertemporal stability. But because we had adopted the ethical principle that we should report results showing any serious problem to a physician designated by the participant, an examination made at the time of enrollment could by itself cause utilization.[9] One could anticipate that hitherto-undetected diseases would be followed up and treated. Moreover, the followup could potentially be more aggressive on the experimental plans with less cost sharing, thereby distorting the observed response to plan.

Our solution to this and similar problems was to split the sample within each plan, with only part of the sample receiving an initial examination. We used the FSM to obtain similar groups to receive or not receive each subexperiment. Because of the great value of the screening examination to the health status outcome analysis, instead of a 50–50 split about 60 percent of the sample was given a screening examination at enrollment and 40 percent was not. Because measurement effects were not a concern at the time of exit, all those leaving the Experiment at the end of their regular enrollment period were asked to take a screening exam; over 99 percent consented to do so.[10]

Timing and Effect of the Health Report Questionnaire

A second data collection instrument, the Health Report, was a questionnaire that asked some information about use that was unavailable on claims forms, as well as information about disability days. This instrument posed two issues: (1) What was the optimal frequency of administration, given that more frequent administration might elicit more accurate data but would be more burdensome to the families and more costly to process? (2) What effect, if any, did it have on utilization? To answer the first question, in the first year the Dayton sample was randomly split 50–50 into two groups, one receiving the form weekly and one receiving it biweekly. Although there appeared to be a modest loss in accuracy (those reporting biweekly reported more utilization in the more recent week), the gain was not worth the cost of weekly administration, and so the administration time was set as every other week. To answer the second question, in the first year in Massachusetts and South Carolina (1976–77) a random 25 percent of the sample did not receive the form at all.[11]

Length of Participation in the Experiment

We enrolled about 70 percent of the participants for three years and the remainder for five. This choice reflected a balance among several considerations, including (1) allowing time for any effects of plan on health to occur, (2) maximizing the number of families, and (3) assessing transitory effects associated with a limited-duration experiment. The rationale for our choices is described more fully in Appendix B.

Choice of Sites

The six sites selected were intended to represent the United States along several dimensions. Because the complexity of the medical care delivery system, especially the percentage of specialists, varies by city size, we thought the nature of medical care and the response to insurance might also differ along this dimension. In addition, we wanted variation by region because use rates such as length of hospital stay were known to differ along this dimension. We thought that responses to insurance plans might also vary by city size and region.

We also wanted variation in the demand conditions facing the primary care delivery system. A national health insurance plan or mandated private health insurance plans with minimal or no cost sharing, if enacted in the 1970s, in all likelihood would have activated non-price rationing mechanisms for ambulatory care. Canadian experience suggested that a principal

Table 2.1 Characteristics of sites

Site	Census region	Population of urbanized area or county (1970)	Primary care physicians per 100,000 population (1972)[a]	Days spent waiting for an appointment with a primary care physician, new patient (1973, 1974)[b]	Median family income (1969 $)	% over age 24 with less than 5 years of education (1970)	% black (1970)	Number of enrollees
Seattle, Wash.	West	1,200,000	59	4.1	$11,800	1.8	3	1,220[c]
Dayton, Ohio	North Central	690,000	41	7.5	11,400	3.3	13	1,140
Charleston, S.C.	South	230,000	33	15.9	8,300	6.2	25	780
Fitchburg-Leominster, Mass.	Northeast	78,000	30	25.0	10,000	4.3	1	724
Franklin County, Mass.	Northeast	59,000	46	9.2	9,900	2.8	1	891
Georgetown County, S.C.	South	34,000	44	0	6,400	20.6	48	1,061
United States	—	—	46	7.1	9,600	5.5	11	—

a. Includes general practitioners, family practitioners, internists, and pediatricians.
b. Physicians who do not use appointment systems and take patients on a first-come, first-served basis are valued as having zero wait time. All physicians sampled in Georgetown County at the time of the survey accepted patients on this basis. For other sites, the values are negligibly changed if only physicians using appointment systems are included.
c. An additional 1,892 participants were enrolled in the Group Health Cooperative of Puget Sound.

mechanism for such rationing would be increased waiting time to an appointment (Enterline et al. 1973). Little was known, however, about the health status consequences of such increased waiting times. By choosing sites with varying waiting times to an appointment, we hoped to discover how much this factor affected similar groups of individuals on the same insurance plan.

Using a telephone survey of physicians, we measured waiting times to an appointment with a primary care physician for both new and established patients (Mathematica Policy Research 1976; Wooldridge 1976). We also measured the percentage of physicians not taking new patients. These various measures, as expected, correlated with one another. We then chose sites to give us variation on these measures.

We wanted both northern and southern rural sites because of variation in their economic and racial characteristics, and at least one site had to have a well-established HMO. Table 2.1 summarizes the characteristics of the sites chosen. Among the areas we sampled, Fitchburg/Leominster had the longest waiting times in the country and the highest percentage of primary care physicians who had closed their practices to new patients.[12] Further details of how we chose sites are given in Appendix B.

Mechanism of Enrollment

We approached families with screening and baseline interviews and subsequently with an offer to enroll. Appendix B describes these interviews and our enrollment techniques. At exit we asked families about their reactions to our enrollment techniques; their answers are given in Chapter 10.

Refusal Rates

Despite the PI—the incentive payment designed to cover the worst-case out-of-pocket cost a family on a given plan could anticipate—refusals to enroll did differ significantly by plan (see Table 2.2). From the participant's perspective, the expected monetary gain was greatest in the 25 percent coinsurance plans; nonetheless, refusal rates were significantly lower on the free-care plan.[13] However, the refusal rates did not affect the distribution of sample member characteristics within plans, so plan comparisons were left unbiased. The data shown in Table 2.3 for adults indicate that the only nominally statistically significant difference (at 5 percent) between the participants on the free-care and other plans is that the proportion of females is lower on the free-care plan than on the cost-sharing plans, although the value for cholesterol level is close to significance. Among the 20 comparisons made in Table 2.3, however, one would be expected to fall in the 5 percent critical region by chance even if there were no true differences between the groups. In any event, all analyses reported below (other than those reporting simple plan means) control for gender, and thus adjust for any bias this differential refusal may cause. Table 2.4 shows the analogous results for children. No differences are significant at the 5 percent level. (For more details on the measures of health described in Tables 2.3 and 2.4, see Chapters 6 and 7.)

A different test for bias is to compare the characteristics of those who refused the enrollment offer with those who accepted. These data are shown by plan in Table 2.5. Those in families who refused the free plan and the 95 percent plan were more likely to be older, and on all plans but the free plan those who refused were more likely to have less education. The number who refused, however, is sufficiently low that these differences do not appear as significant in Table 2.3. In any case, all our analyses other than comparison of simple plan means control for age and education.

With refusal rates averaging 15 percent among the plans, it is reasonable to ask whether the population that enrolled was representative of the nonelderly community. Carl Morris (1985) analyzed data gathered on the baseline interview, and compared the sample enrolled with the sample that completed the baseline interview but was not enrolled, along the following dimensions: physician visits; self-reported health status; self-reported worry attributed to health; self-reported pain attributed to health; age; income; and whether the individual had insurance coverage. These comparisons should

Table 2.2   Percentage of refusals, by plan

Plan	Refusal rate (%)
Free	8
25 and 50% coinsurance	11
95% coinsurance	25
Individual Deductible	17

Note: One can reject the null hypothesis of no difference among the plans at the $p < 0.01$ level.

detect bias that might have been caused either by refusal at any stage or by our inability to obtain details about the person's insurance coverage, which precluded making an offer to enroll.

For the key *dependent* variables analyzed below—physician visits, health status, worry, and pain—the comparison between the group enrolled and the group not enrolled showed smaller differences than would be expected at random. Among the *explanatory* variables analyzed, Morris showed that families that enrolled had a higher proportion of children than families that did not enroll. All analyses reported below (other than comparison of simple plan means) control for this difference, either by restricting the analysis to children or by including age as an explanatory variable.

Attrition

Like initial refusal rates, attrition rates during the Experiment varied by plan (Tables 2.6 and 2.7). The proportion of adults who completed the Experiment and exited after the planned three- or five-year period varied from 94.7 percent on the free-care plan to 84.6 percent on the 95 percent coinsurance plans, a difference that is statistically significant at the 1 percent level. The proportion of children who completed the Experiment is also higher on the free-care plan: 96.7 percent versus 91.7 on all the cost-sharing plans; this difference is also significant at the 1 percent level.

Because all analyses could produce distorted results if those leaving the Experiment prematurely were sicker or healthier than those who did not, it is reassuring that virtually all the differential attrition by adults occurred for reasons unrelated to health.[14] Specifically, attrition from death, institutionalization for health reasons, and becoming eligible for Medicare by virtue of becoming disabled are at low levels (1–2 percent) on all plans, and the rates by plan do not vary significantly. In the analysis of health outcomes, data were recovered from 77 percent of those who left the Experiment prematurely and from 85 percent of those who left prematurely and did not die. Hence, data loss from attrition poses negligible problems for the health outcome analyses described in Chapters 6 and 7.[15]

The analysis of demand is not as sensitive to the problem of attrition as is the analysis of health status, because data were available on utilization up to the time of exit. Thus, we could test whether the rate of use by those who left the Experiment prematurely differed from the rate of use by those

Table 2.3 Values on demographic, study, and health status measures at enrollment, by type of experimental insurance plan, persons 14 years of age or over[a]

Variable and brief description[b]	Cost-sharing plans				Free plan	t-test value[d]
	Family Deductible	Individual Deductible	Other cost sharing	Total cost sharing[c]		
No. of enrollees ≥ 14 years of age	759	881	1,024	2,664	1,294	
Mean age (years)	32.8	33.6	33.8	33.4	33.3	-0.0
Gender (% female)	56.1	53.8	53.5	54.4	52.2	-2.1
Race (% nonwhite)	20.8	18.3	17.4	18.9	16.6	-0.5
Mean family income adjusted for family size (000s of 1991 $)	30.3	32.9	32.2	31.8	31.2	-0.5
% hospitalized in year before enrollment	11.5	12.0	11.2	11.6	11.7	0.1
Mean no. of physician visits in year before enrollment	4.49	4.80	4.23	4.51	4.55	0.2
Mean education (years)	11.9	12.0	12.0	12.0	11.8	-1.4
% taking enrollment screening examination	59.1	58.6	57.8	58.5	62.5	1.6
% enrolled for 3 years	69.8	71.3	67.4	69.5	68.9	-0.3
Physical functioning (mean score, 0–100)	89.6	89.1	88.7	89.1	88.9	-0.2

Role functioning (mean score, %)	94.8	91.8	91.9	92.8	93.1	0.3
Mental health (mean score, 0–100)	73.8	73.7	75.0	74.2	74.7	0.9
Social contacts (mean score, 0–100)	72.8	72.3	72.1	72.4	72.5	0.1
General health perceptions (mean score, 0–100)	70.5	69.4	71.1	70.4	69.7	-1.2
Smoking scale (mean score, 1–2.20)	1.29	1.32	1.30	1.30	1.29	-0.7
Mean standardized weight (kg)	71.5	71.0	71.3	71.3	71.3	0.0
Mean cholesterol level (mg/dl)	207	206	205	206	202	-1.9
Mean diastolic blood pressure (mm Hg)	75.2	75.4	75.3	75.3	74.6	-1.4
Functional far vision (mean no. of lines)	2.28	2.42	2.39	2.37	2.33	-0.9
Risk of dying (mean score)	0.99	1.12	1.05	1.05	1.04	-0.6

a. Values are adjusted for differences according to site.

b. For demographic data, table entries include everyone with valid enrollment data. For health measures, the mean score for enrollees excludes persons who did not have valid enrollment data because of missing data or the study design (e.g., they were not assigned to an initial screening examination). See Chapter 6 for a description of the health measures and family size adjustment to income.

c. Values represent equally weighted averages of the three types of cost-sharing plans.

d. Difference between free and total cost-sharing plans.

Table 2.4   Raw values of demographic, study, and health measures of children
age 0–13 at enrollment, by type of experimental insurance plan[a]

Variable and description[b]	Free plan	Cost-sharing plans	t-test value[c]
No. of enrollees	599	1,245	
Mean age (years)	7.1	7.2	0.54
Gender (% male)	52	52	−0.23
Race (% nonwhite)	21	25	1.37
Mean family income adjusted for family size and site (1991 $)	24,300	26,400	1.65
Mean education of mother (years)	11.8	11.9	0.84
% of children hospitalized in year before enrollment	7.5	7.1	−0.30
Mean no. of physician visits in year before enrollment	3.3	3.1	−0.86
% taking physical screening examination	64	60	−1.56
% enrolled for three years	69	70	0.38
Role limitations: % limited	3.1	3.4	0.30
Mental Health Index (mean score, 0–10)	6.2	6.1	−0.97
General Health Index (mean score, 0–10)	5.9	5.9	0.20
% with low hemoglobin levels	8.6	9.8	0.66
% bothered by plant allergies	9.8	7.7	−1.02
Functional far vision (mean in Snellen lines; higher score represents poorer vision)	2.8	2.8	−0.49
% with hearing impairments	8.6	5.6	−1.46
% with suspected fluid in middle ear	27.9	25.6	−0.66

a. Because the allocation to the free-care plan did not differ markedly by site, these values are not adjusted for site differences in the allocation by plan. For site-specific values, see Valdez (1966), app. E.

b. For demographic data, entries include everyone with valid enrollment data. For health measures, the mean score for the enrollment sample excludes children not assigned to an initial screening examination or missing data. See Chapters 6 and 7 for a description of the health measures.

c. Test of difference between cost-sharing and free plans.

Table 2.5 Characteristics of families in Seattle and Massachusetts, age 14 or over, that accepted and refused enrollment offer, by plan[a]

Characteristic	Free plan		25 and 50%		95%		Individual Deductible		F value[b]
	Accept	Refuse	Accept	Refuse	Accept	Refuse	Accept	Refuse	
Education (years)	12.6	12.1	12.6	11.7[c]	12.8	12.0[c]	12.7	11.7[c]	0.2
No. of physician visits in past year	4.3	4.6	3.6	3.9	3.7	4.5	4.5	3.8	0.9
Income (000s of 1991 $)[d]	31.3	39.0	30.7	27.6	30.7	34.7	31.6	31.0	2.2
% hospitalized in past year	10.6	9.2	9.2	13.2	10.0	13.2	12.3	13.7	0.5
% male	49.3	42.6	48.8	40.5	46.0	43.0	49.7	44.2	0.2
Age (years)	29.1	39.8[c]	29.8	29.9	28.0	34.1[c]	28.6	30.6	2.4
% black	0.9	0.0	2.1	0.5	2.6	0.4	2.2	0.0	0.1
Health Index[e]	9.9	9.8	9.9	9.8	10.0	9.9	9.9	9.6	0.9
No. of families	332	20	234	66	194	65	264	62	
% of families	94	6	78	22	75	25	81	19	

a. Sample consists of individuals in families in Seattle and Massachusetts. (Dayton and South Carolina data for refusals are not available.) Variables are averaged within families; averages presented are averages across families.

b. F-tests are for differences between plans. They have 3 and n degrees of freedom, where n ranges between 1,186 and 1,229, because of missing data. The F-value for significance at the 5% level is approximately 2.60 and at the 10% level approximately 2.08.

c. p < 0.05, using t-test.

d. 1973 dollars adjusted to 1991 dollars using the all-items Consumer Price Index.

e. The Health Index is the sum of responses to one question about the amount of pain (from 1 equals a great deal to 4 equals none), one question about the amount of worry (from 1 = a great deal to 4 = none), and one self-rated health question (1 = poor, 2 = fair, 3 = good, 4 = excellent).

Table 2.6 Numbers of adult enrollees who completed study and reasons for noncompletion, by plan

Category of participation	Family Deductible		Individual Deductible		Other cost sharing		Total cost sharing		Free plan		Grand total	
	No.	%	No.	%	No.	%	No.	%	No.	%	No.	%
Total enrolled	759	100.0	881	100.0	1,024	100.0	2,664	100.0	1,294	100.0	3,958	100.0
Completed enrollment and exited normally	642	84.6	772	87.6	926	90.4	2,340	87.8	1,225	94.7	3,565	90.1
Left experiment voluntarily	83	10.9	53	6.0	43	4.2	179	6.7	5	0.4	184	4.7
Terminated for health reasons[a]	3	0.4	11	1.3	13	1.3	27	1.0	15	1.2	42	1.1
Terminated for non-health reasons[a]	24	3.2	34	3.9	31	3.0	89	3.3	38	2.9	127	3.2
Died	7	0.9	11	1.3	11	1.1	29	1.1	11	0.9	40	1.0
Recovered for health analysis[b]	94	80.3	69	63.3	84	85.7	247	76.2	54	78.3	301	76.6

a. Participation ended because the person no longer fulfilled criteria for eligibility. Health reasons included becoming eligible for disability Medicare and being institutionalized; nonhealth reasons included joining the military and failing to complete data-collection forms.

b. Recovered from enrollees in each plan who did not exit normally. Percentages in this row use denominator of those not exiting normally.

who did not. We found that, with the exception of use by those who died (1 percent of those initially enrolled), there was no statistically significant difference in the rate of use between those who did and those who did not complete the Experiment.[16]

Not surprisingly, use by those who died exceeded use by others. Those who died, however, constituted such a small subsample (for example, a total of 11 people on the free-care plan throughout the Experiment) that we could not conduct a meaningful test of whether the effect of plan differed in that group.

The Group Health experimental group, which was drawn entirely from those not previously enrolled at Group Health, received a different type of offer from the participants in the fee-for-service plans.[17] In the case of the fee-for-service plans, participants were always better off financially from joining the Experiment. Indeed, unless they did not find the monetary payment for completing questionnaires enough to counteract any distaste for filling them out, or did not trust our assurances of confidentiality, or simply did not want to participate, there was no reason to refuse.

We asked the Group Health experimental group, however, to change sharply the terms on which they could see their previous physician(s). Although they paid no out-of-pocket charge for care they received at Group Health, they had to pay 95 cents on the dollar for any care received outside Group Health, except for emergency care outside the area or for services that Group Health did not deliver, such as dentistry or chiropractic. We therefore expected refusals among the Group Health experimental group to be much higher than among the other groups. In fact the

Table 2.7   Number of children who completed Experiment and reasons for noncompletion, by plan

Category of participation	Free plan		Cost-sharing plans	
	No.	%	No.	%
Total enrolled	599	100.0	1,245	100.0
Completed study normally	579	96.7	1,141	91.7
Voluntarily left study early	1	0.2	73	5.9
Terminated from study[a]	19	3.2	26	2.1
Died[b]	0	0.0	5	0.4

a. Participation ended because family no longer fulfilled criteria for eligibility.

b. Three deaths resulted from accidents (fire and asphyxia), one from murder, and one from epileptiform seizure with anoxia.

refusal rate among the Group Health experimental group was only two percentage points above the refusal rate among the cost-sharing plans in Seattle (a difference that is not statistically significant at conventional levels). Possible bias in the Group Health sample from refusal and attrition is discussed further in Chapter 8.

We conclude that neither refusal of the enrollment offer nor withdrawal from the Experiment subsequent to enrollment caused any appreciable bias. Thus, the design, especially the use of the Participation Incentive and the Completion Bonus, and the enrollment techniques were successful in their primary intent—obtaining a sample that was representative of the sites selected for the Experiment, except for intentional differences and the higher proportion of children. (For further discussion of refusal and attrition issues, see Newhouse et al. 1987.)

Data Collection for Utilization

Obtaining valid results depended on obtaining accurate data on the participants' use of services. This section describes the methods for obtaining the data on use that are analyzed in the next three chapters.

Fee-for-Service Participants

Our primary source of utilization data on fee-for-service participants was claim forms.[18] To avoid a high noncompletion rate, we designed these forms to request much the same kind of data as standard claim forms. The four kinds of claim forms corresponded to various types of providers: a hospital claim form; a "physician" claim form, which also served for services of other health professionals except dentists and suppliers; a pharmacy and durable medical equipment claim form; and a dental claim form. A copy of the physician form appears in Chapter 4 as Figure 4.1. (All forms are reproduced in K. Marquis 1977.)

These forms sought information on the procedure(s) or good(s) obtained and the date, place, and price of the service. Physician services and procedures were coded in accordance with the 1974 revision of the California Relative Value Scale, dental procedures in accordance with American Dental Association procedure codes (Council on Dental Care Programs 1972), and drugs in accordance with both the National Drug Code (U.S. Public Health Service 1972) and the American Medical Association therapeutic class code

(American Medical Association 1973). Because there was no established coding system for supplies at that time, we devised our own method of coding them. For each visit the physician was asked to indicate up to four diagnoses, which were coded in accordance with the *Hospital Adaptation of the International Classification of Diseases Adapted for Use in the United States* (H-ICDA-2) (Commission on Professional and Hospital Activities 1973). The physician was also asked to indicate any referring physician and any physician to whom the patient was referred. (All codes used are described in Nelsen and Edwards 1986.)

In addition to the information sought on standard insurance forms, we included several nontraditional data items on our claim forms:

- Each procedure or service for which a physician billed, except the visit itself, was to be linked to a diagnosis or diagnoses. This information permitted us to implement process measures of quality of care (see Chapter 5), as well as to allocate procedures to particular episodes in cases of visits that involved multiple problems (see Chapter 4).
- The physician was asked to link any drugs or supplies prescribed to a particular diagnosis. These data also enabled us to assess quality of care and to allocate costs to specific episodes, as well as to test for compliance.
- The patient was asked the major symptom or reason for the visit. This information was recorded using codes developed by the National Ambulatory Medical Care Survey and was used in the analysis of mental health services.
- The physician was asked to indicate the nature of the medical problem for which the patient sought care on the basis of the following categories: initial acute, initial chronic, repeat acute, chronic routine, chronic flareup, and well care. These codes were used to group visits and services into episodes of illness (described further in Chapter 4).

The claims data formed the basis for most of the analyses of demand. In addition, certain data pertaining to utilization that would not normally be found on claim forms were collected through a questionnaire, the Health Report, which was filled out biweekly by the participant. The utilization data gathered on the Health Report included:

- Telephone visits. We asked the person on whose behalf the call was made, the reason for the call, and with whom the problem was discussed. We were interested in whether additional cost sharing caused participants to substitute telephone visits, for which there was customarily not a charge (and thus would produce no claim form), for office visits.[19]

- Whether any hospitalization or physician or dental visit had occurred, or whether any prescription had been filled. If so, the person was asked whether a claim form had been left with the provider or was being submitted directly by the participant. If the participant indicated that a claim form had been left with the provider but it had not been received within six weeks following the date of use, the provider was queried about the form. The intent of this arrangement was to create a semi-independent utilization reporting system that would both minimize underfiling and detect at least some of any underfiling that might be occurring. (To minimize underfiling the families were clearly instructed at enrollment to file all claims; after the first year in Dayton participants in all plans received at least a 5 percent payment for filing claims.)
- In the case of physician and dental visits, the person was asked how many days ahead the appointment was made, the amount of travel time to the office or clinic, and the time the physician (dentist), nurse (dental hygienist or assistant), and medex or nurse practitioner spent with the patient. The identities of any accompanying family members were also requested, in order to better establish the true cost of the visit to the family.[20]
- Purchases of nonprescription medicines (which, with the exceptions described earlier, were not covered) were asked about. The intent was to determine whether those with high cost-sharing plans substituted self-care with over-the-counter drugs for prescription drugs.

HMO Participants

The Group Health Cooperative sample filed claim forms only for use outside Group Health. As a result, the basic source of information about utilization within Group Health was the medical record. We abstracted data from the medical record onto forms that resembled claim forms, except, of course, there was no charge by service. Our intent was to make the Group Health data as comparable as possible with the data from fee-for-service providers.[21] (For details on how we abstracted data from the medical record, see Chapter 8.)

The Group Health sample, both experimentals and controls, did fill out Health Reports. For practical purposes the Health Reports filled out by the Group Health sample collected the same information as those filled out by the fee-for-service sample. Thus there was no issue of comparability for the data that came from the Health Report.

Part II

Effects of Cost Sharing
on Use of Medical Services

The next three chapters analyze the use of medical services by fee-for-service participants during the Experiment. Chapter 3 focuses on the most inclusive measure of use, total annual expenditure per person, as well as major components of that total, including outpatient, inpatient, dental, and mental health expenditure. Chapter 4 analyzes episodes of illness. Chapter 5 analyzes more narrowly defined components of use, such as emergency room visits and utilization for specific diagnoses.

Chapter 3

Total Annual Per-Person Expenditure

This chapter estimates the effect of the Experiment's health insurance plans on overall use of and expenditure on medical, dental, and mental health services. Our more reliable estimates of the effects of cost sharing come from a statistical model, but those estimates are reasonably close to the ones calculated only from per-person expenditure by plan (simple plan means). Two possible methods effects—differential underfiling of claims by plan and instrumentation effects—do not materially affect the analysis.

Medical Services

The Sample

The sample used in the analysis of annual expenditure includes enrollees during each full year of participation, as well as the partial years for those who died or were born during the Experiment.[1] If a person voluntarily or involuntarily left the Experiment midway through year 2 (other than by dying), for example, data are included from the first year but not from the second. Usually for newborns, the data from the birth year are omitted; subsequent complete-year data are included. All inpatient expenses for newborns associated with the birth itself are included in the expenditure of the mother.

We excluded partial-year cases because the statistical models used in our analysis require equal time periods for each observation.[2] Since, as noted in the previous chapter, expenditure rates for partial-year participants cannot be distinguished from expenditure rates for others, with the exception of those who died, omission of the partial-year data causes no serious bias. The number of person-years used in our analysis is just over 20,000, distributed among the plans as shown in Table 3.1.

Dependent Variables

Medical expenditure includes all services except dental and outpatient mental health expenditures. In addition to expenditure, we analyze the annual number of face-to-face visits, the probability of any use of medical services, and the hospital admissions rate. Inpatient mental health expenditure is included with inpatient expenditure on medical services because it is very rare, but when it occurs it is large and varies widely. Combining it with outpatient mental health expenditure would therefore have produced results that would have been hard to interpret.

Explanatory Variables

In our regression analysis we use three groups of explanatory variables: insurance plan, health status, and sociodemographic and economic measures.

Insurance plan. We group the insurance plans into five categories: (1) the free plan (no out-of-pocket cost to the family); (2) 25 percent coinsurance rate plans for medical services (including the plans with 50 percent coinsurance for dental care and mental health); (3) 50 percent coinsurance rate plans for medical services; (4) 95 percent coinsurance rate plans for medical services; and (5) the plan with a 95 percent coinsurance rate for outpatient services (subject to a limit of $150 per person or $450 per family per year) and free inpatient care (Individual Deductible). In the estimated equa-

Table 3.1   Sample size used in annual expenditure analysis

Plan	Person-years
Free	6,822
25%, all MDE levels[a]	4,065
50%, all MDE levels	1,401
95%, all MDE levels	3,727
Individual Deductible	4,175
Total	20,190

a. Plan with 50% coinsurance for mental health and dental services and 25% coinsurance for all other services is grouped with 25% coinsurance.

tions predicting use, each of these groups is represented by a dummy variable. Thus, we do not impose a functional form on the plan response.

These five groups do not differentiate plans by the size of the limit on annual out-of-pocket expenses (MDE). In the analysis of episodes reported in the next chapter we estimate the effect of variation in the MDE and conclude that the differences between the 5 and 15 percent upper-limit groups for a given level of coinsurance is less than 4 percent of the plan mean.[3] Thus, ignoring the MDE variation in our analysis here poses no major problem.

In the analysis of inpatient use, we group the insurance plans into only three categories: free, family pay, and Individual Deductible. The family pay plans consist of all plans with a coinsurance rate of 25, 50, or 95 percent. Earlier analysis of the first 40 percent of experimental data (Newhouse et al. 1981) found no appreciable or statistically significant differences in inpatient use among the family pay plans. This lack of detectable difference in inpatient use is not surprising, because 70 percent of those with any inpatient use on the family pay plans exceeded the MDE amount, irrespective of plan. For these families, therefore, the price of a hospital admission did not depend on the coinsurance rate; for example, for those with a $1,000 MDE the price was $1,000 (assuming no previous expenditure). Furthermore, the price to them of an additional day, test, or procedure was zero, irrespective of plan.

Health status. We use four measures of health status to increase the precision of our estimates of the consumption of medical services: (1) a General Health Index; (2) the presence of physical or role limitations; (3) chronic disease status; and (4) a Mental Health Index. Each of these measures is based on a self-administered Medical History Questionnaire for individuals 14 years or older. Measures for children (13 years and younger) are based on questionnaires filled out by parents. All the health status data used in our analysis in this chapter were collected at the beginning of the Experiment; a summary description of each measure is presented below. (For more detailed descriptions of health measures see Part III.)

1. The General Health Index, a subjective assessment of personal health status, refers to health in general and does not specify a particular component such as mental health. It is a continuous score (0–100), based on 22 questionnaire items for individuals aged 14 and over and 7 items for children, measuring perceptions of current, past, and future health. The items also measure perceived resistance to illness and to worries about health.

The reliability and validity of the Index have been extensively studied and documented (Ware 1976; Eisen et al. 1980; Davies and Ware 1981) and are described further in Part III. One way to interpret the Index is to show how it is affected by chronic diseases. For example, those with hypertension, everything else equal, have Index scores 5 points lower than those without, and those with diabetes are 10 points lower (Brook et al. 1984). The Index predicts subsequent mortality; the death rate during the Experiment was 25/1,000 for those with an Index score below 63, 6/1,000 for those with scores from 63 to 76, and 1/1,000 for those with scores from 76 to 100.

2. The physical or role limitations measure is scored dichotomously (1 = limited, 0 = otherwise) to indicate the presence of one or more limitations due to poor health. Based on 12 questionnaire items for adults and 5 for children, it assesses four categories of limitations: self-care (eating, bathing, dressing); mobility (confined or able to use public or private transportation); physical activity (walking, bending, lifting, stooping, climbing stairs, running); and usual role activities (work, home, school). The reliability and validity of these measures have been studied and documented by Stewart et al. (1977, 1978, 1981) and Eisen et al. (1980).

3. The disease measure is a simple count of the number of diseases or health problems out of a possible 26, for individuals 14 or older (Manning, Newhouse, and Ware 1982). The list includes kidney disease and urinary tract infections, eye problems, bronchitis, hay fever, gum problems, joint problems, diabetes, acne, anemia, heart problems, stomach problems, varicose veins, hemorrhoids, hearing problems, high blood pressure, hyperthyroidism, and 10 other diseases or problems.

4. The Mental Health Index for adults is a continuous score (0–100) based on 38 questionnaire items measuring both psychological distress and psychological well-being, as reflected in anxiety, depression, behavioral and emotional control, general positive affect, and interpersonal ties. The reliability and validity of this measure have been studied and documented by John E. Ware and colleagues (Ware, Johnston, and Davies-Avery 1979; Ware, Davies-Avery, and Brook 1980; Williams, Ware, and Donald 1981; Veit and Ware 1983) (see Part III). A similar construct has been developed for children aged 5–13, based on 12 questionnaire items (Eisen et al. 1980).

Sociodemographic and economic measures. The model used in our analysis also included covariates for age, gender, race, family income, and family size. With the exception of family size and income, these data were collected before or at enrollment in the Experiment. The value for family size varies by year. Family income data are from 1975 in Dayton, 1978 for the three-year group in South Carolina, and 1976 for all other participants.[4]

Although we have not tested for all possible interactions among covariates, we did test for some that are particularly important for policy purposes, such as whether the effect of plan differed by income. Our search suggested that the following interactions were important: between plan and being a child in the inpatient and outpatient use equations; between plan and income in the probabilities of any use of medical services and of any inpatient use, given some use; and between gender and age. The remaining interactions that we examined were neither significant nor appreciable, and thus have been omitted.

Unit of Analysis

The unit of analysis is a person-year. We use the year as the time frame because the upper limit on out-of-pocket expenses is annual. We use the person as the unit of observation because the major determinants of service use are individual (such as age, gender, and health status) rather than family (such as insurance coverage and family income) characteristics.

Statistical Methods

We use analysis of variance (ANOVA) techniques, as well as a four-equation model, to estimate the demand for medical services. We use ANOVA to provide sample means for the use of medical services. We augment these results with more robust estimates based on the four-equation model developed by Duan et al. (1982, 1984). We chose this model because the distribution of medical expenses is not normal (that is, not a bell-shaped curve). Three characteristics account for this non-normality: one-sixth to one-third of the participants use no medical services during the year; the distribution of expenses among users is skewed or long-tailed; and the distribution of medical expenses is different for individuals with only outpatient use than for individuals with some inpatient use.

Because of these characteristics, ANOVA and analysis of covariance (ANOCOVA) techniques yield imprecise, though consistent, estimates of the effects of health insurance, health status, and socioeconomic status on the use of medical services, even for a sample size as large as 20,000 observations. As Duan et al. (1982) have shown, a four-equation model that exploits the three characteristics of the medical expense distribution yields more precise and more robust estimates than sample means.

The Four-Equation Model

We modeled the distribution of medical expenses by dividing the participants into three groups: nonusers, users of only outpatient services, and users of any inpatient services. The model examines the expenses of the two groups of users separately.

The first equation of the model is a probit equation for the probability that a person will receive any medical service during the year from either inpatient or outpatient sources. Thus it separates users from nonusers and addresses the first characteristic of non-normality described above—that a large proportion of the population does not use medical services during the year. The second equation is a probit equation for the conditional probability that someone who has used some medical service during the year will have at least one inpatient stay. This equation separates the two user groups and thus addresses the third characteristic of non-normality noted above—different distributions of medical expenses for inpatient and outpatient users. The third equation is a linear regression for the logarithm of total annual medical expenses of outpatient-only users. The fourth equation is a linear regression for the logarithm of total annual medical expenses for the users of any inpatient service. This last equation includes both outpatient and inpatient expenses for users of any inpatient services.

The logarithmic transformation of annual expenses practically eliminates the skew in the distribution of expenses among users, and thus addresses the second distributional characteristic noted above. It yields nearly symmetric and roughly normal error distributions. Results in Duan et al. (1982) and in Manning et al. (1987) show that the estimates from this model are more precise than those obtained by either ANOVA or ANOCOVA techniques on the untransformed expenses.

The first equation is a probit equation for the dichotomous event of zero versus positive medical expense:

$$(3.1) \quad I_{1i} = x_i \beta_1 + \epsilon_{1i},$$

$$(3.2) \quad (\epsilon_{1i} | x_i) \sim N(0, 1),$$

where medical expense is positive if $I_{1i} > 0$, zero otherwise.

The second equation is a probit equation for having zero versus positive inpatient expense, given that the person is a positive user of medical services:

$$(3.3) \quad I_{2i} = x_i \beta_2 + \epsilon_{2i},$$

$$(3.4) \quad (\epsilon_{2i} | x_i, I_{1i} > 0) \sim N(0, 1),$$

where inpatient expenses are positive if $I_{1i} > 0$ and $I_{2i} > 0$, and zero if $I_{1i} > 0$ and $I_{2i} \le 0$. (The equation is defined only for $I_{1i} > 0$. There are outpatient expenses only if $I_{1i} > 0$ and $I_{2i} \le 0$.)

The third equation is a linear model on the log scale for positive medical expenses if only outpatient services are used:

$$(3.5) \quad \ln(\text{medical expenditure} | I_{1i} > 0 \text{ and } I_{2i} \le 0) = x_i \beta_3 + \epsilon_{3i},$$

where

$$(3.6) \quad E(\epsilon_{3i} | x_i, I_{1i} > 0, I_{2i} \le 0) = 0.$$

The fourth equation is also a linear model on the log scale for positive medical expenses if any inpatient services are used:[5]

$$(3.7) \quad \ln(\text{medical expenditure} | I_{1i} > 0 \text{ and } I_{2i} > 0) = x_i \beta_4 + \epsilon_{4i},$$

where

$$(3.8) \quad E(\epsilon_{4i} | x_i, I_{1i} > 0, I_{2i} > 0) = 0.$$

For the last two equations, the errors are not necessarily assumed to be normally distributed.

The likelihood function for this model is multiplicatively separable because of the way the conditional densities are calculated. The separability does *not* depend on any assumption of independence among errors in the four equations; in fact the errors may be correlated (Duan et al. 1984). Separability implies that estimating the four equations by maximum likelihood *separately* provides the global full information maximum-likelihood estimates (Duan et al. 1982, 1984). We therefore estimate the four equations separately.

Despite our use of the logarithmic transformation of expenditure to approximate the normal assumption as closely as possible, the error distributions for the two levels of expense equations deviate appreciably from the normal assumption. As a result, if we used the normal theory retransformations $[\exp(\sigma_\epsilon^2/2)]$ to estimate spending in dollars rather than the logarithm of dollars, the predictions would be inconsistent. (See Duan et al. 1982, 1984; and Manning et al. 1988 for a comparison of normal theory and nonparametric retransformations.) Instead we use a nonparametric estimate of the retransformation factors, the smearing estimate, developed by Duan (1983). In this case the smearing estimate is the sample average of the exponentiated least-squares residuals:

$$(3.9) \quad \phi_j = \Sigma_i \exp(\hat{\epsilon}_{ij})/n_j, \quad j = 3,4$$

where n_j = sample size for equation j,

$$\hat{\epsilon}_{ij} = \ln(y_{ij}) - x_{ij}\hat{\beta}_j, \hat{\beta}_j = \text{OLS estimate of } \beta_j.$$

The smearing estimate is weakly consistent (asymptotically unbiased) for the retransformation factor if the error distribution does not depend on the characteristics x_i.[6] In the results presented below, the smearing factors for the log level of expense for outpatient-only users are estimated separately by plan and year to allow for heteroscedasticity (that is, greater variance in plans with higher coinsurance rates and in later years). For the log level of expenses for users of any inpatient services, the smearing factor is a constant.

A consistent estimate of the expected medical expense for medical services based on the four-equation model is given by

$$(3.10) \quad E(\text{medical expenditure}) =$$
$$(1/n) \Sigma p_i [(1-\pi_i) \exp(x_i\hat{\beta}_3) \phi_3 + \pi_i \exp(x_i\beta_4)\phi_4]$$

where n = number of people over which the expectation is taken,

$p_i = \phi(x_i\hat{\beta}_1)$ = estimated probability of any medical use,

$\pi_i = \phi(x_i\hat{\beta}_2)$ = estimated conditional probability for a medical user to have any inpatient use,

$\exp(x_i\beta_3)\phi_3$ = estimate of the conditional expense for medical services if there is only outpatient expenditure,

$\exp(x_i\hat{\beta}_4)\phi_4$ = estimate of the conditional expense for medical services if there is any inpatient expenditure,

ϕ_3, ϕ_4 = estimated retransformation factor of the error terms $\exp(\epsilon_3)$ and $\exp(\epsilon_4)$.

Our estimates of predicted expenditure presented below are based on Eq. (3.10). We use Eq. (3.10) to predict medical expenditure for each person we enrolled, alternatively placing that person on each plan by successively turning on the relevant plan dummy variables in the x-vector.[7] We then average within plans over each predicted value to obtain a mean value for each plan. Standard errors of the predicted values are obtained by the delta method (Duan et al. 1982, pp. 40, 48). The regression equations underlying our predicted values are presented in Manning et al. (1988).

Eqs. (3.5) and (3.7) group together all expenditures of a person, in contrast to an alternative specification with a more straightforward interpretation, namely, all outpatient expenditure and all inpatient expenditure. That is, outpatient use by inpatient users is estimated in Eq. (3.7), whereas it might seem more natural to estimate it in Eq. (3.5). This is done to minimize correlation between the error terms of Eqs. (3.5) and (3.7). Had outpatient use by those with some inpatient use been grouped in Eq. (3.5), the error terms in the two equations would have been correlated because inpatient and outpatient expenditure within persons is correlated. Reducing the correlation to negligible levels makes the calculation of standard errors for expected expenditure (Eq. 3.10) more tractable.

Correlation in the Error Terms

Although we have observations on more than 20,000 person-years of data, we do not have the same number of *independent* observations, because of substantial positive correlations in the error terms among family members and among observations on the same person over time. These correlations exist in all equations. Failure to account for them in the analysis would yield inefficient estimates of the coefficients and statistically inconsistent estimates of the standard errors. In other words, the inference statistics (t, F, and χ^2), calculated in the usual way, without adjusting for these correlations, would be too large. In the results presented below, we have used a nonparametric approach to correct the inference statistics for this positive correlation. The correction is similar to that for the random effects least-squares model, or equivalently the intracluster correlation model (Searle 1971). The method is described in Brook et al. (1984), based on work by Huber (1967) on the variance of a robust regression.

Selection Models

The econometric literature provides an additional class of models for continuous but limited dependent variables. These models include the Tobit model (Tobin 1958), the adjusted Tobit model (van de Ven and van Praag 1981), and sample selection models (Maddala 1983). Like our four-equation model, these are multiequation models, with one equation, typically a probit, for whether there is a positive amount, and another equation for the level of the positive amount. These models differ from ours in that they explicitly model the correlation between the probability of any use and the level of use.

Manning et al. (1988) discuss these models in more detail and compare their behavior with ANOVA and the four-equation model, but a few remarks are in order here. First, our four-equation model is not nested within the class of selection models (Duan et al. 1984). Second, we believe that our model is preferable. On a split-sample analysis, we cannot detect a difference in mean squared error between the sample selection and the four-equation models, but we can detect significantly greater bias in the sample selection than in the four-equation model. The bias is on the order of 10–25 percent of the mean in the case of the selection model, compared with about 2 percent of the mean (and insignificantly different from zero) in the case of the four-equation model. Finally, in Monte Carlo studies a variant of the four-equation model performed as well as or better than the selection model, even when the true model was a selection model (Manning, Duan, and Rogers 1987).

Results for Main Effects of Insurance Plan

ANOVA Estimates

Use of medical services responds unequivocally to changes in the amount paid out of pocket. Table 3.2 lists the sample means and standard errors by plan for several measures of use of services—the probability of being treated, visit and admission rates, and total expenses. The measures are ordered by their underlying variability (the "noise index"), with the least variable measure on the left.

Per capita expenses on the free plan (no out-of-pocket costs) are 45 percent higher than those on the plan with a 95 percent coinsurance rate and an upper limit of $1,000 or less on out-of-pocket expenses (982/679 = 1.45).

Table 3.2 Annual use of medical services per capita, by plan (standard errors in parentheses)[a]

Plan	Likelihood of any use (%)	Outpatient expenditures (1991 $)	Face-to-face visits	One or more admissions (%)	Total expenditures (1991 $)	Total admissions	Inpatient expenditure (1991 $)	Number of person-years
Free	86.8	446	4.55	10.3	982	0.128	536	6,822
	(0.8)	(14)	(0.17)	(0.45)	(50.7)	(0.0070)	(42)	
25%	78.7	341	3.33	8.4	831	0.105	489	4,065
	(1.4)	(20)	(0.19)	(0.61)	(69.2)	(0.0070)	(56)	
50%	77.2	294	3.03	7.2	884	0.092	590	1,401
	(2.3)	(22)	(0.22)	(0.77)	(189.1)	(0.0166)	(182)	
95%	67.7	266	2.73	7.9	679	0.099	413	3,727
	(1.8)	(16)	(0.18)	(0.55)	(58.7)	(0.0078)	(49)	
Individual Deductible	72.3	308	3.02	9.6	797	0.115	489	4,175
	(1.5)	(16)	(0.17)	(0.55)	(60.3)	(0.0076)	(55)	
$\chi^2(4)$[b]	144.7	85.3	68.8	19.5	15.9	11.7	4.1	
p-value for χ^2	2.8×10^{-30}	1.3×10^{-17}	4.1×10^{-14}	0.0006	0.003	0.02	n.s.	
p-value for free vs. 95% contrast[c]	1.6×10^{-22}	2.0×10^{-17}	1.0×10^{-13}	0.00037	0.000051	0.0028	0.027	
Noise index[d]	0.009	0.032	0.037	0.044	0.052	0.055	0.078	

a. The values in the table are sample means by plan. All standard errors are corrected for intertemporal and intrafamily correlation using an approach due to Huber; see text. Dollars are expressed in 1991 dollars. Visits are face-to-face contacts with M.D., D.O., or other health providers and exclude visits for only radiology, anesthesiology, or pathology services. All data exclude dental services and outpatient psychotherapy services. The sample includes children born into the study except for the year of birth and excludes partial years except for deaths.

b. Testing null hypothesis of no difference among plans.

c. p-value comes from 1-tail t-test.

d. Value shown is coefficient of variation in free-care plan.

Spending rates on plans with an intermediate level of cost sharing lie between these two extremes.

Cost sharing affects the number of medical contacts but not their intensity. In other words, the differences in expenditure across plans reflect real variation in the number of contacts rather than an increase in the intensity or charge per service.[8] For example, outpatient expenses on the free plan are 68 percent higher than those on the 95 percent plan (446/266 = 1.68), and outpatient visit rates to physicians and other health providers are 67 percent higher (4.55/2.73 = 1.67). A similar but weaker pattern holds for inpatient care; for example, inpatient expenses are 30 percent higher on the free plan than on the 95 percent plan, and admission rates are 29 percent higher.

The largest decrease in use of outpatient services occurs between the free and 25 percent plans, with smaller but significant differences between the 25 percent and other family coinsurance (pay) plans [$\chi^2(2) = 9.48$, $p < .01$].[9] As described in Chapters 4 and 11, this comes about because the dampening effect of the MDE increases as the coinsurance rate rises.

There are no significant differences among the family pay (25, 50, and 95 percent) plans in the use of inpatient services. For the probability of any inpatient use, total admission rates, and inpatient expenses, the contrasts between the 25, 50, and 95 percent plans have p values greater than 0.50. As noted above, this lack of a significant difference probably reflects the effect of the upper limit on out-of-pocket expenses, because 70 percent of people with inpatient care exceeded their upper limit. Hence the out-of-pocket cost of a hospitalization was at most $1,000 (in current dollars) and did not vary much among the pay plans except in the Individual Deductible plan.[10] Moreover, for the 30 percent who did not exceed the MDE there are potentially offsetting effects. For any given stay, coinsurance at the margin should reduce expenditure relative to free care; however, when one averages across stays by plan, this effect can be offset if the incremental cases admitted in the free plan are less costly than average.

The Individual Deductible plan exhibits a somewhat different pattern from the other cost-sharing plans. This plan has free inpatient care but a 95 percent coinsurance rate up to an annual maximum for outpatient services of $150 per person or $450 per family. Total expenditure on this plan is significantly less than on the free plan ($t = -2.34$, $p < .02$). This overall response is the sum of a one-third reduction in outpatient expenses ($t = -6.67$) and a less than one-tenth reduction in inpatient expenses ($t = -0.68$). Thus the Individual Deductible plan looks like a combination of the 50 or 95 percent plans for outpatient care and the free or 25 percent plan for inpatient care. The admission rate for the Individual Deductible plan lies roughly midway between the free plan and family pay plan rates, suggesting a nontrivial cross-price elasticity between inpatient and outpatient services.

Four-Equation Estimates

Because sample means are sensitive to the presence of individuals with large expenditure, we used the four-equation model to provide more robust estimates of the plan responses.[11]

The use of covariates in these equations removes the relatively minor imbalances across plan, including the site imbalance (see Appendix B, Table B.2). Table 3.3 presents estimates from this model of plan response for the probability of any use of medical services, the unconditional probability of any inpatient use, and total medical expenses.

Mean predicted expenditure in the free-care plan is 46 percent higher than in the 95 percent plan ($p < .001$), almost exactly the difference found in the sample means. This may seem to be a trivial result following simply from the orthogonality of plan and covariates. Such is not the case, however, because of the nonlinear transformations in the four-equation model. Using the logarithm of expenditure plus $5 as a dependent variable, for example, instead of the four-part model would lead to a much larger estimate of plan response, one that is biased upward. (See Duan et al. 1982; Manning et al. 1988.)

Like the sample means in Table 3.2, the more robust estimates in Table 3.3 indicate that the largest response to plan occurs between free care and the 25 percent plan, with smaller decreases thereafter.[12]

Not surprisingly, given the approximate orthogonality of plan and covariates, adding covariates does not change the estimated probability of any use of medical services from the sample mean; 87 percent of the free-plan participants are predicted to use some service during the year, in contrast to only 68 percent of the 95 percent plan participants. These differences among plans in the likelihood of receiving any care account for over three-fifths of the overall response to cost sharing. Virtually all of the remaining response is attributable to the effect of cost sharing on hospital admissions.

As was seen in the data on means (Table 3.2), cost sharing for outpatient services only—the Individual Deductible plan—produces a different pattern

Table 3.3 Predicted mean annual use of medical services for a standard population (standard errors in parentheses)[a]

Plan	Probability of any medical use (%)		Probability of any inpatient use (%)		Medical expenses per person (1991 $)	
	Mean	t vs. free	Mean	t vs. free	Mean	t vs. free
Free	86.7 (0.67)	—	10.37 (0.42)	—	1,019 (43)	—
25%	78.8 (0.99)	-6.69	8.83 (0.38)	-2.74	826 (38)	-4.05
50%	74.3 (1.86)	-6.33	8.31 (0.40)	-3.57	764 (43)	-4.91
95%	68.0 (1.48)	-11.57	7.75 (0.35)	-4.80	700 (35)	-6.74
Individual Deductible	72.6 (1.14)	-10.69	9.52 (0.53)	-1.28	817 (45)	-3.78

a. Estimates are predicted values from the four-equation model. Medical services exclude dental and outpatient psychotherapy. The predictions are for the enrollment population carried forward through each year of the Experiment. The standard errors are corrected for intertemporal and intrafamily correlation. These t-statistics are larger than those one would compute from the standard errors shown in Table 3.2 because use of the standard errors ignores the positive covariance between the two predicted plan means from the shared $X\beta$ term. The difference in expenses between the 25% and 50% plans is significant at the 5% level ($t = 1.97$), and between the 50% and 95% plans is significant at the 6% level ($t = 1.93$). The parameter estimates underlying these predictions are available in Manning et al. (1988).

of utilization from cost sharing for all services. According to the more precise estimates from the four-equation model, outpatient-only cost sharing reduces expenditures relative to free care ($p < .0001$), largely by reducing the likelihood of any use ($p < 10^{-30}$). Outpatient-only cost sharing also reduces inpatient use, but by an insignificant amount ($p = .20$ for the probability of any inpatient use).

This last result is the only important change arising from analyzing all the data rather than the first 40 percent of the data that became available (reported in Newhouse et al. 1981). Using only the first 40 percent of the data, one could reject at the 5 percent level the hypothesis that the free plan and Individual Deductible plan means for inpatient use were the same (in favor of the hypothesis that the Individual Deductible plan reduced the admission rate). This difference may have been due to the fact that inflation in the late 1970s reduced the real value of the deductible, which was kept fixed at $150 (that is, in nominal dollars); it may also have been due simply to chance. The replication of almost all the results in a subsample, however, means that they are robust.

Use by Subgroups

An important goal of the Experiment was to study how the response to cost sharing varied across subgroups. In particular, we were interested in differences in responses among income groups, between adults and children, and between the sickly and the healthy; we were also interested in differences across time (for example, any transitory surges in use as insurance changed) and in differences across medical markets (for example, short versus long wait to an appointment).

Income groups. Different measures of the use of medical services exhibit different plan responses by income group. Table 3.4 gives the results for each plan for each third of the income distribution for three measures of use.[13]

Because other variables are not held constant, the observed differences in use are due both to income directly and to the effects of variables correlated with income. We did not hold other variables constant, because we were interested in whether cost sharing had a larger effect among the poor.

The probability of any use of medical services significantly increases with income for each of the five plans, with larger increases for the family pay (25, 50, and 95 percent) and Individual Deductible plans than for the free plan. In contrast, the (unconditional) probability of any use of inpatient services declines with income for the family pay plans, but is not significantly different across income groups for the two plans with free inpatient care (the free and Individual Deductible plans). Because of these two conflicting effects of income—positive on outpatient use but negative on inpatient use—the net result on medical expenditure is a shallow U-shaped response to income for the family coinsurance plans, and little income response on the free plan.

Table 3.4   Predicted annual use of medical services by income group for a standard population[a]

	Lower third	Middle third		Higher third	
Plan	Mean	Mean	t vs. lower third	Mean	t vs. lower third
Probability of any use (%)					
Free	82.8	87.4	4.91	90.1	5.90
25%	71.8	80.1	5.45	84.8	6.28
50%	64.7	76.2	4.35	82.3	4.86
95%	61.7	68.9	3.96	73.8	4.64
Individual Deductible	65.3	73.9	6.09	79.1	7.09
Probability of any inpatient use (%)					
Free	10.63	10.14	−0.91	10.35	−0.35
25%	10.03	8.44	−2.95	7.97	−2.75
50%	9.08	8.06	−1.78	7.77	−1.66
95%	8.77	7.38	−2.79	7.07	−2.46
Individual Deductible	9.26	9.44	+0.31	9.88	+0.68
Expenses (1991 $)					
Free	1,033	965	−1.78	1,060	+0.53
25%	891	771	−3.17	817	−1.47
50%	800	721	−1.89	773	−0.49
95%	762	648	−3.09	691	−1.41
Individual Deductible	798	778	−0.57	878	+1.38

a. Predictions for the enrollment population carried forward for all years of the study. Standard errors corrected for intertemporal and intrafamily correlation.

Our estimate of the differences by income group of the family-pay plans is influenced by the income-related upper limit on out-of-pocket expenses. In particular, the response is a combination of two conflicting factors: the direct response to income, which would raise expenditures among high-income families; and a countervailing price effect, because families with lower incomes are more likely to exceed their limit and to receive free care for part of the year.[14] In the case of the positive effect of income on the probability of any use, the direct income effect is more important, because most individuals do not exceed their upper limit. In the case of inpatient use, however, most individuals who use inpatient care do exceed their limit, and so the limit has relatively more influence. Partly for that reason we observe a negative income effect on the probability of any inpatient use.

The Individual Deductible plan provides a test of non-income-related cost sharing. We observe an insignificant 10 percent increase in medical expenses between the bottom and top third of the income distribution. The effect of income is limited to an increased likelihood of using any services, but inpatient services are free on this plan.

The results in Table 3.4 compare use among people in different income groups rather than examining the partial effect of income. In comparing income groups some of the differences are due to the partial effect of income (that is, its effect with all else held constant), and some are due to health, age, and family size variables that are correlated with income.[15] Income has a moderately significant (at $p < .10$) and positive partial effect on use in all but the inpatient expenditure equation; in the level of outpatient-only expenditures, the income coefficients are of mixed sign.[16]

Overall (that is, for total expenditure) partial income elasticities are in the range of 0.2 to 0.4, depending on plan.

Age groups. We found a different response to insurance plan for children (under age 18) from the response for adults: for inpatient services we cannot reject the hypothesis that children have no inpatient response to insurance coverage (Table 3.5).[17] Adults, by contrast, have significantly lower use of inpatient services on the family pay plans than they do on the free plan.[18] There are no significant differences among the three family pay plans for adults.[19]

For outpatient services we observe a very similar pattern of plan responses for children and adults (results not shown). On the 25 percent plan, adults spend 78 percent as much on outpatient services and children 74 percent as much as they would on the free care plan. On the 95 percent plan, adults spend 60 percent as much and children 59 percent as much as they would on the free plan. On the Individual Deductible plan, children spend 70 percent as much as they would on the free plan, and adults spend 67 percent as much. Only the 50 percent plan does not follow this pattern; adults spend 59 percent as much and children 89 percent as much as they would on the free plan.

Health status. Although health status was a strong predictor of expenditure levels, we observed no differential response to health insurance coverage between the healthy and the sickly. Using ANOVA methods, we found no significant plan interactions with perceived health, defined as site-specific thirds of the distribution of the General Health Index, our best summary health measure, $[\chi^2(8) = 5.18$ for total expenditures, $p > 0.70)$. We obtained similar results for the other measures of use of medical services.[20] We also obtained this result with the four-equation model.

Some might expect the sickly to be less responsive to insurance coverage than the healthy, on the grounds that their use of services is less discretionary. The failure to find such a difference among groups in different health status suggests that this is not the case.

Table 3.5   Predicted annual use of medical services by age group for a standard population[a]

Plan	Probability of any medical use (%)		Probability of any inpatient use (%)		Medical expenses (1991 $)	
	Mean	*t* vs. free	Mean	*t* vs. free	Mean	*t* vs. free
Children (< 18)						
Free	84.0	—	5.33	—	454	—
25%	75.1	−6.72	4.98	−0.55	376	−2.16
50%	70.3	−6.48	4.62	−1.13	366	−2.20
95%	63.5	−11.64	4.23	−1.81	309	−4.10
Individual Deductible	68.5	−10.68	5.86	+0.63	392	−1.42
Adults						
Free	88.6	—	13.9	—	1416	—
25%	81.4	−6.63	11.5	−2.92	1143	−3.70
50%	77.1	−6.19	10.9	−3.64	1045	−4.80
95%	71.2	−11.37	10.2	−4.69	975	−6.07
Individual Deductible	75.6	−10.57	12.1	−1.89	1117	−3.63

a. Predictions for all years of the study for the enrollment population carried forward for all years of the study. Standard errors corrected for intertemporal and intrafamily correlation.

On the contrary, one might infer from our findings that the sickly are in fact more responsive to price than the healthy. If there were an equal response to price, the presence of an upper limit on out-of-pocket expenses should give the appearance of less plan response for the sickly because, all other things being equal, the latter are more likely than the healthy to exceed their upper limit and to receive some free care, especially on the 95 percent plan, on which 35 percent of the families exceeded the upper limit. In other words, the 95 percent plan is a mixture of some individuals with free care (those above the MDE) and some with costly care (those below the MDE), with sicker individuals more likely to have free care. Individuals in the latter group can be expected to behave at the margin as if they were on the free plan, as demonstrated in the next chapter. Hence, even if the true interaction between *price* and the General Health Index were zero, one would observe less response among the sick because of an interaction between *plan* and the Index. Thus the absence of a plan-health interaction is stronger evidence than we might at first think against the hypothesis that the sickly are less responsive to price.

Although we may have failed to detect a small interaction between plan and health status, our conclusion that the sickly are more responsive to price is consistent with the physician discretion suggested by the literature documenting variation in the use of different procedures across areas (Chassin et al. 1987).

Sites. As described in Chapter 2, we selected six sites to reflect a spectrum of city sizes, waiting times to appointment, and physician-to-population ratios to determine whether the response to insurance coverage varied according to the complexity of the medical delivery system or to the excess demand in the medical market (Table 2.1). For example, with longer delays to appointment, there might be a smaller plan response because self-limiting illnesses such as colds are less likely to be seen by a physician before the person recovers. In fact we found no differences among sites in response to insurance coverage.[21]

Although plan response did not appear to differ by site, we did find differences among sites in levels of use. Table 3.6 shows probabilities of service use on the free plan for the six sites.

The data are not consistent with the hypothesis that delays to appointment reduce either the level of spending or the plan response. The site with the longest delay to appointment and lowest physician-to-population ratio (Fitchburg) had the second-highest expenditures per enrollee, the second-highest probability of any use, and the second-highest probability of inpatient use. The first and third phenomena may represent substitution of inpatient for outpatient care (if patients become sicker before treatment because of long waiting times) (McCombs 1984). If delays do matter, the second is difficult to explain in any terms except chance. We did, however, find a consistent relationship between waiting times to an appointment and the likelihood of using the emergency room rather than the physician's office. (See Chapter 5.)

Years. We enrolled families for three or five years to see if the response to insurance either changed over time or was affected by the length of enrollment.[22] We were interested in any initial surge in demand in the more generous plans or in transitory demand at the end of the Experiment as individuals anticipate returning to their (usually) employer-provided plan.

To test for the presence of such plan-related surges for medical services, we compared the use of such services during the middle years of the Experiment with use during the first and last years.[23] We found no significant differences in the medical expenditure response to plan across years.[24] (As we shall see later, there was a surge in dental expenditure.)

We did, however, find an upward drift in mean medical expenses over time in all plans, even after using the medical component of the Consumer Price

Table 3.6   Predicted annual use of medical services by site, free-care plan (standard errors in parentheses)[a]

Plan	Probability of any medical use (%)		Probability of any inpatient use (%)		Medical expenses (1991 $)	
	Mean	*t* vs. Seattle	Mean	*t* vs. Seattle	Mean	*t* vs. Seattle
Seattle	89.2 (0.90)	—	10.5 (0.68)	—	1,131 (60.3)	—
Dayton	89.9 (0.88)	+0.65	10.6 (0.72)	+0.12	1,198 (69.6)	+0.94
Fitchburg	91.4 (1.04)	+1.88	11.0 (0.88)	+0.56	1,190 (86.0)	+0.68
Franklin County	92.0 (0.82)	+2.80	8.9 (0.66)	−1.91	844 (53.7)	−4.31
Charleston	77.2 (1.56)	−7.62	10.0 (0.72)	−0.46	908 (60.7)	−3.19
Georgetown County	79.1 (1.28)	−7.46	11.1 (0.69)	+0.67	835 (48.6)	−4.79

a. Predictions for the enrollment population as if enrolled on the free plan for all years of the study. Standard errors are corrected for intrafamily and intertemporal correlation.

Table 3.7   Predicted annual use of medical services by year, free-care plan
(standard errors in parentheses)[a]

Year	Probability of any medical use (%)		Probability of any inpatient use (%)		Medical expenses (1991 $)	
	Mean	t vs. year 1	Mean	t vs. year 1	Mean	t vs. year 1
1	87.5 (0.71)	—	10.1 (0.52)	—	932 (44.7)	—
2	85.9 (0.78)	−3.17	10.1 (0.52)	+0.08	996 (51.4)	+1.39
3	86.0 (0.77)	−2.94	10.8 (0.56)	+1.33	1088 (54.0)	+3.25
4	87.6 (0.96)	+0.04	10.5 (0.87)	+0.50	1075 (84.6)	+1.77
5	88.1 (0.97)	+0.60	10.6 (0.85)	+0.64	1211 (90.1)	+3.32

a. Predictions for the enrollment population as if enrolled on the free plan. Standard errors
are corrected for intrafamily and intertemporal correlation.

Index to adjust for inflation.[25] Table 3.7 presents the predicted mean
expenses for the standard population for the free plan for each year of the
Experiment. We believe that this upward trend reflects technological change
(see Chapter 11).[26] It is unlikely to be due to the effect of inflation on the
upper limit (which is in nominal terms). The argument is that as medical
prices rise, it becomes easier to exceed the upper limit on the pay plans
(Manning et al. 1988, app. B). Thus, over time, increasing numbers of people
reach their upper limit and receive free care for part of the year. If this were
the explanation, however, we would observe the difference between the free
and pay plans narrowing over time (a plan-by-year interaction), which we do
not. Also this explanation would predict no drift in the free plan expenses,
yet we observe such a drift, albeit a smaller one than occurs on the pay plans.

Dental Services

The Sample

The sample used in analyses of dental utilization is 6,962 individuals,
including both those used in the analyses of medical expenditure and those
enrolled in the HMO experimental group. Because the HMO did not provide

dental services, these individuals were provided free dental services in the fee-for-service system; that is, they had the same dental benefits as the individuals in the free fee-for-service plan. To check our assumption that we could add this group to the sample, we compared their use of dental services with dental service use by sample members on the free-care plan in Seattle. There was no significant difference. We therefore included these individuals as part of the free plan sample when analyzing dental expenditure.

Measures of Use

Our analysis focuses on the number of dental visits and expenditures for dental services. As with medical expenditure, claims filed by participants provide data on the amount and type of utilization. The number of visits is a count of the visits with a nonzero charge—that is, a count of billed visits.

Because the data are derived from claims, the Experiment did not necessarily receive a claim if the dentist did not bill for the visit (typically the case when a course of treatment is billed on a flat-fee basis). To see whether this presented a problem for the analysis, we compared visit rates from the biweekly Health Report, which included zero-charge visits, with visit rates from claims for Seattle in year 1 and Dayton in year 2.

Total visits were 15 percent higher than billed visits. We observed no systematic difference by insurance plan, however. (The difference was 16 percent for the free plan, 20 percent for the 25 percent plan, 7 percent for the 50 percent plan, 11 percent for the 95 percent plan, and 11 percent for the Individual Deductible plan.) Hence, our comparisons of dental-visit rates by insurance plan should not be biased by using a billed-visit definition.

Analytic Methods and Explanatory Variables

In general, we analyzed dental expenditure using methods similar to those used for the analysis of medical expenditure. Instead of a four-equation model, however, we used a two-equation model to estimate dental expenditure. The first equation was a probit equation for any use; the second used as a dependent variable the logarithm of dental expenditure, conditional on some expenditure. As with medical expenditure, the logarithm of dollars was retransformed to dollars using the smearing estimator. (For details, see Manning et al. 1986a.)

Dental visits were estimated using negative binomial regression, a method described at length in the next chapter. We used age, gender, site, family size, income, education, and race as explanatory variables. Experimental insurance plans were specified as dummy variables. The standard errors and test statistics are corrected for intrafamily and intertemporal correlation (that is, for the tendency for the level of use to be positively correlated over time for the same person and among members of the same family at the same point in time) using the same method as for medical expenditure. (Manning et al. 1986a provide the parameter estimates for the visit and expenditure equations separately for the first, middle, and last years of the Experiment.)

One of the major issues in analyzing dental use is the magnitude of any transitory surge in demand for dental services as individuals change to more or less generous insurance coverage.

We expected such a surge for dental use because few Experiment participants had previously had insurance for routine dental care. In most cases their previous coverage had been limited to accident provisions of medical plans. As a result, most families on the free, 25 percent, 50 percent, and Individual Deductible plans had much better dental coverage during the Experiment than they had had before. Most families in the 95 percent plan faced little change unless they exceeded the catastrophic cap on their insurance plan (as 35 percent of them did); beyond that point, all dental services were free to the family for the remainder of the accounting year.

We test for a transitory surge at the outset by comparing each person's use in year 1 with use in year 2; formally, we test whether the average difference in expenditures is zero.[27] We test for a transitory surge at the end of the Experiment in a similar way, comparing use in the last and second-to-last years.

In most analyses we make comparisons among plans as we did for medical expenditure—in terms of predictions for a population with the same set of sociodemographic (nonplan) characteristics as the entire enrollment sample. This approach corrects for the differing proportions of participants on the free plan by site (a higher fraction of the free plan is in Seattle than in the analysis of medical expenditures because of the additional HMO sample) and the imbalance by age, plan, and year in Dayton in insurance coverage because we did not cover dental services for adults on the cost-sharing plans in year 1 (see Appendix B).

Transitory Demand

Table 3.8 presents the sample means and standard errors for each of the dental coinsurance rates during the first two years of dental coverage on the Experiment. The plan with 50 percent coinsurance for dental and mental health services and 25 percent for medical services is grouped with the 50 percent plans for the purpose of analyzing dental care use.

The results for visits and expenditure in Table 3.8 indicate a substantially greater response to dental insurance during the first year of coverage than during the second year of coverage on plans other than the 95 percent coinsurance plan. These year-to-year differences in the response to the free, 25 percent, 50 percent, and Individual Deductible plans (compared with the 95 percent plan) are statistically significant ($p = 0.001$), whether use is measured in dollars or in visits. Because there is little change over the two years in the likelihood of having any dental service use, all the surge is in the intensity of use for people who use dental services.[28] There is no evidence of a surge in demand during the first year for the 95 percent plan; in fact there is (insignificantly) higher use on that plan on all three measures during the second year of dental coverage than during the first.

Table 3.8   Use of dental services by dental plan: sample means (standard errors in parentheses)

Dental insurance plan	Year 1 of dental coverage			Year 2 of dental coverage		
	Probability (%)	Visits	Expenses per enrollee ($)[a]	Probability (%)	Visits	Expenses per enrollee ($)[a]
Free	68.7 (1.19)	2.50 (0.065)	509 (24.1)	66.8 (1.18)	1.93 (0.049)	349 (16.7)
25%	53.6 (3.39)	1.73 (0.138)	300 (43.9)	52.6 (3.34)	1.51 (0.111)	254 (37.5)
50%	54.1 (2.41)	1.80 (0.118)	293 (41.9)	53.0 (2.55)	1.50 (0.103)	237 (43.2)
95%	47.1 (2.59)	1.39 (0.098)	197 (25.0)	48.3 (2.62)	1.44 (0.099)	240 (33.3)
Individual Deductible	48.9 (2.12)	1.70 (0.104)	324 (32.3)	48.1 (2.12)	1.33 (0.080)	212 (27.3)

a. Expenses were converted to January 1984 dollars using the dental fee component of the CPI and then adjusted to 1991 dollars using the overall CPI. There has been no adjustment for regional differences in prices or for differences in population characteristics across plans and years. Standard errors are corrected for intrafamily and intertemporal correlation.

Table 3.9   Predicted steady-state annual use of dental services for a standard
population, by insurance plan (standard errors in parentheses)[a]

Plan	Probability of any use (%)		Visits per enrollee		Expenses per enrollee $	
	Mean	*t* vs. 95% plan	Mean	*t* vs. 95% plan	Mean	*t* vs. 95% plan
Free	66.1 (1.07)	6.77	1.87 (0.045)	5.23	325 (17.4)	3.54
25%	52.3 (2.44)	0.57	1.47 (0.093)	0.63	248 (30.9)	0.69
50%	49.8 (2.07)	−0.25	1.41 (0.084)	0.16	221 (31.7)	−0.04
95%	50.5 (2.07)	—	1.40 (0.077)	—	222 (24.9)	—
Individual Deductible	48.9 (1.72)	−0.60	1.33 (0.069)	−0.65	209 (27.3)	−0.37

a. Predictions are for population of all participants present at enrollment. *t*-statistics adjusted for intrafamily correlation. Expenses are converted to January 1984 dollars using the dental fee component of the CPI and brought forward to 1991 using the overall CPI. Based on data from the middle years of the Experiment; see text.

We conducted a similar analysis using data from the last two years of the Experiment. We found a statistically significant ($p = 0.05$) but smaller surge in use on the free and 25 percent plans in the last year of the Experiment. In contrast, we found no appreciable differences in the use of dental services among the years of the Experiment that were not beginning or ending years (year 2 for the group enrolled for three years and years 2–4 for the group enrolled for five years).

In light of these results, we use only the middle years of the Experiment to estimate the steady-state response to dental insurance. Because there is no middle year of dental coverage for Dayton adults on family coinsurance plans with a three-year period of enrollment, these people are excluded from the steady-state sample.

Steady-State Demand

Table 3.9 presents the steady-state response to dental insurance plans in terms of probability of any use, number of dental visits, and annual expenditures.

The results are for a standardized population with the same mix of character-istics as those initially enrolled on experimental dental plans.

Use increases significantly as generosity of coverage increases. Partici-pants in the free plan had 34 percent more visits and 46 percent higher dental expenses than enrollees in the 95 percent coinsurance plan; the 46 percent difference in expenditure is almost identical with that for total medical expenditure. As in the case of medical expenditure, most of the observed response to insurance plans occurs between the free and the 25 percent plans. Expenditure rates on the other plans differ by a much smaller, and insignificant, amount. Nearly two-thirds of the response to cost sharing occurs in the probability of any use, and about three-quarters of the response to cost sharing is in the number of visits per enrollee rather than in dollars per user.[29]

Only the free plan has significantly higher expenditure rates per enrollee than the 95 percent coinsurance plan. The Individual Deductible plan (with a ceiling of $150 per person or $450 per family per year) does not generate significantly different dental expenditure from the Family Deductible plan (where the MDE can be as much as $1,000).

We also investigated the possibility of a differential response to insur-ance plan between children and adults but could find no persuasive evi-dence of such a differential. For dental expenditures and the likelihood of any visit, we found that the differences were less significant than one would expect at random, and that the point estimates of the plan-by-adult interaction terms exhibited no meaningful pattern. For visits, we observed a one-third higher response (nominally significant at the 5 percent level) for adults on the family coinsurance plans (25, 50, and 95 percent), but an insignificantly smaller response for adults on the Individual Deductible plan. Because of the insignificant results for probability and expenditures, and the contradictory signs for visits, we dropped plan-by-adult interac-tion terms from our equations.

Mix of Services

To examine plan differences in the mix of services more closely, we disag-gregated dental use into the following categories: diagnostic and preven-tive care, restoration (for example, fillings), prosthodontia (for example, dentures), endodontia (for example, root canal) and periodontia (for example, treatment of gum disease), and other dental work. Although a relatively small fraction of the population uses prosthodontic, periodontic, and endodontic services, these accounted for two-fifths of dental expenditures (see Table 3.10).

We also examined the probability of any use of each type of service by plan; the values shown in Table 3.11 are predictions for the enrollment population. The probabilities of any diagnostic/preventive work or of any restorative work show the same response to plan as the overall probability of any use: about one-third higher on the free plan than on the 95 percent plan. Prosthodontia is more responsive to plan than overall use; the probability of any use is 62 percent higher on the free plan than on the 95 percent plan. Endodontia and periodontia exhibit a larger-than-average response, though not as large as prosthodontia; the probability of any use is 50 percent higher on the free plan than on the 95 percent plan.

Effect of Income on Use and Response to Cost Sharing

Table 3.12 presents estimates of the effect of income on the use of dental services and the response to cost sharing. The results are for participants in the upper and lower thirds of the distribution of income and do not hold constant other variables correlated with income. Thus, these results test whether the poor exhibit a greater response to cost sharing than the more well-to-do.

On all three measures of the use of dental services, higher income leads to higher use. The differences are greater for the probability of any use than for either the number of visits or annual expenses. Indeed, the differences in the expenditure rate for the high- and low-income groups are small and insignificant at conventional levels. The smaller response of expenditure to income reflects a fall in expense per user as income increases.

Table 3.10   Disaggregated annual use of dental services, second year of dental coverage[a]

Service	Probability of any use (%)	Share of total dental expense (%)	Expenses per enrollee ($)
Diagnosis/preventive	54	17	46
Restoration	31	35	98
Prosthodontics	6	30	83
Endodontic/periodontic	9	11	29
Other	12	7	19

a. Based on full-year participants. Expenses are converted to January 1984 dollars using the dental fee component of the CPI and brought forward to 1991 using the overall CPI.

Table 3.11 Predicted steady-state probability of any use of dental services for a standard population, by plan, year 2[a]

Plan	Any dental services		Diagnosis/ preventive		Restoration		Prosthodontia		Endodontia/ periodontia	
	Mean %	t vs. 95%	Mean %	t vs. 95%	Mean %	t vs. 95%	Mean %	t vs. 95%	Mean %	t vs. 95%
Free	66.1	6.77	61.3	6.20	35.8	4.57	7.8	3.49	9.7	2.27
25%	52.3	0.57	48.3	0.53	28.4	0.34	6.6	1.45	9.6	2.27
50%	49.8	−0.25	44.5	−0.70	26.1	−0.69	7.2	2.03	6.3	−0.27
95%[b]	50.5	—	46.6	—	27.6	—	4.8	—	6.6	—
Individual Deductible	48.9	−0.60	44.3	−0.84	25.4	−1.08	4.6	−0.27	8.4	1.65

a. Predictions are for population of all participants present at enrollment. t-statistics adjusted for intrafamily and intertemporal correlation.
b. The standard errors for those on the 95% plan are 2.1% for the probability of any use, 2.1% for diagnosis and prevention, 1.6 for restoration, 0.7% for prosthodontia, and 0.7% for periodontia/endodontia.

For visits the response to cost sharing is greater for the low-income than for the high-income group. The low-income group has 46 percent more visits on the free than on the 95 percent plan, whereas the high-income group has only 26 percent more visits. Although this difference is not significant at conventional levels ($p = 0.18$, two-tailed), it is much larger than one would expect at random.[30]

The response of expenditures to plan, however, is almost identical in the two income groups. We explore further the importance of the differences, or lack of them, in responsiveness by income group in Chapters 6 and 7 where we discuss outcomes.

Response to Cost Sharing in Dental Services versus Other Health Services

Although we found that the steady-state response of dental services to cost sharing was similar to that for all health care services, it may be more appropriate to make the comparison only with outpatient services, since both involve ambulatory patients. Here a mixed picture emerges. Table 3.13

Table 3.12   Predicted steady-state annual use of dental services by income tertiles for a standard population for free and 95% plans[a]

Plan	Low-income tertile		High-income tertile		
	Mean	t vs. 95%	Mean	t vs. 95%	t vs. low
Free					
Probability of any use (%)	57.8	5.91	74.7	4.59	9.17
Visits/enrollee	1.69	4.75	2.05	3.31	4.43
Expenditure ($)	317	2.76	339	3.23	1.02
95% plan					
Probability of any use (%)	39.8	—	61.3	—	6.04
Visits/enrollee	1.16	—	1.63	—	3.44
Expenditures ($)	216	—	234	—	0.61

a. Standardized population is all participants present at enrollment. *t*-statistics adjusted for intrafamily and intertemporal correlation. Expenditures standardized to January 1984 dollars using the dental fee component of the CPI and brought forward to 1991 using the overall CPI. Low-income tertile had family incomes below $26,400 in 1991 dollars; high-income tertile had family incomes above $38,400.

shows that dental services are significantly more responsive (that is, they show a larger percentage increase in use for a given decrease in cost sharing) to cost sharing during the first year of dental coverage than are outpatient health services ($p = 0.001$), but are significantly less responsive during the second year ($p = 0.001$).[31]

Outpatient Mental Health Services

The Sample

The sample used for analyzing outpatient mental health expenditure is almost the same as that used to analyze medical expenditure. We have, however, deleted observations from the first year of Dayton for the Family and Individual Deductible plans because psychotherapy was not a covered service for those groups. Thus, for the main substantive results the sample consists of 19,819 person-years of observations. In addition, we carried out a number of methodological studies on a subsample of 12,345 person-years; this smaller sample reflects the lack of data on the three-year group in South Carolina at the time this work was completed.[32]

We classified mental health providers as "formal" or "nonformal" on the basis of their professional training. Table 3.14 describes the distinction between formal and nonformal providers.

For the mental health visit analysis we partitioned the user population into those using only nonformal providers and users of any formal pro-

Table 3.13   Response to cost sharing of dental versus other outpatient care: ratio of plan average to 95% plan average (95% plan = 100)[a]

Nondental/dental coinsurance rates	First year of dental coverage		Second year of dental coverage	
	Nondental	Dental	Nondental	Dental
Free/free	200	252	177	152
25/25	145	158	128	109
25/50	144	181	122	98
50/50	111	118	105	112
95/95	100	100	100	100
Individual Deductible	143	163	124	94

a. Nondental is outpatient medical, mental health, drugs and supplies. Second year of dental coverage sample excludes adults on three-year pay plans in Dayton. The response on each plan is stated as a percentage of the response on the 95% plan.

viders (including those using both nonformal and formal providers). We did not treat the group using both nonformal and formal providers as a separate category because it was too small for reliable estimation.

The Dependent Variable: Defining Mental Health Visits

To estimate the demand for outpatient mental health services, we first had to separate mental health use from use of other health services. The literature suggests that psychiatric diagnoses from insurance claim forms underestimate the use of mental health services because of underreporting or "minimizing" psychiatric diagnoses.[33] Providers may wish to protect patient confidentiality or help them avoid the social stigma of the label of mental illness. Physicians other than psychiatrists also may disguise mental health visits so that they will be reimbursed under the more generous medical benefits of many insurance plans.

To see how sensitive the results are to possible underreporting, we identified mental health visits by four types of claims information: mental health procedure, mental health diagnosis, psychotropic medication, or mental health reason for visit.[34] We believe that these four mental health visit criteria are ranked in descending order of specificity in identifying an actual mental health visit.[35]

Using this information, we developed three definitions of mental health visits. We believe that these definitions can be ordered in terms of increasing probability of false-positive identification of mental health visits. Those def-

Table 3.14   Mental health providers

Formal providers
    Psychiatrists
    Psychologists
    Other mental health specialists
    Alcohol and drug abuse treatment providers
    Psychologically oriented providers (e.g., holistic providers)
    Mental health clinics
    Psychiatric hospitals
    Others[a]

Nonformal providers
    All other providers, including internists and family and general practitioners

a. Includes institutional providers, multispecialty clinics, and providers of unknown professional training, only if the claim includes mental health procedures. See Wells et al. (1982) for additional details.

initions are: (1) presence of any mental health procedure or diagnosis (conservative definition); (2) presence of any mental health procedure, mental health diagnosis, or psychotropic medication (middle definition); and (3) presence of any mental health procedure, mental health diagnosis, psychotropic medication, or mental health reason for visit (liberal definition). Table 3.15 summarizes the relationship between each criterion and the three definitions.

The three definitions of mental health visits are thus nested. For example, a definition based on mental health procedure or diagnosis identifies any visit meeting these criteria as a mental health visit. Adding a new criterion (such as reason for visit) to the definition only adds visits not identified by the previous criteria. (Wells et al. 1982 specifies each criterion in more detail.)

Mental Health Procedure

A visit is classified as containing a mental health procedure if any procedure in that visit is a mental health procedure according to the California Relative Value Studies (California Medical Association 1975). Table 3.16 lists the mental health procedures.

Mental Health Diagnosis

Our list of mental health diagnoses includes the mental disorders section of the H-ICDA-2 (Commission on Professional and Hospital Activities 1973) and several mental health symptoms and psychiatric procedures listed there as diagnoses. A visit is considered to have a mental health diagnosis if any of its diagnosis codes are for a "mental disorder." Table 3.17 summarizes mental health diagnoses.

Table 3.15   Relation of criteria to mental health definitions

Mental health definition			
Conservative	Middle	Liberal	Mental health criterion
X	X	X	Mental health procedure or diagnosis
	X	X	Psychotropic medication
		X	Mental health symptom (reason for visit)

Table 3.16 Mental health procedures

All providers (formal and nonformal)
  Psychotherapy
    Individual
    Family
    Group
  Shock therapy
  Psychological testing
  Others (e.g., supervision, biofeedback)

Formal providers only
  General counseling
  Initial office visits with a deferred
    diagnosis

Psychotropic Medication

We separate psychotropic medications into two categories: (1) antipsychotics and antidepressants, and (2) antianxiety agents and sedative/hypnotics.[36] We include in our analysis any drugs in these two categories that were prescribed by the physician at the visit or administered or injected during the visit.[37] Because psychotropic drugs may be prescribed for physical as well as mental health problems, however, we use psychotropic medication to identify a *mental health* component of a visit only in the absence of justifiable medical indications. If psychotropic medication is prescribed during a visit and is accompanied by an appropriate mental health *and* medical diagnosis, the visit is identified by the mental health diagnosis only and not by the medication. Table 3.18 lists the medical indications for both drug categories.

Mental Health Reasons for Visit

Mental health reasons for visit include the mental health symptoms section of the National Ambulatory Medical Care Survey Symptom Code Index (such as anxiety or depression) and other selected reasons for visit, including a request for psychiatric therapy or "counseling," or poor sleep when the only diagnosis is "sleep disturbance."[38] Visits identified only by mental health reason for visit are less likely to be mental health visits, strictly speaking, because many of the categories are nonspecific (such as "seeking advice") and because emotional symptoms are sometimes manifestations of physical illness. Without confirmation of mental health content from the provider-reported mental health criteria (procedure, diagnosis, medication), these visits could be mental health or medical visits. As a result, inclusion of the mental health reason for visit provides a liberal definition for the analysis of mental health service use.

Outpatient Expenditure: Analytical Methods

In addition to presenting simple means (analysis of variance methods), we used a four-equation model to estimate mental health expenses. The model examines separately the expenses of users of only nonformal providers and the expenses of users of any formal providers. As in the case of medical expenditures, we used a logarithmic transformation of expenditure together with the nonparametric smearing estimator described above to

Table 3.17   Mental health diagnosis[a]

Mental health disorders
    Mental retardation
    Organic brain syndromes
    Psychoses not attributed to
        physical conditions
    Neuroses
    Personality disorders
    Psychophysiologic disorders
    Special symptoms
    Transient situational disturbances
    Behavioral disorders of childhood

Symptoms
    Nervousness
    Hallucinations

Other
    Inadequate psychosocial
        environment
    Self-inflicted injury
    Mental health procedures

a. Excluded are speech disturbance, specific learning disturbance, enuresis, encopresis, and speech therapy procedure (in the absence of other mental health diagnosis). See Wells et al. (1982) for additional details.

Table 3.18   Medical indications for
psychotrophic medications[a]

Hypnotics, anxiolytics[b]
Surgical procedures
Invasive radiography
Acute trauma
Spasticity, muscle tension
Epilepsy
Thyrotoxicosis
Corneal abrasion

Antipsychotics, antidepressants[c]
Surgical procedures
Invasive radiography
Vertigo
Porphyria
Neuralgia
Enuresis
Hiccough
Headaches (including migraine)

a. See Wells et al. (1982) for details.
b. Specific exclusions are hydroxyzine
and diphenhydramine if there are skin or
allergy problems.
c. Compazine is specifically excluded.

retransform the logarithmic values to dollars. Unless otherwise specified, we use the conservative definition (procedure or diagnosis) of mental health visits.

Prevalence of Use according to Alternative Definitions

Table 3.19 shows the number and percentage of enrollees using any mental health service for each of the three visit definitions during year 2 of the Experiment.[39] Between 7.1 and 9.6 percent of enrollees had any mental health visits during year 2, depending on the visit definition.[40]

The total number of persons using mental health services from only formal providers or from both formal and nonformal providers was the same (163), regardless of definition.[41] By contrast, successively more liberal definitions identified additional users in the "nonformal only" category. The multiple-regression model of demand contrasts "any formal" with "nonformal only" use.[42]

Table 3.19 Prevalence of use of mental health services, year 2[a]

Definition	All users		Users of nonformal providers only		Users of formal providers only		Users of formal and nonformal providers only	
	No.	% of enrollees	No.	%[b]	No.	%[b]	No.	%[b]
Conservative	302	7.1	139	46	134	44	29	10
Middle	390	9.2	227	58	128	33	35	9
Liberal	407	9.6	244	60	123	30	40	10

a. Sample size = 4,254.
b. Percent of all users with mental health visits for the same-row definition of a visit (see Table 3.15).

We show elsewhere that the response to important covariates, such as cost sharing or mental health status, is insensitive to the definition of mental health services (Wells et al. 1982).

Intensity of Use for Formal and Nonformal Services

In addition to number of visits, total use also encompasses intensity of use—that is, expenditures per user on mental health services.[43] Although users of formal and nonformal mental health care represent approximately equal proportions of total users of mental health care, formal users have much higher expenses than nonformal users. Table 3.20 presents the median expenditures for formal mental health services for users with *any* formal mental health visit and the median expenditures for nonformal mental health services for users with any nonformal mental health visit.

The lower estimate of expenditures in the table prorates the mental health care charges over the diagnoses related to each service if there are multiple diagnoses.[44] The higher estimate assigns to mental health the total charge for each service related to use of mental health services.[45] As Table 3.20 indicates, regardless of definition or expenditure allocation, the median formal mental health expenditure per user with any formal mental health visit was $280 (current-year dollars). The median nonformal mental health expenditure per user with any nonformal mental health visit ranged

Table 3.20   Median expenditures for mental health users by type of use, year 2[a]

	Users of any formal visit		Users of any nonformal visit	
Definition	Formal mental health expenditures ($)[b]	Prorated ($)[c]	Nonformal mental health expenditures ($)[b]	Prorated ($)[c]
Conservative	280	280	22	14
Middle	280	280	20	11
Liberal	280	280	20	11

a. Sample size = 4,254. Dollars are nominal dollars from the second year of the Experiment, approximately 1976–1978.

b. Includes all charges linked to any mental health diagnosis and the full office charge for any mental health visit.

c. Includes all mental health charges and charges for basic office visits prorated by proportion of associated diagnoses that are mental health diagnoses if there are multiple diagnoses. Medication and reason for visit count as mental health diagnoses for prorating charges for the middle and liberal definitions of a mental health visit (see Table 3.15).

from $11 to $14. This lower expense for nonformal care than for formal care reflects both lower charges per visit and fewer visits per user. (For mean formal and nonformal expenditures per enrollee-year, see Wells et al. 1982, table G.1.)

Frequency of Visits

Only 0.2 percent of enrollees came close to or reached the maximum coverage for mental health visits of 52 visits per year (Table 3.21). This result implies that few people used intensive long-term therapies (such as psychoanalysis), but the 52-visit annual limit itself discouraged entry into such therapies.

Effect of Plan on Use

Although the overall level of spending on mental health services is much lower than spending on medical and dental services, plan has an effect on expenses for ambulatory mental health services. Table 3.22, which limits the definition of use to visits with a mental health procedure (such as psychotherapy), shows that the main source of plan response is in the probability of any use. The effects of plan on provider choice (formal or nonformal) and on any formal expense are statistically insignificant. The effect of plan on the amount of nonformal-only expense is statistically significant (result not shown) but of negligible practical magnitude, because expenses for nonformal providers represent only about 5 percent of total mental health care spending. Thus, even major changes in the level of non-

Table 3.21 Psychotherapy visits, year 2[a]

Number of visits	% of enrollees
0	95.9
1–10	2.5
11–20	0.4
21–30	0.4
31–40	0.4
41–50	0.2
51+	0.2

a. California Relative Value Studies codes 90801–90899 are used to define psychotherapy visits. Sample size = 4,254.

Table 3.22   Effect of plan on use of outpatient mental health procedures
(standard errors in parentheses)[a]

Plan	Probability of any use		Annual expense per enrollee	
	Mean %	t vs. free	Mean $	t vs. free
Free	4.3 (0.48)	—	42.20 (7.10)	—
25/25	3.1 (0.71)	−1.47	28.40 (7.50)	−1.33
25/50	2.9[b] (0.71)	−1.63	32.20[b] (13.10)	−0.66
50/50	1.6[b] (0.46)	−3.89	13.10[b] (8.11)	−2.61
95/95	2.1 (0.46)	−3.36	18.10 (4.56)	−2.85
Individual Deductible	4.1 (0.67)	−0.30	47.70 (10.93)	+0.43
$\chi^2 4$ for plan differences[c]	18.15		10.41	

a. Mental health services defined using only mental health procedures. Nearly all of these are delivered by formal mental health providers. Expenditures are stated in 1991 dollars. Based on full sample. Results are using analysis of variance; inference statistics are corrected for intertemporal and intrafamily correlation. Data from Manning et al. (1986b), inflated to 1991 dollars.

b. If the 25/50 and 50/50 plans were combined, the probability of any use would be 2.35% (s.e. = 0.46, $t = -3.01$ vs. free) and the mean annual expense would be $24.10 (s.e. = 6.17, $t = -1.68$ vs. free).

c. The 25/50 and 50/50 plans have been combined for this test.

formal-only use cannot have much impact on the total expenses for mental health services.

The means reported in Table 3.22 are based on the characteristics of the actual sample in each plan. If plans were perfectly uncorrelated with all other variables, these predictions would yield a "pure" response to plan. Unfortunately, the plans are not balanced by site. The 25/50 plans have more participants in sites with higher use of formal providers (such as Seattle), while the 50/50 plan has more participants in Dayton, a site with lower use of formal providers. Thus, in these results plan and site are partially confounded.

To eliminate this confounding of variables, we use the four-equation model and predict the mean for each plan. Rather than using predictions based on the characteristics of the sample enrolled in each plan, we make predictions on the same population. This approach bases the predictions for all plans on the same mix of sites and other characteristics, thereby eliminating any confounding effect.[46]

Table 3.23 presents the resulting predictions; these data are not exactly comparable to those in Table 3.22, because they come from a sample that excluded many of the South Carolina participants and because they include use defined by a mental health diagnosis as well as by procedure.[47] The predicted probabilities of use fall uniformly as the coinsurance rate increases, except for the statistically insignificant reversal between the 95 percent plan and the 50/50 plan for the probability of using a formal provider. Participants with free care are twice as likely to use mental health services (formal or nonformal) as those on an insurance plan with a 95 percent coinsurance rate.

Table 3.23   Predicted effects of insurance plan on outpatient mental health use, year 2[a]

Plan	Probability of any mental health use		Probability of any formal use		Relative expenditure (free plan = 100)	
	Mean %	t vs. free	Mean %	t vs. free	% of free	t vs. free
Free	8.8[b]	—	5.0[c]	—	100[d]	—
25% medical/ 25% mental	7.5	−0.73	3.8	−1.08	88	−0.36
25% medical/ 50% mental	6.0	−1.45	2.6	−2.15	47	−2.09
50% medical/ 50% mental	4.6	−2.19	1.8	−3.06	19	−3.77
95%	4.3	−3.13	2.4	−2.79	58	−1.74
Individual Deductible	7.7	−0.72	4.2	−0.85	88	−0.51

a. Uses diagnosis or procedure to define mental health use (conservative definition). Expenses are per enrollee-year. Data from Wells et al. (1982), table 6.2. Predictions adjusted for site and other nonplan imbalances. Sample excludes South Carolina three-year group and years four and five of South Carolina five-year group.

b. Standard error = 1.3.

c. Standard error = 0.8.

d. Coefficient of variation = 0.21.

By contrast, predicted probabilities for the Individual Deductible plan are statistically indistinguishable from the probabilities for the free plan.

As with the results in Table 3.22, the effect of plan on total ambulatory mental health expenditures corresponds to the effect of plan on the probabilities of receiving any care. Participants with free care spend nearly three-quarters more than those on an insurance plan with a 95 percent coinsurance rate.

Tables 3.22 and 3.23 show a major reversal in spending between the 50/50 plan and the 95 percent plan, as well as a large drop between the 25/50 and 50/50 plans. We believe that this is an anomaly, one source of which is the confounding of plans with site. Almost all our 50/50 plan participants are in Dayton, a site that also happens to have a low propensity to use formal mental health care providers. Thus, Dayton participants have lower expenditures because they use relatively fewer services from formal providers, who charge more than nonformal providers. In contrast, most of our 25/50 participants are in the Seattle, Fitchburg, and Franklin County sites, which have a higher propensity to use formal providers. Unfortunately, the sample size is too small to test this hypothesis formally.[48]

Implications of Variation in Expenditure by Plan

The response of mental health use to cost sharing has three policy implications.

1. The overall response of the use of mental health services to the Experiment's cost-sharing plans is similar to that observed for ambulatory medical services; Table 3.24 compares ambulatory medical and outpatient mental health expenses.[49] However, as we shall see in the next chapter, the response to price (as opposed to plan) is not the same as for ambulatory medical services. This result provides a reason to cover mental health services less well[50] on the usual insurance principle of less coverage as demand response rises (see Chapter 4).

2. The absolute amount spent on ambulatory mental health care is small: even with very generous health insurance, ambulatory mental health services amount to only 4 percent of total personal health care expenses.[51] Most of these data, however, are from the late 1970s; more recent experience may well differ. Furthermore, use of services appeared to increase steadily through the Experiment; accounting for this increase yields values for steady-state demand in all plans about 30 to 40 percent greater than the values shown here, although the relative effect of plan is not altered (Wells, Keeler, and Manning 1990).

3. The results are not very informative about the effect of different coinsurance rates for mental health than for medical services. Some have argued that more cost sharing for mental health services may actually increase expenditure because participants are more likely to seek care from nonformal providers who do not treat them appropriately—the so-called offset hypothesis. In principle we can test this hypothesis by comparing results on the 25/50, 50/50, and 25/25 plans, but the results are inconclusive. Differences among these plans are not significantly different from zero, although the differences for some of these plan comparisons are large (see Wells et al. 1982, tables E.9–E.12). There are two reasons to suspect that the lack of significance of these results may be due to lack of precision in the Experiment's data. First, the sample size is small for these plans. Second, some of these plans are badly confounded with site. Therefore, it is

Table 3.24   Comparison of expenditure on ambulatory medical and mental health care per enrollee (standard errors in parentheses)[a]

Plan	Ambulatory medical care[b]		Ambulatory mental health care	
	Sample mean ($)	% of free plan	Mean expense ($)	% of free plan
Free care	488 (17)	100	42.20 (7)	100
25% medical/ 25% mental[c]	379 (28)	78	28.40 (7)	67
25% medical/ 50% mental[d]	362 (35)	74	32.20 (13)	76
50% medical/ 50% mental[d]	308 (24)	63	13.10 (8)	33
95%	282 (18)	58	18.10 (5)	43
Individual Deductible	353 (20)	72	47.70 (11)	113

a. Mental health services defined using diagnosis or procedure (conservative definition). Results from Manning et al. (1986b). The sample is the same as that in Table 3.22. The results for ambulatory medical care differ from those in Table 3.2 because the sample excludes the first year of experience in Dayton on the 95% and Individual Deductible plans. This maintains comparability with the mental health results; the first year of experience in Dayton is excluded on those plans because outpatient mental health services were not covered. Dollars are 1991 dollars.

b. Excludes all inpatient and dental expenses.

c. Medical coinsurance rate = 25%.

d. Ambulatory mental health coinsurance rate = 50%.

difficult to disentangle the effects of differential coinsurance rates for medical and psychotherapy services from differences among sites. In sum, the size of the confidence intervals makes it impossible to rule out a meaningful offset effect, but neither is there any support for it.

Effects of Other Covariates

Effects of income and socioeconomic status, health status, age, gender, and site on the use of mental health services are described and discussed in Wells et al. (1982). The following list summarizes some of those findings.

- The probability of choosing a formal provider, given any use of mental health services, increases with education,[52] and education has a dramatic effect on the level of the any-formal expense equation.
- Among the occupation variables, the only one that is statistically significant is that of being a professional or managerial worker, which increases use.
- We do not observe an effect of income on total expenditure when we compare predictions for the upper, middle, and lower thirds of the income distribution.
- We do not find a plan-income interaction; that is, response to plan is similar across income groups.[53]
- Not surprisingly, participants with poorer mental health status (as measured by the Mental Health Index) use more ambulatory mental health services than those with better mental health status (controlled for physical limitation, chronic disease, and the General Health Index). This is one test of the Index's validity; see also Chapter 6.
- We do not find a mental health status–plan interaction; that is, participants with varying mental health status respond similarly to plan.
- Physical and mental health have independent effects on the use of mental health services. With mental health status controlled for, those who are physically limited spend 50 to 100 percent more on mental health services than those who are not.
- Use of mental health services varies greatly with age and gender. This is true whether one adjusts for covariates, such as mental health status, or not. Adjusted for covariates, adult women use three times as many ambulatory mental health services as children and two-thirds again as many as adult men.
- Once we control for the other individual characteristics (such as age, gender, and health status), the sites do not differ significantly in the probability of use of mental health care despite marked differences in the psychiatrist/population ratio.[54]
- We found no transitory (short-term) surge in demand for mental health services.

Underfiling of Claims by Plan

The measures of use reported throughout this book are based on claims filed by participants. But actual use rather than claims filed determines the demand for health care facilities and training (although the claims filed are the relevant figure for an insurer). An implicit working assumption of our analysis above is that any difference in actual use and claims filed is small or related only slightly to plan.

This assumption appears plausible if one compares reported utilization in the various plans with average figures for the country at the time of the Experiment (Newhouse et al. 1981). Because coverage of hospital services was nearly complete and high in comparison with coverage of outpatient services, the admission rate in the nation at that time should lie below the rate in the free plan—at about the rate of the Individual Deductible plan—and above the other cost-sharing plans. In fact, in terms of national rates for 1977, it did. Similarly, the probability of visiting a physician and per-person visit rates lay at about the rates found in the 25 and 50 percent coinsurance plans, a result consistent with the partial coverage in the late 1970s of physician office visits. Finally, per-person expenditure among the noninstitutionalized under 65 lay at about the rate found in the 25 percent coinsurance plan, as it should. Hence there is no reason to suspect gross underreporting in the claims data.

The data also suggest that any plan-related bias from underfiling is small. Underfiling would be most likely to occur on the 95 percent coinsurance plans, because the incentive to file there is weakest. However, we found that the largest percentage reduction in use is between the free and 25 percent coinsurance plans. If that reduction is treated as real and not as an artifact of underfiling, the amount of further reduction in use from 25 percent to 95 percent coinsurance plans appears plausible.[55]

Because of the importance of the issue of underfiling, however, we attempted to verify actual utilization by collecting data from physician and hospital outpatient department billing records. Such data allowed us to estimate the rate of underfiling by plan and to determine the bias, if any, in our estimates of the response to plan.

The billing record survey covered 2,082 participants in the two Massachusetts and the two South Carolina sites. The survey covered each participant's utilization during the first two years on the Experiment. In principle, we could have sampled the records of each physician to look for utilization by each participant. But this approach would have yielded little information and placed an enormous burden on physicians, who would have been given hundreds of names, most of which would have no utilization. Therefore, we used a three-stratum sampling technique based on known utilization. "Mentioned pairs" designated a participant who had named the physician on a baseline survey or a claim in hand from that physician for that participant; "family-mentioned pairs" designated individuals in the same family as participants in mentioned pairs; "unmentioned pairs" designated all other physician-participant pairs. The three groups were sampled at different rates. All mentioned pairs were included; all family-mentioned pairs except those on intermediate (25 and 50 percent) coinsurance plans were included; unmentioned pairs were included at random such that each physician had a total of 150 names. Names were given to the provider in alphabetical order.

For each participant the provider was asked whether the person was a patient and, if the answer was yes, the dates and charges for services. The amount of any bad debt was also ascertained. Fifty-seven percent of providers responded.

Billing records were then matched to claims. Of the 9,361 visits reported in the billing record survey, 7 percent were unmatched, 56 percent were perfectly matched, 10 percent were matched but contained a date error, 20 percent were matched but contained a cost error, 6 percent were matched but contained a provider error, and 1 percent contained multiple errors. We restricted the analysis to visits with positive charges. We assumed that the likelihood of finding an actual visit in the billing records was independent of the likelihood that a claim was filed for it. (See Rogers and Newhouse 1985 for details of the matching rules.)

For each participant-provider pair we calculated five mean-dollar values:

a. Matched billing record and claim (including the matched part if one amount exceeded the other): $53.88.
b. Matched billing record and claim—amount by which claim exceeded record: $37.51.
c. Matched billing record and claim—amount by which billing record exceeded claim: $2.77.
d. Unmatched claims—amount of claim: $96.51.
e. Unmatched billing record—amount of record: $6.50.

The unmatched claims, category d, which have a large dollar value, come from the 43 percent of providers who did not respond to the questionnaire and from out-of-area providers. We therefore ignored this category. Because we were interested in underreporting of claims, we also ignored category b, excess claims.

The category of greatest interest was category e, visits found in the physician's billing records for which we could not find a claim. We further subdivided category e into three groups according to the sampling strata: unmatched mentioned-provider expenses, or category e_1 (which averaged $2.88 across all plans; Table 3.25, row 1); family-mentioned provider expenses, or category e_2 (which averaged $0.78 across all plans; Table 3.25, row 2); and unmentioned provider expenses, or category e_3 (which averaged $2.84 across all plans; Table 3.25, row 3). We then compared these unmatched billing records (category e) with matched records (category a); we also examined excess billing records (category c) by plan.

The results are shown in Table 3.25. In Massachusetts we found $3.96 ($8.38 − 4.42) more unreported expenditures per person on the low-incentive-to-file plans—the 95 percent and Individual Deductible plans—than on the high-incentive-to-file plans—the free, 25 percent, and 50 percent plans. In South Carolina we found $1.66 ($7.23 − 5.57) more. These figures are, respectively, 9 and 7 percent of the matched claims for the low-incentive-to-file plans in these sites. There was no evidence that excess billing records (category c) varied systematically by plan.

Because 9 and 7 percent are small relative to the observed differences in plan means, we conclude that differential underreporting existed, but on such a small scale that none of our conclusions would be changed if we had adjusted for it. For example, we reported earlier in this chapter that predicted expenditure on the 95 percent plan was 69 percent of expenditure on the free-care plan. If this figure were raised 9 percent, we would have concluded that the true use rate was 75 percent as large. None of the interpretations we make would be sensitive to this difference.[56]

The Unimportance of Instrumentation or Transitory Effects

Subexperiments

None of the subexperiments to study instrumentation effects showed a measurable effect on expenditure. Those individuals who took the entry physical examination averaged $58 less a year in medical expenses (in 1991 dollars) than those without the entry examination.[57] The difference is

Table 3.25 Average unmatched and matched billing records, in current dollars (standard errors in parentheses)[a]

	Massachusetts				South Carolina			
	Free	25% and 50%	95%	Individual Deductible	Free	25% and 50%	95%	Individual Deductible
Summary of results								
Mentioned (e_1)	2.44	2.38	3.27	3.43	1.50	3.31	2.97	4.49
Family (e_2)	0.96	0.00	1.13	1.06	1.09	0.00	0.69	1.22
Unmentioned (e_3)	0.98	2.13	5.43	3.39	2.07	3.94	3.17	1.85
Total	4.38	4.51	9.83	7.88	4.66	7.25	6.83	7.56
	(0.91)	(1.27)	(2.52)	(1.48)	(1.35)	(1.84)	(1.84)	(1.65)
Total, pooled by incentive	4.42			8.38	5.57			7.23
	(0.74)			(1.27)	(1.09)			(1.23)
Compared to free and intermediate		3.96[b]					1.66	
		(1.47)					(1.64)	
Disposition of claim[c]								
Matched (a)	73.91	62.20	42.18	46.70	50.85	22.66	27.32	18.58
Unmatched (d)	131.55	84.16	65.24	120.12	85.05	34.62	44.03	42.06
Excess (b)	51.59	44.50	33.80	40.59	22.58	6.86	5.36	4.30
Excess billing (c)	3.04	2.90	2.21	2.99	2.79	1.90	3.04	0.99

a. (a) through (d) and (e_1), (e_2), and (e_3) refer to definitions in text. Standard errors are computed assuming independence. Intrafamily correlation was unimportant in this data set.

b. Significant at the 1% level, z = 2.7. Pooling across sites gives $4.71 for the free and intermediate coinsurance plans, $7.78 for the catastrophic and Individual Deductible plans. A hypothesis test on the difference yields a z value of 2.8 (p < 0.01).

c. These claims cover the same reference period (27 months) as the billing records survey.

not significant ($t = -1.31$). If we limit the analysis to the first year after the examination, to allow the exam to act as a substitute for planned well care, we find positive but insignificant effects on expenditures and visits (all ts less than 0.50).[58] There were no significant interactions between the entry examination and insurance plan.[59]

Although we conducted this subexperiment as a test of our methods, this particular finding represents the effect of a randomized trial of a screening examination in a general population. Thus, we have no evidence that such an examination would save money over a three-to-five-year period by identifying conditions and treating them early.

Individuals who were initially assigned not to file health diaries (Health Reports) had expenditures $20 higher than those who filed weekly, but medical expenditures $8 lower than those who filed biweekly.[60] Nor could we could find significant differences in plan response among those who filed Health Reports never, weekly, or biweekly.[61]

The annual expenditures for the three- and five-year groups differed by an insignificant $5 per person per year (1991 dollars, $t = 0.11$).[62] We also found no significant differences in the plan response between the three- and five-year groups.[63]

The additional lump-sum payment in the next-to-last year of the Experiment (SPI), which was unanticipated by participants, did not have a significant or appreciable effect on utilization. This subexperiment was limited to the 95 percent and Individual Deductible plans. The increase in payments was one-quarter or one-third of the annual lump sum (PI), up to a maximum of $250. To estimate the effect of the additional payment, we subtracted the third-to-last year's utilization from the second-to-last (that is, year 1 from year 2 or year 3 from year 4). This approach is equivalent to using each person as his or her own control. We then compared the difference in expenditures for the groups with and without the extra lump-sum payment. The group with the extra payment had an average 0.20 more visits and 0.024 more admissions per person but $4.50 lower expenditures (1991 dollars) than the group without the payment; the t-statistics on these values are not significant (+0.71, +0.86, and −0.05, respectively).

The results of these subexperiments suggest that our data collection methods did not have an appreciable effect on our findings for medical utilization. The results of subexperiments on dental utilization tell a similar story.[64] (For details on dental utilization see Manning et al. 1986a.)

Transitory Effects

In general, transitory effects for medical services were weak; the three- and five-year groups did not differ measurably in their rates of expenditure. The story for dental use is different, however. Dental utilization on the lower coinsurance plans, especially on the free-care plan, was markedly higher in the first year than in subsequent years (Table 3.8). There was also an upward trend in the use of mental health services.

The final piece of evidence that transitory effects are unimportant for medical services comes from the analysis of episodes reported in Chapter 4. As described there, participants did not do much to anticipate changes in price; for example, spending after exceeding the MDE did not rise above the free plan rate, as it would have if participants had been trying to crowd in services before the end of the accounting year, at which time they would go back to cost sharing. The absence of transitory effects at the end of the Experiment is consistent with this lack of price change anticipation behavior within the Experiment's accounting year.

Summary

Varying the cost-sharing rate induced a substantial change in the use of health care services. Per-person expenditure on the 95 percent plan was about 69 percent of that on the free-care plan; adjustment for underfiling raises this figure to about 75 percent. Intermediate plans had smaller reductions. Thus, cost sharing markedly decreases use of all types of services among all types of people. Although cost sharing in the Experiment was reduced for the poor, decreases in expenditure were similar among the poor and the nonpoor. This similarity reflected a greater response of ambulatory use to cost sharing among the poor and a smaller response of inpatient use. Response to plan was also similar among the sites, despite markedly different medical care systems and waiting times to appointment.

We summarize the results pertaining to plan and price effects on the use of mental health services in the next chapter, in order to incorporate our analysis of mental health spending by episode.

Chapter 4

Episodes of Treatment

The results described in Chapter 3 simply related annual use per person to insurance plan. That analysis did not require or inform any economic theory. Insurance can be thought of as affecting price of health care, however, and this linkage makes it possible to exploit the economic theory that relates price to demand.

In the case of the insurance plans used in the Experiment, economic theory suggests that the natural unit of decision making is an episode of illness. At a minimum, it is more plausible that the consumer makes an initial decision to seek (or not seek) care with some expectation about the cost consequences of the entire episode rather than simply the cost of the initial visit. Perhaps more importantly, analysis of care by episode enables one to generalize more readily to types of insurance plans other than those used in the Experiment — for example, to plans that contain an initial deductible, followed by coinsurance, followed by a ceiling on out-of-pocket expenditures.

If the coinsurance rate were always the same regardless of total expenditure on care, the analysis in this chapter would not add to our knowledge, because using episodes as the unit of observation to estimate how demand responds to plan or price would yield the same results as using dollars per year. The only Experiment plan that keeps price constant as expenditure varies, however, is the free-care plan. Because of the Maximum Dollar Expenditure (MDE) — the cap on out-of-pocket expenditure in the plans with cost sharing — the coinsurance rate (the price facing the service user) does vary with total expenditure in all other plans (between the specified rate below the MDE and zero after the MDE is reached). It is, of course, no accident that the Experiment plans had a cap; an optimal insurance policy would almost certainly have a cap to prevent financial ruin to the insured (Arrow 1963, 1973, 1976). Thus, analyzing behavior in the presence of such caps is important.

To exploit the relevant economic theory, we need to define the price that faces the consumer as total expenditure varies. As is usual in economics, we assume a utility-maximizing consumer. Such a consumer will, when making choices, take into account the likelihood that the coinsurance rate will change as expenditure rises.

Consider a consumer on the Experiment plan with 50 percent coinsurance plan and a $1,000 MDE. In any year, this person will have free care after spending $2,000 on medical services. Suppose the person knows in advance that she will spend at least $2,000; then any additional care she decides to purchase today is, in effect, free. Alternatively, suppose the person knows that she will not spend as much as $2,000; then any additional care she decides to purchase today will cost 50 cents on the dollar because she will not anticipate free care later in the year.

This example suggests a simple rule: the price a utility-maximizing consumer on an experimental plan will use to determine whether a visit (say) was worth its cost is the presenting price of the visit (say $20) minus the product of the probability of exceeding the MDE and the presenting price of the visit. Thus, if there is a 25 percent chance of exceeding the MDE, the effective price (to the consumer) of a $20 office visit is $15 ($20 − $5).[1]

More specifically, using episodes as the unit of observation when the insurance plan has a ceiling has two advantages: (1) it allows us to model the effect of anticipating that any deductible (or upper limit) will be exceeded later in the year; and (2) it allows us to model the effect of any "sale" once the deductible or MDE is exceeded. This sale comes about because the price of medical services is zero for the remainder of the current accounting period (in this case a year) but reverts to a positive level at the beginning of the next accounting period. This ratchet down, then up, provides an incentive to move the consumption of services into the present accounting period and to consume at a rate exceeding that of the free-care plan; we term this a sale effect.

In this chapter we sketch the methods and results of the analysis by episode. (Further details are available in Keeler et al. 1982, 1988; Keeler, Wells, and Manning 1986.)

Since medical and dental episodes and mental health episodes turned out to have different characteristics, we analyze them separately.

Major Findings of the Medical and Dental Episode Analysis

Our analyses of medical and dental episodes produced four major results:

1. Both coinsurance and deductibles have strong effects on use. Taking variation in coinsurance first, we estimate that with no cap on out-of-pocket spending, those with 100 percent coinsurance (that is, no insurance) would spend about half as much as those with free care, those with 50 percent coinsurance would spend about 63 percent as much as those with free care, and those with 25 percent coinsurance would spend about 71 percent as much.[2] Variation in the size of a deductible has effects that are almost as large. For full coverage after an individual deductible, those with a $100 deductible would spend 81 percent as much as those with free care, those with a $500 deductible 73 percent as much, and those with a $1,000 deductible 61 percent as much.[3]

2. Coinsurance reduces the cost per episode slightly, especially on the Family Deductible plan, but its main effect is on the number of episodes.

3. Different episode types represent different decisions. Price has similar effects on all types, but other covariates have quite different effects on different episodes. Acute, chronic, and hospital episodes are strongly related to health status at enrollment, whereas dental and well-care episodes are more closely related to income and education. Acute episodes are less affected than the other types by price changes within the year—presumably people have less ability to defer treatment of acute illnesses to times when the MDE is exceeded. Although plan had more effect on outpatient expenditures than on hospital expenditures, the main reason for this is that people going into a hospital are more likely to have already exceeded their MDE than people starting an outpatient episode.

4. Before we analyzed the data, we thought people might time their medical care purchases to take advantage of the years in which they exceeded the deductible and care was free. However, the rates of spending on the cost-sharing plans remained below the free plan rates for outpatient and dental episodes in the period after the MDE was exceeded. The rates did rise after the MDE was exceeded and for well care approached the free plan rate, but there were no sales sprees that wiped out the pre-MDE reductions in use.

We also thought that people with a small amount of remaining MDE might anticipate having free care later in the year and increase their rate of spending. Except for hospital episodes, however, we could detect no anticipation effects on starting episodes. In particular, for nonhospital episodes there was no difference in spending rates between those with a little and those with a great deal of MDE remaining. For hospital episodes, we saw more spending by those with just a little MDE remaining, but people might well have decided to have these expensive treatments because the out-of-pocket price was low relative to the total price, without thinking about future spending on other episodes. The exact value of the remaining MDE that distinguishes low priced hospital episodes is arbitrary, but this effect is real. The myopic behavior of participants in the Experiment may be another instance of bounded rationality—people may not have the energy to think about their future insurance status, or experience in taking advantage of these temporary changes in price. In any event, such behavior serves to amplify the effect of deductibles on demand.

Major Findings of the Mental Health Services Analysis

Our analyses of mental health services produced five major findings:

1. Use of outpatient mental health care is responsive to cost sharing or to the price paid out-of-pocket by the patient. Moving from a world with no insurance to one with full insurance (free care) approximately quadruples expenses for mental health care.

2. The pure price response (the response to a coinsurance without a cap) for outpatient mental health care is twice as large as that for outpatient medical care over the 25–95 percent range of coinsurance rates. However, over the lower range, 0–25 percent, the two services have the same response to price, assuming a cap at least as large as that used in the Experiment.

3. Even with generous insurance coverage, relatively little was spent on outpatient mental health care at the time the Experiment was conducted. With free care, average annual expenditure per enrollee was only about $42 (1991 dollars), which for the nonelderly in our sample is 9 percent of outpatient medical care spending and 4 percent of all medical care spending.

4. Even with free care, relatively few people use outpatient mental health care. We found that only 4.3 percent used any care from a formal provider in a year, and only 14 percent had any use in five years on the Experimental free plan. Those who did use such care commonly used it over several years. It is possible that the proportion of users today would be higher.

5. Small or modest deductibles have little or no effect on the use of outpatient mental health care.

Defining Episodes of Treatment

To analyze episodes of treatment we developed a system to group the different claims, or Medical Expense Reports (MERs), according to type of episode, which we then dated. The four types of MERs reflect the four broad types of services for which subjects can make a claim: (1) hospital, (2) physician and supplies, (3) pharmacy, and (4) dental. A physician MER is shown in Figure 4.1. As exemplified there, each MER may contain charges, called line charges, for several different services. Providers are asked to date, describe, and link each line charge to a diagnosis and treatment history. These linked line charges are the basic building blocks of the episodes.

Linking

Line charges are linked according to the probable units of decision—that is, treatment of a medical or dental problem—rather than by location or type of services provided. The first action in an episode of spending is taken by the patient, although physicians can encourage that action in previous contacts or over the phone. The subsequent cost of the episode is a result of decisions the physician makes (for example, whether to prescribe a drug), as well as by decisions the patient makes (for example, whether to fill a prescription). Both physician and patient operate under some uncertainty about the ultimate cost of the episode (for example, neither knows before an operation what complications may occur).

Our method groups all charges that reflect decisions about the same medical problem. For example, all expenses surrounding a hospital episode—office visits leading to an admission, and visits and drugs following the admission—are considered to be part of one hospital episode. Similarly, restorations following a dental exam are included with the exam in one episode of spending. Thus our method assumes in effect that at the initial visit, the participant is told of the need for additional care, and the approximate total cost of the episode is negotiated. This assumption may not hold in each case, but it seems to be the most reasonable in the absence of information about how much the physician told the patient or how much the physician knew about the course of the episode at its beginning. This information, of course, is not on the claims records.[4]

The program code for the grouping process is long and complex because of the great variety of types of charges and claims, and because of the complex rules necessary to decide whether or not a new charge is related to some set of previous charges.[5] The grouping is based primarily on the time since the last charge for a given diagnosis, and on how the physician completed the Treatment History Code on the MER. The Treat-

FAMILY HEALTH PROTECTION PLAN

PHYSICIANS, DOCTORS, SUPPLIERS AND OUTPATIENT MEDICAL EXPENSE REPORT

(Use this form for *all* outpatient charges: clinics, surgery, emergency, etc.)

MAIL TO: FAMILY HEALTH PROTECTION PLAN, P.O. BOX 2076, Oakland, CA, 94604

PART 1 PARTICIPANT TO FILL IN ITEMS 1 THROUGH 14 PLEASE PRINT OR TYPE

1 Last Name of Patient	First		M.I.	2. Age	3. Patient's Family No.

4. Patient's Address	City, State, Zip Code		5. Patient's Individual No.

6. What Was The Major Reason or Symptom For This Visit To The Doctor?	8. Was Illness or Injury Employment Related? YES ☐ No ☐	9. Was Illness or Injury Accident Related? YES ☐ NO ☐	10. Date of Injury or Accident / /	11. Describe how and where accident occurred:

7. Date You First Noticed This Symptom (For Illness or Accident):	12. Name of Doctor, Supplier or Outpatient Facility	13. Has the Patient Ever Visited This Doctor, Supplier or Outpatient Facility Before? YES ☐ NO ☐

14 I authorize any holder of medical or other information about the patient to release to the Family Health Protection Plan or its intermediaries any information needed for this or related medical reports. I permit a copy of this authorization to be used in place of the original. In conformance with the Family Health Protection Plan Enrollment Agreement, all health care benefits covering the Patient are hereby assigned to the Family Health Protection Plan.

SIGN HERE ▶ | Signature of Adult Participant or Guardian of Minor Participant | Print Adult's Name | Date Signed

PART 2 DOCTOR OR SUPPLIER TO FILL IN ITEMS 15 THROUGH 29 PLEASE PRINT OR TYPE

15. Full Name of Referring Doctor. If None, Write None. | 16. Full name(s) of Providers to Whom You Referred Patient for Consultation, Lab Tests, or Other Services. If None, Write None.

17. Describe the Primary Problem or Diagnosis Which Brought the Patient To Your Office and Any Other Problem(s) for Which You Supplied Treatment Please List Primary Problem or Diagnosis on Line A.	18. Type of Problem (check one)	19. Treatment History (omit if well care or pregnancy)
A.	☐ Acute ☐ Well Care (or pregnancy)	☐ Flare-up of Chronic ☐ Chronic (not flare-up)	☐ Initial Visit for this episode ☐ Repeat Visit for this episode
B.	☐ Acute ☐ Well Care (or pregnancy)	☐ Flare-up of Chronic ☐ Chronic (not flare-up)	☐ Initial Visit for this episode ☐ Repeat Visit for this episode
C.	☐ Acute ☐ Well Care (or pregnancy)	☐ Flare-up of Chronic ☐ Chronic (not flare-up)	☐ Initial Visit for this episode ☐ Repeat Visit for this episode
D.	☐ Acute ☐ Well Care (or pregnancy)	☐ Flare-up of Chronic ☐ Chronic (not flare-up)	☐ Initial Visit for this episode ☐ Repeat Visit for this episode

KEY **Place of Service Codes:** O = Doctor's Office; IL = Independent Laboratory; H = Patient's Home; IH = Inpatient Hospital; NH = Nursing Home or SNF; OH = Outpatient Hospital, including Hospital Clinic, Emergency, Outpatient Surgery; SC = School Clinic; CC = Company Clinic; OL = Other Location, Including Other Non-Hospital Clinic. **Type of Visit Codes:** 1 = Minimal Service; 2 = Brief Examination; 3 = Limited Examination; 4 = Intermediate Examination; 5 = Extended Examination; 6 = Comprehensive Examination; 7 = Unusually Complex Examination. **SEE DETAILED INSTRUCTIONS ON REVERSE SIDE.** For Inpatient Services, Omit 18, 19, and 21.

20	A. Date Of Service	B. Place of Service Use code above	C. Describe Each Medical or Surgical Procedure and Other Service or Supplies Furnished For Each Date, Including Specific Lab Tests and the Specific Name of Any Drug Injected	D. Type of Office Visit Use code above	E. Relate Treatment to Problem by Ref. to 17 A, B, C or D above	F. Charge	21. Were Any Drugs Prescribed? Were any Supplies Prescribed or Suggested? ☐ Yes ☐ No	
							A. If yes, specify drug(s) and/or supply(ies):	B. Relate to Problem by Reference to 17 A, B, C or D above
1								
2								
3								
4								
5								

22. Name and Address of Doctor or Supplier	23. Social Security or Provider Tax ID Number Telephone Number	24. TOTAL CHARGE
		25. AMOUNT PAID, IF ANY
		26. BALANCE DUE

27. I hereby certify that the services and/or supplies listed above have been provided on the date(s) shown. | Date Signed

PROVIDER'S SIGNATURE ▶

28. I hereby authorize payment directly to the above-named provider of the benefits otherwise payable to me but not to exceed the charges shown. I understand that I am financially responsible for any charges not covered by the Family Health Protection Plan. | Date Signed

PARTICIPANT'S SIGNATURE ▶

HIEI #961 REV. 9-76   **MAIL TO FHPP**   127

Figure 4.1   Physicians, doctors, suppliers, and outpatient medical expense report

ment History Code classifies diagnoses listed on the claim as acute (initial or repeat), chronic (routine or flare-up), well care, or unobtainable (see item 19 in Figure 4.1). These codes are normally filled in by the billing physician's staff, but in some cases they were filled in or corrected by staff at Glen Slaughter and Associates, the health and welfare plan administrator that processed the claims, according to guidelines supplied by project physicians. (Details of the algorithms and methods used to process the claims are given in Keesey, Keeler, and Fowler 1985.)

It may seem that to analyze spending by line charge instead of by episode would greatly increase the sample size; the mean number of line charges per episode is around seven (although the median number is fewer than two). The gain, however, is illusory because of the close connection between charges in the same episode. Treatment is often a package. Operations are often explicitly sold as a package, but even medical treatment of minor acute problems may involve a drug purchase and a followup visit. The high correlation among charges for services (for example, drug charges are much more likely in the days following an office visit than at other times) within an episode complicates analysis by line charge and results in little more precision than use of the smaller number of episodes. (Some hospitalization episodes have hundreds of line charges, and these charges reflect behavior that is very far from a series of independent decisions.) Grouping spending into episodes also avoids some arbitrariness in how followup charges, tests, drugs, and supplies are priced, because aggregating over the episode tends to cancel out cross-subsidies among different types of services connected to the episode.

Dating

We know from their responses to a questionnaire that most participants and their physicians understood the terms of their Experiment insurance policies (see M. S. Marquis 1983). Most patients knew their share of expenses, as well as which medical services were covered. Because each plan had a limit on out-of-pocket spending, the theoretically appropriate price sketched at the beginning of this chapter depended on the amount of medical services already purchased (except for participants on the full coverage or free plan) because that affected the amount of MDE remaining and hence the probability of exceeding the MDE. To ensure that they had information on the MDE remaining, with each claim processed the participants were informed by Glen Slaughter and Associates of that amount.

The fully maximizing economic person, however, does not change his or her other decisions on medical spending on the date of receiving a bill from the provider, but rather on the date he or she decided to incur the expense. Suppose a woman learns she is pregnant and will deliver before the end of the accounting year. Suppose the hospital bill alone at that time will exceed her remaining MDE. She may not wait until delivery to get her new glasses, and she may go more readily to the doctor for minor acute conditions. Because she knows the MDE eventually will be exceeded, she can act as if it already has been because she faces an effective price of zero for additional services.

Thus, for the episode analysis we try to date each charge to the earliest time the participant would have committed himself or herself to paying it. Some spending for chronic conditions such as diabetes or hypertension is presumably anticipated from the first day of the accounting year; routine spending for such episodes are dated to that time. (Flare-ups of chronic conditions are treated differently; see below.) Routine pregnancy costs are dated to the first prenatal visit. Drugs and followup visits for acute conditions are dated to the first office visit for that condition.[6] Dental work is dated to the first in a series of procedures or the immediately preceding examination. We distinguish elective surgery and well care from acute care by the criterion of deferrability, calling the episode acute if the procedure loses most of its value if deferred.

Classifying

Decisions to obtain a routine physical examination are likely to be different from decisions to obtain treatment for a specific condition, such as a broken leg or arthritis. Aggregating decisions that are likely to be affected differently by price and by other covariates such as age could lead to poor predictions if the mix of episodes within category changed, as well as to difficulties of interpretation. Therefore, to understand further the effects of price on health care behavior, we analyzed various types of episodes separately.

Another reason for distinguishing among episode types is that different types might be subject to different coinsurance rates in any health insurance plan. First, there is the standard economic result that more price-responsive categories should be subsidized at a lower rate (Ramsey 1927; Baumol and

Bradford 1970; Zeckhauser 1970; Besley 1988). Second, society may want to subsidize expenditures such as preventive care for small children at higher rates. Finally, to reduce the insured's exposure to risk, it is sensible to insure rare catastrophes more fully than common smaller expenses.

Using these considerations as general guidance about how to classify episodes, we created five types of episodes. (1) All episodes with a hospital stay are classified as hospital episodes. (2) All episodes with a dental procedure are classified as dental episodes. Outpatient episodes are classified as (3) acute, including flare-up of chronic conditions, (4) routine chronic, or (5) well care.

Acute episodes are defined by unforeseen and undeferrable treatment opportunities. From an economic point of view, spending on these episodes will occur only when the patient is temporarily sick.

Chronic episodes comprise foreseen and continuing expenses. Treatment for most chronic diseases is designed to ameliorate the consequences rather than to cure, and people under treatment for such conditions should be able to budget their routine expenditures from the start of the year. Thus we consider all the routine care for each chronic condition within the year as one episode. Some conditions pose a reasonably high chance of complications during the year. That is, someone with a certain chronic condition may expect such a flare-up during the year, just as the owner of a decrepit car knows that sometime during the year a mechanic's services may well be necessary. However, because they probably do not have a good idea of when or how many flare-ups there will be, we assume that these flare-ups are unforeseen and treat them as we do acute spending. Flare-ups are clearly economically different from the drugs and checkup routines normal for those with chronic diseases such as hypertension or diabetes.

Finally, well-care episodes deal with conditions that are deferrable for weeks or even months without great loss. It may seem inappropriate to call this category elective, because it implies a contrast with necessity, and care for minor acute conditions such as colds may be more elective in a true sense than such well-care procedures as immunizations. Indeed, many well-care procedures—such as examinations, immunizations for school, and Pap smears for birth control pills—may be medically deferrable though legally or socially required. But the important distinction economically is not their ultimate necessity but their deferrability in contrast to acute episodes.

Sample and Variables

The Sample

The analysis is based on the three years of experience in each site during which both the three- and five-year enrollees participated.[7] Otherwise the sample is similar to that used for the analysis of annual expenditure in Chapter 3. It includes enrollees who participated for a full year in any of the years, plus those who died or were born during the three-year period. Excluded are the partial years of other individuals. As before, a person who left in year 2 was included in year 1 if she participated for all of year 1, and the hospital expenditures on newborns were allocated entirely to the mother. The exclusions constitute about 5 percent of the total sample. Table 4.1 summarizes the estimation sample by plan.

Dependent Variables

We analyze variation in the number of episodes (for the five episode types) per person-year, and the cost per episode of each type.

Explanatory Variables

Experiment insurance plans are grouped into the same five groups used for the annual expenditure analysis in Chapter 3: the free-care plan; a family medical coinsurance rate of 25 percent; a family medical coinsurance rate of 50 percent;[8] a family medical coinsurance rate of 95 percent (the Family Deductible plan); and the Individual Deductible plan of 95 percent coinsurance up to $150 per person or $450 per family for outpatient care.

Table 4.1   Estimation sample for medical and dental episodes of care

Plan	Person-years
Free	5,768
25%	3,018
50%	1,475
95%	3,130
Individual Deductible	3,650
Total	17,041

An indicator or dummy variable is specified for four of the groups; thus, no functional form is imposed.

We controlled for three other randomized Experiment treatment variables, namely: whether a household was one of the 60 percent given a pre-enrollment screening examination; whether the family was assigned to weekly rather than biweekly Health Reports in the first year in Dayton; and whether the family was enrolled for three rather than five years.

The remaining variables are also similar to those used to analyze annual spending. These include pre-Experiment income, education of head of household, family size, pre-Experiment physician visit rates, race, age, gender, self-reported health, pain, and worry about health and four other measures of health status: (1) the General Health Index, (2) a dichotomous (yes-or-no) measure of physical or role limitation, (3) a count of the number of 26 possible diseases or health problems, and (4) the Mental Health Index. These health status variables are described further in Chapter 6. Pre-enrollment interviews provided data on all these characteristics.

Cost and Annual Frequency of Episodes

Episode cost and frequency together determine annual medical spending. That is,

$$(4.1) \text{ Annual spending} = \sum_i (\text{number of episodes})_i \times (\text{cost per episode})_i,$$

where

$$i = \text{acute, chronic, well, hospital, dental.}$$

We now describe how the cost and the annual frequency of episodes vary by episode type, by insurance plan, and by individual characteristics. Using Eq. (4.1), we can then compare the predictions of annual medical spending deduced from the episode approach with the annual spending predictions obtained in Chapter 3. This comparison serves as a check on the validity of both methods.

We deal first with the cost per episode and tabulate variation in cost by episode type. Next we model an individual's cost per episode as a multiplicative function of his or her attributes. We then analyze the number of episodes per year and, in particular, how numbers vary with episode type, insurance plan, and participant characteristics.

This analysis parallels our approach to estimating annual spending but uses episodes rather than dollars as the dependent variable. Most of our results are based on a negative binomial regression model of episode counts.[9] This model has the advantage of accounting for the greater variation in individual propensities to have episodes than participants' measured variables predict. It also is compatible with two observed characteristics of the distribution, namely, skewedness and a large number of zeros. The measured variables that most affect episode rates are self-assessed health, age, gender, and physician visits in the year preceding the Experiment. Income, plan, and having a regular physician are also important, but less so.

We finally take up the issue of how individuals' behavior varies within the year, describing the effects of within-year price changes, caused by a participant's expenses reaching the MDE before the end of the year, on medical spending.

Cost of Episodes

Descriptive statistics on cost. The distribution of episode cost varies with type of episode. No one family of distributions fits the cost of all five episode types well, but the lognormal distribution is a good approximation for all but dental episodes.

Table 4.2 gives descriptive statistics on the distribution of cost per episode for the five episode types. The table shows statistics from year 2 for acute episodes, from years 2 and 3 for dental, well-care, and chronic episodes, and from all three years for hospital episodes. In the original analysis the medical care Consumer Price Index (CPI) was used to inflate costs from the date incurred (between 1975 and 1981) to 1986 medical dollars. For this book we brought these 1986 dollars forward to 1991 using the overall CPI.

The five episode types differ considerably, both in frequency and in cost per episode. Not surprisingly, hospitalizations are the most costly, averaging $4,770, with the median episode costing $3,030. Other episode types are much smaller, with acute and well-care episodes being the least expensive on average. A comparison of means and medians, as well as an examination of the quantiles, reveals that all five episode types have distributions that are skewed to the right and quite peaked. The bottom four rows of Table 4.2 give the fitted lognormal distribution parameters for the five episode types. The skewedness and kurtosis (peakedness) of the distributions indicate that the distribution of episode costs is roughly lognormal with the exception of dental episodes. The positive skew indicates that there are slightly more very expensive episodes than there would be if the distribution were truly lognormal. These very expensive episodes have little impact on inferences about the effect of covariates, but, especially in the case of hospital episodes, they have a large impact on predicted expenses.[10]

Table 4.2   Summary of the distribution of cost per episode, by type of episode (rounded 1991 $)[a]

			Outpatient		
Item	Hospital	Dental[b]	Acute	Chronic	Care
Number of episodes[c]	1,969	12,267	10,379	6,577	6,870
Quantiles					
100% (maximum)	$201,000	$18,970	$4,990	$7,040	$3,680
90	8,100	639	260	525	249
75	5,150	179	124	217	156
50 (median)	3,030	76	59	81	65
25	1,950	46	31	34	41
10	1,190	32	15	16	28
0 (minimum)	270[c]	5	2	1	2
Moments					
Mean	4,770	298	119	244	119
Standard deviation	20,110	780	206	644	158
Skewedness[d]	12	8	7	12	7
Kurtosis[d]	236	90	73	257	96
Lognormal parameters[e]					
Mean	7.85	4.45	3.91	4.27	4.11
Standard deviation	0.8	1.2	1.1	1.3	0.9
Skewedness[d]	0.2	1.1	0.3	0.3	0.1
Kurtosis[d]	1.4	1.0	0.2	−0.0	0.2

a. Original dollars brought forward to September 1986 using the medical care CPI and then brought forward to 1991 using the overall CPI. This accounts for the discrepancy with the $194,000 figure given for the largest hospitalization in Chapter 3.

b. Excludes data from year 1 in Dayton because dental care for adults was not covered there except on free plan.

c. Hospital statistics are based on all three years of data, acute on year 2 only, and the others on years 2 and 3. Hospital spending is truncated on the left at $270.

d. The skewedness and kurtosis are based on the third and fourth moments of the empirical distribution. They can be regarded as measures of how nonnormal the distribution is. Values of zero correspond to normality. See Kendall and Stuart (1961), vol. 1, chap. 3, for details. Based on September 1986 medical dollars.

e. Based on September 1986 dollars, rounded.

Table 4.3   Mean episode costs by type and plan (1991 $)

Insurance plan	Hospital	Total medical outpatient	Acute	Chronic	Well care	Dental[a]
Free	4,532	153	119	235	122	320
Cost sharing	4,878	153	117	250	112	280
t-test on difference	−1.1	0.1	1.1	−0.9	2.6	2.7

a. Excludes data from first year in Dayton because adults on cost-sharing plans there were not covered for dental services.

Plan differences controlling for other factors. We turn now to analyzing how episode cost varied with insurance plan—one of our primary goals. For each of the five episode types, we looked at whether the cost per episode is the same across the five insurance plans.

Table 4.3 presents the mean cost for each type of episode for the free plan and for the cost-sharing plans. The rare large expenditures make these means somewhat noisy; still, well-care and dental episodes are about 10 percent larger with free care, and the differences are statistically significant at conventional levels.

Although the participants assigned to each insurance plan are approximately balanced with respect to their relevant measured characteristics, the people with episodes may not be balanced by plan because of varying rates of initiating episodes. For this and three other reasons we carried out a more detailed analysis by including covariates. Those additional reasons are: (1) We use these models below to simulate streams of medical episodes. It is important to include any systematic variation in cost per episode in the simulation model. (2) The simulation model can be used to estimate a particular group's portion of the total costs of health care if covariates are included. Such a capability is helpful in estimating health insurance premiums in other contexts. (3) Controlling on an individual basis for the effect of covariates leads to more precise estimates of the plan effects, if any, on cost per episode.

Given the approximate lognormality of the distribution of episode costs, our primary tools for modeling the effects of participant attributes are regression models that estimate the logarithm of cost. Table 4.4 gives the means and standard deviations of the covariates. Table 4gives results of our regression analysis.

Table 4.4   Covariates used in regression

Name of variable	Mean[a]	Standard deviation	Comments
Dayton	0.20	(0.4)	
Fitchburg	0.12	(0.4)	Variable = 1 for people that site, 0
Franklin	0.16	(0.4)	otherwise (Seattle is omitted site)
Charleston	0.13	(0.3)	
Georgetown	0.18	(0.4)	
Free	0.33	(0.4)	The omitted insurance plan; full coverage
Ind. Ded.	0.22	(0.4)	$150 Individual Deductible plan
P25	0.20	(0.4)	25% coinsurance for medical service plan
P50	0.07	(0.2)	50% coinsurance for medical service plan
P95	0.19	(0.4)	95% coinsurance (Family Deductible plan)
PD25	0.11	(0.3)	25% coinsurance for dental
PD50	0.15	(0.4)	50% coinsurance for dental
Age 0–2	0.03	(0.2)	Age categories are based on age at end of
3–5	0.06	(0.2)	study
6–17	0.27	(0.4)	
Woman, age 18–40	0.22	(0.4)	Woman, age 18–40
Woman 41–65	0.12	(0.3)	Woman, age 41–65
Man 46–55	0.04	(0.2)	Man, age 46–55
Man 56–65	0.03	(0.2)	Man, age 56–65
Health	4.0	(2.4)	Health–pain–worry; three enrollment scales added so that best health is 7, worst health is –2
Ghindx	73	(14.0)	General Health Index, scored so 100 is best, 0 worst
Mhi	77	(12.0)	Mental Health Index, scored so 100 is best, 0 worst
Disease	11.2	(7)	Count of number of diseases reported
Physlm	0.13	(0.3)	Set to 1 if physically limited, 0 if not limited
Log (M.D. visits)	1.2	(1.0)	The logarithm of M.D. visits in year preceding Experiment (set at 0 if there were no visits)
Linc	8.8	(0.8)	Log income in year preceding Experiment
Lfam	1.2	(0.5)	Log family size at start of Experiment
Exam	0.58	(0.5)	1 if took exam at start of Experiment, 0 otherwise
Educ	12	(3)	Years of education of self for adults or female adult in household for children
Black	0.09	(0.3)	1 if head of family is black, 0 otherwise
Socioeconomic status (SES)	0.00	(1.1)	Linc + 0.2 Educ – 0.5 Lfam – 10.51
Sick	0.00	(0.1)	–0.004 Ghindx + 0.16 Physlm + 0.008 Disease + 0.027
Coin*SES	0.01	(0.73)	(on family coinsurance plans) × SES
PidS*ES	0.00	(0.52)	(on ID plan) × SES
Kid*Pay	0.24	(0.43)	(Age ≤ 17) × (1 – free)
Sick*Pay	0.00	(0.10)	Sick × (1 – free)

a. Values in year 1 of 5,904 individuals who were in sample at least six months.

Because of the intrafamily correlation among residuals of log costs for some episode types, we employed the same generalized regression method (similar to the random-effects model) used in Chapter 3 to correct the inference statistics.

The first column of figures in Table 4.5 gives the selected coefficients from the fitted regression equation for the logarithm of the cost of hospital episodes. In all these regressions the omitted category against which comparisons are made is Seattle, white, no screening exam, free plan, and male 18–45 years old. The squared multiple correlation (R^2) for the cost of hospital episodes is 0.11, so most of the variance remains unexplained. Plan effects are scattered, with the median cost of hospital episodes in the 95 percent coinsurance plan 12 percent smaller than that of the free plan: [exp(−.13) = .88]. However, the raw mean of a lognormal variable depends on the standard deviation of the logarithm as well as on the mean of the logarithm. The standard deviation is larger in the 95 percent plan, and in the cost-sharing plans generally, than in the free plan; this result narrows the difference in the raw means.[11] We conclude that plan effects on the cost per hospitalization are small to nonexistent.

Cost sharing does seem to affect the cost of other types of episodes, causing slight reductions in most types. The reductions are greater for the 50 and 95 percent coinsurance plans than for the 25 percent plan, about 6 percent less for both medical outpatient and dental episodes and close to significant at the 5 percent level. Although only a small fraction of the variance is explained by the other variables, there are large differences by site and age, with plan controlled for, with Seattle being more expensive, especially for episodes other than hospital, and with children and healthier people having cheaper episodes. For dental episodes, being black or of lower socioeconomic status, with plan controlled for, leads to much more expensive episodes; these groups have significantly fewer episodes, however, so total expenditure differs for these groups much less than do episode costs. Intrafamily correlations for all episode types are positive but small. Even these small correlations have an impact on the significance tests, however, because families have many episodes of the same type. For example, for medical outpatient episodes, uncorrected t-statistics on insurance plan are 50 percent larger than those corrected for these correlations.

Refinements. In the fitted regression models reported in Table 4.5, some dependencies in the data were assumed away. Episode cost and annual episode frequency may be related, for example, perhaps because those with large episodes are more likely to exceed the MDE. Because this effect

Table 4.5 Selected coefficients from regression equations for predicting log episode cost, rounded[a]

Variable	Hospital	All medical outpatient[b]	Acute	Chronic	Well	Dental[c]
Intercept	7.953	4.436	4.503	4.436	4.741	5.503
Dayton	0.13[d]	-0.16[e]	-0.21[e]	-0.11	-0.23[e]	-0.42[e]
Fitchburg	0.12	-0.24[e]	-0.26[e]	-0.12	-0.34[e]	-0.47[e]
Franklin	-0.00	-0.26[e]	-0.26[e]	-0.19	-0.35[e]	-0.62[e]
Charleston	0.20[d]	-0.11[d]	-0.18[e]	-0.10	-0.06	-0.20[d]
Georgetown	-0.18[d]	-0.16[e]	-0.17[e]	0.01	0.15[e]	-0.41[e]
Health	-0.023[d]	-0.02[d]	-0.018[d]	-0.032[d]	-0.017[d]	-0.029[e]
Socioeconomic status	0.03	-0.01	-0.04[d]	0.05	0.00	-0.13[e]
Log(M.D. visits)	-0.03	0.01	0.00	0.09[d]	-0.03	-0.03
Exam	-0.10[d]	-0.01	-0.01	0.03	0.01	0.04
Black	0.14[d]	0.03	0.01	-0.16	0.00	0.52[e]
P25	0.07	-0.03	-0.05	-0.07	-0.01	0.05
P50	0.02	-0.06	-0.14[d]	-0.13	-0.02	-0.05
P95	-0.13[d]	-0.06	-0.03	-0.10	-0.11[d]	-0.08
Individual Deductible	-0.03	0.01	-0.03	0.02	0.03	-0.03

Age 0–2	−0.63[e]	−0.68[e]	−0.55[e]	−0.75[e]	−0.89	−1.76[e]
Age 3–5	−0.64[e]	−0.59[e]	−0.51[e]	−0.46[d]	−0.88[e]	−0.79[e]
Age 6–17	−0.30[e]	−0.42[e]	−0.39[e]	−0.40[e]	−0.53[e]	−0.60[e]
Woman, age 18–65[f]	0.11	−0.14[e]	−0.15[e]	−0.23[d]	−0.07	−0.08[d]
Man, age 46–65[f]	0.26[d]	0.02	−0.08	−0.00	0.21[e]	0.01
R^2	0.11	0.04	0.04	0.03	0.18	0.12
Sample size[g]	1,967	17,012	10,359	6,576	6,852	12,267
Intrafamily correlation	0.02	0.06	0.07	0.11	0.07	0.14

a. Estimated using September 1986 medical dollars. If we had brought these forward to 1991 using the overall CPI, the intercepts would be 0.208 larger. For the full regression see Keeler et al. (1988), table 3.5.

b. Sum of acute, chronic, and well episodes in the second year of the Experiment. Differs from sum of acute, chronic, and well columns by amount of chronic and well episodes in year 3.

c. Omitting data from the first year in Dayton.

d. $t > 1.96$, $p < 0.05$

e. $t > 3.29$, $p < 0.001$.

f. Age groups have been collapsed from those shown in Table 4.4; the coefficients of the more disaggregated age groups were similar.

g. The sample sizes differ slightly from those in Table 4.2 because we deleted cases with missing data for covariates.

would not occur without an MDE, we do not use episode frequency to predict episode cost here. Also, cost per episode may be affected by whether people have exceeded their MDE. If the cost per episode after exceeding the MDE resembles cost per episode on the free plan, then the differences shown here understate the impact of a pure coinsurance rate (one with no MDE) on episode size. We used a rough correction for this effect in the simulation model, with details shown in Keeler et al. (1988, app. F). Because three-fourths of the episodes occur in the pre-MDE period, it is unlikely that this MDE effect is large, and the statistical problems involved in estimating the logarithm of costs controlling for MDE effects are great. (Later in the chapter we describe a model of MDE effect on episode frequency.)

Conclusions about episode costs. So far, we have estimated plan effects on the cost of an episode controlling for other factors by fitting regression equations to the logarithm of episode cost using dummy variables for insurance plan, and using other independent variables to capture participant characteristics. From these regressions, we conclude that cost sharing reduces spending per nonhospital episode by 5 to 8 percent. Because large hospital episodes do not seem to be affected by cost sharing, price effects on the costs of hospital episodes are probably small. For practical purposes the cost per episode (hospital and nonhospital) can be treated as only weakly related to insurance plan.

Annual Episode Frequencies

Since plan effects on the size of episodes are much smaller than the differences in total expenditure by plan described in Chapter 3, plan-related differences in demand for medical care lie primarily in differences in the number of episodes. We now investigate how price and other explanatory variables affect the frequency of treated episodes. This section analyzes annual rates of episode occurrence, ignoring for the moment what happens as the price changes during the year.

As with total annual expenditure, episode rates differ most between full coverage and the other plans, with smaller differences between low and high levels of coinsurance. Differences are also smaller across plans for hospital episodes than for the other episode types.

Episode frequency by type and plan. The number of episodes per person varies greatly. Table 4.6 presents descriptive statistics on the 5,904 people who were eligible for six months or more; most were eligible for the three full years of the analysis period. Although the average number of outpatient medical episodes was only 3 per year, one person had 76 acute episodes over the three-year period (25.33 per year), over two per month.

Acute outpatient episodes are the most common. Chronic episodes encompass a number of distinct chronic conditions under treatment, because all routine chronic care for a given chronic condition during a year is grouped into one episode. Sizable numbers of participants had no episode of any type; 11.8 percent of participants incurred no medical care spending at all in the three-year analysis period.

Table 4.7 shows the mean number of various episode types by plan. Not surprisingly, given the large plan differences in total expenditure and small differences in cost per episode, there are substantial differences in responses to plan in number of episodes. These responses appear for all five episode types.

There are fewer statistical problems associated with analyzing the number of episodes than with analyzing annual expenditure. First, there are fewer problems with outliers, because the distribution of episode occurrences is considerably less skewed—much of the variance of dollar expenses comes from the size of episodes, not from their number. Second, zeroes need not be modeled separately as they are for annual expenses, and experience over several years is straightforward to model.[12]

In analyzing the counts of episodes, ordinary least-squares regression is not the preferred method; among other problems, the variance increases with the number of episodes. Rather, as discussed in Keeler et al. (1982),

Table 4.6   Annualized episode frequencies, by type (5,904 participants, up to three years)

Item	Hospital	Total medical out-patient	Medical outpatient		Well care	Dental[a]
			Acute	Chronic		
Mean number	0.118	3.05	1.83	0.57	0.65	1.07
Standard deviation	0.31	2.83	1.84	0.98	0.81	1.02
Maximum	5.67	29.67	25.33	13	7.82	7

a. Dental figures are based on 5,881 participants, excluding 23 participants who dropped out during year 1 in Dayton. Also excludes data from year 1 in Dayton (i.e., there are only two years of data on dental episodes for most Dayton participants).

Table 4.7 Annualized episode frequencies, by type and plan (5,904 participants, up to three years)

Plan	Statistic	Hospital	Medical outpatient	Acute	Chronic	Well care	Dental[a]
Free	Mean	0.133	3.77	2.29	0.70	0.79	1.33
	Standard deviation	(0.35)	(3.00)	(2.01)	(1.09)	(0.85)	(1.05)
Total cost sharing	Mean	0.110	2.68	1.60	0.51	0.58	0.94
	Standard deviation	(0.29)	(2.66)	(1.69)	(0.91)	(0.78)	(0.98)
25%	Mean	0.109	2.96	1.78	0.54	0.64	1.06
50%	Mean	0.099	2.83	1.60	0.51	0.72	0.97
95%	Mean	0.098	2.42	1.44	0.46	0.51	0.88
Individual Deductible	Mean	0.125[b]	2.61	1.56	0.52	0.53	0.89

a. Dental figures are based on 5,881 participants, excluding those who dropped out of the experiment in the first year in Dayton. Dental figures also exclude data from year 1 in Dayton because only the free plan covered dental services for adults in that year, and there appears to be underreporting of dental services by adults on the pay plans in that site and year.

b. Inpatient care is free in this plan.

we view the number of episodes for an individual as Poisson distributed (conditional on his or her expected number), with individuals having different expected numbers of episodes.

Our results are consistent with other analyses of episodes that have found that a negative binomial distribution fits well (Kilpatrick 1977). The negative binomial can be generated by a Gamma distribution of underlying expected number of episodes, with the number of episodes being Poisson conditional on the underlying expected number (Johnson and Kotz 1969). This "mixing" interpretation of the negative binomial distribution has been exploited by workers in a number of fields for situations in which the distribution of counts results from combining counts for individuals, each generating counts according to his or her own Poisson process. Applications include accidents (Greenwood and Yule 1920), crimes (Rolph, Chaiken, and Houchens 1981), patents (Hausman, Hall, and Griliches 1984), and insurance claims (Ferreira 1974).

Effect of individual characteristics on episode frequency. In understanding our model of how a participant's expected number of episodes of a particular type varies with the person's characteristics, think of one episode type (such as acute) and let λ_i be the expected number of episodes of that type for individual i in a year. We call λ_i the person's episode *propensity* and distinguish it from the person's *observed* rate, n_i, in a given year. Then, conditional on λ_i, n_i has a Poisson distribution with mean λ_i. Of course, λ_i is unobservable. We model λ_i as $\lambda_i = \delta_i u_i$, where δ_i is predicted from individual i's attributes (including plan) and u_i is a random component. We assume that $\log(\delta_i) = X_i \beta$, where X_i is a vector of individual i's attributes and β is a vector of regression coefficients to be estimated. We also assume that u_i is Gamma distributed with mean 1 so that the marginal distribution of n_i, given δ_i, is negative binomial with mean δ_i.

In perhaps more familiar terms, we can write an individual's expected number of episodes λ_i as a multiplicative regression equation. That is,

$$\log(\lambda_i) = \log(\delta_i) + \log(u_i) = X_i\beta + \text{individual error.}$$

The error term reflects the negative binomial distribution discussed above. The vector of regression coefficients is estimated by the method of maximum likelihood.

This multiplicative form is especially convenient for comparison with results on annual expenditure. Taking the log of Eq. (4.1), and assuming that the same variables affect cost and frequency,[13] we obtain:

$$\log(\text{expenditure}) = \log(\text{cost per episode}) + \log(\text{number of episodes})$$

$$= X\beta_1 + e_1 + X\beta_2 + e_2$$

$$= X(\beta_1 + \beta_2) + (e_1 + e_2).$$

Because both components are modeled multiplicatively, the proportional change in spending caused by, say, income can be obtained by adding the regression coefficients of income in the two regressions. This sum is analogous to coefficients in a regression of log(expenditure). We do not account for the correlation between e_1 and e_2. There is a statistically significant correlation only for well-care episodes. Accounting for this correlation would have little practical effect but would considerably increase the analytic complexity of the exercise.

Relative to estimating an equation for each year separately, we do not lose much information when we add together three years of episode counts and regress these on predictor variables that come from data at the start of the Experiment. The advantage of this procedure is that it eliminates worry about year-to-year correlations. There are three justifications for aggregating the three years of data: (1) the regression coefficients are stable over time, (2) the explanatory variables are stable over time, and (3) the episode counts are independent over time. In addition, the negative binomial distribution fits the data on the number of episodes by length of enrollment quite well. (See Keeler et al. 1982, app. F, for the analysis leading to these conclusions.)

The same explanatory variables are used to predict episode counts as were used for the cost per episode regressions shown in Table 4.4.

Table 4.8 gives selected coefficients from the regressions of the annual rate of episodes, by type, for the 5,904 fee-for-service participants who were enrolled for at least six months. (Equations for the other coefficients, including site, age, and health variables, are presented in Keeler et al. 1988.) The fitted equations vary considerably across episode types. The coefficients should be interpreted as indicating how much the logarithm of the episode rate can be expected to change when the variable is increased one unit. Hence, exponentiating the coefficient gives the proportional change with a one-unit increase in the predictor. For example, the estimated coefficient of −0.54 on the dummy variable for black (black = 1, other = 0) in the acute episode equation means that blacks on average have 58 percent [exp(−0.54)] as many treated acute episodes as nonblacks, all other variables being equal.

Table 4.8   Selected coefficients from negative binomial regression equations for predicting number of episodes (5,904 fee-for-service participants, up to three years)[a]

	Hospital		Acute		Chronic		Well		Dental coeff.[b]	
P25	-0.21	-2.1	-0.28	-7	-0.37	-5	-0.24	-5	-0.22	-4
P50	-0.30	-2.0	-0.46	-7	-0.49	-5	-0.29	-4	-0.34	-7
P95	-0.30	-3.0	-0.49	-9	-0.52	-6	-0.50	-9	-0.36	-7
Ind. Ded.	-0.17	-1.8	-0.42	-9	-0.41	-5	-0.46	-9	-0.39	-7
Ghindx	-0.012	-4.2[c]	-0.0052	-5.2	-0.0075	-3.8	0.0027	2.53	—	—
Disease	0.0025	0.5	0.011	5.6	0.015	4.8	0.0062	3.1	—	—
Physlm	0.34	3.3	0.11	2.64	0.17	2.48	0.052	1.1	—	—
Log(M.D. visits)	0.25[c]	7	0.28	17	0.31	11	0.12	7	0.03	2.1
Linc	0.04	0.6	0.04[c]	1.5	0.13	2.5	0.08	2.3	0.16	5
Educ	-0.03	-2.1	-0.02	-2.8	0.01	1.0	0.03	4	0.04	5
Black	-0.20	-1.6	-0.54	-8	-0.40	-3.2	-0.29	-2.9	-0.16	-1.6
Coin*SES	-0.02	-0.2	0.07	2.3	0.06	1.2	0.07	1.7	0.04	1.0
PID*SES	0.03	0.4	0.15	4	0.20	3.1	0.16	3.4	0.06	1.0
Kid*Pay	0.23	1.3	0.07	1.4	0.03	0.4	0.13	2.3	-0.04	-0.8
Sick*Pay	0.57	1.2	0.22	1.2	1.06	3.4	—	—	—	—
(α)[d]	0.71	-3.5	1.99	19	0.82	-4	4.77	17	2.64	15
Intrafamily correlation	0.04		0.22		0.08		0.21		0.27	

a. See Table 4.4 for explanation of variables. For the full regression see Keeler et al. (1988), table 3.8.

b. Dental coefficients are based on 5,881 participants, excluding those who dropped out during year 1 in Dayton. Also excludes data from year 1 in Dayton because only the free plan covered adults in that year.

c. These values correct errors in Keeler et al. (1988), table 3.8.

d. α is the shape parameter of the Gamma mixing distribution. The t-statistic test was actually done on ln(α) and tests the null hypothesis that ln(α) = 0, which is why the values of α < 1 have negative t-statistics. The values of α shown are exp(ln[α]); if α = 1, the coefficient of variation of the Gamma is 1.

Not surprisingly, given the approximate independence of plan from other covariates, the estimated regression coefficients show that the raw plan differences reported in Table 4.7 hold up after individual attributes are accounted for. As before, the free plan participants generate more episodes of every type, and the biggest difference is between free plan participants and those with some cost sharing. The coefficients across the pay plans differ in the expected order. Plan has the smallest effect on hospital episodes.

The influence of the other variables on episode frequency varies with the type of episode being considered. The more important determinants of number of episodes appear to be physician visits in the year preceding the Experiment, age, measures of health status before the Experiment, whether the participant is a woman over 17, and site. (Of these variables, the table shows regression coefficients only for prior physician visits and measures of health status.) Generally, log income, being black, log family size, and education are also moderately important.

Other variables were tested in developing the model but proved to be unimportant, including marital status, life events in the preceding year (a measure of stress), size of the MDE as percentage of income, whether the participant was in the Experiment for three or five years, the Mental Health Index, and AFDC status.[14]

The interaction of plan with socioeconomic status measures how much more (or less) people of lower socioeconomic status are affected by coinsurance than better-off people. Because cost sharing on the Individual Deductible plan does not vary with income, whereas it does on the other plans, it may show a different interaction with socioeconomic status (SES) from the other plans. For this reason, a separate variable (PID*SES) has been included. Consistent with the annual expenditure results for the income tertiles, people of lower socioeconomic status were more affected by cost sharing for outpatient services, and especially by the non-income-related Individual Deductible plan. (The generally positive coefficients on Coin*SES and PID*SES mean that better-off groups have less negative plan effects.)

Children were slightly less affected by cost sharing, as were sick people (see the coefficients of Kid*Pay and Sick*Pay). Other interactions were tested but found to be insignificant. These included insurance by the following variables: time on study, previous utilization, gender, examination at enrollment, as well as three-way interactions of insurance plan with poor-sick and with poor children.[15]

The five episode types fall into two groups, according to the regression equations. Hospital, acute, and chronic episodes are heavily affected by enrollment health (the General Health Index, a count of diseases, and an indicator variable for physical limitations) and previous visits to a physician; well-care and dental episodes are heavily affected by education and income. Well-care episodes are concentrated among women and children, and chronic episodes among older participants.

The estimated values for α in Table 4.8 show the extent to which individuals differ in unmeasured ways in their propensities to have treated episodes. The small values (less than one) for hospital and chronic episodes show that people have varying propensities that are not captured by the explanatory variables. And the large value for well-care episodes implies that most individual differences are captured by the measured explanatory variables.[16]

There is substantial residual correlation among counts of the different episode types over individuals. Table 4.9 shows that acute and chronic episode counts are particularly correlated. This may reflect the assignment of chronic flare-ups to the acute category, where, from an economic theory point of view, they belong. Correlation on the pay plans was considerably higher for all episode-type pairs, owing to MDE effects. That is, individuals who exceeded the MDE tended to increase their spending on all episode types. These correlations do not affect predictions of per capita total spending on the Experimental plans, which is still the sum of the averages of the individual episodes types, but they are important for simulation of different deductible plans. Because the full distribution of expenditures determines who will exceed the deductible, the correlations must be considered. In the simulation work discussed later in the chapter, we use a random procedure that accounts for the correlation.

Table 4.9   Correlation of residuals of episode counts, by plan and type of episode[a]

| | Free plan | | | | Pay plans | | | |
Type	Acute	Chronic	Well care	Hospital	Acute	Chronic	Well care	Dental
Hospital	0.18	0.16	0.03	−0.04	0.29	0.30	0.15	−0.04
Acute	1	0.40	0.22	0.20	1	0.50	0.35	0.34
Chronic		1	0.16	0.18		1	0.27	0.22
Well care			1	0.18			1	0.29

a. Correlations are of residuals from the predictions presented in Keeler et al. (1988), table E.1. The correlations are based on three years of data for the full free-plan sample. All correlations greater than 0.1 are significant at $p < 0.01$.

Changes during the Year in Episode Frequencies: Within-Year Price Effects

Analyzing annual counts of episodes is interesting in its own right, but it misses a major advantage of episodic data. If we knew how people behave as price changes *through the year,* we would have a better understanding of the demand for medical care, as well as the effects of deductibles on demand, and could use this knowledge to extrapolate the Experiment's results to different kinds of insurance plans. In this section we analyze price changes through the year. We then use the results to predict spending on plans with a range of deductibles.

We face both economic and statistical problems in analyzing the effects of price changes within the year. The chief economic problem is the definition of the marginal price of services for a family facing a cap on out-of-pocket expenditure.[17] The effective marginal price will differ from the nominal price if families anticipate exceeding the cap and so begin to consume services at a higher rate. Keeler et al. (1982) showed how we adapted the theory of Keeler, Newhouse, and Phelps (1977) to model this effect. In fact, few participants proved able to anticipate exceeding the MDE, which allowed us to ignore this factor and to obtain a much more tractable estimation problem. Anticipation might be important with smaller deductibles than those in the Experiment, however.

For hospital or other large episodes, a small remaining MDE may have another effect. Because the out-of-pocket price is limited to the MDE remaining, a small remaining MDE makes the price of an expensive episode relatively low. We show below that the size of the remaining MDE is important in the decision to initiate hospital episodes, but not to initiate other episode types.[18]

The statistical problem arises because "sickly" people, who tend to seek more care and to exceed the MDE, will face lower prices on average than will others. Causality thus runs from use to price. If unaddressed, this reverse causation will make our estimated response to price too large; in effect, response that is properly attributable to sickliness will be wrongly attributed to price.

To separate price effects from sickliness effects, we begin by assuming that unobservable individual propensities to spend are constant over the year, an assumption we tested. We then compare behavior before and after the MDE is exceeded with behavior on the free plan, where presumably there are no within-year price effects because price does not change.

The Economic Problem

When the coinsurance rate for medical services can change, the current out-of-pocket price is not necessarily the effective price, because the economically rational (or utility-maximizing) family accounts for the effects of current spending on future prices. Families may anticipate future spending in two ways. First, they may anticipate continued treatment of such things as dental problems found at a previous examination, or continuing care for diabetes. Second, a large family with only a few dollars left on its MDE early in the year can be fairly certain that it will exceed the MDE with a new episode, even if it does not know precisely how or when that will occur.

Neither of these forms of anticipation importantly changes the results presented thus far. Continued treatment of known problems is already taken into account by the program that groups charges into episodes. The program assumes in its linking and dating procedures that such spending is fully anticipated. Keeler et al. (1982) showed that the second form of anticipation cannot be important because it rarely occurs.

Thus, except for episodes already begun, participants were rarely in a position to anticipate exceeding their MDE or deductible because of new episodes. For this reason, we could estimate price effects by simply computing the average rate of spending before the deductible was exceeded (accounting, however, for all the expenditure in an episode). In effect this would group all pre-MDE situations together in the analysis; however, our analysis is not quite this simple.

High-priced episodes. For hospital and other costly episodes, having a treatment episode is more attractive when a small amount of MDE is remaining. Keeler et al. (1982) showed that people were rarely in a position with less than $100 of MDE remaining, but that initiating a relatively high-cost episode could be influenced even with larger amounts of MDE remaining. An examination of MDE left at various times during the year in three years of Massachusetts data revealed that about 20 percent of the time participants had $0–400 left on their MDE. This is an adequate sample for estimating whether the amount of the MDE remaining influences behavior, so we divided the situations before exceeding the MDE into those with more or less than $400 (approximately 1978 dollars) of MDE remaining.[19] For sufficiently large hospital bills, the price of initiating the episode is independent of the coinsurance rate on the 25, 50, and 95 percent plans because the total price is the MDE remaining.

Indeed, if the episode is large enough, average price might seem low even if the full $1,000 of MDE remains. In Keeler et al. (1988, app. B) we show the results of a study of catastrophic hospital expenses. The rate of hospitalizations per person-year that cost more than $13,500 (1991 dollars) was the same (0.6 percent) on the coinsurance and free plans. In our simulations, therefore, we will assume such catastrophic episodes are unaffected by price.[20]

Sales. Families with changing coinsurance rates can schedule deferrable treatment episodes at a time when out-of-pocket prices are low. Thus, families with care that is temporarily free have medical care "on sale," and have more incentive to spend during that period than do families with permanently free care. We can ascertain the importance of this phenomenon by examining the experience on the free plan at the start and finish of the Experiment, as well as by comparing the behavior of families in the months just after the time they satisfy their deductible with families on the free care plan.

The most deferrable types of treatment are dental and well care. In Keeler et al. (1982), which analyzed data from the Dayton site, we saw an initial "catch-up" surge on the free plan in the first quarter of year 1 for dental and well care and a somewhat smaller "store-up" surge at the end of year 3. However, during the Experiment we did not see an analogous surge after the MDE was exceeded by those on pay plans. Instead, rates on the pay plans for outpatient episodes were slightly lower than free plan rates after the MDE was exceeded. This finding may reflect ignorance about MDE status or difficulty in making short-run changes (for example, moving to a more interventionist physician). Because there were no measurable sales effects on pay plans in Seattle either, we decided to group together all situations after the MDE was exceeded.

Chosen procedure. We estimate spending rates for three economic periods in each accounting year: the period in which the remaining MDE is greater than $400 (current-year dollars from the Experiment, approximately 1978 dollars), the period in which the remaining MDE is $0–400, and the rest of the year. We call these the big MDE period, the small MDE period, and the free period. In most outpatient episode analyses, we merge the two pre-MDE periods.

The Statistical Problem

For health insurance plans with deductibles, prices are lower on average for those with more episodes. We call such people "sickly" although they may differ from others in attitudes about going to physicians as well as in health. Sicklier families tend to consume relatively more care early in the year and hence are more likely to exceed their deductibles or MDEs. This sickliness effect means that high users face lower effective prices. It does not affect the analysis of annual expenditure by plan, because the design of the Experiment caused participants to be balanced among plans by propensities to spend. But plan subgroups based on price determined by spending within the year, such as the three MDE groups we just defined, become unbalanced as the year goes on.

Table 4.10 shows the actual fraction of days per person, the actual fraction of episodes, and the predicted fraction of episodes in the post-MDE period for each plan. The predicted episodes use free plan data. They take account of several demographic characteristics (see Keeler et al. 1988, app. E), but because they are entirely based on free plan data they do not incorporate any price effect from exceeding the MDE. As can be seen, the proportion of predicted episodes is equal to or greater than the proportion of time after the MDE is exceeded (rows 2 and 5 are equal to or greater than rows 1 and 4), and the number of actual episodes is even larger (rows 3 and 6). The predicted fraction may understate the actual either because

Table 4.10   Fraction of annual episodes occurring after the MDE is exceeded

Event	Insurance plan (coinsurance rate)				
	25%	50%	95%	Individual Deductible	Test of methods[a]
Outpatient time over MDE[b]	0.10	0.13	0.22	0.24	0.17
Predicted outpatient episodes[c]	0.10	0.13	0.24	0.25	0.22
Actual outpatient episodes	0.13	0.19	0.37	0.40	0.25
Hospital time over MDE[b]	0.08	0.11	0.19	0.21	0.15
Predicted hospital episodes[c]	0.10	0.12	0.21	0.22	0.19
Actual hospital episodes	0.28	0.34	0.41	0.42	0.31

a. An imaginary MDE of either $1,000 (two-thirds of families) or $300 (one-third of families) and a coinsurance rate of 40% were applied to participants on the free-care plan to test for methods effects; see text.

b. Time is transformed to account for carryover episodes on the first day of the accounting year. Actual days after the first day are multiplied by 0.94 for outpatient and 0.8 for hospital, which is why the fraction of time over the MDE differs for the two types.

c. Values assume that families spend at same rate before and after MDE is exceeded; see Keeler et al. (1988) for prediction equations.

of some unmeasured propensities to have episodes (those who exceed the MDE are sicker) or because of price effects (more episodes because care is free over the MDE). Our methods are designed to untangle these two causes. Table 4.10 also contains the results from a "test-of-methods" plan, which we describe below after describing our methods in more detail. By construction, however, there can be no price effects on this plan; hence, the excessive predicted or actual episodes (relative to the proportion of time over the MDE) show that those who exceed the MDE are indeed more sickly.

In Keeler et al. (1982) we developed a model to separate sickliness and price effects—that is, to disentangle the degree to which high use causes low prices and low prices cause high use. The model allows us to compute the ratio of the episode rates in the three periods defined by MDE status relative to what those rates would have been on the free plan. The model relies on four critical assumptions:

1. Non-price-related propensities to have episodes are constant over the accounting year. These propensities are determined by measured and unmeasured characteristics; the measured characteristics do not vary within the year. Individuals have an expected number of episodes on the free plan that depends on their measured nonplan individual covariates. We can add up the predicted number of episodes for each person to get a predicted number of episodes for family k which we call δ_k. Because our information about families is limited, they can also be expected to have propensities that will not be captured by measured characteristics. That is, we would expect the actual episode counts of individual families to be consistently over- or underpredicted by the δ_k. To account for this unmeasured variation, we assume that each family has an unmeasured propensity, u_k, which is constant from year to year. The family's actual propensity is the product $\delta_k u_k$. The u_k are assumed to be drawn from a Gamma distribution. The Gamma distribution can take a variety of shapes and has computational advantages. To insulate the estimates of u_k from price effects, we used only free plan data to fit both the prediction equations and the distribution of unmeasured propensities.

2. The year is split into three periods by MDE status, and within these periods the effects of price are constant. In effect, we estimate three ratios (π_{ij}; $i = 1, 2, 3$) for each coinsurance plan j. These price ratios are defined as the ratio of the expected number of episodes in period i for a family on plan j to the expected number of episodes in period i for that family if care were always free. That is, it is the ratio of pay plan propensity to the free plan propensity to generate episodes. The three periods are the big MDE period ($> \$400$

remaining), the little MDE period (more than zero but less than or equal to $400 remaining), and the free period (use already at or above the MDE).

3. Episode rates on the free plan can be considered constant over time. This is a corollary of assumption 1 with empirical support. Further data analysis confirms the results in Keeler et al. (1982) that episode rates for all types of episodes are uniform over time except for the sales effects of exceeding the MDE on the cost-sharing plans, the first day of the year, and a tendency for chronic episodes to occur early in the year. The additional episodes on the first day of the year can be attributed to carryover episodes from the preceding year. In effect, in the process of defining episodes we split one medical episode into two accounting episodes. Similarly, the tendency for chronic episodes to be dated earlier in the year follows from our convention that all routine chronic care is dated to the first date of treatment (if not already under treatment). Except for the sales effects, these effects should be the same on all plans. To counteract these effects we transform time so that episode rates are uniform.[21]

4. Occurrences of episodes are independent over time. Individuals have different propensities, but conditional on these propensities, episode occurrences do not appear to be bunched or spread more than random. Thus, they can be modeled as being Poisson distributed.[22] This is convenient for purposes of comparison because the Poisson distribution is infinitely divisible; that is, the episodes in any fraction of the year also follow a Poisson distribution.

To summarize the four assumptions: a family k on plan j in MDE status i for an effective period of time t_{ik} will have n_{ik} episodes, where n_{ik} follows a Poisson distribution with mean $\pi_{ij}\delta_k u_k t_{ik}$. Table 4.11 summarizes the notation and assumptions made thus far in specifying the model.

To estimate the parameters of the price-effects model, we define $f_k = \delta_k u_k$, where δ_k is the predictable family component and u_k is the remaining unpredictable component. First, we estimate the predictable family component, δ_k, from individual covariates and free plan data. Free plan data ensure that there will be no price effects. Next, we estimate the parameters of the distribution of u_k. Finally, we use a maximum-likelihood procedure to estimate the price effects, π_i. We describe our methods in more detail before presenting the numerical estimates.

Recall that δ_k is the predicted annual number of episodes for family k if care were free. This is estimated by d_k, which is obtained by summing individual regression predictions based on free plan data of annual episode rates over the individuals in the family.[23] We assume negligible interactions between within-year price effects and other covariates, so that all the effects of measured covariates other than price on numbers of episodes are summarized by δ_k.

We are assuming that family k has an unmeasured multiplicative factor, u_k, with u_k having a Gamma distribution with shape and scale parameters α and β. Given the value u_k, the annual rate for family k is assumed to be $\delta_k u_k$ if care were free. This can be regarded as the Poisson regression ana-

---

Table 4.11   Notation and assumptions

Notation:

π_{ij} = ratio of occurrence rates for period i on plan j to free-plan rate; $i = 1,2,3$ (the price effect).

δ_k = predictable component of expected annual episode occurrence rate under free plan for family k (a function of the covariates of individuals in family k).

u_k = multiplicative component of expected annual occurrence rate for family k if care were free that is due to unmeasured family propensities to have episodes.

$\delta_k u_k$ = expected annual occurrence rate for family k if care were free $\delta_k u_k = f_k$).

t_{ik} = time spent by family k in period i. Period 1 = the time when family k has more than \$400 of MDE remaining, period 2 the time with 0–\$400 MDE remaining, and $t_{3k} = 1 - t_{1k} - t_{2k}$ is the proportion of time after the MDE is exceeded.

n_{ik} = number of episodes that family k has during period i.

Assumptions:

1. Episodes occur during period i to family k on plan j, according to a Poisson process with intensity function $\pi_i \delta_k u_k$.

2. Thus $n_{ik} | t_{ik}, \pi_{ij}, \delta_k u_k \sim$ Poisson $(\pi_{ij} \delta_k u_k t_{ik})$.

3. u_k is independently and identically distributed, Gamma (α, β). That is, the unmeasured component is modeled as being drawn from a Gamma distribution independently for each family.

Table 4.12   Estimates of dispersion of unmeasured family characteristics (based on 1,990 free-plan family-years)

| Episode type | Average of separate family years | | All three years together, estimated α |
	Estimated α	Estimated αβ	
Acute	2.77	0.998	3.08
Chronic	2.03	0.995	1.79
Dental	3.94	0.997	3.71
Well care	6.96	0.995	7.08
Hospital	1.10	1.03	1.70

logue to random-effects models in the analysis of variance. We use the negative binomial regression model described in Table 4.8 on the all-sites free plan sample to estimate α and ß. The dependent variable is the number of episodes. Because the "adjusted time" for family k is set to be $\delta_k t_k$, no covariates are needed beyond those included in δ.

The resulting α and ß show the unmeasured differences between families in episode rates in the absence of price effects. The larger the unobservable or unmeasured differences between families, the higher the variance of the mixing distribution, and the lower the value of α.[24]

Price effects of occurrence are estimated on the nonfree plan data, by maximum likelihood, as shown in Keeler et al. (1982, app. H).

Estimation of Alpha and Beta from Free Plan Data

By definition there can be no price effects within the free plan, and our assignment methods assure that participants on the free plan are representative of those on other plans. We can therefore use the free plan to estimate the parameters of the Gamma distribution, α and ß. Equations predicting the number of episodes based on the free plan experience were estimated for each site separately and, when we could not reject homogeneity across sites, were pooled. The variance of unmeasured characteristics between families was computed from the negative binomial model. The maximum likelihood values of α and αß for the Gamma distribution are given in Table 4.12. Because αß was never significantly different from 1, we chose $ß = 1/α$ in all price ratio regressions. As can be seen from the values of α, the largest unmeasured differences between people occur in hospital care (α is smallest), and the least in well care.

As a test of MDE effects, we estimated α and ß for the 2,695 pay plan family-years. The value of α for acute episodes dropped to 1.53, and for hospital episodes to 0.64. Thus there was a substantially greater dispersion across individuals in the number of episodes on the pay plans. This result comes from the MDE effect—that is, from the difference in episode rates between one subgroup within the plan whose care is influenced by having to pay at the margin and another subgroup that, after exceeding the MDE, has free care at the margin.

The dispersion in characteristics based on all three years of experience combined (Table 4.12, far right column) is similar to that based on single years, except for hospital episodes. Families may have single-year peaks in hospitalizations that are not sustained over three years. Because our estimation and prediction are mainly annual, we use the annual estimates of α in further calculations.

Occurrence Ratios for Outpatient Episodes

Whether large (>$400) or small (≤ $400) MDEs remained did not much affect occurrence ratios (rates of episodes relative to free rates) for outpatient episodes (Table 4.13). To increase the sample for this comparison, we combined all coinsurance plans except the Individual Deductible. Table 4.13 shows that the biggest difference in occurrence ratios between the two MDE periods was for acute episodes (0.65 versus 0.70). Because of the small difference between occurrence ratios in the big and small MDE periods, we combined these two and called the resulting period the pay period. Thus, the pay period is the time before the MDE is exceeded, and the rest of the year is the time during which additional care is free (the sale period).

Table 4.13   Estimated occurrence ratios (π) for outpatient episodes in combined coinsurance plans

	Type of episode			
MDE remaining	Acute	Chronic	Well care	Dental
>$400[a]	0.65	0.63	0.68	0.67
$0–$400[a]	0.70	0.67	0.69	0.64
$0	0.84	0.89	0.98	0.91

a. The $400 figure is in current-year dollars from the Experiment; the years are centered on about 1978.

Table 4.14 presents estimated occurrence ratios or price effects under this classification for outpatient episodes. Because 5/6 of the experience occurred before the MDE was exceeded, the standard errors for the pay period (pre-MDE) ratios are smaller than those for the rest-of-the-year ratios.

For each outpatient episode type, the estimated pay period occurrence ratios decline with increased coinsurance. The 25 percent plan rates are about halfway between free care (1.0) and the 95 percent plan rates (0.51–0.57). In other words, if there were no MDE, outpatient episodes would be treated just over half as often on the 95 percent plan as on the free-care plan.

As a test of whether our methods separate sickliness from price, we computed the "effects" of a fictitious MDE for the free plan. We randomly assigned two-thirds of the free care families to an initial high fictitious MDE ($1,000), and the other third to an initial fictitious low MDE of $300. All the families were given a fictitious coinsurance rate of 40 percent.

The actual occurrence of episodes on the free plan was such that these assumptions lead to a distribution of fictitious remaining MDE that roughly matches the actual pay plan experience throughout the year. We can observe what happens to behavior when the families approach and exceed their fictitious MDE. Because in fact care was free throughout for them, there can be no real price effects within the year, so any estimated price response to this fictitious MDE must be an artifact of our methods. In other words, any observed response will occur because a low price is being imputed to those with higher propensities to spend for unmeasured reasons.

As Table 4.15 shows, the occurrence ratios on the fictitious MDE plan are never very different from 1.0, and none by a statistically significant amount. Thus, we believe our methods satisfactorily distinguish between price and sickliness.

The occurrence ratios after the MDE is exceeded (the "rest of year" columns in Table 4.14) seem similar on all three plans. If people did not plan ahead but were aware of their current insurance status, we might expect a ratio of 1, the free plan rate. Initial low use on the pay plan could have two offsetting effects on use after the MDE is exceeded. It might lead to a demand for treatments that were deferrable (the sale effect), but it might also reflect a habit of not going to the physician that would carry over into the later period. Also, there may be some delay in real time before people realize that medical care is now free, which would dampen the sale effect. Indeed, 15 of the 16 estimated rest-of-year coefficients in Table 4.14 are less than 1; this result implies that ignorance of exceeding the MDE or a

Table 4.14   Occurrence ratios (π) for episodes in outpatient categories relative to free plan (standard errors in parentheses)[a]

Type of episode	25% coinsurance		50% coinsurance		95% coinsurance		Individual Deductible	
	Pay period	Rest of year	Pay period	Rest of year	Pay period	Rest of year	Pay period	Rest of year
Acute	0.76 (0.02)	0.84 (0.04)	0.61 (0.02)	0.78 (0.06)	0.55 (0.01)	0.84 (0.03)	0.62 (0.01)	0.85 (0.02)
Chronic	0.71 (0.02)	0.90 (0.06)	0.61 (0.04)	0.86 (0.13)	0.57 (0.02)	0.88 (0.04)	0.64 (0.02)	0.96 (0.04)
Well care	0.80 (0.02)	0.92 (0.05)	0.75 (0.03)	1.08 (0.10)	0.51 (0.02)	0.98 (0.04)	0.56 (0.02)	0.98 (0.04)
Dental[b]	0.80 (0.03)	0.91 (0.08)	0.70 (0.02)	0.77 (0.05)	0.54 (0.02)	0.96 (0.04)	0.58 (0.01)	0.89 (0.03)

a. Here and in subsequent tables, ratios are given relative to the free plan; i.e., the free plan rate is 1. The values are the maximum likelihood estimate of π. Standard errors of π are given by the asymptotic variance of the maximum-likelihood estimate. These standard errors are underestimated, most likely by a factor of less than two; see Keeler et al. (1988).

b. Year 1 Dayton was omitted for dental. The plan with 25% medical insurance, 50% dental insurance is put with 50% coinsurance for dental.

habit of not seeking care dominated any sale effect. The post-MDE ratios for well care, however, are close to 1.

The standard errors computed using maximum-likelihood theory look quite low, with values around 0.02 for the pay period and 0.05 in the rest-of-year period. There are theoretical reasons why these standard errors are underestimated (Keeler et al. 1988). As a result, we studied the bias in the estimated standard errors and concluded that the true standard errors were most likely between one to two times those shown in Table 4.14.

Occurrence Ratios for Hospital Episodes

The occurrence ratios or price effects for hospital episodes follow a different pattern from outpatient episodes. Table 4.16 shows that the large MDE period results are essentially the same, around two-thirds, on all the coinsurance plans. The small MDE period has a rate closer to 1, and the free period ratio is much larger than 1. The free period findings imply large apparent sale effects for hospitalizations (that is, more spending than on the free plan). It is surprising to see such large sale effects, both because there were not many purely elective hospitalizations and because we did not find sale effects for well care and dental care, where they would be more likely. Further examination, however, shows that these results are an artifact of some assumptions of the model, and that adjustments should be made in the free period values in order to extrapolate to the population.

Although there appears to be a sale effect of 48 percent on the pay plans (row 3, column 1 of Table 4.16), there also appears to be a sale effect of 31 percent on the test-of-methods plan. Since there can be no true sale effect on the test-of-methods plan, the sale effect must be largely an artifact.

The explanation for this artifact appears to be the correlation between hospital and other types of episodes. Those with their first hospital episode are more likely to be already over the MDE than those with their first outpatient

Table 4.15   Effects of a fictitious MDE on free-plan rate of episodes to test methods

Period	Type of episode			
	Acute	Chronic	Well care	Dental
> $400	0.99	1.01	1.01	1.00
≤ $400	0.97	0.95	0.95	1.02
$0	1.05	1.03	1.01	0.96

Table 4.16 Occurrence ratios for hospital episodes (standard errors in parentheses)[a]

Period	Total coinsurance	Coinsurance rate			Individual Deductible	"Test of methods" plan[b]	Adjusted coinsurance/ coinsurance free[c]
		25%	50%	95%			
MDE > $400 (large MDE)	0.64 (0.04)	0.65 (0.05)	0.62 (0.09)	0.63 (0.06)	— —	0.92 (0.06)	0.70
0 < MDE ≤ $400 (small MDE)	0.87 (0.07)	0.94 (0.11)	0.72 (0.21)	0.85 (0.13)	0.71 (0.05)	0.98 (0.08)	0.89
MDE = 0 (free period)	1.48 (0.10)	1.91 (0.21)	1.56 (0.34)	1.22 (0.11)	1.62 (0.13)	1.31 (0.09)	1.13

a. The standard errors are too low, most likely by less than a factor of two; see text.
b. An imaginary MDE of either $1,000 (two-thirds of families) or $300 (one-third of families) and a coinsurance rate of 40% were applied to free-plan participants to test for methods effects.
c. Total coinsurance/test of methods.

episode because they are likely to have had outpatient spending before the hospitalization, whereas those with outpatient episodes are not likely to have been hospitalized. But our methods control only for being over the MDE because of earlier occurrences of the same type of episode, because each type is estimated separately.

For purposes of simulation, we assume that the apparent sale effect for hospital episodes is an artifact and adjust the coefficients shown in Table 4.16 to eliminate the sale effect and to make the total number of episodes for the plan correct. Because approximately 15 percent of hospital days are in the over-MDE period, hospital price ratios of 0.72 for the large MDE period, 0.9 for the small MDE period, and 1 for the over-MDE period will keep the overall episodes equal to 80 percent of free plan number, consistent with the analysis of hospital admissions presented in Chapter 3. Thus, hospital spending is less responsive to price than are other medical services.

Pure Price Effects

We can now compute the overall effect of price on medical spending in the absence of deductibles or limits. We assume that this "pure" effect of price is approximated by behavior of people in the large MDE period. To compute these estimates we allow for dependence among episode types (as described in Keeler et al. 1988, app. C).

We have already shown that cost sharing leads to a substantial decline in the rate of initiating episodes and to somewhat less costly episodes when they occur. We combine smoothed estimates of the effects on cost of episodes shown in Table 4.5 with the effects on number of episodes shown in Table 4.14 for outpatient episodes and Table 4.16 for inpatient episodes. These results are shown in Table 4.17 as a percentage of spending with free care.[25]

The reductions in the cost of episodes that we estimate to be caused by cost sharing are only marginally important. If price really had no effect on the cost of an episode, the values for all medical services would change from the 71, 63, and 55 shown in the next-to-last column of Table 4.17, to 73, 68, and 64, and the total outpatient values would rise to 75, 63, and 55.

The pure price effects shown in Table 4.17 are, of course, larger than the plan effects on annual expenditure shown in Chapter 3 because they exclude the MDE effect. In other words, these values show the effect of a plan with a given coinsurance rate and no MDE. Thus, the pure 95 percent rate approximates the effect of being uninsured.

In Chapter 3 the 25 percent plan is estimated to have total medical spending at 81 percent of the free plan rate, the 50 percent plan at 75 percent, and the 95 percent plan at 69 percent, ignoring the modest rate of underfiling. The difference from the pure effects computed in Table 4.17 is largest for the 95 percent plan—69 percent versus 55 percent—because more people (35 percent) exceeded the MDE on that plan than on the other two plans (21 percent in each plan).[26]

For comparison with the economic literature on demand for medical services, which generally gives results in terms of price elasticities, we have computed the elasticities implied by our results in Table 4.18. These estimates are in fact estimates of price elasticities, based on the usual definition of an elasticity, whereas most estimates in the literature are based on an average coinsurance rate. For comparison purposes we made a different estimate of price elasticities, using the annual data from Chapter 3 and the average coinsurance rates by plan. The alternative method yielded an estimate for total medical services of the 0–25 percent elasticity as –0.10 and the 25–95 percent elasticity as –0.14 (Manning et al. 1987), or about 60 percent as large as the values in Table 4.18.

Table 4.17   Estimated spending on medical services for plans with no MDE as a percentage of spending on the free-care plan (standard errors in parentheses)[a]

Pure coinsurance rate	Acute	Chronic	Well care	Total outpatient[b]	Hospital	Total medical[b]	Dental
Free	100	100	100	100	100	100	100
25%	72	67	75	71	71	71	79
	(4)	(6)	(4)	(3)	(7)	(4)	(6)
50%	56	56	69	58	68	63	68
	(5)	(7)	(6)	(4)	(13)	(7)	(5)
95%	49	51	45	49	60	55	50
	(3)	(5)	(4)	(2)	(7)	(4)	(3)

a. Standard errors are computed assuming errors in the estimation of reductions in episode size and rate are independent. Source is Keeler et al. (1988), table 4.9.

b. Computed assuming estimates weighted by shares of spending during the big MDE period. For total medical these shares are: hospital 0.54, acute 0.23, chronic 0.15, well care 0.08. For total outpatient the shares are acute 0.50, chronic 0.33, well care 0.17.

Table 4.18   Arc price elasticities of medical spending (standard errors in parentheses)[a]

Range	Acute	Chronic	Well	Total out-patient	Hospital	Total medical	Dental
0–25	−0.16	−0.20	−0.14	−0.17	−0.17	−0.17	−0.12
	(0.02)	(0.04)	(0.02)	(0.02)	(0.04)	(0.02)	(0.03)
25–95	−0.32	−0.23	−0.43	−0.31	−0.14	−0.22	−0.39
	(0.05)	(0.07)	(0.05)	(0.04)	(0.10)	(0.06)	(0.06)

Source: Keeler et al. (1988), table 4.10.
a. For the method of computation of standard errors see Keeler et al. (1988).

These alternative values are, however, biased by the use of the average coinsurance rate in the pay plans. For small total expenditures the true coinsurance rate is well above the average rate (the MDE has not been exceeded), whereas for large expenditures (those exceeding the MDE) the true coinsurance rate at the margin is zero. Thus, for small expenditure the elasticity is overestimated (the price change compared with the free plan is underestimated), and conversely. Apparently the large expenditures dominate. A third estimate, using an indirect utility function, yields an elasticity estimate of −0.18 for all care in the 25–95 percent range (Manning 1988), or about 80 percent as large as the value in Table 4.18.[27]

The values in Table 4.18 lie at the low end of the range of earlier estimates of price elasticities in the literature. (See Manning et al. 1987 for more discussion of the literature and the implications of these estimates.)

The Simulation Model

We constructed a simulation model so that the Experiment's results could be generalized to types of health insurance plans not included in the Experiment and to crossvalidate the models and ideas developed above. The simulation uses the models of episode frequency and cost described in this chapter to estimate annual individual and family expenditures by type of episode for different types of health insurance plans. We use a randomly drawn sample of 970 families from the March 1984 Current Population Survey (CPS) to make these simulations. The CPS provides data on family composition, the age and gender of each family member, and the income and ethnic status of the family.

The simulation model compares the effects of different health insurance plans on family expenditures, holding constant the health problems faced by the family during the year. The plans whose effects we model are characterized by an initial deductible period (possibly zero) in which the patient must pay 100 percent of the cost of care, a cost-sharing phase in which the patient pays a share of the cost that equals the coinsurance rate and the plan pays the remaining portion, and either an individual or family maximum-dollar expenditure (MDE) limit on out-of-pocket expenditures, beyond which the plan pays 100 percent. For plans with family MDE limits, the expenditures of all family members contribute to the maximum. When the family maximum is exceeded, the plan pays 100 percent of the care of all family members. Plans with individual MDE limits will pay for all of an individual's costs once he or she has exceeded the limit. The model also accommodates "hybrid" plans in which different deductibles, coinsurance rates, or MDEs apply to different types of episodes within a plan.

All insurance plan experience is considered relative to free care—that is, an insurance plan that pays for all medical care expenditures. The model first estimates annual expenditures for each family on the free plan and then subsequently estimates how the family would have responded to the same health problems if it had each of the other insurance plans. To provide a benchmark at the other extreme, we have also included a full-pay plan on which the family must pay the entire cost of its care.

Demand for Episodes of Care on the Free Plan

We have already estimated the distribution of the number of episodes of each type to be negative binomial (Table 4.8). The negative binomial distribution may be interpreted as a compound Poisson process, which is a Poisson process in which the intensity parameter λ is a random variable. In the case of the negative binomial distribution, the intensity variable has a Gamma distribution. The number of episodes of a given type that an individual has, or his or her episode intensity, varies with personal characteristics. These individual episode propensities are assumed to have a constant measured component determined by observable characteristics, such as age and gender (δ in our notation above, d in our notation in this section), and a variable unmeasured Gamma component that includes unobservable factors such as recent changes in health status. In our notation above, the unobservable factor was denoted u and was individual specific; here we make it family specific and denote it as U.

A convenient feature of Poisson processes is that the sum of several independent Poisson processes with intensities λ_1, λ_2, ..., λ_n is also a Poisson process with intensity $\lambda = \lambda_1 + \lambda_2 + \ldots + \lambda_n$. We use this property to generate a single episode stream for the family.

The simulation model processes one family at a time by first estimating an overall family propensity for episodes of all types. This family propensity is estimated by summing each family member's individual propensity for episodes of each type. The constant measured components of the individual propensities are computed from the negative binomial regression equations described above and reported fully in Keeler et al. (1988).[28] We do not include dental episodes in the simulations because most health plans at the time of the Experiment did not include dental care as part of the common medical deductible.

Let d_{ij} represent the predicted number of episodes of type j from the regression equation for family member i in a family of size n. U_j represents the family's unobserved component for episode type j. Person i's propensity for episodes of type j is given by

$$\lambda_{ij} = d_{ij}U_j,$$

where U_j is distributed as $G(\alpha_j, \beta_j)$; that is, U_j is randomly drawn from a Gamma distribution with scale parameter β_j and shape parameter α_j. The Gamma parameters are given in Table 4.12. The family's propensity for episodes of type j is given by

$$\Sigma_i d_{ij}U_j$$

and the family's propensity for all j types of episodes is given by

$$\lambda_f = \Sigma\Sigma_{ij}\lambda_{ij} = \Sigma\Sigma_{ij}d_{ij}U_j,$$

where j ranges from 1 to 4.

Correlation among Episode Types

We noted that after controlling for the effect of observable characteristics on episodes, the number of episodes that an individual had of one type was correlated with the number of other types of episodes (Table 4.9). Specifically, hospital episodes were correlated with acute and chronic episodes, and all outpatient episodes were correlated. To replicate this correlation structure across types of episodes, we calculated U_j as the sum of three Gamma variates: one to introduce the correlation between hospital, acute, and chronic episodes; the second to replicate the correlation across outpatient episodes; and the third to represent the effects unique to the jth type of episode.

Episode Generation

Because the occurrence of episodes is modeled as a Poisson process with family episode propensity λ_f, we know that the time between episodes has an exponential distribution with mean $1/\lambda_f$. The simulation model generates episodes by computing the time between episodes from this exponential distribution.

To determine the type of episode and the family member who had it we observe that the probability that this is an episode of type j occurring to family member i is given by λ_{ij}/λ_f. We map these probabilities onto the unit interval and draw a uniform random variate to determine the family member with the episode and the episode type.

Cost of Treatment on the Free Plan

Once the model determines the type of episode and the person to whom it occurs, we use the logarithmic cost regression equations from Table 4.5 to predict the mean logarithmic expenditure for this individual. Using the mean and the variance predicted from the overall regression equation, we generate a random variate from a lognormal distribution with this mean and variance. We use stochastic variate generation methods discussed in Fishman (1973 chap. 8).

We observed earlier in the chapter that the lognormal distribution fit the observed episode costs reasonably well but that the actual distribution has a positive skew. To correct for this, we augment the size of large episodes. When a large random variate is drawn, defining large by the number of standard deviations above the mean (column 1 of Table 4.19), we increase its value (by the factor shown in column 2 of Table 4.19). No correction is made for well-care episodes. Use of these factors makes the simulated distribution of costs resemble the actual distribution. (A discussion of the derivation of these values is found in Keeler et al. 1988, app. A.)

Censoring Pay Plan Episodes

We have already shown that the higher the coinsurance rate, the larger the reduction in both the number and, to a lesser degree, the cost of episodes. For families on the cost-sharing plans we simulate, the amount of cost sharing will generally vary throughout the year. For example, the cost sharing is 100 percent during any deductible period, drops to the coinsurance rate (say 20 percent) during the cost-sharing phase, and declines to nothing beyond the MDE limit.

Earlier in this chapter we described a model that divides the year into three periods that differ in the price the consumer faces. We estimated a price effect (occurrence ratio) as the ratio of the number of episodes of treatment obtained by individuals with a specific cost-sharing rate relative to the number of episodes observed when individuals have no cost sharing. We now interpret these price effects as the binomial probability that an individual with cost sharing will seek treatment for the same episode for which an individual with no cost sharing would certainly seek care. We fit a model of the form $\pi_j = \exp[b_j r^{a(j)}]$, where r is the coinsurance rate, j is type of episode, and a and b are estimated. We then use the predicted π to simulate the effect of plan. (See Keeler et al. 1988 for a formal treatment.)

The Reduced Size of Pay Plan Episodes

Because the cost-sharing plans had less expensive as well as fewer episodes, the episodes observed on those plans were adjusted downward in size. Instead of using the equations in Table 4.5, we used an adjustment estimated analogously to that just described for occurrence ratios. (See Keeler et al. 1988 for details.)

Table 4.19   Episode cost expansion factors

	Standard deviations above the mean	Multiplicative factor
Hospital	1.8	1.28
Acute	1.8	1.31
Chronic	1.6	1.42
Dental	1.4	2.03

Catastrophic Hospitalizations

We have already noted that very expensive hospitalizations—those above $13,500 in 1991 dollars—were experienced with the same relative frequency on the free plan and on the cost-sharing plans. In addition, such episodes on the cost-sharing plans were similar in size to those on the free plan. As a result, within the simulation model, hospital episodes that occur on the free plan and exceed $13,500 are assumed to occur at the same rate and size on all plans.

Hospital Episodes with Low Out-of-Pocket Cost

We showed in Table 4.16 that when the amount of out-of-pocket expenditures needed to meet the MDE limit is small, rates of hospital (but not outpatient) episodes are larger than when the amount of out-of-pocket expenditures needed is large. The probable reason is that families may realize that the total out-of-pocket cost of the hospital episode is limited to the amount of MDE remaining.[29] Our data suggest that this change occurs when people come within $400 of the MDE. On the basis of the far right column of Table 4.16 (adjusted coinsurance/free), we assumed that 10 percent of the hospital episodes are censored when a person is within $400 of the maximum out-of-pocket expenditure for that plan. The remaining 90 percent of such hospital episodes are assumed to be as large as those experienced on the free plan. That is, cost sharing does not affect the cost of the hospital episode when people are in the low MDE period, because the marginal cost of additional hospital care will be zero.

Basic Simulation Model Flow

The simulation model generates a year of health experience for one family by generating episodes one at a time, in each case computing a random time to next episode. The type of episode, its cost, and the person experiencing it are recorded for the free plan. For pay plans the episode is censored using the current predicted price (occurrence) ratio for that plan; episodes not censored are reduced in size as just described.

Both total and out-of-pocket expenditures are recorded. The plan status is tracked through four periods as the year progresses: the deductible period, the cost-sharing or coinsurance period, the low-cost period for hospital episodes (the period within $400 of the MDE), and the period beyond the MDE. Each family member is in one of these four states in each of the pay plans. After an episode is recorded, the insurance state is updated. In general, different coinsurance rates are associated with each of these states. New episodes are generated and recorded until the year has elapsed. At this stage a new family is input and the process repeated.

The statistics reported here are based on four replications through the input file of 970 families. Statistics and confidence limits were calculated using sequential estimation methods described in Fishman (1978, pp. 68–72). (A complete set of output statistics is shown in Keeler et al. 1988, app. G.)

Variance Reduction Techniques

We used several features in the design of the simulation (described in Keeler et al. 1988) to help reduce the variance of our estimates of plan differences. These had the effect of reducing the confidence limits on plan differences by a factor of 20 relative to calculating experience on different plans independently.

Overall Plan Comparisons: Expenditures, Value, and Risk

We use several measures to compare the different health insurance plans. Obvious measures of interest are total family and individual health expenditures. Comparing total expenditures across plans gives a direct measure of the effect of different cost-sharing arrangements on medical care use. Individual and family out-of-pocket expenditures provide information about the effect of these plans on the family's economic position.

In addition, we have estimated the value to the family of services purchased and the risk associated with each plan's coverage. Our measure of risk is a multiple of the variance of out-of-pocket expenditures.[30] Plans with large variability in out-of-pocket expenses provide less protection against large financial losses than plans with the same average out-of-pocket expenditures and more predictable out-of-pocket expenses. The value to the family of the additional services is assumed to be measured by what a family would pay out-of-pocket for the service; in general this amount is less than the price of the service because of insurance. (For a brief exposition of the welfare economic theory underlying these measures, and details of our method, see Keeler et al. 1988, app. D.)

Model Validation

The model was tested to determine whether it could in fact generate health expenditure experience that looked like the actual experience of the

Experiment families. We used the Seattle sample to validate the model. We constructed plans similar to the Experiment plans and compared the average numbers of episodes generated by the model with actual data. These comparisons are shown in Table 4.20 for the free plan. The match is good.

In addition, using the demographic characteristics of the Seattle experimental population, we created pseudoclaims corresponding to the utilization experience generated by the model. These claims were then used to estimate the parameters described earlier in the chapter. Comparison of the Gamma parameter estimates derived using the pseudoclaims and those developed from actual experimental data shows that the two estimates fall within 1.3 standard errors of the difference for all four episode types. This result further validates the simulation model.

Simulation Model Results and Discussion

How Total Expenditures and Other Measures Vary with Different Coinsurance and MDE Limits

Keeler, Newhouse, and Phelps (1977) hypothesized that the demand for medical services as a function of the maximum out-of-pocket expenditure was shaped like a logistic or backward S: people with small deductibles behave as if they have no deductible (because with high probability they will exceed it), and people with large deductibles behave as if they have no insurance (because with high probability they will not exceed it). For deductibles near zero or extremely large, variation should have little effect

Table 4.20   Comparison of actual data and simulated data at the family level, free plan (standard errors in parentheses)

	Actual Seattle	Simulated data
Probability of hospitalization	0.32	0.33
	(0.03)	(0.03)
Acute episodes	6.17	5.83
	(0.25)	(0.30)
Chronic episodes	2.02	1.88
	(0.09)	(0.10)
Well-care episodes	1.73	1.70
	(0.08)	(0.08)

on the probability of exceeding the deductible, but for some middle range, variation in the deductible should have a substantial effect on the probability of exceeding and hence on demand.

To test this idea, we used the simulation model to compare expenditures on 28 different insurance plans. We used a simple structure for the plans: no initial deductible; cost sharing of 25, 50, or 100 percent up to the MDE; and no cost sharing beyond. The MDE was an individual MDE with no limit on family out-of-pocket expense. We used MDEs of $50, $100, $200, $500, $1,000, $1,500, $2,000, $3,000, and no limit (the dollars are 1983 dollars).[31] All plans were compared with the free care plan and with no insurance. The 100 percent coinsurance plans with varying MDEs, of course, represent varying deductibles.

Our results were somewhat different from what we anticipated. The upper panel of Figure 4.2 graphs per capita total expenditures against the MDE for plans with each of the three coinsurance rates, as well as free care and no insurance.[32] In the case of free care, per capita total spending is $860, and for no insurance it is $494. (Both are horizontal lines because the MDE is irrelevant in these two situations.) For the three plans with coinsurance, total expenditure falls as the MDE increases.

What we did not anticipate was that expenditures decline less steeply as the MDE increases from $200 to $1,000 than from $50 to $200. Beyond $1,000 we observe only small changes, which we did anticipate.

The expenditure level for large MDEs differs significantly across the different coinsurance rates. A $1,000 individual MDE and a coinsurance rate of 25 percent reduces average per capita expenditures by only 57 percent of the difference between the free care and no insurance rates. A 100 percent coinsurance rate and a $1,000 individual MDE, in contrast, reduce per capita expenditures by more than 90 percent of the difference between free care and no insurance.

The upper panel of Figure 4.2 also shows the sensitivity of spending to an alternative definition of the low-cost hospitalization region; if the region of increased spending on hospital care is only half as large ($300, 1983 dollars), the spending rate is somewhat less.[33]

The decline in total expenditures is quite sharp as the MDE increases from $0 (free care) to $200 for all three coinsurance rates, especially between $0 and $50. (The three lines are not connected between $0 and $50, but expenditure drops by about $100 when moving from free care to a $50 MDE.) Coinsurance, even with a small MDE, is an effective deterrent to total spending.

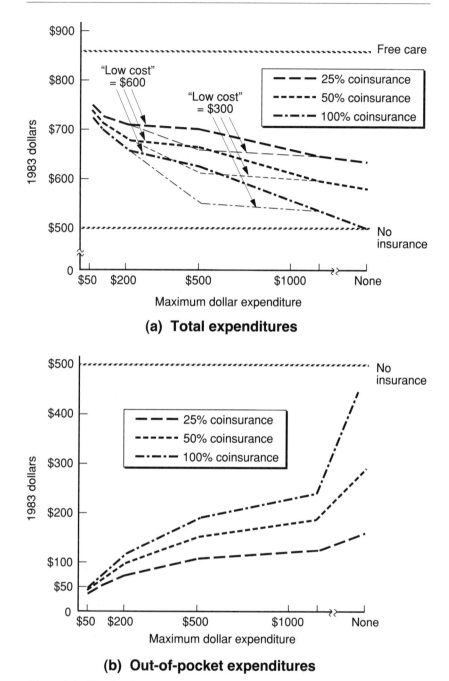

(a) Total expenditures

(b) Out-of-pocket expenditures

Figure 4.4   Simulated per capita total and out-of-pocket expenditures with individual MDEs. Low cost in the upper figure refers to the size of a low-cost hospitalization.

The probability that individuals will exceed the MDE for the three coin-surance rates is graphed in Figure 4.3. The average amount of time beyond the MDE for people exceeding the MDE is about half the year on average for each of the rates. With a $50 MDE, 50 to 70 percent of people exceed the MDE depending on the coinsurance rate; at a $1,000 MDE, fewer than 10 percent of people in any plan exceed the limit.

Conventional economic analysis assumes that the patient values services at an amount equal to the last dollar spent and that there are no externali-ties. Although both assumptions may be violated in our application, in this chapter we make conventional welfare economic calculations based on those assumptions. (The assumptions are discussed further in Chapter 11.)

On these assumptions, the average value of services used in each of the plans is graphed against total per capita expenditures in Figure 4.4. The value is assumed to be less than the spending because of the subsidy from the coinsurance and the MDE. Calculating the value with no MDE and just a change in the coinsurance rate results in the usual welfare triangle calculation, because a change in coinsurance is just like a change in unit price. A change in the MDE is not as straightforward, but the principle is

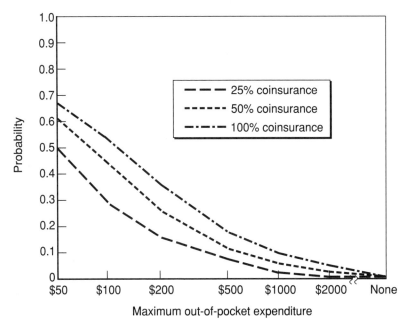

Figure 4.3   Probability of exceeding the maximum individual MDE, 1983 dollars

the same: integrate under the demand curve for the incremental change in demand to get the value of services used.[34]

For plans with 25 percent coinsurance in the cost-sharing phase (top center), the average value of services used does not vary much as the MDE varies, from $1,000 to $50; the average value rises only from $581 to $588 (shown on the vertical axis). The average per capita expenditure changes by considerably more, from $641 to $750 (shown on the horizontal axis, as well as in the upper panel of Figure 4.2). For the 50 percent coinsurance plans, the average value of services increases from $561 to $582 with the increase in total expenditures as the MDE falls from $1,000 to $50.[35] For plans with 100 percent coinsurance, both total expenditures and the average value of services vary more widely with the MDE. The average value of services and average expenditure increase sharply as one moves from no insurance (corresponding to spending and value of $494) to a $500 MDE (a $500 per person deductible). As the deductible falls further to $50 per person, the value of services used continues to increase, but at a slower rate. The lower total expenditures are associated with plans with more cost sharing and little or no protection against major expense.

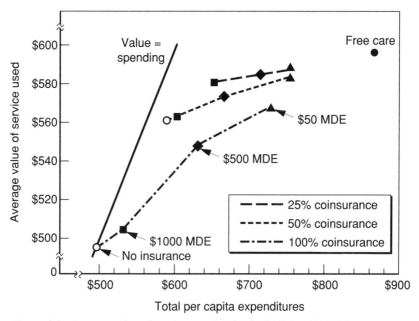

Figure 4.4   Average value of services used, individual MDEs, 1983 dollars

For these plans, relatively valuable services are being forgone, a result that follows from the assumption that the consumer values the expenditure at an amount equal to the last dollar spent. On the 100 percent coinsurance plans with a high MDE, for example, few consumers have their marginal dollar subsidized.

The average cost of risk for each plan's coinsurance rate and out-of-pocket limit is plotted in Figure 4.5. Minimal risk is associated with any of the plans with maximum out-of-pocket limits less than or equal to $500, because the variance in out-of-pocket spending is kept down by the low MDE. Beyond $500, risk levels increase rapidly. The rate of increase is higher for plans with larger coinsurance rates.

Comparisons between Individual and Family MDE Limits

Many health insurance plans in the United States have limits on the maximum out-of-pocket expenditures that an individual faces, sometimes known as a stop-loss feature. However, it is the family's economic welfare that is affected by these individual expenses. Just as insurance pools risks

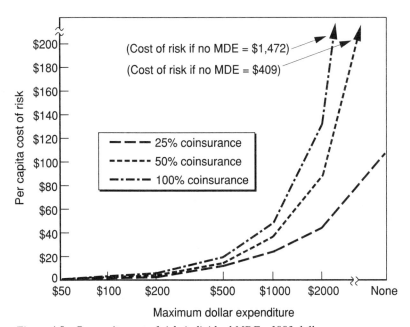

Figure 4.5   Per capita cost of risk, individual MDEs, 1983 dollars

over a group of people, health insurance plans could pool risks over the family by creating plans with family maximum out-of-pocket limits instead of individual out-of-pocket limits.

To compare plans with individual and family MDE limits, we began by looking at plans with the same average per capita expenditures.[36] For each set of individual limits, we can find a family limit with the same expected spending for the set of people in the simulation. Figure 4.6 shows for a family of four the relationship between the individual MDE limit and the family limit with the same total expected per capita expenditure, which is the number shown next to the five points in the Figure. (For example, expected expenditure with an individual MDE of $50 or family MDE of $350 is $604.) We show only the results for the 25 percent coinsurance plans; results for plans with 50 percent and 100 percent coinsurance are very similar.

As the figure shows, small individual MDE limits correspond to much larger family limits (these results clearly depend on family size). Individual MDEs of $50 yielded average expenditures equivalent to a four-person family limit of $350, almost twice as large as the four combined individual

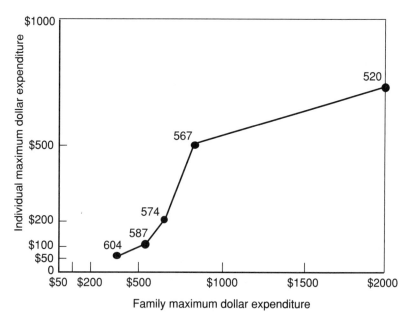

Figure 4.6   Individual and family MDEs with equal expected total expenditures, 25 percent coinsurance, four-person families

MDEs. Results were similar for $100 individual MDEs, but the relationship changed markedly at the $200 individual MDE level, where a family limit of $657 yielded the same expected medical expenditure for the family of four. This change reflects our assumption about low-cost hospital episodes; plans with small MDEs are always in the low-cost range. As family MDEs increase above $600, families begin their health insurance year without low-cost hospital episodes and consequently spend at reduced rates. Hence the family MDE does not have to increase as fast as the individual MDE to keep expected spending the same. As the individual MDE rises above $600, both individual and family limit plans have lower spending rates.

Figure 4.7 displays the relationship between risk and out-of-pocket expenditure for these "equivalent" plans. Risk costs are always higher for the family limit plans than for the equivalent individual limit plan, where equivalence means the same average total expenditures. In other words, the family limit plans are riskier. Average out-of-pocket expenditures are generally higher for family limit plans. The exception is the middle range of limits, where the individual limit plan has a small enough limit to

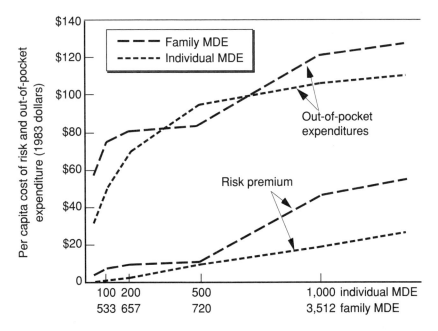

Figure 4.7   Equivalent individual MDE and family MDE plans, 25 percent coinsurance.

always be in the low-cost hospital episode phase but the family limit plan
does not initially have low-cost hospital episodes. Thus, on these two
dimensions individual MDE plans appear superior to equivalent family
MDE plans. (These results also imply that equivalent shorter accounting
periods are probably better than longer ones.)[37]

The advantage of individual limits derives from three empirical points. First,
with individual limits, lower-priced care is better targeted at the sick. The
probability that individuals exceed the limit is lower with the individual
limit than with the equivalent family limit. The reason is that with an individual limit family members who go to the hospital take only themselves
over the limit, but with a family limit they carry the other healthier family
members with them. Thus the group of people over the limit with individual
limits is smaller and sicker than the group with family limits on average.
Second, individual limits are less risky. Family limits are generally much
larger than equivalent individual limits (Fig. 4.6). The financial risk of an
expensive episode is cut short by the individual limit but may be considerable with the family limit. Even when the average out-of-pocket spending is
similar on both plans, the risk is higher with the family plan. Third, individual limits are easier to administer because there is no need to keep track
of who is in the family. For these reasons the preceding figures considered
only individual limits.

The Effect of Initial Deductibles on Expenditures

We looked at the effect of initial individual deductibles of $100, $200 and
$300 on both 25 percent and 50 percent coinsurance plans with individual
MDEs of $500 or more. In these comparisons the MDE remains constant
but the patient pays 100 percent of the initial spending (for example,
$200), in contrast to the previous estimates, where cost sharing started
with the first dollar of health care purchased. For 25 percent plans with a
$500 MDE, total per capita expenditures fell 19 to 22 percent, depending
on the size of the deductible, when compared with a plan with no initial
deductible (that is, coinsurance started with the first dollar of spending).
For larger MDEs the drop was 14–19 percent.[38] Thus, the smaller the
MDE, the greater the percentage drop for any given initial deductible.

Optimal Insurance Plan Design

Standard economic theory indicates that a well-designed health insurance
policy is one that best trades off the risk borne by the insured and the welfare loss from excess spending (Zeckhauser 1970; Besley 1988).[39] The

welfare loss is defined as the difference between the total cost to society and the value of the medical services that are purchased (see Fig. 4.4). In Table 4.21 we use this measure (in the far right column) to compare alternative insurance plan structures. We make the assumption that the charge we and the participant jointly paid represents the resource cost to society and that the additional services consumed do not affect the utility of non-family members. Our health status results (described in Part III) give some plausibility to the latter assumption. (See Chapter 11 for a discussion of these assumptions.) For comparison purposes, all the plans have a $1,000 individual MDE but differ in the initial deductible ($0, $100, $200, or $300) and in the coinsurance rate (25, 50, or 100 percent).

If we consider only plans with no initial deductible ($0), the 100 percent coinsurance plan is preferred (with combined risk and welfare loss of $73) to either the 25 percent coinsurance plan ($93) or the 50 percent coinsurance plan ($74). The introduction of initial deductibles of $100, $200, or $300 markedly improves the plans with lower coinsurance rates. The table makes clear that the "best" plans (with welfare loss plus risk equal to $45–50) are the 25 percent coinsurance plans with any of the initial deductibles. Such plans are quite similar in structure to actual insurance plans offered by many employers throughout the country—or at least were before the advent of managed care.

Sensitivity of Results to Assumptions about Catastrophic Events

The assumption that people with catastrophic events (defined as hospitalizations costing more than $13,500 in 1991 dollars) do not respond to cost sharing increases total expenditures $30–70 per person, depending on the coinsurance rate. This assumption has only modest effect on risk for plans with limits on maximum out-of-pocket expenditures; it has a large impact on risk for plans without these limits.

Implications for Insurance Design

One benefit of insurance is protection against rare financial catastrophe. Another likely benefit is the transfer of money from states or times when one is healthy to times when one is sick. The economic cost is the waste associated with overuse by the insured (moral hazard or welfare loss). If insured patients buy services they do not value enough to buy at full price, society is not using resources efficiently.[40] In this light our results for insurance design have several implications:

Table 4.21   Plan comparisons for optimal insurance design (1983 $)[a]

Coinsurance rate	Deductible	MDE	Per capita total expenditures	Out-of-pocket expenditures	Value of services[b]	Cost of risk[c]	Welfare loss plus risk
0%	0	0	860	0	595	0	265
	100	100	696	68	562	1	135
	200	200	659	112	555	3	107
25%	0	1,000	650	126	581	24	93
	100	1,000	557	154	528	22	51
	200	1,000	536	180	516	25	45
	300	1,000	529	199	510	29	48
50%	0	1,000	601	185	563	36	74
	100	1,000	543	197	522	35	56
	200	1,000	531	211	512	37	56
	300	1,000	526	222	508	39	57
100%	0[d]	1,000	529	243	505	49	73
No insurance			494	494	494	1,472	1,472

a. 1991 dollars are approximately 37% higher than 1983 dollars, using the all-items CPI. For details on how numbers were calculated see Keeler et al. (1988), table 5.7. Results differ slightly from those in Keeler et al. (1988), table 5.6, because they are based on eight replications and do not use antithetic variates.

b. No insurance is assumed to be valued at out-of-pocket cost. Value of incremental expenditures in other plans is measured as out-of-pocket cost plus consumer surplus, assuming no externalities.

c. Risk is 0.0005 times the variance of spending.

d. 100% coinsurance and a $1,000 MDE could equally be referred to as a $1,000 deductible, but we have shown this as zero to compare with zero deductibles and other coinsurance rates.

1. Even fairly small deductibles curb demand. We had hypothesized that the graph of purchased medical services as a function of deductibles would have a backward S shape (Keeler, Newhouse, and Phelps 1977). Starting from a zero deductible we thought there would be a flat initial section where deductibles would be so small that they would have little effect on behavior, followed by a steep fall in demand in the region of middle-sized deductibles, followed finally by another flat section where deductibles became so large that all participants would act essentially as if they had no insurance. However, we did not observe any initial flat section; the data showed decreased rates of outpatient spending even for variation in small MDEs. Our simulations, reflecting these data, showed a fairly smooth decline in spending throughout the range of small- and medium-sized deductibles. Thus, we would predict that even $150 deductibles (in 1991 dollars) would be effective in curbing demand. Relatively small deductibles suffice to keep down outpatient spending, and since hospital spending is less responsive to price, even large deductibles do not reduce hospitalization much. Deductibles above $1,500 (in 1991 dollars) have little effect on demand, whereas the financial risk they impose starts to increase rapidly. Thus there is little reason to have deductibles much bigger than $1,500.

2. Individual deductibles are better than family deductibles. They are easier to administer because insurers do not need to keep track of family composition. Furthermore, with a family deductible one hospitalized individual can take a whole family into a period of free care; as a result, family deductibles need to be considerably larger than individual deductibles to keep expected expenditures equal, which increases the financial risk relative to a set of smaller individual deductibles. For the same reason, short accounting periods (or possibly even visit fees) may be better than an actuarily equivalent deductible over a longer accounting period.

3. The group insurance market does quite well in offering desirable insurance policies by our criteria. According to our calculations, the best policy has a small individual deductible, 25 percent coinsurance, and a cap of about $1,500 on out-of-pocket expense. We did not simulate the more common 20 percent coinsurance rate or the (usually) larger observed caps.

Implications for Health Services Research

Cost Sharing Affects Patients but Not Doctors

What inferences can be drawn about patient and physician behavior from the limited effects of cost sharing on the similarity of costs per episode?

Assuming the severity of treated illness was similar on different plans, cost sharing did not much affect the course of treatment.[41] There are several reasons why this result may not be surprising. Tort liability tends to enforce a common standard of care. Many physicians may believe it improper to offer less-expensive or lower-quality care to patients who have to pay cost sharing. Although they may confer with their physicians about whether to go to a hospital in the first place, hospitalized patients have even less opportunity to influence the cost of their episode than ambulatory patients. Finally, some physicians are unaware of the fraction of charges paid by the patient.[42]

Episodes Are Useful in Analysis

Aggregating care into episodes has been shown to be useful for studying quality of care, reimbursement, planning, and HMO management (Hornbrook, Hurtado, and Johnson 1985; Lohr et al. 1986b). In addition, as shown here, they can be useful in economic analysis. Episodes of treatment are well-behaved statistically. They appear to be roughly independent over time, and roughly lognormal in size. Negative binomial models appear to fit the number of counts well, permitting analysis of factors influencing the rate of episodes. Moreover, a study of episodes yields insights into the determinants of care seeking. Unfortunately, as Hornbrook, Hurtado, and Johnson (1985) note and as we found in the Experiment, we need different kinds of episodes for different purposes, and creating episodes is not an easy task.

Limitations

Even the 17,000 person-years of experience studied here leave some imprecise estimates. We face a fundamental problem of health econometrics that 1 percent of the sample accounts for about one-quarter of the spending and 5 percent for about half (Manning et al. 1987; Newhouse 1987). We were not able to establish by normal statistical standards what size, if any, of catastrophic episodes was so large that price has a negligible effect on whether and how the episode is treated. Unfortunately, our estimates are moderately affected by our assumptions. For example, in plans with very large deductibles, estimated demand can decrease by about 15 percent if we assume that catastrophically large episodes are affected by insurance.

The sample size was also too small to discover any effects of almost being over the MDE (for example, having $20 left in possible out-of-pocket expenditures). This gap in knowledge, however, is unimportant, because very small (for example, $20) deductibles are not found in actual insurance policies.

Hospital episodes were more frequent when the remaining MDE was small, but they were sufficiently rare that we were unable to estimate with any precision how much remaining MDE could be considered small. Therefore, we worked with a simple classification of the remaining deductible as large or small. We made $400 (approximate 1978 dollars) the dividing line between large and small, but presumably decisions depend in a continuous fashion on the amount of MDE remaining. Unfortunately, our data could not support finer divisions.

The patterns of welfare losses in our simulations show that the large differences in welfare lie between those with some insurance and those with none (Table 4.2 This finding is reinforced by the finding that the health consequences of losing all insurance can be severe for the poor (Lurie et al. 1984). As we demonstrate in subsequent chapters, use of initial cost sharing for the bulk of the population—especially those covered by employment-based insurance—can save money at a low cost in health outcomes. Most employment-based insurance, however, already uses at least some cost sharing. Partly for that reason and partly because of the health status consequences among the poor (described in Part III), the largest gains in welfare will probably result not from adding to initial cost sharing, but from extending insurance coverage to those who currently have none.

Analysis of Outpatient Mental Health Episodes

Our methods for analyzing outpatient mental health episodes differ somewhat from those just described. (Further details on our methods and results are available in Keeler et al. 1986; Manning et al. 1989.)

The mental health analyses described in Chapter 3 resulted in some controversy in the literature as to whether medical and mental health services responded to price to the same degree (Ellis and McGuire 1984; Manning et al. 1984). The question is of some interest, since greater responsiveness could explain why mental health services are usually less well insured than medical services.[43] The response across plans observed in Chapter 3 is an amalgam of response to variation in the coinsurance rate and to the upper limit on family out-of-pocket expenses, the MDE. The higher coinsurance rates tend to reduce demand for services, but they also increase the proportion of families exceeding the MDE; hence they differentially increase demand on the high coinsurance plans. By examining episodes of mental health care, we can estimate the "pure" response to coinsurance, just as we did for medical services earlier. Thus, in this section we estimate how plans with no MDE would affect demand for mental health services.

We limit our study to an analysis of outpatient episodes because there were only 116 inpatient mental health episodes in the entire Experiment, too few for a separate analysis.[44] We also limit this analysis to episodes treated by formal mental health providers (psychiatrists, psychologists, and psychiatric social workers; see Chapter 3) because such episodes account for over 95 percent of mental health expenditures.

Definition of Mental Health Episodes and Statistical Methods

When grouping claims for various medical services into episodes, the analyst must determine whether a service on a given day belongs to an existing episode or signals the beginning of a new one. In the case of acute medical episodes, we did this by looking at the number of days that had elapsed since the last treatment for the problem. Specifically, we defined an acute medical episode as ending 16 days after the last treatment (28 days for a chronic flare-up). Thus, the first service delivered more than 16 days after the last treatment defined the start of a new episode. By contrast, for routine chronic problems we grouped all services for the year into one episode.

Defining medical episodes in this way facilitated the analysis of spending described earlier in this chapter. Decomposing spending per year into the number of episodes per year times the cost per episode, we found that the number of episodes defined in this fashion varied greatly by insurance plan, but that cost per episode was not much affected by plan. This finding greatly simplified the analysis.

Unfortunately, the methods we had used to analyze medical episodes did not perform as well for mental health episodes. Defining an episode by the end of treatment seemed more problematic; when treatment stopped, was that a temporary interruption because the patient or provider went on vacation, or was it the end of an episode? Because there were few long gaps without treatment among the Experiment patients using mental health services, we tried defining the end of an episode as eight weeks without treatment. But when we applied this definition, decomposed spending into the number of episodes per year and the cost per episode, and tried to analyze each component, we encountered serious problems. Few people had more than one mental health episode per year, which meant there was little variation in the number of episodes. Moreover, those who did have more than one episode had a lower cost per episode. Indeed, the annual spending by persons with multiple episodes was similar to the spending by persons with one episode.

Because annual spending did not appear to be much influenced by the number of episodes in a year, we aggregated all mental health spending for the year into one episode (treating it, in effect, as a chronic condition). We then used a different decomposition from the one we had used for medical spending:

> Expected annual mental health spending = $\sum_n$prob(start spending at day n) $\times$ $(365 - n)$ $\times$ $E(\$$ spent per day$|$care starts at day n).

If the expected amount spent per day, the last term, does not depend on when treatment starts, annual spending depends only on when treatment starts. If one controls for certain covariates, this turns out to be the case, which helps simplify the analysis. (The amount spent per day, for example, would not depend on when treatment started if a person saw a psychotherapist once a week from the time in the year when treatment began.)

This decomposition is also helpful in resolving the controversy in the literature over the responsiveness of mental health spending to price or coinsurance. To determine whether the demand for mental health services was more responsive to coinsurance than was the demand for medical services, we needed to examine response when there was a great deal of MDE remaining, which we defined in the same way as for medical episodes, as more than $400 (approximate 1978 dollars). Our decomposition allows us to relate the decision to initiate treatment to the amount of MDE remaining at the time that decision was taken, and thus assess the response of mental health demand to variation in coinsurance when a great deal of MDE remained. We next sketch our analysis of when in the year treatment began and our analysis of the rate of spending after that date.

Our statistical method for estimating the time at which treatment starts is to estimate a hazard model as a function of plan; we have estimated both a nonparametric (Kaplan-Meier) and a parametric (Weibull regression) model. We show in Keeler, Wells, and Manning (1986) that the Weibull regression model fits the data well. The sample used in this section is similar to the sample used for much of the chapter, the 18 largest site-years of data in the Experiment, namely, the 3 years of data in which both three- and five-year participants were enrolled in each site.

Our model and assumptions are also similar to those used in the medical analysis, except that hazard estimation of time to start an episode replaces the regression on episode frequencies. Thus, the plan effects (relative to the free plan) are hazard rates relative to the free plan. Unmeasured characteristics of families are assumed to be distributed as a Gamma distribution, as in the case of medical episodes.[45] We also used the same three periods within the year (over $400 of MDE remaining; less than $400 of MDE remaining; MDE exceeded) to estimate price effects, and to separate the underlying propensity to have episodes from the likelihood that a family is over the MDE (families with high propensities to have episodes will be differentially over the MDE) we estimated the rate of episodes on the free plan as a function of individual characteristics. Time is transformed by taking its logarithm, so that the hazard rate for beginning an episode on the free plan is approximately constant.

Estimated Rates for Starting Treatment Episodes by Plan

The estimated hazard ratios are shown in Table 4.22. The results of major interest are those of the first row, because they most closely approximate behavior with no MDE. These results show a considerable response of the hazard rates to coinsurance: the likelihood of initiating an episode in any given period with 95 percent coinsurance and more than $400 of MDE remaining is only one-quarter as large as on the free-care plan. Because most mental health episodes start early in the accounting year and because most families do not exceed their MDE, there is more experience in the large MDE period than in the other two periods (except for the Individual Deductible plan); this result is reflected in the larger standard errors in the small and over-MDE periods and in the instability of the estimated coefficients for those periods.

To test our methods, we again estimated price effects on a "test-of-methods" plan.[46] That is, we estimated the effects of an imaginary MDE among those on the free plan, knowing there can be no true MDE effect on the free plan. Thus, a value for this "plan" differing from 1.0 would suggest a problem.

Table 4.22 Hazard ratios for mental health episodes relative to free plan (standard errors in parentheses)[a]

MDE Period	Insurance plan (coinsurance rate)				Total cost sharing	Test of methods[b]
	Individual Deductible	95%	50%	25%		
Large (> $400)[c]	—[d]	0.24	0.37	0.79	0.42	0.95
	—	(0.05)	(0.07)	(0.14)	(0.04)	(0.12)
Small (≤ $400)[c]	0.74	0.46	1.16	0.61	0.73	1.06
	(0.10)	(0.16)	(0.31)	(0.26)	(0.08)	(0.16)
Over MDE	1.08	1.54	0.84	0.76	1.10	1.07
	(0.24)	(0.34)	(0.34)	(0.37)	(0.15)	(0.23)

a. Based on 18 large site years, the first three years in the four non–South Carolina sites and the last three years in the two South Carolina sites. Standard errors are understated, probably by a factor of 1.5; see Keeler et al. (1986), pp. 149–150. Hazard ratios predicted from Weibull regression model.

b. See text.

c. $400 is a current-year figure from the Experiment; the years are centered on approximately 1978.

d. There was never more than $150 of MDE remaining in this plan.

The values in the last column of Table 4.22 suggest a mild bias in our methods in the direction of showing a price effect. Although the 0.95 value is insignificantly different from 1.0, we are inclined to believe there may be a mild bias, because our methods do not account for the correlation between medical spending and mental health spending. In light of this finding, when we simulate pure price effects we divide the relevant hazard ratio by the estimate for the test-of-methods plan for the large MDE period (that is, by 0.95).

Hazard rates greater than one in the over-MDE period, the last row of Table 4.22, would indicate the presence of a sale effect. Although the point estimate for the combined cost-sharing plans is greater than 1.0 (1.10), it is within one standard error of 1.0. Thus, these data provide no strong evidence of a sale effect. The data do, however, suggest an anticipation effect; the hazard rate in the small MDE period is notably larger than in the large MDE period (0.73 versus 0.42).

Estimated Cost per Treatment Episode by Plan

There are no clear trends in the cost of episodes by plan. None of the differences in cost shown in Table 4.23 is significant at conventional levels. Nonetheless, when we examined the behavior of (the logarithm of) cost per episode in the large MDE period only, controlling for site and year, there was suggestive evidence of a coinsurance rate effect (Keeler, Wells, and Manning 1986, table 9.10).[47] As a result, we simulate the effects of plans with no MDEs in two different ways, alternatively assuming that there is a coinsurance rate effect on cost per episode and that there is none.

Table 4.23   Costs of outpatient mental health episodes, by plan[a]

Mental health episodes	Insurance plan (coinsurance rate)					
	Individual Deductible	95%	50%	25%	Total cost sharing	Free
Number	144	66	58	51	329	226
Costs ($)	536	379	404	440	463	447
Log costs	5.53	5.32	5.07	5.46	5.39	5.44

a. Based on the same sample as used in Table 4.22. Episodes costing less than $20, fewer than 5% of the episodes, have been set equal to $20. Differences among plans in cost are not statistically significant at conventional levels. Costs are in current dollars from the year in which they were incurred (1974–1982).

Table 4.24   Expected number and costs of mental health episodes for pure
coinsurance plans (no MDE)[a]

Mental health episodes	Pure coinsurance plans			
	Free	25%	50%	95%
Annual probability (expected number of episodes)	0.039	0.034	0.018	0.012
Cost per episode ($)	659	540	536	534
Total costs per enrollee ($)	25.80	18.20	9.70	6.60

a. Predictions from regression equation based on 18 largest site years of data; see Table 4.22.
Predicted levels are for rates and costs in year 2 in Seattle (1977). The total costs and annual
probability are derived first, and the cost per episode is obtained by dividing total costs by
probability. The overall CPI in 1991 was 2.25 times as high as in 1977; simply multiplying the
cost figures in the second row by 2.25, however, will yield a value based on Seattle prices and
usage patterns.

Our base case assumes that there is an effect of 18 percent; this assumption comes from the regression analysis controlling for site and year.[48]

Costs on Plans with No MDEs

We can use the estimated effects of plan on initiating episodes and on cost
per episode to estimate the overall effects of price on mental health
spending in the absence of deductibles or limits. As with medical episodes,
we assume that the pure price effect is approximated by the behavior of
people in the large MDE period. In Table 4.24 we show the annual probability, or equivalently the expected number of episodes, for the four coinsurance rates in the study.[49] The rates decline sharply with cost sharing,
with the 95 percent plan having only 32 percent as many episodes in a year
as the free plan (.32 = .0124/.0391). When the reduction in cost per episode is taken into account, the pure 95 percent coinsurance plan is estimated to spend at 26 percent of the free plan rate (.26 = 6.60/25.80), and
the pure 50 percent coinsurance plan does not have much larger expenditure, spending at 38 percent of the free plan rate (.38 = 9.70/25.80). The
spending with a pure 25 percent coinsurance rate is 70 percent of that of
the free plan rate, within rounding error of the 67 percent value observed
on the actual 25 percent plan (Table 3.24); that the value for the pure 25

percent plan was much closer to the actual than the value for the pure 95 percent plan is not surprising, because considerably fewer families on the 25 percent plan exceeded the MDE.

These estimates are based on our best guesses about the effects of price on hazard ratios and on cost per episode. Because the model is made up of these two distinct pieces, we cannot easily compute an exact overall standard error of the estimates. To provide some indication of the precision of our estimates, Table 4.25 shows the results of varying some of the parameters that go into the final model. The top row (derived from the last row of Table 4.24) gives our best-guess estimates of the effect of the coinsurance rate on outpatient mental health services spending. The next row shows the result of modifying these estimates by assuming that coinsurance has no effect on cost per episode.

The last two rows show the possible effects of sampling errors in estimating price effects. To derive these estimates, we assume that the errors in the estimates of price on episode rates are independent of those on cost per episode. We can then estimate a combined standard error.[50] If the other parameters in the model are accurate, there is a 68 percent chance that the true price effects lie between the values in the last two rows. The range those values span indicates substantial uncertainty in the estimates.

Table 4.25   Sensitivity of predicted mental health costs to assumptions for pure coinsurance plans (no MDE)

Assumptions	Pure coinsurance plan			
	95%	50%	25%	0
Base case	0.257	0.375	0.704	1.000
Cost/episode changes:				
No difference in cost/episode	0.312	0.462	0.865	
Effects of sampling errors in coinsurance effects:[a]				
Base +1 combined std. dev.	0.323	0.460	0.855	
Base −1 combined std. dev.	0.204	0.306	0.578	

a. Assumes independence between errors in hazard rate estimation and cost per episode. Uses hazard rate errors that are 1.5 times as large as those shown in Table 4.22 for plan effects and assumes other coefficients are correct.

Table 4.26   Comparison of price effects for outpatient mental health and
outpatient medical spending (free plan = 100)

	Coinsurance rate				Arc elasticity	
	0	25%	50%	95%	0–95%	25%–95%
Pure coinsurance (no MDE)						
Mental health	100	70	38	26	0.59	0.79
Outpatient medical	100	71	58	49	0.34	0.31
HIE plans						
Mental health	100	67	76, 33[a]	43	0.40	0.37
Outpatient medical	100	78,74[a]	63	58	0.27	0.23

Source: Keeler et al. (1986), table 9.13. Also Tables 3.24, 4.17, and 4.18 in this book.
a. The first element in the pair is for the 25/50 plan; the second is for the 50/50 plan.

We can now try to determine whether outpatient mental health care is more responsive to price than outpatient medical care. Table 4.26 gives cost ratios and arc elasticities for both outpatient mental health and medical spending by plan and by pure coinsurance.

Although there is little difference between the mental health and medical responses over the range of zero to 25 percent cost sharing, larger amounts of cost sharing have a larger effect on use of mental health services than on use of medical services. The estimated mental health spending with a pure 95 percent coinsurance plan is about 55 percent of what it would be if the price response were the same as for outpatient medical spending as a whole.

The estimated pure price elasticity is larger than the estimates that use the Experiment plans as proxies for pure prices and ignore the MDE effect. Comparing the last two rows of Table 4.26 with the first two, we see that the MDE feature mutes the impact of coinsurance on spending. This holds for both mental health and medical spending, but especially so for mental health spending. Since both medical and mental health episode rates increased after the MDE was exceeded, the plan effect is a mixture of coinsurance and free prices. Although the mental health spending itself did not usually cause a family to exceed the MDE, about two-thirds of families with mental health spending did exceed the MDE, compared with only 30 percent of families with no mental health spending, which explains why there is a larger difference between mental health spending with pure coinsurance and spending observed on the Experiment plans (rows 1 and 3) than there is for outpatient medical spending generally (rows 2 and 4).

Although the estimated arc elasticity for mental health services is larger than would be computed if the MDE feature were ignored (row 1 versus row 3 and row 2 versus row 4), it is smaller than most estimates from observational studies (Keeler, Wells, and Manning 1986).

Summary of Price Effects and Mental Health Services

We found that outpatient mental health use was somewhat more responsive to price than medical expenditures, but not as responsive as most observational studies had indicated. Our best guess is that use of mental health services with no insurance coverage would be about one-quarter that of free care, that care with 50 percent coinsurance is about two-fifths that of free care, and that care with 25 percent coinsurance is about 70 percent that of free care. Price elasticities are about 50 percent higher for mental health spending than for outpatient medical expenditures as a whole.

Economic considerations also seemed to play a larger role in other ways in decisions about care for mental health problems than in decisions about medical problems. Unlike medical care users, mental health users showed some anticipation of exceeding the MDE; spending in the period when the remaining MDE was small was considerably more than when the remaining MDE was large (Table 4.22). Because only about one-quarter of families exceed the MDE and mental health use generally starts early in the year, there is not much precision in the small MDE and over-MDE rates for each coinsurance rate, but when all cost sharing plans are combined, the anticipation effect comes through clearly.

We also conducted an analysis of the welfare loss from various coinsurance rates and upper limits, similar to the one we performed for medical services. The assumptions of an informed consumer and no externalities, which are necessary for this analysis, may be even shakier than for medical services. Given these limitations, we conclude that optimal coinsurance rates for mental health services would be around 25 to 50 percent, depending on the length of period considered. The value is 50 percent if only one year is considered, a higher value than for medical services, in part because of the greater price response. However, over longer periods the optimal coinsurance rate falls because of the tendency for episodes to persist, thereby adding to the variance of expenditure. Finally, it is more critical for mental health services than for medical services to have a cap on out-of-pocket expenditures in a year. We estimated the optimal cap for individuals to be about $1,400 ($1,000 in 1986 dollars) for all health services, and for families about $2,000.[51] (Further details on the optimal cap are available in Manning et al. 1989.)

Chapter 5

Specific Types of Use

The ultimate metric for assessing the differences in use analyzed in Chapters 3 and 4 is outcomes — a topic covered in some detail in Chapters 6 and 7. Here we examine how plans affect specific kinds of utilization that are generally thought to be particularly desirable or undesirable: emergency department use for more and less urgent problems; use for specific diagnoses, and especially for diagnoses for which medical care is thought to be more or less efficacious; use of prescription drugs; use of antibiotics by type of condition; appropriate and inappropriate use of the hospital; and preventive care.

Emergency Department Use

We studied emergency department use among participants enrolled in Dayton, Seattle, and the two Massachusetts sites (the data from South Carolina were not available when we performed this analysis). Our analysis includes data from three- and five-year participants in their first three years in these sites (11,456 person-years of data on 3,988 persons). When analyzing expenditure, we include only individuals with completed years of experience, as in Chapter 3. Our method for analyzing visits is similar to the one used to study frequency of episodes in Chapter 4, negative binomial regression; this method allows us to include people with partial years of participation. (Further details are available in O'Grady et al. 1985.)

The effect of insurance plan on the rate of emergency department visits did not differ significantly between those who left the study before three years and those who completed three years: $[\chi^2(4) = 3.32]$. Thus the plan predictions from our expenditure model, which are made for a standardized population, are not appreciably biased by the differential sample loss among plans described in Chapter 2. As a result, we have made no adjustment for sample loss.[1]

Differences in Use among Plans

Expenditure for emergency department services decreases as cost sharing increases (Table 5.1). Expenditure on the 95 percent plan is 70 percent of that on the free-care plan. Thus, the response of emergency room use to plan is similar to that of outpatient use (Chapter 3); in fact emergency room use is about 14 percent of total ambulatory use on each plan.[2]

The effect of cost sharing on annual expenses can be decomposed into the effect on the decision to use any emergency department services and the effect on the amount of services used, given any use. Doing so shows that almost all the cost-sharing effect is on the decision to use. The probability of any use on the 95 percent plan is 70 percent of the probability of any use on the free-care plan (15 percent versus 22 percent).

Differences among plans in the number of emergency department visits per 1,000 persons show a similar pattern. With respect to the likelihood of a visit and the number of visits, the reversals of order involving the 50 percent plan are not statistically significant (for example, in the first column 90 percent versus 86 percent). (Because fewer people were assigned to the 50 percent plan, the mean values for that plan are less precise.)

Table 5.1   Adjusted annual emergency department use per person (cost-sharing plans use shown as % of free-plan use)[a]

Plan	Expense (1991 $)	Probability of any use	Visits per 1,000 persons
Free	100% = $42	100% = 0.22	100% = 304
25%	86%	85%[b]	79%[c]
50%	90%	92%	82%
95%	70%[c]	70%[c]	65%[c]
Individual Deductible	82%[d]	81%[b]	80%[b]

a. Results shown on each plan are for a standardized population with the same age, gender, race, geographic site, income, education, and health status characteristics as the population actually enrolled throughout year 1 of the Experiment.

b. The contrast with the free plan is significant at the 0.05 level.

c. The contrast with the free plan is significant at the 0.01 level.

d. The contrast with the free plan is significant at the 0.10 level.

About one-tenth of the visits result in hospitalization. Although these visits are presumptively for serious problems, an assessment of them alone reveals that they too respond to cost sharing. People on the 25, 50, and 95 percent plans make only two-thirds as many emergency department visits resulting in hospitalization as do those with free care (Table 5.2); that is, people making visits resulting in hospitalization have the same response to cost sharing as those making other emergency department visits: $[\chi^2(4) = 1.80]$. Although one might assume that visits resulting in hospitalization are of a more serious nature, the results presented later in the chapter about the appropriateness of hospitalization cast some doubt on that assumption.

Because the Individual Deductible plan provided free care for any emergency department visits resulting in admission, we expected that people on that plan might respond differently from those on the coinsurance plans. In fact, however, the response does not differ, probably because the benefit information given to participants did not mention that they would receive free care under those conditions. Thus we cannot infer from the response to the Individual Deductible plan whether cost sharing deters hospital admission following an emergency department visit by influencing the patient's decision to come to the emergency department or by influencing the physician's decision to hospitalize the patient once he or she gets to the emergency department.

We also examined diagnosis data to get another reading on whether responsiveness to plan varies with the kinds of medical problems for which patients use the emergency department, and in particular whether the responsiveness is greater for less urgent or serious problems. Ninety-one

Table 5.2   Annual rate of emergency department visits resulting in hospitalization[a]

Plan	Visits per 1,000 persons[b]	% of free plan
Free	32 (3.5)	100
25%, 50%, and 95%	21 (2.1)[c]	67
Individual Deductible	22 (3.5)[c]	68

a. Visit rates shown are simple means.

b. Figures in parentheses are the standard errors of the mean uncorrected for intrafamily or intertemporal correlation. The true standard errors are slightly larger.

c. $p < 0.05$ for the contrast with the free plan.

percent of visits involved one or more diagnoses recorded by the physician on the claim form. We grouped the more frequent diagnoses into categories, 26 of which each accounted for 1 percent or more of all emergency department visits. We then asked a panel of four emergency department physicians to rate these diagnostic categories as either "more urgent" or "less urgent" on the basis of the seriousness of the diagnosis and the need for immediate care. Fifteen categories were rated more urgent and eleven were rated less urgent, with complete agreement for all categories except three—otitis media, sprain, and "abdominal pain, no other diagnosis" (Table 5.3).

Table 5.3   Response to plans, by diagnosis[a]

Diagnosis	Annual visits per 10,000 persons		Visits on cost-sharing plans as a proportion of visits on free plan
	Cost-sharing plans (25%, 50%, 95%, Individual Deductible)	Free plan	
More urgent diagnoses			
Fracture/dislocation	134	168	0.80
Miscellaneous serious trauma[b]	57	67	0.85
Asthma	30	83	0.36
Otitis media	40	78	0.51
Chest pain/acute heart disease	59	57	1.04
Cellulitis/abscess/ wound infection	36	39	0.92
Surgical abdominal disease[c]	42	38	1.11
Head injury	36	33	1.09
Urinary tract infection	22	43	0.51
Acute eye injury/ infection	34	34	1.01
Obstetrical	29	31	0.94
Allergic reaction	26	26	1.00
Acute alcohol/drug related	27	20	1.35
Burn, second degree/ complicated	19	22	0.86
Visits with any of the above diagnoses	991	1,280	0.77[d]

Emergency department use involving any of the more urgent diagnoses is 23 percent lower on the plans with any cost sharing than on the free plan ($p < 0.01$). By contrast, use involving only less urgent diagnoses is 47 percent lower on the cost-sharing plans than on the free plan ($p < 0.01$). Stated differently, as compared with the cost-sharing plans, free care is associated with 90 percent higher use for the less urgent diagnoses but only 30 percent higher use for the more urgent diagnoses. This difference is highly significant—[$\chi^2(4) = 17.10$, $p < 0.01$]—and its significance is not changed by recategorizing the diagnoses for which opinions about the level of severity differed.

Table 5.3   (continued)

Diagnosis	Annual visits per 10,000 persons		Visits on cost-sharing plans as a proportion of visits on free plan
	Cost-sharing plans (25%, 50%, 95%, Individual Deductible)	Free plan	
Less urgent diagnoses			
Abrasion/contusion	228	403	0.54
Sprain	164	249	0.63
Upper respiratory infection	92	190	0.51
Influenza/viral syndrome	40	61	0.65
Gastroenteritis/diarrhea	36	67	0.62
Abdominal pain (no other diagnosis)	34	65	0.53
Back/neck pain	32	67	0.45
Arthritis/bursitis	30	63	0.45
Headache	8	59	0.11
Acute bronchitis	14	36	0.42
Burn, first degree	7	28	0.28
Visits involving only the above diagnoses	663	1185	0.53[d]

a. Equal partial weights were used to count visits involving multiple diagnoses. For example, if a visit resulted in three diagnoses, each diagnosis was credited with one-third of a visit.

b. Includes foreign bodies, ingestions, ligamentous ruptures, and internal, neurovascular, and crush injuries.

c. Includes cholecystitis, gastrointestinal bleeding, appendicitis, intestinal obstruction, and peptic ulcer disease.

d. $p < 0.01$ for the difference between cost-sharing plans and the free plan, and for the difference between visits involving more urgent diagnoses and visits involving only less urgent diagnoses.

Table 5.4   Annual visit rates per 10,000 persons for sutured and unsutured
lacerations under free-care and cost-sharing plans (standard
errors in parentheses)[a]

Plan	Sutured lacerations	Unsutured lacerations
Free	205 (1.9)	248 (2.3)
25%, 50%, and 95%	207 (2.0)	152 (1.7)[b]

a. The Individual Deductible plan is included with free care.
b. $p < 0.01$ for the difference between visits involving unsutured lacerations under free care and such visits under cost sharing.

For less urgent visits, nearly all the observed response to cost sharing occurs between free care and the 25 percent coinsurance plan. There is very little difference among the 25, 50, and 95 percent plans. By contrast, visits involving urgent diagnoses continue to decrease as cost sharing increases. For these visits, use on the 25 percent plan is 85 percent of the free plan rate, whereas use on the 95 percent plan is only 65 percent of the free plan rate.

To test further the hypothesis that a disproportionate amount of the additional use associated with free care involved less serious medical problems, we classified visits for lacerations—the single most frequent diagnosis—by whether or not they were sutured. We found a sharp contrast: whereas the rate of visits for sutured lacerations does not differ between the free and cost-sharing plans (Table 5.4), visits for unsutured lacerations are 63 percent higher on the free-care plan than on any cost-sharing plans ($p < 0.01$).

Insurers sometimes provide more generous coverage for emergency department visits related to accidents than for those related to illness. For this reason we compared the response to cost sharing for visits with accident-related diagnoses and for visits with other diagnoses. Accident-related visits are 69 percent as frequent on the coinsurance plans as on the free plan, and visits unrelated to accidents are 66 percent as frequent as on the free plan. This difference is not significant at the 0.10 level: [$\chi^2(3) = 0.83$]. Thus, with free care accident-related visits increase about as much as illness-related visits.

Differences in Use by Income Group and Site

With insurance plan controlled for, persons in the lower third of the income distribution have emergency department expenses 66 percent higher than those of persons in the upper third of the income distribution, with those in the middle third intermediate (Table 5.5). As income falls, emergency department services also constitute an increasingly large proportion of all ambulatory care expenses.

Despite their greater use of the emergency department, however, the poor are not measurably more sensitive to cost sharing. We compared the responses to cost sharing of persons in the lower third and persons in the upper two-thirds of the income distribution with respect to the probability of any emergency department use. We could not reject the hypothesis of an equal response at a 0.10 significance level.

Emergency department use varies markedly by site. Table 5.6 shows that emergency department expenses in Franklin County and Fitchburg are

Table 5.5 Annual emergency department expense per person, by income tertile (1991 $)[a]

Income tertile	Expense ($)	% of total ambulatory expense
Upper	33	8
Middle	41	11[b]
Lower	54[b]	16[b]

a. Results shown are controlled for the insurance plan but are not adjusted for differences among income tertiles in terms of age, gender, race, geographic site, education, or health status. Income, however, has a significant ($p < 0.10$) effect on emergency department expense independent of its association with these other demographic variables.

b. The contrast with the highest-income tertile is significant at the 0.01 level.

Table 5.6 Annual emergency department expense per person, by site

Site	Free plan spending rate ($)[a]	Wait for new patient appointment, 1973–74 (number of days)
Seattle	37	4
Dayton	34	7
Franklin County	46[b]	9
Fitchburg	63[b]	25

a. Spending rates are for a population with the demographic characteristics of the population actually enrolled in each site in year 1 of the Experiment, but are standardized to the free plan. Expenses are expressed in 1991 dollars and are adjusted for regional differences in cost of living.

b. The contrast with Seattle is significant at the 0.01 level.

about 25 and 70 percent higher, respectively, than those in Seattle, even after adjustment for differences in the cost of living. Table 5.6 also presents the number of days that a new patient must wait for an appointment with a primary care physician, as measured in 1973–74—a measure of demand pressure on the ambulatory care system. The relationship between waiting times and emergency department use seems clear; we infer that if it is more difficult to see a primary care, office-based physician, people rely more heavily on the emergency department.

An analogous finding in the literature strengthens our belief in the validity of this finding. As Medicaid physician fees fall relative to Medicare physician fees, with a resulting fall in physician participation in Medicaid, use of the emergency department, and especially use of the clinic, by Medicaid eligibles increases; overall visit rates, however, do not change (Long, Settle, and Stuart 1986). Thus, as it becomes harder for Medicaid eligibles to see a private physician, they shift their use to the emergency department.

Implications for Insurance Design

Different levels of insurance coverage for different kinds of care can be justified on several different grounds. One argument from economic theory supports more generous coverage of services whose demand is less affected by insurance (Baumol and Bradford 1970; Zeckhauser 1970). Historically, this has probably been an important rationale for the more generous coverage of emergency department care relative to other ambulatory care. Our results indicate that more generous insurance coverage of emergency department care cannot be justified on this basis. The same may be said for providing differential coverage of accident-related and illness-related emergency department visits—a type of coverage that seems to be disappearing.

Use for Specific Diagnoses

For emergency room use, cost sharing appeared to have the effect predicted by standard economic theory; that is, it appeared to reduce selectively the least valuable care. Such was not the case, however, for a number of other types of care. We begin with an analysis of whether any care was sought by people with different diagnoses. (Our analysis is reported in much greater detail in Lohr et al. 1986b.)

Using data from year 2 of the Experiment in all sites, we performed separate analyses for adults and children, and for individuals in poor and nonpoor households. For these purposes we defined as "poor" those in the lowest income tertile in our sample.[3] Thus, the poor and nonpoor households differ in characteristics other than income, such as education.

We grouped all claims from year 2 of the study according to one of 150 diagnostic categories, selecting for further analysis those categories in which at least 2 percent of the sample (or subsample of interest) had some medical care contact. We then analyzed the probability of any contact as a function of plan. In making tests of significance we applied a modified Bonferroni test to adjust for the multiple comparisons we were making (and hence the increased likelihood of finding a test statistic that fell in any given size critical region by chance).[4] Because the Bonferroni test is conservative (that is, it may have low power), we used a 10 percent level of significance when adjusting for multiple comparisons.

Of the 150 categories, we examined 14 frequently occurring ones using logistic regression methods to adjust for the minor imbalances of plan with respect to site, age, and gender distributions, and an initial measure of health (the General Health Index). For each individual we predicted the probability of any contact in year 2 for the condition in question; these predicted values were then averaged over the cost-sharing and income groups to produce the values reported here.

In addition, we classified diagnostic groups according to our view of the effectiveness of medical care. Specifically, physicians who were part of the Experiment team grouped conditions into the categories shown in Table 5.7. We then examined whether cost sharing differentially affected the likelihood of contact in particular categories, and specifically whether cost sharing had less effect on conditions where medical care was thought to be highly effective.

Tables 5.8 and 5.9 list the diagnoses that exhibit a significantly lower likelihood of contact for poor and nonpoor adults and children on cost-sharing plans. For all diagnoses shown one can reject the hypothesis of no relationship between cost sharing and use at a 5 percent level of significance (unadjusted for multiple comparisons). Diagnoses listed with a note b are significant at a 10 percent level of significance with a Bonferroni correction for multiple corrections.

The difference in the cost-sharing response between poor and nonpoor children is particularly striking. For children, there is no response to cost sharing for the nonpoor except for acute upper respiratory infections, and even the statistical significance of that finding does not survive a correction for multiple comparisons (see the right side of Table 5.9). For poor children, by contrast, there are significant differences for 14 diagnoses, and 5 of these 14 conditions survive a multiple comparison correction.

For adults, cost sharing reduces the probability of seeking care for more conditions among the nonpoor than among the poor, but the two income groups respond in a similar way for several conditions: general medical

Table 5.7   Medical effectiveness groupings[a]

Group One: Highly Effective Treatment by the Medical Care System
  1. Medical Care Highly Effective: Acute Conditions
     Eyes—conjunctivitis
     Otitis media, acute
     Acute sinusitis
     Strep throat
     Acute lower respiratory infections (acute bronchitis)
     Pneumonia
     Vaginitis and cervicitis
     Nonfungal skin infections
     Trauma—fractures
     Trauma—lacerations, contusions, abrasions
  2. Medical Care Highly Effective: Acute or Chronic Conditions
     Sexually transmitted disease or pelvic inflammatory disease
     Malignant neoplasm, including skin
     Gout
     Anemias
     Enuresis
     Seizure disorders
     Eyes—strabismus, glaucoma, cataracts
     Otitis media, not otherwise specified
     Chronic sinusitis
     Peptic and nonpeptic ulcer disease
     Hernia
     Urinary tract infection
     Skin—dermatophytoses
  3. Medical Care Highly Effective: Chronic Conditions
     Thyroid disease
     Diabetes
     Otitis media, chronic
     Hypertension and abnormal blood pressure
     Cardiac arrythmias
     Congestive heart failure
     Chronic bronchitis, chronic obstructive pulmonary disease
     Rheumatic disease (rheumatoid arthritis)

examination, abdominal pain, skin rashes (these three even with a multiple comparison correction), chest pain, vaginitis, and lacerations.

Cost sharing does not have a differential effect according to the effectiveness of care (Table 5.10); it is just as likely to lower use when care is thought to be highly effective as when it is thought to be only rarely effective—a very different finding from emergency department use. For adults and children, cost sharing is associated on average with a statistically significant lower likelihood ($p < 0.10$, two-tailed test, with multiple comparisons correction) of at least one medical encounter for nearly all

Table 5.7   (continued)

Group Two: Quite Effective Treatment by the Medical Care System
     Diarrhea and gastroenteritis (infectious)
     Benign and unspecified neoplasm
     Thrombophlebitis
     Hemorrhoids
     Hay fever (chronic rhinitis)
     Acute pharyngitis and tonsillitis
     Acute middle respiratory infections (tracheitis, laryngitis)
     Asthma
     Chronic enteritis, colitis
     Perirectal conditions
     Menstrual and menopausal disorders
     Acne
     Adverse effects of medicinal agents
     Other abnormal findings

Group Three: Less Effective Treatment by the Medical Care System
     Hypercholesterolemia, hyperlipidemia
     Mental retardation
     Peripheral neuropathy, neuritis, and sciatica
     Ears—deafness
     Vertiginous syndromes
     Other heart disease
     Edema
     Cerebrovascular disease
     Varicose veins of lower extremities
     Prostatic hypertrophy, prostatitis
     Other cervical disease
     Other musculoskeletal disease
     Lymphadenopathy
     Vehicular accidents
     Other injuries and adverse effects

the effectiveness categories.[5] Decreases prompted by cost sharing are not uniformly stronger for adults than for children; nor is there any obvious trend suggesting that cost sharing deters care seeking more as one moved "down" the effectiveness ranking.

To see whether these effects were similar for the poor and the nonpoor, we restricted the analyses to the two ends of the effectiveness spectrum: "medical care highly effective: acute conditions" and "medical care rarely effective but self-care effective." Both have substantial sample sizes (around one-third of adults and children getting care in year 2) and significant cost-sharing effects for the average person.

Table 5.7   (continued)

Group Four: Medical Care Rarely Effective or Self-Care Effective
    1. Medical Care Rarely Effective
        Viral exanthems
        Hypoglycemia
        Obesity
        Chest pain
        Shortness of breath
        Hypertrophy of tonsils or adenoids
        Chronic cystic breast disease
        Other breast disease (nonmalignant)
        Debility and fatigue (malaise)
    2. Over-the-Counter (OTC) or Self-Care Effective
        Influenza (viral)
        Fever
        Headaches
        Cough
        Acute upper respiratory infection (URI)
        Throat pain
        Irritable colon
        Abdominal pain
        Nausea or vomiting
        Constipation
        Other rashes and skin conditions
        Degenerative joint disease
        Low back pain diseases and syndromes
        Bursitis or synovitis and fibrositis or myalgia
        Acute sprains and strains
        Muscle problems

a. Classifications are for medical care technology as of the time of the Experiment, approximately the late 1970s.

Table 5.8   Summary of diagnostic groups with significantly lower observed probabilities of an episode of care for adults on cost-sharing plans, by income group[a]

Poor adults	Nonpoor adults
Hay fever	
	Obesity
Anxiety neurosis[b]	
Chronic sinusitis[b]	
	Peripheral neuropathy, neuritis, and sciatica
Vision examinations[b]	
General medical examination[b]	General medical examination[b]
	Influenza
Acute pharyngitis	
Chest pain	Chest pain
Abdominal pain[b]	Abdominal pain[b]
	Acne
	Nonfungal skin infections
Skin rashes and other skin diseases[b]	Skin rashes and other skin diseases[b]
Vaginitis or cervicitis	Vaginitis or cervicitis
	Urinary tract infection
	Degenerative joint disease
	Disc displacement or derangement
	Low back pain diseases and syndromes[b]
Bursitis and fibrositis	
Lacerations, contusions, and abrasions	Lacerations, contusions, and abrasions
	Fractures
	Other gastrointestinal disease
	Other injuries and adverse effects
Other signs and symptoms	

a. All diagnostic groups shown had significantly ($p < 0.05$) lower "observed" probabilities with cost sharing.

b. The effect was significant at $p < 0.10$, two-tailed test, even with multiple comparisons correction. See Lohr et al. (1986b), app. C, tables C.3–C.6, for details.

For adults, cost sharing significantly affects both poor and nonpoor for both effectiveness categories (Table 5.11). The reduction tends to be larger for poor adults, but not significantly so.

The pattern is different for children (Table 5.12): cost sharing significantly decreases care seeking for the "rarely effective" category for both poor and nonpoor children, and rather more so for the poor. In contrast, for "highly effective" care there is a significant decrease in care seeking among the poor but not among the nonpoor. Moreover, the probability of at least one episode of "highly effective" outpatient care for poor children facing cost sharing is 56 percent of the level for those with free care, in marked contrast to 85 percent for nonpoor children, a statistically significant difference.

Use of Prescription Drugs

Data on how cost sharing affects use of prescription drugs come from claims forms filed by participants during the first year of the Experiment in Dayton, Seattle, and the two Massachusetts sites (the South Carolina data were not available when this analysis was done).[6]

Participants' expenditures on drugs averaged $65 (in 1991 dollars), ranging from $82 on the free care plan to $46 on the 95 percent coinsurance plan (Table 5.13). The national per capita expenditure for those under 65 in 1983 (in 1991 dollars) was $49. Because most Americans in 1983

Table 5.9   Summary of diagnostic groups with significantly lower observed probabilities of an episode of care for children on cost-sharing plans, by income group[a]

Poor children	Nonpoor children
Vision examination	
General medical examination[b]	
Otitis media, not otherwise specified	
Otitis media, acute	
Influenza	
Acute upper respiratory infection (URI)[b]	Acute upper respiratory infection (URI)
Acute pharyngitis	
Streptococcal sore throat[b]	
Acute bronchitis	
Diarrhea and gastroenteritis	
Skin rashes and other skin diseases	
Acute sprains and strains	
Lacerations, contusions, and abrasions[b]	
Other injuries and adverse effects[b]	

a. All diagnostic groups shown had significantly ($p < 0.05$) lower "observed" probabilities with cost sharing.

b. The effect was significant at $p < 0.10$, two-tailed test, even with multiple comparisons correction. See Lohr et al. (1986b), app. C, tables C.9–C.12, for details.

Table 5.10   Predicted percentages of adults and children with an episode of care, by medical effectiveness categories and plan

Medical care effectiveness category	Adults (N = 3,643)			Children (N = 1,830)		
	Free	Cost sharing	Cost sharing as % of free	Free	Cost sharing	Cost sharing as % of free
Highly effective						
Acute	28.4	19.0	67[a]	32.0	23.1	72[a]
Acute/chronic	16.8	13.3	79[a]	19.4	16.1	83
Chronic	12.6	10.7	85	4.7	2.4	52[a]
Quite effective	23.2	17.6	76[a]	22.4	17.6	79[a]
Less effective	25.0	18.6	74[a]	12.9	9.7	76
Rarely effective	10.5	7.4	70[a]	5.1	3.4	67
Rarely effective but self-care effective	38.8	29.2	75[a]	35.6	23.9	67[a]

a. Effect of cost sharing significant at $p < 0.05$.

Table 5.11   Predicted percentages of adults with an episode of care, by medical effectiveness category, income, and plan[a]

Medical care effectiveness category	Poor adults (N = 1,303)			Nonpoor adults (N = 2,340)		
	Free	Cost sharing	Cost sharing as % of free	Free	Cost sharing	Cost sharing as % of free
Medical care highly effective for acute conditions[b]	28.4	16.8	59[c]	26.9	19.2	71[c]
Medical care rarely effective, but over-the-counter or self-care effective[d]	38.7	27.2	70[c]	38.8	30.1	78[c]

a. Predictions are for individuals who, except for income, have the characteristics of an average adult.

b. For example, otitis media, acute bronchitis, vaginitis, lacerations. See Table 5.7.

c. Effect of cost sharing significant at $p < 0.05$.

d. For example, acute URI, low back pain syndromes, acute sprains and strains. See Table 5.7.

Table 5.12   Predicted percentages of children with an episode of care, by medical effectiveness category, income, and plan[a]

Medical care effectiveness category	Poor children (N = 807)			Nonpoor children (N = 1,023)		
	Free	Cost sharing	Cost sharing as % of free	Free	Cost sharing	Cost sharing as % of free
Medical care highly effective for acute conditions[b]	34.3	19.2	56[c]	30.3	25.8	85
Medical care rarely effective, but over-the-counter or self-care effective[d]	35.3	19.3	54[c]	35.8	27.1	76[c]

a. Predictions are for individuals who, except for income, have the characteristics of an average child.

b. For example, otitis media, lacerations. See Table 5.7.

c. Effect of cost sharing significant at $p < 0.05$.

d. For example, acute URI, acute sprains and strains. See Table 5.7.

Table 5.13   Prescription drug utilization per person, by plan

Plan	Prescription expenditures			Number of prescriptions			Ambulatory visit index (free=100)[b]
	1991 $[a]	Index (free=100)	t vs. free	No.	Index (free=100)	t vs. free	
Free	$82	100	—	5.4	100	—	100
25%	63	76	3.28	4.4	82	2.77	73
50%	49	60	4.47	4.3	80	3.25	67
95%	46	57	6.31	3.6	67	4.80	60
Individual Deductible	60	73	3.32	4.3	79	1.78	66

a. Expenditure values are predicted from a two-equation model (likelihood of any use; logarithm of expenditure conditional on use); see Leibowitz et al. (1985) for further details.

b. Ambulatory visits are face-to-face visits and reflect data from all five years of the Experiment. See Table 3.2.

were not covered by insurance for their drug expenditure, our data appear reasonably consistent with national data. In particular, there does not appear to be serious underreporting of expenditure on drugs, which was certainly a possibility given the rather modest pecuniary reward for filing a claim on the 95 percent coinsurance plan (for example, for a $10 prescription the participant would have received $.50 for filing a claim). (See Chapter 3 for a further discussion of underreporting.)

A comparison of expenditure on drugs with rate of visits indicates that the variation in expenditure stems largely from the visit rate per plan, not from the expenditure on drugs per visit; the number of prescriptions per enrollee does not vary quite as much across plans as expenditure on drugs. This result appears to imply that expenditure per prescription is higher on the free care plan, but in fact average cost per prescription is not significantly related to plan at the 5 percent level ($F = 1.85$, d.f. = 4,2359). Moreover, the proportion of generic drugs among all prescriptions does not differ by plan. Thus, there is no evidence that less generous insurance stimulates patients to search for generic drugs. This finding is analogous to another finding—that less generous insurance does not motivate participants to search for lower-cost physicians (M. S. Marquis 1985).

At first the finding that expenditure per visit on drugs does not vary much by plan may seem to imply that physicians are equally likely to write a prescription on the free-care and cost-sharing plans, but in fact the data cannot be interpreted in this way. Facing a patient in the office, the physician may in fact be more likely to write a prescription if the drug is fully covered by insurance, but any tendency to do so may be offset by the tendency for additional visits on the free-care plan to be for less serious reasons, and thus less likely to result in a prescription.

Expenditure and number of prescriptions filled reflect the likelihood that the participant filled the prescription, as well as the likelihood that a physician wrote a prescription. Consistent with the rather similar response of visits and expenditure on drugs, the probability that a prescription was filled varied little by plan, although it did vary by the nature of the problem for which the drug was prescribed (for example, markedly higher for antihypertensive medication than for anti-acne medication).

Use of Antibiotics

To shed light on the appropriateness of prescribing behavior, we analyzed oral antibiotic use for 5,765 adults and children during their second year of participation in the Experiment as a function of insurance plan. We included all prescriptions for antibiotics filled by patients who were not in a hospital or nursing home, with each antibiotic linked to a specific diagnosis. Generally this linkage was established by the prescribing physician, who recorded the diagnosis on the claims form (see Fig. 4.1). In a few cases the physician recorded multiple diagnoses and did not link the antibiotic to a specific diagnosis. In these cases a physician at RAND, George A. Goldberg, assigned the most probable diagnosis. A diagnosis was available for 97 percent of the claims (3,793 of 3,903). We grouped the diagnoses into four categories for which antibiotics might be appropriately or inappropriately prescribed, according to whether an illness was likely to be bacterial (for example, streptococcal sore throat) or viral (for example, influenza) or one for which antibiotics are standard therapy (for example, acne). (For further details see Foxman et al. 1987.)

We used negative binomial regression methods to estimate the number of antibiotics purchased in the 12-month period. The quantity of pills per prescription and dosage levels does not vary by plan; hence the number of antibiotics purchased differs from the total quantity of antibiotics consumed, if at all, by differential rates of compliance with the prescribed dosage once the prescription has been filled. Because of the time and trouble to fill a prescription, it is plausible that the participant would not fill the prescription unless he or she intended to take the antibiotic. Hence we believe that compliance, once the antibiotic is purchased, does not vary by plan and that our data reflect actual use in our population.

The regression methods include as covariates age, age squared, gender, income, a dummy variable for cost sharing, and three interaction terms with the cost-sharing dummy variable: income, age × income, and age squared × income.[7] The three interaction terms are all significant at conventional levels (*t*-statistics of 3.2, 3.7, and 2.4, respectively). We use the estimated equation to derive predicted values for individuals with particular characteristics.

Cost sharing makes a substantial difference. On average, antibiotic use per person in the free care plan is 85 percent greater than in the cost-sharing plans.[8] Table 5.14 shows predicted rates of oral antibiotic use for individuals with differing characteristics. The effect of free care is strong for poor adults (more than a factor of three for both males and females); even with free care, however, antibiotic use differs by income level.

To shed some light on the issue of appropriate use we examined whether the effect of insurance differed by diagnosis. The results of grouping antibiotic use into four broad categories are shown in Table 5.15. The effect of free care on antibiotic use is roughly similar across the four categories. In particular, the use for viral conditions, where the indications for antibiotic use are equivocal at best, is 97 percent higher in the free care plan; the increase in use for bacterial conditions, where antibiotic use would generally be indicated, is very similar, 95 percent higher. Thus free care appears to have a general, nonspecific effect on increasing antibiotic use. This finding is similar to those for diagnosis-specific use but differs from the finding for emergency room use.

The randomized nature of the Experiment allows us to presume that the incidence of illness was unrelated to plan. Thus, the increase in use for bacterial conditions can be presumed to be generally appropriate. The increase in use for viral conditions, by contrast, can be presumed to be generally inappropriate. From published epidemiologic data on the incidence of adverse reactions by drug class, we calculated that the prescribed antibiotics would cause 5 serious adverse effects per 1,000 persons enrolled on the cost-sharing plan and 10 on the free plan. Eighteen percent of those reactions (across all plans) would be associated with antibiotics given for viral conditions. Additionally, the antibiotics would cause 39 milder adverse effects on the cost-sharing plan per 1,000 persons enrolled and 55 on the free plan. Thus, cost sharing reduces the likelihood of an individual's suffering an adverse effect related to antibiotic use. Cost sharing, however, also reduces appropriate antibiotic use; a method that more selectively reduces inappropriate use would clearly be desirable.

Table 5.14   Predicted annual per-person rate of oral antibiotic use for persons of different family income, gender, and age, by plan[a]

Gender and age	Free plan		Cost-sharing plans	
	Low income	High income	Low income	High income
Female				
4 years	1.82	2.48	1.06	1.14
45 years	0.49	0.67	0.14	0.53
Male				
4 years	1.15	1.57	0.67	0.72
45 years	0.31	0.42	0.09	0.33

a. Per-person rates are predicted by using a negative binomial model, holding health status and geographic site constant.

Table 5.15 Number and percentage of all antibiotics and rate of use per person per year, by diagnostic category and insurance plan

Diagnostic category	Free plan (N = 1,935)			Cost-sharing plans (N = 3,830)			Ratio of free to cost sharing (95% confidence interval)[a]
	Number of antibiotics purchased	%	Number per person enrolled in plan	Number of antibiotics purchased	%	Number per person enrolled in plan	
All viral conditions	320	17	0.17	321	16	0.08	1.97 (1.70, 2.28)
Acute upper respiratory infection	195	10	0.10	222	11	0.06	1.74 (1.45, 2.09)
Influenza	43	2	0.02	39	2	0.01	2.18 (1.42, 3.35)
Cough	19	1	0.01	13	1	0.003	2.89 (1.43, 5.84)
Throat pain	20	1	0.01	22	1	0.01	1.80 (0.98, 3.29)
Chronic rhinitis	15	1	0.01	10	<1	0.003	2.97 (1.34, 6.60)
Viral rashes, exanthems	28	2	0.01	15	1	0.004	3.69 (1.98, 6.89)
All viral-bacterial conditions	301	16	0.16	382	19	0.10	1.56 (1.36, 1.80)
Acute pharyngitis	191	10	0.10	245	12	0.06	1.54 (1.28, 1.85)
Acute laryngitis	14	1	0.01	21	1	0.01	1.32 (0.67, 2.59)
Acute bronchitis	96	5	0.05	116	6	0.03	1.64 (1.26, 2.14)
All bacterial conditions	905	49	0.47	919	45	0.24	1.95 (1.81, 2.10)
Respiratory conditions	337	18	0.17	412	20	0.11	1.62 (1.42, 1.85)
Nonrespiratory conditions	568	31	0.29	507	25	0.13	2.22 (2.00, 2.47)
All other conditions	289	16	0.15	356	17	0.09	1.61 (1.39, 1.86)
Total[b]	1,857	98[b]	0.96	2,046	97[b]	0.53	1.80 (1.75, 1.86)

a. Taylor's series 95% confidence intervals; ratio and confidence intervals calculated using 8 significant digits.
b. Numbers shown for the four main diagnostic categories do not sum to the total because diagnoses were unknown for 42 claims on the free plan and 68 claims on the cost-sharing plans.

Appropriate and Inappropriate Use of Hospitalization

We have already shown (Chapters 3 and 4) that insurance plan affects the rate of hospitalization. Here we ask whether the additional admissions on the free care plan were primarily appropriate or inappropriate.

We were able to obtain hospital charts for 1,132 of the 1,268 medical-surgical adult hospitalizations that occurred during the Experiment (89 percent). We excluded psychiatric and maternity cases. Two physicians then independently applied the Appropriateness Evaluation Protocol (AEP) to these charts (Gertman and Restuccia 1981). The AEP consists of a previously validated list of criteria that define patients who benefit medically from being in the hospital. We accounted separately for surgical procedures that could have been done on an outpatient basis if facilities had been available. Thus, we classified admissions as inappropriate if hospitalization was of no medical benefit—that is, if no acute services were required or rendered. We did not judge the appropriateness of any procedure performed, only whether it was appropriate for a patient undergoing such a procedure to be hospitalized. We also reviewed a random day during each stay, using the AEP to determine if that day was appropriate.

Although our definition of appropriateness used a medical criterion only, some admissions that we classified as medically appropriate may have been economically inappropriate; that is, the costs may have exceeded the benefits. Thus, our figures probably understate the proportion of economically inappropriate admissions.

The reliability of appropriateness determination was good. Fully 84 percent of the time the two physician reviewers agreed on whether their admission was appropriate, inappropriate, or avoidable by use of outpatient surgery ($\kappa = 0.72$). If this three-way classification scheme is collapsed to a two-way scheme by combining the first and third categories, the percentage of agreement rises to 92 percent ($\kappa = 0.76$). Reliability for classification of the random day as appropriate was slightly less.

In order to shed more light on the nature of inappropriate admissions, the two physician reviewers also assigned a severity stage (modified from Horn's Patient Severity Index) to each admission. The intent was to determine whether an increasing rate of inappropriate admissions was associated with increased proportions of less severe illness.

For this analysis we grouped the insurance plans into three groups: the free care plan, the Individual Deductible plan, and all other cost-sharing plans. All other cost-sharing plans were grouped together because there were no significant differences among them in overall admission rates (Chapter 3). Because no free-standing outpatient surgery facilities were available in any of the six sites during the study years, our analyses treat outpatient surgery admissions as appropriate when they are not distinguished as a separate category. (Further details can be found in Siu et al. 1986; Siu, Manning, and Benjamin 1990.)

Overall, 60 percent of the admissions in the sample were appropriate, 23 percent inappropriate, and 17 percent could have been avoided by use of outpatient surgery. Although the overall admission rates differ by plan (Chapter 3), the *proportion* of inappropriate admissions and appropriate days does not (Table 5.16, rows 9 and 10). Thus, cost sharing reduces both

Table 5.16   Rates of adult medical-surgical hospitalizations by insurance plan[a]

	Free plan	Cost sharing for all services	Individual Deductible
Enrollees (no.)	1,098	1,535	780
Admissions (no.)	486	504	278
Response rate (%)[b]	90.5	88.5	88.5
Total medical-surgical admissions[c]	126 ± 19	96 ± 13[d]	109 ± 20
Appropriate admissions[c]	96 ± 15	75 ± 11[d]	82 ± 17
Inappropriate admissions[c]	30 ± 7	22 ± 5[e]	26 ± 9
Total hospital days[c]	830 ± 159	640 ± 110	842 ± 241
Inappropriate days[c]	292 ± 83	213 ± 53[f]	324 ± 107
Inappropriate admissions (%)	24 ± 4	22 ± 4	24 ± 7
Inappropriate days (%)	35 ± 6	34 ± 6	38 ± 10
Inappropriate days per admission	2.3 ± 0.6	2.2 ± 0.5	3.0 ± 0.8

a. 95% confidence intervals are presented for all plans.

b. Percent of admissions.

c. Per 1,000 person-years.

d. $p < 0.05$ vs. free plan.

e. The significance of this difference between the free and cost-sharing plans is sensitive to the method of analysis used. If only simple means are analyzed, $p = 0.06$; however, $p = 0.015$ when a multiple regression model is used.

f. The significance of the difference between the free and cost sharing plans is sensitive to the method of analysis used. If only simple means are analyzed, $p = 0.11$; however, $p = 0.02$ when a multiple regression model is used.

appropriate and inappropriate days by about the same amount, similar to its nonspecific effect on antibiotic use and diagnosis-specific seeking of care.

This result is contrary to theoretical expectations. Although standard economic theory would predict that cost sharing would reduce some admissions that by these clinical criteria might be considered appropriate—namely, those whose benefits are positive but less than the costs—it would also predict that the reduction in inappropriate admissions would be greater than the reduction in appropriate admissions.[9]

Our finding of a rather general, nonspecific effect on appropriate and inappropriate admissions is confirmed by an analysis of the stage of disease in the three types of cost-sharing arrangements (Table 5.17). If the additional admissions on the free care plan were primarily inappropriate, one would expect more stage 1 (least severe) cases on the free plan and a smaller proportion of stage 3 and 4 (most severe) cases. Clearly, however, this is not the pattern shown.

Substantial variation does appear across sites in the percentage of inappropriate admissions and days (Table 5.18). The percentage of inappropriate admissions ranges from 10 in Seattle to 35 in Georgetown, and the proportion of inappropriate days from 20 in Seattle to 44 in Dayton.

Table 5.17 Stage of disease presentation, by plan (% of plan total in parentheses)[a]

	Free plan	Cost sharing for all services	Individual Deductible[b]
Stage 1. Asymptomatic manifestations	121 (27.5)	157 (30.8)	70 (38.5)
Stage 2. Moderate manifestations	259 (58.9)	271 (53.1)	89 (48.9)
Stage 3. Major manifestations	58 (13.2)	74 (14.5)	20 (11.0)
Stage 4. Catastrophic manifestations	2 (0.4)	8 (1.6)	3 (1.6)
Total	440 (100)	510 (100)	182 (100)

a. Chi-square = 3.2 (d.f. = 2), p = NS for 3 x 2 table of free plan vs. cost sharing for all services with Stages 3 and 4 combined.

b. Chi-square = 7.42 (d.f. = 2), $p < 0.05$ for 3 x 2 table of free plan vs. Individual Deductible plan with Stages 3 and 4 combined.

Table 5.18 Rates of adult medical-surgical hospitalization by site[a]

Site	Seattle	Dayton	Fitchburg	Franklin County	Charleston	Georgetown County
Enrollees (no.)	781	685	415	524	442	566
Admissions (no.)	256	277	168	163	146	258
Response rate (% of admissions)	88.3	79.1	94.6	90.2	93.2	95.0
Months from exit to solicitation of consent	5 or 25	24 or 48	4 or 31	4 or 31	0	0
Total medical-surgical admissions[b]	101 ± 21	106 ± 21	122 ± 36	91 ± 22	100 ± 23	139 ± 25[c]
Appropriate admissions[b]	91 ± 19	74 ± 17	103 ± 32	75 ± 18	72 ± 19	90 ± 18
Inappropriate admissions[b]	10 ± 5	32 ± 10[c]	18 ± 10	17 ± 6	28 ± 11[c]	48 ± 12[c]
Inappropriate admissions (%)	10 ± 4	30 ± 8[c]	15 ± 7	18 ± 5[d]	28 ± 9[c]	35 ± 7[c]
Total hospital days[b]	495 ± 130	801 ± 176[c]	926 ± 386[d]	591 ± 170	811 ± 272[d]	983 ± 248[c]
Inappropriate days[b]	99 ± 41	348 ± 103[c]	306 ± 191[d]	199 ± 92	265 ± 113[c]	398 ± 104[c]
Inappropriate days (%)	20 ± 7	44 ± 8[c]	33 ± 11	34 ± 11[d]	33 ± 13	40 ± 8[c]

a. 95% confidence intervals are presented for all sites.
b. Per 1,000 person-years.
c. $p < 0.01$ vs. Seattle.
d. $p < 0.05$ vs. Seattle.

This variation in inappropriate use, however, is not significantly correlated with the overall admission rate; the correlation *(r)* of the admission rate with the percentage across the six sites is only 0.45 (*p* = .38). This finding is similar to that of Chassin et al. (1987) that the proportion of three different procedures that were inappropriate does not vary with the overall rate of the procedure.

Although we do not estimate the cost savings that might be achieved by reducing inappropriate admissions, the inappropriate hospitalizations do not involve disproportionately short-stay cases. The 23 percent of the cases that we label inappropriate (that is, treating the outpatient surgery cases as appropriate) account for about one-third of the hospital days.

What patient characteristics predict inappropriate hospitalization? Women are at greater risk of inappropriate hospitalization (excluding maternity cases): 27 percent of their hospitalizations are inappropriate, compared with 18 percent of male hospitalizations. Patients of older physicians— those who had been licensed for 15 or more years—are also at greater risk (27 versus 20 percent), as are patients of non-board-certified physicians (28 versus 21 percent) (Siu, Manning, and Benjamin 1990).

Thus, our results show that many nonelderly adult hospitalizations in the late 1970s were potentially avoidable; indeed, given the availability of outpatient surgery, nearly 40 percent of the patients who were hospitalized had no clinical reason to be in the hospital, and undoubtedly some additional percentage derived benefits from their stay that were less than the social costs. The drop in hospital admissions that occurred in the 1980s, around a quarter, is consistent with these findings (see Table 11.2).

Preventive Care

Preventive care by its nature is designed to reduce future illness and cost. Some believe that any preventive services can be economically justified, and that therefore any reduction caused by "financial barriers" is wrong. This position is clearly too extreme because not all services may be worth their cost (Russell 1986; Wagner, Hardman, and Alberts 1989). In this section we analyze how cost sharing affected the use of preventive services during the first three years of the Experiment and how that use compares with standards of preventive care use.

We analyzed data from the Seattle, Dayton, and two Massachusetts sites (data from South Carolina were not available at the time we performed the analysis).[10] Only the 3,823 individuals who participated for the entire three years and newborns who participated for at least 18 months were included. The analysis is based on all claims for face-to-face, outpatient visits in which "preventive services" were provided.

For children, we defined preventive visits as all those associated with the diagnosis or procedure codes for well-care examinations, immunizations, or tuberculosis tests. For adults, we defined preventive visits as all those associated with claims for the following diagnoses and procedures: immunizations, annual physical examinations, administrative examinations, general medical examinations, multiphasic screening examinations, routine gynecologic examinations, and office visits listed only as well-care visits. Pap smears, mammography, and sigmoidoscopy were considered to be preventive services only if the diagnoses (other than well-care) listed on the claim form associated with the visit could not conceivably have been the reason for the laboratory test. Each laboratory test was linked with the visit at which it was requested according to a set of rules based on provider and dates of service (Lillard et al. 1986).

Visits were classified as preventive or nonpreventive according to the type of services delivered. Visits were classified as both preventive and nonpreventive if a preventive service was provided during a nonpreventive visit. Charges were allocated according to the proportion of diagnoses and procedures that were preventive or nonpreventive.

Because physicians rarely bill separately for counseling about health habits, we could not examine the amount or nature of this activity. We also did not examine prenatal or maternity care. (For an analysis of preventive dental care, see Chapter 3.)

We compared use of services with a standard derived from recommendations of the Canadian Task Force, the American Cancer Society, the American College of Physicians, and the American Academy of Pediatrics. For children the standard was: diphtheria-pertussis-tetanus (DPT) and polio immunization at 2, 4, 6, and 18 months. We modified this criterion to three rather than four doses because three doses are often considered adequate and because administration of the vaccine may be delayed because of viral illness. In the case of measles-mumps-rubella, the standard was vaccination at 12–18 months, and for tuberculosis it was skin testing at 12–18 months. For adults the standard was: tetanus immunization every 10 years; influenza vaccine yearly for high-risk adults (whom we defined as adults 45–64 with chronic obstructive pulmonary disease); Pap smears every 3 years for women 17–64; mammography every 1–3 years for women over age 45; sigmoidoscopy every 3 years for men and women over age 45.

For all types of preventive care except well-child care examinations, the amount of preventive care consumed by participants in the Experiment was much less than what is generally recommended (Table 5.19). The seemingly wide disparity between the standards and behavior cannot be attributed primarily to cost sharing in the Experiment plans. Although Chapters 3 and 4 have shown that cost sharing does reduce the use of preventive care, its effect, as shown in Tables 5.20 and 5.21, is not so large that it could account for the kinds of discrepancies shown in Table 5.19. The percentage of persons using any preventive service was only marginally higher on the free plan. And even on the free plan, the majority of adult males used no preventive services at all for the entire three-year period.

Table 5.19   Compliance with preventive care recommendations

Procedure	Population	% complying with standard	% that should have complied with standard
Immunization	Newborns		
DPT, 3+ doses		44	100
Polio, 3+ doses		45	100
Measles-mumps- rubella		60	100
Tuberculosis skin testing	Newborns	55	100
Well-care examination, one or more visit(s)	Newborns	93	100
Vaccinations			
Tetanus	Adults 17–64	1[a]	30[b]
Influenza	Adults 45–64	3	8[c]
Pap smears	Women 17–44	66	100
	Women 45–64	57	100
Mammography	Women 45–64	2[d]	100
Sigmoidoscopy	Adults 45–64	<1[e]	100

a. 4% if accident-related vaccines are included.

b. Based on 3 years of observation with vaccination every 10 years as standard.

c. Percentage of sample with chronic obstructive pulmonary disease.

d. 8% if nonpreventive tests are included.

e. 3% if nonpreventive tests are included.

Table 5.20   Effect of cost sharing on preventive care, adults

Age group and type of care	Percent with any preventive care in 3 years		
	Free plan	Family coinsurance plans	Individual Deductible
Males 17–44			
Preventive care	27.2	23.1	17.2[a]
Males 45–64			
Preventive care	39.1	27.4	18.8[a]
Females 17–44			
Pap smears	72.2	65.8	54.8[a]
Preventive care	83.7	76.9[b]	71.1[a]
Females 45–64			
Pap smears	65.0	52.8[b]	50.0[b]
Preventive care	76.9	65.3[b]	68.6

a. Significantly different from the free plan ($p < 0.01$).
b. Significantly different from the free plan ($p < 0.05$).

Table 5.21   Effect of cost sharing on preventive care, children

Age and type of care	Percent with any preventive care in 3 years		
	Free plan	Family coinsurance plans	Individual Deductible
0–6 years			
Immunizations	58.9	48.7[a]	50.4
Preventive care	82.5	73.7[a]	77.9
7–16 years			
Immunizations	21.2	21.7	16.1
Preventive care	64.8	59.6	53.2[a]

a. Significantly different from the free plan ($p < 0.05$).

We also estimated the cost that would have been incurred over a three-year period had the standards described in Table 5.19 been satisfied for childhood immunization, Pap smears, and mammography. The cost for immunizations (1984 dollars inflated to 1991 using the Medical Care Price Index), averaged over all children less than 18 months, is about $22 per child more than is now spent; the average additional cost if every woman aged 17–65 had a well-care visit with a Pap smear every three years would be about $15 per woman; and if mammography were performed every three years for women aged 45–65, the average cost for women in this age group would rise $161. The methods for estimating cost are described in Lillard et al. (1986) and Lurie et al. (1987).

Summary

With the exception of emergency room visits, our analyses suggest that cost sharing has a nonspecific effect on the use of medical services. In particular, it reduces appropriate and inappropriate services—or highly efficacious and relatively inefficacious services—by the same proportion. This is the case for the use of antibiotics, for the medical advantage from being hospitalized, and for particular diagnoses for which medical care should be of substantial and little effect. Cost sharing also reduces the use of preventive services, but even with free care this use falls far short of widely accepted standards.

These findings, again excepting those for emergency room visits, appear to be at odds with the theory behind the welfare loss calculations in Chapter 4, namely, that cost sharing reduces the least-valued services. Some have interpreted this nonselective effect as an indictment of cost sharing, but such a verdict should not be accepted without some evidence on outcomes. We now turn to what all these use differences mean for health outcomes.

Part III

Effects of Cost Sharing
on Health Outcomes

A major objective of the Experiment was to determine how the additional services received by participants with lower coinsurance rates affected their health. In Chapter 6 we describe our measures of adult health status, the data upon which they were based, their reliability and validity, and the effects of plan on them. We conclude with a brief analysis of patient satisfaction. Although we touch on some results for children in Chapter 6, most of the analysis of pediatric health occurs in Chapter 7.

Chapter 6

Adult Health Status
and Patient Satisfaction

Developing Measures of Adult Health

We developed or adapted a variety of measures to evaluate the effect of cost sharing on health status, starting with the World Health Organization (WHO, 1948) definition of health—a state of complete physical, mental, and social well-being, not merely the absence of disease or infirmity. The measures were grouped into five distinct categories: general health, including physical, mental, and social health; physiologic health (presence and effect of various chronic diseases); health habits; prevalence of symptoms and disability days; and risk of dying from any cause related to various risk factors. In each category, especially those of physiologic health and health habits, we emphasized measures that would be most commonly encountered in a general population and could be expected to show change as a function of differences in the quantity and quality of medical services consumed during the three- or five-year duration of the Experiment.

General Health

We used four measures of general health: physical health, mental health, social health, and the General Health Index (GHI; health perceptions).[1] The questions asked of the participants and the details of scoring for each scale are found in Davies et al. (1988).

Physical health. We used two summary measures to analyze physical health.

1. The Personal Functioning Index (PFI) is a 21-item scale of physical functioning that includes items related to self-care, mobility, physical activities, and physical capacities. Consistent with the WHO definition's statement that health is not merely the absence of disease, the physical

functioning measure assesses both the negative aspect of physical health (for example, "Are you in bed or a chair for most or all of the day because of your health?") and the positive aspect (for example, "Does your health limit the kind of vigorous activities you can do, such as running, lifting heavy objects, or participating in strenuous sports?"). The second summary measure is a dichotomous measure of role limitations ("Does your health keep you from working at a job, doing work around the house, or going to school?")

The functional status items, which assess limitations due to poor health regardless of duration, are derived from studies by Hulka and Cassel (1973), Patrick, Bush, and Chen (1973), and the National Center for Health Statistics (1974). Although most limitations were present for more than three months, both acute and chronic limitations were captured.

Associations among subscales measuring self-care, mobility, and physical activities were very strong and indicated a cumulative relationship among limitations in the various categories. For example, people unable to perform self-care tasks were also limited in mobility and in performing more strenuous physical activities. Thus, from the perspectives of both the content of the measures and empirical studies of their associations, a summary index of functioning was justified. However, because many individuals with role limitations do not have limitations in personal functioning, physical and role limitations could not be summarized in a single index without considerable loss of information.

Initially we constructed separate scales to measure self-care, mobility, physical activity, role limitations, and physical capacities. But tests of scalability indicated that a PFI could be constructed according to Guttman criteria by aggregating all the measures except role limitations (Stewart, Ware, and Brook 1981, 1982a, 1982b). The PFI defines six levels, transformed to a 0–100 scale to reflect differences in impact on health.

We generally followed the convention that a higher score indicates better health; thus a score of 100 indicates no limitations in self-care, mobility, physical activity, and physical capacities. Intermediate values were determined by estimating mean General Health Index scores (described below) for persons at each of the six levels of PFI. The highest and lowest of the six values were transformed to 100 and zero, respectively, and values in between were expressed as a proportion of the observed range in GHI scores. A ten-point difference on this scale is equivalent to having chronic mild osteoarthritis, controlling for age and gender.

2. Role Functioning Index (RFI) was developed from a negatively oriented dichotomous Role Limitations Index. Thus, persons who were completely free of limitation in their usual role activities were assigned a score of 100 on the Role Functioning Index. Those reporting one or more limitations in role performance because of poor health were assigned a score of zero. Hence, a one-point difference in the scale is equal to a one percentage point higher probability of being limited in the performance of one's major role.[2]

Mental health. The concept of mental health as surveyed in general population studies evolved from items that confounded measures of different dimensions of health to items that focus more exclusively on symptoms of psychological distress (Ware, Johnston, and Davies-Avery 1979). A typical mental health measure fielded before 1970 aggregated questions about physical symptoms, physical functioning, general health perceptions, health habits, and some symptoms of psychological distress. Consistent with a new generation of general population mental health survey instruments, the Experiment's Mental Health Inventory (MHI) measured psychological distress and psychological well-being and was purged of other health status concepts, which were scored and interpreted separately.

In its first mental health survey during enrollment at the Dayton site, the Experiment fielded a 22-item adaptation of Dupuy's General Well-Being Schedule (Veit and Ware 1983) plus 50 items to measure the history of emotional problems and treatment (Ware, Johnston, and Davies-Avery 1979; Ware, Davies-Avery, and Brook 1980). Following studies of the scalability of all these items and tests of reliability and validity, we retained 15 items from the Dayton enrollment instrument and added 23 others selected to increase the comprehensiveness of the instrument and the precision of some MHI subscales. Some of these new items came from Dupuy's experimental items; others were constructed from scratch. (These additional items were very similar to items in instruments developed by Zung 1965; Beck 1967; Costello and Comrey 1967; Comrey 1970; and Dohrenwend et al. 1980.)

The 38 MHI items well represent the most prevalent symptoms of psychological distress (such as anxiety and depression), as well as loss of behavioral/emotional control and a general positive affect (in accordance with the WHO definition). Each item asks about a psychological construct during the past month and is associated with a six-choice response scale that varies the frequency and/or intensity of that construct (for example, "How much of the time, during the past month, have you felt downhearted and blue?" with six choices ranging from "all of the time" to "none of the time").[3]

A three-point reduction in the mental health scale is equivalent to the effect of being fired or laid off from a job.

Social health. Measures of social contacts extend the concept of health beyond the physical and mental status of the individual to include interpersonal contacts such as visits with friends and relatives. Such measures reflect social functioning (Donald et al. 1978; Donald and Ware 1982, 1984). To measure social health in the Experiment, we developed an 11-item battery that was administered annually.

The social well-being items were adapted from measures used by J. K. Myers and colleagues (Myers et al. 1972) in their studies of social activity, life events, and mental status, and by Dohrenwend, Dohrenwend, and Cook (1973) in their studies of role functioning of psychiatric patients. Three items measuring social contacts were selected from the 11-item battery to represent the social well-being concept and form a Social Contacts Scale (SCS). These items measured the frequency with which study participants got together with friends or relatives, visited with friends at their homes, and visited with friends at their friends' homes. Each item was accompanied by six or seven standardized response categories indicating the frequency of occurrence.[4]

A five-point difference in the scale predicts a one-point change in the exit value of the MHI, controlling for its value at enrollment.

General Health Index. Self-ratings of general health are among the more commonly fielded measures of health status (Ware 1976). An example is the rating of health as "excellent," "good," "fair," or "poor." These ratings are considered measures of *general* health because they do not focus on a specific health status attribute and because they have been linked empirically to a wide range of physical and mental health concepts as well as to health and illness behaviors.[5]

The Experiment administered 29 general health items to all study participants annually (Davies and Ware 1981); 26 were taken from the Health Perceptions Questionnaire (HPQ) developed by Ware and colleagues (Ware and Karmos 1976; Ware, Davies-Avery, and Donald 1978). HPQ items were worded as complete statements of opinion about personal health (for example, "I have been feeling bad lately"; "I expect to have a very healthy life") and were accompanied by five standardized response categories defining a true-false continuum. These HPQ items were used to score six subscales that assessed the following dimensions of health perceptions: three time-bounded perceptions of health (past, present, and future), health-related worry and concern, resistance versus susceptibility to illness, and the tendency to view illness as part of life.

Twenty-two HPQ items were used to compute the General Health Index, a favorably scored summary of health perceptions (Davies and Ware 1981). The GHI was scored using a simple summated ratings method and then transformed to a 0–100 scale, with higher scores representing a better rating of one's health. In a general population, scores are roughly symmetrically distributed. At enrollment one or more adults was observed at 80 GHI levels.

A five-point reduction in the GHI is equivalent to being diagnosed as hypertensive.

Physiologic Health

Physiologic health is useful in predicting future health; for example, those with high blood pressure (hypertension) are at increased risk of stroke. Specifically, measures of physiologic health have been shown to predict future mortality, thereby mitigating the problem that the number of deaths during the Experiment is too small to detect plan effects on mortality directly.

The physiologic dimension of health for adults comprised 16 chronic or quasi-chronic "tracer" conditions (plus dental conditions) that met five criteria:

- They are common.
- They can be defined concretely in terms with which most physicians would be comfortable.
- They can be measured easily and accurately, without an invasive or potentially embarrassing procedure.
- They can cause substantial discomfort, disability, morbidity, or premature death.
- They are disorders for which appropriate medical care offers considerable symptom relief and control of physiologic status, if not outright cure.

Table 6.1 lists the 16 conditions used, along with an indication of how their presence and severity was measured.[6]

Table 6.1   Diseases or conditions studied in the Health Insurance Experiment

Disease or tracer	Measure of abnormal physiology impact
Chronic obstructive airway disease	Forced expiratory volume in 1 second from spirometric testing as % of predicted FEV_1, best of three tries; see reference 19 in Keeler et. al. (1987)
	Self-reported shortness of breath, based on dyspnea questionnaire, ranging from 0 = no shortness of breath to 4 = severe shortness
	Chronic phlegm production, self reported phlegm production during at least three months of previous year, 1 = present, 0 = absent
Congestive heart failure	Self-reported shortness of breath, see above
Hay fever	Self-reported time bothered, on a natural log scale ranging form 0 = none to 6.4 = 180 days or more
Angina pectoris/ ischemic heart disease	Modified Rose Scale (see Berman et al. 1981); presence of one or more of the following ECG abnormalities: intraventricular conduction abnormality, ventricular enlargement (including LVH), atrial fibrillation, ST-segment and T-wave changes, Q-wave abnormalities, ventricular dysrhythmias, artificial pacemaker rhythm
Varicose veins (surgical)	Severity of varicose veins, 1 = absent, 2 = spider angiomata, 3 = minimal, 4 = moderate, 5 = severe
Hypertension	Diastolic blood pressure (mm/Hg)
Hypercholesterolemia	Serum cholesterol (mg/dl)
Joint	Self-reported symptoms of mild to moderate joint disorders
	Diagnosis of gout, 1 = present, 0 = absent
	Number of seconds to walk 50 feet
	Grip strength, measured three times in both hands with dynamometer; best try of weaker hand; mm/Hg
Peptic ulcer disease	Self-reported stomach pain or ache in past three months with previous physician diagnosis and X-ray confirmed ulcer or presence of symptom pattern characteristic of ulcer; 1 = present, 0 = absent
	Self-reported dyspepsia; 1 = present, 0 = absent

Table 6.1   (continued)

Disease or tracer	Measure of abnormal physiology impact
Vision	Functional far and near vision; measured in Snellen lines, 1 = 20/15, 2 = 20/20, 3 = 20/25, 4 = 20/30, higher numbers worse; functional refers to vision using whatever correction, if any, used by person to improve vision
Hearing	Simple averages of hearing thresholds at 500, 1000, and 2000 Hz, calculated for left and right ears separately
Diabetes mellitus	Random glucose (mg/dl)
Thyroid	T7 outside the normal range except T4 at Dayton enrollment, excluding women who are pregnant or on birth control pills
Anemia	Hemoglobin (g/100ml)
Urinary tract infection	Urine culture with growth $\geq$/ 100,000/ml of one or more pathogens, and patient not on medication for UTI
Acne	Severity of acne based on reading of facial photo by dermatologist, 0 = no acne, 1 = 1 comedo or papule, 2 = extensive comedos or papules, 3 = pustules, 4 = inflammatory cysts, 5 = acne conglobata
Dental conditions	Number of decayed, missing, and filled teeth (DMFT)
	Russell's Periodontal Index with modified scoring, 0 = negative, 1 = mild gingivitis, 2 = gingivitis, 3 = gingivitis with pocket formation, 4 = advanced destruction with loss of masticatory function

Dental Health

Dental conditions—especially decayed, missing, and filled teeth, as well as a measure of periodontal health—were also included. Table 6.1 describes the indices used. (For a more detailed discussion see Spolsky et al. 1983.)

Health Habits

We analyzed several health habits known to affect health, either positively or negatively, in order to establish how additional medical care use might affect such habits. Table 6.2 lists the health habits.

Prevalence of Symptoms and Disability Days

We analyzed the prevalence of various symptoms, which we grouped into serious and minor symptoms (Table 6.3). This grouping was derived from a larger list of symptoms compiled on two bases: (1) ratings by nine physicians of the seriousness of the symptoms and the proportion of patients with such symptoms who, in the judgment of the physicians, should seek care; and (2) the effect of the symptom, other factors being equal, on the

Table 6.2   Health habits studied in the Health Insurance Experiment

Habit	Measures of habits
Weight[a]	1.75(weight/height^2) for men; 1.65(weight/height$^{1.5}$) for women; height measured in meters
Exercise (level of physical activity)	Self-reported measure of physical activity, from 1 = not very active to 4 = strenuous activity most days
Smoking	Scaled as overall mortality relative to never or ex-smoker, 1.00 = never or ex-smoker; 1.06 = pipe or cigar smoker; 1.57 = less than 1 pack/day; 1.79 = about 1 pack per day; 2.07 = about 2 packs/day; 2.20 = more than 2 packs per day
Alcohol consumption	Ounces of ethanol per month
Use of relaxants	Number of days per month on which sleeping pills or tranquilizers are taken
Seat belt use	Self-reported frequency (0 to 100%)
Most recent rectal exam	1 = rectal exam by a physician within the past two years, 0 = more than two years or never
Most recent Pap smear	1 = within past 12 months, 0 = more than 12 months or never
Frequency of breast self-examination	"How often do you check your own breasts for lumps?" 1 = every month or almost every month, 0 = several times a year or less
Oral health habits	Oral health habits, frequency of brushing, flossing, flouride use, consumption of cariogenic foods

Note: For further information, see Stewart, Brook, and Kane (1979); Brook et al. (1984); and Keeler et al. (1987).

a. Excludes pregnant women. Weight measured in kilograms.

Table 6.3   Symptoms studied in the Health Insurance Experiment

During the past 30 days did you have any of the following symptoms?

Serious symptoms
1. Chest pain when exercising?
2. Bleeding (other than nosebleed or periods) not caused by accident or injury?
3. Loss of consciousness, fainting, or passing out?
4. Shortness of breath with light exercise or light work?
5. A weight loss of more than 10 pounds (unless you were dieting)?

Minor symptoms
1. A cough without fever, which lasted at least 3 weeks?
2. Your nose stopped up, or sneezing or allergies for 2 weeks or more?
3. Stomach "flu" or virus (gastroenteritis) with vomiting or diarrhea?
4. An upset stomach, for less than 24 hours?

General Health Index. (Further details are available in Shapiro, Ware, and Sherbourne 1986.)

Disability days were measured in two ways: (1) Participants reported about each day on a (usually) biweekly form, the Health Report (see Chapter 2). They first answered screening questions pertaining to disability days (Table 6.4). If they answered yes to any of the screening questions, they were asked to name the family member with the disability day and to circle the day(s) in the 14-day period that corresponded to the disability day(s). (2) In addition, at enrollment and at exit from the Experiment participants reported how often in the past three months their health had kept them from performing the same kinds of activities as other people their age and how many bed days they had had in the preceding 30 days. (Further details are available in Brook et al. 1979, app. D.)

Risk of Dying

The risk-of-dying index is derived from measures of systolic blood pressure, cholesterol, and smoking. Index values are calculated according to a specific formula based on findings from several major epidemiologic studies of cardiovascular disease (see McGee and Gordon 1976):

[exp(Index)/(1 + exp(Index)], where Index is equal to: 1.28 (smoking scale) + 0.0023 (cholesterol) + 0.023 (systolic blood pressure) − 9.52.[7]

The smoking scale and cholesterol variables are measured as described in Table 6.1; systolic blood pressure is measured in millimeters of mercury (mm Hg). The resulting value was normalized so the average person would have a value of 1.00 percent, which is roughly the probability that a 40-year-old male will die in the next three years.

Sources of Data

Three major sources of data underlie our analyses of health status:

1. Self-administered medical history questionnaires (the Medical History Questionnaire) were administered at enrollment and at exit; an abbreviated version was administered at annual intervals during the Experiment. These questionnaires were the source of data for the physical, mental, and social health scales and the GHI measure. They were also the data source on health

Table 6.4   Screening questions for disability days

During this two-week period, did any persons age 17 and over (including yourself) who have a job

    1. ... miss work for one-half day or more because of their own illness or injury?

    2. ... have to cut down on things they usually do for one-half day or more on nonworking days because of their own illness or injury?

    3. ... miss any work to go to a doctor, dentist, clinic, etc., or to take another family member to a doctor, dentist, clinic, etc.?

    4. ... miss work for one-half day or more to care for another family member who was sick or injured?

    5. ... take any paid sick leave hours for any reason?

During this two-week period, did anyone age 17 and over (including yourself) who does not have a job

    6. ... have to cut down on things they normally do for one-half day or more because of their own illness or injury?

During this two-week period, have any children age 16 and under in your family unit

    7. ... missed school for one-half day or more because of their own illness or injury?

    8. ... had to cut down on things they usually do for one-half day or more on nonschool days because of their own illness or injury? (Include information about preschool children and children on vacation from school here.)

Table 6.5   Reliability and stability estimates for Experiment general health status
measures

Measure	k^a	Reliability[b]	One-year stability[c]
Personal Functioning Index	21	0.97[d]	0.59
Role Limitations Index	2	0.92[d]	0.50
Mental Health Index	38	0.96	0.64
Social Contacts Scale	3	0.72	0.55
General Health Index	22	0.89	0.68

a. Number of items.

b. Internal-consistency reliability estimated by Cronbach's (1951) alpha, unless otherwise noted.

c. Product-moment correlation between scores obtained approximately one year apart.

d. Coefficient of reproducibility.

habits and symptom prevalence. In the analyses discussed here, data from the abbreviated version were used only if exit data were missing.

2. A screening examination, required of a random 60 percent of participants at enrollment and all participants at exit, was the source of the physiologic data for the tracer conditions described in Table 6.1. (The rationale for the particular tests administered at the examination is discussed further in Smith et al. 1978.)

3. Biweekly self-administered questionnaires (the Health Report) were the source of most of our data on disability days.[8]

Reliability and Validity of Physical, Mental, Social, and General Health Measures

We found our measures of physical, mental, social, and general health reliable and valid according to the usual norms of the field.[9]

Reliability. We checked reliability using both test-retest and internal consistency methods. In the case of physical health measures, for which a Guttman scale was used, we estimated a coefficient of reproducibility. Table 6.5 summarizes the reliability of the various measures.

Validity of the physical health measures. Both summary measures—the PFI and RFI—well represented the content of functional status measures identified in the published literature (Stewart et al. 1978; Stewart, Ware, and Brook 1982a). Their validity has also been established in empirical terms. Multivariate studies of correlations among the Experiment's functional status measures and other health and health-related measures strongly supported their discriminant validity as measures of physical functioning (Ware, Davies-Avery, and Brook 1980). They have also been shown to predict medical expenditures and mental health expenditures in models that control for a wide range of health-related variables (Manning, Newhouse, and Ware 1982; Ware et al. 1984).

Validity of the mental health measure. Several strategies were employed to evaluate the validity of the Experiment's mental health measures. The first studies of validity focused on the relationships among the mental health subscales and their associations with other conceptually related variables also measured by self-administered questionnaire. The subscales were substantially intercorrelated, but because the intercorrelations were well below their reliability coefficients, we aggregated the subscales to define the MHI. Subscales can differ in interpretation, as is reflected in differing correlations with other variables (Ware, Davies-Avery, and Brook 1980).

Factor-analytic studies of the mental health subscales and numerous other health and health-related variables demonstrate that the mental health measures are distinct from both physical and social factors (Ware, Davies-Avery, and Brook 1980). Furthermore, as would be expected for valid measures, they have been linked to life events, social contacts and resources, chronic diseases, acute physical symptoms, and general health perceptions (Davies and Ware 1981; Williams, Ware, and Donald 1981; Donald and Ware 1982; Manning, Newhouse, and Ware 1982).

Subsequent Experiment validity studies focused on data gathered from sources other than the questionnaire containing the mental health items. For example, controlling for other health and attitudinal variables, we showed that the mental health subscales significantly predicted subsequent general medical expenditures (Manning, Newhouse, and Ware 1982) and outpatient mental health expenditures (Ware et al. 1984).

Validity of the social health measure. Items in the Social Contact Scale (SCS) satisfied our discriminant validity criterion; the items correlated more highly with the specific social well-being construct they were intended to measure than with other health constructs. Correlations between the SCS and other Experiment social well-being items and measures were significant and positive, supporting the validity of the scale. The low correlations, however, indicate that social well-being constructs are only weakly related. The magnitude of positive associations between social contacts and psychological well-being suggested that the SCS may be more predictive of positive emotional states and general views about life than of negative emotional states or general states of health. Findings from a longitudinal analysis of Experiment data suggested a direct positive effect of social contacts on mental health (Williams, Ware, and Donald 1981). This effect has been demonstrated for men and women separately, as well as for employed and unemployed men and women.

Validity of the general health measure. The validity of the GHI and its subscales has been substantiated in numerous investigations. Norms are available for elderly and nonelderly general adult populations (Ware, Davies-Avery, and Donald 1978; Davies and Ware 1981). Cross-sectional and longitudinal analyses have been conducted for general and targeted populations to address questions about:

- the kinds of individual differences in health status measured by the GHI
- similarities and differences in results compared with other widely used health status measures
- sensitivity to the impact of different diseases
- sensitivity to individual differences in disease severity
- sensitivity to changes in health status over time, owing to treatment, aging, and other factors
- predictive validity in relationship to the use of medical services, future morbidity, and survival
- who, in sociodemographic terms (for example, age, gender), scores high and low on the GHI and its subscales

Initial validity studies examined the factor structure of the early version of the GHI described above, the Health Perceptions Questionnaire (HPQ) (Ware and Karmos 1976; Ware, Davies-Avery, and Donald 1978). These studies examined the factor structure of the HPQ and the correlations between HPQ subscales and other survey measures of health status and health-related behaviors in four general population studies. The factor structure of the HPQ was very similar across populations, indicating that the HPQ had construct validity; it included six correlated health percep-tions factors, the basis for the six HPQ health subscales. The HPQ sub-scales correlated substantially with survey measures of physical and mental health and with self-reported use of health services (Ware, Davies-Avery, and Donald 1978; Davies and Ware 1981). A pattern of differences related to age and gender has also been consistently replicated: women and older persons score lower than others on the GHI.

Subsequent validity studies provided the psychometric basis for the GHI summary score. They examined correlations between the GHI (and HPQ subscales) and 35 measures of health status and health-related validity variables using data from all Experiment sites (Davies and Ware 1981). These studies expanded the list of validity variables measured by self-report, and they also added measures of chronic disease based on clinical examinations and subsequent use of health services reported on Experiment insurance claim forms. Results indicated that the GHI is a sensitive indicator of individual differences in disease status, limitations in physical and role functioning owing to poor health, acute physical and psychosomatic symptoms, and mental health (symptoms of psychological distress and psychological well-being). Correlations between the GHI and measures of social contacts and resources were statistically significant but very weak. Experiment analyses reported in Chapters 3 and 4 show that the GHI is related to subsequent use of ambulatory medical and mental health services and that it has considerable incremental validity in these predictions; that is, it adds information not contained in the other health status measures listed above (see also Manning, Newhouse, and Ware 1982; Ware et al. 1984).

Reliability and Validity of Physiologic Measures

Extensive analyses, based on a test-retest procedure, confirmed the reliability of the physiologic measures. For a number of the tests on the screening examination, a random subsample of participants, usually around 8 percent of the entire sample, was retested. In general, the mean among the retested group was insignificantly different from the mean among the tested group. In the case of each test, the reliability of the screening examination was deemed to be adequate for the purposes for which it was to be used.[10]

We assessed the validity of the screening examination results by comparing the disease prevalence rates or the results of various tests among the participants with those found in other general adult populations. Most often the comparison sample was from the Health Examination Survey of the National Center for Health Statistics. Sometimes we used results from other specialized studies, such as the Tecumseh study for blood glucose and hay fever (Broder et al. 1974; Ostrander, Lamphiear, and Block 1976).

In all cases we concluded that our results were valid for the purpose of making comparisons across insurance plans. (Urinary tract infection was the single exception, because it was impossible to make a comparison with the results in the literature.) In a number of cases, however, our estimated prevalence rates differed from those in the literature because of differing definitions of disease (such as more conservative thresholds) or different testing methods.

Estimation Methods

Although we could and sometimes did compare the mean values of the various health status measures across plans at exit, in general we compared predicted values from regression equations estimated using several covariates, including dummy variables for insurance plan. Using predicted values rather than simple means improved the precision with which we could measure plan effects. The most important covariate in predicting the value of the health status measure at exit was typically the value of the same measure at enrollment. Other covariates included age, gender, family income adjusted for family size and composition and the site cost of living,[11] and experimental variables such as length of the enrollment period and whether the individual took an enrollment screening examination. We included interactions between plan and both income and health status. (Further details are available in Brook et al. 1984, app. E.)

We then used the estimated equation for exit health status to predict values for each participant in the sample. For each plan we first predicted a value for each person in the entire sample, then averaged these predicted values within plan. In effect, we based our predictions on the demographic characteristics of the entire sample. This approach enabled us to correct for the small imbalances across the plans that came from allocating a finite sample. When we predicted for the low-income group, we used individuals in the lowest fifth of the income distribution (adjusted for family size) at enrollment, and for the high-income group we used individuals in the highest two-fifths (similarly adjusted). When we predicted for the "sick" group for each health status variable, we used individuals in the lowest quarter of the distribution of that variable at enrollment. All statistical tests have been corrected for correlation of the error term within the family and for nonconstant variance of the error term. Unlike the case of utilization, these corrections were generally small.

Results

Physiologic Measures

.In comparing results within the group of cost-sharing plans, we could detect no differences among the plans; therefore, we have generally combined

Table 6.6 Predicted exit values for an average person according to measure and plan[a]

Health status measure	Cost-sharing plans	Free plans	Predicted difference (free minus cost sharing)[b]	Direction and magnitude of effect[c]	Raw mean difference (free minus cost sharing)	Sample size[d]
Respiratory system						
FEV_1 (% of predicted)[e]	94.8	95.0	0.1±1.1	F	0.9	3,225
Shortness of breath	0.20	0.19	-0.01±0.04	F	-0.03	3,497
Chronic phlegm production (% of sample)	8.5	9.1	0.5±1.8	C	-0.0	3,523
Severity of hay fever	0.16	0.21	0.05±0.06	C+	0.03	3,540
Circulatory system						
Rose Scale[f]	0.03	0.03	0.004±0.02	C	0.005	1,434
All ECG abnormalities (% of sample)[f]	10.0	9.3	-0.7±3	F	-0.4	1,360
Severity of varicose veins[g]	2.21	2.15	-0.06±0.09	F+	0.01	1,624
Diastolic blood pressure (mm Hg)	78.8	78.0	-0.8±0.7	F++	-0.9	3,495
Cholesterol (mg/dl)	202	203	0.7±2	C	-1.3	3,381
Musculoskeletal system						
Chronic joint symptoms (% of sample)[f]	31.6	30.0	-1.6±5	F	-0.7	1,435
Walking speed (seconds)[g]	10.11	10.05	-0.06±0.3	F	-0.4	514
Grip strength (mm Hg)[e,g]	233.8	232.5	-1.3±5	C	-1.2	516

Gastrointestinal system					
Active ulcer (% of sample)	3.0	3.3	0.3±1	C	0.7	3,539
Dyspepsia (% of sample)	7.9	9.9	2.0±2.1	C+	2.1	3,540
Vision/hearing					
Functional far vision (Snellen lines)	2.52	2.42	−0.10±0.06	F++	−0.13	3,465
Functional near vision (Snellen lines)[f]	2.44	2.35	−0.09±0.08	F++	−0.07	1,410
AHTL, right ear (dB)	12.25	12.28	0.03±0.5	C	0.03	3,267
AHTL, left ear (dB)	12.46	12.84	0.38±0.5	C+	0.07	3,270
Endocrine system					
Glucose (mg/dl)	94.2	94.7	0.5±1.5	C	0.7	3,395
Abnormal thyroid level (% of sample)	1.7	2.4	0.7±1.0	C+	0.9	3,373
Other systems					
Hemoglobin (g/100 ml)[e]	14.45	14.46	0.01±0.1	F	0.03	3,390
Positive urine culture (% of sample)[h]	2.9	3.5	0.6±2	C	0.0	1,796
Severity of acne[i]	0.32	0.37	0.05±0.07	C+	0.1	2,478
Health practices[j]					
Weight-height index	0.27	0.27	0.005±0.04	C	0.005	3,087
Level of physical activity[e]	2.24	2.21	−0.03±0.06	C	−0.03	3,056
Smoking scale	1.29	1.29	−0.002±0.02	F	−0.01	3,037
Monthly alcohol consumption (oz/mo)	13.4	13.7	0.3±2	C	0.3	3,062

Table 6.6   (continued)

Health practices (cont.)						
Use of relaxants	1.69	2.09	0.40±0.5	C+	0.53	3,070
Seat belt use (%)[e]	28.5	29.2	0.7±2	F	−0.02	3,062
Rectal exam within past two years (%)[e,k]	52.6	56.7	4.1±6	F+	4.0	1,057
Pap smear within past 12 months (%)[e,h]	59.7	63.4	3.8±5	F+	3.4	1,679
Breast self-examination almost every month (%)[e,h]	50.8	53.4	2.6±5	F	2.6	1,679

Source: Keeler et al. (1987).

Note: FEV_1 is forced expiratory volume in 1 second; ECG is electrocardiogram; AHTL is average hearing threshold level.

a. For detail of measures, see Table 6.1.

b. Number following predicted difference represents the width of the 95% confidence interval, i.e., 1.96 (standard error).

c. F++, F+, F represent differences that favor the free plan at two-tailed $p < 0.05$, $0.05 < p < 0.20$, and $0.20 < p$, respectively; C++, C+, C represent differences that similarly favor the cost-sharing plans. These p-values do not account for multiple comparisons.

d. Numbers of persons included in the analyses vary because of differences in the number of persons with valid data for the health status measures, and restrictions on age and gender applied to some of the measures.

e. For this condition, a higher value denotes better health.

f. Limited to persons 35 or older.

g. Limited to females.

h. Limited to persons 35 or older who reported joint discomfort.

i. Limited to persons less than 45.

j. Limited to persons 18 or older.

k. Limited to persons 40 or older.

cost-sharing plans and compared them with the free plan, although we present some results for specific coinsurance rates within the cost-sharing group.

For the average person there were no substantial benefits from free care (Table 6.6). There are beneficial effects for blood pressure and corrected vision only; ignoring the issue of multiple comparisons, we can reject at the 5 percent level the hypothesis that these two effects arose by chance, but we do not believe the caveat about multiple comparisons to be important in this case. We investigate below the mechanisms by which these differences might have arisen; the results from these further analyses strongly suggest that the results did not occur by chance.

For most health status measures the difference between the means for those enrolled in the free plan and those enrolled in the cost-sharing plan did not differ at conventional levels. Many of these conditions are rather rare, however, raising the possibility that free care might have had an undetected beneficial effect on several of them. To determine whether this was the case we conducted an omnibus test, the results of which make it unlikely that free care had any beneficial effect on several conditions as a group that we failed to detect when we considered the conditions one at a time.

If the various conditions are independent and if free care were, for example, one standard error better than cost sharing for each measure, then of the 23 physiologic measures in Table 6.6 we would expect to see four measures significantly better on the free plan (at a 5 percent level using a two-tail test), and none significantly worse. Among the insignificant comparisons, 15 would favor free care and only 4 would favor cost sharing. In fact three measures *are* significantly better on the free plan and none is significantly worse, but 13 of the 23 measures rather than the predicted 4 favor the cost-sharing plan. Hence it is very unlikely that free care causes one standard error of difference in each measure. If the independence assumption is violated, the violation is probably in the direction of positive dependence, in which case accounting for such dependencies would only strengthen our conclusion. Moreover, one standard error of difference is not a very large difference — about half of the 95 percent confidence intervals shown in the fourth column of Table 6(equal, for example, to one milligram per deciliter (mg/dl) of cholesterol).

The same qualitative conclusions hold for persons at elevated risk (Table 6.7). In this group, those on the free plan had (nominally) significantly higher hemoglobin but worse hearing in the left ear. Again outcomes on 13 of 23 measures favored cost sharing.

Table 6.7 Predicted exit values for an elevated-risk person, according to measure and plan[a]

Health status measure	Mean value at enrollment for elevated risk group[b]	Cost-sharing plans	Free plan	Predicted difference (free minus cost sharing)[c]	Direction and magnitude of effect[d]
Respiratory system					
FEV_1 (% of predicted)[e]	78.0	77.0	78.2	1.2±2	F
Shortness of breath	0.67	0.57	0.53	-0.04±0.1	F
Chronic phlegm production (% of sample)	33.4	22.5	24.2	1.7±5	C
Severity of hay fever	0.56	0.5	0.7	0.18±0.20	C+
Circulatory system					
Rose scale[f]	0.16	0.09	0.06	-0.03±0.07	F
All ECG abnormalities (% of sample)[f]	68.6	25.0	17.8	-7.3±8	F+
Severity of varicose veins[g]	3.1	3.56	3.55	-0.01±0.2	F
Diastolic blood pressure (mm Hg)	87.2[h]	88.3	87.6	-0.7±1.5	F
Cholesterol (mg/dl)	242[h]	243	244	2±5	C
Musculoskeletal system					
Chronic joint symptoms (% of sample)[f]	90.0	64.7	64.4	-0.3±10	F
Walking speed (seconds)[i]	10.7	12.3	12.5	0.3±1	C
Grip strength (mm Hg)[e,i]	199.4	206.1	203.3	-2.8±15	C
Gastrointestinal system					
Active ulcer (% of sample)	12.5	9.6	10.6	1.0±4	C
Dyspepsia (% of sample)	48.0	17.5	18.4	0.9±5	C

Vision/hearing				
Functional far vision (Snellen lines)[h]	3.4	3.36	3.20	−0.16±0.22	F+
Functional near vision (Snellen lines)[f]	4.5	2.99	2.86	−0.12±0.3	F
AHTL–right ear (db)	23.7	20.6	21.2	0.6±1.4	C
AHTL–left ear (db)	21.3	20.5	22.0	1.5±1.4	C++
Endocrine system				
Glucose (mg/dl)	125.9	107.0	108.0	1.1±5	C
Abnormal thyroid level (% of sample)	1.6	4.6	6.6	1.9±3	C
Other systems				
Hemoglobin (g/100 ml)[e]	12.3	13.00	13.14	0.14±0.12	F++
Positive urine culture (% of sample)[g]	22.6	8.7	9.3	0.6±6	C
Severity of acne[j]	1.76	0.92	1.08	0.16±0.22	C+

Source: Keeler et al. (1987).

Note: FEV$_1$ is forced expiratory volume in one second; ECG is electrocardiogram; AHTL is average hearing threshold level.

a. For more detail of measures, see Table 6.1.

b. Elevated-risk groups are the least healthy 25% of the sample defined with respect to the individual health measure at enrollment.

c. Number following predicted difference represents the width of the 95% confidence interval, i.e., 1.96 (standard error).

d. F++, F+, F represent differences that favor the free plan at two-tailed $p < 0.05$, $0.05 < p < 0.20$, and $0.20 < p$, respectively; C++, C+, C represent differences that similarly favor the cost-sharing plans. These p-values do not account for multiple comparisons.

e. For this condition, a higher value denotes better health.

f. Limited to persons 35 or older.

g. Limited to females.

h. Predicted exit values.

i. Limited to persons 35 or older who reported joint discomfort.

j. Limited to persons less than 45.

Hypertension and vision. Further examination shows that the improvements for hypertension and far vision are concentrated among those low-income enrollees at elevated risk (Table 6.8). Indeed, there was virtually no difference in diastolic blood pressure readings across the plans for those at elevated risk who were in the upper 40 percent of the income distribution.

Because the low-income, elevated risk group is small (usually between 5 and 10 percent of the original sample depending on the health status measure), the outcome differences for that group between the free and cost-sharing groups have relatively large standard errors. These results might be taken to mean that we missed beneficial effects for the low-income, elevated risk group for certain measures. But although this might be the case for a small number of measures, it is unlikely to be generally true. If we apply the same omnibus test just described to the low- and high-income groups shown in Table 6.8, we would expect that if there were a true one standard error favorable difference for the free plan for each measure, 2 of the 13 comparisons in Table 6.8 would be significantly positive and 2 would be negative, but none would be significantly negative. Of the 9 that would be insignificantly positive at the 5 percent level, 6 would have values of significance between 5 and 20 percent. The data in Table 6.8 show that for the low-income group, none (rather than 2) of the 13 comparisons is significantly positive at the 5 percent level; 4 (rather than 6) are significant at the 20 percent level; and 4 (rather than 2) are negative, one (acne) significantly so. For the high-income group, 7 of the 13 results favor the free-care plan, and the results are even "less significant" than one would expect at random (that is, one would have expected 2 or 3 differences "significant" at the 20 percent level among 13 comparisons, even if there were no true difference, whereas only one comparison was significant at this level).

Symptomatic relief. People who knew they had a condition were asked if they were worried about it or if symptoms caused them pain. We had expected that the additional medical care on the free plan might yield benefits in lower anxiety levels or in symptomatic relief, even if the underlying pathology was untreatable. However, there was no evidence to support this expectation; if anything, the data support the opposite hypothesis (Tables 6.9 and 6.10). Of the 11 conditions described in Table 6.9, persons with all but 2 reported more worry on the free plan when the comparison was some worry versus no worry (columns 1 and 2, $p < .033$ using a sign test, if the conditions are independent). Among those reporting some worry about the

Table 6.8 Differences between free and cost-sharing plans in predicted exit values for an elevated-risk person, by measure and income[a]

Health status measure	Low income[b]	Direction and magnitude of effect[c]	High income[b]	Direction and magnitude of effect[c]
Respiratory system				
FEV_1 (% of predicted)[d]	2.6±2.9	F+	−0.1±3.4	C
Shortness of breath	−0.06±0.2	F	−0.03±0.2	F
Chronic phlegm production (% of sample)	−4.0±10	F	4.6±7	C+
Severity of hay fever	0.19±0.4	C	0.16±0.3	C
Circulatory system				
Severity of varicose veins[e]	0.02±0.4	C	−0.03±0.3	F
Diastolic blood pressure (mm Hg)	−2.3±2.6	F+	0.1±2.1	C
Cholesterol (mg/dl)	−0.4±9	F	2.8±6	C
Other systems				
Chronic joint symptoms (% of sample)[f]	3.8±20	C	−2.0±12	F
Dyspepsia (% of sample)	−3.5±9	F	4.0±8	C
Functional far vision (Snellen lines)	−0.33±0.35	F+	−0.07±0.30	F
Functional near vision (Snellen lines)[f]	−0.02±0.4	F	−0.16±0.3	F
Hemoglobin (g/100ml)[d]	0.166±0.169	F+	0.101±0.185	F
Severity of acne[g]	0.31±0.28	C++	−0.05±0.333	F

Source: Keeler et al. (1987).

Note: FEV_1 is forced expiratory volume in one second.

a. Elevated-risk groups are the least healthy 25% of the sample defined with respect to the individual health measure. Low-income families are those in the lowest one-fifth of the income distribution in the sample; high-income families are those in the highest two-fifths of the income distribution. For more detail on measures, see Table 6.1.

b. Number following predicted difference represents the width of the 95% confidence interval, i.e., 1.96 (standard error).

c. F++, F+, F represent differences that favor the free plan at two-tailed $p < 0.05$, $0.05 < p < 0.20$, and $0.20 < p$, respectively; C++, C+, C represent differences that similarly favor the cost-sharing plan. These p-values do not account for multiple comparisons.

d. For this condition, a higher value denotes better health.

e. Limited to females.

f. Limited to persons 35 or older.

g. Limited to persons under 45.

Table 6.9 Frequency of reported worry and mean level of reported worry for selected health conditions at exit, by plan

Condition	% of sample reporting worry due to condition			Mean level of worry[a]		
	Cost-sharing plans	Free plan	t-test value[b]	Cost-sharing plans	Free plan	t-test value[c]
Phlegm production, chronic bronchitis, or emphysema	6.8	8.3	2.27	1.23	1.27	0.56
Hay fever	9.6	10.0	1.32	1.35	1.36	0.20
Chest pain[d]	14.1	15.2	0.19	1.41	1.43	0.18
Varicose veins[e]	7.9	10.9	1.55	1.30	1.41	1.17
Chronic joint disorders[d]	25.9	25.8	-0.42	1.56	1.66	1.22
Dyspepsia	8.9	9.7	0.03	1.50	1.56	0.73
Vision disorders	36.1	36.4	-0.44	1.36	1.28	-1.52
Kidney disease[e]	7.4	10.1	1.12	1.52	1.50	-0.13
Acne[f]	13.0	14.7	0.52	1.36	1.36	0.06
Shortness of breath, enlarged heart or heart failure[g]	16.4	14.7	0.05	1.49	1.40	-0.60
Hemorrhoids	6.6	7.7	1.55	1.21	1.24	0.47

Source: Keeler et al. (1987).

a. Based on those who reported worrying at least a little about the condition at exit; 1 = a little worry, 2 = some worry, 3 = a great deal of worry.

b. Based on a significance test for the coefficient representing insurance plan (1 = free, 0 = cost sharing) in the logistic equation for report of any worry at exit. Because of differences in initial prevalence, which are controlled for, this value may be in a different direction from the raw percentages shown in the table.

c. Based on a significance test for the difference between sample means.

d. Limited to persons 35 or older.

e. Limited to females.

f. Limited to persons under 45.

g. Limited to persons 45 or older.

Table 6.10   Frequency of reported pain and mean level of reported pain for selected health conditions at exit, according to plan

Condition	% of sample reporting pain due to condition			Mean level of pain[a]		
	Cost-sharing plans	Free plan	t-test value[b]	Cost-sharing plans	Free plan	t-test value[c]
Phlegm production, chronic bronchitis, or emphysema	4.0	4.6	1.34	1.25	1.25	0.0
Hay fever	13.2	12.5	0.47	1.37	1.38	0.23
Chest pain[d]	15.4	14.8	-0.70	1.41	1.34	-0.76
Varicose veins[e]	6.6	8.6	1.26	1.30	1.42	1.15
Chronic joint disorders[d]	30.6	29.4	-0.93	1.75	1.82	0.87
Dyspepsia	10.6	12.8	1.39	1.56	1.60	0.47
Vision disorders	17.5	19.8	0.82	1.40	1.24	-2.32
Kidney disease[e]	7.8	11.3	1.80	1.58	1.60	0.14
Acne[f]	7.2	8.2	0.13	1.24	1.15	-1.38
Shortness of breath, enlarged heart, or heart failure[g]	10.6	10.9	0.71	1.51	1.42	-0.56
Hemorrhoids	9.0	10.7	1.90	1.28	1.36	1.38

Source: Keeler et al. (1987).
a. Based on those who reported at least a little pain from the condition at exit; 1 = a little pain, 2 = some pain, 3 = a great deal of pain.
b. Based on a significance test for the coefficient representing insurance plan (1 = free, 0 = cost sharing) in the logistic equation for report of any pain at exit. Because of differences in initial prevalence, which are controlled for, this value may be in a different direction from the raw percentages shown in the table.
c. Based on a significance test for the difference between sample means.
d. Limited to persons 35 or older.
e. Limited to females.
f. Limited to persons under 45.
g. Limited to persons 45 or older.

condition, the mean level of worry is greater on the free plan for all but 3 of the conditions (columns 4 and 5, $p < .114$ using a sign test, if the conditions are independent). Moreover, for one of the conditions for which less worry was reported on the free plan (with initial prevalence controlled for), vision disorders, we found that free care actually improved functional vision; this result only underscores the negative findings for the remaining 10 conditions.

Similar findings hold for reported pain; of the eleven conditions described in Table 6.10, all but two report more pain on the free-care plan when the comparison is some pain versus no pain (with initial prevalence controlled for), and all but 4 report more pain conditional upon reporting some pain. We noted in the previous chapter that the additional medical care on the free plan may have caused both adverse and beneficial effects. We regard these findings of possibly greater amounts of worry and pain on the free-care plan as examples of adverse effects that additional care may have induced.[12]

Health Practices

No effects of plan on health practices were detectable (lower portion of Table 6.6). In particular, we can rule out any substantial favorable effect on smoking habits from the additional medical care on the free plan, perhaps because only one-quarter of the smokers reported that a physician had advised them to stop smoking.

General Health and Risk of Dying

No effects of plan on the general health measures — physical, mental, and social health and the GHI — were detectable, that is, statistically significant at the 5 percent level (Table 6.11). This was also true in the low-income, initially ill-health group (Table 6.12). The rather small confidence interval for the difference in the GHI reinforces the inference made in conjunction with the analysis of the physiologic measures that we did not miss a widespread favorable effect for free care.

There was no measurable effect on risk of dying for the average person, but there was an effect among high-risk individuals, especially the poor (Table 6.13). For the high-risk group the change in the Index value — or the probability of death — is about 10 percent (0.2 percentage points). Thus, a person with a 2.1 percent chance of dying on the cost-sharing plans would

Table 6.11 Predicted exit values and raw mean differences of five general health status measures for an average person, by measure and plan (95% confidence intervals in parentheses)

Health status measure	No.[a]	Cost-sharing plans				Free plan	Predicted mean difference (free minus cost sharing)	Raw mean difference (free minus cost sharing)
		95%	25%, 50%	Individual Deductible	Total			
Physical functioning[b]	3,862	86.0	85.0	84.9	85.3	85.3	0.0 (−1.6,1.5)	−0.3 (−2.3,1.7)
Role functioning[c]	3,861	95.5	95.0	94.7	95.1	95.4	0.3 (−0.6,1.2)[d]	−0.3 (−2.2,1.6)[d]
Mental health[e]	3,862	75.6	75.5	75.8	75.6	75.5	−0.2 (−1.1,0.8)	−0.1 (−1.1,1.0)
Social contacts[f]	3,827	69.3	70.2	69.8	69.8	69.4	−0.3 (−2.3,1.6)	−0.2 (−2.4,2.0)
General Health Index[g]	3,943	68.1	68.0	67.9	68.0	67.4	−0.6 (−1.5,0.3)	−0.9 (−2.1,0.3)

a. Numbers of persons in various parts of the analysis are dissimilar because of differences among measures in the number of persons with valid enrollment or exit data.

b. A ten-point difference equals the effect of chronic mild osteoarthritis.

c. % not limited.

d. Approximate confidence interval.

e. A three-point difference equals the effect of being laid off or fired.

f. A five-point difference at enrollment is associated with a one-point difference on the mental health scale.

g. A five-point difference equals the effect of being diagnosed as hypertensive.

have that chance reduced to about 1.9 percent on the free-care plan. This effect is attributable entirely to the effect of free care on blood pressure control. The other two factors that affect the Index, cholesterol and smoking, were unaffected by the additional medical care that free care induced.

In light of the importance of the blood pressure finding for mortality, one might ask whether there is any other way to achieve it. We analyzed the effect of having a screening exam and found that the estimated effect of the exam within the cost-sharing group, 0.6mm Hg diastolic, is almost as large as the effect of free care; this result suggests that a screening exam might be an effective alternative.[13] We return to this option in Chapter 11.

Table 6.12   Predicted exit values of five general health status measures, according to measure, plan, income, and initial health status

	Total cost sharing	Free plan	Free minus cost sharing
Low income and initial ill health[a]			
Physical functioning	60.3	65.9	5.6 (−2.9,14.0)
Role functioning	69.0	46.3	−22.7 (−53.2,7.8)
Mental health	65.6	67.0	1.4 (−1.8,4.7)
Social contacts	51.8	55.3	3.5 (−5.2,12.2)
General Health Index	54.2	54.6	0.3 (−3.0,3.7)
Low income and initial good health			
Physical functioning	89.8	91.2	1.4 (−1.6,4.4)
Role functioning	95.0	96.1	1.1 (−1.8,4.0)
Mental health	81.1	79.3	−1.8 (−4.1,0.6)
Social contacts	77.7	77.9	0.2 (−4.1,4.5)
General Health Index	74.7	72.4	−2.3 (−4.8,0.1)
High income and initial ill health[a]			
Physical functioning	59.9	55.6	−4.3 (−9.8,1.2)
Role functioning	60.3	56.0	−4.3 (−24.1,15.5)
Mental health	63.3	64.5	1.3 (−1.6,4.1)
Social contacts	47.3	47.6	0.3 (−5.0,5.5)
General Health Index	52.8	52.1	−0.7 (−3.1,1.7)
High income and initial good health			
Physical functioning	92.6	91.9	−0.6 (−2.8,1.6)
Role functioning	96.3	96.3	−0.0 (−2.0,1.6)
Mental health	82.7	82.1	−0.6 (−1.9,0.7)
Social contacts	82.2	80.1	−2.1 (−5.1,1.0)
General Health Index	77.7	77.8	0.1 (−1.4,1.6)

Source: Brook et al. (1984).

a. In this analysis, initial ill health is the lowest fifth of the distribution on the measure at enrollment.

Table 6.13   Risk of dying index as a function of plan[a]

	Cost sharing	Free plan	Free minus cost sharing (95% confidence interval)
All persons	1.00[b]	0.99	−0.01[b](−0.05,0.02)
All elevated-risk persons (risk > 1.42)	2.10[b]	1.90	−0.19[b](−0.37,−0.02)[c]
Elevated-risk and low-income persons	2.12[b]	1.83	−0.28 (−0.58,−0.02)[d]
Elevated-risk and high-income persons	2.09	1.96	−0.13 (−0.4,0.1)

a. See text for definition of index. Values have been normalized to 1.00 for all persons. A 40-year-old man has a 1% chance of dying in a three-year period.

b. Value corrected from figures in Brook et al. (1983, 1984).

c. $t = 2.19; p = 0.03$.

d. $t = 1.97; p = 0.05$.

Disability

The direction of the overall effect of cost sharing on disability—defined as restricted activity and work loss—is not theoretically clear. Cost sharing could increase disability through reducing care seeking that would prevent illness or treat it more promptly. But cost sharing could also reduce restricted activity and work loss directly by reducing time spent in doctors' offices, reducing prescribed and labeled disability ("take two aspirin and go to bed"), or reducing iatrogenic consequences of additional tests, hospital stays, or misprescribing.

Disability status was measured in the Experiment by restricted activity days (RADs) and work loss days (WLDs).[14] We collected RAD data by asking respondents the following screening question (Table 6.4): "During this past two-week period, did anyone in your family unit have to cut down on usual activities for more than half a day because of illness, injury, medical treatment, or some other health problem?" For an employed person, a RAD would involve missing work for reasons of illness or injury; for a nonemployed person or student, it would involve not engaging in a usual activity (including school-loss days) for reasons of health. A respondent who answered the screening question affirmatively was asked to list the name of the person experiencing the disability and circle the days on which the disability occurred. A similar procedure was used for work loss. Work loss required a "yes" response to the screening question "During this two-week period, did anyone in your family unit take any time off from work because of illness, a visit to the doctor, emergency treatment, or for any other health reason?"

For a person with no missing data, we constructed an annualized measure of RADs and WLDs by combining the biweekly data. For a person with some missing data, we estimated the missing part using data adjacent to those that were missing, as well as information on the person's site, age, gender, and the time of year. No data were available for about 1 percent of the enrollment sample.

After imputing the missing data, we estimated the effect of plan using a square-root transformation of the annualized RADs and WLDs. This transformation reduced the effect of statistical fluctuations from very sick people and from random errors in estimating disability day rates for people with missing data. The square root of the data was nearly normally distributed. The transformed RADs and WLDs were then averaged over the years in which the person participated in the Experiment. We then transformed the square root of RADs and WLDs to their original units (days per year) using Duan's retransformation smearing estimate (Duan 1983 and Chapter 3).

We also tested whether the effect of cost sharing on disability days was greater for low-income groups and for those who began the Experiment in poor health. An income variable (log of income adjusted for family size at enrollment), a health variable (predicted RAD or WLD level at enrollment based on a combination of enrollment demographic and health status measures such as physical health and self-perceived health status), and interaction terms involving those two variables and insurance plan were included in the regression equation.[15] To determine how different income and sickness subgroups were affected by plan, we then evaluated the regression equation at several levels of sickness and income. Income was defined as follows: the lowest 20 percent were termed "low," the next 40 percent "medium," and the top 40 percent "high." In a similar fashion "poor health" was defined as the bottom 20 percent of the predicted RAD or WLD distribution, "average health" as the next 40 percent, and "good health" as the highest 40 percent.

Using predicted RADs at enrollment as the health status variable in the RAD equation allowed us to combine adults and children in the analysis, even though other health status variables collected for the two groups were different. When we report results for the total group (adults and children), the sick subgroup refers to the lowest 20 percent of the entire population. When we report results for children and adults separately, sick refers to the lowest 20 percent for each group as appropriate.

Cost sharing turned out to decrease restricted activity days (Table 6.14). Among the three plans with some cost sharing, however, the rate of RADs was similar. Therefore, we combined data from those plans when analyzing the effect of plan by health-income subgroup (Table 6.15). Not surprisingly, health status is strongly associated with RADs; people in poor health—the lowest 20 percent—have about four times as many RADs as those in good health. By contrast, income appears to have little effect on RADs after health status is controlled for.

No systematic plan effects on RADs were observed for those in good health, but there were plan effects for those with average or poor health, especially among the nonpoor. Higher RADs were reported for those in the free plan in eight of the nine subgroups; only the most advantaged group, those with high income and good health, was an exception.

Results for adults and children are shown in Tables 6.16 and 6.17, respectively. The trends found for all persons appear for adults, but because of the smaller sample sizes the confidence intervals for adults are

Table 6.14   Restricted activity days per person per year, by plan[a]

Plan	Mean	Standard error of mean	95% confidence interval	Mean no. face-to-face physician visits[b]	No. of persons
Free	9.77	0.56	8.67 to 10.87	4.55	1,883
Intermediate (25% and 50%)	8.61	0.59	7.45 to 9.77	3.25	1,504
Individual Deductible	8.00	0.55	6.92 to 9.08	3.02	1,245
Family Deductible (95%)	8.15	0.65	6.88 to 9.42	2.73	1,094

a. Free vs. Family Deductible and free vs. Individual Deductible contrasts are significant at $p < 0.05$; F-statistic to test null hypothesis of equal means among all plans (d.f. = 3,5721) is 8.17 ($p < 0.01$).

b. Face-to-face contacts with M.D., D.O., or other health provider, excluding visits for only radiology, anesthesiology, or pathology services. From Table 3.2.

Table 6.15 Predicted restricted activity days per person per year for free *vs.* cost-sharing plans, by income and health status, all persons

Income/health status	95%	25%, 50%	Individual Deductible	Cost-sharing plans (total)	Free plan	95% confidence interval, free minus cost sharing	
High income							
Good health	4.3	4.6	4.1	4.4	4.0	-2.09	1.45
Average health	8.1	8.8	7.9	8.3	9.8	-0.27	2.72
Poor health	16.2	18.2	16.0	16.9	23.6	-0.36	13.17
Medium income							
Good health	4.0	4.6	3.8	4.1	4.1	-1.19	1.09
Average health	7.8	8.4	7.6	8.0	9.2	-0.39	1.99
Poor health	16.4	16.6	16.0	16.3	20.9	-0.67	8.57
Low income							
Good health	3.5	4.5	3.3	3.8	4.2	-1.37	2.10
Average health	7.5	7.7	7.1	7.5	8.2	-0.37	1.85
Poor health	16.7	14.2	15.8	15.4	17.0	-3.29	6.46

Table 6.16 Predicted restricted activity days per person per year for free vs. cost-sharing plans, by income and health status, adults

Income/health status	95%	25%, 50%	Individual Deductible	Cost-sharing plans (total)	Free plan	95% confidence interval, free minus cost sharing	
High income							
Good health	3.55	3.65	3.36	3.52	3.03	-2.76	1.77
Average health	6.35	7.14	6.38	6.66	7.55	-0.66	2.45
Poor health	14.33	17.57	15.25	15.85	22.61	-2.38	15.90
Medium income							
Good health	3.43	3.82	3.23	3.51	3.38	-1.56	1.31
Average health	6.44	7.09	6.29	6.64	7.49	-0.14	1.85
Poor health	15.25	16.59	15.44	15.82	20.49	-0.99	10.33
Low income							
Good health	3.26	4.09	3.03	3.48	3.93	-1.81	2.70
Average health	6.59	7.02	6.17	6.61	7.40	-0.78	2.37
Poor health	16.65	15.21	15.71	15.78	17.59	-6.39	10.01

Table 6.17   Predicted restricted activity days per person per year for free and cost-sharing plans, by income and health status, children

Income/health status	95%	25%, 50%	Individual Deductible	Cost-sharing plans (total)	Free plan	95% confidence interval, free minus cost sharing	
High income							
Good health	7.10	8.08	4.45	6.44	8.12	-1.89	5.23
Average health	10.37	15.00	10.47	11.84	14.21	-1.59	6.33
Poor health	14.19	23.86	18.87	18.73	21.85	-5.71	11.95
Medium income							
Good health	6.36	10.16	4.16	6.66	7.12	-2.16	3.08
Average health	12.37	15.31	9.60	12.31	13.70	-1.37	4.16
Poor health	20.21	21.39	17.13	19.53	22.26	-3.57	9.01
Low income							
Good health	5.15	14.40	3.67	7.05	5.52	-5.52	2.47
Average health	16.32	15.86	8.15	13.15	12.84	-4.23	3.60
Poor health	33.41	17.36	14.27	20.98	22.98	-6.81	10.80

wider than among all persons. For children, confidence intervals are generally wider still, but in seven of the nine subgroups higher RADs were reported on the free care plan.

In contrast, we found no significant differences in WLDs by type of plan, although the qualitative pattern was similar to that of RADs (Table 6.18). Comparisons holding income and health status constant also showed little differences in reported WLDs by plan (Table 6.19). As in the case of RADs, WLDs increased as health status declined, and no significant income effect was noted.

In sum, cost sharing decreased RADs and had no significant effect on WLDs. Given that WLDs are a subset of RADs, one can infer that the increased RADs in the free plan are found disproportionately in the nonworking segments of the population.[16]

As noted, more generous health insurance plans may stimulate restricted activity through the direct loss of time spent in doctors' offices. Because differences in visit rates among plans are of the same general magnitude as differences in RADs (Table 6.14), one might infer that the visits themselves could account for the differential in RADs. If this hypothesis is the explanation, however, the additional visits are, on average, not having a beneficial effect on disability. That is, prescribed disability or the higher risk of suffering an adverse medication effect on the free care plan offsets any reduction in disability and restricted activity due to the benefits of free care.[17]

Table 6.18   Work loss days per employed person per year, by plan[a]

Plan	Mean	Standard error of mean	95% confidence interval	No. of persons
Free	5.47	0.42	4.65–6.29	1,136
Intermediate (25%, 50%)	4.82	0.37	4.09–5.55	983
Individual Deductible	4.54	0.36	3.83–5.25	787
Family Deductible (95%)	4.82	0.53	3.78–5.86	600

a. F-statistic to test null hypothesis of equal means among all plans (d.f. 3,3482) is 1.03 ($p < 0.38$).

Table 6.19   Predicted work loss days per employed person per year, by income and health status

Income/health status	95%	25%, 50% plan	Individual Deductible	Cost-sharing plans (total)	Free plan	95% confidence interval, free minus cost sharing	
High income							
Good health	4.71	2.06	3.37	3.30	4.81	−1.42	4.49
Average health	5.82	5.72	5.15	5.54	5.14	−2.42	1.52
Poor health	7.08	11.34	7.36	8.41	5.47	−7.10	1.24
Medium income							
Good health	4.00	2.17	2.76	2.92	3.88	−0.66	2.56
Average health	5.12	5.26	5.20	5.19	5.18	−1.38	1.35
Poor health	6.42	9.79	8.48	8.18	6.69	−4.44	1.47
Low income							
Good health	3.01	2.36	1.95	2.39	2.63	−2.26	2.74
Average health	4.13	4.59	5.28	4.69	5.24	−1.74	2.83
Poor health	5.46	7.63	10.36	7.83	8.81	−7.37	9.32

Prevalence of Symptoms

We asked participants annually and at entrance and exit whether they had had any of certain symptoms (see Table 6.3) during the past 30 days and, if so, whether they had seen a physician for that symptom. There was no difference among plans in the prevalence of five serious and five minor symptoms at enrollment, but there was a difference between free care and the cost-sharing plans in the prevalence of the serious symptoms at exit from the Experiment (Shapiro, Ware, and Sherbourne 1986). Moreover, this difference was concentrated among participants in the lowest 40 percent of the distribution for both socioeconomic status and family income. Specifically, 29 percent of cost-sharing participants reported such symptoms during the Experiment, versus 24 percent of those on the free plan. Uncorrected for multiple comparisons, the probability that this result will occur at random is less than 1 percent. There was no measurable difference in the prevalence of minor symptoms.

A natural interpretation of this result is that it reinforces the results among the poor sick for hypertension and vision reported above. A skeptic, however, may question the degree to which additional medical care can prevent such symptoms, and attribute these results to chance.

Dental Health

The sum of decayed, missing, and filled teeth did not differ across plans. For adolescents and young adults (ages 12–34) there was roughly one less decayed tooth on the free plan than on the 95 percent plan, but this was balanced by one more filled tooth on the free plan (Tables 6.20–6.23). The number of missing teeth did not respond to plan.[18]

The Periodontal Index was lower (better oral health) for adolescents on the free care plan. The free-care plan also had the lowest value for the two other age groups, although generally the differences were not significant (Table 6.24). Even for adolescents, the improvement in the free plan is modest—0.12 of a scale point—between the free plan and the average of all the cost-sharing plans. Such a change would come about, for example, if 12 adolescents out of every 100 improved their periodontal health from mild gingivitis to no gingivitis.

These plan effects were greater for groups with below-average and average education (defined as those whose education was less than 1 standard deviation above the average, roughly the lowest 84 percent of the education distribution) and for those with teeth that had average or higher-than-average decay rates at enrollment and low or average rates of filled teeth (Tables 6.25 and 6.26). Interactions with income were small and insignificant. The effect on periodontal disease was also concentrated in adolescents with average and low education and average and high periodontal disease (Table 6.27).

Preventive dental behaviors—including brushing, flossing, and, for children, even consumption of cariogenic foods—was affected by plan. For adults (age 14 and over), there was more frequent brushing and

Table 6.20　Mean number of decayed teeth at exit from the Experiment, by plan and age group[a]

	Age group		
Plan	12–17 (N = 744)	18–34 (N = 1,794)	35–64 (N = 1,437)
Free	1.8	1.3	1.5
25%	1.7	1.7	1.6
50%	2.3	1.5	1.5
95%	3.2[b]	2.0[b]	1.6
Individual Deductible	2.6[b]	1.9[b]	1.6
All cost-sharing plans	2.5[b]	1.8[b]	1.6

a. Values shown are predicted from regression equation.
b. $p < 0.01$, one-tailed test. Hypothesis tests compare the free with cost-sharing plans.

Table 6.21　Mean number of filled teeth at exit from the Experiment, by plan and age group[a]

	Age group		
Plan	12–17 (N = 744)	18–34 (N = 1,794)	35–64 (N = 1,437)
Free	7.9	12.0	10.3
25%	6.1[b]	10.7[b]	9.3
50%	7.0	11.0[b]	9.7
95%	6.4[b]	10.2[b]	8.8[b]
Individual Deductible	7.1	10.6[b]	8.9[b]
All cost-sharing plans	6.7[b]	10.5[b]	9.1

a. Values shown are predicted from regression equation.
b. $p < 0.01$, one-tailed test. Hypothesis tests compare the free with cost-sharing plans.

Table 6.22 Mean number of missing teeth at exit from the Experiment, by plan and age group[a]

Plan	Age group		
	12–17 (N = 744)	18–34 (N = 1,794)	35–64 (N = 1,437)
Free	1.0	3.2	8.3
25%	0.8	3.4	7.8
50%	1.2	2.9	8.0
95%	1.3	3.2	8.5
Individual Deductible	1.1	3.3	8.5
All cost-sharing plans	1.1	3.2	8.2

a. Values shown are predicted from regression equation.

Table 6.23 Mean number of DMF28 teeth at exit from the Experiment, by plan and age group[a]

Plan	Age group		
	12–17 (N = 744)	18–34 (N = 1,794)	35–64 (N = 1,437)
Free	10.6	16.1	19.4
25%	8.9[b]	15.9	18.5
50%	10.8	15.6	19.2
95%	11.1	15.3[b]	19.1
Individual Deductible	10.9	15.7	19.3
All cost-sharing plans	10.6	15.6	19.0

a. Values shown are predicted from regression equation.. DMF28 = the sum of decayed, missing, and filled teeth, using 28 teeth as a base.

b. $p < 0.01$, one-tailed test. Hypothesis tests compare the free with cost-sharing plans.

flossing on the more generous plans (Table 6.28). For children, there was more frequent flossing and less frequent intake of cariogenic foods on the free-care plan (Table 6.29).

Despite these changes in preventive behaviors, there was no evidence of a preventive effect of insurance plan on the decayed, missing, and filled teeth index. An increased number of decayed teeth were filled on the free-care plan, but the total number of decayed, missing, and filled teeth did not differ by plan (Table 6.23). We infer that these changes in preventive behaviors had at best a modest effect on outcomes, at least for the three-to-five-year period that we observed.

Table 6.24   Mean scores for the peridontal index at exit from the Experiment, by plan and age group[a]

| | Age group | | |
Plan	12–17 (N = 734)	18–34 (N = 1,759)	35–64 (N = 1,293)
Free	0.84	0.96	1.12
25%	0.94[b]	1.08[b]	1.17
50%	0.98[b]	1.04	1.17
95%	0.95	0.99	1.12
Individual Deductible	1.01[b]	1.01	1.21
All cost-sharing plans	0.96[b]	1.02	1.16

a. Values shown are predicted from regression equation. Index scores were rescaled from original values of 0, 1, 2, 6, and 8 to 0, 1, 2, 3, and 4 for regression equation; lower scores indicate better periodontal health. See Table 6.1 for interpretation of scale values.

b. $p < 0.01$, one-tailed test. Hypothesis tests compare the free with cost-sharing plans.

Table 6.25   Education subgroups with significantly better oral health outcomes at exit from the Experiment when enrolled in the free (versus all cost-sharing) plan[a]

| | Oral health measure | | | |
Age group	Decayed teeth	Missing teeth	Filled teeth	DMFT[b]
6–11[c]	Average and low	d	Average and low	d
12–17	Average and low	Low	Average and low	d
18–34	No significant plan differences by subgroup			
35–64	No significant plan differences by subgroup			

a. Average years of schooling of household head, by age group (standard deviation in parentheses): 6–11, 12.0 (2.4); 12–17, 11.4 (2.9). High (low) subgroups are one standard deviation above (below) the average. Thus, the low education group for those age 6–11 is 9.6 years of education or less (9.6 = 12.0 - 2.4). Plan difference significant at $p < 0.01$, two-tailed test.

b. Decayed, missing, and filled teeth.

c. Results for this age group are discussed in Chapter 7.

d. No significant plan differences by subgroup.

Table 6.26   Enrollment oral health status subgroup with significantly better oral health outcomes at exit from the Experiment when enrolled in the free (versus all cost-sharing) plan[a]

Age group	Oral health measure			
	Decayed teeth	Missing teeth	Filled teeth	DMFT[b]
6–11[c]	High and average	d	High and average	d
12–17	High and average	d	Average	d
18–34	High and average	d	Average and low	Low
35–64	No significant plan differences by subgroup			

a. Enrollment oral health status, average (standard deviation in parentheses), by age group: Decay: 6–11, 1.04 (1.28); 12–17, 2.76 (2.60); 18–34, 2.69 (2.64); Filled: 6–11, 0.76 (1.18); 12–17, 4.07 (3.38); 18–34, 9.19 (5.12). High (low) subgroups are more than (less than) one standard deviation from the average. Plan difference significant at $p < 0.01$, two-tailed test.

b. Decayed, missing, and filled teeth.

c. Results for this age group are discussed in the text of Chapter 7.

d. No significant plan differences by subgroup.

Table 6.27   Education and enrollment oral health status subgroups with significantly better periodontal health at exit from the Experiment when enrolled in the free (versus all cost-sharing) plan[a]

Age group	Education	Level of periodontal disease at enrollment
12–17	Average and low	High and average
18–34	No significant plan differences	
35–64	No significant plan differences	

a. Average years of schooling, by age group (standard deviation in parentheses): 12–17, 11.32 (2.9); 18–34, 12.7 (2.4); 35–64, 12.1 (3.2). Enrollment periodontal index, average (standard deviation in parentheses), 12–17, 1.06 (.26); 18–34, 1.13 (.32); 35–64, 1.23 (.43). High (low) subgroups are one standard deviation above (below) the average. Plan differences significant at $p < 0.01$, two–tailed test.

Table 6.28   Predicted mean scale scores for adult oral health behaviors at exit from the Experiment, by type of plan[a]

Behavior[b]	Free	25%	50%	Individual Deductible/ 95%	t-statistic for plan variable[c]
Brushing	4.44	4.44	4.45	4.36	−2.06
Flossing	2.96	2.77	2.82	2.83	−2.15
Eating cariogenic foods	1.66	1.65	1.59	1.69	0.01
Eating between meals	2.90	2.94	2.92	2.93	−0.42

a. Predicted from a regression equation with the following covariates: (1) the natural logarithm of one plus the coinsurance rate (defined on a 0 to 95 scale); (2) the corresponding oral health habit entrance value; (3) number of years of education (for adults, own education; for those under 18 years, education of female head of household); (4) gender and race (nonwhite); (6) age at exit from the study, adults represented by three groups, ages 17–20, 21–34, and 35–64; children represented by four groups, ages 5–8, 9–10, 11–13, and 14–16; (7) pre-enrollment family income and family size (entered as logarithmic transformations); (8) length of enrollment in the experiment; (9) experimental site; (10) data quality variables.

b. Behavior scale ranges from 1 = less to 5 = more.

c. t-value on log(1+coinsurance) in regression equation explaining outcomes. *F*-value on null hypothesis of all means equal for brushing is 3.02 (d.f. 3,2767), $p < 0.05$, and for flossing 1.79 ($p > 0.05$).

Table 6.29   Predicted mean scale scores for oral health behaviors in children at exit from the Experiment, by cost-sharing plans[a]

Behavior[b]	Free	25%	50%	Individual Deductible/ 95%	t-statistic for plan variable[c]
Brushing	4.50	4.47	4.47	4.45	−0.71
Flossing	2.62	2.36	2.20	2.20	−4.15
Eating cariogenic foods	2.07	2.18	2.64	2.32	2.57
Eating between meals	3.80	3.73	3.77	3.83	0.50

a. For the variables included in the predictive equation, see Table 6.28, note a.

b. Behavior scale ranges from 1 = less to 5 = more.

c. t-value on log (1 + coinsurance) in regression equation explaining outcomes. *F*-value on null hypothesis of all means equal for brushing is 3.35 (d.f. 3,1228), $p < 0.05$, and for cariogenic foods eaten 2.79 ($p < 0.05$).

Quality of Medical Care

The foregoing analyses of outcome could be thought of as the ultimate arbiter of the quality of care in different insurance plans. However, the process of medical care, another measure of quality, is controlled directly by the physician or dentist. We conducted two different types of analyses to augment our understanding of the level and variation in quality of care: (1) For the two medical conditions in which plan affected adult outcomes—hypertension and vision—we conducted further analyses of the mechanism by which plan had its effect. (2) We conducted global analyses of process quality of care measures that we designated at the beginning of the Experiment for both ambulatory medical care and dental care.[19] These analyses sought in particular to determine whether the process of care differed by plan.

Treatment of Hypertension

Having established that outcomes of care differed among plans for hypertensives, we asked the degree to which this outcome difference was attributable to patient behavior (for example, the patient's not seeking care on the cost-sharing plans) and, alternatively, the degree to which the difference was attributable to physician behavior (for example, different prescribing patterns on the cost-sharing plans). To answer this question we examined where in the possible process of blood pressure control the plans may have differed. (Our methods and results are described more fully in Keeler et al. 1985.)

We defined two cohorts of hypertensive individuals on the free-care plan (one that was hypertensive at enrollment and another that was hypertensive only at exit) and analogous cohorts on the cost-sharing plans. Participants were defined as hypertensive at enrollment if:

1. They reported taking antihypertensive drugs.
2. They had a repeat systolic blood pressure over 160 or diastolic blood pressure over 95 at the examination.
3. They had a repeat systolic blood pressure over 140 or diastolic over 90 *and* reported that their doctor had previously told them they had hypertension.

4. They reported that a physician had told them more than once that they had hypertension and either were assigned not to take the examination or had systolic blood pressure over 130 or diastolic blood pressure over 80.

Others were classified as hypertensive at exit if they met criteria 1, 2, or 3 at that time or if:

5. They had both repeat enrollment and exit systolic blood pressure over 140 or diastolic over 90.
6. A physician had reported hypertension on an insurance claim form and the participants reported having been diagnosed as hypertensive, or the physician had reported hypertension on two or more insurance claim forms.

Strictly speaking, using criteria to define hypertension that depend on data collected during or at the end of the Experiment introduces potential biases when one analyzes the effect of insurance plan on blood pressure control. If more persons on the free plan are labeled hypertensive because of more physician visits or more use of antihypertensive drugs, then comparisons of outcomes as a function of plan based on the foregoing definitions may be biased because the additional hypertensives so labeled might have a milder disease. Excluding hypertensives we could not identify at enrollment, however, risks missing genuine plan effects because of inadequate sample size.

We had two options: we could use the unbiased group (those classified as hypertensive at enrollment), or we could test for bias in the total hypertensive group (using all criteria) to determine if the percentage of hypertensives was greater on the free than on the cost-sharing plans. This latter test was done, and the prevalence of hypertension was similar across plans (Table 6.30, last column). Moreover, the mean entry diastolic blood pressure level on the free-care plan was insignificantly lower than on the cost-sharing plans at entry and insignificantly higher at exit. If labeling bias were important, one would expect the free-care plan to have more hypertensives at exit with lower blood pressure levels. We conclude that labeling bias cannot be large and so use the total hypertensive group in our analysis.

Among this cohort, hypertensives on the free plan at exit had diastolic blood pressure levels 1.67 mm Hg lower than hypertensives on the cost-sharing plans. (Results in this section differ slightly from those reported earlier in the chapter for diastolic blood pressure, because the second or repeat measurement rather than the first measurement was used in this analysis.) To determine how the lower blood pressure came about, we decomposed the effect by looking down the tree of events involved in hypertension control: hypertensive awareness, treatment, and control. Table 6.31 shows numbers of and average exit diastolic blood pressure for all hypertensives on each plan and for the four subgroups defined as those who answered "no" to one of the three questions in the figures, or those under care at exit (that is, having a visit for hypertension in the year preceding exit). Initially, 34 percent (294/856) of the hypertensives were on the free plan, the same percentage of all participants in that plan.

Over the course of the study, 42 of the 856 hypertensives never visited a physician, but only 5 of these 42 were on the free-care plan—significantly fewer than would be expected if visit behavior were unrelated to plan. Despite their small number, the 42 people with no visits accounted for one-third (0.56/1.67) of the differential in exit blood pressure found between the free and pay plans, with those who made no visits on the pay plans having an average exit diastolic blood pressure of 96.4 mm Hg, nearly 12 mm Hg higher than those who made no visits on the free plan. The lower values for the 5 untreated people on the free plan imply that most of them are false positives, whose blood pressure was temporarily high at the entry screening examination. Among the 37 people with no visits on the cost-sharing plans, however, are more true hypertensives.

Of those with a physician visit, a larger percentage on the cost-sharing plan were never diagnosed as hypertensive (47 versus 38 percent). This feature of cost sharing accounted for most of the overall difference (1.47

Table 6.30 Prevalence of hypertension in adults 14 and older who completed the Experiment, by definition used and by plan

| Plan | Total | Hyper-tensive at enrollment (%) | Hypertensive at exit only[a] | | Total hyper-tensive (%) |
			Con-trolled (%)	Uncon-trolled (%)	
Free plan	1,191	14.2	3.8	6.7	24.7
Cost-sharing plans					
Individual Deductible	755	13.5	2.1	9.3	24.9
25% and 50% coinsurance	917	13.0	3.3	7.3	23.6
95% coinsurance	632	13.3	3.0	8.7	25.0
Total %	100	13.6	3.1	7.8	24.5
Total number	3,495	474	110	272	856

a. Includes mainly people not assigned to the screening examination at enrollment.

Table 6.31 How plan affects care for blood pressure: Was diagnosis made and care provided?

	Free plan			Cost-sharing plans			Difference between cost sharing and free in DBP[a]
	Number answering yes	Number answering no	Average exit DBP	Number answering yes	Number answering no	Average exit DBP	
Total hypertensives	294		89.0	562		90.6	1.67
Physician visit?	289	5 (2%)	84.8[b]	525	37 (7%)[c]	96.4[b]	0.56
Any diagnosis of high blood pressure?	178	111 (38%)	86.6[b]	278	247 (47%)[c]	90.3[b]	1.47
Under care at exit?[d]		44 (25%)	86.7[b]		60 (22%)	88.6[b]	0.30
Under care at exit	134 (46%)[e]		91.9	218 (39%)[d]		90.7	−0.66

Note: DBP = diastolic blood pressure (mm/Hg)
a. A positive value shows that the free plan did better with this subgroup. Calculated assuming free plan average is the standard as follows: −(84.8 − 89.0) ×
5/294 + (96.4 − 89.0) × 37/562 = 0.56; −(86.6 − 89.0) × 111/294 + (90.3 − 89.0) × 247/562 = 1.47.
b. Average for those answering no.
c. Proportion in group is significantly different from those leaving free plan ($p < 0.01$).
d. At least one visit for hypertension in the year preceding exit.
e. % of total hypertensives. Test for difference has $p = 0.06$.

mm of the 1.67 mm net change) in blood pressure control between the plans at the end of the study. Those on the free plan who saw a physician but were not diagnosed as hypertensive had exit blood pressure levels 4 mm Hg lower than the corresponding group on the cost-sharing plans (86.6 versus 90.3). Nearly half the people diagnosed as hypertensive were under care at exit.

Unfortunately, we cannot make a simple inference from these data about whether the beneficial effect of free care that we observed was attributable to patient or physician behavior. It is clear that the 0.56 mm of the differential attributable to never seeking care is a patient-related phenomenon. The bulk of the difference, however, is the 1.47 mm attributable to any diagnosis of hypertension. This differential may stem from either physician or patient behavior. Suppose that on any given visit there is some probability p that the physician detects hypertension. We know that among those with visits, there are about 1.1 more visits per person per year (about 27 percent more) by those on the free-care plan than by those on the cost-sharing plans (see Chapter 3). If p were the same across plans, these additional visits could account for the effect, in which case the effect would be attributable to patient behavior. But p could also be higher on the free-care plan (that is, a physician effect). Our data do not allow us to distinguish between these hypotheses.

The size of the blood pressure effect can be interpreted by setting it against the effect of the screening examination. Those in cost-sharing plans who took the initial screening examination had an exit diastolic blood pressure 0.6 mm Hg lower than those who did not ($p = .07$) and a systolic blood pressure that was 1.2 mm Hg lower ($p = .03$).[20] Thus, as noted above, the effect of the screening exam on blood pressure was more than half as large as the effect of free care.

Treatment of Vision

We analyzed vision disorders in a fashion similar to that just described for hypertension. The population of interest in this analysis consisted of the 2,399 participants with natural vision impairment at entry or exit.[21] Because virtually no one in the Experiment underwent a procedure to improve natural vision, such as cataract removal, we could assume that those with natural impairment at the beginning also had natural impairment at the end of the Experiment and that such impairment was not

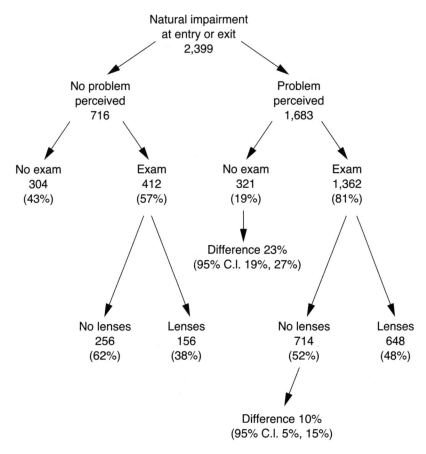

All percentages use as a denominator the number on the preceding branch.
Exam refers to eye examination during the Experiment.
Difference refers to difference between free and cost-sharing plan rates for
that subgroup.
C.I. = confidence interval

Figure 6.1 Relationship of percieved vision problem to likelihood of obtaining lenses

affected by insurance plan. (The methods and results of our analysis are described more fully in Lurie et al. 1989.)

At the top of the vision tree (Fig. 6.1) are all those with a natural impairment. The first branch distinguishes between participants who did or did not perceive a vision problem, as defined by answers to the Enrollment Medical History Questionnaire. Identical percentages of those on the free plan and cost-sharing plans perceived a vision problem (Table 6.32), but those who perceived themselves to have a vision problem were more likely to obtain an examination if care was free (90 versus 76 percent). Among those who perceived that they had a problem and had an examination, however, similar percentages in both the free and cost-sharing plans purchased lenses (48 and 47 percent). Additionally, among the 30 percent of the participants who did not perceive their vision to be a problem, participants on the free-care plan were somewhat more likely to obtain lenses (41 versus 36 percent).

Thus, as was the case with diastolic blood pressure, the outcome gain in the free-care plan was achieved by treatment of those who were not under care at the beginning of the study; once the person was under treatment there was no detectable difference among the plans. In other words, the primary difference between the free-care and other plans was whether the person had an eye examination; this was true even though 70 percent of the participants perceived that they had a problem. Evidently those on the cost-sharing plans, especially those of low income, did not believe the perceived problem was worth remedying.

In the case of vision services, the process of care can be related to outcomes. The effect of plan on obtaining an eye exam was more pronounced among the poor (Table 6.33), as were differences in vision outcomes.

Table 6.32   Effect of cost sharing on process of care for vision problems (sample size in parentheses)

Measure	% on free plan	% on cost-sharing plans
Had natural impairment and perceived vision problem	70 (579)	70 (1,104)
Had eye examined *if* problem perceived	90 (519)	76[a] (843)
Purchased lenses *if* problem perceived *and* had eye exam	48 (250)	47 (398)
Purchased lenses *if* problem not perceived but had eye exam	41 (67)	36[b] (89)

a. 95% confidence interval for difference (6–22).
b. 95% confidence interval for difference (0.1–9.9).

Table 6.33   Effects of cost sharing on vision care for poor and nonpoor
enrollees

	Free			Cost sharing		
	Poor	Nonpoor	Difference	Poor	Nonpoor	Difference
% with natural impair- ment having eye exam	78 (215)[a]	86 (466)[a]	8 (3–13)[b]	59 (285)[a]	74 (808)[a]	15 (9–21)[b]

a. Sample size.
b. 95% confidence interval for difference.

Process Measures of Care

Ambulatory medical care. We examined process measures of the quality of care for 13 chronic adult conditions (acne, anemia, angina pectoris, chronic obstructive pulmonary disease, congestive heart failure, diabetes, hay fever, hearing loss, hypercholesterolemia, hypertension, joint disorders, active peptic ulcer, and near- and far-vision disorders) and 4 chronic childhood conditions (anemia, asthma, eczema, and hay fever). We compared process measures for participants on the free-care plan and participants on all cost-sharing plans. For some relatively prevalent diagnoses (hay fever, joint disorders, acne, vision disorders, hypertension) we also compared the quality of care for the poor and the nonpoor, with a poor family defined as one that, at enrollment, was in the lower one-third of the income distribution adjusted for family size.

The quality-of-care measures used in this analysis were selected from those developed at the beginning of the project and were acceptable to physicians in both the fee-for-service and prepaid group practice systems.

The process measures of quality of care dealt with (1) the appropriate use of visits and diagnostic tests and (2) the appropriateness of therapeutic interventions once care was sought. Visit criteria included mainly statements about whether a visit or test in a symptomatic or asymptomatic person would be useful to establish a diagnosis or would be essential to monitor a patient's course of illness. For example, one measure of quality was whether a person who had hypertension at exit reported seeing a physician in the six months before completing the Experiment. Therapeutic process criteria were usually applied to patients who had already entered the medical system (for example, we asked if an antihypertensive medication was given to a person who had been diagnosed as having hypertension). Brook et al. (1990) contain a complete list of criteria, as well as the number of people to whom the criteria apply, the number who met each criterion, and additional details of this analysis.

The quality-of-care criteria were applied to each enrollee who met the definitional criteria for each disease at enrollment, exit, or during the Experiment. Therapeutic process criteria applied only to persons who sought care for that condition; hence there should be little or no bias from the inducement that free care provided to seek care. (Visit process criteria are by definition affected by this inducement, of course.)

For each of the 17 conditions we developed 2 to 21 process criteria. Many of the criteria applied only to those who sought care for the condition. Depending on the disease, 18 to 65 percent of the process criteria were applicable to an individual patient.

Not surprisingly given the results of Chapters 3 and 4, visit process criteria were met more often in the free care plan, 59 percent versus 52 percent in the cost-sharing plans (summary row of Table 6.34). But there was scarcely any difference in the percentage of times the therapeutic process criteria were met—67 percent of the time in the free-care plan and 65 percent in the cost-sharing plans. We do not attempt to compute the statistical significance of this difference, because of the complicated pattern of intercorrelation within the criteria for a given person with a given disease. (The same person could appear on multiple criteria.) However, even if the difference were statistically significant, we judge it practically to be small.

It is perhaps more noteworthy that the therapeutic process criteria were satisfied much more often for children than for adults—85 and 64 percent, respectively. This result, however, may not be robust, because there are many fewer observations for children and because the results for children are dominated by hay fever, which receives two-thirds of the weight.

For visit criteria, the spread between the free and cost-sharing plans is higher for the poor than for the nonpoor (Table 6.35). For therapeutic criteria the differences are smaller for both groups. The differential spread in the visit criteria is consistent with the results in Chapter 3 regarding the percentages of poor and nonpoor who sought care in various plans.

In order to shed further light on quality of care, we had a physician employed by the Experiment examine those participants at exit who were under active treatment for any of seven diseases (angina, arthritis, chronic

Table 6.34   Percentage compliance with quality of care criteria, by disease, type of criterion, and insurance plan (sample size in parentheses)[a]

Age group and disease	Visit		Therapeutic	
	Free	Cost sharing	Free	Cost sharing
Adults				
Acne	19	7	94	95
	(178)	(271)	(409)	(530)
Anemia	34	21	55	41
	(113)	(151)	(104)	(122)
Angina	41	42	58	52
	(66)	(90)	(143)	(208)
Chronic obstructive	58	50	44	46
pulmonary disease	(48)	(88)	(997)	(1,957)
Congestive heart	77	53	78	70
failure	(39)	(97)	(106)	(255)
Diabetes	76	64	65	58
	(152)	(289)	(162)	(304)
Hay fever	78	79	93	94
	(285)	(477)	(351)	(651)
Hearing loss	33	34	—	—
	(64)	(106)		
Hypercholesterolemia	29	22	68	61
	(294)	(525)	(301)	(545)
Hypertension	60	55	58	56
	(877)	(1,599)	(1,313)	(2,533)
Joint disorders	54	35	88	78
	(132)	(230)	(247)	(335)
Ulcer	35	21	76	83
	(72)	(121)	(144)	(230)
Vision impairments	80	70	71	71
	(694)	(1,433)	(1,591)	(2,966)
Children				
Anemia	27	11	59	62
	(77)	(159)	(17)	(16)
Asthma	41	38	93	88
	(22)	(37)	(39)	(56)
Eczema	17	60	33	27
	(6)	(5)	(18)	(22)
Hay fever	77	82	94	93
	(57)	(84)	(124)	(208)
Summary	59	52	67	65
	(3,176)	(5,759)	(6,066)	(10,938)

a. The number of observations were calculated by summing the number of persons for whom each criterion was applicable across all criteria.

Table 6.35   Percentage compliance with quality of care criteria, by income group, disease, type of criterion, and insurance plan (sample size in parentheses)

Income group and disease	Visit		Therapeutic	
	Free	Cost sharing	Free	Cost sharing
Poor[a]				
Acne	14	4	93	96
	(81)	(108)	(152)	(195)
Hay fever	79	72	94	95
	(112)	(117)	(127)	(181)
Hypertension	59	52	55	56
	(268)	(452)	(427)	(762)
Joint disorders	52	30	96	82
	(42)	(71)	(54)	(89)
Vision	79	67	65	64
	(291)	(573)	(557)	(896)
Summary	64	55	69	67
	(794)	(1,321)	(1,317)	(2,123)
Nonpoor				
Acne	23	9	95	95
	(97)	(163)	(257)	(335)
Hay fever	78	82	92	94
	(173)	(360)	(224)	(470)
Hypertension	60	56	59	56
	(609)	(1,147)	(886)	(1,771)
Joint disorders	54	37	86	77
	(90)	(159)	(193)	(246)
Vision	81	72	74	73
	(403)	(860)	(1,034)	(2,070)
Summary	65	61	73	71
	(1,372)	(2,689)	(2,594)	(4,892)

a. Poor is defined as those in the lowest third of the enrollees' income distribution.

obstructive pulmonary disease, congestive heart failure, diabetes, hypertension, and peptic ulcer). Active treatment was defined as having had a specified number of physician visits for that problem in the 18 months before the end of the Experiment. The physician made an independent determination of whether the patient definitely or probably had the disease, if side effects were being experienced from the current regimen, and if a change in regimen would be desirable (to improve health status or reduce side effects). The results are shown in Table 6.36.

Table 6.36 Percentage of positive responses for issues addressed at physician evaluation, by disease and insurance plan (sample size in parentheses)

Disease	No. of visits required in previous 18 months to define active treatment[a]	Examinee definitely or probably has the disease		No side effects being experienced from current therapy		No, minimal, or minor improvement expected from therapeutic change		No change in current therapy suggested	
		Free	Cost sharing	Free	Cost sharing	Free	Cost sharing	Free	Cost sharing
Angina	2	67 (15)	75 (17)	67 (15)	67 (17)	62 (15)	60 (17)	22 (15)	25 (17)
Arthritis	3	64 (69)	64 (96)	70 (69)	70 (96)	87 (69)	85 (96)	38 (69)	38 (96)
Chronic obstructive pulmonary disease	3	65 (37)	68 (50)	76 (37)	76 (50)	40 (37)	38 (50)	27 (37)	30 (50)
Congestive heart failure	3	100 (3)	100 (4)	67 (3)	75 (4)	67 (3)	75 (4)	33 (3)	50 (4)
Diabetes	2	90 (20)	91 (23)	65 (20)	70 (23)	85 (20)	78 (23)	35 (20)	44 (23)
Hypertension	1	76 (68)	86 (104)	84 (68)	88 (104)	71 (68)	62 (104)	26 (68)	26 (104)
Peptic ulcer	3	94 (12)	96 (15)	81 (12)	83 (15)	81 (12)	74 (15)	25 (12)	26 (15)
Summary		72 (224)	77 (309)	75 (222)	77 (309)	72 (224)	67 (309)	30 (224)	32 (309)

a. For example, a person was examined if he or she had had two visits with a diagnosis of angina in the previous 18 months.

The independent physician concluded that therapeutic change would bring about no improvement or only a minor improvement about 70 percent of the time. There were no important differences between the free-care and cost-sharing plans. Likewise, there were no important differences between free care and cost sharing in the frequency with which side effects were experienced. Even so, the independent physician suggested a change in current therapy more than two-thirds of the time.

Dental care. Similar process criteria were developed for dental care. This analysis was carried out on the 1,933 individuals enrolled for three years in all but the two South Carolina sites. (The effect by plan is analyzed in Bailit et al. 1984.)

Explicit process (and outcome) criteria were developed and reviewed by numerous dentists. They focused on the major conditions dentists treat: caries, periodontal disease, and missing teeth. The process criteria dealt with the technical quality of restorations and the treatment planning dimension of care; and the necessity and appropriateness of service, including measures of both underutilization and overutilization relative to professional norms. Here we present selected, representative results. The results pertaining to overtreatment could well be affected by the prior authorization requirement for any treatment plan that exceeded $500 (except in case of emergency) or for replacement of crowns, bridges, or dentures.

1. *Treatment of caries.* Restorations to sound teeth constitute one form of overtreatment. Fewer than 1 percent of sound teeth (that is, caries free, no fillings) at enrollment received a Class I or V restoration in the 6 months following the entrance examination (Table 6.37). This share increased to about 1.5 percent at 12 months (data not shown). There were no significant plan effects.

Another form of overtreatment is to provide restorative crowns for teeth having simple (one-surface) fillings. Over the three years of the Experiment, this occurred in about 2 percent of teeth in the free, 25, and 50 percent plans (Table 6.37). The incidence in the free plan was significantly different from that in the 95 percent and Individual Deductible plans.

In light of the large number of decayed teeth seen at the exit examination (Table 6.20), undertreatment of carious teeth appears to be more of an issue than overtreatment. It is also evident in the percentage of decayed teeth that were restored within 12 months of enrollment: in the 95 percent plan, only 12 percent of carious teeth were treated at 12 months (Table 6.37); even in the free plan only 30 percent of carious teeth were treated (a difference that is statistically significant). Even after 24 months (data not shown), only about 40 percent of enrollees in the free plan—a plan under which 75–80 percent of eligibles received at least some dental care in a two-year period—had their decayed teeth restored.

2. *Periodontal disease.* To assess possible overtreatment further, we investigated the percentage of enrollees (aged 12–64) with no more than mild gingivitis (Periodontal Index < 1.2) who nonetheless received advanced treatment (such as scaling/curettage or surgery) within 12 months of enrollment. None of the subjects with this level of periodontal disease received surgery, and about 5 percent received scalings/curettage. These percentages did not differ systematically by plan (Table 6.38).

There was some undertreatment of periodontal disease. Most free plan enrollees (70 percent) with no more than mild gingivitis received appropriate care (prophylaxis) within 12 months (Table 6.38), but significant reductions were observed between the free and the 25 and 95 percent

Table 6.37   Percentage of teeth receiving restorations, by plan and type of restoration[a]

Criterion	Free	25%	50%	95%	Individual Deductible
Sound teeth receiving Class I or V fillings within six months of enrollment, age 6–64	1.0 (4,698)	0.7 (1,676)	0.6 (1,958)	0.9 (3,187)	0.9 (3,275)
Teeth with Class I fillings receiving crowns within 36 months of enrollment, age 18–64	2.5 (626)	2.0 (244)	2.8 (250)	0.0[b] (364)	0.7[b] (454)
Decayed teeth restored within 12 months of enrollment, age 3–64	30.0 (663)	25.5 (243)	20.7[c] (391)	11.7[c] (522)	25.9 (563)

a. Total number of teeth in plan category included in this analysis shown in parentheses.
b. $p < 0.05$ versus free plan.
c. $p < 0.01$ versus free plan.

Table 6.38 Percentage of enrollees age 12–64 who received appropriate levels of periodontal care within 12 or 36 months of enrollment, by plan[a]

Criteria	Free	25%	50%	95%	Individual Deductible
PI < 1.2, did not receive scaling or surgery	94.2 (207)	90.6 (64)	97.7 (88)	98.1 (105)	91.1 (135)
PI < 1.2, received prophylaxis	70.1 (207)	50.0[b] (64)	61.4 (88)	41.0[b] (105)	60.7 (135)
PI > 1.2, received prophylaxis and scaling	9.7 (62)	6.5 (31)	0.0 (27)	6.1 (49)	4.6 (44)
PI > 1.9, dentist told had gum disease	34.1 (44)	35.7 (14)	16.7 (18)	21.4 (28)	30.3 (33)

Note: PI = Periodontal Index.
a. Total number of teeth in plan category included in this analysis shown in parentheses.
b. $p < 0.01$ vs. free plan.

plans. Furthermore, for the relatively small numbers of subjects with more than mild gingivitis (Index > 1.2), only a few (less than 10 percent) received both prophylaxes and scalings. No plan effects were seen for any of the free versus cost-sharing plan comparisons.

A related aspect of underutilization is the number of people with moderate or severe disease who knew they had periodontitis. Across all plans fewer than 30 percent of these subjects reported being informed by their dentist that they had gum disease. Thus, most people with moderate to severe periodontal disease were not aware of their condition. Because of the small number of people with advanced disease, however, these estimates should be viewed cautiously.

3. Radiographs. The American Dental Association's radiation safety guidelines state that full-mouth radiographs should not be taken more than once every 36 months. In order to be conservative in determining excess numbers of radiographs, we set the limit at 30 months. About 2–5 percent of enrollees who visited the dentist received more than one set of radiographs in 30 months (Table 6.39), but there were no clear plan effects.

We performed the same type of analysis for bite-wing radiographs. About 1 percent of enrollees had bite-wings taken more than once within 5 months, and there were no plan effects in this case either. In both instances the multiple radiographs may have been taken by different dentists.

4. Treatment restorations. The technical fit of restorations is an important aspect of dental care quality. The examination of amalgam restorations at exit from the Experiment indicated that about 90 percent were rated adequate for marginal integrity and 96 percent for overhanging margins (Table 6.40). For cast crowns, most ratings exceeded 95 percent adequate for integrity of margins and contour. Pontics were less well done, but 80–90 percent were rated adequate. There were no clear plan effects for any of the criteria.

5. Timeliness of treatment. Cost sharing had a major effect on the timeliness of needed treatment. Over a twofold difference was seen between the free and 95 percent plans in the percentage of teeth filled within 12 months of enrollment (Table 6.37). Similarly, subjects with moderate to advanced periodontal disease, poorer oral hygiene, and two or more carious teeth received more appropriate curative or preventive treatments if they were in the free rather than the pay plans. These findings provide indirect evidence that the improved dental health outcomes associated with less cost sharing may be related to more timely treatment.

On an absolute basis, the evidence indicates substantial undertreatment. Even in the free plan, within 12 months of enrollment only 30 percent of decayed teeth were restored (Table 6.37), and only 10 percent of enrollees with Periodontal Index scores greater than 1.2 received prophylaxes and scalings (Table 6.38). The factors responsible for this level of undertreat-

Table 6.39   Percentage of enrollees age 3–64 receiving overly frequent full-mouth and bitewing radiographs, by plan (sample size in parentheses)[a]

Criterion	Free	25%	50%	95%	Individual Deductible
> 1 full-mouth set of radiographs taken within 30 months	4.8 (1,166)	2.8 (214)	1.8[b] (278)	2.7 (339)	4.4 (474)
> 1 bitewing set of radiographs taken within 5 months	1.4 (293)	1.3 (75)	0.7 (74)	0.9 (107)	0.9 (161)

a. Among enrollees who had at least one dental visit in 30 or 5 months, respectively. This includes persons who saw more than one dentist in that period.

b. $p < 0.05$ vs. free plan.

Table 6.40   Percentage of restorations with no defects at the exit examination, by plan and type of restoration[a]

Criterion	Free	25%	50%	95%	Individual Deductible
Fillings with no defects	(2,035)	(475)	(852)	(1,003)	(1,048)
No open margins	89.4	92.4[b]	86.0[c]	87.2	90.7
No overhangs	95.3	97.4	93.2	95.4	96.7
Crowns with no defects	(457)	(98)	(92)	(205)	(246)
No open margins	97.4	99.0	93.4[b]	95.6	95.1
Not overcontoured	91.6	94.9	95.5	94.6	89.3
Pontics with no defects	(89)	(27)	(26)	(55)	(70)
Not overcontoured	80.6	96.3[c]	92.3	87.3	87.1

a. Data are available only on five-year enrollees. Numbers in parentheses are the number of tooth restorations in plan category.

b. $p < 0.05$ vs. free plan.

c. $p < 0.01$ vs. free plan.

ment are not known, but in light of the free plan results it cannot be accounted for by financial barriers to care.

The impact of free care on overtreatment was minimal. Reduced cost sharing caused no significant increase in unnecessary one-surface fillings, scalings, and periodontal surgery. There was a statistically significant increase in restorative crowns, but the absolute difference between the free and 95 percent plans over a three-year period was minimal (15 crowns). These are important results because they suggest that reduced cost sharing is not a major cause of overtreatment, at least for the types of unnecessary care assessed in this study, and given our prior authorization procedures.

Subject to the caveat that prior authorization provisions were in place, the limited overtreatment seen also suggests that this type of abuse is probably not a serious cause of iatrogenic disease or unnecessary expenditures. This conclusion is reinforced by the substantial amounts of untreated disease seen.

Patient Satisfaction

In order to measure patient satisfaction, we used a 43-item short form of the Patient Satisfaction Questionnaire, developed by Ware and colleagues (Ware, Snyder, and Wright 1976); Ware, Davies-Avery, and Stewart 1978; Ware et al. 1983). The battery was self-administered by all adults 17 and

Table 6.41   Operational definitions of satisfaction measures

Category/measure	Sample item	Score range[a]
Accessibility		
Answers to questions	If I have a medical question, I can reach someone for help without any problem.	1–5
Appointment waits	It's hard to get an appointment for medical care right away.	1–5
Emergency care	In an emergency, it's very hard to get medical care quickly.	1–5
Office hours	Office hours when you can get medical care are good for most people.	1–5
Office waiting time	People are usually kept waiting a long time when they are at the doctor's office.	1–5
Parking arrangements	Parking is a problem when you have to get medical care.	1–5
Travel time/ convenience	It takes me a long time to get to the place where I receive medical care.	2–10
Availability		
Family doctors	There are enough family doctors around here.	2–10
Hospitals and specialists	More hospitals are needed in this area.	3–15
Finances		
Costs of care	The amount charged for medical care services is reasonable.	2–10
Quality of care		
Facilities	I think my doctor's office has everything needed to provide complete medical care.	2–10
Interpersonal aspects	Doctors respect their patients' feelings.	8–40
Technical quality	Doctors aren't as thorough as they should be.	6–30
Overall		
General satisfaction	I'm very satisfied with the medical care I receive.	4–20
Other		
Provider continuity	I see the same doctor almost every time I go for medical care.	2–10
Recommended annual exam	Most people are encouraged to get a yearly exam when they go for medical care.	1–5

a. The lowest possible score is equal to the number of items in the scale. Respondents' instructions say: "On the following pages are some statements about medical care. Please read each one carefully, keeping in mind the medical care you are receiving now. If you have not received medical care recently, think about what you would expect if you needed care today. On the line next to each statement circle the number for the opinion which is closest to your own view. This is not a test of what you know. There are no right or wrong answers. We are only interested in your opinions or best impression." Responses are: strongly agree, agree, don't know, disagree, strongly disagree.

older before the Experiment began, and biennially throughout the Experiment by all enrollees 14 and older. Analyses using both Experiment data and other administrations of this instrument indicate that consumers can evaluate several separate dimensions of satisfaction, shown in Table 6.41. The reliability and validity of the patient satisfaction scales have been demonstrated with Experiment data, as well as in other general population samples (Ware, Snyder, and Wright 1976; Marquis, Davies, and Ware 1983; Ware et al. 1983).

For the fee-for-service sample, with data from all sites, there were no differences in overall satisfaction among plans. This finding is consistent with what is known about utilization—namely, that the individuals on the different plans for the most part used the same providers (M. S. Marquis 1985) and were treated quite similarly in terms of the medical content of the illness episode (see also Chapter 4 and Lohr et al. 1986b, app. E). Moreover, it is unlikely that the same physician would alter his or her interpersonal manner or features such as convenience in response to plan. Thus, the patient satisfaction analysis is of greater interest when comparing the fee-for-service system with the HMO (Chapter 9) than when comparing alternative fee-for-service plans.

Summary

Our results show that the 40 percent increase in services on the free-care plan had little or no measurable effect on health status for the average adult. The additional care had beneficial effects on blood pressure levels for the poor with high blood pressure, with an associated gain in predicted mortality for this group. However, a one-time screening examination achieved most of the gain in blood pressure that free care achieved. There were modest gains in correctable vision, also concentrated among the poor, and gains in periodontal health. Caries were more likely to be filled on the free plan. The sick poor reported fewer serious symptoms on the free plan, but restricted activity days due to sickness or illness were higher on the free-care plan. Why free care did not have a more beneficial effect on outcomes is a subject we return to in Chapter 11.

Chapter 7

Pediatric Health Status

For our child health analysis we used data on children who were age 13 and under at enrollment. Because families were enrolled for at most five years, the oldest child included in the analysis was 18. Health concerns and needs are different for children from those for adults, so we had to use a different set of health measures. Some apply to children through age 18, while some apply only to children age 5 and above. As in the case of adults, our measures include both physiologic and perceived health measures.

Health Measures

In choosing physiologic measures for our analysis of pediatric health status, we sought measures that are readily detected, are relatively prevalent, are amenable to medical treatment, and have important adverse side effects if left unattended. Of a set of 12 conditions we tested for at enrollment, we selected the 5 that met this set of criteria best: anemia, hay fever, fluid in the middle ear, hearing loss, and visual acuity.[1] We also used measures of perceived physical role limitations, mental health, and general health perceptions. Tables 7.1 and 7.2 provide further information about the health measures.[2]

Data Collection Methods

Physiological function. These measures came from the screening examination. Table 7.3 shows the number and ages of children screened.

Perceived health. As in the case of adult health, information on perceived health was collected at enrollment and at exit three or five years later by means of the Medical History Questionnaire, as well as on an abbreviated version of this questionnaire annually. To measure perceived health we

Table 7.1   Definitions of health status measures and percent at risk of illness: physiologic measures and parental worry

Health variable and definition	Specific scoring	% with condition at enrollment

Anemia status: A dichotomous (0,1) indicator of low hemoglobin, adjusted for age and gender	Defined as having anemia if hemoglobin falls below the following limits (in g/100ml of blood):
	Boys and girls:
	  6 mos.–2 years 10.0
	  2–12 years 11.0
	Boys only: 13–18 years 12.0
	Girls only: 13–18 years 11.5
		9.4

Hay fever status: A dichotomous (0,1) indicator of whether the child is bothered by hay fever or other plant allergies	Based on responses to medical history for children 5 years or older	8.4
Functional far vision: Visual acuity with usual correction in better eye (i.e., glasses or contacts), measured in Snellen lines	Visual impairment indicated if score is > 2; (2 = 20/20, 3 = 20/25, 4 = 20/30)	29.2
Hearing loss: A dichotomous (0,1) indicator of hearing impairment in the better ear	Hearing impaired if average hearing threshold level in better ear (tested at 500, 1,000, 2,000, and 4,000 Hz) is > 15 dB	6.6
Fluid in middle ear: A dichotomous (0,1) indicator of fluid in either or both middle ears	Tympanometry results indicate effusion or probable effusion according to the following criteria:	26.4

Air pressure (mm H_2O)	Compliance (Madsen units)	Slope
−400 to −100	5 to 10	All
−100 to 50	5.5 to 10	All
−100 to 50	5.5 to 4.5	Flat or rounded
−400 to −100	0 to 5	Flat or rounded
50 to 300	5.5 to 10	Flat or rounded

Table 7.1   (continued)

Health variable and definition	Specific scoring	% with condition at enrollment
Parental worry: A four-point scale measuring worry associated with anemia, hay fever, vision, or hearing loss	The highest level of worry expressed about one of the physiologic conditions examined (1 = not at all 4 = a great deal)	20.9[a]

a. Percentage whose parent expressed any worry. Parents of children with hearing loss = 1 score 0.36 points higher on this scale.

designed age-appropriate questionnaires to gather information on infants and toddlers (0–4 years) and children aged 5–13 (Eisen et al. 1980; Davies and Ware 1981; Ware, Johnston, and Davies-Avery 1979; Ware et al. 1984). For the health status measures shown in Table 7.2, the Experiment relied on parental assessments (usually the mother's) for all children under 14 and on self-reports for adolescents who were 14 or older at exit.

Reliability and Validity

The reliability, validity, and precision of the child health status measures have been reported in detail elsewhere.[3] We summarize those findings briefly here.

Physiological function. The physiologic screening tests were selected on the basis of logistics of performance, acceptability to participants, and acceptability to the medical community, including the participants' physicians.[4] During the Experiment's screening examination of children, test-retest measurements were taken for visual acuity, tympanometry (responsiveness of the eardrum to air pressure changes), and audiometry (hearing threshold). Duplicate blood samples were drawn on 5–10 percent of participants. Each child also had at least one of the other tests repeated about one hour after the first test. Test-retest evaluations yielded the following results:

- Hemoglobin measurement: The difference between the first and second measurement of hemoglobin ranged from −2.4 to 1.1 grams/100 milliliters; the mean difference was 0.04g and the standard deviation of the mean difference, 0.42g.
- Vision: For natural far vision, the difference between the first and second measurements was never greater than 2 lines, and the mean absolute differ-

ence was 0.20 line. For natural near vision, the difference was never greater than 1 line, and the mean absolute difference was 0.02 line.

- Tympanometry: Of the 43 ears retested, 41 (95 percent) were classified the same (impaired or not) at both tests. Of course, some agreement would have been expected by chance alone. To account for this, the data were evaluated according to the κ statistic and found highly significant ($\kappa = 0.85$, $p < 0.001$).

Table 7.2   Definitions of health status measures: health perceptions measures

Health variable and definition	Typical item	Meaning of a high score
Role limitations:[a] A dichotomous (0,1) measure that indicates whether child can play, go to school, or take part in usual activities free of limitations due to poor health.	Is this child limited in the amount or kind of other activities (such as playing, helping around the house, hobbies) because of health?	Child is limited in role activities because of poor health.
Mental Health Index:[b] A standardized (0–10) scale that measures anxiety, depression, and psychological well-being during the past month. A high score represents a positive level of mental health.	During the past month, did this child seem to be anxious or worried?	Child is relaxed and cheerful. Children with moderate to severe hearing problems score 0.41 points lower than those without such problems.[d]
General Health Index:[c] A standardized (0–10) scale that assesses perceptions of the child's health in the past, present, and future and susceptibility to illness.	In general, would you say this child's health is excellent, good, fair, or poor?	Child is in excellent health. Children suffering from mild hay fever score 0.51 points lower than those without hay fever; children with moderate to severe hearing problems score 1.1 points lower than those without such problems.[d]

a. Constructed from 2 items for children under 5 years and 3 items for children 5 and older.

b. This battery was not administered to children under 5; it was constructed from 12 items for children under 14 and 38 items for those 14 or older (the adult scale).

c. Constructed from 7 items for children under 14 and 22 items for children 14 and older (the adult scale).

d. Moderate to severe hearing loss means Hearing Loss variable = 1.

- Hearing: The mean difference between the first and second average hearing threshold levels for the better ear was 0.91 decibels, with a standard deviation of 2.84 dB.

Although these errors in measurement degrade our ability to detect differences among plans, for our sample sizes the amount of degradation by plan is small. For example, for the free plan sample size of 600, the additional error variance for hemoglobin would be about .04 of a standard deviation, or .017g of hemoglobin. We concluded that the reliability of the experimental physiologic measures was acceptable for our analyses.

Parent-assessed measures of perceived health. Table 7.4 summarizes the findings for the reliability and stability of our measures of perceived health. In general, the scores produced by the General Health Index (GHI) and the other mother-assessed measures provide adequate reliability for group comparisons, despite their use of fewer items than their counterparts for adults. We estimated internal-consistency reliability coefficients (that is, average interitem correlations) for the children's General and Mental Health Indexes. Scores were sufficiently reliable for group comparisons (Cronbach's $\alpha > 0.50$). The reliability coefficients were considerably higher than what would have been achieved with single-item measures.

Table 7.3   Medical screening tests and eligible population[a]

Disease condition	Screening test	Population screened	Exit only	Enrollment and exit
Anemia	Hematocrit Hemoglobin	Children 6 mos.– 18 years	639	906
Hearing loss	Pure-tone threshold audiometry	Children 4–18 years	775	695
Fluid in middle ear except those with surgery in past 6 months	Tympanometry	Children 4–13 years	627	360
Visual disorder	Near vision, with and without correction; far vision, with and without correction; Pinhole Acuity Correction	Children 5–18 years	795	796

a. Numbers differ by test because of different age criteria, missing medical history questionnaires, and missing date of screening.

Table 7.4 Reliability and stability estimates for parent-assessed health status
measures

Measure	Medical History Questionaire[a]	Number of items	Reliability[b]	One-year stability[c]
General Health	I	7	0.77	0.49
Index	P	7	0.76	0.64
Mental Health	P	12	0.87	0.52
Index				
Role limitations	I, P		[d]	0.35

a. I = infants 0–4 years; P = children 5–13 years.

b. Internal-consistency reliability estimated by Cronbach's (1951) alpha.

c. Product-movement correlation between scores obtained approximately one year apart.

d. Because attempts to create summated rating scales failed for children, dichotomous
scores were assigned to children with one or more role activities limitations.

We were unable to create a multi-item scale for the three role limitation
questions for children, because the sample was small and limitations rare.
Therefore, we assigned scores indicating whether the child reported
having one or more of these limitations. As a result, our role limitation
data suffer from lack of variability. Role limitations due to poor health are
relatively rare (under 5 percent) in general populations of children
(National Center for Health Statistics 1990), and improvements in health
are difficult to detect with such a measure. Power calculations published in
Eisen et al. (1980) indicate that the differences would have to be moderate
to large to be detected with our sample size. We were unwilling to exclude
the possibility of a moderate or large effect of cost sharing a priori, however, so we included this measure in our analyses. Other Experiment measures are sufficiently variable to detect smaller effects.

Stability of scores across repeated measurements a year apart was generally high. Stability estimates range from a low of 0.35 for role limitations to a high of 0.64 for the GHI.

The Experiment produced a number of findings supporting the validity
of the perceived-health measures. For example, the parent-assessed measures successfully differentiate between well children and those with
chronic serious conditions or acute illnesses. The association between the
GHI and the presence of chronic conditions was statistically significant for
those in the 5–13 age group (Gamma statistic = -0.32, $p < 0.05$, two-tailed
test). The association was also significant but lower between the GHI and

the frequency of acute illnesses. In fact, all parent-assessed measures discriminated between well children and children with some type of illness (see Eisen et al. 1980, table 58). It thus appears that the parent-assessed measures are valid indicators of changes in health status during the Experiment.

The measures also exhibit content validity. The content of the items was based on Eisen et al. (1980), which contains an extensive review of content validity for child health measures. The only significant shortcoming in the content of the Experiment measures used at enrollment was the absence of any reference to child behavior problems. We corrected this omission in the fall of 1978 by adding to the medical history questionnaires a comprehensive battery of multi-item scales measuring behavior problems, based on the work of T. M. Achenbach (1978, 1979).

Methods of Analysis

The methods used to analyze health outcome data on children were similar to those used on data from adults; specifically, we used regression analysis to predict health status at exit as a function of insurance plan, health status at enrollment (that is, the enrollment value of the exit measure that was being predicted), and family income (adjusted for family size and site cost of living) (see Chapter 6). We also included variables to control for other experimental manipulations (for example, taking the screening examination, three- or five-year enrollment, questionnaire form, and respondent), as well as demographic characteristics (education of the mother, race, gender, and site).[5]

As in the case of adults, we looked at predicted values for both the average child and the at-risk child. For parental-assessed measures (for example, the GHI) we defined the at-risk child as a child in the lowest quartile of children at enrollment. For physiologic conditions we defined the at-risk child to be one with a given physiologic condition at enrollment (for example, classified as anemic). We imputed values to children who were missing enrollment screening examination values because they had not been assigned to take an enrollment exam; these imputations were made using explanatory variables observed at enrollment. Observations with imputed values were downweighted in the analysis to account for the error introduced by the imputation (Dagenais 1971).

Also as in the adult analysis, we compared effects for children in families with varying incomes. Those from families in the bottom quarter of the income distribution at enrollment were designated as poor, and those from families in the upper half of the distribution were designated as nonpoor.[6] In generating predicted values for the subgroups (for example, children at risk in poor families) we used mean values for the explanatory variables in the subgroup; in the linear models considered here, that is equivalent to predicting the mean for the subgroup. The correlation of the error term within family and the nonconstant variance of the error term were corrected using the same methods as for adults.

Results

Health Status of the Average Child

For the average child participant, we could not discern significant differences in health status between those who received free care and those on the cost-sharing plans (Table 7.5). Only the difference in the probability of having hay fever approached conventional statistically significant levels ($p = .08$ without correction for multiple comparison), and this measure suggested a greater prevalence of hay fever on the free-care plan (17 percent versus 12 percent). Nor were any differences observed within the group of cost-sharing plans. When all the measures were taken together, the direction of estimated effects favored neither the free plan nor the cost-sharing plans.

For all measures the confidence intervals for the difference between free and cost-sharing plans were fairly narrow, making it unlikely that substantial differences would have been detected in a larger sample. For example, the 95 percent confidence interval for the GHI is approximately plus or minus 0.2. This can be compared with the effect of having hay fever on the Index, -0.5. Thus, a reasonable upper bound on the effect of free care is less than half the effect of having hay fever, and the most likely effect of free care is none.

Health Status of At-Risk Children

For both poor and nonpoor children at risk of illness because of an existing condition, we observed no statistically significant difference (at the 5 percent level of significance) between the free and cost-sharing plans for any of our measures (Table 7.6). Nevertheless, among the poor families, those at-risk children on the free plan appeared less likely to have anemia at the conclusion of the Experiment than those on the cost-sharing plans (8 versus 22 percent). Although this difference was not statistically significant at conventional levels ($p = 0.12$, without correction for multiple comparison), a true difference of this size would have clinical importance.

Confidence intervals among the at-risk children are broader than those among all children because of the smaller sample size, so they are more likely to mask some clinically important differences. Therefore, we are less certain of our conclusion that health effects did not differ between plans for the medically at-risk child than we are for the case of the average child.

Table 7.5   Predicted exit values of health status measures for a child with average characteristics, by measure and plan

Health status measure	Number[a]	Free plan	Cost-sharing plans	Free minus cost sharing[b]
Parental-assessed measures				
General Health Index[c]	1,506	5.5	5.5	−0.01 (−0.20, 0.18)
Mental Health Index[c]	1,048	5.8	5.9	−0.13 (−0.37, 0.11)
Role limitations (%)	1,480	2.6	2.6	0.0 (−7, 7)
Physiologic measures				
Anemia (%)	1,538	1.9	2.1	−0.20 (−1.8, 1.4)
Hay fever (%)	1,378	17	12	5.0 (0, 10)[d]
Hearing loss (%)	1,463	7.2	6.2	1.0 (−1.7, 3.7)
Fluid in middle ear (%)	987	25	25	0.0 (−7, 7)
Functional far vision[e]	1,591	2.6	2.7	−0.07 (−0.21, 0.07)
Parental worry about physio-logic conditions[f]	1,535	1.40	1.35	0.05 (−0.02, 0.12)

a. Sample sizes differ because the number of children included in each health status analysis differs due to age restrictions or missing data.

b. 95% confidence intervals in parentheses; approximate confidence intervals for dichotomous indicator variables.

c. 0–10 scale; a higher value denotes better health.

d. $t = 1.74$; $p = 0.08$.

e. In Snellen line values: 2 = 20/20, 3 = 20/25, 4 = 20/30.

f. 4-point scale: 1 = not at all, 2 = a little, 3 = somewhat, 4 = a great deal.

Table 7.6   Predicted exit values of health status measures for children with preexisting conditions, by measure, plan, and income

Health status measure	Poor			Nonpoor		
	Free plan	Cost-sharing plans	Free minus cost sharing[a]	Free plan	Cost-sharing plans	Free minus cost sharing[a]
Parental-assessed measures						
General Health Index[b]	4.8	4.6	0.17 (−0.22, 0.56)	4.8	4.9	−0.11 (−0.42, 0.20)
Mental Health Index[b]	5.0	5.2	−0.20 (−0.61, 0.21)	5.3	5.4	−0.10 (−0.43, 0.23)
Role limitations (%)	22	30	−8 (−35, 19)	24	21	3 (−19, 25)
Physiologic measures						
Anemia (%)	8	22	−14 (−31, 3)[c]	12	8	4 (−7, 15)
Hay fever (%)	61	44	17 (−10, 44)	71	66	5 (−16, 26)
Hearing loss (%)	35	43	−8 (−35, 19)	36	27	9 (−15, 33)
Fluid in middle ear (%)	56	57	−1 (−18, 16)	55	55	0 (−15, 15)
Functional far vision[d]	3.2	3.2	−0.05 (−0.32, 0.22)	3.1	3.2	−0.07 (−0.29, 0.15)

a. 95% confidence intervals in parentheses; approximate confidence intervals for dichotomous indicator variables.
b. 0–10 scale; higher value indicates better health status.
c. $t = 1.55$, $p = 0.12$.
d. In Snellen line values: 2 = 20/20, 3 = 20/25, 4 = 20/30.

Health Status of Poor Children

Our analyses on children classified as both poor and at risk used small samples that yielded wide confidence limits around the estimates of health effects. In order to narrow the confidence intervals, we contrasted health outcomes for all poor children with outcomes for all nonpoor children. Table 7.7 compares mean values of relevant variables at enrollment for

Table 7.7   Values of demographic, study, and health measures of children age 0–13 years at enrollment, by income level and type of plan

	Poor		Nonpoor	
	Free plan	Cost-sharing plans	Free plan	Cost-sharing plans
Number of enrollees	187	367	270	590
Mean age (yrs.)	6.9	7.1	7.7	7.3
Gender (% male)	48.1	48.5	53.0	54.4
Race (% nonwhite)	49.2	61.8	8.7	6.6
Mean family income (000s of 1991 $)	7.9	9.2	41.8	42.9
Mean education of mother (yrs.)	10.8	10.5	12.3	12.8
Enrollment screening exam (%)	57.8	55.0	67.8	62.7
Enrollment for 3 years (%)	71.7	69.5	71.1	65.1
Role limitations (%)	5.8	3.6	1.9	3.3
Mental Health Index	6.2	6.1	6.3	6.1
General Health Index	5.2	5.4	6.4	6.2
Anemia (%)	9.5	12.2	10.1	9.5
Hay fever (%)	7.1	4.4	10.9	11.7
Hearing loss (%)	5.7	10.5	7.8	4.5
Fluid in middle ear (%)	35.2	26.3	25.2	26.2
Functional far vision	2.80	2.77	2.81	2.63

these two groups.[7] Although poor children are much more likely to be nonwhite, in general the plans appear balanced within income group.

Differences between predicted health status measures at exit for poor and nonpoor children are not pronounced (Table 7.8)[8] . For example, the GHI—one of our most reliable and valid health status measures—does not vary significantly by plan, and the confidence intervals are quite small. The only (nominally) significant difference at the 5 percent level is for anemia, with low-income children on the cost-sharing plan more likely to suffer from anemia at the conclusion of the study, as was suggested in our analysis of the poor at-risk sample. Nonetheless, given the number of statistical comparisons that we have made, one must guard against overinterpreting a single finding that is "significant."

Effect of the Maximum Out-of-Pocket Payment

The observed results indicate that the Experiment insurance plans generally do not affect the health of poor children any more than they affect the health of average children, even though, as Part II showed, poor families' use of outpatient visits responds more to plan than does outpatient use by high-income families. Interpretation of these results is complicated by the fact that the required maximum out-of-pocket payment was defined as a percentage of family income (5, 10, or 15 percent) up to a maximum of $1,000. Thus, low-income families were eligible to receive free care after spending a smaller absolute amount than high-income families had to spend. Moreover, as the coinsurance rate increased, a smaller gross expenditure was needed to exceed the cap. For example, at a 50 percent coinsurance rate and a $1,000 maximum a gross expenditure of $2,000 was needed to exceed the cap, whereas at a 95 percent coinsurance rate and a $1,000 maximum a gross expenditure of only $1,053 (1,000/0.95) was needed. Table 7.9 shows how the percentage of families exceeding the cap and receiving free care for part of the year increased with the coinsurance rate. It also shows that for a given coinsurance rate, families whose incomes were low enough that their MDE was less than $1,000 per year were more likely to exceed their cap than other families. Over 40 percent of such families on the 95 percent coinsurance plans exceeded the cap, for example, in contrast to 27 percent of families whose incomes were high enough to give them an effective MDE of $1,000.

The analysis of expenditure by families who exceeded the MDE (described in Chapter 4) indicates that they used care at a higher rate after

Table 7.8 Predicted exit values of health status measures for poor and nonpoor children, by health status measure and plan

	Poor			Nonpoor		
Health status measure	Free	Cost sharing	Free minus cost sharing[a]	Free	Cost sharing	Free minus cost sharing[a]
Mental Health Index	5.6	5.9	−0.33 (−0.75, 0.09)	5.9	5.9	0.01 (−0.34, 0.36)
General Health Index	5.5	5.4	0.07 (−0.27, 0.41)	5.4	5.5	−0.09 (−0.33, 0.15)
Role limitations (%)	2.5	4.0	−1.52 (−4.58, 1.54)	2.6	2.3	0.33 (−1.61, 2.27)
Physiologic measures						
Anemia (%)	1.5	4.6	−3.12[b](−6.01,−0.23)	2.1	1.4	0.73 (−0.99, 2.45)
Hay fever (%)	14.9	8.0	6.97 (−1.02, 14.96)	20.0	15.9	4.11 (−2.98, 11.2)
Hearing loss (%)	9.0	13.1	−4.02 (−9.98, 1.94)	10.8	7.1	3.71 (−0.43, 7.85)
Fluid in middle ear (%)	24.4	24.5	−0.16 (−9.33, 9.01)	25.8	25.9	−0.16 (−7.80, 7.48)
Vision[c]	2.6	2.7	−0.05 (−0.29, 0.19)	2.6	2.6	−0.08 (−0.25, 0.09)

a. Values in parentheses are 95% confidence intervals; approximate confidence intervals for dichotomous variables.

b. Statistically significant at $p < 0.05$.

c. Functional far vision in Snellen line values: 2 = 20/20, 3 = 20/25, 4 = 20/30.

Table 7.9   Percentage of families exceeding MDE, by plan and MDE status

Coinsurance rate	Below $1,000 MDE	$1,000 MDE
25%	33.8	11.2[a]
50%	25.9	18.4
95%	41.4	27.3

a. For most sites and years the $1,000 MDE was reduced to a maximum of $750 in the 25% coinsurance plan. See Chapter 2, note 2.

than before exceeding the MDE. Indeed, use of services after exceeding the MDE is within 10 or 15 percent of the free plan use rate. Thus, the lower MDE for poor families may help explain why we did not see greater differences by insurance plan in health status among poor children.

Another puzzle is why the result found in Chapter 5—that cost sharing caused marked reductions in use among poor children with conditions where medical care is generally thought to be efficacious—did not affect observed health status. We take up this issue in Chapter 11.

Dental Health

Measures of dental health for children were similar to those for adults. We have already discussed in Chapter 6 results for persons age 12 and over. Here we discuss results for decayed, missing, and filled teeth (DMFT) for children age 6–11 and decayed, extracted and filled (def) primary teeth for those age 3–5.

Both the methods used and the results are similar to those in the analysis of adults. More generous coverage of dental services reduced the number of decayed teeth at exit and increased the number of filled teeth; the difference between the free-care plan and the 95 percent coinsurance plan was about half a tooth on average in both age groups (Tables 7.10 and 7.11). In the age 6–11 group the combined decayed, missing, and filled index was nearly constant across the plans, as it was for adults. In the age 3–5 group, as would be expected, there were very few filled (primary) teeth; 83 percent of the sample on the free plan had no filled teeth, and 90 percent of the sample on the 95 percent and Individual Deductible plans had no filled teeth. There was, however, a difference in the decayed rate, with the net result that the combined decayed, extracted, and filled index was 0.8 to 0.9 of a tooth less on the free-care plan than on the plans with cost sharing for the age 3–5 group. Hence, for the preschool group, there was an effect of plan on the *prevention* of decay in primary teeth, although this effect was not observed for the older age groups with permanent teeth.

If we aggregate the cost-sharing plans and compare results by income group (high being defined here as more than one standard deviation above the average, low as more than one standard deviation below, and the rest defined as middle), we find that the benefits of the free plan for 3-to-5-year-olds are statistically significant in the low- and middle-income groups, whereas for the high-income group the absolute difference is smaller and not statistically significant (Table 7.12). This result contrasts with the Chapter 6 finding, that for those age 6–11 the effects are concentrated in

Table 7.10   Predicted decayed, filled, and missing teeth at exit, age 6–11[a]

Plan	Decayed	Filled	Missing	DMF28[b]
Free	1.2	3.5	0.5	5.3
25%	1.5	3.3	0.4	5.1
50%	1.9[c]	2.3[c]	0.7	5.3
95%	1.6[c]	2.7[c]	0.5	5.2
Individual Deductible	1.5	2.7[c]	0.4	4.6
All cost-sharing plans	1.6[c]	2.7[c]	0.5	5.1

a. Values shown are predicted from a regression equation. See Bailit et al. (1985) for details. The total sample is 840.

b. The sum of decayed, missing, and filled teeth using 28 teeth as a base.

c. $p < 0.01$, one-tailed test. Hypothesis tests compare the free with the cost-sharing plans.

Table 7.11   Predicted mean number of decayed primary teeth and percentage of children (age 3–5) free of caries at exit, by plan[a]

Plan	Sample size	Mean no. of decayed teeth	Mean no. of DEF [b]
Free	93	0.33	.80
25% and 50%	63	0.81[c]	1.67[c]
95% and Individual Deductible	108	0.82[c]	1.57[c]

a. Values are predicted from a regression equation. See Bailit et al. (1986) for details.

b. The sum of decayed, extracted, and filled deciduous teeth.

c. $p < 0.05$; hypothesis tests compare the free with the various cost-sharing plans.

Table 7.12   Mean number of decayed primary teeth at exit, by family income and cost-sharing plans, age 3–5[a]

Plan	No. of subjects	Family income		
		High	Average	Low
Free	93	.19	.33	.47
Cost sharing	171	.44	.82[b]	1.20[b]

a. Values are predicted from regression equations. See Bailit et al. (1986) for details. High income is more than one standard deviation above average and similarly for low income.

b. $p < 0.05$; hypothesis tests compare the free with the cost-sharing plans.

the groups whose parents have average and low educations rather than low incomes—a result that resembles the findings for 12-to-17-year-olds.

Summary

We observed little difference in health outcomes for children as a function of plan. The results suggest the possibility of a beneficial effect of free care for anemia among poor children and indicate a favorable effect on caries in the deciduous teeth of preschool children. Otherwise, the substantial increase in acute and preventive services induced by free care did not manifest itself in measurable improved health outcomes for children.

Part IV

Results at the Health Maintenance Organization

The next two chapters analyze data from the health maintenance organization (HMO) included in the Experiment. The key research questions we addressed are: (1) Does the HMO have a representative mix of health risks, or is there selection? (2) Does the HMO deliver fewer services when the mix of risks is similar? (3) If the HMO does deliver fewer services, is there any effect on health outcomes or patient satisfaction? Chapter 8 addresses the first two questions. Chapter 9 addresses the third.

Chapter 8

Use of Services

Samples

As described in Chapter 2, 1,149 individuals who had used the fee-for-service sector throughout the previous year were randomly assigned to health care coverage through the Group Health Cooperative of Puget Sound (GHC) in Seattle, Washington. GHC is a well-established staff model health maintenance organization (HMO).[1] We call these 1,149 persons the experimentals. In addition, 733 individuals who were already GHC members were randomly selected as controls. Since these GHC members had previously chosen HMO coverage, their expense provides a benchmark against which to assess how, if at all, the mix of risks among those who selected HMO coverage differed from the mix of risks among those who chose the fee-for-service system.

The analysis also compares HMO experimentals with the 431 fee-for-service participants enrolled in the free-care plan in Seattle. The experience of those in the free-care plan provides a benchmark to measure the "pure" effect of HMO membership on use and health status (that is, the HMO effect with cost sharing and the nature of the population enrolled held constant). The 782 fee-for-service participants assigned to cost-sharing plans in Seattle were also used in some comparisons.

Our total sample thus includes 3,095 persons. Their average length of participation was 3.3 years, with moves from the Seattle area accounting for more than half the partial years of participation. People who moved from the Seattle area could, as a practical matter, no longer receive services at GHC. To maintain comparability with the two GHC groups, those in the fee-for-service groups who left the area were also omitted from our analyses starting at the time of their move (Table 8.1).

The choice to limit the fee-for-service comparisons to Seattle involved a tradeoff between potential bias and precision. Using the fee-for-service sample in Seattle minimizes bias because it was drawn from the same population as the GHC experimental group. Using data from all sites for comparison would require us to rely on statistical controls to eliminate any differences in sample characteristics. To the degree that those controls were imperfect, our results would be biased.[2] But limiting the sample to Seattle participants implies some loss of precision because of small sample sizes. Because the Seattle group sample sizes yielded results sufficiently precise for our purposes, we took the conservative course of using only Seattle data.

Some may regard comparing the GHC experimentals with participants on the free-care plan as biasing the comparison in favor of the HMO, because free care in the fee-for-service system is highly unusual. We believe that this comparison is the most appropriate choice because it keeps factors other than the delivery system—in particular the very important factor of cost sharing—constant. If there were cost sharing in the HMO, the utilization we observed there would presumably have been less.[3] We also compare the HMO results with results for the Seattle cost-

Table 8.1   Reasons for not completing study in the Seattle area, by plan (%)

Reason	GHC experimental	GHC control	Free fee-for-service	Pay fee-for-service
Voluntarily withdrew	4.4	11.9	0.2	9.6
Terminated because of failure to meet study obligations	2.5	20.6[a]	3.0	3.2
Died	0.3	0.3	0.2	0.8
Moved from area	22.3[b]	10.5	20.7[b]	12.9[b]
Other	0.5	0.8	0.2	0
Completed normally	70.1	55.9	75.6	73.5

a. Includes loss of eligibility for GHC (e.g., because of employment change).

b. These individuals were kept in the Experiment; the GHC experimentals, however, were switched to the free fee-for-service plan once they moved from the Seattle area. For reasons explained in the text, this group is included in the analysis only for the period they lived in Seattle. Once control families moved from the Seattle area, they were dropped.

sharing sample in this chapter. Readers may make their own comparisons with the results from all sites, on both free and cost-sharing plans, by referring back to Chapter 3.

Because differential refusal rates can lead to biased results, we investigated the pattern of refusals across plans and related issues. There is no evidence of measurable bias.

As in the case of the fee-for-service portion of the Experiment, most people who refused to participate in the HMO portion of the Experiment did so before we made assignments to experimental treatments. In all, 29 percent of those originally contacted in Seattle refused to participate in preliminary interviews. In most sites those who participated were not very different from the entire population of those who received baseline interviews. In Seattle, however, those who refused tended to be older (Morris 1985, tables 1.1–1.3). This differential refusal does not pose a problem of bias in our analysis, however, because age is entered as a covariate.

Of the persons to whom an offer to participate was made in Seattle, 5 percent refused to participate in the free fee-for-service group, 21 percent refused to participate as the GHC experimentals, 16 percent refused to participate as GHC controls, and 19 percent refused the cost-sharing plans.[4] (Those who refused were not reassigned to another plan.)

If these refusals occurred at random our results would not be biased. The raw differences in the refusal rates among plans suggest that bias may have been introduced, although refusals appear mostly random with respect to measurable characteristics (Table 8.2).[5] In any case, the differences that appear are quantitatively small, and correcting for them in order to generalize to the Seattle population leaves our qualitative findings unaffected. For reasons of parsimony, therefore, we do not report the corrected results.

A comparison across plans of those who accepted the offer supports our conclusion that there was minimal bias (Table 8.3). Across the three groups randomly assigned to plan status—the two fee-for-service groups and the GHC experimentals—neither the family variables nor the person variables differed significantly.[6] The GHC controls did differ significantly from the GHC experimentals in both individual and family characteristics ($p < .001$)—being somewhat older, better off, and better educated.[7] Because the control group was not randomly assigned to HMO status, however, these differences almost certainly reflect true differences between people who select GHC and the remainder of the Seattle population.

Table 8.2 Average characteristics at baseline of those who accepted and refused offer to enroll, by plan (standard errors in parentheses)[a]

	Free fee-for-service		Pay fee-for-service		GHC experimentals		GHC controls		F-statistic[b]
	Accept	Refuse	Accept	Refuse	Accept	Refuse	Accept	Refuse	
Family variables									
Number of families	154	10	311	77	434	111	128	43	
Family size	2.6	2.3	2.4	2.4	2.5	2.8	2.4	2.7	1.0
	(0.1)	(0.5)	(0.1)	(0.2)	(0.1)	(0.1)	(0.1)	(0.2)	
Income	29.6	40.3	28.7	29.3	28.6	37.6	33.7	33.7	7.9c
(000s of 1991 $)	(1.4)	(5.8)	(0.8)	(2.2)	(0.8)	(1.7)	(1.1)	(3.0)	
Person variables									
Number of persons	431	23	782	191	1149	310	733	145	
Age in years	25.2	34.5	25.8	26.8	24.4	28.7	25.6	26.7	5.0c
	(1.1)	(4.7)	(0.7)	(1.6)	(0.6)	(1.3)	(0.8)	(2.0)	
Female (%)	51.1	47.8	50.4	57.8	51.0	50.0	52.8	52.6	0.7
	(2.6)	(10.6)	(1.9)	(3.6)	(1.6)	(2.9)	(2.1)	(4.7)	
Black (%)	1.7	0.0	2.9	1.7	1.6	3.3	4.0	5.9	1.0
	(1.1)	(0.0)	(0.8)	(1.2)	(0.7)	(1.3)	(1.2)	(4.8)	
Education of persons 21 and over	13.0	13.2	13.1	12.3	13.1	12.8	13.9	14.3	1.8
	(0.2)	(0.7)	(0.1)	(0.3)	(0.1)	(0.2)	(0.2)	(0.4)	
Self-rated health status[d]	1.5	1.7	1.5	1.5	1.5	1.5	1.4	1.5	0.8
	(0.0)	(0.2)	(0.0)	(0.1)	(0.0)	(0.1)	(0.0)	(0.14)	
Amount of pain due to health[e]	3.3	3.1	3.3	3.4	3.3	3.3	3.2	3.2	1.5
	(0.0)	(0.3)	(0.0)	(0.1)	(0.0)	(0.1)	(0.0)	(0.1)	

Measure									F
Amount of worry due to health[d]	3.2 (0.1)	3.5 (0.2)	3.3 (0.0)	3.2 (0.1)	3.4 (0.1)	3.2 (0.0)	3.2 (0.0)	3.1 (0.1)	1.7
Physician visits in previous year	3.9 (0.4)	2.5 (0.4)	3.5 (0.2)	4.1 (0.5)	4.0 (0.2)	3.4 (0.3)	4.5 (0.3)	5.4 (0.9)	1.7
% hospitalized in previous year	10.6 (1.6)	4.3 (10.0)	9.8 (1.4)	14.3 (3.1)	10.4 (1.1)	8.4 (1.7)	9.3 (1.3)	11.4 (3.7)	1.1
Dental visits in previous year	2.1 (0.2)	2.4 (0.4)	2.0 (0.2)	1.7 (0.2)	1.8 (0.1)	2.0 (0.2)	2.2 (0.2)	1.9 (0.3)	0.9
% on AFDC program	12.0 (2.0)	0.0 (0.0)	6.1 (0.2)	11.0 (0.2)	5.2 (0.1)	3.9 (0.2)	2.2 (0.2)	1.8 (0.3)	0.7
% with group insurance	77.6 (3.4)	78.3 (13.3)	77.8 (2.4)	80.8 (4.5)	78.7 (2.1)	88.0 (2.8)	73.4 (2.9)	60.5 (7.1)	3.8[c]
% with nongroup insurance	10.4 (2.7)	17.4 (10.0)	14.0 (2.0)	9.3 (4.0)	12.0 (1.6)	10.3 (2.7)	37.7 (3.1)	51.8 (7.5)	0.4
% with public insurance	9.6 (1.8)	0.0 (0.0)	5.1 (1.1)	15.5 (3.7)	4.7 (1.0)	3.9 (1.5)	2.4 (0.8)	0.9 (0.4)	3.0[c]

a. The values are based on measures collected at the baseline interview (three to nine months before enrollment) in order to maintain comparability between the Accept and Refuse groups. No imputations for missing data have been made. For all but the Group Health control group, about 5% of the cases had missing data; for the control group the value is 20%. There are minor discrepancies (approximately 1%) between the number accepting enrollment shown here and the number on the Public Use Files because of subsequent data cleaning. We present here the analysis using the original data. Income is 1974 income inflated to 1991 using the all-items Consumer Price Index.

b. F-statistics are for Accept vs. Refuse (4 degrees of freedom in the numerator). An F of 2.4 is significant at the 5% level.

c. Significant at $p < 0.05$.

d. Response to how would you rate your health? 1 = excellent; 2 = good; 3 = fair; 4 = poor.

e. Responses to how much pain (worry) does your health cause you? 1 = lots; 2 = some; 3 = a little; 4 = none.

Table 8.3 Comparison of means among study populations at enrollment (standard errors in parentheses)[a]

	Free fee-for-service		GHC experimentals		GHC controls		Pay fee-for-service	
Family variables								
AFDC (%)	6.0	(1.9)	6.1	(1.2)	3.6	(1.2)	4.7	(1.3)
Black (%)	1.9	(1.1)	2.3	(0.7)	4.0	(1.1)	3.2	(1.0)
Family size	2.7	(0.13)	2.6	(0.07)	2.4	(0.08)	2.5	(0.08)
Income (000s of 1991 $)	34.6	(1.6)	30.6	(0.8)	37.9	(1.3)	31.3	(1.0)
Person variables								
Age (years)	25.2	(0.79)	24.6	(0.45)	26.6	(0.60)	26.1	(0.59)
Female (%)	49.7	(2.4)	51.0	(1.5)	52.7	(1.8)	51.0	(1.8)
Number of chronic complaints[b]	6.5	(0.35)	6.9	(0.22)	7.5	(0.26)	7.0	(0.26)
General Health Index[c]	72.9	(0.77)	73.5	(0.47)	72.8	(0.57)	74.5	(0.55)
Mental Health Index[d]	75.8	(0.68)	75.8	(0.41)	75.2	(0.51)	75.9	(0.52)
% with physical or role limitation	16.8	(1.8)	15.9	(1.1)	14.6	(1.3)	14.1	(1.24)
M.D. visits[e]	3.8	(0.28)	4.0	(0.17)	4.5	(0.21)	3.6	(0.2)
Hospitalized in previous year (%)[e]	10.3	(1.48)	10.5	(0.92)	9.4	(1.09)	10.0	(1.08)
Education (years)[f]	12.7	(0.12)	12.8	(0.07)	13.8	(0.09)	12.8	(0.08)
Number enrolled	431		1,149		733		782	

a. Means and standard errors are calculated with the family as the unit of observation for family variables and with the person as the unit of observation for person variables. The values differ from those in Table 8.2 because imputations for missing data have been made using data collected at enrollment. (Such imputations could not be made for the Refuse group in Table 8.2.) The income measure used is based on 1976 income; we believe the methods used to ascertain the 1976 income resulted in greater accuracy than the 1974 income measure in Table 8.2, but 1976 income data cannot be used in Table 8.2 because they are not available for the Refuse group.

b. Applies to individuals 14+ at enrollment. See Chapter 6 for details.

c. A higher value reflects better health. See Chapter 6 for details.

d. Applies to individuals 5+ at enrollment. See Chapter 6 for details.

e. Year before the beginning of the Experiment. We have no definitive explanation for the seemingly high GHC control hospitalization rate.

f. Own education if age 18 or older, otherwise education of female head of household (if present, otherwise male) head of household.

Methods of Analysis

We examine visit rates, hospital use, and expenditure. For all but expenditure we present simple means (analysis of variance) for each experimental treatment because adjusting for participant characteristics does not materially change our results. In the case of expenditure, however, we present results from a multiple-regression model using plan, age, and gender as covariates because such controls substantially increase the precision of the estimates.[8] (More details are available in Manning et al. 1985.)

In the analysis of visit and admission rates, we weight observations to correct for the length of an individual's participation in the study in the Seattle area. This method would be biased if the participants who left the study early did not come from the same distribution as the stayers. We ran a number of statistical tests and are persuaded that they did indeed come from the same or nearly the same population.[9]

When we calculate the percentage of participants using one or more services in a year and impute expenditure, we use only participants who completed a full year in the Seattle area plus those who died during a year. In the case of the percentage using any service, including data on people who completed only part of a year makes interpretation of the results difficult. In the case of expenditure, the statistical methods we used in this analysis did not permit including participants who did not complete a full year.[10] The expenditure values we show come from averaging, within each group, the predicted values from regression equations using the actual age and gender of each individual in that group.

Measurement of Use

Data on HMO in-plan use (number and type of visits, procedure use, and number and type of admissions) came from GHC records (Goldberg 1983). Data on out-of-plan use by the GHC groups, as well as all data on use by the fee-for-service participants, came from claim forms filed with the Experiment.

Our results omit drugs and supplies. Because of the expense involved, we did not code drugs prescribed at GHC. Prescription drugs were only 8 percent of expense in the fee-for-service system (see Tables 3.2 and 5.13), and it therefore seems unlikely that accounting for drugs and supplies could materially alter our conclusions. We consider the use of mental health services separately.

Imputing Expenditures

Comparing the number of visits and the number of admissions among the various groups does not allow us to detect any differential intensity of service per visit or per admission between GHC and fee-for-service participants. Because actual expenditures are not available at GHC, in order to measure HMO intensity we constructed a measure for imputing expenditure. Our imputation method differed for hospital and physician services. For admissions at the GHC hospitals, we used the dollar figure that GHC would have charged had it billed the case to a payer outside GHC. (GHC does bill for some admissions; two common instances are emergency admissions of a nonenrollee at a GHC hospital and workers' compensation cases.) For admissions at fee-for-service hospitals, we used the hospital's actual billed charges.

In the case of physician services, we compared the number of California Relative Value Studies (CRVS) units that GHC and fee-for-service physicians delivered (California Medical Association 1975). To arrive at an imputed expenditure figure, we valued units in both systems at the same dollar figure.

We coded physician procedures, whether inpatient or outpatient, as well as services of other providers such as speech therapists, from the GHC medical record and the fee-for-service claim form. Each procedure was associated with a number of CRVS units. Because the units are not commensurate across different types of services (for example, medical, surgical), one cannot simply tally the units. Hence, we established a common denominator in order to aggregate different types of CRVS units. GHC has established charges to other payers for each type of CRVS unit; this charge per unit was applied to each unit delivered by both GHC and fee-for-service providers, and an estimate of total physician charges was calculated. The estimated total charges for the fee-for-service system, when calculated in this fashion, did not equal the actual total; we therefore multiplied both the estimated GHC and fee-for-service total charges by the same proportionality factor, which was set so as to equate the estimated and actual fee-for-service charges.

One problem we faced in applying this method was that not all procedures could be associated with CRVS units. In particular, some procedures were so new that their relative value had not yet been established, and some were assigned no fixed unit value. For all such procedures a physician member of the research team (George A. Goldberg) assigned a number of units. In so doing he was blind to whether the procedure was from GHC or fee for service. Once a value was determined, it was used for all instances of the procedure, whether from GHC or fee for service. The number of units so assigned amounted to 10 percent of the total.

We tested our procedure for imputing physician charges by calculating the degree of correlation between actual charges and imputed charges for each person receiving fee-for-service care. To do so, we computed a correlation coefficient between the logarithm of the actual charges and the logarithm of the imputed charges for each person with some use for each year of the study. We found that the CRVS structure we employed quite accurately mirrored the actual structure of fee-for-service charges. For outpatient care, the lowest of the five annual correlation coefficients was 0.97; for inpatient care, the lowest correlation coefficient was 0.93.

In addition to comparing the rates at which the participants saw physicians, we also compared the rates of preventive care visits in the various plans. Preventive care includes any well-care service other than vision, hearing, and prenatal care. Well-care services were defined by the physician's diagnosis, by the use of certain procedures (for example, immunizations), or by a well-care treatment history code in conjunction with the patient's indicating that the reason for visit was well care. We included the patient's reason for visit as a category to counteract the possibility that some fee-for-service physicians might have failed to label some visits as preventive (because many standard health insurance plans do not reimburse for preventive services). Any such failure in labeling would bias a comparison of the amounts of preventive care the various groups received.

Use of Medical Services

Not only did the GHC experimental and control groups differ in imputed expenditure on medical services; both also differed markedly from the free fee-for-service group (Table 8.4).[11] Imputed expenditures were 28 percent less for the GHC experimental group ($p < 0.01$) and 23 percent less for the GHC control group ($p < 0.05$) than for the free fee-for-service group.

The magnitude of the imputed expenditure reduction at GHC is comparable to that achieved by 95 percent coinsurance in the fee-for-service system, although the means by which expenditure is reduced are considerably different. At GHC, the percentage of enrollees seeking care was comparable to or even exceeded the percentage in the free fee-for-service plan: GHC reduced expenditure more than free fee-for-service because fewer enrollees were admitted to the hospital. With 95 percent coinsurance, the percentage seeking care as well as the percentage admitted to the hospital was notably lower than on the free fee-for-service plan (Chapter 3). The expenditure rate on the individual deductible plan was lower than on the 95 percent plan, but that result appears to be an anomaly of the Seattle sample (see Table 3.2 for results from all sites).

The differences between GHC and the free fee-for-service plans come even more sharply into focus when we examine admissions, hospital days, and visit rates (Table 8.5). There were 40 percent fewer admissions ($p <$ 0.01) and hospital days in the two GHC groups than in the free fee-for-service plan, although face-to-face visits occurred at approximately similar rates in all three plans.[12] By contrast, participants in all the cost-sharing plans had both lower admission rates and lower visit rates than those in the free-care plan.

Although the overall face-to-face visit rates were similar between the two GHC groups and the group in the free-care plan, the number of pre-

Table 8.4   Comparison of likelihood of using any service, likelihood of hospitalization, and imputed annual expenditure (standard errors in parentheses)[a]

Plan	% using inpatient or outpatient service in year	% with one or more hospitalizations in year	Imputed annual expenditure per participant (1991 $)[b]
GHC experimental	86.8 (1.0)	7.1 (0.50)	600 (34)
GHC control	91.0 (0.8)	6.4 (0.55)	641 (60)
Fee-for-service			
Free	85.3 (1.6)	11.1 (1.17)	833 (90)
25%	76.1 (2.7)	8.8 (1.37)	848(141)
95%	68.4 (3.4)	8.5 (1.18)	628 (98)
Individual Deductible	73.9 (2.4)	7.9 (0.96)	565 (70)

a. The sample consists of all participants present at enrollment while they remained in the Seattle area. Except for decedents, observations on partial years of participation are deleted.

b. Values include both in-plan and out-of-plan use by GHC participants. The method of imputing expenditure is described in the text. The t-statistics to test the difference in imputed expenditure between the GHC experimental and the five groups below it in the table are 0.87, 3.22, 2.22, 0.30, and −0.56, respectively. Because age and gender are included as covariates, these t-statistics are larger than those that would be calculated from the standard errors shown in the table.

Table 8.5   Admission and face-to-face visits, annual rates
(standard errors in parentheses)[a]

Plan	Admission rate/ 100 persons[b]	Hospital days/ 100 persons	Face-to-face visits[c]	Preventive visits[d]
GHC	8.4	49	4.3	0.55
experimental	(0.67)	(9.6)	(0.14)	(0.02)
GHC control	8.3	38	4.7	0.60
	(1.01)	(9.0)	(0.17)	(0.02)
Fee-for-service				
Free	13.8	83	4.2	0.41
	(1.51)	(26)	(0.25)	(0.03)
25%	10.0	87	3.5	0.32
	(1.43)	(28)	(0.35)	(0.03)
95%	10.5	46	2.9	0.29
	(1.68)	(9.9)	(0.34)	(0.04)
Individual	8.8	28	3.3	0.27
Deductible	(1.20)	(5.1)	(0.33)	(0.03)

a. The sample includes all participants present at enrollment while they remained in the Seattle area. For GHC controls and experimentals, the data include both in-plan and out-of-plan use.

b. A count of all continuous periods of inpatient treatment.

c. Includes all visits with face-to-face contact with health providers for which a separate charge would have been made in fee-for-service. Excludes radiology, pathology, and pre-and postnatal, pre-and postoperative, speech therapy, psychotherapy, dental, chiropractic, podiatry, Christian Science healer, and telephone visits.

d. Includes well-child care, immunizations, screening examinations, routine physical and gynecological examinations, and visits with Pap smears (other than for cancer). Excludes prenatal, vision, and hearing visits. In the case of GHC, includes in-plan and out-of-plan visits.

ventive visits was significantly higher in the two GHC groups than in the free fee-for-service group (Table 8.5). Cost sharing further reduces preventive visits below the values in the free fee-for-service plan.

Non-HMO use by the two GHC groups was relatively small (Table 8.6). Experimentals were more likely than controls to seek non-HMO care. This result is not surprising given that experimentals were formerly fee-for-service clients who were assigned to HMO status, whereas controls chose to join an HMO. About 2 percent of the experimental group each year sought care exclusively from ancillary providers such as chiropractors, Christian Science practitioners, and podiatrists. Half the out-of-plan inpatient admissions were related to accidents or to psychiatric diagnoses.

Our Findings Compared with Those in the Literature

The comparison of medical care use among the HMO controls with use among the fee-for-service groups resembles analogous comparisons in the literature and thus lends support to the validity of the HMO experimental results.

Harold Luft's reviews of several noncontrolled studies (Luft 1978, 1981, 1982) found that traditional prepaid group practices hospitalized 15–40 percent less than fee-for-service practices. In the analogous comparisons from our study, HMO controls were 40 percent less likely to go into the hospital than those in the free fee-for-service group and 20 to 30 percent less likely to be admitted than those in the cost-sharing groups (see Table 3.3).

Table 8.6   Annual use outside GHC (standard errors in parentheses)[a]

Type of use	GHC experimentals	GHC controls
Hospital admissions per 100[b]	0.74 (0.26)	0.21 (0.087)
Hospital days per 100 persons	15[c] (9)	1.4 (0.8)
Ambulatory face-to-face visits per person[b,d]	0.14 (0.02)	0.076 (0.02)
Chiropractor, podiatrist, Christian Science practitioner visits per person[e]	0.72 (0.12)	0.12 (0.06)
Speech therapist visits per person	0.0002 (0.0002)	0.007 (0.006)
Expenditures per person (1991 $)[e]	118 (25)	29 (10)

a. The sample includes all participants present at enrollment, while they remained in the Seattle area.

b. Comparison significant at $p < 0.05$.

c. One case accounts for two-thirds of this mean. Inpatient psychiatric cases account for one-sixth of this mean.

d. A face-to-face visit is one for which a separate charge would have been made in fee-for-service. Excludes radiology, pathology, pregnancy, speech therapy, psychotherapy, chiropractic, podiatric, and Christian Science practitioner visits.

e. Comparison significant at $p < 0.01$.

It is plausible that the difference in admission rates between the HMO control group and the free fee-for-service group is at the high end of those observed in the literature. The free fee-for-service plan had better ambulatory benefits than virtually all fee-for-service plans studied in the literature, and more extensive coverage of ambulatory services appears to lead to more hospitalization among those using fee-for-service physicians (see Table 3.3). In the Experiment cost-sharing plans, the coverage of ambulatory services was at most equal to and probably less than coverage in plans studied in the literature, and coverage of hospital services was also probably less. To the degree that this lesser ambulatory coverage depressed hospitalization rates, the difference between the admission rates in the HMO control group and in the cost-sharing plans should be near the low end of Luft's range.

Outpatient visit rates among GHC controls were higher (though not significantly higher) than in the free fee-for-service group and significantly higher than in the cost-sharing group ($p < 0.01$ for Seattle data). Luft found roughly similar results in a variety of studies (Luft 1981).

Use of Mental Health Services

We define a mental health visit to be any encounter between a patient and a provider with a mental health procedure or diagnosis (see Chapter 3). HMO expenditures on mental health services were imputed as for medical services.[13]

HMO outpatient mental health use differs from the fee-for-service pattern. In a single year the proportion of people using mental health specialists was about the same in the two delivery systems (shown as "% any formal use" in Table 8.7), but the fee-for-service system provided much more intensive therapy per user, nearly three times as much in imputed expenditure in the free-care plan as in the HMO environment (Table 8.7 for visits and Table 8.8). The cost-sharing plans also showed higher imputed expenditure per user, although the differences were not statistically significant at conventional levels.

The difference in annual expenditures on mental health is thus made up primarily of differences in the number of visits per user to mental health specialists. The number of visits was more than three times as large for those using the fee-for-service system (16.9 versus 4.7).[14] Moreover, the HMO made greater use of group therapy than did the fee-for-service

Table 8.7 Annual use of outpatient mental health services per enrollee (standard errors in parentheses)[a]

Use	GHC experimental Mean	GHC control Mean	t	Free Mean	t	Family pay Mean	t	Individual Deductible Mean	t
% any use	13.9 (0.94)	13.2 (1.06)	−0.46	9.2 (1.48)	−2.70	5.5 (0.97)	−6.24	7.9 (1.58)	−3.25
% any formal use	6.5 (0.70)	6.9 (0.87)	+0.40	6.3 (1.42)	−0.13	3.3 (0.80)	−3.05	5.6 (1.36)	−0.57
% any informal use	9.7 (0.68)	8.8 (0.75)	−0.89	4.2 (0.63)	−5.95	3.0 (0.51)	−7.96	3.2 (0.86)	−5.96
Average no. of formal visits	0.31 (0.065)	0.33 (0.076)	+0.20	1.1 (0.3)	+2.28	0.5 (0.16)	+1.27	1.0 (0.35)	+1.91
Average no. of informal visits	0.23 (0.037)	0.18 (0.024)	−1.18	0.18 (0.061)	−0.66	0.05 (0.013)	−4.54	0.08 (0.032)	−3.14

Note: Free = free fee-for-service. Family pay = 25%, 50%, and 95% coinsurance plans. Formal use = formally trained mental health specialists (psychiatrists, psychologists, social workers). Informal use = general medical providers.

a. ts are for contrast with the GHC experimental group. Standard errors and t-statistics are corrected for intrafamily and intertemporal correlation. Visits identified by mental health diagnoses or procedures.

system; 45 percent of the HMO participants who used the services of a mental health specialist had some family or group psychotherapy, in contrast to only 20 percent of fee-for-service participants. Over a three-year period, those who used mental health services at GHC were less likely to receive a psychotropic drug (28 versus 40 percent, $t = 3.09$), a difference that was concentrated in the category of antipsychotics (3 percent versus 10 percent).

Although in a year the proportion of the population using mental health specialists was about the same in the two systems, over a three-year period the proportion of people seeing a mental health specialist in the HMO was about 50 percent greater than in the free fee-for-service plan (14.4 percent for the experimentals, 15.4 percent for the controls, 10.3 percent for the free-care plan).

The proportion of HMO enrollees who saw a general medical provider for a mental health service was greater than the proportion of fee-for-service enrollees who did so. Indeed, visits to non–mental health specialists, primarily general or family practitioners, accounted for 36 percent of expenditure on mental health services at the HMO, whereas the comparable figure for the fee-for-service plans in Seattle was only 9 percent. Moreover, the HMO made much greater use of mental health personnel other than psychiatrists. Among users of formally trained mental health providers, in the fee-for-ser-

Table 8.8. Imputed annual expenditures for outpatient mental health services (standard errors in parentheses)[a]

	Expenditures per person ($)	
Plan	Mean	t vs. GHC experimental
Group Health Cooperative plans		
Experimentals	34 (5.30)	—
Controls	32 (4.80)	−0.28
Fee-for-service plans		
Free	95 (26.80)	+2.23
Family pay[b]	48 (13.50)	+0.96
Individual Deductible	92 (34.30)	+1.67

a. Standard errors and t-statistics corrected for intrafamily and intertemporal correlation. Use is identified by mental health procedure or diagnosis.

b. Family pay = 25%, 50%, and 95% coinsurance plans.

vice system 64 percent were to psychiatrists, compared with 35 percent at the HMO. The HMO made greater use of psychologists (25 percent of users at GHC versus 19 percent in fee-for-service) and markedly greater use of psychiatric social workers (57 percent versus 18 percent). (Some patients saw more than one type of provider.)

Thus, the HMO was providing a less intensive intervention to a greater number of people than was the fee-for-service system. Mental health use among the experimentals was similar to that among the controls, implying little or no favorable selection with respect to mental health at the HMO.[15] The absence of selection is also borne out by the Mental Health Index of the two groups at enrollment; the value for the controls was 75.2, less than the value for the experimentals and fee-for-service groups (75.8, about a one standard error difference; see Table 8.3).

Use of inpatient mental health services was too uncommon to permit comparisons among groups.

The Key Research Questions

Selection

Our results showing minor and generally insignificant differences between the GHC experimental and control groups imply that selection effects were minimal at this HMO. In particular, imputed expenditures in the experimental group were 6 percent less than in the control group. Given that the standard errors for these expenditure figures are 5–10 percent of the mean, it is unlikely that there is a large difference in expected health services use between these two groups.

Reasons for the Lower HMO Hospitalization Rate

GHC delivered fewer services to a similar group of enrollees than did the fee-for-service system, with the reduction concentrated in hospital services. Because services delivered in a hospital accounted for 40 percent of all expenditure on personal health services in the United States in 1978, the markedly lower HMO rate invites closer scrutiny. Two not mutually exclusive explanations of these reductions are (1) greater use of preventive care at the HMO or (2) a treatment style that favors outpatient use over hospitalization. We believe that the data favor the latter explanation.

The HMO did deliver more preventive care than the fee-for-service system, but this did not reduce the number of doctor visits, as might have been expected if HMO enrollees were truly healthier. Further, there was more preventive care in the free fee-for-service plan than in the cost-sharing plans, yet the free plan had a higher hospitalization rate than the cost-sharing plans (Chapter 3). Moreover, two-thirds of the preventive visits were for well-child care and gynecologic examinations. Because gynecologic and pediatric admissions account for a minority of hospitalizations, it seems unlikely that preventive care could account for much of the large difference in hospitalization rates. Indeed, despite the concentration of preventive care among children, the percentage reduction in admission rates among children at the HMO was roughly similar to (and insignificantly different from) the percentage reduction among adults (Table 8.9).

The immediate reduction in hospital use among the experimentals is more consistent with a "style-of-care" explanation because one would expect the effects of preventive care to be delayed. The similarity of outpatient visit rates among the two HMO groups and the free fee-for-service group could thus reflect a treatment style involving more intensive outpatient treatment of those whom fee-for-service physicians would hospitalize, combined with less intensive treatment of those who would not be admitted in any event. As we shall see in the next chapter, the results on outcomes also favor a style-of-care explanation.

Table 8.9 Percentage of sample with one or more admissions per year, children and adults (standard errors in parentheses)[a]

Plan	Children (under 18)	Adults (18 or over)
GHC experimental	3.5 (0.56)	9.2 (0.68)
GHC control	3.6 (0.70)	7.8 (0.73)
Fee-for-service		
Free	6.2 (1.13)	13.7 (1.71)
25% plan	5.8 (1.92)	10.6 (1.62)
95% plan	3.2 (1.08)	11.6 (1.62)
Individual Deductible	6.0 (1.64)	8.7 (1.26)

a. The sample consists of all participants present at enrollment while they remained in the Seattle area. Except for decedents, observations on partial years of participation are deleted. A chi-squared value for comparability of response between children and adults is 3.83 with 5 d.f., $p > 0.50$.

Savings Achieved through Increasing HMO Enrollment

The difference in imputed expenditure between the HMO experimental plan and the free fee-for-service plan is striking—28 percent (Table 8.4). Although a different set of prices to impute expenditure could yield a different number, it seems unlikely that with any reasonable set of prices the true difference could be much less than 25 percent. Ambulatory visit rates were similar for the two groups, but both admissions and total hospital days at the HMO were 40 percent below the rate on the free fee-for-service plan.

As a rough check on the accuracy of the 28 percent figure, we can go through the following exercise of how many dollars such a reduction in use might save. Suppose the 40 percent reduction in admissions was random; that is, it happened irrespective of the severity of the case or the length of the hospital stay. In that case inpatient expenditure, which accounted for somewhat over half of total expenditure in the Experiment (see Chapter 3), would fall by 40 percent. If ambulatory expenditure in the two systems were similar, total expenditure would fall by about one-fourth, as our imputed figures indicate.

Now suppose the 40 percent reduction in admissions was not random, but rather was made up disproportionately of short-stay admissions. Such a pattern would imply that the HMO also reduced the length of stay among those it did admit.[16] A combination of reduced admissions and reduced length of stay that together yielded a 40 percent reduction in hospital days could well have caused a true reduction in expenditure on the order of one-fourth.

Our estimates of HMO savings do not account for any efficiencies that the HMO may have enjoyed in the delivery of physician services—such as greater substitution of paramedical personnel. To estimate the magnitude of such efficiencies, if any, would require a study of costs within each system, which we did not attempt. Thus, the true difference in resource use may have been even greater than we estimated.

Skeptics might object that comparing HMO use with free fee-for-service use is not realistic, since most insured individuals do face some cost sharing. How much of the HMO reduction in utilization would be preserved if we compare the HMO experience with national means? The annual likelihood of one or more hospitalizations among Americans under 65 in 1977 was 9.5 percent. This result is identical with the value for the Individual Deductible plan (Table 3.3) and well above the HMO rates of

7.1 and 6.4 percent for the experimentals and controls, respectively. Thus, as of 1977 most of the reduction would have been preserved.

By 1987, however, the national rate for the under 65 had fallen to 7.3 percent, and 5.8 percent if deliveries are excluded (National Center for Health Statistics 1988).[17] How did GHC fare over this period? The only GHC figures we have are admission rates for those 62 and under (also excluding newborns and deliveries). These are by definition higher than the likelihood of one or more admissions because someone with multiple admissions is counted multiple times. GHC admission rates remained relatively constant from 1980 to 1987 at 45 to 48 per 1,000, dropping thereafter (Table 8.10). By comparison, admission rates among people under 65 nationwide (excluding newborns and deliveries) fell from 121.1 per 1,000 in 1980 to 80.6 per 1,000 in 1988 (Table 11.2). Thus, treatment styles in the nation appear to be converging toward GHC's style, although national admission rates were still about twice as high as GHC's rate in 1988.

Summary

During the Experiment, a group of individuals assigned to a well-established staff model HMO were admitted to a hospital 40 percent less frequently than

Table 8.10   Admission rates per 1,000 at Group Health Cooperative, enrollees age 62 and under[a]

Year	Rate excluding short stays	Rate including short stays
1980	46	58
1981	46	58
1982	47	59
1983	48	60
1984	46	60
1985	45	62
1986	47	66
1987	45	64
1988	42	63
1989	36	57
1990	39	60

Source: Personal communication from Edward H. Wagner.
Note: Short stay is same-day discharge and is primarily day surgery.
a. Rates exclude newborns and deliveries and are for GHC's central region, primarily Seattle. Sample size is 80,000–100,000.

a comparable group of individuals in the fee-for-service system. Neither group faced any cost sharing. A similar reduction in use observed among a group who had chosen to enroll at the HMO implies that there is little selection bias in the HMO/fee-for-service comparisons. Ambulatory use was similar for the HMO and fee-for-service groups. We estimate the dollar savings from the reduced hospital use to be about 25 percent, similar to the savings from cost sharing in the fee-for-service system. Subsequent national trends in use suggest that the United States has moved toward the less hospital-intensive style of care observed in the Experiment's HMO, but hospital admission rates nationwide remain almost twice as high as those at the HMO.

Chapter 9

Health and Satisfaction Outcomes

Did the greatly reduced hospitalization rate among the HMO experimental group and other differences in service delivery such as greater use of allied health personnel and less intense mental health services affect health outcomes? That question is the main subject of this chapter, which also compares satisfaction with care among the fee-for-service group, the HMO experimentals, and the HMO controls.

Methods

The measures of health and satisfaction used to evaluate HMO health outcomes are similar to those used to evaluate outcomes among the various fee-for-service plans (Chapters 6 and 7), and the groups whose outcomes we discuss in this chapter are the same as those described in the previous chapter. The major comparison is between the HMO experimental participants and the free plan participants in Seattle. This choice is deliberate, in order to keep the populations sampled and the cost-sharing conditions comparable. As in the previous chapter, we have included results from the cost-sharing group in Seattle for the sake of completeness, but for comparisons within the set of fee-for-service plans it is more appropriate to use data from all sites rather than just those from Seattle (see Chapters 6 and 7).[1]

Adult Health Outcomes

Physiologic Outcomes

In numerous comparisons of physiologic outcomes for the average person at the HMO and in the free fee-for-service plan, no strong evidence was found favoring one system over the other. Table 9.1 lists nominal significance

Table 9.1 Predicted exit values for an average person, by measure and system of care

Health status measure	HMO	Fee-for-service Free	Fee-for-service Cost sharing	HMO minus free[a]	Direction of effect[b]	HMO minus cost sharing[a]	Direction of effect[b]	Sample size
Respiratory system								
FEV_1 (% of predicted)[c]	100.3	99.6	100.1	0.6±2.5	H	0.2±2.1	H	1,284
Shortness of breath[d]	0.18	0.15	0.15	0.04±0.06	F	0.03±0.05	C	1,450
Chronic phlegm production (% of sample)	9.6	11.3	8.2	-1.7±4	H	1.4±3	C	1,457
Severity of hay fever[e]	0.23	0.20	0.19	0.03±0.12	F	0.05±0.09	C	1,466
Circulatory system								
Modified Rose Scale[f]	0.03	0.03	0.04	-0.003±0.06	H	-0.01±0.07	H	544
ECG abnormalities (% of sample)[f]	12.0	9.3	11.6	2.8±7	F	0.4±6	C	506
Severity of varicose veins[g]	2.25	2.00	2.14	0.25±0.2	F++	0.11±0.2	C	629
Diastolic blood pressure (mm Hg)	77.0	77.1	77.7	-0.1±1.5	H	-0.7±1.2	H	1,439
Cholesterol (mg/dl)	202	206	204	-4.1±6	H+	-1.9±4	H	1,405
Musculoskeletal system								
Chronic joint symptoms (% of sample)[h]	31.4	35.5	33.2	-4.1±10	H	-1.9±7	H	546
Walking speed[h]	9.7	9.8	9.7	-0.15±0.5	H	-0.01±0.5	H	193
Grip strength (mm Hg)[c,h]	229.7	231.0	237.4	-1.2±11	F	-7.7±10	C+	190
Gastrointestinal system								
Active ulcer (% of sample)	3.1	2.4	3.3	0.8±2	F	-0.2±2	H	1,464
Dyspepsia (% of sample)	8.7	8.8	7.8	-0.1±4	H	0.9±3	C	1,465

Vision and hearing							
Functional far vision (Snellen lines)	2.4	2.3	2.5	0.07±0.10	F+	−0.087±0.09	H+	1,433
Functional near vision (Snellen lines)[f]	2.3	2.2	2.3	0.08±0.12	F+	−0.05±0.13	H	534
AHTL right ear (dB)	10.4	10.8	10.8	−0.5±0.9	H	−0.4±0.9	H	1,297
AHTL left ear (dB)	10.3	10.2	10.0	0.1±0.9	F	0.3±0.9	C	1,297
Endocrine conditions							
Glucose (mg/dl)	89.7	89.2	89.6	0.5±2.6	F	0.1±2.0	C	1,409
Abnormal thyroid level (% of sample)	2.6	3.5	2.5	−1.0±2.3	H	0.1±1.7	C	1,401
Other chronic conditions							
Hemoglobin (g/100 ml)[c]	14.62	14.61	14.58	0.02±0.14	H	0.04±0.11	H	1,407
Positive urine culture (% of sample)[g]	2.9	3.6	0.6	−0.8±3.5	H	2.2±2.0	C++	714
Severity of acne[i]	0.28	0.23	0.19	0.05±0.12	F	0.095±0.098	C+	1,012

Note: HMO = health maintenance organization; FEV_1 = forced expiratory volume in 1 second; ECG = electrocardiogram; AHTL = average hearing threshold level.

a. Number following predicted difference represents width of the 95% confidence interval, that is, 1.96 (standard error).

b. H++, H+, and H represent differences that favor the health maintenance organization at $p < 0.05$, $0.05 \leq p \leq 0.20$, and $0.20 < p$, respectively; F++, F+, and F represent differences that favor the free plan at $p < 0.05$, $0.05 \leq p \leq 0.20$, and $0.20 < p$ respectively; C++, C+ and C represent differences that favor the cost-sharing plan at $p < 0.05$, $0.05 \leq p \leq 0.20$, and $0.20 < p$ respectively.

c. For this condition, a higher value denotes better health.

d. Scale value ranging from 0 (no shortness of breath) to 4 (severe shortness of breath).

e. Self-reported amount of time per year bothered by hay fever, on log scale from zero (none) to 6.4 (6 months or more): See Chapter 6.

f. Limited to persons 35 or older.

g. Limited to women. Severity scale for vaicose veins: 1 = absent, 2 = spider angiomata, 3 = minimal, 4 = moderate, 5 = severe.

h. Limited to persons 35 or older who reported joint discomfort. Seconds to walk 50 feet for walking speed; mm/Hg using dynamometer for grip strength.

i. Limited to persons under age 45.   Scale from 0 = no acne, 1 = one comedo or papule, to 5 = acne conglobata.

values, but because of the large number of comparisons, the actual likelihood that any single "significant" difference will occur in the absence of any true difference is considerably higher than the nominal value of 5 percent. For example, of the 46 comparisons shown in Table 9.1, two would be expected to be "significant" at the 5 percent level by chance even with no true difference. Nine would be expected to be "significant" at the 20 percent level by chance. In fact, 2 are significant at the 5 percent level, both favoring fee-for-service (varicose veins with free care and a positive urine culture with cost sharing). Eight are significant at the 20 percent level, 2 of which favor the HMO. Thus, the results could easily have arisen with no true differences in outcomes between the HMO and the fee-for-service system.

If we limit the comparisons to groups at elevated risk, defined as the least healthy 25 percent of the enrollment population on the particular measure, we find no differences even nominally significant at the 5 percent level. Nor does a sign test favor one system over the other (see Sloss et al. 1987, table 2). Further limiting the sample to those at elevated risk in the lowest one-fifth of the income distribution as one group and those at elevated risk in the highest two-fifths as another also produces no evidence favoring one system over the other (see Sloss et al. 1987, table 3). Because of the large confidence intervals, however, we cannot conclude definitively that there are no major differences in physiologic outcomes between the two types of systems for the highly disadvantaged population.

Other Outcomes

In addition to physiologic measures, we compared health habits and several measures of general health, using the same measures as in Chapter 6. As was the case for the physiologic measures, we find little reason to favor one system over the other for the average person.[2] The two exceptions are differences for bed days and serious symptoms, both of which favor the fee-for-service system (see Tables 9.2a and 9.2b for operational definitions of the outcome measures and Table 9.3 for the results).

As with our comparisons of a variety of measures, it is important to examine the likelihood that we would have observed this degree of difference in our sample if there were no true difference in any measure. To perform such a test, we estimated a set of seemingly unrelated regressions using as dependent variables the nine measures shown in Table 9.2 plus blood pressure, cholesterol, and functional far vision.[3] We then tested the null hypothesis that the coefficient on the HMO variable was zero in all the regressions. We found we could reject this hypothesis at the 5 percent level: $[F(12,13140) = 1.97]$. Thus we can be reasonably confident that the differences reported in Table 9.3 are not simply an artifact of making comparisons with several measures. It is worth examining the differences involving bed days and serious symptoms more closely because the differences for these measures not only are nominally significant but are much greater in the low-income initially sick group than in the high-income initially sick group (Table 9.4).

A different measure of disability days that we regard as more reliable gives modest additional support to the bed day results. The measure of bed days reported in Tables 9.3 and 9.4 is based on the number of bed days during the past 30 days, as reported on the annual Medical History Questionnaires. Subsequent to performing the analyses with that measure, we also analyzed data on restricted activity days and work loss days from the biweekly Health Report. We regard the data from the Health Report as more reliable because (1) they were collected continuously over much of the Experiment, thus giving us many observations; (2) they are based on two-week rather than 30-day recall; and (3) they are based on a diary that could have been kept contemporaneously (it was mailed out for receipt at the beginning of the two-week period and mailed back at the end of the period).

The data from the Health Report on restricted activity days among the sick poor are consistent with the results on bed days reported in Tables 9.3 and 9.4. The Health Report did not ask about bed days, but it did ask about restricted activity days and work-loss days (see Table 6.4; bed days are a subset of restricted activity days). Unlike bed days, restricted activity days show no main effect of plan; when the population is divided into thirds by income and health (health is measured using the GHI), in four of the nine subgroups the free plan rate exceeds the Group Health rate (Table 9.5). As with the bed day result, however, the sick and poor group at the HMO have about one-third more restricted activity days than its fee-for-service counterpart. Nonetheless, the *t*-statistic on this difference, 1.3, is not significant at conventional levels, and within the sick and poor group the difference is found only for adults (Table 9.6).

In the case of work loss days, the results tend to support fee for service as yielding the better health outcomes. The HMO experimental participants had more work loss days (in comparison with the free-care plan) in

Table 9.2a   Operational definitions and enrollment value of health status measures used to define subgroups for prediction analyses, by selected health variables: general health measures

Health concepts and operational definitions	Typical item	Mean value for adults at enrollment		Interpretation of effect size
		"Good" health[a]	"Ill" health[b]	
Physical functioning: A standardized (0–100) scale (23 items) that indicates the degree of limitation in self-care, mobility, or physical activities.	Do you have any trouble either walking one block or climbing one flight of stairs because of your health?	100	44.8	10-point difference: effect of having chronic, mild osteoarthritis[c,d]
Role functioning: A dichotomous measure (2 items) that indicates whether the person can do work, school, or housework activities free of limitations due to poor health. Mean probabilities are expressed as percentages.	Does your health keep you from working at a job, doing work around the house, or going to school?	100	0	1-point difference: 1 percentage point higher probability of being limited in the performance of one's major role
Mental Health: A standardized (0–100) scale (38 items) that measures anxiety, depression, emotional ties, behavioral/emotional control, and psychological well-being during the past month.	How much of the time, during the past month, have you felt downhearted and blue?	86.4	52.3	3-point difference: impact of being fired or laid off
Social contacts: A standardized (0–100) scale (3 items) that mea-	About how often have you visited with friends at their homes	94.3	29.1	5-point difference: a 1-point increase in the Mental Health Index.

sures contacts with friends and relatives during the past month or year.	during the past month? (Do not count relatives.)			
General Health Index: A standardized (0–100) scale (22 items) that measures the person's perceptions of past, present, and future health, susceptibility to illness, and worry about health.	My health is excellent.	83.6	47.8	5-point difference: effect of having been diagnosed as hypertensive.[e]
Bed days: Estimate of the number of days in bed due to poor health during one year; based on reports gathered annually throughout the Experiment.	During the past 30 days, how many days has your health kept you in bed all day or most of the days?	f	f	Not available.
Serious symptoms: Estimate of the probability of one or more serious symptoms during one month; based on reports gathered annually throughout the Experiment for five symptoms rated as serious by physician panel.	Chest pain when exercising (during the past 30 days).	f	f	23-point difference: effect of serious airway obstruction disease.[g]

a. Mean of the healthiest 40% of the distribution at enrollment for measure analyzed.

b. Mean of the sickest 20% of the distribution at enrollment for measure analyzed.

c. Among participants in the Experiment, adjusted for age and gender.

d. Classifications based on responding yes to questions about age and gender.

e. Effect size interpretation based on responding yes to questions about ever having acute or chronic pain, aching, swelling, or stiffness in fingers, hip, or knee. Classifications based on responding yes to a question about ever being diagnosed as having high blood pressure and yes to a question about being so diagnosed more than once or to a question about having been prescribed pills or medicines for high blood pressure.

f. "Good" and "ill" health groups for analysis of bed-days and serious symptoms were the same sample as used in the analysis of General Health ratings.

g. Classification based on forced expiratory volume in one second or less of 65% of predicted controlling for age, gender, and height.

Table 9.2b   Operational definitions and value of health status measures used to define subgroups for prediction analyses, by selected health variables: health habits

Health concepts and operational definitions	Mean value of persons at specific elevated risk[a]	Scoring	
Smoking: A six-level measure of the risk of death due to smoking relative to not smoking.	1.89	Never smoked/ex-smoker	1.00
		Pipe/cigar smoker only	1.06
		Cigarette smoker	
		<1 pack/day	1.57
		1 pack/day	1.79
		2 packs/day	2.07
		>2 packs/day	2.20
Weight (kg)[b]	88.4	Standardized for height (in meters) by multiplying by $(1.75/height^2)$ for men and by $(1.65/height^{1.5})$ for women. Standardized for gender by summing 0.5 (average value for men) and 0.5 (average value for women).	

a. Mean of the sickest 25% of the distribution at enrollment.
b. Excludes those 14–17 and pregnant women.

Table 9.3 Predicted health outcomes for a typical person according to variable and system of care (95% confidence intervals in parentheses)[a]

Variable (direction of better health)	Group Health Cooperative	Fee-for-service		GHC minus free	GHC minus cost sharing
		Free	Cost sharing		
Health habits					
Smoking (−)	1.28	1.31	1.24	−.02 (−.06, .01)	.04 (.01, .07)[c]
Weight (−)	72.3	72.4	72.1	−0.1 (−1.1, 0.8)	0.1 (−0.6, 0.9)
General health					
Physical functioning (+)	85.6	84.8	86.1	.77 (−2.4, 4.0)	−0.56 (−3.0, 1.9)
Role functioning (+)	94.8	96.6	96.3	−1.8 (−6.7, 3.1)	−1.5 (−6.2, 3.2)
Bed days (−)	4.0	3.3	3.4	0.7 (0.1, 1.4)[b]	0.6 (0.04, 1.2)[b]
Serious symptoms (−)	16.1	11.6	14.2	4.5 (1.1, 7.8)[c]	1.9 (−1.0, 4.7)
Mental health (+)	75.8	75.7	75.4	.1 (−1.7, 2.0)	.4 (−1.1, 1.9)
Social contacts (+)	69.8	68.8	69.9	1.1 (−2.6, 4.7)	−.07 (−3.0,2.9)
General health (+)	69.4	68.1	70.0	1.2 (−0.6, 3.1)	−65 (−2.1,0.8)

a. For interpretation of scales, see Tables 9.2a and 9.2b.
b. $p < 0.05$, two-tailed test.
c. $p < 0.01$, two-tailed test.

Table 9.4 Predicted outcomes of general health indices according to variable, system of care, income, and initial health status (95% confidence intervals in parentheses)[a]

Variable (direction of better health)	Group Health Cooperative	Free	Cost sharing	GHC minus free	GHC minus cost sharing
Low income and initial ill health					
Physical functioning (+)	64.1	57.8	60.3	6.3 (−8.4, 20.9)	3.8 (−8.0, 15.7)
Role functioning (+)	60.7	64.0	64.2	−3.3 (−29.2, 22.6)	−3.5 (−28.3, 21.3)
Bed days (−)	9.6	5.9	9.2	3.7 (0.5, 7.4)[b]	0.4 (−3.0, 4.5)
Serious symptoms (−)	34.7	21.8	24.0	12.9 (2.8, 23.1)[b]	10.7 (−0.9, 22.3)
Mental health (+)	64.4	67.2	65.5	−2.8 (−8.1, 2.5)	−1.1 (−6.1, 3.9)
Social contacts (+)	46.6	52.6	46.9	−6.0 (−17.5, 5.4)	−0.4 (−14.5, 13.8)
General health (+)	55.1	57.8	55.9	−2.7 (−7.8, 2.4)	−0.8 (−5.3, 3.7)
High income and initial ill health					
Physical functioning (+)	55.4	52.7	64.7	2.7 (−10.3, 15.7)	−9.3 (−19.2, 0.61)
Role functioning (+)	69.6	70.6	76.6	−1.0 (−24.0, 22.0)	−7.0 (−27.0, 13.0)
Bed days (−)	7.3	7.7	5.3	−0.4 (−2.9, 2.3)	2.0 (−0.4, 4.7)
Serious symptoms (−)	25.7	20.3	27.1	5.4 (−4.8, 15.7)	−1.4 (−10.8, 8.0)
Mental health (+)	63.2	67.3	63.1	−4.1 (−10.2, 2.0)	0.05 (−4.8, 4.9)
Social contacts (+)	53.1	48.9	46.2	4.2 (−4.8, 13.3)	6.9 (−0.87, 14.7)
General health (+)	56.6	49.5	55.4	7.1 (2.4, 11.9)[c]	1.2 (−2.5, 4.9)

a. For interpretation of scales, see Tables 9.2a and 9.2b.
b. $p < 0.05$, two-tailed test.
c. $p < 0.01$, two-tailed test.

all but one of the nine subcategories; interestingly, the exception is the sick and poor group (Table 9.7). In three of these nine categories, the result is nominally statistically significant, those three being the average and poor health group among the high-income third and the average health group among the middle-income third.

To sum up, for 2 types of measures—disability days (bed days and work loss days) and serious symptoms—participants with free care in the fee-for-service system may have had better outcomes than those in the HMO, although for more than 20 others they did not. In comparison with the free fee-for-service plan, the HMO experimental group had more bed disability days as measured by the exit interview for disability days in the prior 30 days. This excess was found almost exclusively in the group that was poor and scored poorly on the General Health Index before the Experiment

Table 9.5   Predicted restricted activity days per year for Seattle participants, by tertiles of income and health[a]

	Cost-sharing plans	Free plan	GHE	GHE minus free	95% confidence interval			
					GHE minus free		GHE minus cost sharing	
High income								
Good health	4.7	2.7	5.7	3.0	−1.2	7.1	−1.7	3.6
Avg. health	9.1	8.7	9.9	1.2	−0.9	3.4	−1.4	3.0
Poor health	18.5	24.2	18.6	−5.6	−22.2	11.0	−9.6	9.8
Medium income								
Good health	4.4	3.9	4.3	0.4	−2.1	2.7	−1.7	1.5
Avg. health	8.9	9.4	9.5	0.1	−1.4	1.6	−0.8	1.9
Poor health	18.9	22.0	21.4	−0.6	−10.2	8.9	−3.7	8.6
Low income								
Good health	3.9	6.4	2.5	−3.9	−7.4	−0.5	−3.7	0.9
Avg. health	8.7	10.6	8.9	−1.7	−4.1	0.8	−1.6	2.1
Poor health	19.6	18.8	26.1	7.3	−3.7	18.3	−1.7	14.7

Note: GHE = Group Health Cooperative experimental.

a. Good, average, and poor health are measured using the General Health Index. Restricted activity days are predicted from a regression of the square root of annual restricted activity days on plan, log of income, adjusted for family size, and predicted restricted activity days at enroll-ment based on a combination of enrollment demographic and health status measures such as physical health and the General Health Index. The square root transformation was retrans-formed back to days using Duan's (1983) smearing method.

began. Measures of restricted activity days and work loss days over the course of the Experiment—which may be more reliable than the measure of bed disability because of the greater period over which the data were collected—show more work loss days for the HMO. This effect is not found among the group that is both sick and poor, however. Among that group alone, the HMO group lost fewer work days than the group on the fee-for-service plan. By contrast, for restricted activity days there were no statistically significant effects for the average person, but a large, though still not statistically significant, difference favored fee-for-service among the sick poor.

On balance, the 40 percent reduction in hospital rates for the HMO experimental sample seems to have had little ultimate effect on health outcomes. The plausibility of this finding is supported by the over 20 percent reduction in discharges in nonfederal short-stay hospitals from 1981 through 1987 (National Center for Health Statistics 1990, table 72), which also occurred with seemingly little or no measurable deleterious effect on the nation's health.[4]

Table 9.6   Predicted restricted activity days per year for adult Seattle participants, by tertiles of income and health[a]

	Cost-sharing plans	Free plan	GHE	GHE minus free	95% confidence interval			
					GHE minus free		GHE minus cost sharing	
High income								
Good health	4.5	1.4	5.0	3.6	−1.1	8.4	−2.7	3.8
Avg. health	8.0	5.9	8.0	2.1	−0.2	4.5	−2.3	2.4
Poor health	17.9	24.0	16.1	−7.9	−30.0	14.1	−14.4	10.8
Medium income								
Good health	3.7	3.0	3.7	0.7	−2.2	3.6	−2.0	1.9
Avg. health	7.3	7.2	7.8	0.6	−1.0	2.2	−1.1	1.9
Poor health	18.0	20.6	20.2	−0.4	−13.1	12.4	−6.4	11.0
Low income								
Good health	2.8	6.8	2.1	−4.7	−8.7	−0.8	−2.7	1.3
Avg. health	6.4	9.5	7.4	−2.1	−5.1	1.0	−1.0	2.9
Poor health	18.0	15.9	27.6	11.7	−4.5	27.9	−0.7	19.7

Note: GHE = Group Health Cooperative experimental.

a. Good, average, and poor health are measured using the General Health Index. Days are predicted using the method described in Table 9.5.

Table 9.7   Predicted work loss days per year for Seattle adult participants[a]

	Cost-sharing plans	Free plan	GHE	GHE minus free	95% confidence interval			
					GHE minus free		GHE minus cost sharing	
High income								
Good health	3.3	4.8	5.1	0.3	−2.7	3.3	−0.4	4.0
Avg. health	5.5	5.1	7.3	2.2	0.2	4.2	0.0	3.5
Poor health	8.4	5.5	9.9	4.4	0.3	8.6	−2.1	5.2
Medium income								
Good health	2.9	3.9	4.9	1.0	−0.7	2.7	0.6	3.4
Avg. health	5.1	5.2	6.7	1.5	0.1	2.9	0.4	2.7
Poor health	8.1	6.7	8.8	2.1	−0.6	4.9	−1.9	3.4
Low income								
Good health	2.3	2.6	4.5	1.9	−1.1	4.9	0.9	3.5
Avg. health	4.6	5.2	5.8	0.6	−1.9	3.0	−0.3	2.8
Poor health	7.6	8.8	7.2	−1.6	−9.9	6.8	−4.0	3.4

Note: GHE = Group Health Cooperative experimental.

a. Good, average, poor health are measured using the General Health Index. Work loss days are predicted using the method described in Table 9.5.

The Control Group

We have emphasized the experimental/free plan comparison, partly because any comparisons with the self-selected control group have inherently fewer implications for policy, and partly because the higher attrition from the control group reduces the reliability of any comparisons. But we did compare results between the control group and the other plans and present a brief summary here. (The results are given in detail in Ware et al. 1987, app. D.)

The only noteworthy control group result is for the General Health Index. Controlling for initial values of the Index, as well as several other variables including age, gender, and income, those in the HMO control group ended the Experiment with a 1.85 point higher Index value than those in the HMO experimental group ($t = 2.17$, 2105 d.f., $p < .05$). In other words, HMO members in the control group profited in terms of general health more by belonging to Group Health than did HMO members in the experimental group, even though aggregate measures of utilization were similar for the two groups. One possible explanation is that those who chose HMO status made more appropriate use of care than did those assigned to HMO status. If this is so, then more appropriate use may have stemmed either from greater familiarity with GHC's practice patterns and how to use them optimally, or from other unmeasured differences between the control group and the general Seattle population.

Pediatric Health Outcomes

The measures we used to evaluate child health at the HMO are the same as those used to evaluate child health across the various fee-for-service insurance plans in Chapter 7.[5]

The Experimental Group

Just as with the comparison of these measures across fee-for-service plans with varying cost sharing, we find no significant differences for children between the average outcome for the HMO experimental group and the average outcome on the fee-for-service free plan (Table 9.8). Two results, corrected vision and the General Health Index, approach nominal statistical significance and favor the fee-for-service system. The difference in the General Health Index—about 0.4 of a scale point on a 0–10 scale—is about 80 percent the size of the impact on the Index of mild to moderate hay fever and about one-third the size of a moderate hearing problem.

Interestingly, mothers of children on the fee-for-service free plan were less worried than mothers at the HMO about their children's health. These effects—a higher General Health Index in the fee-for-service plans and lower parental worry in the fee-for-service plans—were found in both high- and low-income groups.

By contrast with the General Health Index, five of the seven physiologic function measures studied favored the HMO.

Like the children participating in the fee-for-service free plan, children in fee-for-service cost-sharing plans also achieved a better result on the General Health Index than the HMO experimentals, a difference that is nominally significant at the 5 percent level, although the magnitude of difference is about the same, 0.4 of a scale point, as the insignificant result for the free plan/HMO experimentals comparison. As with the free-care plan, comparisons of physiologic health favored the HMO over the cost-sharing plans, but none of the differences was significant.

One possible explanation for the adverse effects on the GHI and greater parental worry found at the HMO is a labeling effect. There was a 21 per-

Table 9.8   Predicted exit values of health status measures for the typical child, by plan[a]

Health status measure	Fee-for-service		GHE	Free minus GHE[b]	Cost sharing minus GHE[b]
	Cost sharing	Free			
Reported health					
Role limitations (%)	2.8	2.5	1.9	0.6 (−2.6, 3.8)	0.9 (−2.6, 4.4)
Social relations[c]	8.23	8.33	8.52	−0.2 (−65, .27)	−0.3 (−68, 0.1)
Behavior problems[d]	15.6	17.0	17.6	−0.6 (−3.4, 2.2)	−2.0 (−4.2, 0.28)[e]
Mental health[c]	5.70	5.73	5.61	0.1 (−23, 47)	0.1 (−20, .38)
General health[c]	5.72	5.70	5.33	0.4 (−.02, .76)[e]	0.4 (.08, .7)[f]
Physiologic measures					
Vision, corrected[g]	2.7	2.3	2.6	−0.3 (−57, .01)[e]	0.1 (−.07, 43)
Hearing (%)	5.6	7.3	4.3	3.0 (−3.0, 9.0)	1.3 (−3.3, 5.9)
Middle ear fluid (%)	39.2	42.6	28.7	13.9 (−4.5, 32.3)	10.5 (−3.4, 24.4)
Anemia (%)	3.4	0.9	0.8	0.1 (−1.9, 2.1)	2.6 (−0.32, 5.52)[f]
Hay fever (%)	17.1	16.2	18.4	−2.2 (−12.9, 8.5)	−1.3 (−10.8, 9.2)
Polio booster (%)	95.9	95.5	97.7	−2.2 (−9.3, 4.9)	−1.8 (−6.8, 3.2)
Tetanus booster (%)	95.3	87.5	96.9	−9.4 (−21.2, 2.4)	−1.6 (−7.4, 4.2)
Parental concern					
Parental worry[h]	1.6	1.4	1.6	0.2 (−38, −.02)[f]	0 (−17, .13)

Notes: GHE = Group Health Cooperative experimental, prepaid group practice. Fee-for-service = 25% and 95% coinsurance plans; free = 0% coinsurance plan.

a. Sample sizes across measures vary because of differing age restrictions or missing data.

b. 95 percent confidence intervals in parentheses; approximate confidence intervals (cost sharing) for dichotomous indicator variables.

c. 0–10 scale; a higher value denotes better health.

d. 0–100 scale; a higher value denotes poorer health.

e. p < 0.10.

f. p < 0.05.

g. In Snellen line values: 2 = 20/20, 3 = 20/25, 4 = 20/30.

h. 4-point scale: 4 = a great deal, 3 = somewhat, 2 = a little, 1 = not at all.

cent higher visit rate among children at the HMO, a greater use of services that may have led parents to judge their child as ill more quickly and to feel greater concern. An alternative explanation is a different mix of providers on the fee-for-service plans. Among children 16 and younger in Dayton and Seattle combined, for example, 62 percent who sought care saw a specialist (80 percent of them saw a pediatrician), whereas most children at the HMO received care from a family practitioner or a pediatric nurse practitioner.[6] We did not study whether ratings of worry or general health differed by provider type.

Whatever the explanation, we judge the differences in the measures of reported health to be small and the confidence intervals around them to be rather tight. In the case of the physiologic measures, by contrast, the confidence intervals are sufficiently large so as to include clinically important differences in a number of instances, which lie in different directions depending upon the measure. Corrected vision favors free fee-for-service, for example; fluid in the middle ear favors the HMO. Finding a difference on the latter measure, however, may mean less than we thought it would when we chose the physiologic measures for the Experiment, because it is less clear now that medical care can prevent middle ear effusion.

Table 9.9 shows that if anything, children had fewer days of restricted activity at the HMO, but neither the main effect nor any of the subgroup comparisons is significant at conventional levels.

Our overall results support the hypothesis that, as in the case of adults, no serious negative health effects exist for children receiving care at the one HMO (a staff model prepaid group practice) we studied.

The Control Group

Table 9.10 shows comparisons of the HMO control and experimental group children at exit. These results should be interpreted with caution because they may reflect self-selection, differential attrition between the two groups, or differences in plan coverage. The last is especially likely to be a factor for the differences in vision outcomes; the experimental group was fully covered for vision services, whereas the control group was not. Thus, cost sharing probably caused differences in vision outcomes within the HMO as well as among fee-for-service plans. The lower level of worry and lower prevalence of fluid in the middle ear among the control group may reflect the control group's preference for, comfort with, and possibly greater mastery of the Group Health system. Such an explanation is consistent with the control children's greater use of medical services.

Process Measures of Ambulatory and Inpatient Care

We undertook an analysis of the process of care at the HMO similar to that conducted among the set of fee-for-service plans and described in Chapter 6 (Brook et al. 1990 provides further details). Our three comparison groups are, again, free fee-for-service, cost-sharing fee-for-service, and HMO experimental. Like the other analyses reported in this chapter, we use the Seattle sample.

The sample sizes were sufficiently large to conduct this analysis for only three conditions—hay fever, hypertension, and vision impairments (Table 9.11). The frequency with which outcome quality-of-care criteria were met was generally the same for the HMO as for the fee-for-service plans. For process measures the frequency for the HMO was higher, primarily because a markedly lower percentage of persons in the cost-sharing

Table 9.9   Predicted restricted activity days per year for child participants, by tertiles of income and health[a]

	Cost-sharing plans	Free plan	GHE	GHE minus free	95% confidence interval GHE minus free		GHE minus cost sharing	
High income								
Good health	5.8	8.1	7.7	−0.4	−3.7	2.8	−1.7	5.4
Avg. health	11.7	14.2	14.4	0.2	−3.3	3.8	−0.5	6.0
Poor health	19.4	32.9	23.1	−9.8	−28.6	9.1	−3.8	11.1
Medium income								
Good health	6.7	7.1	6.5	−0.6	−3.0	1.7	−2.4	2.0
Avg. health	12.2	13.7	13.3	−0.4	−2.9	2.0	−1.1	3.2
Poor health	19.4	22.3	22.3	0	−5.7	5.7	−1.6	7.4
Low income								
Good health	8.3	5.5	4.6	−0.9	−4.6	2.8	−8.2	0.9
Avg. health	13.2	12.8	11.3	−1.5	−5.1	2.1	−5.4	1.6
Poor health	19.2	23.0	20.8	−2.2	−10.0	5.6	−5.7	8.8

Note: GHE = Group Health Cooperative experimental.

a. Good, average, and poor health are measured using the General Health Index. Days are predicted using the method described in Table 9.5.

plans received an eye examination during the Experiment.[7] But outcomes for corrected vision differed little among the three groups. This finding emphasizes the importance of obtaining outcome data for full interpretation of the findings, a point to which we return in Chapter 11. Among the remaining criteria, there is no pattern.

We also conducted a study of the appropriateness of HMO hospitalization using methods similar to those used for studying appropriateness of hospitalization in the fee-for-service system (Chapter 5).[8] In particular, we compared 122 inpatient charts of HMO experimental participants who had

Table 9.10   Predicted health outcomes for the typical child, by whether prior GHC enrollee[a]

Health status	GHE	GHC	GHC minus GHE[b]
Health perceptions			
Role limitations (%)	1.9	2.9	1.0 (–2.5, 4.5)
Social relations[c]	8.52	8.26	–0.26 (–.69, .17)
Behavior problems[d]	17.5	16.8	–0.7 (–3.8, 2.3)
Mental health[c]	5.61	5.64	0.03 (–.34, .40)
General health[c]	5.33	5.47	0.14 (–.27, .55)
Physiologic measures			
Vision, corrected[e]	2.6	3.0	0.4 (.13, .67)[f]
Hearing (%)	4.5	5.5	1.0 (–4.3, 6.3)
Middle ear fluid (%)	27.9	14.3	–13.6 (–26.9, –0.3)[f]
Anemia (%)	0.8	1.4	0.6 (–2.3, 3.6)
Hay fever (%)	18.7	14.9	–3.8 (–15.6, 8.0)
Polio booster (%)	97.4	97.9	0.5 (–5.8, 6.8)
Tetanus booster (%)	96.9	98.4	1.5 (–3.8, 6.8)
Parental concern			
Parental worry[g]	1.6	1.4	–0.2 (–.41, –.01)[f]

Note: GHE = Group Health Cooperative experimental; GHC = Group Health Cooperative control (self-selected).

a. Sample sizes across measures vary because of differing age restrictions or missing data. The small differences in predicted GHE scores from Table 9.8 are due to differences in modeling the fee-for-service plans; specifically, children in cost-sharing plans are excluded from the sample used to estimate these equations.

b. 95 percent confidence intervals in parentheses; approximate confidence intervals for dichotomous indicator variables.

c. 0–10 scale; a higher value denotes better health.

d. 0–100 scale; a higher value denotes poorer health.

e. ln Snellen line values: 2 = 20/20, 3 = 20/25, 4 = 20/30.

f. $p < 0.05$.

Table 9.11 Frequency with which quality-of-care criteria were met for people randomized into a health maintenance organization (HMO) and those enrolled in the fee-for-service sample in Seattle (%)(sample size in parentheses)[a]

| | Outcomes | | | | | | | | | Process | | | | | |
| | Total | | | Physiologic | | | Impact[b] | | | Visits | | | Therapeutic | | |
	HMO	Free	Cost sharing	HMO	Free	Cost sharing	HMO	Free	Cost sharing	HMO	Free	Cost sharing	HMO	Free	Cost sharing
Hay fever	87 (683)	84 (264)	87 (588)	93 (100)	92 (39)	91 (91)	86 (488)	82 (184)	86 (419)	86 (95)	83 (41)	85 (78)	—	—	—
Hypertension	65 (603)	61 (305)	65 (510)	48 (106)	43 (53)	48 (85)	76 (200)	79 (101)	77 (173)	65 (91)	58 (45)	64 (78)	64 (206)	55 (106)	63 (174)
Vision impairments	82 (3,865)	81 (1,621)	79 (2,907)	83 (1,591)	84 (656)	81 (1,197)	81 (1,331)	82 (552)	82 (1,008)	86 (313)	79 (131)	64 (231)	77 (630)	74 (282)	73 (471)
Total	81 (5,151)	79 (2,190)	78 (4,005)	81 (1,797)	82 (748)	80 (1,373)	82 (2,019)	82 (837)	82 (1,600)	82 (499)	75 (217)	68 (387)	74 (836)	69 (388)	70 (645)

a. The sample sizes were calculated by summing the number of persons for whom each criterion was applicable across all criteria. Standard errors and tests of significance could not be computed because of the complex correlations among the criteria; the same person could be observed on multiple criteria.

b. Patient self-reports at end of Experiment concerning pain, worry, activity restriction, or days in bed attributable to the condition.

been hospitalized and 122 charts of randomly chosen participants from the free fee-for-service plan in Seattle who had been hospitalized.

In addition to the definition of appropriateness based on the Appropriateness Evaluation Protocol (which rated only whether it was appropriate to hospitalize the patient given what was done; see Chapter 5), we had two physicians independently rate the medical appropriateness or indications for the hospital services rendered. The physicians used a scale of 1 to 9, assigning 1 to 3 points for cases that were inappropriate and not efficacious, 4 to 6 for services possibly appropriate, and 7 to 9 for services clearly efficacious and appropriate. We summed the scores of the two physicians and determined the percentage of cases for which the sum was less than 7 (clearly inappropriate in the judgment of both physicians) and less than 13 (possibly or clearly inappropriate).

In both the HMO and fee-for-service systems, 12 percent of cases were judged inappropriate by the Appropriateness Evaluation Protocol (Table 9.12). When we expanded the definition of appropriateness to include physician judgments of appropriateness of services delivered, however, the percentage inappropriate rose by more in the fee-for-service than in the HMO system. Using the more conservative of the two physician definitions of appropriateness (sum of physician ratings less than 7) raised the proportions of inappropriate hospitalizations to 33 percent (fee for service) versus 27 percent (HMO). Using the more liberal definition of appropriateness (sum of physician ratings less than 13) raised the proportions to 50 percent and 37 percent, respectively.

Table 9.12   Percentage of inappropriate admissions, free fee-for-service and HMO[a]

Appropriateness criterion	Fee-for-service (N = 122)	HMO (N = 122)
AEP[b]	12	12
AEP or rating < 7[c]	33	27
AEP or rating < 13[d]	50	37

a. For further details, see Siu et al. (1988).

b. Standard is Appropriateness Evaluation Protocol; see Chapter 5.

c. A rating less than 7 means two physicians both judged the services delivered during the hospitalization as inappropriate and not efficacious.

d. A rating less than 13 means two physicians both judged the services delivered as less than clearly appropriate. The *t*-statistic in the comparison, when corrected for intracluster correlation, is 1.62, not significant at the 5% level.

Table 9.13   Predicted hospitalization rates per 1,000 person-years, by category, free fee-for-service and HMO[a]

Category	Fee-for-service (N = 122)	HMO (N = 122)
Overall[b]	102	55
Surgical nondiscretionary	20	18
Surgical discretionary[c,d]	22	7
Medical nondiscretionary[d]	34	15
Medical discretionary[c,d]	30	14

a. For further details, see Siu et al. (1988).

b. Excludes admissions for pregnancy-related causes, psychiatry, alcohol rehabilitation, ophthalmology, and oral surgery. The difference is significant at $p < 0.01$.

c. Discretionary means inappropriate as judged by Appropriateness Evaluation Protocol or physician rating < 13.

d. The difference between fee-for-service and the HMO is significant at $p < 0.01$.

When we looked at whether the reductions in admissions the HMO achieved were disproportionately in discretionary or inappropriate categories, we found reductions in all categories except nondiscretionary surgical cases (Table 9.13). Although we had expected to find reductions in admission rates for discretionary or inappropriate cases, we did not expect to find a substantial reduction in medical admissions that we considered nondiscretionary. When we examined these cases more closely, however, this finding appeared attributable partly to random events, such as more accidents among the fee-for-service group, and partly to HMO delivery of certain types of care (most notably chemotherapy) on an outpatient basis that we had considered appropriate for admission (Siu et al. 1988). As a result, we would expect little observable difference in outcomes from the lower rate of nondiscretionary medical admissions at the HMO.

Thus, our findings on the appropriateness of hospitalization among HMO and fee-for-service participants seem generally consistent with our finding of no adverse outcome effect from the substantial reductions in hospitalization at the HMO.

Patient Satisfaction

Patient satisfaction is of greater significance in comparing the HMO and fee-for-service systems than in comparing plans within the fee-for-service system because the nature of the service differs to a greater degree (for example, the HMO offers less hospital care and greater use of allied health personnel). Thus, we used the measures of patient satisfaction described in Table 6.41 to compare satisfaction between the Group Health experimentals, the Group Health controls, and all fee-for-service participants. Because there were no measurable differences in patient satisfaction among the fee-for-service plans, we have combined all fee-for-service plans for the purpose of this analysis. We do, however, limit the analysis to participants in Seattle.[9] Table 9.14 summarizes the (statistically significant) differences.

Overall, fee-for-service participants were more satisfied with their care than were those assigned to the HMO experimental group. Moreover, those who had chosen the HMO—the HMO controls—were more satisfied than those assigned to HMO experimental status. This result is not surprising, since a substantial portion of those randomly assigned to HMO status had had an earlier opportunity through their place of employment to

Table 9.14   Summary of results for patient satisfaction

Feature of care	GHC experimentals more satisfied	Similiar satisfaction	Fee-for-service more satisfied
Access	Office waits[a]	Office hours[a]	Appointment waits[a]
		Answers to questions	Parking
			Travel time
		Care in emergencies	Convenience
Availability		Family doctors[a]	Hospitals[a]
			Specialists
Finances	Costs of care	Technical quality[a]	Continuity of care[a]
Quality of care		Facilities	Interpersonal aspects
Overall			General satisfaction

a. Features of care for which both self-selected (control) and experimental comparisons produced the same conclusions regarding differences between HMO and fee-for-service in attitudes toward care. All differences are significant at $p < 0.05$.

choose GHC coverage and had passed it up.[10] Although those in fee-for-service plans were more satisfied overall than those assigned to HMO status, there was no measurable difference in satisfaction between those in fee-for-service plans and those who had chosen the HMO.[11]

Cost

Both HMO groups were more satisfied with the costs of care than the fee-for-service group. This is not surprising in the case of the HMO controls, who presumably saved money as a result of GHC's low-cost style of medicine (see Chapter 8).[12] It is surprising in the case of the experimentals, however, because neither the experimental nor the free plan participants paid for care, and the participation incentive payments compensated those on the cost-sharing plan for any costs. One possible explanation is that those in the fee-for-service plans did not like either having to file claims or (even on the free plan) being out of pocket for the provider's fee until they were reimbursed (see also Table 10.4).

Wait Times

Fee-for-service participants were more satisfied than HMO members with their waits to appointment; but both HMO groups were more satisfied with waiting time in the office than were fee-for-service participants. This result mirrors the usual pattern of GHC and other mature HMOs, which tend to make patients wait longer for an appointment than the fee-for-service providers but have shorter waits once the patient is in the office.

Access

Those assigned to the HMO viewed themselves as having less access to hospital and specialty care. Access to hospital care is a major source of cost savings at the HMO, and the substitution of generalists for specialists that GHC engaged in is presumptively another major source of savings. Thus, it is not surprising that the experimentals, a substantial portion of whom had previously elected not to receive care at GHC, would not be satisfied with these aspects of care. There had to be something about fee-for-service care that made its additional costs worthwhile to those who chose it over HMO care, and the perception of better access to hospital and specialty care appears to be that something.

Summary

Few adverse effects were observed as a result of the reduction in hospitalization at GHC, with the exception of possibly more disability days. There were scattered indications of adverse outcomes among the group that began the Experiment both poor and sick, but these may well have arisen by chance. Experimental participants assigned to the HMO were less satisfied overall with their care than participants assigned to the fee-for-service system. By contrast, those who had self-selected the HMO were as satisfied with their care as those in the fee-for-service system.

Part V

Lessons from the Health Insurance Experiment

Chapter 10

Administrative Lessons

The previous chapters have presented the design and substantive results of the Experiment. In this chapter we address administrative issues. We begin by summarizing lessons learned about administering income-related health insurance benefits. We then discuss lessons learned about operating a social experiment, beginning with issues related to participant reactions and their effect on data quality and then proceeding to management issues. The final section provides tips for the prospective experimenter.

Unfortunately, the Experiment provides little guidance in estimating the administrative costs of an ongoing health insurance program, because it incurred substantial additional costs of coding for research purposes. Insurers of existing programs must encode the amount of the bill, but encoding the diagnosis or the specific nature of the services provided has historically been discretionary. For the Experiment, in sharp contrast, patient diagnoses were coded in accordance with the H-ICDA-2 (Commission on Professional and Hospital Activities 1973); services provided were coded in accordance with the California Relative Value Studies (California Medical Association 1975) or American Dental Association codes (Council on Dental Care Programs 1972); drugs were coded in accordance with the National Drug Code (U.S. Public Health Service 1972); and supplies were coded in accordance with a system developed by the Experiment. There were no noteworthy lessons learned from this coding effort, except that physicians will provide data that link procedures to diagnosis (in the case of multiple diagnoses) and will also link drugs and supplies to diagnoses.

Administering Income-Related Benefits

When we began the Experiment, Martin Feldstein (1971) was advocating income-related deductibles. Many skeptics believed that the administrative costs of such a scheme would be exorbitant. The Experiment offered some insights into the potential problems in administering income-related benefits, including definition of the insured unit, definition of income, and definition of the accounting period over which expenditures would be counted.[1]

Definition of the Insured Unit

The Experiment related income to health insurance benefits through a cap on total out-of-pocket expenditure, called the Maximum Dollar Expenditure. An income-related MDE can, in principle, either relate an individual's medical expenditure to some measure of the individual's income, or relate a family's medical expenditure to a measure of family income. We opted for the latter, which meant we had to define a family unit for the purpose.

Our decision to pool income and medical expenditure across a family unit was driven fundamentally by the pooling of income within families and the difficulty of imputing income to an individual within the unit.[2] If we had the decision to make again, however, we would be inclined to base the limit on the individual, because with the experimental data one can now estimate actuarially equivalent individual and family deductibles (Chapter 4). That is, one can relate family income to a family deductible, or MDE, which in turn would correspond to an individual MDE.

When we were discussing how to define the insured unit, an argument against the family approach was that it forced us not only to define a family unit—something that had an element of arbitrariness—but also to monitor changes in the unit, which was costly and had an inevitable element of error. Indeed, one of the most important administrative lessons we learned was to change the definition of the family unit only on an annual basis. Recognizing family unit changes when they actually occurred (for example, on the date of a separation) would have had led to frequent changes for some families within a given year. For example, a child might leave her parents to live with her grandparents and return to her parents two months later. It would have been costly, cumbersome, and confusing to have adjusted the parents' MDE downward during the time the child was living with the grandparents, and to have imputed an income to the child for two months and given the child an MDE (which would have been set on the presumption that the child would reside with the grandparents for the remainder of the accounting year and would then have had to be changed after the two-month period). Such adjustments would also have yielded data that would be virtually impossible to analyze, because the degree to which the family unit change was anticipated in advance would be unknown. Our actual rule was that if the family unit changed during the middle of an accounting year, that change was recognized at the beginning of the next accounting year. Thus, in the example above, the MDE would be fixed for twelve months, and if the child was living with her parents at the beginning of the accounting year, the child's and the parents' expenditure would be counted toward a common MDE based on their common income.

An argument for using the family rather than the individual as the relevant unit was that under certain assumptions—most notably zero price elasticity—the variance of payments by the insured is less with a family deductible than with an equivalent individual deductible (equivalent in the sense of having the same expected out-of-pocket expenditure for the sum of the individual deductibles as for the family deductible) (Keeler, Relles, and Rolph 1977a, 1977b). In the event, price responsiveness turned out to be considerable, and the results described in Chapter 4 show that the more desirable arrangement is an individual MDE rather than a family MDE. Thus, a choice made for administrative reasons, which at the time had analytic support, was revealed to have been misplaced.

In defining the family unit, we tried to approximate as well as possible the group of individuals who drew out of a common income pool to finance their medical expenditures. Thus, the basic unit included: (1) the head of the family, defined as a person age 18–61 (three-year plan) or 18–59 (five-year plan) who was not dependent for more than half of his or her support on any other member of his household,[3] (2) the spouse of the head, (3) unmarried minors (under 18) related to the head, and (4) any other members of the head's household who were dependent on the head for more than half of their support. A person could be "related" to the head through blood, marriage, or adoption.

Two qualifications to the dependency and relationship criteria exemplify practical issues that must be addressed by any health insurance plan using a family relationship. First, all natural or adopted children of the head were assigned to the head's family if they were unmarried and under 18. All other unmarried persons under 18 related to the head were assigned to the head's unit unless they were more closely related to another economic family unit head who was living in the same household.[4] This qualification of the relationship criterion prevented, for example, the assignment of a child to her uncle's family when her own parents were part of that same household. Second, only *unmarried* minors were assigned to the head's family unit. This distinction between married and unmarried minors was drawn to avoid assigning a married minor who was dependent on his or her own spouse to another head's family.

Definition of Income

The intent of income-relating the benefits in the Experiment was that cost sharing should be a function of ability to pay; hence, we wished to have as comprehensive a definition of income as was practicable, given the need to have income sources with standard definitions that are easily identifiable. Practicality dictated that we begin with gross income as reported on federal income tax returns, which in turn implied a twelve-month accounting period for income. We added three categories of nontaxable income to the Internal Revenue Code's definition of income: (1) welfare payments, including Aid to Families with Dependent Children and Supplemental Security Income; (2) court-ordered child support payments; and (3) the portion of dividends at that time excluded from taxable income.

Information on income was collected annually, on a form mailed in mid-April, just after the filing date for the federal income tax. The format of this form, the Annual Income Report, was keyed to the federal income tax form, so that in most cases the respondent had merely to copy figures from the federal income tax form.

Use of the federal income tax form implied that the Experiment's income measure was retrospective rather than current. Use of current income, though more sensitive to current ability to pay, would have required a forecasted income, which would have given participants an incentive to overstate their income because of the associated higher Participation Incentive (Chapter 2).

In general, we calculated income by summing the incomes of all the members in the economic unit; however, because some of these units contained individuals ineligible for the Experiment (such as nonrelated dependents of the head or an elderly spouse), we developed a formula for adjusting the unit's income for this eventuality. This was in fact the same formula used in Chapter 6 to adjust the analytical measure of income for family size and is described there.

Definition of Accounting Period

That income was measured over a 12-month period did not necessarily imply that the MDE had to be calculated on an annual basis, but we chose this approach for its simplicity. We could, for example, have assigned quarterly MDEs based on annual income. However, this would have increased administrative costs, seemingly to no good purpose, because the measure would not, in any case, be sensitive to short-term fluctuations in income.

Administering a Social Experiment

Participant Reactions

The evaluation questionnaire. At the end of the Experiment, one individual from each enrolled family filled out an evaluation questionnaire. With this instrument we sought to test the validity of some of the principles we had used in designing and operating the Experiment, as well as to gather information on some choices we had made with little or nothing to guide us. Of the 2,845 people to whom questionnaires were given, 2,772 completed the form, for a response rate of 97 percent.

Enrollment techniques. Our enrollment strategy centered on the issue of how to market the offer, which might appear "too good to be true." To convince the families we were attempting to enroll of our legitimacy, and thus minimize the refusal rate, we relied upon three tactics:

1. We wrote statements describing the offer, including the nature of the insurance plan, that were substantially simpler and clearer than the typical statement of insurance benefits. Figure 10.1 shows a sample page from the Certificate of Benefits.[5] We also had the enroller explain to the families how they would benefit under various scenarios. In general, we tried to eschew a hard sell (including discouraging families from enrolling at the time they heard the offer) and let the facts speak for themselves.
2. We established a list of local contacts; Figure 10.2 shows a sample list from Seattle. These generally included the local office of the congressman, the mayor's office, the Better Business Bureau, and the county medical society.
3. We gave the families a pledge of confidentiality (Figure 10.3).

Our strategy succeeded. Refusal of the offer, though (surprisingly to us) related to plan, did not generally lead to detectable bias (see Chapters 2 and 8). The effort to describe the plan in clear language appears to have been well worth the effort. During the Experiment we asked families questions about how much they would pay for medical care services net of the

DETAILED DESCRIPTION OF BENEFITS

A. HOSPITAL CARE — INPATIENT

While a Participant is an inpatient* in a hospital* (general, maternity or mental), the Plan shall provide coverage for the following items for an unlimited number of days for treatment of illness, injury, or pregnancy according to the terms described in your Benefits Statement:

1. The hospital's standard charges for accommodations when the Participant occupies other than a private room.

2. The hospital's standard charges for a private room, intensive care unit, or isolation room if the attending physician* certifies such occupancy as medically necessary* or if the hospital administrator certifies that no semi-private room was available. (If a private room is occupied on an elective basis, the benefit will be an amount equal to the hospital's charges for a semi-private room for the period of such occupancy.)

3. The hospital's standard charges for medically necessary or prescribed supplies** and services furnished to a patient (excluding personal convenience items such as television, telephone, beauty or barber services). Such services include:

   a. Use of operating room
   b. Anesthetic supplies
   c. Surgical supplies, dressings, and cast materials
   d. Physical therapy
   e. Drugs
   f. X-ray and laboratory services
   g. Private duty nursing services if medically necessary.

(Note: See restrictions on cosmetic surgery, Section E; dental care benefits, Section I; vision care benefits, Section J; hearing care benefits, Section K; and sterilization, Section O.)

B. HOSPITAL CARE — OUTPATIENT

If any Participant is an outpatient* in the emergency room or outpatient department of a hospital, according to the terms described in your Benefits Statement, the Plan shall provide for the hospital's standard charges for services performed and supplies provided in conjunction with the diagnosis or treatment of any illness or injury of the Participant.

(Note: See restrictions on cosmetic surgery, Section E; outpatient psychiatric services, Section G; dental care benefits, Section I; vision care benefits, Section J; hearing care benefits, Section K; and sterilization, Section O.)

---

* See Definitions, pages 11-12.

** See Section O, page 9 for limitations on prosthetic devices.

Figure 10.1 Sample page from Certificate of benefits

HEALTH INSURANCE STUDY
COMMUNITY LEADER CONTACT LIST
SEATTLE, WASHINGTON

United States Congressman
Brock Adams
(206) 442-7478 (Seattle)

United States Congressman
Joel Prichard
(206) 442-4220 (Seattle)

Better Business Bureau
(206) 622-8066 (Seattle)

John D. Spellman
County Executive, KING COUNTY
(206) 344-4040 (Seattle)

State Representative
Peggy Joan Maxie
(206) 753-7946 (Olympia)

A. G. Vande Wiele
Office of the State Insurance Commissioner
(206) 464-6290 (Seattle)
(206) 753-3381 (Olympia)

HEALTH INSURANCE STUDY Local Office: (206) 323-3410 (Seattle)

Figure 10.2   Local contact list

WHAT HAPPENS TO THE INFORMATION THAT IS GATHERED AS
PART OF THE HEALTH INSURANCE STUDY?

All information which would permit identification of individuals or families participating in the Health Insurance Study, or which might be identified with such individuals or families, will be regarded as strictly confidential, will be used only for the purposes of evaluating and operating the Health Insurance Study, and will not be disclosed or released for any other purposes without prior written consent of such individuals or heads of families, except as required by law. For the purpose of research, all information which would identify individuals will be deleted from interview materials. Identifying information will be destroyed after the conclusion of the Study.

Figure 10.3   Confidentiality pledge

insurance payment (for example, "How much would you pay of a $20 physician visit charge?"); they answered correctly about 80 percent of the time in most plans (M. S. Marquis 1981).

Families found the materials easy to understand and relied on them in the enrollment process; the most frequently cited aid in deciding that the enrollment offer was honest was the Questions and Answers booklet (Table 10.1).[6] Cited nearly as often were the interviewer's persuasion and funding by the federal government. The contact list was used by half the families, and most of those said it was helpful. The importance of the written materials given the families is attested by the fact that 80 percent still had their Enrollment Agreement and Certificate of Benefits at the end of the Experiment.

One-third of the participants indicated that the main reason they enrolled was either interest in national health insurance or a chance to be a good citizen. Given the strong incentive for respondents to show themselves in a favorable light, we hesitated to accept this reason at face value. Accordingly, we controlled for such an incentive by including a variable to measure the Socially Desirable Response Set. Regressing an indicator variable for these responses on a measure of Socially Desirable Response Set showed that this motive was indeed present (Table 10.2), but its quantitative effect in the response is not large.[7]

The ethics of experimentation dictate that data be kept confidential; hence the confidentiality pledge. The pledge played a practical role in enrollment decisions as well as in decisions to complete questionnaires: more than half the participants said the confidentiality pledge was important in their decision to enroll, and over 60 percent said it was important in convincing them to answer questions. The magnitude of this response provides some ex post justification for our decision to expend considerable resources to support the pledge. Among other things, we built a system of linking identifying numbers, with the links held in different places. The subcontractor who processed claims and kept family unit change information held a list of names, addresses, and one set of identifying numbers. The RAND analytical group held the data base, which used a different identifying number and had no names and addresses.

The importance of confidentiality to participants implies a responsibility on the part of social science researchers; a few well-publicized examples of a researcher's failure to protect confidential data could jeopardize future efforts.

Table 10.1   Families' perceptions at exit of the enrollment process and enrollment materials

Questions	Answers (%)		
Please think back to the time when you enrolled in the Family Health Protection Plan. Did you find it hard to understand any of the following enrollment materials?	Hard to understand	Not hard to understand	Don't remember
A. Enrollment agreement	6	83	10
B. Certificate of benefits	8	82	10
C. Questions and answers booklet	4	88	7
Do you think the following things were adequately explained at the time of enrollment?	Yes	No	Don't remember
A. Insurance benefits	86	7	7
B. Participation incentive payments	87	7	6
C. How to fill out claims forms	88	8	4
Which of the following items helped you decide the FHPP was making an honest offer?	Helped	Did not help	Did not use
A. Statements in the questions and answers booklet	80	9	11
B. Talk with a local official an the contact list	43	7	51
C. The fact that the FHPP is paid for by the U.S. government	72	14	14
D. Talked with a friend or community leader not on the contact list	19	11	70
E. The interviewer's persuasion	74	13	13
F. Talk with your doctor	19	13	68
G. Call to better business bureau	10	8	82
Do you still have your enrollment agreement?	Yes	No	Not sure
	80	3	17
Do you still have your Certificate of Benefits?	82	3	15

Table 10.1 (continued)

Questions	Answers (%)
The FHPP has pledged to protect your privacy by not releasing personal information about you to others. Was this pledge important to you in deciding to enroll in the FHPP, in answering questions, in filling out forms, or in any other way? (Circle all that apply.)	
A. Not important in any way	21
B. Important in deciding to enroll	55
C. Important in answering questions	61
What was the main reason that you enrolled in the FHPP? (Circle one)	
A. Good medical and dental benefits	45
B. Participation incentive payments	8
C. Interested in national health insurance	27
D. Chance to be a good citizen	6
E. Unhappy with previous health insurance	2
F. Another family member wanted to enroll	5
G. Other	8

Table 10.2   Socially Desirable Response Set affects the indicated reason for enrolling (asymptotic *t*-statistics in parentheses)

Logit of probability of responding that reason for enrollment was interest in national health insurance or chance to be a good citizen.	$= -1.10 + 0.0085$ Socially Desirable Response Set (7.37) (3.38) + Vector of site dummies, $\chi^2 = 25.6$ (5 d.f.)

Note: The sample contains 2,053 observations; the Dayton site is not represented because Socially Desirable Response Set measures are not available for that site. The method of estimation is maximum likelihood. The vector of site dummy variables has a χ^2 value of 15.5, significant at the 0.005 level. The measure of Socially Desirable Response Set is the number of extreme responses to eight questions; e.g., "How often do you eat too much?" (Extreme response is "never") or "Are your table manners at home just as good as they are when you are invited out to dinner?" (Extreme response is "Yes, always just as good"), transformed linearly to a 0–100 scale. The eight items were adapted from the Comrey Personality Scales (Comrey 1970) and are further described in Davies et al. (1988), p. 57. Socially Desirable Response Set is measured at enrollment.

Methods to improve reliability of information. After enrolling the families, we faced a challenge scarcely unique to social experimentation—trying to ensure that the forms were completed and that the information collected was accurate. Our techniques were not new. We relied principally upon paying families: four dollars to fill out a relatively simple questionnaire (the Health Report) every other week, and five dollars per head of family to fill out most other questionnaires, including an annual questionnaire about health status, the annual questionnaire about income (based primarily on responses to the Internal Revenue Service Form 1040 or 1040A), and a one-time questionnaire on assets and liabilities.

By conventional standards our response rates were high; even after five years, 85–90 percent of the biweekly Health Report forms were returned each period. How much response rates might have fallen with less payment is open to conjecture. Reliability of most constructed scales was around 0.9, even in the least educated groups (see Chapter 6).

At exit we asked the families about the payments, our interviewing techniques, and their reactions to specific questionnaires (Table 10.3). Most respondents answered that the payments were fair or more than fair, but self-selection bias may have somewhat inflated these percentages. An upper bound on selection bias, however, can be obtained by assuming the 10 percent who dropped out of the Experiment thought that the payment was too little. Even in this case, a large majority would have regarded the payments as fair.

Of greater interest, perhaps, are the participants' responses to the method of interviewing. We relied heavily on self-administered forms because they are far less expensive than personal interviews and because we thought respondents might be willing to put down sensitive health status information on a self-administered form that they might not be willing to tell an interviewer. (We did not use telephone interviews except as a last resort.) Our participants overwhelmingly preferred self-administered questionnaires to personal interviews, by a margin of six to one. Given the additional expense of personal interviews and the demonstrated quality of the data obtained from self-administered forms, analogous future efforts should use self-administered forms.

Generally we sent out the self-administered interview instruments separately. We did not experiment with sending out all questionnaires together because response rates were sufficiently high for our purposes, and there was no marked cost difference. Because it wasn't broke, we didn't try to fix it.

Table 10.3 Families' perceptions of techniques to obtain data

Questions	Answers (%)		
In general, do you think the amount you were paid to fill out questionnaires was more than fair, a fair amount, or less than fair?	More than fair	Fair	Less than fair
A. Biweekly questionnaire	23	75	2
B. Annual health questionnaire	20	76	4
C. Annual income report	20	74	6
When providing the Experiment with information, do you prefer questionnaires that you fill out yourself, or interviews where an interviewer asks the questions and records the answers?	Prefer to fill out forms myself	Prefer interviewer to fill out forms	No preference
	70	12	19
As a reminder to mail your questionnaires, do you prefer a letter, a phone call, or do you have no preference?	Letter	Phone call	No preference
	22	30	48
When different kinds of questionnaires are scheduled for the same month, do you prefer that they all come together in one package, that different kinds arrive in separate packages with a short delay in between, or do you have no preference?	Arrive together	Separate packages	No preference
	38	17	45
Did the calendar provided to you by the FHPP help you to fill out your biweekly questionnaire?	Yes	No, or never used	
	71	29	
At the top of the claims form is a flap called a visit record. Did this visit record help you to fill out the biweekly questionnaire?	Yes	No, or never used	
	78	22	

Almost half the families had no preference between receiving several questionnaires at the same time or separately, but of those who expressed a preference, around two-thirds preferred all questionnaires in a given month to come as a package. The expression of such a preference, of course, does not mean that response rates would be similar under the two options, but given these stated preferences, an experiment to ascertain what response rates would be seems worthwhile.

The families were given printed forms to aid them in completing questionnaires. The forms allowed people to record information at the time of the event (for example, the time the doctor spent with the patient, the exact day that a child was home sick from school) for copying onto an interview form later. Roughly three-quarters of the families indicated that they used these printed forms, strongly suggesting the value of recall aids.

Factors that might cause attrition. Despite the low attrition (see Chapters 2 and 8), 15 percent of families said they had considered dropping out, and nearly half of these (6 percent) cited the burden of filling out forms as a problem (Table 10.4). The questions most resented were those on income, assets, and liabilities. Nearly one-third of the participants thought that filling out the annual income report was the single worst thing about the Experiment. Indeed, it was the most commonly cited negative feature. One can only guess at the implications of this result for the burden taxpayers incur to assemble data for and fill out federal and state income tax forms. Finally, nearly two-thirds of the sample disapproved of the redundancy that we built into a number of the health status scales in order to improve reliability.

Conclusions. The participants told us a considerable amount about how they viewed us, the designers and operators of the Experiment. Here are the more salient findings:

1. Clear, simple written materials were useful in decisions whether to enroll and were retained for future reference.
2. The persuasiveness of the enroller appears to have been important in obtaining a high enrollment rate. Persuasiveness in our context, however, was more a matter of explaining the facts and letting them speak for themselves than of hyperbolic or pressuring language.
3. A pledge of confidentiality was important to more than half the participants in deciding to enroll and subsequently complete questionnaires.
4. Families overwhelmingly preferred self-administered questionnaires to personal interviews.

5. There was a mild preference for receiving several self-administered forms at once rather than spread out over time, but we have no hard data on how such bunching might affect the completion rate. That rate was high, even though the forms were typically mailed separately.

6. Information on income, assets, and liabilities appears to have been considerably more burdensome than information on health problems. The redundancy needed to achieve relatively high reliability in scales of health status also was rather widely resented, although it does not appear to have had much influence on attrition or form noncompletion, both of which were modest.

Table 10.4   Families' perceptions of burdens of participation

Questions	Answers (%)	
	Yes	No
Did you ever think about dropping out of the study?	15	85
If yes, why did you consider dropping out? (% of families answering yes to previous question)		
A. Forms in general are overwhelming, too much, too difficult, too detailed, too complex	31	
B. Unspecified complaint about paperwork, forms, questionaires	3	
C. Obtaining information to complete forms too much trouble	3	
D. Getting forms in on time, having to meet deadlines for questionnaire	4	
Did you ever have any of the problems listed below when filling out FHPP forms?		
A. Questions were too personal	22	78
B. Afraid the information might be used against me	9	91
C. Thought the questions repeated each other	64	36
What was the worst thing about the FHPP?		
A. Filling out annual income reports	31	
B. Filling out claims forms	16	
C. Filling out the biweekly questionnaire	14	
D. Filling out other forms	9	
E. Forms are overwhelming (this was volunteered)	2	
F. No problem or complaint (this was volunteered)	10	
G. Getting forms in on time (this was volunteered)	1	
H. Other	15	

Management Issues

The administration of a social experiment requires implementation of a good many management principles.[8]

Organizational design. Because social experiments typically involve several institutions and extend over several years, the experimenter must explicitly consider organizational design from the outset. The apportionment of responsibility and authority is important, not only at the outset but throughout the experiment.

Although many organizational arrangements can be suitable for a social experiment, a single organization should have ultimate responsibility and authority for completing all the work—from experimental design through program operation and research. The importance of this tenet derives from the generally large scale of social experiments and the broad range of skills required, which frequently lead to the formation of consortia and partnerships. These can be viable organizational forms, but the high degree of coordination required in any successful experiment suggests that authority should be unambiguous. None of the difficulties in assembling the requisite mixture of talent and job assignments should be allowed to weaken the concept of a sole source of accountability.

The team approach. Even though one organization should have ultimate responsibility, a team approach to implementing an experiment is an absolute necessity. Henry Riecken and Robert Boruch (1974) have identified six roles in the social experimentation process: initiator, sponsor, designer-researcher, treatment administrator, program developer, and audience-user. Charles Field and Larry Orr (in Boruch and Riecken 1975) have pointed out that the initiator and sponsor are often one and the same, and that the roles of designer-researcher, treatment administrator, and program developer may be executed by people from the same organization. The primary reason for defining specific roles is to stress the variation in perspective, motivation, and skills required in an experiment. It is unlikely that the staff of any one institution will have all the necessary skills. Even if it does, the task of coordinating these skills is far from trivial.

The team approach is designed to overcome the most frequent source of dissonance cited by those who have analyzed social experiments: a conflict between the perspective of the designer-researchers and of those who must carry out the day-to-day activities—that is, conflict between the "research" team and the "action" team (Riecken et al. 1974).

The conflict is easy enough to describe, but harder to resolve success-fully in practice. One important strategy for averting or at least minimizing conflict is to have representatives of each team participate fully and as early as possible in the experimentation process. In particular, the "action" per-spective (including the data processing group) should be represented in the design phase because the choice of experimental treatments must include assessments of their operational feasibility. Treatments that the action team has not considered will have a lower probability of success, not only because of potential objective difficulties in implementation, but also because the action team has less stake in their success.

Another essential strategy is to cultivate and perpetuate mutual respect for each perspective within and across participating organizations. Strong disagreements inevitably arise, and little can—or, in our view, should— be done to suppress them. Instead, the experiment's manager should turn them into productive exercises that in the end contribute to the success of the experiment. Close, daily communication between the head of the research team and the head of the action team is essential.

Third, routine—as opposed to ad hoc—mechanisms must be designed for resolving differences. Such mechanisms not only promote contact between action and research team members but also broaden the perspec-tives of both parties; routine interaction also helps keep decisions and actions consistent and can defuse conflict and tensions before they become intolerable.

Fourth, although sustained interaction among groups is essential, team members and groups must be given as much latitude as possible to carry out their designated tasks without interference. Considerable division of labor is necessary in a social experiment. Some of this division can and will take place naturally, but some must be managed—even forced. Mem-bers or groups within teams ultimately derive their value from the special talents they contribute to team performances. Too much interference by one team in the activities of the others is likely in the long run to be detri-mental to the exercise of that talent—and thus to the experiment.

Preserving the integrity of treatments. Of all the managerial challenges, perhaps the most compelling is the need to preserve the integrity of the experimental treatments in the face of both operational and analytic diffi-culties and opportunities. Whenever that challenge arose, we tried to apply a fundamental test: To what extent would alternative courses of action strengthen or threaten the integrity of the experimental treatments? This test may seem to belabor the obvious, but it is easy to lose sight of when confronting the unanticipated issues of mounting an experiment.

In the absence of other guidelines, many operational decisions will be made to suit administrative convenience. However, social experimentation also requires considering the decision's effect on participant behavior and the resulting ability of the analyst to make inferences. Thus, the action team must think about research implications as well as the most convenient or expedient methods to accomplish a task. We do not deny the utility of administrative simplicity, but research implications are the *raison d'être* of the endeavor.[9]

Taking account of research implications is neither easy nor always successful, but the rewards for doing so (as well as the penalties for not doing so) are high.[10] Training, well-thought-out procedures, and an organizational structure that facilitates sustained interaction between the action and research groups throughout the operation of the experiment will keep research considerations at the forefront. Such a simple matter as placing the research and action teams in close physical proximity has proved very helpful. At a more general level, frequent use of the question "How will my actions affect participant behavior?" has been a helpful guideline for decision making by the action team. Not fruitful are unrealistic expectations such as assuming that the action team is trained in statistical inference or that it has more than a moderate appreciation of the technical research skills that will be used to analyze the experimental data.

Most social experiments involve field operations so extensive that written procedures cannot cover every situation, and virtually all experiments have crises that require immediate action. Although it is unrealistic to expect the research team to participate in all the day-to-day decision making of the field staff, there is a great danger that field decisions may be made without considering the possible impact on analysis. Consequently, mechanisms must be designed to trigger communication between the teams when important issues arise. A useful guideline to help the action team distinguish situations that are innocuous from an analytic viewpoint from those that may threaten research goals is for the action team to ask: "Will these actions affect participant behavior in a fashion not already known to be accounted for?" If the question is raised, the proper disposition will usually be clear.

Adaptability. Transformation of any experimental design into a field operation is likely to generate unanticipated consequences. Both the research design and operations plan must be adaptable. Rigid protocols are doomed to failure as the action team struggles to force human behavior into the prescribed treatment. Operations plans, carried out strictly in accordance with administratively precise procedures that later prove inappropriate, can irreversibly compromise the possibility of valid treatment comparisons before the first set of data reaches the research team.

Expecting the unexpected, the experimenter must know when to modify design or operating procedures. Standard administrative performance measures are of little help here. The goal is consistent treatment of participants, uniform application of data collection procedures, careful organization and delivery of services according to specifications, and effective early warning systems of potential flaws in the design. Unfortunately, conventional efficiency measures such as cost per unit output, number of units processed per month, or number of complaints per unit of output are of little help. Instead, the experimenter must design measures to judge the effect of operations on participant behavior and the integrity of experimental treatments, so that the manager can make "mid-course" corrections. If performance measures are ill defined or badly reported, the manager simply cannot know when to intervene. Performance measures are also needed to monitor the effect of any intervention. The manager must know if making an adjustment in one part of the system wreaks havoc with other parts. Such knowledge requires performance measures that allow sufficient oversight and control to confirm that global experimental objectives are being met.

Creating timely feedback and establishing a basis for understanding participant behavior can help in the design of such measures. At the time of the Experiment, traditional methods of data collection systems entailed considerable preparation and editing to produce machine-readable data that could be batch-processed. This time-consuming process often led to delays of many months between initial collection and analysis by the research team. In the intervening period, the manager needed mechanisms to get a quick reading on the success of data collection activities. We used devices such as weekly progress reports, periodic system audits, site observation, and analysis of hand-tallied data to provide faster feedback about the progress of experimental operations.

Quality control. Quality control systems are common to survey research and data processing—two key activities in any social experiment. Here we focus on quality control as one aspect of designing performance measures of both data quality and administration.

Quality control plays two important roles in a social experiment. Because of the long interval between data collection and analysis, field quality control operations must carry the principal burden of maintaining data quality. Most decisions regarding data quality will effectively be made at the time of collection—with little prospect for reversibility. Therefore, the research team should participate fully in designing data quality control checks and in monitoring the results.

Establishing a quality control system offers an opportunity for productive cooperation between the action and research teams. It is an especially difficult challenge for the researcher, who will be required to make judgments without having been able to analyze data in any sophisticated manner, and who may be forced to make decisions that run some risk of compromising analytic possibilities. But intensive participation by the researcher at the data collection stage of an experiment can preserve analytic options that may otherwise be unintentionally foreclosed. In addition, the greater the participation of the researcher, the better the chances for appropriately adapting to changing or unforeseen circumstances.

Quality control procedures also permit the researcher to communicate intended outcomes to the action team in a concrete manner that facilitates real understanding. Quality control instructions signal to the action team what is important in the field operation, and they help the action team react to field circumstances in a way that minimizes research risk.

Planning and managing the information flow. Experimental operations generate a large amount of information that requires prompt action, something which will be unfamiliar to many researchers. The information flow, when properly structured, can provide a written record of what has already transpired in the experiment. Especially if administration of the treatments is complex and the experiment runs for several years, it is nearly impossible for researchers to retain information needed for decision making in their memories. A written record can help counter both threats to consistent application of the experimental program and changing perspectives as the experiment matures.

A well-structured, written record helps in another way. Many decisions cannot be reduced to small, discrete issues susceptible to unilateral consideration. As a result, several parties will participate, requiring more thorough and detailed information to support the decision-making process than would be the case if decisions were made unilaterally.

The management information system should not only provide timely, relevant information but also simplify accounting for the effects of change in one part of the system on other parts. In communicating the consequences of changes in design or procedures to various teams, large-scale experiments will be forced to adopt some bureaucratic trappings; few experiments can be run in the collegial style familiar to academic researchers. The need to structure information flow, accept considerable division of labor, purposefully design communication and decision-making procedures to account for the variety of activities and actors involved, and make decisions on a timely basis must be recognized at the outset.

Skill requirements. A wide set of skills—none of them mysterious, but all of them necessary—will be drawn upon during a social experiment.

1. Financial management skills. Financial skills include budgeting, cost estimation, accounting, cash-flow management, and financial auditing. If the research or the treatments involve considerable uncertainty, as will almost certainly be the case, "the" budget is likely to consist of many budgets, adjusted over time to reflect changing costs, the operating environment, and research progress.

One key difficulty facing the experiment manager is how to trade off research possibilities in the face of uncertainty about field operation costs. Overly pessimistic cost estimates may lead a manager to cut back activities prematurely. Overly optimistic estimates may force later compromises to the research design. Thus, without careful management, cost estimates and budget realities can end up dictating the course of the experiment to a much greater degree than might be imagined. Because the manager's tradeoffs between cost and research possibilities may have more irreversible consequences than many other decisions, a high premium attaches to sound cost information. The timing of adjustments to research plans, and consequently to field operations, can profoundly affect the richness of experimental outcomes. We offer three examples of real-time design adaptations made during the Experiment to keep within a budget: reducing the ceiling on the Maximum Dollar Expenditure in the 25 percent coinsurance plans from \$1,000 to \$750, not keeping the MDE constant in real terms, and suspending administration of Health Reports to much of the sample in 1978. All these decisions had consequences for the analysis or interpretation of the data.

The most important features of a budget are good cost-estimating procedures. Cost uncertainty is likely to arise in both the administration of the experimental treatments and whatever survey activities are undertaken—

to say nothing of the cost of the research. Managing an experiment therefore involves scores of cost estimates for various components and periodic projections of the total cost. Revised budgets have to be issued frequently. The more common practice of constructing an annual budget does not suffice.

Accounting and auditing skills are also important. Especially for experiments funded with public monies, it is essential to design financial systems that are easily audited and that organize expenditures into standard systems of accounts. Owing to the peculiarities of government contracting and accounting in the United States, grants or contracts may not be audited and "closed out" until several years after expenditures have been made. Actions taken by the manager in the "heat of the battle" should be supported routinely by sound accounting practices to preclude questions of liability later.

Cash-flow management is also necessary. When large sums of money are involved, timing the transfer of funds from one agency or unit to another can have important consequences. Managing that flow wisely can effectively increase the budget of the experiment.

2. Coordination skills. Most social experiments call for skills in planning, scheduling, and project management. Not only do schedules and project plans affect costs; they inevitably dictate the pace of the analytic effort. Long-range planning should be an inherent part of the experimental design process. But just as a social experiment is likely to have many budgets, so is it likely to have many plans. The primary skill required is to integrate each component of experiment operations into the larger design of the experiment with detailed projections of resource needs, environmental constraints, task definitions, task completion times, and interrelationships.[11]

Scheduling activities will prove to be a nontrivial task, and at the very least Gantt charts and similar scheduling tools will be necessary. Many organizational units may require detailed schedules of their own, with relevant unit outputs or needed inputs forming the basis for a more global project schedule.

The particular technique used is less important than careful planning and scheduling to minimize delays and inefficiencies. All plans and schedules also require monitoring and updating, especially when operations have uncertain outcomes or when the design of future activities depends on results from preceding activities.

3. Other executive skills. Other skills that may be needed at one time or another during a social experiment include not only good written and oral communication but also public relations, personnel management, and legal services.

Because social experiments focus on people and their behavior, experimenters have invariably found it necessary to design, take part in, or at the minimum approve campaigns to "sell" their program. In announcing the undertaking to a wide audience, the experiment team will want to explain clearly their purposes, the details of treatments, the obligations of participants and cooperators, and a myriad of other details. Some programs may use multimedia campaigns to recruit participants. Researchers do not necessarily have the skill or the time to mount successful public relations campaigns. Especially when cooperation of various actors in the environment is essential, at least some team members must have good public relations skills.

Relations with the sponsor are also important. In experiments dealing with questions of public policy, the researcher may find it hard to maintain the longer-term, more reflective view of the scientist if the sponsor is pressing for shorter-term results that are directly relevant to policy. Thus, during the study the experimenter is likely to need communication skills other than those that suffice for writing journal articles or final reports.

The presence of many diverse personnel in some experiments requires more time and attention to personnel management than the researcher may be accustomed to. Also, a good deal of personnel turnover may occur in both the action and research teams over the life span of long experiments. The inevitable turnover emphasizes the need for a written record of decisions and policies. Although much of the personnel function may be delegated to others, the experiment manager is likely to spend considerable time seeing that staff members have comfortable working conditions, appropriate compensation, and challenging responsibilities. Because many people will outgrow the jobs they held at the beginning of a long experiment, the manager must provide for their growth and development and find replacements for them when they move up or leave. These functions consume a great deal of time, energy, and concern—more than a researcher may expect.

Legal skills are used throughout most social experiments. Since legal advice usually is more valuable before the trouble or problem develops than after, the experimenter should be alert to situations in which legal advice is helpful and learn how to use it. Many field operations involve routine legal processes such as obtaining business licenses, filing reports with regulatory or other administrative agencies, and checking for compliance with local laws. Because subcontracting is common in social experiments, legal aid may be needed for writing and negotiating contracts, assuring conformance with government or other sponsor procurement regulations, and resolving disputes among parties. At least in the United States, an attorney is likely to be a standard member of the experiment team.

Perhaps most important, legal help may be needed in establishing procedures to protect the confidentiality of data provided to the experiment. U.S. statutes, regulations, case law, and common practice do not provide unambiguous guidelines. Many experimenters aim to protect from third parties both the identity of participants and any personally identifiable data that they provide. In addition to its ethical desirability, such protection may reduce refusal rates and improve the quality of data provided. Except in certain narrowly defined circumstances, however, full protection is not available in the United States; information provided to an experiment can be subpoenaed and may have to be made available to others. Disclosure can be minimized, but establishment of proper procedures, including the wording of any promises of confidentiality, requires legal help.

4. Data processing capability. Data processing capability is crucial to the success of a social experiment. Data processing design and management requires:

- organization of a data base in which all data collected by the experiment are stored
- creation of a sample maintenance system to keep track of the status of individuals or institutions participating in or cooperating with the experiment
- design of a system to match the status (for example, married, divorced) of persons, families, or institutions to the data collected from them
- design of an efficient method of extracting data and status information for many different combinations of variables of interest to the researcher
- provision for dissemination of the data base to other researchers

Two types of data are typically collected in an experiment: survey data and program (treatment administration) data. Survey data include responses to self-administered questionnaires or personal interviews conducted at one time or at intervals to gather sociodemographic, economic, or attitude information. Program data include information collected in the process of administering the experimental treatment (such as medical care expenditure information and income support payments). Program data may be reported sporadically at the participant's initiative (for example, when a participant files a medical insurance claim) or collected routinely for program monitoring (for example, monthly income reporting as part of the calculation of monthly income maintenance benefits). Usually survey data are collected at the initiative of the experimenter. Although the data collection forms and procedures may be quite varied, at some point the data need to be archived in a consistent, easy-to-access, machine-readable form. This is a significant task that requires skills in data base design and management.

An even greater challenge is to design a sample maintenance system for keeping track of the status of each participant. At any particular point a number of variables (for example, age, gender, employment status, marital status, location) define a person's status for the analyst. During an experiment the status of individuals may change, and rather more frequently than one might expect. For example, people may move or change jobs, become separated or divorced, have children, decide to leave the experiment, or die.

The design of such a tracking system is enormously important to an experiment's success. For example, suppose a three-person family is receiving health insurance benefits as an experimental treatment. The benefits are related to family income and are paid when a member of the family files a health insurance claim. During the course of a year the family splits up and forms two new families, one with two members and one with one member. However, no one informs the experiment of the split until later. In the meantime the experiment has paid some health insurance claims as if the original family were intact. Once the experiment learns of the change in family composition, how does it identify data collected between the time of the change and when it learned of the change?

Alternative associations of family status with the program data present different pictures to the researcher. The ideal system provides information that enables the researcher to define family status in the manner most appropriate to the specific analysis at hand. However, providing for a wide range of options is complicated and imposes additional costs.

Even with a good data base design and sample maintenance system, researchers confront the problem of matching the program and survey data to relevant participant status variables. Generally, the program data collection system cannot gather a full range of sociodemographic information (status variables) every time some program information is collected (for example, is the participant employed on a certain date?). Some of this information will have been gathered from survey data or from periodic checks of program data. Typically, the analyst faces uncertainty in associating data gathered from one form at one point in time with data gathered from another form at another point in time. The better the system for matching dates to status variables (that is, for tracking status across time), the higher the quality of analysis.

Most experiments have analytic agendas requiring different combinations of data for different analytic tasks. Even given consistent, efficient storage of data and ready matching to status variables, researchers must be able to extract different combinations of data for different tasks easily and cheaply.

In the United States, one of the selling points of experimentation has been the creation of large, longitudinal data bases that other researchers can eventually use to validate or extend the experiment's findings for use in research on new topics. This value is lost if later researchers find it prohibitively expensive or complex to extract data for their own uses.

Tips for the Prospective Experimenter

Create a pilot sample. When purchasing a fleet of new aircraft, it is wise to "fly before you buy"—to develop a prototype to determine cost and feasibility before committing to a full-scale production run. Similar considerations apply to social experimentation.

Typically feeling pressed to produce results as soon as possible, the experimenter may be tempted to proceed rapidly with implementation of the full study. Nevertheless, even if data from a pilot sample will not be useful for formal analysis, as will usually be the case, such a sample, preceding the regular sample by several months, has other important uses: In particular, a pilot sample can:

1. Establish the feasibility of enrolling participants. It may even be possible to estimate two or three points on a "supply curve" of participants—that is, discover how the refusal rate varies as a function of payments or obligations required of participants. Such knowledge may prevent either excessive refusal rates or excessively high payments to participants to induce them to enroll. Techniques for enrolling participants may also be tested.
2. Establish the ability to resolve procedural and definitional difficulties with the treatment, such as apparent legal problems. For example, when

we began the Experiment, we did not know whether it would be subject to state insurance regulation, and if so, what the consequences would be. (In fact the Experiment was not subject to insurance regulations, since no premiums were paid.)

3. Provide a population for pretesting interviews and other data collection instruments—an axiomatic procedure in survey design.

The pilot sample should be used to test operational feasibility but should not be expected to serve as the first step in a sequential experimental design. There is a good chance that the experimenter will wish to change the protocol (and maybe even the treatment) after obtaining the pilot sample. (Indeed, we made such changes even after obtaining the regular sample; see Chapter 2.) Thus data from the pilot sample are unlikely to be comparable to data generated later.

Build in an ability to measure effects that are an artifact of the experiment (methods or Hawthorne effects). At the conclusion of an experiment, those conducting it can expect to face the common criticism that participant behavior might have been different in a real program because experiments and programs differ, if only in the amount of data collection. Anticipating that criticism, the experimenter can often build into the experimental design, at relatively little expense, the ability to detect and measure effects that may be peculiar to the experiment (see Chapters 2 and 3), and so insulate the estimated outcomes from artifactual distortions.

Design the experiment to keep refusal and attrition low. The desirability of keeping refusal and attrition at low levels is obvious, the means to do so less obvious. One useful strategy is to design the experiment so that no one is financially worse off as a result of participating. In addition, payment for interviews can compensate the participant for the time and trouble taken to provide data. Any payments made to minimize refusal and attrition rates, however, cannot be conditional upon behavior the experimenter seeks to measure, if the results are to be free of bias.

Do not attempt to eliminate all bias. Although an experimental design must try to keep refusal and attrition—and thus possible bias—at a low level, it is almost certainly not desirable to attempt to eliminate all bias: the expense entailed is likely to be high, and the money used to reduce additional small sources of bias could probably be used to greater advantage elsewhere.

Bias can arise in an attempt to ensure that the distribution of families within treatments is as similar as possible for each treatment. To achieve this balance, it is necessary to collect and process information about candidate families, and return to them later with an offer to participate in a specified program. Unresolved issues of sampling are raised if the family's composition changes in the interim (someone moves in with the family, the heads separate, the family moves out of the area; see Morris, Newhouse, and Archibald 1979 for detailed discussion of these problems). For this and other reasons it is virtually impossible in practice to maintain an unbiased sample frame. To do so would require following families who move from the area. Although that may be practical once the families have been enrolled in the experiment (using self-administered interview instruments), it is expensive to do so prior to enrollment. The amount of bias, if any, introduced in the sample by not following movers out of the area prior to enrollment (and, say, substituting in the sample the family that has moved into the dwelling) is almost certain to be small in most applications; it therefore does not make sense to use funds to eliminate it.

Balance the sample across treatments unless there are strong reasons not to. Balancing the sample—ensuring that the characteristics of participants assigned to each treatment are as similar as possible to those of participants assigned to other treatments—will minimize the need to adjust for differences across experimental treatments in the analysis phase. We used the Finite Selection Model for this purpose, as described in Chapter 2, and commend its use to others.

Do not strongly oversample a group whose membership is not well defined. The experimenter is often especially interested in a program's effect on one particular subgroup of a population—in our case, low-income families. It is appropriate to oversample the subgroup of interest (the favored group) if it can be defined with little error (for example, people over 65). But if a favored group can be defined a priori only with substantial error (for example, families who will consistently have annual incomes under $5,000), disproportionate sampling can reduce the experimenter's precision of estimation, even for the favored group (Morris, Newhouse, and Archibald 1979). We recommend that the experimenter ascertain the reliability of any measures used for disproportionate sampling before setting sampling fractions, and that sampling fractions not depart far from proportionality if the classification contains nontrivial measurement error.

Inform participants as fully and clearly as possible about the treatment. Informed consent should be an ethical precept for an experimenter. It is also a matter of self-interest. First, informing the participants fully at enrollment about the details of an experimental treatment will help minimize refusal rates and attrition. Refusals should be few because proper experimental design and full information should make it clearly in the participant's interest to participate. Attrition should be low because participants will receive no unpleasant surprises after enrollment. Second, the experiment will almost certainly last for only a limited time (rarely more than a few years). If behavior under the experiment is to be generalized to behavior under some kind of permanent or open-ended program, it is important that participants understand the experiment as fully as they will the later programs.

Do not attempt too much. Most experiments have multiple objectives and use interdisciplinary research teams. Data gathered to serve one discipline or type of analysis may not be suitable for another. Because resources are scarce, tradeoffs are inevitable. The needs of the sponsor, the skills and preferences of the analyst, and the feasibility of alternative courses of action inevitably affect decisions about allocating resources. But attempting to do too much with one experiment poses the risk of accomplishing too little. The experiment manager should concentrate principally upon data collection activities that support sound analysis of treatment comparisons. Only after that is assured should one invest in potentially interesting methodological studies or auxiliary data use.

Such a warning sounds banal. But our experience suggests that the unique setting of most social experiments can induce those responsible for managing it to overextend themselves. And once activated, the cycle of mistakes can be unforgiving. An increased research agenda usually demands increased field operations. In all social experiments we know about, operation staffs have functioned under extreme time pressure and severe budget constraints. If the research agenda is not carefully defined and controlled, performance in field operations can deteriorate severely. Indeed, the field operations may not be able to recover from an overambitious research design, thus risking contamination of the primary treatment comparisons.

An experimenter should resist the powerful temptation to collect too much data. In a multiyear research project it may not be clear at the outset what the ultimate budget constraint really is.[12] Thus, the temptation to allocate the early-year resources disproportionately to data collection on the assumption that one can always find money later to analyze the data can be hard to resist. Budget constraints have a way of becoming more rather than less limiting; resources may simply not be available later to analyze the rich data collected early on.

The problem of underestimating the budget constraint is compounded by the difficulty of keeping the research team together near the end of the project. Team members may well seek or accept employment before the analysis has been completed. Thus, the analyst who argued passionately for collecting some specific piece of data at the beginning may have simply disappeared by the time the research plan called for analyzing the data, and those remaining may not be able or willing to perform the necessary analysis.

The problems of keeping a team together at the end of an experiment are compounded by lack of professional rewards for documenting data and producing public use files. It is certainly more stimulating intellectually, and perhaps more lucrative, for the researcher to move on to a new research project rather than document data files from the experiment. But any failure to document compounds the problem of team members' leaving the project early, because their expertise may not be duplicated among the remaining members.

Other powerful forces also push the experimenter to overallocate funds to data collection early in the project. There may well be uncertainty about just what data may ultimately be wanted for the analysis, and a decision not to collect something is often irreversible. Thus, there is a temptation to collect the data "just in case."

We certainly did not entirely avoid overcollecting data. For example, several of our analyses in this book do not include data from some of the later sites and years, especially the South Carolina sites, which have not been fully analyzed.[13] Although the temptation to collect too much data is virtually unavoidable, it can be mitigated by requiring that the research team have a written analytic plan for all data being collected. Such a plan not only protects against unnecessary data collection but also may identify other data that need to be collected.

Chapter 11

Central Findings and Policy Implications

The effects of cost sharing on health care service use and health status was the central focus of the Experiment. This chapter summarizes our findings on the effects of cost sharing in the fee-for-service sector and their principal policy implications; our findings on use and health status differences between an HMO environment and fee-for-service medicine, and *their* principal policy implications; and the lessons that our results suggest for health care financing.

Effects of Cost Sharing

Effects on Use

In the Experiment we observed the consequences of varying the amount of initial cost sharing — that is, the amount families (excluding the elderly) had to pay out-of-pocket for medical services up to a specified annual limit.

The more families had to pay out of pocket, the fewer medical services they used. Families on the plan with the most cost sharing had to pay 95 cents of every dollar (95 percent coinsurance) up to a $1,000 limit (which did not rise with inflation from 1974 to 1982) on annual family out-of-pocket expenditure. The limit was reduced for low-income families. This amount of cost sharing reduced expenditure about 25 to 30 percent relative to a plan in which care was free to the family (Chapter 3).

All types of service — physician visits, hospital admissions, prescriptions, dental visits, and mental health service use — fell with cost sharing. There were no striking differences among these services in how their use responded to plan, with the exception of hospital admissions of children, which did not respond to plan. Another partial exception was demand for

338

mental health services—which, the results indicate, would have been more responsive than other services to cost sharing had there been no cap on out-of-pocket expenditure.

Responsiveness matters because of the standard economic argument that services for which demand is less responsive should have less cost sharing (Ramsey 1927; Baumol and Bradford 1970; Zeckhauser 1970; Besley 1988).[1] Thus, with the possible exception of mental health services, our results suggest that decisions about how much to cover various services need not be importantly influenced by the responsiveness of demand to coverage.[2] Rather, such decisions should be influenced by other factors such as the loading charge or administrative cost of covering the service more or less extensively compared with the amount of risk borne by the family. Coverage of hospital expenses fares well on this criterion; coverage of routine office care services does not. Perhaps this is why hospital expenditures have historically been better covered than routine office expenditures. Some have argued that covering the more intensive services better than the less intensive services has the perverse effect of increasing total expenditure by raising the relative use of the more expensive (hospital) service. Our results do not support this argument; with hospital coverage held constant, better coverage of office services increases total expenditure (Chapter 3).

Effects on Health

The reduced service use under the cost-sharing plans had little or no net adverse effect on health for the average person (Chapters 6 and 7). Indeed, restricted activity days fell with more cost sharing.

Health among the sick poor—approximately the most disadvantaged 6 percent of the population—was adversely affected, however. In particular, the poor who began the Experiment with elevated blood pressure had their blood pressure lowered more on the free care plan than on the cost-sharing plans. The effect on predicted mortality rates—a fall of about 10 percent—was substantial for this group. In addition, free care marginally improved both near and far corrected vision, primarily among the poor, and increased the likelihood that a decayed tooth would be filled—an effect found disproportionately among the less well educated. Health of gums was marginally better for those with free care. And serious symptoms were less prevalent on the free plan, especially for those who began the Experiment poor and with serious symptoms. Finally, there appeared to be a beneficial effect on anemia for poor children. Although sample sizes made it impossible to detect any beneficial effects that free care might have had on relatively rare conditions, it is highly improbable that there were beneficial effects (one standard error of the mean changes) that we failed to detect in the physiologic measures of health taken as a group. Moreover, the confidence intervals are tight enough to rule out any important beneficial effect of free care on the General Health Index, our best summary measure of health. Measures of pain and worry also showed little or no effect of plan.

Effects on Different Income Groups

The percentage reduction in expenditure caused by cost sharing did not differ strikingly by income group, but which services fell did. Ambulatory services were more responsive to cost sharing for the poor than for the well-to-do; the opposite was true for hospital services (Chapter 3).

The ultimate test of a reduction in use, however, is its effect on outcomes, and these did differ by income group.[3]

How a Large Increase in Demand Would Affect Rationing of Services

When we began planning the Experiment, policymakers were talking simultaneously about the possibility of a national health insurance plan with no cost sharing and a physician shortage. In this environment, it was clear that free medical care would lead to additional nonprice rationing of services, but little was known about the rationing—who might be let into a physician's office and how that person might be treated (Newhouse, Phelps, and Schwartz 1974).

In the early 1990s there is much talk about physician glut and less advocacy of plans with no cost sharing. Thus, concern about excess demand has changed into concern about excess supply, although many experts believe that the excess supply is limited to specialists and that there are still too few primary care physicians (Schroeder 1992). In this environment it is sensible to ask the reverse question of the one we started with: If physicians were to become more plentiful relative to demand, how would patterns of care change?

We studied this question by conducting an observational study within the Experiment—choosing sites that differed markedly in the number of days one had to wait for an appointment with a primary care physician.

Our interest in appointment delays stemmed from Canadian experience, which suggested that delays were a key mechanism for rationing services when cost sharing was reduced (Enterline et al. 1973).

Despite substantial variation across sites in waiting times, there were few differences by site in the responsiveness of use to plan (Chapter 3).[4] However, the likelihood of going to the emergency room was higher in sites where it was more difficult to see a primary care physician. Thus, if the supply of primary care physicians grows relative to demand and if nothing else changes—especially the amount and nature of insurance coverage and the sociodemographic makeup of the population—we would forecast a reduction in emergency room use.

Policy Implications

Because publication of our results began in December 1981 and continued steadily through the 1980s, their policy implications have already taken shape in practice. As the results emerged, large employers substantially increased initial cost sharing, especially cost sharing for hospital services, and also made more frequent use of stop-loss provisions like the Maximum Dollar Expenditure (Table 11.1). Whether these changes were a direct effect of the Experiment's results must remain a largely speculative issue; but we do have some anecdotal evidence that our findings may have influenced increased initial cost sharing. For example, the Xerox Corporation in 1983 increased its annual deductible from $100 per person or $200 per family to 1 percent of earnings per family and its coinsurance from zero to 20 percent, and decreased the maximum out-of-pocket expense from 6 percent of earnings to 4 percent of earnings. In explaining the charges to its employees, it said in a brochure:

> Experience indicates that when employees share in the costs of services, they help to avoid uneconomical and unnecessary medical care . . . Recent research has demonstrated that the patient/consumer can have an impact on medical costs. According to a study by the RAND Corporation, when consumers are required to increase their share of medical costs, there is a significant decrease in the total amount spent for these services. Furthermore, this study—and other similar studies—does not indicate that the health of the employees was affected adversely by the decrease in costs.

It is equally plausible that the Experiment contributed to the increased use over this period of stop-loss features like the MDE. Such caps increase the effective coverage of large bills, which may explain why the percentage of hospital expenditure paid out of pocket did not change much in this period, despite the increased initial cost sharing. In particular, the percentage of the hospital bill paid out of pocket rose only from 7.6 percent in 1982 to 8.7 percent in 1984 (Levit et al. 1985),[5] whereas the percentage of physician bills paid out of pocket in these two years actually fell from 27 to 22 percent. The latter change reflects two trends—more policies covering physician services as well as additional stop-loss provisions.

The higher initial cost sharing would have been expected to decrease hospital admissions, and indeed admission rates among persons under 65 dropped substantially after 1983 (Table 11.2). How much of the drop should be attributed to the increased cost sharing is difficult to say, but the Experiment results suggest that at least some part of it should be.

If a linkage does exist between publication of the Experiment's results and increased initial cost sharing, the Experiment affected hospital use in the United States through a reduction in admissions. But there may have been other causes of this reduction. Medicare's Prospective Payment

Table 11.1   Elements of insurance plan changes, 1980–1984

Elements	% of plans sampled		
	1980	1982	1984
Plans requiring front-end deductible for inpatient hospital charges	—	30	63
Plans requiring front-end deductible for inpatient surgical charges	—	34	59
Plans with an annual deductible of $200 or more per family[a]	—	4	21
Plans paying 100% of first day's stay in hospital	—	67	42
Plans paying 100% of surgical fee	—	42	26
Group major medical plans with limits on out-of-pocket expense	78	—	98

Sources: Hewitt Associates, "Company Practices in Health Care Cost Management—1984," cited in Goldsmith (1984); 1,185 companies sampled. Group major medical plans with limits: Health Insurance Association of America (1980, 1986).

a. The Wyatt Company (1986), in a survey of 1,185 firms (though possibly not a different survey), gives the following data on the percentage of comprehensive major medical plans with deductibles (strictly) greater than $100: in 1982, 9%; in 1984, 39%; in 1986, 55%.

Table 11.2   Hospital admission rates (per 1,000 civilian resident population) among persons under 65, excluding deliveries, by year

Year	Age group		
	0–14	15–44	45–64
1975	70.1	119.0	191.6
1976	69.9	117.2	192.0
1977	71.5	121.7	195.0
1978	66.9	117.2	189.4
1979	70.5	116.4	191.8
1980	71.3	114.2	194.7
1981	72.6	111.9	195.2
1982	70.9	108.4	195.5
1983	70.6	103.9	192.2
1984	61.7	97.3	183.3
1985	57.0	90.7	169.4
1986	53.3	85.8	162.2
1987	51.1	81.0	156.9
1988	49.0	71.2	140.5

Sources: National Center for Health Statistics, *Utilization of Short Stay Hospitals: Annual Summary for the United States*, National Health Survey, Series 13, nos. 31, 37, 41, 46, 60, 64, 72, 78, 83, 84, 91, 96, 99, and 106 (DHHS pub. nos. HRA 77–1782, PHS 78–1788, 79–1792, 80–1797, 82–1721, 82–1725, 83–1733, 84–1739, 85–1744, 86–1745, 87–1752, 88–1757, 89–1760, 91–1767). Data on civilian resident population, 1975–1980: National Center for Health Statistics, *Adjustment of Hospital Utilization Rates*, National Health Survey, Series 13, no. 81, 1984 (DHHS pub. no. PHS 85–1742) (Washington, D.C.: U.S. Government Printing Office).

System (PPS), which began to be phased in during October 1983, was associated with a reduction in admissions among the over-65. This drop—a surprise to the many analysts who expected the opposite—is usually attributed to the review of over-65 admissions done by the peer review organizations employed by Medicare for this purpose. Although these organizations did not review admissions among the privately insured under-65 group, their influence could have spilled over to this group. Alternatively, an under-65 effect from additional cost sharing could have spilled over to the over-65 group. That PPS was not the only cause of the decline is suggested by the much greater fall in admissions among the under-65 group, to whom the Medicare PPS did not apply.[6] For example, from 1980 through 1986 admission rates among the over-65 fell by only 4 percent, in contrast to 23 percent among the under-65 (National Center for Health Statistics 1990, table 70; U.S. Bureau of the Census 1991, table 22).

Whatever the cause of the admission decline, it clearly saved many billions of dollars. Total expenditure on hospital care among the under-65 was approximately $127 billion in 1987 (Waldo et al. 1989). Even if the percentage reduction in cost was much less than the 23 percent reduction in admissions, the savings surely accounted for billions of dollars annually.

Was this reduction a good thing? Or did the benefits forgone exceed the costs saved? The Experiment results imply that for the average person the cost in terms of health outcomes was minimal, but three additional points should be made in this connection:

1. We observed certain adverse health consequences in the Experiment from cost sharing, concentrated among the sick poor. The majority of the employed population, however, is neither sick nor poor. As a result, we can virtually rule out any substantial adverse effect among the group subject to increased initial cost sharing.

2. For those with chronic health problems—and many among the group subject to increased cost sharing have such problems—any increase in initial cost sharing repeats year after year. Some regard it as unfair to subject those whose health forces them to use health care to pay more out of pocket. Economists may term this a market failure—that is, a difference in initial endowments of health that should be insurable.[7] For example, a healthy young adult just entering the labor force may wish to insure against the costs of developing later in life a chronic disease that will require ongoing treatment. It is possible to provide some protection, for example by waiving a deductible if it is satisfied frequently enough, but doing so will dilute the cost savings.[8]

3. It may well be that the health benefits among the sick and poor could be achieved at substantially lower cost than free care for all services. This is almost surely the case for the vision and dental effects. An insurance benefit covering only those services can obtain the health gains, if they are worth their costs, without incurring the costs of covering all other medical services. High blood pressure, however, poses a more difficult problem. Efforts targeted at hypertension reduction might achieve some of the benefits that free care did, though certainly not all, as we discuss below.

Subject to these limitations, discussed in more detail later in the chapter, our results suggest that the increases in initial cost sharing among the employed population and the concomitant fall in admissions were warranted.

Increased initial cost sharing is unlikely to affect the rate of cost increases in the health care system, however, other than temporarily. Initial cost sharing and a stop-loss feature seem unlikely to change much the steady-state rate of expenditure increase, which appears mainly to reflect the enhanced capabilities of medicine (Newhouse 1992).

Our results also seem to have had implications for public programs, especially the Medicaid program, which covers many poor individuals: since 1982 federal law has permitted nominal cost sharing in the Medicaid program; before 1982 cost sharing was permitted in only a limited number of demonstration projects.[9]

Policymakers and experts take one of two basic positions on the issue of nominal cost sharing in Medicaid. Those on the political left tend to argue that it should be eliminated. This position assumes that health benefits for the sick poor justify the costs of free care, and that the cost sharing now present in the Medicaid program is not "in the neighborhood" of free care in its effect on use. Those on the political right tend to advocate at least token cost sharing and reject one or both of the assumptions above. There seems to be no advocacy for increasing the amount of real cost sharing in Medicaid.

Clearly, our results show a greater effect on health outcomes among the sick poor (and among all poor children in the case of anemia). Whether the health effects we found among the sick poor justify free care for that group, we leave to others to decide.[10]

The issue of allowing some individuals to remain completely uninsured seems much more serious, irrespective of one's views on nominal cost sharing in Medicaid.[11] Strictly speaking, our results have nothing to say about uninsured individuals, because all groups in the Experiment were insured. Nonetheless, the outcome differences we found between the free and the cost-sharing plans would presumably be still greater between the free plan and lack of any insurance; some evidence suggests they could be much greater (Lurie et al. 1984, 1986). We return to this point later.

We cannot say much about cost sharing among those over 65, because Medicare eligibles were excluded from our sample. We would speculate that our findings apply to the younger elderly because we detected no difference in the responses of those in our sample who were close to age 65 and those who were younger. It is, however, problematic to generalize our findings to the older old with multiple chronic problems.

Health Management Organization Results

Selection

Subject to the crucial qualification that we studied only a single, well-established staff model HMO, the Experiment results are quite clear: there was negligible or no risk selection at the HMO. Utilization among a group previously using fee-for-service care but randomly assigned to the HMO during the Experiment was similar to that of a group that had chosen to enroll in the HMO.

Effects of Reduced Use on Health Outcomes and Patient Satisfaction

Among comparable groups of individuals with comparable benefits randomly assigned to the HMO and to the fee-for-service system, the HMO group had 39 percent fewer hospital admissions and 28 percent lower estimated expenditures (Chapter 8). Preventive service use was higher among both groups at the HMO.

For people in good health at enrollment in the Experiment, we observed little difference at the end of the Experiment between those in the HMO and those in the fee-for-service system. There were more work loss days in the HMO group, however, for all but the sick poor (Chapter 9).

For individuals in poor health some differences appeared between the HMO and the fee-for-service groups, and they seemed to go in opposite directions among high- and low-income individuals. The low-income sick assigned to the HMO had significantly more bed days (about 3.5 per person per year) and a greater prevalence of serious symptoms (about 13 percentage points more) than did their counterparts in the fee-for-service system. The bed day result, however, may have been an anomaly because an analysis of restricted activity days did not support the bed days result (Chapter 9). Thus, the poor sick may have had worse outcomes at the HMO, but the evidence supporting that view is thin.[12]

The high-income sick, by contrast, did better at the HMO than did their fee-for-service counterparts, with a difference of 7 scale points in the General Health Index. (A difference of 5 points is equivalent to a diagnosis of hypertension, other factors equal.) There were no significant differences in measures of physical, mental, or social health. High-income individuals with high cholesterol levels receiving care at the HMO reduced those levels 16.7mg/dl more than comparable persons receiving care in the fee-for-service system. Differences in smoking habits, though not statistically significant, also favored the HMO.

Individuals who were already enrolled at the HMO at the beginning of the Experiment gained about two points more on the General Health Index during the Experiment than those whom we randomly assigned to the HMO. This result may have reflected a better ability to use services at the HMO. No other differences in outcomes could be detected between the group who selected the HMO and the group we randomly assigned to it.

Patient satisfaction for individuals who selected the HMO was on average similar to satisfaction for individuals in the fee-for-service system. For individuals whom we randomly assigned to the HMO, however, satisfaction was less.

Satisfaction with HMO care also differed according to the dimension of care being rated. Two dimensions—waits at the office and costs of care—were rated more favorably by both groups at the HMO than by those in the fee-for-service system, but several other dimensions, including appointment waits, availability of hospitals, access to specialists, and continuity of care, were rated more favorably in the fee-for-service system.[13] Interpersonal aspects of care at the HMO were also rated less well by those who were randomly assigned to it, and this factor carried a large weight in their overall rating of satisfaction with services.

Policy Implications

The implications of the HMO results are necessarily more tentative than those pertaining to cost sharing because the Experiment was designed primarily to look at cost sharing in the fee-for-service system and only secondarily to answer questions about HMOs. As a result, only one HMO was studied, and the sample assigned to the HMO was much smaller than the sample used in the fee-for-service portion of the Experiment. The results are correspondingly less precise.

These qualifications, especially that we studied only one HMO, are important. Nonetheless, the results give encouragement to group and staff model HMOs. Cost savings are apparent, and, with the possible exception of those poor who began the Experiment in ill health, these savings do not appear to cause negative health effects. Confidence intervals on outcome effects for the average person are reasonably narrow, indicating that, despite the small sample size, we did not miss important effects.

Implications for the private sector. Membership in HMOs grew from about 5 percent of the population in 1980 to 7 percent in 1984 and to 13 percent in 1989, although little of the growth occurred at staff or group model HMOs of the type we studied (National Center for Health Statistics 1990). The role played by publication of the Experiment's results in bringing about this growth is, however, problematic; HMO utilization results were not released until June 1984, initial health status results in May 1986, and child health status results in 1989.

The results on patient satisfaction, however, suggest why the market share for traditional group and staff model HMOs is still far below 50 percent even in those areas where they are readily available. Many individuals prefer greater choice of physicians, and particularly specialists, than group or staff model HMOs offer. How much more individuals are willing to pay to obtain this greater choice we do not know. This continuing small market share and our satisfaction results however, make it seem unlikely that most individuals will choose to enroll in a staff or group model HMO.[14]

The growth of so-called point-of-service plans and preferred provider organizations is consistent with our findings. In these arrangements a person who seeks care outside the organization can usually have most of the expense reimbursed, whereas in a traditional group or staff model HMO none of it is reimbursed. This difference would clearly appeal to someone concerned about access to specialty care and hospitals. Whether these new arrangements can achieve cost savings comparable to those of group and staff model HMOs is still an open question.

Implications for the public sector. Many states are now making efforts to channel Medicaid enrollees into capitated or HMO-like arrangements. Although our findings about the sick poor might appear at first to raise a note of caution about this initiative, such a conclusion does not necessarily follow, because the Experiment's fee-for-service plans paid physicians at market rates, whereas Medicaid typically does not. Thus, even if one were to interpret our results as showing that the free fee-for-service plan was better than the HMO plan for the sick poor, one could not infer that fee-for-service Medicaid with its below-market rates would be better for this group.

Our results do suggest that healthy Medicaid beneficiaries enrolled in group or staff model HMOs will use fewer services with little or no adverse effect on health. Most of the population receiving Aid to Families with

Dependent Children (AFDC) may fit the description of poor but healthy. Many of the disabled and medically needy, however, do not; and the AFDC population accounts for only just over half of the Medicaid dollars spent on hospital and physician services in 1989 (that is, excluding chronic long-term care in nursing homes and institutional care for the mentally retarded), and about one-quarter of total Medicaid spending. Finally, even if the sick poor did better in fee-for-service plans—and we regard our evidence as only suggestive—and even if the gains were large enough to justify the additional cost, our HMO results among the sick poor might have been better had special outreach programs been implemented.

Because of these caveats, and because our results come entirely from one HMO, we believe that programs to enroll Medicaid beneficiaries in capitated organizations should be implemented in a way that enables the new arrangements to be evaluated against the traditional Medicaid program. Ideally, states would employ some type of randomized design—for example, keeping a group on conventional Medicaid—in an effort to learn more about the effects of capitation in this segment of the population before rushing wholesale into capitation.

Implications of the Findings for the Debate over Free Medical Care

The Debate at the Start of the Experiment

In the early 1970s, at the beginning of the Experiment, many American economists considered the issue of free medical care in terms of the tradeoff between inefficiency or moral hazard (that is, induced overconsumption) and risk protection (that is, the desire of individuals to be insured against large financial losses) (Arrow 1968; Pauly 1968; Zeckhauser 1970; Feldstein 1973). These economists typically concluded that there should be some initial cost sharing and some upper limit on out-of-pocket losses; most of these arguments were theoretical rather than empirical. The results in Chapter 4 on the value of risk protection support this conclusion in two ways: (1) the gains in reduced risk from eliminating initial cost sharing are modest, and (2) limiting out-of-pocket expense yields a large gain in reduced risk relative to no insurance (see Table 4.21).

An additional argument for cost sharing in the form of initial deductibles was that such cost sharing preserves the competitive properties of markets: it weeds out costly suppliers, provided most consumers do not satisfy the deductible and therefore remain sensitive to price differences among suppliers (Newhouse 1981). Existing markets that fit this definition include those for eyeglasses and retail prescription drugs; many insurance policies do not cover eyeglasses and drugs, and even if they do, the deductible is often not satisfied.

The case for initial cost sharing, however, has never been universally accepted. Some economists, especially outside the United States, emphasized that benefits from one person's consumption of medical care can also accrue to others because you may feel remorseful enough about my inability to pay for care to subsidize my medical services (Lindsey 1969; Culyer 1971; Evans 1984).[15] Unfortunately, they provided no direct evidence of the magnitude of any such externalities. (Some even appeared to make the tautological argument that the existence of free care in countries such as the United Kingdom must mean that the externalities are large enough to justify free care.) Nonetheless, this group maintained that one could not presume overconsumption simply from the existence of a subsidy.[16]

Other economists who favored free care emphasized consumer ignorance rather than externalities, arguing that consumer ignorance removes the presumption that the additional services in the free plan are of little value. They offered two possible reasons for this stance. First, consumers might need to be induced to consume more medical care for their own good. This paternalistic logic was applied especially to cost sharing for ambulatory care. The feared scenario was that persons might put off seeking care at an early stage of illness because of ignorance, when intervention might be more effective and treatment less costly (Roemer et al. 1975). Second, consumer ignorance might permit physicians to prompt demand that an informed consumer would not want; that is, the physician might act as an imperfect agent for the patient. Such services might well be of little value, but nonetheless observed demand could not be taken as a valid indicator of what demand for medical services "should" be.

Finally, advocacy groups argued that medical care is a right and therefore that medical services, or at least efficacious medical services, should be free at the time of use. Put into economic terms, this argument has analogies with the externalities argument about the benefits to others of one individual's consumption of medical care.[17]

The Experiment sought to cut through these abstract arguments by measuring both the cost and the health benefits of initial cost sharing versus those of free care. If cost proved minimal or health benefits large, the scale would tip toward free care. Conversely, if the health benefits of free care were minimal, one could infer that externalities would be less important and paternalism would be unnecessary. Hence there would be a stronger argument for cost sharing.

In fact the Experiment provides some support for both free care and initial cost sharing. For most individuals the cost of free care seems substantial and health benefits minimal. As a result, there is a good case for initial cost sharing for the majority of the population. But for the 6 percent of our sample who were both sick and poor, the health benefits of free care were measurable. These findings prompt the question: Is it feasible to have cost sharing for most individuals but (1) to exempt the conditions for which free care shows measurable benefits over insurance with cost sharing or (2) to exempt the poor from cost sharing?

Exemptions for the Sick?

With the exception of our findings on serious symptoms, which may be a chance result,[18] all the beneficial effects of free care that we detected share the following characteristics:

- They occur for relatively common conditions.[19]
- The standard diagnostic test is relatively inexpensive (for example, measuring blood pressure, giving a vision refraction, taking an X-ray of a tooth).
- The treatment is well-known, inexpensive, and efficacious relative to the treatment of many medical conditions.

In such circumstances could programs targeted at these conditions achieve the benefits we identified at lower cost than free care for all conditions?

The answer is that it depends on the condition. Dental and vision care contrast sharply with hypertension.

For dental and vision care, the benefits observed on the free plan could almost certainly be achieved more cheaply with a targeted benefit—that is, free care for just these conditions.[20] First, dental or vision problems are often assessed by specific providers (for example, dentists, ophthalmologists, optometrists), so free care across the board would not be necessary to identify the problems.[21] Second, because the treatment is not transferable from one condition to another, there is no temptation for the service provider to distort the diagnosis in order to enable the patient to be reimbursed. If well care or mental health care is not covered, for example, there is a natural temptation for a service provider to substitute a covered diagnosis with similar treatment courses for an uncovered one. The issue for policymakers is not whether a targeted benefit would achieve the gains we identified; it would. Rather, the issue is whether the modest gains we found under free care justify the cost of a targeted benefit.[22]

In sharp contrast to vision and dental care, the Experiment results make it highly unlikely that an insurance benefit for hypertensives alone could reduce high blood pressure as much as free care for all. Virtually all the improvement in blood pressure control brought about by free care occurred as a result of better identification of hypertensives (Chapter 6). Control, once the person was diagnosed, was not measurably affected by cost sharing. Thus, free care—by inducing individuals to have more contact with physicians for reasons potentially unrelated to hypertension— raised the likelihood of detection in a way that a specific benefit for hypertensives would not.

The Experiment can also shed some light on the benefits of screening the population for high blood pressure. The Experiment divided those in the cost-sharing plans into two groups: one group was randomly assigned to a screening examination at enrollment and was tested for blood pressure at that time; those in the other group did not receive an initial screening exam. Three to five years later, the screened group had lower diastolic pressure than those in the other group—an improvement that was more than half as large as the improvement caused by free care (Chapter 6) for a much lower cost than free medical care. These results indicate that a screening examination might be an attractive alternative to free care. The problem is that large-scale screening for hypertension is not cost effective in general populations (Weinstein and Stason 1976). Screening programs in communities with a high prevalence of the disease, such as black communities, however, have much higher cost-effectiveness ratings than screening programs in general populations, provided proper followup and treatment are done; thus some targeted screening programs may well be desirable.

Exemptions for the Poor?

If it is difficult to target a benefit for hypertensives, what would be the effect of eliminating cost sharing for the poor? In answering this question we start from the premise that substantial cost sharing for the poor is simply not an option. Rather, the choice is one between little or no cost sharing for the poor and free or nearly free care for everyone.

Exempting the poor from cost sharing is clearly possible—as the Medicaid program demonstrates—but it raises several well-known issues. First, exempting the poor may imply identification procedures that are demeaning or stigmatizing. We gathered no evidence on this issue. But it is worth noting that the degree of stigma may well depend on whether there is an entirely separate program for the poor, as in Medicaid, or income-related cost sharing in a more universal plan.[23]

A second well-known issue is the "notch" problem. A strict cutoff, based on income, for defining who is eligible for free care provides a strong incentive not to cross just above the cutoff, because the value of the forgone free care exceeds the small additional income from being above the cutoff. In effect, there is a much greater than 100 percent tax rate on the first dollar of income above the cutoff. This problem has historically existed for Medicaid benefits. A woman receiving AFDC assistance who contemplates taking a job without health insurance would be foolish not to weigh heavily the cost of losing her Medicaid benefits. Recent modifications to federal law provide a temporary continuation of Medicaid benefits in this situation, but after these benefits expire, the notch returns.

One can avoid a strict cutoff by tapering benefits as income rises, but the effect is to impose a tax rate on income over and above formal income tax rates. Consider a family in the Experiment plans with a Maximum Dollar Expenditure (MDE) of 10 percent of income. For this family, earning an additional $10 raises the MDE by $1; hence there is a tax on the $10 of income equal to $1 times the probability of exceeding the MDE (the tax comes out to something less than 10 percent).

Thus the implicit tax outcome associated with tapering benefits increases any distortions or inefficiencies from taxes in the first place. For example, taxing earnings induces people to allocate hours to produce services themselves—for example, caring for an elderly parent, repairing a clogged sink, changing a car's motor oil—rather than allocating hours to earning money to purchase the service, because the "output" of the hour that produced the service is not taxed. If it takes more time to produce the service oneself, the tax induces inefficiency.[24] One must, however, compare the magnitude of the inefficiency from the implicit tax associated with the tapering benefits against the magnitude of the inefficiency from financing free care for all. Insofar as free or nearly free medical care is financed through taxes on income or other types of taxes, the induced inefficiency is potentially much larger than the inefficiency from income-related cost sharing.

Other problems with exempting the poor from cost sharing have to do with classifying people on the basis of income. Many of these are also well-known:

1. Income must be defined. The complexity of the Internal Revenue Service code testifies to the difficulty of this task. Especially difficult to account for is income in kind rather than in cash (for example, housing services from equity in a home).

2. Income must be reported. Many of the poor do not file an income tax return; and among those who do, income is thought to be substantially unreported.[25]

3. An accounting period must be defined. The accounting period is a year in the case of the income tax and a month in the case of AFDC. Shorter periods are more sensitive to changes in circumstances but leave more scope for avoidance behavior and unequal treatment of persons whose incomes fluctuate. An example of avoidance behavior is concentrating medical expenditures in the year in which the deductible is satisfied. The Experiment results (Chapter 4) suggest that this is not an important problem for cost sharing. Persons who exceeded the MDE (and therefore had free care for the rest of the year) spent at somewhat less than the free-care plan rate—not in excess of it as would have been the case if they had been shifting expenditures *into* that period. An example of fluctuating income is a person who earns $40,000 in one year and nothing in the next, and is on a plan with an MDE of $1,000 or 10 percent of income, whichever is less. Such a person will have cost sharing in the first year and free care in the next, whereas a person who earns $20,000 in each of two years will have cost sharing in both years, yielding a less valuable plan overall.

4. A family unit must be defined. We defined the family as the unit that shares income. In such a system, it is to the family's advantage to split into smaller units. Doing so in a plan with a *family* limit can never decrease reimbursement to the family as a whole and may increase it.[26] Moreover, one must determine what to do when the family unit changes for legitimate reasons. The Experiment fixed a family unit for an entire year even if living arrangements changed—for example, the husband and wife divorced—because the operational problems of any other strategy were insuperable (Chapter 10).

The importance of these income-defining problems can be reduced by limiting the number of persons or families for whom the definition of income matters. This approach argues for restricting any income-related feature to an upper limit on cost sharing, or so-called back-end protection, and leaving any initial cost sharing unrelated to income because many more families will be affected by initial cost sharing. This point may seem obvious. We mention it because the Ford administration's proposal for national health insurance, introduced around the beginning of the Experiment, called for income-relating not only an out-of-pocket ceiling but also premiums, initial deductibles, and coinsurance.

An alternative solution is to keep the cost sharing unrelated to income, as was done, for example, in the Experiment's Individual Deductible plan. The chief drawback of this strategy is that it may excessively limit the amount of cost sharing for the average person while imposing excessive cost sharing for the poor person.

In sum, exempting the poor from cost sharing is operationally feasible. Several other issues need to be considered however, before reaching a judgment on which (if any) groups should be exempt from cost sharing, in particular billing costs and the burden of cost sharing on the chronically ill.

Billing Costs

Relative to free care, cost sharing potentially generates additional billing costs. To be paid, a fee-for-service provider must generate at least one bill for each service or group of services. One transaction is needed if care is free to the user and if the provider bills the insurer directly, as is usually the case for Medicaid. There may also be only one transaction if there is a deductible that is not exceeded, because the provider simply bills the patient.[27] Two transactions are needed if the patient is responsible for part of the bill. Either the provider bills the insurance company for part of the bill and the patient for the other part, or the provider bills the patient for everything and the patient bills the insurer for part of the bill.[28] The Experiment gathered no data on the incremental cost of a second transaction, but it seems inconceivable that it would be major by comparison with the savings in reduced use on the cost-sharing plans.[29] Furthermore, cost sharing provides an incentive to the patient to scrutinize the bill for error or fraud—for example, services that are billed but not delivered.

The Burden on the Chronically Ill

Cost sharing forces those with a chronic health problem to pay the initial cost sharing each year. But individuals may wish to insure themselves against the risk of contracting a chronic problem that would force them to pay substantial amounts of cost sharing each year.[30] Paying the initial cost sharing year after year may also be viewed as inequitable—that is, as a tax on the sick (Evans 1984).

This problem can be addressed, albeit imperfectly, by exempting persons who exceed the MDE a specified number of years from cost sharing (or reducing their cost sharing in future years). Alternatively, cost sharing could be waived or reduced if a person had certain chronic conditions.

A Right to "Free" Care?

For many, free medical care embodies a "right to medical care," irrespective of whether cost sharing affects health status or not. Such individuals should ask themselves what is really being bought by medical care that is free at time of treatment. Clearly, free care is costly because of the additional use it stimulates. What benefits are bought for these extra costs?

The results in Chapters 6 and 7 suggest that free care offers little benefit for the average person, but a skeptic might believe that the health status measures used there were imperfect. Such a person might emphasize the results in Chapter 5, which showed that cost sharing appeared to discourage medical care in some instances in which it would have been efficacious. An analogy to Pascal's argument may be invoked: Free care may induce some wasted visits, but even a few instances of additional efficacious care—and both the results in Chapter 5 and common sense strongly suggest that such instances do exist—more than offset the costs of those contacts and average out to an overall gain in health. Indeed, some have ignored the results on outcomes and cited the results that cost sharing reduces appropriate and inappropriate care in about the same way as an argument *for* free care.

Our view is different because we are confident that our health status measures were sufficiently accurate and comprehensive to have captured any important gain in health status. We interpret the proportionate changes in appropriate and inappropriate care to mean that the benefits of the additional appropriate care were offset by the additional inappropriate care received by those with full coverage. In other words, the increased inappropriate care was not just zero-benefit care; it actually had negative effects. Examples of such care include prescribing antibiotics for viral infections, thus incurring side effects in some fraction of cases for no gain; inappropriate hospitalization; and labeling effects—recall that free care induced an increase in restricted activity days (see Chapter 6). In addition, other studies have shown that one-sixth to one-third of certain medical procedures do not produce a benefit sufficient to justify the clinical risk (Chassin et al. 1987) and that close to 4 percent of hospital admissions result in a iatrogenic treatment-induced injury that prolongs the stay or causes a disability that lasts past the stay (Brennan et al. 1991).

Our argument is reminiscent of Lawrence Henderson's well-known remark that it was not until the second decade of the twentieth century that "for the first time in human history, a random patient with a random disease consulting a doctor chosen randomly stood better than a 50–50 chance of benefiting from the encounter" (quoted in Somers and Somers 1961, pp. 136–137). Our interpretation requires the following amendment: the *additional* random patient with a random disease who sees a random doctor when care is free has only about a 50–50 chance of benefiting. For the sick poor, however, the additional care induced on the free plan had substantially better than 50–50 odds of helping.

Thus, those who believe that free medical care is a right need to confront two related arguments: (1) the issue is the efficacy of the *additional* medical services induced by free care, not the efficacy of any medical service; and (2) although medical services are beneficial in many instances, in some instances they are not. Just as a right to food does not preclude overeating, a right to medical care does not preclude overtreatment.

Our judgment is that for most of the American population, free medical care in an "unmanaged" fee-for-service system is not worth its costs. The burden on the poor and on persons (particularly the poor) with chronic conditions is a separate issue and should be dealt with as such.[31]

What about cost sharing in a managed or budget-constrained system, a subject of greater policy interest today than at the time we conducted the Experiment? A key issue here, of course, is how much cost sharing in such circumstances would reduce highly beneficial care relative to care with low or negative benefits. If the rationing mechanisms called forth by a global budget or inherent in managed care principally reduce low or negative benefit care, the argument for cost sharing loses force.[32]

The Experiment shed no direct light on how a global budget would ration care. But the finding that the percentage of inappropriate care varies hardly at all with the overall rate of services offers no support for the notion that a global budget will selectively reduce low or negative-benefit care or leave it at negligible levels (Chapter 5 and Chassin et al. 1987). The finding that inappropriate hospitalization increased less at the HMO than in the fee-for-service sector as the definition of inappropriateness became more inclusive is more encouraging (Chapter 9). But lack of experience with global budgets in the United States leaves great uncertainty on this point.

The Nature of Cost Sharing

Accepting cost sharing in the fee-for-service sector does not end the debate. Important questions still remain, the first of which is the form cost sharing should take: higher coinsurance rates, higher MDE, or both?[33]

The level of the coinsurance rate. Consider first the variation in coinsurance rates given an MDE, the issue on which the Experiment is most informative. Use declined as coinsurance rose, but at a declining rate. Relative to the free care plan the 25 percent and Individual Deductible plans reduced use about 20 percent; the 50 percent coinsurance plan about 25 percent; and the 95 percent coinsurance plan about 30 percent.

Does this result mean that the coinsurance rate should be above zero but rather modest? Not necessarily. The apparent fall in the effect of cost sharing stems from the increased percentage of individuals who exceeded the MDE in plans with higher coinsurance rates (Table 11.3). The reason is simple: persons on higher coinsurance plans had to consume fewer medical services to exceed the MDE. Fully one-third of those on the 95 percent plan faced free care for their last dollar of spending. One way to think about the 95 percent plan, therefore, is as a combination of two plans. On one plan, people pay for virtually all the care they receive; two-thirds of the people on the 95 percent plan are on this plan. On the other, people pay for care up to a certain point, past which they receive free care; one-third of the people on the 95 percent plan are on this plan.[34]

Because of the MDE, therefore, the differences among plans in the effective cost-sharing rate are much less than the differences in the nom-

Table 11.3   Percentage of families exceeding MDE

Coinsurance rate	% exceeding limit
25%	20.8[a]
50%	21.5
95%	35.0

a. The maximum MDE in this plan for many of the site-years was $750, whereas it was $1,000 in the other plans; see Chapter 2, note 3.

inal coinsurance rates suggest. The average coinsurance rate in the 25 percent plans was 16 percent, for example, compared with 31 percent on the 95 percent plans.[35] Thus, although the nominal coinsurance rate in the 95 percent plans was nearly four times as high as in the 25 percent plans, the average coinsurance rate was only twice as great. In short, increased coinsurance has a diminishing effect on use simply because fewer people are subject to the coinsurance for the whole accounting period.[36]

Despite its diminished potency, increased coinsurance did continue to reduce the use of services. The higher coinsurance caused additional risk, but under conventional assumptions of welfare economics that risk did not offset the gains from reducing the use of low-valued services (Chapter 4). And an initial moderate deductible, followed by coinsurance, followed by an individual cap appeared to be even better than initial coinsurance with no deductible—this form of cost sharing is in fact common.

Still, many would not accept the applicability of the conventional assumptions that lie behind the calculations in Chapter 4—that the consumer can judge the value of services and that those services do not affect the welfare of those outside the family. For those who are uncomfortable with these assumptions it may be relevant that the additional coinsurance within the cost-sharing group of plans did not appear to affect health adversely. This appears to be an argument for the superiority of an initial deductible followed by coinsurance and an MDE over lesser amounts of cost sharing, but the uncertainty about this conclusion is greater than the uncertainty about the superiority of some initial cost sharing relative to free care.

In particular, confidence intervals in comparing health outcomes among the various cost-sharing plans, especially the 50 percent plan, are wider than the comparisons between the free care plan and all cost-sharing plans taken together (because the free care plan had a larger sample than the other coinsurance rate plans). Hence, the likelihood that clinically important differences between the 95 percent plan and other cost-sharing plans were not detected because of sampling error is greater than for the free care/cost-sharing comparison.

Whether health outcomes would be better at a 25 or 95 percent coinsurance rate, even setting aside the issue of possible iatrogenesis from additional services on the 25 percent coinsurance rate plan, remains uncertain, however. The reason is that those with costly illnesses are more likely to have free care at the margin on the 95 percent plan (because it takes less gross expenditure to satisfy any given level of MDE) and that this group may benefit the most from free care.

Another issue that remains in doubt is whether the additional 10 percentage point reduction in utilization on the 95 percent plan relative to the Individual Deductible plan is worth the administrative costs of income-relating the MDE. We would judge that it is, but this is inevitably a value judgment.[37]

The size of the Maximum Dollar Expenditure. The Experiment is less well suited to address the level of the MDE than the level of the coinsurance rate. The only variation was in the 5, 10, and 15 percent-of-income limits to a maximum of $1,000. This variation induced small differences in spending (Chapter 4). The modest spending differences together with our small sample sizes made it impossible to determine whether health outcomes were affected,[38] but given the small effect on spending, important effects on health seem unlikely. Moreover, our estimates indicate that the additional risk as the MDE rises over this range is not very large. These results suggest that, at least over this range, for the nonpoor the MDE should be set at the high end—that is, at the equivalent of $1,000 per family in late 1970s prices.[39]

Many participants, however, did not necessarily agree with our assessment; on self-administered questionnaires they indicated that they would have bought supplemental insurance if it had been available (Marquis and Phelps 1985). At a 15 percent loading fee,[40] 40 percent said they would have liked full supplementation and 77 percent said they would have liked at least some supplementation. Although this seems like an argument for a lower MDE (indeed, seemingly an argument against any cost sharing), the argument is not as strong as at first may appear. The premium quoted was based on the mean health cost, and the questions were asked retrospectively. Assuming a 15 percent loading, about 40 percent of the participants would in fact have been ahead financially given their above-average expenditures (even ignoring risk aversion) if they had purchased supplemental insurance. In other words, although in hindsight the families may have wanted insurance, it is not certain that ex ante they would have given the same answer as they did ex post.

What about a public plan combining a very high limit with the possibility of private supplementation for those who choose it? Two arguments militate against such an arrangement: (1) the supplementary insurance would inevitably incur high loading fees relative to a single public plan simply because two plans are not as cheap to administer as one; and (2) whether a supplementary insurance market could sustain itself is not clear.

If the supplementary insurance were bought predominantly by those with above-average expenditure, its premium would of necessity be above the average expenditure, which in turn might induce those who had the lowest expected expenditure among those purchasing insurance to drop the coverage, with a further rise in premium for those wanting the insurance.[41]

In any case, a sufficiently high MDE effectively loses any resemblance to insurance, and the health consequences of no insurance relative to some insurance may be larger than any of the variations in health outcomes that we saw. Nicole Lurie et al. (1984, 1986), for example, studied a cohort of Medically Indigent Adults who had been under treatment at the UCLA Medical Center but whose coverage there was terminated. Services were subsequently covered only at Los Angeles County medical facilities, most of which were several miles away from UCLA, entailing time and travel costs that in effect raised the cost of health care substantially.

The adverse health effects observed in this cohort after coverage was terminated were much greater than any observed in the Experiment. To be sure, this is not the same as adding an uninsured group to those studied in the Experiment, because the cohort studied by Lurie and her colleagues was under treatment for chronic problems, and thus not representative of the population as a whole. Consequently, the potential for damaging health effects from termination of coverage was considerably greater than it would have been in a representative sample. Nonetheless, the magnitude of the effects observed suggests that for a subgroup of the population lack of insurance could have catastrophic consequences.

In sum, there is an optimal level of MDE that is considerably greater than zero, but the Experiment's design does not provide much information about what it is. We evaluated family MDEs of up to $1,000 in late 1970s dollars, which would probably be in the vicinity of $2,000 in 1991 dollars. In the tradeoff among increased risk and possible wasteful use of services, an income-related $1,000 MDE appeared better than smaller ones. It is clear, however, that MDE amounts above a certain level are bad policy for two reasons: (1) they impose more risk than much of the population wishes to bear; and (2) at a level at which they effectively become no insurance, they can have serious health consequences.

The question also arises whether the MDE should be individual or family based. The analysis of demand and risk in Chapter 4 showed that individual MDEs more effectively concentrated insurance benefits on the sicker population. Moreover, they are administratively simpler. Thus our analysis suggests that any MDE should be individual rather than family based.[42] And in fact individual MDEs are now the rule in most employment-based plans with an MDE.

Another issue is whether the MDE should be related to either income or earnings. Some employment-based plans, such as the Xerox plan described earlier, do relate the MDE to earnings; others do not. In the context of a universal public plan, it may be feasible to relate an *individual* MDE to *family* income. One can in principle relate an individual MDE to family income in a fashion that makes it actuarially equivalent to an income-related family MDE; in Chapter 4 we calculate how such a schedule would look (see Figure 4.6).

In light of the administrative difficulties of relating cost sharing to income, one may well wish to use non-income-related individual MDEs for most of the population, probably no cost sharing for the lowest part of the income distribution, and income-related individual MDEs for those with income just above the lowest part of the distribution.

Deciding What Services Should Be Covered

At the time the Experiment began the great majority of Americans were covered for hospital services. Ambulatory coverage was becoming more widely available, but coverage for dental care, prescription drugs, and mental health services was relatively rare. Throughout the 1970s and 1980s coverage for all of these increased.

In this section we take up issues pertaining to the coverage of these four types of services, as well as emergency room services. The data from the Experiment are not ideally suited to making decisions about what services should be covered because all plans applied the same coinsurance rate to all services (with the two exceptions of the Individual Deductible plan and the plans with 50 percent coinsurance for dental and mental health services and 25 percent coinsurance for all other services).

Ambulatory physician services. Most health insurance plans today cover ambulatory services, though sometimes less well than hospital services. The reasons hospital services were the first to be covered by health insurance and tend still to be the most extensively covered are not hard to find: they pose the largest expenditure risk, and the loading or retention (as a percentage of payout) is least for them because claims-processing costs do not rise proportionately with the size of the claim. In addition, it may have been thought—somewhat erroneously in light of the Experiment's findings—

that hospital services were less discretionary and hence had lower price elasticities, with the result that coverage would stimulate less additional demand.

Some have criticized preferential coverage of hospital services, arguing that cost sharing for ambulatory services and not for hospital services deters some consumers from seeking care at a time when their illness could be treated relatively cheaply (Roemer et al. 1975). Others are critical on the grounds that physicians, acting as the patient's agent, may hospitalize a patient who could be treated at least as effectively on an ambulatory basis, in order to avoid the ambulatory cost sharing.

The findings from the Individual Deductible plan largely refute these criticisms. Although cost sharing does appear to deter efficacious care for low-income hypertensives and children, when compared to a plan in which all services are free, cost sharing for ambulatory services only reduces total expenditure. It certainly reduces visits, and it may well reduce admissions (Chapter 3).

Emergency room visits. Some health insurance policies give preferential coverage to emergency room services relative to physician office visits, perhaps because emergency room visits are thought to be less price elastic. The Experiment's results, however, do not support such reasoning; emergency room visits show roughly the same response to plan as office visits (Chapter 5).

Mental health services. Employers have traditionally tended to exclude mental health services from coverage altogether or to cover them less generously than other services. (Indeed, the greater frequency of 50 percent coinsurance rates for mental health than for other medical services was a reason for the Experiment to include the plans with 50 percent coinsurance for mental health and dental services and 25 percent coinsurance for everything else; see Appendix B.) Reasons given for differential coverage include fear of adverse selection (that is, that individuals who desire to use mental health services would seek employment with the first few employers who covered such services) and the view that such services are more responsive to price than are medical care services.

In response to the fact of differential coverage, the mental health community advanced the so-called offset hypothesis. This hypothesis held that poorer coverage of mental health services resulted in patients inappropriately seeking care from non–mental health professionals, thereby leading to both poorer health outcomes and higher costs (Follette and Cummings 1967, 1968).

The Experiment results bear on this issue in two ways. First, the split coinsurance rate plan (25 percent coinsurance for medical services, 50 percent for mental health or dental) was designed to test the offset hypothesis directly. This test unfortunately proved uninformative because confidence intervals were too large to permit any inference about expenditures or health outcomes. Second, the Experiment also compared price responses among services and found a somewhat greater price response for mental health than for medical services (see Table 4.26). Interestingly, the Experiment price response for mental health was much lower than the response found in observational studies (Reed 1974), implying that those who have a higher demand for mental health services obtain better coverage. Thus the fear of adverse selection is well founded.

The outstanding fact about mental health utilization in the Experiment, however, was how little there was. Mental health expenditures were 4 percent of other medical expenditures, even less if dental expenses are included (see Tables 3.1, 3.2, and 3.22). This may not be a steady-state estimate, because demand for mental health services appeared to rise during the Experiment. But even if we take as our estimate the 30–40 percent higher use that characterized the latter part of the Experiment (Manning et al. 1989), the 4 percent figure needs to be adjusted only to 5 or 6 percent.[43] Not surprisingly, with so little use of services, there was no detectable effect of plan either on the mental health status indices (Chapters 6 and 7) or on the subscales of positive well-being and psychological distress. It is worth noting, however, that with the increase of substance abuse treatment programs, during the last decade, these figures may no longer be valid.

Dental services. Expenditures on dental services were much higher than expenditures on mental health services. Indeed, they were approximately a third as much as the expenditures on all medical services in year 2 and subsequent years. Dental services were the one part of the Experiment in which transitory demand was noticeable; demand on the free care plan in year 1 was about 50 percent higher than in year 2 except in the 95 percent plan. In steady state the price responsiveness of dental services to insurance plans was similar to that of outpatient medical services.

As described in Chapters 6 and 7, the additional use of dental services induced by less cost sharing did improve oral health; some of the measures of oral health used, however, especially the filling of decayed teeth, make such a finding almost tautological. Whether these benefits are worth their additional costs remains to be decided by policymakers. By professional norms, however, even on the free care plan undertreatment was substantial and overtreatment minimal. The minimal overtreatment may reflect the requirement that any treatment plan costing more than $500 have prior authorization.

Just as with medical services, decisions about scope of coverage are necessary for dental services. Some plans cover preventive dental services more extensively and often with no cost sharing; others exclude certain types of care such as prosthodontics (for example, dentures and fixed bridges). This latter choice is consequential; prosthodontic services accounted for 30 percent of dental expenditures in the second year of the Experiment and are more responsive to the variation by plan than other dental services (see Table 3.11); preventive services respond to the plan variation like other services.

Drugs. Outpatient drugs have traditionally been poorly covered by health insurance plans and are still not covered by Medicare, perhaps because of the relatively high loading fees to cover them. We did not measure loading fees, since claims processing costs in a research project with extensive coding could provide little useful information about the costs of an operating insurance plan. Nor did we measure the effect on demand or health outcomes of not covering drugs (or of covering them less well than other medical services) while covering other medical services.

Nonetheless, some of our findings are relevant to issues of drug coverage. First, about 8 percent of total spending was for drugs. Second, other than through its effect on visits, plan did little to alter drug use; that is, plan did not much affect either the physician's tendency to prescribe for a patient in the office or the patient's tendency to fill the prescription (Leibowitz, Manning, and Newhouse 1985; Lohr et al. 1986b). Third, although we saw evidence of medically inappropriate overprescribing, the proportion of inappropriate prescribing did not vary much by plan (Foxman et al. 1987). Fourth, cost sharing reduced the use of both prescription and nonprescription drugs; there was no evidence of substitution of over-the-counter drugs for prescription drugs as cost sharing increased (Leibowitz 1989).

Given the small demand response (other than through the visit effect), we see no strong reason to exclude drugs from coverage completely. If a paper claim must be processed for each prescription, however, the loading fees to cover drugs will be substantial. Under such conditions, if drugs are covered, there should probably be a sizable deductible.[44] If electronic billing becomes widespread and lowers loading charges, this conclusion could change.

Validity and Generalizability of Results

The findings of any empirical research project are inevitably tied to concerns about validity. Some of these concerns relate to internal validity: Did refusal of the enrollment offer or attrition from plans bias the results? Did behavior during the Experiment differ from that of an actual program—either because of the very observation of participants (Hawthorne effects) or because of transitory effects related to the fixed time span of the Experiment? Other concerns relate to external validity: Were the sites chosen representative of the country as a whole? Do results derived largely in an earlier period still apply? And are results derived from a small-scale Experiment applicable to a possible large-scale change in cost sharing?

Internal Validity

Refusal and attrition. Any bias from refusal or attrition in the Experiment was minimal (Chapters 2 and 8). Although both refusal and attrition were higher on the cost-sharing plans, the additional refusal and attrition appear to have been random with respect to the characteristics of the participants, and therefore free of bias. In particular, we found no evidence that those who were less healthy or who were high users of medical care differentially refused or withdrew from cost-sharing plans. We also found no reason to believe that refusal or attrition materially affected the HMO results.

Hawthorne effects and transitory effects. Any bias from Hawthorne and transitory effects was also minimal. The design of the Experiment permitted numerous tests of the possibilities that people who are being observed behave differently from people who are not (a Hawthorne effect), and that the Experiment's limited duration might induce them to pile up or postpone services. As described in Chapter 3, these tests suggested no important Hawthorne or transitory effect except for dental care. In addition, the average utilization for the national under-65 population, which reflects the distribution of actual insurance in the population, fell plausibly within the range of utilization across the insurance plans in the Experiment.

External Validity

Representativeness of sites. The six sites for the Experiment were not chosen as a national probability sample; rather, they were chosen to be representative of the four census regions, to vary in city size, to include urban and rural areas, and to vary in waiting times to appointment (Chapter 2). The question thus arises whether results based on these sites apply to the country as a whole. We believe they do, for three reasons.

First, we detected no difference across the sites in the response to plans. Although six sites is a small sample, the differences among them on a number of dimensions makes this similarity of response particularly striking. Second, on many important characteristics the characteristics of the Experiment's sample do not depart markedly from national averages (Table 11.4).[45] Third, with the exception of admission rates for children, we detected no important interactions of plan with demographic variables; thus, differences between the sample and the national population in demographic characteristics, especially small differences, are unlikely to generate important discrepancies in response to plan.

Continuing validity of data from an earlier period. We believe that if the Experiment were to be repeated in the 1990s, the implications of the results would be largely unchanged (although there would be an increase in the absolute level of spending in all plans). This conclusion, however, must remain somewhat speculative, and in fact there are a number of reasons why inferences from 1974–1982 data might no longer be valid.

First and most obviously, medical technology has changed; for example, admission rates to hospitals have declined (see Table 11.2) and new methods of treatment have appeared, such as thrombolytic therapy for acute myocardial infarction. Second, the nature of disease has somewhat changed, most clearly perhaps with the advent of Acquired Immune Deficiency Syndrome. The current applicability of the results is difficult to address because no data exist on the response to plan with current medical technology. Nonetheless, we observed no plan by year interaction during the Experiment.[46] Using the medical care component of the Consumer Price Index as a deflator, we did observe an upward trend in mean expense but not in median expense over time; that is, the right tail of the expenditure distribution became thicker over time. This trend may well have reflected the spread of new and more expensive technology and procedures (for example, coronary artery bypass surgery, computed axial tomography).[47] Spending in the far right tail was, however, not sensitive to variation across the plans because of the MDE (Chapter 4). Thus we doubt that the differences we found among plans are much affected by the increase in high-technology medicine.

Because mental health expenditure increased substantially in the 1980s, we suspect that if the Experiment were repeated today, expenditures for these services would be substantially higher than we observed.[48]

Finally, if managed care (not of the group or staff model HMO type) succeeds in reducing primarily low-benefit care, our conclusions about the desirability of cost sharing for the bulk of the population could change.

Table 11.4   Comparison of Experiment sample with national averages[a]

	United States		Experiment sample
	1970	1980	1974–1977[b]
Age[c]			
< 20	42	36	41
20–44	35	42	40
45–64	23	22	19
Female	51	50	51
Black	11	12	13
Education[d]			
< high school	48	34	34
< 5 years	5.5	3.6	2.1
Median household income[e]	$10,090		$10,814
AFDC eligible	—	6.5	5.9

Sources: National data: U.S. Bureau of the Census (1988). Experiment sample data: S. M. Polich et al. (1986).

a. All values except median household income are percentages.

b. Experiment values include data for noneligibles.

c. The values are age at enrollment; because those 62 and over were ineligible, the 45–64 age group is somewhat underrepresented in the Experiment. Those 62 and over at enrollment in the Experiment were generally ineligible persons in households with eligible members.

d. National data are for 25 and over and include the over-65. Experiment data are for 18 and over in Dayton, 16 and over in other sites.

e. National figure is 1974 household median income, deflated to 1973 dollars using Consumer Price Index. Experiment figures are 1973 family income for Dayton, 1974 family income for Seattle and Massachusetts, and 1975 for South Carolina, all in 1973 dollars. Income is summed from components; for method of construction see Polich et al. (1986).

Moving from the small scale to the large scale. The Experiment was a small-scale intervention that caused no major perturbation in the health care market at any site. Even in the site with the highest proportion of the population enrolled (Georgetown County), less than 2 percent of the population was enrolled in the Experiment. Moreover, in all sites some participants had more cost sharing relative to their preexisting insurance policies and some had less.

A universal plan, however, would create the possibility of a major perturbation. If demand changed in some major way, how might the Experiment results change? A simple but probably not very helpful way to think about the problem is to imagine that medical care is like the marketplace portrayed in economics textbooks; in that event, one would want to know the shape of the supply curve. The more elastic or flat the curve, the less the Experiment results would change.

A more realistic approach is to recognize that in many medical markets price tends to be set between the third-party payer and the provider; especially in a universal plan, such a price need not be set at the point where supply and demand curves intersect. As a result, price may be only one of the mechanisms—and perhaps not a very important one—used to equilibrate medical markets; some other forms of nonprice rationing of medical services may well serve to bring the market into equilibrium. Indeed, it was for this reason that we chose sites with widely varying degrees of excess demand.

The potential importance of non-price rationing is related to the argument that one cannot generalize from a small-scale increase in cost sharing to a large-scale increase because physicians would induce new demand to offset the effect of the cost sharing. Three Canadians, among others, have put forward this view (Barer, Evans, and Stoddart 1979).[49] Usually the assumption is that an informed consumer would not value the induced demand at its cost. This assumption, however, need not be valid. For example, if one of the nonprice mechanisms used to equilibrate the market is time spent per patient, which certainly seems plausible on a day-to-day basis as a physician's patient load fluctuates, a decrease in overall demand from greater cost sharing may lead physicians to spend more time per patient and bill for longer visits. This might be termed supplier-induced demand—but patients might prefer it, depending on whether the visit time initially was optimal. Turning the argument around, suppose overall demand increases because of less cost sharing, with a resultant decrease in time spent per patient. If patients preferred longer visits (and were willing to pay for them), should this be termed a supplier-induced decrease in demand?

Although the literature has not achieved consensus with respect to the magnitude of undesirable supplier-induced demand, two pieces of evidence indicate that physicians cannot fully offset the decrease in demand from increased cost sharing. The first is the diffusion of physicians into smaller cities as their numbers have increased, a phenomenon observed in both the United States and Canada (Newhouse et al. 1982a, 1982b; Dionne, Langlois, and Lemire 1987). If doctors could fully control demand and their locational preferences were unchanged, new cohorts would locate exactly where old cohorts did, but this has clearly not happened. The alternative hypothesis—that location preferences have changed and that physicians now prefer smaller cities—is not very persuasive, because the changes in location are very systematic by size of specialty. Members of smaller specialties, such as dermatologists, diffused into towns of 20,000–30,000 in the 1970s but rarely into smaller ones, whereas members of larger specialties, such as internists, diffused into towns as small as 5,000–10,000. A successful argument that changes in location preferences account fully for the data would have to explain the differential way in which these tastes have changed by specialty.

The second piece of empirical evidence is simply the behavior of hospital admissions in the United States. As shown in Table 11.2, admissions have fallen in recent years among those under 65, as has length of stay. This decline is inconsistent with simple accounts of supplier-induced demand.[50] One might counter that supplier-induced demand should apply only to physicians' services and not to hospital services; but such an argument concedes that cost sharing could affect the demand for hospital services.[51]

As a test of the importance of supplier-induced demand we can ask whether the magnitude of the recent downward trend in hospital admissions in the United States is consistent with the Experiment results. A decline that was much smaller than would be predicted from the Experiment data would suggest that induced demand was important. Among "large firms," the proportion introducing an initial deductible for inpatient services rose from 30 percent in 1982 to 63 percent in 1984, and the percentage paying all of the first day's stay fell from 67 to 42 (see Table 11.1).[52] It is not known what the corresponding share was for small firms; most likely the change was less because they were less likely to provide full coverage in the first place.

Suppose, nonetheless, that an additional 30 percent of the under-65 faced an initial deductible for inpatient services in 1984. On the basis of the finding that the admission rate in the Individual Deductible plan was 90 percent as large as the rate in the free care plan (Chapter 3), the data from the Experiment yield an estimated reduction in admissions among the under-65 of around 3 percent.[53] If the percentage of the under-65 who newly faced an initial deductible was less than an additional 30 percent, the 3 percent figure would be lower.

In fact discharges decreased by 7.8 percent from 1982 through 1984 (American Hospital Association 1985) (see also Table 11.2). The size of the discrepancy is large enough to suggest either that other factors contributed to the decline in admissions or that the 3 percent estimate is too crude, but it provides no support for the argument that physicians can fully offset changes in demand.[54]

Other empirical findings from the supplier-induced demand literature also suggest that physicians do not act in a way that is close to fully offsetting a fall in demand (Fuchs 1978; Rossiter and Wilensky 1983; McCarthy 1985; Stano 1985; Cromwell and Mitchell, 1986).[55]

The evidence thus seems convincing to us that a widespread increase in cost sharing would reduce demand and use, just as it did when employed on a small scale in the Experiment. Whether the reduction would be of the magnitude observed in the Experiment is less certain, but that question may have limited relevance. In 1990 the average coinsurance rate in the United States was 20 percent, between the average coinsurance rate of the 25 and 95 percent Experiment plans (Levit et al. 1990). As a result, it seems unlikely that there will be any substantial increase in cost sharing in the United States; the more relevant issue is whether there will be a large-scale decrease to free or nearly free care.[56] If there were to be a large-scale decrease, we believe the Experiment results are a good rough guide to the magnitude of the consequent increase in demand on the delivery system.

Appendix A

Health Insurance Study Publications

Public Use File Documentation

The overall guide to the public use files is listed first.

Taylor, Christine d'Arc, et al. 1987. *User's Guide to HIE Data*. HIE Reference Series, vol. 3. Santa Monica: RAND Corporation (Pub. no. N-2349/3-HHS).

Bloomfield, Ellen S., Liza Y. Weissler, and Alicia M. Bell. 1987. *Dental Examinations: Codebook for Adults and Children at Enrollment and Exit*. Santa Monica: RAND Corporation (Pub. no. N-2506-HHS).

Bloomfield, Ellen S., Liza Y. Weissler, and A. B. Holland. 1986. *Codebooks for Insurance Preference Files: Relation between Expense Limit and Premium*. Santa Monica: RAND Corporation (Pub. no. N-2508-HHS).

Edwards, Carol A., et al. 1986a. *Codebooks for Adults at Enrollment and Exit, Form A*. Medical History Questionnaire Series, 1. Santa Monica: RAND Corporation (Pub. no. N-2485/1-HHS).

——— 1986b. *Codebooks for Adults at Enrollment and Exit, Form B*. Medical History Questionnaire Series, 2. Santa Monica: RAND Corporation (Pub. no. N-2485/2-HHS).

——— 1986c. *Codebooks for Children at Enrollment and Exit*. Medical History Questionnaire Series, 3. Santa Monica: RAND Corporation (Pub. no. N-2485/3-HHS).

——— 1986d. *Codebooks for Infants at Enrollment and Exit*. Medical History Questionnaire Series, 4. Santa Monica: RAND Corporation (Pub. no. N-2485/4-HHS).

Nelsen, Mark, and Carol A. Edwards. 1986. *Codes Used in HIE Claims — Diagnoses, Symptoms, Procedures, Drugs, and Supplies*. HIE References, vol. 1. Santa Monica: RAND Corporation (Pub. no. N-2349/1-HHS).

Operskalski, Belinda H., et al. 1987. *Codebook for Adults at Enrollment and Exit.* Medical Disorder Series, vol. 1. Santa Monica: RAND Corporation (Pub. no. N-2446/1-HHS).

Petersen, Christine E., Mark M. Nelsen, and Ellen S. Bloomfield. 1986. *Codebook for Fee-for-Service Annual Expenditures and Visit Counts.* Aggregated Claims Series, vol. 1. Santa Monica: RAND Corporation (Pub. no. N-2360/1-HHS).

Petersen, Christine E., Mark M. Nelsen, and D. L. Wesley. 1986. *Codebooks for HMO and Seattle Fee-for-Service Visits—Outpatient and Inpatient.* Aggregated Claims Series, vol. 4. Santa Monica: RAND Corporation (Pub. no. N-2360/4-HHS).

Petersen, Christine E., Christine D. Taylor, and Ellen S. Bloomfield. 1986. *Codebooks for Fee-for-Service Treatment Episodes and Annual Episode Counts.* Aggregated Claims Series, vol. 3. Santa Monica: RAND Corporation (Pub. no. N-2360/3-HHS).

Peterson, Christine E., et al. 1986a. *Codebooks for Fee-for-Service Claims.* Claims Line-Item Series, vol. 1. Santa Monica: RAND Corporation (Pub. no. N-2347/1-HHS).

———1986b. *Codebooks for Fee-for-Service Visits—Outpatient, Inpatient, and Dental.* Aggregated Claims Series, vol. 2. Santa Monica: RAND Corporation (Pub. no. N-2360/2-HHS).

———1986c. *Codebook for HMO and Seattle Fee-for-Service Annual Expenditures.* Aggregated Claims Series, vol. 5. Santa Monica: RAND Corporation (Pub. no. N-2360/5-HHS).

———1986d. *Codebooks for Health Maintenance Organization Claims.* Claims Line-Item Series, vol. 2. Santa Monica: RAND Corporation (Pub. no. N-2347/2-HHS).

———1986e. *Codebooks for Seattle Fee-for-Service Claims for Comparison with HMO Claims.* Claims Line-Item Series, vol. 3. Santa Monica: RAND Corporation (Pub. no. N-2347/3-HHS).

Polich, Suzanne M., Mark M. Nelsen, and D. L. Wesley. 1987. *Providers Cited in HIE Data.* HIE Reference Series, vol. 2. Santa Monica: RAND Corporation (Pub. no. N-2349/2-HHS).

Polich, Suzanne M., and Christine d'Arc Taylor. 1986. *Codebook for Eligibility-Family Changes File.* Master Sample Series 1. Santa Monica: RAND Corporation (Pub. no. N-2264/1-HHS).

Polich, Suzanne M., et al. 1986. *Codebook for Full Sample Demographic File,* vol. 2. Santa Monica: RAND Corporation (Pub. no. N-2264–2).

———1987a. *Codebook for Supplemental Data File.* Master Sample Series 3. Santa Monica: RAND Corporation (Pub. no. N-2264/3-HHS).

———1987b. *Disability Days: Codebook for Adults and Children.* Santa Monica: RAND Corporation (Pub. no. N-2507-HHS).

Sloss, Elizabeth M., et al. 1986. *Codebooks for Adults and Children at Enroll-ment and Exit.* Health Status and Attitude Series, vol. 1. Santa Monica: RAND Corporation (Pub. no. N-2447/1-HHS).

———1987. *Codebook for Children at Enrollment and Exit.* Medical Disorder Series, vol. 2. Santa Monica: RAND Corporation (Pub. no. N-2446/2-HHS).

Other Publications

Abrahamse, Allen, and Arnold Kisch. 1975. *Health Status Age: An Age Pre-dictive Health Status Index.* Santa Monica: RAND Corporation (Pub. no. R-1626-OEO).

Acton, Jan P. 1972. *Site Selection for a Health Insurance Experiment.* Santa Monica: RAND Corporation (Pub. no. R-1095-OEO).

———1973. *The Demand for Care among the Urban Poor with Special Emphasis on the Role of Time.* Santa Monica: RAND Corporation (Pub. no. R-1151-OEO/NYC).

———1974. *Demand for Health Care When Time Prices Vary More than Money Prices.* Santa Monica: RAND Corporation (Pub. no. R-1189-OEO/NYC).

———1975. "Nonmonetary Factors in the Demand for Medical Services: Some Empirical Evidence." *Journal of Political Economy* 83:595–614.

Acton, Jan P., Lindy J. Clark, and Robert J. Young. 1973a. *Population Health Survey for 1968: Codebook and Marginals.* Santa Monica: RAND Corpora-tion (Pub. no. R-1096-NYC/OEO).

———1973b. *Population Health Survey for 1969–70: Codebook and Mar-ginals.* Santa Monica: RAND Corporation (Pub. no. R-1162-NYC/OEO).

Afifi, A. A. 1972. *Thoughts on the Experimental Design for the Health Insur-ance Experiment.* Santa Monica: RAND Corporation (Pub. no. P-4892).

André, Carolyn D. 1979. *Payment Incentives in a Social Experiment.* Santa Monica: RAND Corporation (Pub. no. P-6410).

———1980. *Do Payment Incentives Affect Response Time in a Social Experi-ment?* Santa Monica: RAND Corporation (Pub. no. N-1473-HEW).

Archibald, Rae W., and Joseph P. Newhouse. 1988. "Social Experimentation: Some Why's and How's." In *Handbook of Systems Analysis,* vol. 2, ed. Hugh J. Miser and Edward S. Quade. New York: Elsevier. Also available from Santa Monica: RAND Corporation (Pub. no. R-2479-HEW), 1980.

Arrow, Kenneth J. 1973a. *Optimal Insurance and Generalized Deductibles.* Santa Monica: RAND Corporation (Pub. no. R-1108-OEO).

———1973b. *Welfare Analysis of Changes in Health Coinsurance Rate.* Santa Monica: RAND Corporation (Pub. no. R-1281-OEO).

———1975. *Two Notes on Inferring Long-Run Behavior from Social Experi-ments.* Santa Monica: RAND Corporation (Pub. no. P-5546).

Avery, Allyson D., et al. 1976. *Quality of Medical Care Assessment Using Outcome Measures: Eight Disease-Specific Applications.* Santa Monica: RAND Corporation (Pub. no. R-2021/2-HEW).

Bailit, Howard L., and Willard G. Manning. 1988. "The Need and Demand for Periodontal Services: Implications for Dental Practice and Education." *Journal of Dental Education* 52:458–462.

Bailit, Howard L., et al. 1984. "The Effect of Cost Sharing on the Quality of Dental Care." *Journal of Dental Education* 48:597–604.

———1985. "Does More Generous Dental Insurance Coverage Improve Oral Health? A Study of Patient Cost-Sharing." *Journal of the American Dental Association* 110:701–707. Also available from Santa Monica: RAND Corporation (Pub. no. N-2591-HHS), 1987.

———1986. "Dental Insurance and the Oral Health of Preschool Children." *Journal of the American Dental Association* 113:773–776.

———1987. "Is Periodontal Disease the Primary Cause of Tooth Extraction in Adults?" *Journal of the American Dental Association* 114:40–45.

Beck, Sjoerd, et al. 1981a. *Conceptualization and Measurement of Physiologic Health for Adults: Hay Fever.* Santa Monica: RAND Corporation (Pub. no. R-2262/13-HHS).

———1981b. *Conceptualization and Measurement of Physiologic Health for Adults: Hearing Loss.* Santa Monica: RAND Corporation (Pub. no. R-2262/14-HHS).

———1983. *Conceptualization and Measurement of Physiologic Health for Children.* Vol. 1: *Allergic Conditions.* Santa Monica: RAND Corporation (Pub. no. R-2898/1-HHS).

Berman, Daniel M., et al. 1981. *Conceptualization and Measurement of Physiologic Health for Adults: Angina Pectoris.* Santa Monica: RAND Corporation (Pub. no. R-2262/4-HHS).

Brook, Robert H. 1975. *Policy Issues in Quality Assurance.* Santa Monica: RAND Corporation (Pub. no. P-5517).

Brook, Robert H., and Allyson D. Avery. 1975. *Quality Assurance Mechanisms in the United States: From There to Where?* Santa Monica: RAND Corporation (Pub. no. P-5520).

———1976a. *Quality Assessment: Issues of Definition and Measurement.* Santa Monica: RAND Corporation (Pub. no. P-5618-HEW).

———1976b. *Quality of Medical Care Assessment Using Outcome Measures: Executive Summary.* Santa Monica: RAND Corporation (Pub. no. R-2021/3-HEW).

———1977a. *Mechanisms for Assuring Quality of U.S. Medical Care Service: Past, Present, and Future.* Santa Monica: RAND Corporation (Pub. no. R-1939-HEW).

————1977b. *Quality Assurance and Cost Control in Ambulatory Care.* Santa Monica: RAND Corporation (Pub. no. P-5817).

Brook, Robert H., Rudy L. Brutoco, and Kathleen N. Williams. 1975. "The Relationship between Medical Malpractice and Quality of Care." *Duke Law Journal* 6:1197–1231. Also available from Santa Monica: RAND Corporation (Pub. no. P-5526).

Brook, Robert H., Caren J. Kamberg, and Kathleen N. Lohr. 1982. "Quality Assessment in Mental Health." *Professional Psychology* 13 (special issue): 34–39. Also available from Santa Monica: RAND Corporation (Pub. no. N-1206-HEW), 1979.

Brook, Robert H., and Kathleen N. Lohr. 1980. "Quality of Care and Episodes of Respiratory Illness among Medicaid Patients in New Mexico." *Annals of Internal Medicine* 92:99–106.

————1981a. "Quality of Care Assessment: Its Role in the 1980s" (editorial). *American Journal of Public Health* 71:681–682.

————1981b. Review of Avedis Donabedian, *The Definition of Quality and Approaches to Its Assessment. Health Services Research* 16 (Summer).

————1982a. "Quality Assurance in Medical Care: Lessons from the U.S. Experience." In *Quality Assessment of Medical Care,* ed. H. K. Selbmann and K. K. Uberla, Gerlingen: Bleicher Verlag. Also available from Santa Monica: RAND Corporation (Pub. no. P-6571), 1980.

————1982b. "Second Opinion Programs: Beyond Cost-Benefit Analyses" (editorial). *Medical Care* 20:1–2.

————1985. "Efficacy, Effectiveness, Variations, and Quality: Boundary-Crossing Research." *Medical Care* 23:710–722.

————1986. "Will We Need to Ration Effective Health Care?" *Issues in Science and Technology* 3:68–77.

Brook, Robert H., Kathleen N. Lohr, and George A. Goldberg. 1982. *Conceptualization and Measurement of Physiologic Health for Adults: Thyroid Disease.* Santa Monica: RAND Corporation (Pub. no. R-2262/9-HHS).

Brook, Robert H., and Kathleen N. Williams. 1975. "Evaluating Quality of Health Care for the Disadvantaged: A Literature Review." *Journal of Community Health* 1:132–156. Also available from Santa Monica: RAND Corporation (Pub. no. R-1658-HEW).

————1976a. "Assessment of Medical Care" (letter to the editor). *New England Journal of Medicine* 295:118.

————1976b. "Effect of Medical Care Review on the Use of Injections: A Study of the New Mexico Experimental Medical Care Review Organization." *Annals of Internal Medicine* 85:509–515. Also published as *The Impact of the New Mexico Experimental Medical Care Review Organization on the Quality of the Use of Injections,* Santa Monica: RAND Corporation (Pub. no. P-5761).

————1976c. "Evaluation of the New Mexico Peer Review System, 1971 to 1973." *Medical Care* 14 (Suppl.):1–122. Also published in Santa Monica: RAND Corporation (Pub. no. R-2110-HEW/RC), 1977.

————1978. "Malpractice and the Quality of Care" (editorial). *Annals of Internal Medicine* 88:836–837.

Brook, Robert H., Kathleen N. Williams, and Allyson D. Avery. 1976. "Quality Assurance in the 20th Century: Will It Lead to Improved Health in the 21st?" In *Quality Assurance in Health Care,* ed. R. H. Egdahl and P. M. Gertman. Germantown, Md.: Aspen Publications. Also available from Santa Monica: RAND Corporation (Pub. no. P-5530), 1975.

Brook, Robert H., Kathleen N. Williams, and John E. Rolph. 1978a. "Controlling the Use and Cost of Medical Services: The New Mexico Experimental Medical Care Review Organization—A Four-Year Study." *Medical Care* 16 (Suppl.). Also available from Santa Monica: RAND Corporation (Pub. no. R-2241-HEW).

————1978b. "Use, Costs, and Quality of Medical Services: Impact of the New Mexico Peer Review System." *Annals of Internal Medicine* 89:256–263.

Brook, Robert H., et al. 1976. *Quality of Medical Care Assessment Using Outcome Measures: An Overview of the Method.* Santa Monica: RAND Corporation (Pub. no. R-2021/1-HEW).

————1979. "Overview of Adult Health Status Measures Fielded in Rand's Health Insurance Study." *Medical Care* 17 (Suppl.):1–131. Also published as *Conceptualization and Measurement of Health for Adults in the Health Insurance Study: Overview,* Santa Monica: RAND Corporation (Pub. no. R-1987/8-HEW).

————1980a. *Conceptualization and Measurement of Physiologic Health for Adults: Acne.* Santa Monica: RAND Corporation (Pub. no. R-2262/2-1-HHS).

————1980b. *Conceptualization and Measurement of Physiologic Health for Adults: Hypertension.* Santa Monica: RAND Corporation (Pub. no. R-2262/3-HHS).

————1981a. *Conceptualization and Measurement of Physiologic Health for Adults: Diabetes Mellitus.* Santa Monica: RAND Corporation (Pub. no. R-2262/7-HHS).

————1981b. *Conceptualization and Measurement of Physiologic Health for Adults: Hypercholesterolemia.* Santa Monica: RAND Corporation (Pub. no. R-2262/11-HHS).

————1984a. "Does Free Care Improve Adults' Health?" *New England Journal of Medicine* 310:1468–70. (Response to letters to editor.)

————1984b. *The Effect of Coinsurance on the Health of Adults: Results from the RAND Health Insurance Experiment.* Santa Monica: RAND Corporation (Pub. no. R-3055-HHS). Abridged version published as "Does Free Care

Improve Adults' Health? Results from a Randomized Controlled Trial," *New England Journal of Medicine* 309 (8 December 1983):1426–34.

————1990. "Quality of Ambulatory Care: Epidemiology and Comparison by Insurance Status and Income." *Medical Care* 28:392–410.

Brown, Marie E. 1984. *Lessons Learned from the Administration of the Rand Health Insurance Experiment.* Santa Monica: RAND Corporation (Pub. no. R-3095-HHS).

Buchanan, Joan, and Shan Cretin. 1986. "Fee-for-Service Health Care Expenditures: Evidence of Selection Effects among Subscribers Who Choose HMOs." *Medical Care* 24:39–51. Also available from Santa Monica: RAND Corporation (Pub. no. R-2241-HHS).

Buchanan, Joan L., et al. 1991. "Simulating Health Expenditures under Alternative Insurance Plans." *Management Science* 37:1067–90.

Cave, Jonathan. 1984. *Equilibrium in Insurance Markets with Asymmetric Information and Adverse Selection.* Santa Monica: RAND Corporation (Pub. no. R-3015-HHS).

Chow, Winston K., and S. Bjerve. 1984. "A New Method of Power Approximation with Application to the Wilcoxon Statistics." *Scandinavian Journal of Statistics* 11:29–37.

Clasquin, Lorraine A. 1973. *Mental Health, Dental Services, and Other Coverage in the HIS.* Santa Monica: RAND Corporation (Pub. no. R-1216-OEO).

Clasquin, Lorraine A., and Marie E. Brown. 1977. *Rules of Operation for the Health Insurance Study.* Santa Monica: RAND Corporation (Pub. no. R-1602-HEW).

Danzon, Patricia M., Willard G. Manning, and M. Susan Marquis. 1984a. "Factors Affecting Laboratory Test Use and Prices." *Health Care Financing Review* 5(4):23–32.

————1984b. *Factors Affecting Laboratory Test Use and Prices: Executive Summary.* Santa Monica: RAND Corporation (Pub. no. R-2987-HCFA).

Davies, Allyson R., Howard L. Bailit, and Susan Holtby. 1985. "Oral Health Status and Use of Dental Services: Will Improved Health Lead to Decreased Demand?" *Journal of Dental Education* 49:427–433.

Davies, Allyson R., and John E. Ware, Jr. 1981a. *Measuring Health Perceptions in the Health Insurance Experiment.* Santa Monica: RAND Corporation (Pub. no. R-2711-HHS).

————1981b. "Measuring Patient Satisfaction with Dental Care." *Social Science and Medicine* 15A:751–760. Abridged version published as *Development of a Dental Satisfaction Questionnaire for the Health Insurance Experiment,* Santa Monica: RAND Corporation (Pub. no. R-2712-HHS).

Davies, Allyson R., et al. 1986. "Consumer Acceptance of Prepaid and Fee-for-Service Medical Care: Results from a Controlled Trial." *Health Services Research* 21:429–452.

————1987. *Explaining Dental Utilization.* Santa Monica: RAND Corporation (Pub. no. R-3528-NCHSR).

————1988. *Scoring Manual: Adult Health Status and Patient Satisfaction Measures Used in RAND's Health Insurance Experiment.* Santa Monica: RAND Corporation (Pub. no. N-2190-HHS).

Donald, Cathy A., and John E. Ware, Jr. 1982. *The Quantification of Social Contacts and Resources.* Santa Monica: RAND Corporation (Pub. no. R-2937-HHS).

————1984. "The Measurement of Social Support." In *Research in Community and Mental Health,* ed. J. F. Greenley. Westport, Conn.: JAI Press.

Donald, Cathy A., et al. 1978. *Conceptualization and Measurement of Health for Adults in the Health Insurance Study: Social Health.* Santa Monica: RAND Corporation (Pub. no. R-1987/4-HEW).

Doyle, B. J., and John E. Ware, Jr. 1977. "Physician Conduct and Other Factors That Influence Patient Satisfaction." *Journal of Medical Education* 52:793–801. Also available from Santa Monica: RAND Corporation (Pub. no. P-5670).

Duan, Naihua. 1982. "Models for Human Exposure to Air Pollution." *Environment International* 8:305–309. Also available from Santa Monica: RAND Corporation (Pub. no. N-1884-HHS).

————1983. "Smearing Estimate: A Nonparametric Retransformation Method." *Journal of the American Statistical Association* 78:605–610.

Duan, Naihua, et al. 1982. *A Comparison of Alternative Models for the Demand for Medical Care.* Santa Monica: RAND Corporation (Pub. no. R-2754-HHS). Abridged version published in *Journal of Business and Economic Statistics* 1 (April 1983):115–126.

————1984. "Choosing between the Sample-Selection Model and the Multi-Part Model." *Journal of Business and Economic Statistics* 2:283–289.

————1986. "Comments on Selectivity Bias (Response to G. S. Maddala)." In *Advances in Health Economics and Health Services Research,* ed. Richard Scheffler and Louis Rossiter. Vol. 6. Westport, Conn.: JAI Press.

Dunn, William C., and Beatrice Yormark. 1974. *Use and Maintenance of a Data Dictionary.* Santa Monica: RAND Corporation (Pub. no. P-5324).

Eisen, Marvin B., et al. 1979. *Measuring Components of Children's Health Status.* Santa Monica: RAND Corporation (Pub. no. P-6218). Abridged version published in *Medical Care* 17:902–921.

————1980. *Conceptualization and Measurement of Health for Children in the Health Insurance Study.* Santa Monica: RAND Corporation (Pub. no. R-2313-HEW).

Fowler, William, Emmett Keeler, and Joan Keesey. 1981. *The Episodes-of-Illness Processing System.* Santa Monica: RAND Corporation (Pub. no. N-1745-HHS).

Foxman, Betsy, Kathleen N. Lohr, and Robert H. Brook. 1983. *Measurement of Physiologic Health for Children.* Vol. 5: *Anemia.* Santa Monica: RAND Corporation (Pub. no. R-2898/5-HHS).

Foxman, Betsy, R. Burciaga Valdez, and Robert H. Brook. 1986. "Childhood Enuresis: Prevalence, Perceived Impact, and Prescribed Treatments." *Pediatrics* 76:482–487.

Foxman, Betsy K., et al. 1982. *Conceptualization and Measurement of Physiologic Health for Adults.* Vol. 8: *Chronic Obstructive Airway Disease.* Santa Monica: RAND Corporation (Pub. no. R-2262/8-1-HHS).

————1986a. "Chronic Bronchitis: Prevalence, Smoking Habits, Impact, and Antismoking Advice." *Preventive Medicine* 15:624–631.

————1986b. *Measurement of Physiologic Health of Children.* Vol. 6: *Urinary Tract Infection.* Santa Monica: RAND Corporation (Pub. no. R-2898/6-HHS).

————1987. "The Effect of Cost Sharing on the Use of Antibiotics in Ambulatory Care: Results from a Population-Based Randomized Controlled Trial." *Journal of Chronic Diseases* 40:429–437. Also available from Santa Monica: RAND Corporation (Pub. no. N-2712-HHS/RC).

Goldberg, George A. 1983. *The Health Insurance Experiment's Guidelines for Abstracting Health Services Rendered by Group Health Cooperative of Puget Sound.* Santa Monica: RAND Corporation (Pub. no. N-1948-HHS).

Held, Philip J. 1985. *Site Selection Criteria for the Health Insurance Study.* Santa Monica: RAND Corporation (Pub. no. N-2266-HHS).

Helms, L. Jay, Joseph P. Newhouse, and Charles E. Phelps. 1978. "Copayments and Demand for Medical Care: The California Medicaid Experience." *Bell Journal of Economics* 9:192–208. Also available from Santa Monica: RAND Corporation (Pub. no. R-2167-HEW).

Hurley, Jeanne S. 1975. *Application of Data Base Concepts in Operationalizing the Archiving and Retrieval of Panel Study Data.* Santa Monica: RAND Corporation (Pub. no. P-5605).

Johnston, Shawn A., and John E. Ware, Jr. 1976. "Income Group Differences in Relationships among Survey Measures of Physical and Mental Health." *Health Services Research* 11:416–429. Also available from Santa Monica: RAND Corporation (Pub. no. P-5716).

Kamberg, Caren J., et al. 1982. *Conceptualization and Measurement of Health for Adults: Use of Hypnotic and Anxiolytic Drugs.* Santa Monica: RAND Corporation (Pub. no. R-2723-HHS).

————1983. *Measurement of Physiologic Health for Children.* Vol. 3: *Seizure Disorders.* Santa Monica: RAND Corporation (Pub. no. R-2898/3-HHS).

Keeler, Emmett B. 1992. "Effects of Cost-Sharing on Use of Medical Services and Health." *Medical Practice Management.*

Keeler, Emmett B., and Shan Cretin. 1983. "Discounting of Life-Saving and Other Nonmonetary Effects." *Management Science* 29:300–306. Also published as *Discounting of Nonmonetary Effects,* Santa Monica: RAND Corporation (Pub. no. N-1875-HHS), 1982.

Keeler, Emmett B., and Joan Keesey. 1985. *The Episodes-of-Illness Processing System.* Santa Monica: RAND Corporation (Pub. no. N-1745-1-HHS).

Keeler, Emmett B., Willard G. Manning, and Kenneth B. Wells. 1988. "The Demand for Episodes of Mental Health Services." *Journal of Health Economics* 7:369–392. Also published under the same title, Santa Monica: RAND Corporation (Pub. no. R-3432-NIMH), 1986.

Keeler, Emmett B., Daniel W. Morrow, and Joseph P. Newhouse. 1977. "What Will the Market Be for Supplementary Insurance under National Health Insurance?" *Journal of Political Economy* 85:789–802. Also published as *Demand for Supplementary Health Insurance, or Do Deductibles Matter?* Santa Monica: RAND Corporation (Pub. no. R-1958-HEW), 1976.

Keeler, Emmett, Joseph Newhouse, and Charles Phelps. 1974. *Deductibles and the Demand for Medical Services: The Theory of the Consumer Facing a Variable Price Schedule under Uncertainty.* Santa Monica: RAND Corporation (Pub. no. R-1514-OEO/NC). Revised and published as "Deductibles and Demand: A Theory of the Consumer Facing a Variable Price Schedule under Uncertainty," *Econometrica* 45 (April 1977):641–655.

Keeler, Emmett B., Daniel A. Relles, and John E. Rolph. 1975. *The Choice between Family and Individual Deductibles in Health Insurance.* Santa Monica: RAND Corporation (Pub. no. R-1393-HEW). Abridged version published in *Journal of Economic Theory* 16 (1977):220–227.

———1977. "An Empirical Study of the Differences between Family and Individual Deductibles in Health Insurance." *Inquiry* 14:269–277.

Keeler, Emmett B., and John E. Rolph. 1983. "How Cost Sharing Reduced Medical Spending of Participants in the Health Insurance Experiment." *JAMA* 249:2220–22.

———1988. "The Demand for Episodes of Treatment in the Health Insurance Experiment." *Journal of Health Economics* 7:301–422.

Keeler, Emmett B., Kenneth B. Wells, and Willard G. Manning. 1988. "Markov and Other Models of Episodes of Mental Health Treatment." In *Advances in Health Economics and Health Services,* ed. Richard Scheffler and Louis Rossiter. Vol. 8. Westport, Conn.: JAI Press.

Keeler, Emmett B., et al. 1982. *The Demand for Episodes of Medical Services: Interim Results from the Health Insurance Experiment.* Santa Monica: RAND Corporation (Pub. no. R-2829-HHS).

———1985. "How Free Care Reduced Hypertension in the Health Insurance Experiment." *Journal of the American Medical Association* 254:1926–31. Also available from Santa Monica: RAND Corporation (Pub. no. R-3326-HHS).

————1986. *The Demand for Episodes of Mental Health Services.* Santa Monica: RAND Corporation (Pub. no. R-3432-NIMH).

————1987. "Effects of Cost Sharing on Physiological Health, Health Practices, and Worry." *Health Services Research* 22:279–306.

————1988. *The Demand for Episodes of Medical Treatment in the Health Insurance Experiment.* Santa Monica: RAND Corporation (Pub. no. R-3454-HHS).

————1989. "The External Costs of a Sedentary Life Style." *American Journal of Public Health* 79:975–981.

Kisch, Arnold, and Paul Torrens. 1974. "Health Status Assessment in the Health Insurance Study." *Inquiry* 11:40–52.

Leibowitz, Arleen. 1979. *Estimating the Errors in Hours of Work and Wage Rates.* Santa Monica: RAND Corporation (Pub. no. P-6276).

————1983. "Fringe Benefits in Employee Compensation." In *The Measurement of Labor Cost,* ed. Jack E. Triplett. Studies in Income and Wealth, no. 48. Chicago: University of Chicago Press for the National Bureau of Economic Research. Also available from Santa Monica: RAND Corporation (Pub. no. N-1827-HHS).

————1984. *Measuring the Value of Time in Medical Care Analyses.* Santa Monica: RAND Corporation (Pub. no. N-2127-HHS).

————1985. "Research and Development and Its Role in Policy Development." In *Preventive Health Care for Children and Cost Containment: Proceedings of a Conference Held in Phoenix, Arizona, October 28–30, 1984.* Washington, D.C.: Center for Policy Research and National Governors Association.

————1989. "Substitution between Prescribed and Over-the-Counter Medicines." *Medical Care* 27:85–94.

————1990. "The Response of Births to Changes in Health Care Costs." *Journal of Human Resources* 25:697–711.

Leibowitz, Arleen, et al. 1985a. "The Demand for Prescription Drugs as a Function of Cost Sharing." *Social Science and Medicine* 21:1063–70. Also available from Santa Monica: RAND Corporation (Pub. no. N-2278-HHS).

————1985b. "Effect of Cost Sharing on the Use of Medical Services by Children: Interim Results from a Randomized Controlled Trial." *Pediatrics* 75:942–951. Also available from Santa Monica: RAND Corporation (Pub. no. R-3287-HHS).

Lillard, Lee A., et al. 1986. *Preventive Medical Care: Standards, Usage, and Efficacy.* Santa Monica: RAND Corporation (Pub. no. R-3266-HCFA).

Lohr, Kathleen N. 1980a. *Quality of Care in Episodes of Common Respiratory Infections in a Disadvantaged Population.* Santa Monica: RAND Corporation (Pub. no. P-6570).

————1980b. "Test Reduction" (letter to the editor). *British Medical Journal* 281:1285.

————1983. *Quality Assurance for Health Administrators.* Santa Monica: RAND Corporation (Pub. no. P-6933).

————1985. "Concepts and Tools for an Effective Quality-Assurance Program." *Health Management Quarterly,* Spring: 2–5, 17.

————1985–86. "Professional Peer Review in a 'Competitive' Medical Market." *Case Western Reserve Law Review* 36:1175–89.

Lohr, Kathleen N., and Robert H. Brook. 1981. "Quality Assurance and Clinical Pharmacy: Lessons from Medicine." *Drug Intelligence and Clinical Pharmacy* 15:758–765.

————1984. *Quality Assurance in Medicine: Experience in the Public Sector.* Santa Monica: RAND Corporation (Pub. no. R-3193-HHS). Abridged version published in *American Behavioral Scientist* 27:583–607.

Lohr, Kathleen N., Robert H. Brook, and Michael A. Kaufman. 1980. "Quality of Care in the New Mexico Medicaid Program (1971–1975)." *Medical Care* 18 (Suppl.):1–129. Also published under the same title, Santa Monica: RAND Corporation (Pub. no. R-2513-HEW).

Lohr, Kathleen N., and M. Susan Marquis. 1984. *Medicare and Medicaid: Past, Present, and Future.* Santa Monica: RAND Corporation (Pub. no. N-2088-HHS/RC).

Lohr, Kathleen N., et al. 1983. *Measurement of Physiologic Health for Children.* Vol. 2: *Middle Ear Disease and Hearing Impairment.* Santa Monica: RAND Corporation (Pub. no. R-2898/2-HHS).

————1986a. "Chronic Disease in a General Adult Population: Findings from the RAND Health Insurance Experiment." *Western Journal of Medicine* 145:537–545. Also available from Santa Monica: RAND Corporation (Pub. no. R-2262/1-HHS).

————1986b. *Conceptualization and Measurement of Physiologic Health for Adults: Overview of Chronic Disease in a General Adult Population.* Santa Monica: RAND Corporation (Pub. no. R-2262/1-HHS).

————1986c. "Use of Medical Care in the Rand Health Insurance Experiment: Diagnosis- and Service-Specific Analyses in a Randomized Controlled Trial." *Medical Care* 24 (Suppl.): S1–87. Also available from Santa Monica: RAND Corporation (Pub. no. R-3469-HHS).

Lurie, Nicole, et al. 1987. "Preventive Care: Do We Practice What We Preach?" *American Journal of Public Health* 77:801–804.

————1989. "How Free Care Improved Vision in the Health Insurance Experiment." *American Journal of Public Health* 79:640–642.

Manning, Willard G. 1983. *The Use of Pathology Services: A Comparison of Fee-for-Service and a Prepaid Group Practice.* Santa Monica: RAND Corporation (Pub. no. R-2919-HCFA).

Manning, Willard G., Naihua Duan, and William H. Rogers. 1987. "Monte Carlo Evidence on the Choice between Sample Selection and Two-Part Models." *Journal of Econometrics* 35:59–82.

Manning, Willard G., Lee A. Lillard, and Charles E. Phelps. 1984. "Preventive Medical Care and Its Consequences: The Effect of a Randomly Assigned Physical Examination." In *Proceedings of the Third International Conference on Systems Science in Health Care,* ed. W. van Eimeren, R. Engelbrecht, and Charles Flagle. New York: Springer Verlag.

Manning, Willard G., and M. Susan Marquis. 1989. *Health Insurance: Trade-off between Risk Sharing and Moral Hazard.* Santa Monica: RAND Corporation (Pub. no. R-3729-NCHSR).

Manning, Willard G., Jr., Joseph P. Newhouse, and John E. Ware, Jr. 1982. "The Status of Health in Demand Estimation: Beyond Excellent, Good, Fair, and Poor." In *Economic Aspects of Health,* ed. Victor R. Fuchs. Chicago: University of Chicago Press. Also available from Santa Monica: RAND Corporation (Pub. no. R-2696-1-HHS), 1981.

Manning, Willard G., and Charles E. Phelps. 1979. "Dental Care Demand: Point Estimates and Implications for National Health Insurance." *Bell Journal of Economics* 10 (Autumn). Also available from Santa Monica: RAND Corporation (Pub. no. R-2157), 1978.

Manning, Willard G., and Kenneth B. Wells. 1992. "The Effect of Psychological distress and Psychological Well-Being on the Use of Medical Services." *Medical Care* 30:541–553.

Manning, Willard G., Kenneth B. Wells, and Bernadette Benjamin. 1986. "Use of Outpatient Mental Health Care: Trial of a Prepaid Group Practice versus Fee-for-Service." *Journal of Human Resources* 21:293–320. A longer version with the same title is available from Santa Monica: RAND Corporation (Pub. no. R-3277-NIMH).

———1987. "Use of Outpatient Mental Health Services over Time in a Health Maintenance Organization and Fee-for-Service Plans." *American Journal of Psychiatry* 144:283–287.

Manning, Willard G., et al. 1980. *Effects of Mental Health Insurance: Evidence from the Health Insurance Experiment.* Santa Monica: RAND Corporation (Pub. no. R-3741-NCHSR).

———1981. "A Two-Part Model of the Demand for Medical Care: Preliminary Results from the Health Insurance Study." In *Health, Economics, and Health Economics,* ed. Jacques van der Gaag and Mark Perlman. Amsterdam: North Holland. Also available in Santa Monica: RAND Corporation (Pub. no. R-2705-HHS).

———1984a. *A Controlled Trial of the Effect of a Prepaid Group Practice on the Utilization of Medical Services.* Santa Monica: RAND Corporation (Pub. no. R-3029-HHS). Abridged version published in *New England Journal of*

Medicine 310:1505–10, 1984; reprinted in *Evaluation Studies Review Manual,* vol. 10, ed. Linda Aiken and Barbara Kehrer, Beverly Hills: Sage, 1985.

————1984b. "Cost Sharing and the Use of Ambulatory Mental Health Services." *American Psychologist* 39:1077–89.

————1984c. "A Response to Drs. Ellis and McGuire." *American Psychologist* 39:1197–99.

————1985. "The Demand for Dental Care: Evidence from a Randomized Trial in Health Insurance." *Journal of the American Dental Association* 110:895–902. Also available from Santa Monica: RAND Corporation (Pub. no. R-3225-HHS).

————1986. "How Cost Sharing Affects the Use of Ambulatory Mental Health Services." *JAMA* 256:1930–34.

————1987. *Health Insurance and the Demand for Medical Care: Evidence from a Randomized Experiment.* Santa Monica: RAND Corporation (Pub. no. R-3476-HHS). Abridged version published in *American Economic Review* 77:251–277.

————1989a. *The Effects of Mental Health Insurance: Evidence from the Health Insurance Experiment.* Santa Monica: RAND Corporation (Pub. no. R-3815-NIMH/HCFA).

————1989b. "The Taxes of Sin: Do Smokers and Drinkers Pay Their Way?" *Journal of the American Medical Association* 261:1604–09.

Marquis, Kent H. 1977. *The Methodology Used to Measure Health Care Consumption during the First Year of the Health Insurance Experiment.* Santa Monica: RAND Corporation (Pub. no. R-2126-HEW).

————1978a. *Inferring Health Interview Response Bias from Imperfect Record Checks.* Santa Monica: RAND Corporation (Pub. no. P-6159).

————1978b. *Record Check Validity of Survey Responses: A Reassessment of Bias in Reports of Hospitalizations.* Santa Monica: RAND Corporation (Pub. no. R-2319).

————1979a. *Evaluation of Health Diary Data in the Health Insurance Study.* Santa Monica: RAND Corporation (Pub. no. N-1212-HEW).

————1979b. *Some Implicit Assumptions in Survey Measurement Error Estimation Using Record Checks.* Santa Monica: RAND Corporation (Pub. no. P-6341).

————1981. "Hospital Stay Response Error Estimates for the Health Insurance Study's Baseline Survey." In *Health, Economics, and Health Economics,* ed. Jacques van der Gaag and Mark Perlman. Amsterdam: North Holland. Also available from Santa Monica: RAND Corporation (Pub. no. R-2555-HEW), 1980.

Marquis, Kent H., M. Susan Marquis, and Joseph P. Newhouse. 1976. "The Measurement of Expenditures for Physician and Dental Services: Methodological Findings from the Health Insurance Study." *Medical Care* 14:913–

931. Also available from Santa Monica: RAND Corporation (Pub. no. R-1883-HEW).

Marquis, M. Susan. 1979. *The Costs, Financing, and Distributional Effects of a Catastrophic Supplement to Medicare.* Santa Monica: RAND Corporation (Pub. no. R-2431-HEW).

———1982a. "The Distributive Impact of a Medicare Catastrophic Benefit." In *Economics of Health Care,* ed. Jacques van der Gaag, William B. Neenan, and Theodore Tsukahara. New York: Praeger.

———1982b. *Laboratory Test Ordering by Physicians: The Effect of Reimbursement Policies.* Santa Monica: RAND Corporation (Pub. no. R-2901-HCFA).

———1983. "Consumers' Knowledge about Their Health Insurance Coverage." *Health Care Financing Review* 5(1):65–80. Also available from Santa Monica: RAND Corporation (Pub. no. R-2753-HHS).

———1985. "Cost-Sharing and Provider Choice." *Journal of Health Economics* 4:137–157. Also published as *Cost Sharing and the Patient's Choice of Provider,* Santa Monica: RAND Corporation (Pub. no. R-3126-HHS).

———1986. *Characteristics of Health Insurance Coverage: Descriptive and Methodological Findings from the Health Insurance Experiment.* Santa Monica: RAND Corporation (Pub. no. N-2503-HHS).

———1992. "Adverse Selection with a Multiple Choice among Health Insurance Plans: A Simulation Analysis." *Journal of Health Economics* 11:129–151.

Marquis, M. Susan, and Joan L. Buchanan. 1989. *Mandating Health Insurance Benefits for Employees: Effects on Health Care Use and Employer Cost.* Santa Monica: RAND Corporation (Pub. no. N-2911-DOL).

———1992. "Subsidies and National Health Care Reform: The Effect on Workers' Demand for Health Insurance Coverage." In *Health Benefits and the Workforce.* Washington, D.C.: U.S. Government Printing Office.

Marquis, M. Susan, Allyson R. Davies, and John E. Ware, Jr. 1983. "Patient Satisfaction and Change in Medical Care Provider: A Longitudinal Study." *Medical Care* 21:821–829. Also available from Santa Monica: RAND Corporation (Pub. no. N-1859-HHS).

———1985. "Change in Medical Provider: A Causal Analysis of the Consequences of Patient Dissatisfaction." *Advances in Consumer Research,* 12. Westport, Conn.: JAI Press.

Marquis, M. Susan, and Ellen R. Harrison. 1992. "Health Status and Health Care Use of Uninsured Workers." In *Health Benefits and the Workforce.* Washington, D.C.: U.S. Government Printing Office.

Marquis, M. Susan, and Martin R. Holmer. 1986. *Choice under Uncertainty and the Demand for Health Insurance.* Santa Monica: RAND Corporation (Pub. no. N-2516-HHS).

Marquis, M. Susan, and Kent H. Marquis. 1977a. *Measurement Evaluation of the Health Insurance Study Screening Interview.* Santa Monica: RAND Corporation (Pub. no. R-2107-HEW).

———1977b. *Survey Measurement Design and Evaluation Using Reliability Theory.* Santa Monica: RAND Corporation (Pub. no. R-2088-HEW).

Marquis, M. Susan, and Charles E. Phelps. 1985. *Demand for Supplementary Health Insurance.* Santa Monica: RAND Corporation (Pub. no. R-3285-HHS).

———1987. "Price Elasticity and Adverse Selection in the Demand for Supplementary Health Insurance." *Economic Inquiry* 25 (April):299–313.

Mills, Helene R. 1978a. *Rand Master Input Tape (RMIT): Description.* Santa Monica: RAND Corporation (Pub. no. RCC-1550/11).

———1978b. *Rand Master Input Tape Generator System (RMITGEN): System Description.* Santa Monica: RAND Corporation (Pub. no. RCC-1550/12).

———1979. *Rand Master Input Tape Generator System (RMITGEN): User's Manual.* Santa Monica: RAND Corporation (Pub. no. RCC-1550/13).

Mitchell, Bridger M. 1976. *Basic Elements of Financing National Health Insurance.* Santa Monica: RAND Corporation (Pub. no. P-5610).

Mitchell, Bridger M., and Charles E. Phelps. 1976. "National Health Insurance: Some Costs and Effects of Mandated Employee Coverage." *Journal of Political Economy* 84:553–511. Also published as *Employer-Paid Group Health Insurance and the Costs of Mandated National Coverage,* Santa Monica: RAND Corporation (Pub. no. R-1509-HEW), 1975.

Mitchell, Bridger M., and William B. Schwartz. 1976a. "The Financing of National Health Insurance." *Science* 192:621–636. Also available from Santa Monica: RAND Corporation (Pub. no. R-1711-HEW).

———1976b. "Strategies for Financing National Health Insurance: Who Wins and Who Loses." *New England Journal of Medicine* 295:866–871.

Mitchell, Bridger M., and Ronald Vogel. 1975. "Health and Taxes: An Assessment of the Medical Deduction." *Southern Economic Journal* 41:660–672. Also available from Santa Monica: RAND Corporation (Pub. no. R-1222-OEO), 1973.

Morris, Carl N. 1979. "A Finite Selection Model for Experimental Design of the Health Insurance Study." *Journal of Econometrics* 11:43–61.

———1980. *Nonresponse Issues in Public Policy Experiments, with Emphasis on the Health Insurance Study.* Santa Monica: RAND Corporation (Pub. no. N-1346) Also published in Committee on National Statistics, National Research Council, *Symposium on Incomplete Data: Preliminary Proceedings, Panel on Incomplete Data,* Washington, D.C., 1979; in *Incomplete Data in Sample Surveys,* vol. 3, chap. 15, 313–325, New York: Academic Press, 1983.

———1985. *Sample Selection in the Health Insurance Experiment: Compar-*

ing the Enrolled and Nonenrolled Populations. Santa Monica: RAND Corporation (Pub. no. N-2354-HHS).

Morris, Carl, and Bradley Efron. 1975. "Data Analysis Using Stein's Estimator and Its Generalization." *Journal of the American Statistical Association* 170:311–319. Also available from Santa Monica: RAND Corporation (Pub. no. R-1394-OEO), 1974.

Morris, Carl N., Joseph P. Newhouse, and Rae W. Archibald. 1979. "On the Theory and Practice of Obtaining Unbiased and Efficient Samples in Social Surveys and Experiments." In *Experimental Economics,* vol. 1, ed. Vernon L. Smith. Westport, Conn.: JAI Press. Reprinted in *Evaluation Studies Review Annual,* vol. 5, ed. Ernst Stromsdorfer and George Farkas, Beverly Hills: Sage, 1980. Also available from Santa Monica: RAND Corporation (Pub. no. R-2173-HEW), 1980.

Murata, Paul J., and Robert L. Kane. 1987. "Do Families Get Family Care?" *Journal of the American Medical Association* 257:1912–15.

Newhouse, Joseph P. 1974a. "A Design for a Health Insurance Experiment." *Inquiry* 11:5–27.

————1974b. *The Health Insurance Study: A Summary.* Santa Monica: RAND Corporation (Pub. no. R-965-1-OEO).

————1974c. "The Health Insurance Study: Response to Hester and Leveson." *Inquiry* 11:236–241.

————1974d. "Informed Consent and Social Experimentation." In *Ethical and Legal Issues of Social Experimentation,* ed. Alice M. Rivlin and P. Michael Timpane. Also available from Santa Monica: RAND Corporation (Pub. no. P-5088).

————1974e. *Issues in the Analysis and Design of the Experimental Portion of the Health Insurance Study.* Santa Monica: RAND Corporation (Pub. no. R-1484-OEO). Also published in *Proceedings of the Social Statistics Section,* American Statistics Association, 1973.

————1975. "Forecasting Demand for Medical Care for the Purpose of Planning Health Services." In *Systems Aspects of Health Planning: Proceedings of the IIASA Conference, Baden, Austria, August 20–22, 1974,* ed. Mark Thompson and Norman T. Bailey, Amsterdam: North Holland. Also available from Santa Monica: RAND Corporation (Pub. no. R-1635-OEO).

————1976a. "Comments on Evaluation of Social Experiments." In *The Evaluation of Social Programs,* ed. Clark Abt. Beverly Hills: Sage.

————1976b. "Health Care Cost Sharing and Cost Containment." In *National Health Insurance.* Vol. 3: *Major Issues. Hearings before the Subcommittee on Health and the Environment of the Committee on Interstate and Foreign Commerce,* U.S. House of Representatives, 94th Cong., 2d sess. (Serial 94-91). Also available from Santa Monica: RAND Corporation (Pub. no. P-5615).

————1976c. "Inflation and Health Insurance." In *Health: A Victim or Cause of Inflation,* ed. Michael Zubkoff, New York: Milbank Memorial Fund. Also available from Santa Monica: RAND Corporation (Pub. no. P-5331), 1975.

————1977. "Medical Care Expenditure: A Cross-National Survey." *Journal of Human Resources* 12:115–125. Also published as *Income and Medical Care Expenditure across Countries,* Santa Monica: RAND Corporation (Pub. no. P-5608-1), 1976.

————1978a. "Insurance Benefits, Out-of-Pocket Payments, and the Demand for Medical Care: A Review of the Literature." *Health and Medical Care Services Review* 14:1, 3–5. Also available from Santa Monica: RAND Corporation (Pub. no. P-6134).

————1978b. "National Health Insurance." In *The Report of the National Commission on the Cost of Medical Care.* Vol. 2: *Collected Papers,* Chicago: American Medical Association. Also available from Santa Monica: RAND Corporation (Pub. no. P-5920), 1977.

————1979. "Medical Costs and Medical Market: Another View." *New England Journal of Medicine* 300:855–856. Also available from Santa Monica: RAND Corporation (Pub. no. P-6319).

————1980a. "Cost Sharing as a Cost Containment Strategy: Comments on Laurence Seidman's Paper." In *National Health Insurance: What Now, What Later, What Never?* ed. Mark Pauly. Washington, D.C.: American Enterprise Institute. Also available from Santa Monica: RAND Corporation (Pub. no. P-6387), 1979.

————1980b. *Rationing of Medical Services: Professional Ethics, Governmental Regulation, or Markets?* Santa Monica: RAND Corporation (Pub. no. P-6551). Also published as "Rationing of Medical Services: Comments on Culyer, Maynard, and Williams; Reinhardt; and Stahl," in *A New Approach to the Economics of Health Care,* ed. Mancur Olson, Washington, D.C.: American Enterprise Institute, 1981.

————1981a. "The Demand for Medical Care Services: A Retrospect and Prospect." In *Health, Economics, and Health Economics,* ed. Jacques van der Gaag and Mark Perlman. Amsterdam: North Holland. Also available from Santa Monica: RAND Corporation (Pub. no. R-2691-HHS).

————1981b. "The Erosion of the Medical Marketplace." In *Advances in Health Economics and Health Services Research,* vol. 2, ed. Richard Scheffler, Westport, Conn.: JAI Press. Nontechnical version published as "The Structure of Health Insurance and the Erosion of Competition in the Medical Marketplace," in *Competition in the Health Care Sector: Past, Present, Future,* ed. Warren Greenberg, Germantown, Md.: Aspen Systems Corporation, 1978; nontechnical version reprinted in *Profile of Medical Practice 1979,* Chicago: American Medical Association.

—————1982a. "Assessing the Impact of Cost Sharing in Health Care Utilization and Expenditures: Interim Results from the Rand Study." In National Health Policy Forum, *Competition in Health Care.* Washington, D.C.

—————1982b. "Austerity in Public Medical Care Programs: Miserliness or Economic Response?" *Journal of Health Economics* 1:210–214. Also available from Santa Monica: RAND Corporation (Pub. no. N-1912-HHS).

—————1982c. "Is Competition the Answer?" *Journal of Health Economics* 1:109–116. Also available from Santa Monica: RAND Corporation (Pub. no. P-6744).

—————1982d. *Should Medical Care Be Free? Cost Sharing and Health Financing Policy.* Santa Monica: RAND Corporation (Pub. no. P-6784).

—————1982e. "A Summary of the RAND Health Insurance Study." *Annals of the New York Academy of Sciences* 387:111-114.

—————1983. *Proposed New Cost Sharing and the Costs of Medicare: Statement to the Committee on Aging and the Committee on Finance,* U.S. Senate, April 13, 1983, and May 16, 1983. Also available from Santa Monica: RAND Corporation (Pub. no. P-6863).

—————1984. "Cost Sharing for Medical Care Services." Testimony before the Subcommittee on Defense of the Senate Appropriations Committee, 12 June 1984. Also available from Santa Monica: RAND Corporation (Pub. no. P-6997).

—————1985. "Experimentation as Part of a Social Science Research Strategy." Testimony before the Committee on Science and Technology, U.S. House of Representatives, 18 September 1985. Santa Monica: RAND Corporation (Pub. no. P-7141).

—————1986. "Using Social Science Experiments to Improve the Appraisal of Social Programs." *Project Evaluation* 1:39–42.

Newhouse, Joseph P., and Rae W. Archibald. 1978. *Overview of Health Insurance Study Publications.* Santa Monica: RAND Corporation (Pub. no. P-6221).

Newhouse, Joseph P., and Lindy J. Friedlander. 1980. "The Relationship between Medical Resources and Measures of Health: Some Additional Evidence." *Journal of Human Resources* 15:200–218. Also available from Santa Monica: RAND Corporation (Pub. no. R-2066-HEW), 1977.

Newhouse, Joseph P., and George A. Goldberg. 1976. *Allocation of Resources in Medical Care from an Economic Viewpoint: Remarks to the XXIX World Assembly of the World Medical Association and Commentary.* Santa Monica: RAND Corporation (Pub. no. P-5590).

Newhouse, Joseph P., and M. Susan Marquis. 1978. "The Norms Hypothesis and the Demand for Medical Care." *Journal of Human Resources* 13 (Suppl.):159–182. Also available from Santa Monica: RAND Corporation (Pub. no. R-2289-HEW), 1980.

Newhouse, Joseph P., and Charles E. Phelps. 1974. "Price and Income Elasticities for Medical Care Services." In *The Economics of Health and Medical Care: Proceedings of a Conference of the International Economics Association,* ed. Shigeto Tsuru and Mark Perlman. London: Macmillan. Also available from Santa Monica: RAND Corporation (Pub. no. R-1197-NC).

——1976. "New Estimates of Price and Income Elasticities for Medical Care Services." In *The Impact of Health Insurance on the Health Services Sector,* ed. Richard Rosett. New York: National Bureau of Economic Research.

——1980. "On Having Your Cake and Eating It Too: An Analysis of Estimated Effects of Insurance on Demand for Medical Care." *Journal of Econometrics* 13:365–390. Also available from Santa Monica: RAND Corporation (Pub. no. R-1149-1-NC), 1979.

Newhouse, Joseph P., Charles E. Phelps, and William B. Schwartz. 1974. "Policy Options and the Impact of National Health Insurance." *New England Journal of Medicine* 290:1345–59; reprinted in *Benefit-Cost and Policy Analysis, 1974,* ed. Richard Zeckhauser, Chicago: Aldine, 1975; and in *Public Expenditure and Policy Analysis,* 2d ed., ed. Robert H. Haveman and Julius Margolis, Chicago: Rand McNally College Publishing Company, 1977. Also available from Santa Monica: RAND Corporation (Pub. no. R-1528-OEO-HEW).

Newhouse, Joseph P., John E. Ware, Jr., and C. A. Donald. 1981. "How Sophisticated Are Consumers about the Medical Care Delivery System?" *Medical Care* 19:316–328. Also available from Santa Monica: RAND Corporation (Pub. no. R-2693-HHS).

Newhouse, Joseph P., et al. 1979. "Design Improvements in the Second Generation of Social Experiments: The Health Insurance Study." *Journal of Econometrics* 11:117–129. Also published as *Measurement Issues in the Second Generation of Social Experiments: The Health Insurance Study,* Santa Monica: RAND Corporation (Pub. no. P-5701), 1976.

——1980. "The Effect of Deductibles on the Demand for Medical Care Services." *Journal of the American Statistical Association* 75:525–535. Also published as *An Estimate of the Impact of Deductibles on the Demand for Medical Care Services.* Santa Monica: RAND Corporation (Pub. no. R-1661-HEW), 1978.

——1982a. "Does the Geographical Distribution of Physicians Reflect Market Failure?" *Bell Journal of Economics* 13:483–505. Also available from Santa Monica: RAND Corporation (Pub. no. R-2734-HHS).

——1982b. Some Interim Results from a Controlled Trial of Cost Sharing in Health Insurance. Santa Monica: RAND Corporation (Pub. no. R-2847-HHS). Abridged version in *New England Journal of Medicine* 305 (17

December 1981):1501–07; and in *Evaluation Studies Review Annual,* vol. 10, ed. Linda H. Aiken and Barbara H. Kehrer. Beverly Hills: Sage, 1985.

———1982c. "Where Have All the Doctors Gone?" *Journal of the American Medical Association* 247:2392–96. Also published as *How Have Location Patterns of Physicians Affected the Availability of Medical Services?* Santa Monica: RAND Corporation (Pub. no. R-2872-HJK/HHS/RWJ).

———1983. "A Controlled Trial in Dental and Medical Insurance." *Journal of the American Dental Association* 106:173–177.

———1985. "Are Fee-for-Service Costs Increasing Faster than HMO Costs?" *Medical Care* 23:960–966.

———1987. "The Findings of the Rand Health Insurance Experiment—A Response to Welch et al." *Medical Care* 25:157–179.

———1989. "Adjusting Capitation Rates Using Objective Health Measures and Prior Utilization." *Health Care Financing Review* 10(3):41–54.

O'Grady, Kevin, et al. 1985. "The Impact of Cost-Sharing on Emergency Department Use." *New England Journal of Medicine* 313:484–490. Also available from Santa Monica: RAND Corporation (Pub. no. N-2376-HHS).

Phelps, Charles E. 1973. *The Demand for Health Insurance—A Theoretical and Empirical Investigation.* Santa Monica: RAND Corporation (Pub. no. R-1054-OEO).

———1976a. "Benefit-Cost Analysis of Quality Assurance Programs." In *Quality Assurance in Health Care,* ed. Paul Gertman and Richard Egdahl. New York: Aspen Systems.

———1976b. "The Demand for Reimbursement Insurance." In *The Role of Health Insurance in The Health Services Sector,* ed. Richard N. Rosett. New York: National Bureau of Economic Research.

———1978a. *Experience Rating in Medical Malpractice Insurance.* Santa Monica: RAND Corporation (Pub. no. P-5877-1).

———1978b. "Illness Prevention and Medical Insurance." *Journal of Human Resources* 13 (Suppl.):183–207.

———1978c. *Insurance Benefits and Their Impact on Health Care Costs.* Santa Monica: RAND Corporation (Pub. no. P-5844).

———1980. "National Health Insurance by Regulation: Mandated Employee Benefits." In *National Health Insurance: What Now, What Later, What Never?* ed. Mark V. Pauly. Washington, D.C.: American Enterprise Institute. Also available from Santa Monica: RAND Corporation (Pub. no. P-6391).

———1983. *Taxing Health Insurance: How Much Is Enough?* Santa Monica: RAND Corporation (Pub. no. P-6915).

Phelps, Charles E., and Joseph P. Newhouse. 1972a. "The Effects of Coinsurance: A Multivariate Analysis." *Social Security Bulletin* 35(6):20–29.

———1972b. *The Effects of Coinsurance on Demand for Physician Services.* Santa Monica: RAND Corporation (Pub. no. R-976-OEO).

———1974. "Coinsurance, the Price of Time, and the Demand for Medical Services." *Review of Economics and Statistics* 56:334–342. Revised version published as *Coinsurance and the Demand for Medical Services,* Santa Monica: RAND Corporation (Pub. no. R-964-1-OEO).

Rogers, William H., and Joseph P. Newhouse. 1985. "Measuring Unfiled Claims in the Health Insurance Experiment." In *Collecting Evaluation Data: Problems and Solutions,* ed. Leigh Burstein, Howard E. Freeman, and Peter H. Rossi. Beverly Hills: Sage.

Rogers, William H., Kathleen N. Williams, and Robert H. Brook. 1979. *Conceptualization and Measurement of Health for Adults in the Health Insurance Study.* Vol. 7: *Power Analysis for Health Status Measures.* Santa Monica: RAND Corporation (Pub. no. R-1987/7-HEW).

Rolph, John E. 1975. "Choosing Shrinkage Estimators for Regression Problems." *Communications in Statistics—Theory and Methods* A5(9):789–802. Also available from Santa Monica: RAND Corporation (Pub. no. R-1640-OEO).

———1981. "Some Statistical Evidence on Merit Rating in Medical Malpractice Insurance." *Journal of Risk and Insurance* 48:247–260. Also available from Santa Monica: RAND Corporation (Pub. no. N-1725-HHS).

Rosenthal, Marc, et al. 1981. *Conceptualization and Measurement of Physiologic Health for Adults.* Vol. 5: *Congestive Heart Failure.* Santa Monica: RAND Corporation (Pub. no. R-2262/5-HHS).

Rubenstein, Randi S., and Kathleen N. Lohr. 1983. "Use of Survey Questions to Measure Presence of Visual Impairment: Findings from the Rand Health Insurance Experiment." *American Journal of Public Health* 73:1331–32.

Rubenstein, Randi S., et al. 1982. *Conceptualization and Measurement of Physiologic Health for Adults.* Vol. 12: *Vision Impairments.* Santa Monica: RAND Corporation (Pub. no. R-2262/12-HHS).

———1983. *Conceptualization and Measurement of Physiologic Health for Adults.* Vol. 15: *Surgical Conditions.* Santa Monica: RAND Corporation (Pub. no. R-2262/15-HHS).

———1984. "Psychosocial Characteristics of Candidates for the Prospective Evaluation of Radial Keratotomy (PERK) Study." *Archives of Ophthalmology* 102:1187–92.

———1985. *Measurement of Physiologic Health for Children.* Vol. 4: *Vision Impairments.* Santa Monica: RAND Corporation (Pub. no. R-2898/4-HHS).

Schwartz, William B., et al. 1980. "The Changing Geographic Distribution of Board-Certified Physicians: Facts, Theory, and Implications." *New England Journal of Medicine* 303:1032–38. Also available from Santa Monica: RAND Corporation (Pub. no. R-2673-HHS/RC).

Scott, Bonnie, et al. 1980. *Conceptualization and Measurement of Physiologic Health for Adults.* Vol. 6: *Anemia.* Santa Monica: RAND Corporation (Pub. no. R-2262/6-HEW).

———1981. *Conceptualization and Measurement of Physiologic Health for Adults: Joint Disorders.* Santa Monica: RAND Corporation (Pub. no. R-2262/10-HHS).

Seda, Martin, and Joan Keesey. 1980. *The Finite Selection Model: Description and User's Guide.* Santa Monica: RAND Corporation (Pub. no. N-1183-HEW).

Shapiro, Martin F., John E. Ware, Jr., and Cathy D. Sherbourne. 1986. "Effects of Cost Sharing on Seeking Care for Serious and Minor Symptoms: Results of a Randomized Controlled Trial." *Annals of Internal Medicine* 104:246–251.

Shekelle, Paul G., and Robert H. Brook. 1991. "A Community-Based Study of the Use of Chiropractic Services." *American Journal of Public Health* 81:439–442.

Sherbourne, Cathy D. 1988. "The Role of Social Supports and Life Stress Events in Use of Mental Health Services." *Social Science and Medicine* 27:1393–1400.

Siu, Albert L., Willard G. Manning, and Bernadette Benjamin. 1990. "Patient, Provider, and Hospital Characteristics Associated with Inappropriate Hospitalization." *American Journal of Public Health* 80:1253–56. Also available from Santa Monica: RAND Corporation (Pub. no. R-3741-NCHSR).

Siu, Albert L., et al. 1986. "Inappropriate Use of Hospitals in a Randomized Trial of Health Insurance Plans." *New England Journal of Medicine* 315:1259–66.

———1988. "Use of the Hospital in a Randomized Trial of Prepaid Care." *Journal of the American Medical Association* 259:1343–46.

Sloan, Frank A. 1973. *Supply Responses of Young Physicians.* Santa Monica: RAND Corporation (Pub. no. R-1131-OEO).

Sloss, Elizabeth M., et al. 1987. "Effect of a Health Maintenance Organization on Physiologic Health: Results from a Randomized Trial." *Annals of Internal Medicine* 106:130–138. Also available from Santa Monica: RAND Corporation (Pub. no. R-3526-HHS).

Smith, Lisa H., et al. 1978. *The Health Insurance Study Screening Examination Procedures Manual.* Santa Monica: RAND Corporation (Pub. no. R-2101-HEW).

Spolsky, Vladimir, et al. 1983. *Measurement of Dental Health Status.* Santa Monica: RAND Corporation (Pub. no. R-2902-HHS).

Stewart, Anita L. 1982. "The Reliability and Validity of Self-Reported Weight and Height." *Journal of Chronic Diseases* 35:295–309.

Stewart, Anita L., Robert H. Brook, and Robert L. Kane. 1979. *Conceptualization and Measurement of Health Habits for Adults in the Health Insur-*

ance Study: Smoking. Santa Monica: RAND Corporation (Pub. no. R-2374/ 1-HEW).

——1980. *Conceptualization and Measurement of Health Habits for Adults in the Health Insurance Study: Overweight.* Santa Monica: RAND Corporation (Pub. no. R-2374/2-HEW). Abridged version published as "Effects of Being Overweight," *American Journal of Public Health* 7 (1982):250–261.

Stewart, Anita L., John E. Ware, Jr., and Robert H. Brook. 1977a. "The Meaning of Health: Understanding Functional Limitations." *Medical Care* 15:939–952.

——1977b. *A Study of the Reliability, Validity, and Precision of Scales to Measure Chronic Functional Limitations Due to Poor Health.* Santa Monica: RAND Corporation (Pub. no. P-5660).

——1981. "Advances in the Measurement of Functional Status: Construction of Aggregate Indexes." *Medical Care* 19:473–488.

——1982a. *Construction and Scoring of Aggregate Functional Status Indexes,* vol. 1. Santa Monica: RAND Corporation (Pub. no. R-2551-1-HHS). A preliminary version was published as "Advances in the Measurement of Functional Status: Construction of Aggregate Indexes," *Medical Care* 19 (May 1981):473–488.

——1982b. *Construction and Scoring of Aggregate Functional Status Indexes.* Vol. 2: *Appendixes.* Santa Monica: RAND Corporation (Pub. no. N-1706-1-HHS).

Stewart, Anita L., et al. 1978. *Conceptualization and Measurement of Health for Adults in the Health Insurance Study: Physical Health in Terms of Functioning.* Santa Monica: RAND Corporation (Pub. no. R-1987/2-HEW).

Stewart, David H. 1974. *A Design for Information Processing in the Health Insurance Study.* Santa Monica: RAND Corporation (Pub. no. P-5229).

Stewart, David H., and Martin Seda. 1978. *Data Processing in the National Health Insurance Study.* Santa Monica: RAND Corporation (Pub. no. P-5926).

Valdez, R. Burciaga. 1986. *The Effects of Cost Sharing on the Health of Children.* Santa Monica: RAND Corporation (Pub. no. R-3270-HHS).

——1989. *The Effect of a Prepaid Group Practice on Children's Medical Care Use and Health Outcomes Compared to Fee-for-Service Care.* Santa Monica: RAND Corporation (Pub. no. N-2618-HHS).

Valdez, R. Burciaga, et al. 1985. "Consequences of Cost Sharing for Children's Health." *Pediatrics* 75:952–961.

——1986. "Health Insurance, Medical Care, and Children's Health." *Pediatrics* 77:124–128.

——1989. "Prepaid Group Practice Effects on the Utilization of Medical Services and Health Outcomes for Children: Results from a Controlled Trial." *Pediatrics* 83:168–180.

Van Riesen, Kathleen. 1975. *Experiences in Conducting a Review of Statistical Program Packages.* Santa Monica: RAND Corporation (Pub. no. P-5491).

Veit, Clarice T., and John E. Ware, Jr. 1982. "Measuring Health and Health-Care Outcomes: Issues and Recommendations." In *Values and Long-Term Care,* ed. R. L. Kane. Lexington, Mass.: D. C. Heath/Lexington Books.

————1983. "The Structure of Psychological Distress and Well-Being in General Populations." *Journal of Consulting and Clinical Psychology* 51:730–742.

Ware, John E., Jr. 1976a. *The Conceptualization and Measurement of Health for Policy Relevant Research in Medical Care Delivery.* Santa Monica: RAND Corporation (Pub. no. P-5599).

————1976b. *The Reliability and Validity of General Health Ratings.* Santa Monica: RAND Corporation (Pub. no. P-5720). Also published as "Scales for Measuring General Health Perceptions," *Health Services Research* 11:396–415.

————1978. "Effects of Acquiescent Response Set on Patient Satisfaction Ratings." *Medical Care* 16:327–336. Also available from Santa Monica: RAND Corporation (Pub. no. P-5676).

————1981. "How to Survey Patient Satisfaction." *Drug Intelligence and Clinical Pharmacy* 15:892–899.

Ware, John E., Jr., and Allyson R. Davies. 1983. "Behavioral Consequences of Consumer Dissatisfaction with Medical Care." *Evaluation and Program Planning* 6:291–297.

Ware, John E., Jr., Allyson Davies-Avery, and Robert H. Brook. 1980. *Conceptualization and Measurement of Health for Adults in the Health Insurance Study.* Vol. 6: *Analysis of Relationships among Health Status Measures.* Santa Monica: RAND Corporation (Pub. no. R-1987/6-HEW).

Ware, John E., Jr., Allyson Davies-Avery, and Cathy A. Donald. 1978. *Conceptualization and Measurement of Health for Adults in the Health Insurance Study: General Health Perceptions.* Santa Monica: RAND Corporation (Pub. no. R-1987/5-HEW).

Ware, John E., Jr., Allyson Davies-Avery, and Anita L. Stewart. 1978. "The Measurement and Meaning of Patient Satisfaction: A Review of the Literature." *Health and Medical Care Review* 1:1–15. Also available from Santa Monica: RAND Corporation (Pub. no. P-6036), 1977.

Ware, John E., Jr., Shawn A. Johnston, and Allyson Davies-Avery. 1979. *Conceptualization and Measurement of Health for Adults in the Health Insurance Study: Mental Health.* Santa Monica: RAND Corporation (Pub. no. R-1987/3-HEW).

Ware, John E., Jr., and J. Young. 1979. "Studies of the Value Placed on Health." In *Health: What Is It Worth?* ed. Selma Mushkin. New York: Pergamon Press, 1979. Also available from Santa Monica: RAND Corporation (Pub. no. P-5987).

Ware, John E., Jr., et al. 1978. *Associations among Psychological Well-Being and Other Health Status Constructs.* Santa Monica: RAND Corporation (Pub. no. P-6213).

————1980. *Conceptualization and Measurement of Health for Adults in the Health Insurance Study.* Vol. 1: *Model of Health and Methodology.* Santa Monica: RAND Corporation (Pub. no. R-1987/1-HEW).

————1981. "Choosing Measures of Health Status for Individuals in General Populations." *American Journal of Public Health* 71:620–625. Also available from Santa Monica: RAND Corporation (Pub. no. N-1642-HHS).

————1983. "Defining and Measuring Patient Satisfaction with Medical Care." *Evaluation and Program Planning* 6:247–263.

————1984. "Health Status and the Use of Outpatient Mental Health Services." *American Psychologist* 39:1090–1100.

————1987. *Health Outcomes for Adults in Prepaid and Fee-for-Service Systems of Care.* Santa Monica: RAND Corporation (Pub. no. R-3459-HHS). Abridged version published as "Comparison of Health Outcomes at a Health Maintenance Organisation with Those of Fee-for-Service Care," *Lancet* 1 (1986):1017–22.

Wells, Kenneth B. 1984. "The Sensitivity of Mental Health Use Estimates to Methods Effects." *Medical Care* 22:783–788.

————1985. "A Summary of Cost Sharing and the Demand for Ambulatory Mental Health Services." *Professional Psychologist* 9:1–3, 22–23.

Wells, Kenneth B., Emmett Keeler, and Willard G. Manning. 1990. "Patterns of Outpatient Mental Health Care over Time: Some Implications for Estimates of Demand and for Benefit Design." *Health Services Research* 24:773–790.

Wells, Kenneth B., Willard G. Manning, and Bernadette Benjamin. 1986a. "A Comparison of the Effects of Sociodemographic Factors and Health Status on Use of Outpatient Mental Health Services in HMO and Fee-for-Service Plans." *Medical Care* 24:949–960.

————1986b. "Use of Mental Health Services in HMO and Fee-for-Service Plans—Results of a Randomized Controlled Trial." *Health Services Research* 21:453–474.

Wells, Kenneth B., Willard G. Manning, Jr., and R. Burciaga Valdez. 1989. "The Effects of Insurance Generosity on the Psychological Distress and Psychological Well-being of a General Population." *Archives of General Psychiatry* 46:315–320. Longer version published as *The Effects of Insurance Generosity on the Psychological Distress and Well-Being of a General*

Population: Results from a Randomized Trial of Insurance, Santa Monica: RAND Corporation (Pub. no. R-3682-NIMH).

————1990. "The Effects of a Prepaid Group Practice on Mental Health Outcomes." *Health Services Research* 25:615–625. Longer version published as *The Effects of a Prepaid Group Practice on Mental Health Outcomes of a General Population: Results from a Randomized Trial,* Santa Monica: RAND Corporation (Pub. no. R-3834-NIMH/HCFA), 1989.

Wells, Kenneth B., et al. 1982. *Cost Sharing and the Demand for Ambulatory Mental Health Services.* Santa Monica: RAND Corporation (Pub. no. R-2960-HHS). Abridged version published in *American Psychologist* 39 (October 1984):1090–1100.

————1986a. "Sociodemographic Factors and Use of Outpatient Mental Health Services." *Medical Care* 24:75–85.

————1986b. "Use of Outpatient Mental Health Services by a General Population with Health Insurance Coverage." *Hospital and Community Psychiatry* 37:1119–25.

————1987. "Cost Sharing and Use of General Medical Providers for Outpatient Mental Health Care." *Health Services Research* 22:1–18.

Williams, Ann W., John E. Ware, Jr., and Cathy A. Donald. 1981. "A Model of Mental Health, Life Events, and Social Supports Applicable to General Populations." *Journal of Health and Social Behavior* 22:324–336.

Williams, Kathleen N. 1975. *Issues of Physician Migration from the Perspective of the Recipient Countries.* Santa Monica: RAND Corporation (Pub. no. P-5499).

————1976. *Implementation of Professional Standards Review Organizations: A Theoretical Discussion.* Santa Monica: RAND Corporation (Pub. no. P-5757).

Williams, Kathleen N., and Robert H. Brook. 1975. "Foreign Medical Graduates and Their Impact on the Quality of Medical Care in the United States." *Milbank Memorial Fund Quarterly: Health and Society* 53:549–581. Also available from Santa Monica: RAND Corporation (Pub. no. R-1698-HEW), 1976.

————1978a. "Quality Measurement and Assurance: A Literature Review." *Health and Medical Care Services Review* 3:1, 3–15.

————1978b. "Research Opportunities in Primary Care." *Mount Sinai Journal of Medicine* 45:663–672. Also available from Santa Monica: RAND Corporation (Pub. no. P-6020).

Wooldridge, Judith. 1976. "Report on the Physician Capacity Utilization Telephone Surveys." Princeton: Mathematica Policy Research.

Yormark, Beatrice, and David H. Stewart. 1973. *A Data Management System Evaluation for the HIS.* Santa Monica: RAND Corporation (Pub. no. P-5181).

Zielske, John V., et al. 1981. *Conceptualization and Measurement of Physiologic Health for Adults: Urinary Tract Infection.* Santa Monica: RAND Corporation (Pub. no. R-2262/16-HHS).

————1982. *Conceptualization and Measurement of Physiologic Health for Adults: Stomach Pain and Peptic Ulcer Disease.* Santa Monica: RAND Corporation (Pub. no. R-2262/17-HHS).

Further Explanation of Design Decisions

Rationale for Plan Choices

The rationale for our plan choices was as follows:

1. The greater the variation in the out-of-pocket prices consumers faced, the better we would be able to measure the effects of cost sharing. The 0–95 percent coinsurance range gave us almost maximal variation on this dimension. We assigned the sample to four coinsurance rates rather than to many rates between 0 and 95 percent for two reasons. First, in any design in which the response can be approximated by a low-order polynomial it is optimal to have design points at the extremes of the range (0 and 95) and one more design point than the order of the polynomial. Thus, four design points permitted estimation of a cubic response function, which seemed general enough (although we subsequently chose not to analyze the data in this fashion in order not to impose a functional form). Second, the interior points were selected at 25 and 50 percent because many private insurance plans at that time had rates of 20 or 25 percent, and some occasionally had 50 percent coinsurance for some services.

2. Choosing MDE levels was more arbitrary than choosing coinsurance levels because there was no natural upper bound (such as 100 percent in the case of the coinsurance rate). We believed that 5–15 percent of income encompassed a reasonable range of variation and that few individuals would accept a plan with a markedly higher limit because of the risk such a limit would entail. We also placed a design point at 10 percent in order to measure any nonlinearity in the 5–15 range; theory suggested that the

response to an MDE would be nonlinear. (See Keeler, Newhouse, and Phelps 1977; and Chapter 4.)

3. Because we guaranteed that no one would be worse off financially from participating in the Experiment (discussion in text), high maximum out-of-pocket limits were expensive. Thus, for a given experimental budget, we faced a tradeoff between the size of the MDE and the size of the sample. Accordingly we capped the limit at $1,000. Although our original intent was to adjust the $1,000 limit in line with inflation (to keep it constant in real terms), budget constraints led us not to do so (that is, the limit was constant in nominal terms).

4. We included the plans with 50 percent coinsurance for outpatient mental health and dental services and 25 percent coinsurance for all other services for two reasons: (a) 50 percent coinsurance was much more common in private insurance for those two services than for other medical services; and (b) comparison of these plans with the "pure" 25 percent and 50 percent coinsurance plans would generate some evidence on the so-called offset hypothesis. This hypothesis, widely discussed in the mental health literature, holds that if mental health services are less well covered than other medical services, improving their coverage will reduce the amount spent on medical services (Follette and Cummings 1967, 1968). Strong versions of the hypothesis hold that the reduction in medical expenditure will equal or exceed the additional amount spent on mental health services, so that the additional mental health coverage comes at no net cost or even at a net savings.[1]

5. We included the plan with 95 percent coinsurance for outpatient services (to a $150 per person per year maximum) and free inpatient services for two reasons. (1) We wished to test the hypothesis that more generous coverage of outpatient services could reduce expenditure on inpatient services. Although one controlled experiment failed to support this hypothesis (Hill and Veney 1970; Lewis and Keairnes 1970), a natural experiment appeared to support it (Roemer et al. 1975; Helms, Newhouse, and Phelps 1978), and the issue was being debated at the time the Experiment began (Chen 1976). (2) This plan approximated coverage among existing employer-based plans, which tended to cover inpatient services well (frequently in full) and outpatient services much less well or not at all.

Approximating typical coverage among existing plans was useful because the fee-for-service portion of the Experiment ultimately lacked a control group. The Experiment began in Dayton, Ohio, with a control group—a random sample from the same population as the experimental groups who remained on their existing insurance plans. Although we were interested mainly in comparisons among the experimental groups, comparison with a control group could in principle show how much change from existing arrangements an experimental plan would cause. However, experience showed what seemed to be substantial underreporting of use in the control group (Table B.1). Control families reported visits on the "Health Report"—a diary filed weekly or biweekly—at less than two-thirds the rate of experimental families and filed claims at one-quarter to one-half the rate. Since the amount of use reported by Experiment families appeared consistent with data from the Health Interview Survey of the National Center for Health Statistics, we made the judgment that the problem was underreporting by controls rather than overreporting by experimentals.

We concluded that the underreporting among the control group stemmed from the burden—for both them and their physicians—of filing two claims forms, one with the Experiment and one with their own insur-

Table B.1   Reported utilization rates by experimentals and controls, Dayton, year 1 (mean per person per year)

	Experimental	Control	National Health Interview Survey, North Central Region[a]
Experimental-control data health reports[b]			
Physician and dentist visits	6.2	3.8	6.6
Hospital admissions	0.22	0.10	0.13
Nonresponse	3.2%	10.4%	—
Experimental-control data from claims[b]			
Physician visits	5.9	1.5	4.9
Dental visits	1.2	0.5	1.6
Hospital admissions	0.19	0.03	0.13
Pharmacy claims	3.1	1.3	—

a. Data for North Central metropolitan areas other than Chicago and Detroit, population under 65 years of age, calculated from National Center for Health Statistics, *Health Characteristics by Geographic Region, Large Metropolitan Areas, and Other Places of Residence, United States, 1973–1974* (Washington, D.C.: Government Printing Office, 1977) (Pub. no. PHS 78-1540), tables 11, 15, 17.

b. Health Reports were self-administered weekly or biweekly reports of utilization and morbidity. Statistics based on 36 weeks of Health Reports data from Dayton at annualized rates. Missing Health Reports were assumed to have no utilization. Claims statistics based on three months of data from Dayton at annualized rates.

ance company. The experimental group, in contrast, filed claims forms only with the Experiment because it acted as their insurance company. This problem appeared to have no remedy, so we dropped the control group in Dayton after little more than a year and did not enroll a fee-for-service control group in any other site.[2]

Rationale for Choice of Covered Services

By covering the same services on each insurance plan, we undermined our ability to achieve the first objective of the Experiment listed in Chapter 1, which was to discover the consequences of covering or not covering a service. The number of services, however, was too great to permit experimental variation by covering different services in different plans without compromising the ability to infer effects about cost sharing. More important, leaving some services uncovered would create a substantial risk that participants would not file claims forms for uncovered services, thereby biasing upward the estimated effect of insurance on total use.

We approximated lack of coverage for a service by using the 95 percent coinsurance plans. This attempt was jeopardized by the MDE feature, however, in that those who exceeded the MDE—just over one-third of those on these plans—had all additional services fully covered, potentially increasing demand over what it would have been if the service had not been covered at all. We used three different methods to extrapolate from our plans to what the demand for various services would have been with no insurance (see Chapter 4).

The rationale for not covering dental services for adults on the nonfree plans in the first year in Dayton was that dental coverage was expensive, and at that time relatively unusual. Hence, if all individuals filed claims when they did use dental services, we would be able to infer demand at the two extreme points of coverage, (usually) no coverage and full coverage. By the end of the first year in Dayton, however, increasing numbers of private-sector insurance plans began to offer partial coverage of dental care. Therefore, in the second year in Dayton and in all other sites the Experiment covered dental services for adults like any other service.

Outpatient mental health services, the other exceptional service during the first year in Dayton, did not count toward the MDE in that year, on the rationale that they might be part of a separate insurance plan; that is, expenditure on such services might not count to satisfy a deductible in a plan covering medical services. However, it later seemed to us more likely that mental health services would be part of a common deductible, and in the second year in Dayton and in all other sites they were covered like any other service.

Exclusions from the Sample

In addition to the elderly, the following groups were excluded:

1. Those with incomes in excess of $25,000 (in 1973 dollars, more like $77,000 in 1991 dollars); the income test was applied at the initial interview.[3] A family whose income rose later remained eligible. This rule excluded about 3 percent of the households we contacted. Its rationale was twofold: the federal government did not wish to make transfer payments to very high-income families, and no one believed that omission of this small group could measurably bias the estimated response of the population as a whole.[4]

2. Individuals participating in the Supplemental Security Income (SSI) program. (Families participating in the Aid to Families with Dependent Children were eligible.) SSI individuals constitute about 1 percent of the national population under 62 years of age. They were excluded because a waiver from the Social Security Administration to exclude the participation incentive payments (see the text) from the income used to calculate the SSI payments did not reach us before our implementation began.

3. Veterans with service-connected disabilities. These individuals also constitute about 1 percent of the national population. They have the highest priority for obtaining care in Veterans Administration facilities, and we assumed that many would continue to use those facilities for their care even if insured by the Experiment, thereby distorting the experimental data on responses to cost-sharing incentives. Although other groups also had access to Veterans Administration facilities, their lower priority made it less important to exclude them from the Experiment's data base.

4. Those eligible for the military medical care system, including active-duty military, their dependents, and retired military personnel. For our purposes, this group's situation was similar to that of veterans with service-connected disabilities. Because they can use the military system, the effect of cost sharing in the "civilian" fee-for-service system should be different for active-duty military and their dependents than for the civilian population. Military retirees under age 62 constitute about 0.5 percent of the under-62 population.

5. Persons residing indefinitely in institutions that assume responsibility for their medical care (such as nursing homes and prisons). Institutionalized individuals under 62 constitute about 0.5 percent of the under-62 population.

6. Because we sampled dwelling units, we also excluded the homeless. However, we do not believe that homelessness was quantitatively important in our sites in the mid-1970s.

Details of Oversampling

The difference in sampling across sites reflects a progression in our understanding of the statistical implications of various methods of oversampling.

In Dayton we divided the population into three equal groups based on income distribution. Each group was sampled at a different rate. We oversampled the lowest third (below $9,000, 1973 dollars) by an amount equal to one-third; thus, families in the lowest income group were to account for about 44 percent of the Dayton sample ($44 = 1.33 \times 33$). The middle third ($9,000–15,000) was undersampled by an amount equal to one-third; thus, families in this stratum were to account for about 22 percent of the sample. The top third was proportionately sampled.

Our purpose in undersampling the middle third was to shift observations away from the mean—in order to increase the precision with which we could estimate both the main effect of income and the extent to which income level affected the response to different cost-sharing plans.

After selection of the Dayton sample we realized that oversampling on an unstable or unreliable measure such as income limited the gain in precision and might actually reduce it even if we were interested only in the oversampled group, in this case the poor (Morris, Newhouse, and Archibald 1979). We deemed that the reliability of two years of income data was sufficiently low to justify only mild oversampling.[5] As a result we did not oversample at all in Seattle.

At the request of the Department of Health and Human Services (DHHS) we returned to oversampling in the last four sites—the two in Massachusetts and the two in South Carolina—using a simpler method than the one we used in Dayton. In these four sites families whose incomes were below 150 percent of the poverty line (for their family size) had a one-third greater chance of being included in the sample.[6] Overall, then, in addition to the exclusion of the highest 3 percent of the income distribution in the six sites, there was a moderate oversampling of the low-income population. Because we did not wish to generalize to the population of the six sites, in our analyses we did not correct for the oversampling of the low-income population.[7]

Calculation of the PIs

Experimental families did not use their previous insurance plans for the three- or five-year period of their participation.[8] Several Experiment plans, however, potentially left families at greater risk than their previous plan had. If this risk were realized, the participant could be expected to exercise his or her right to withdraw from the Experiment and return to the previous plan. For example, an individual assigned to a 50 percent coinsurance plan with a $1,000 MDE was liable for half of his or her medical bills up to $1,000 in any 12-month period. Under the person's previous policy, the liability might well have been less; a hospitalization, for example, might have been fully covered. This situation was common on the cost-sharing plans, although few individuals could be worse off on the free-care plan than they had been on their previous policy.[9] As a result, if there were no side payment to the participant the cost-sharing plans would clearly be less appealing than the free-care plan to those anticipating or experiencing large expenditures, and such people would be more likely to refuse an offer to enroll in the cost-sharing plans than similarly circumstanced individuals offered enrollment in the free-care plan. To the extent that such selection bias occurred, the experimental results would overestimate the response of use to cost sharing. The PI was designed to prevent such bias.

We began by computing the maximum loss in the experimental plan relative to the existing plan. In general, the maximum loss occurred at an expenditure that was equal to the MDE on the best-covered service in the participant's existing policy. For example, if someone's major medical policy had covered hospitalization with a $100 deductible and a 20 percent coinsurance rate, and we wished to assign the individual to a 25 percent coinsurance rate plan with a $1,000 MDE, the largest difference in favor of the old plan would occur if the individual were hospitalized and had a bill that totaled exactly $4,000. Under the Experiment plan the participant would be out of pocket $1,000, compared with only $880 ($880 = 100 + 0.2 [4,000–100]) under the preexisting plan. For hospital bills above or below $4,000, the difference in out-of-pocket expenditures would be less (and for hospital bills below $1,600 or above $4,600, the Experiment plan would be better).[10] The intent of the PI was to reimburse the participant the worst case, which in the example above is $120 per year.

The worst-case reimbursement was implemented in the following fashion: If participants had had to pay any out-of-pocket premium for their previous insurance, those payments were made by the Experiment, and the amount was deducted from the amount paid to the participants (although the amount paid never became negative).[11] In the example above, with a worst-case payment of $120, suppose the person paid premiums of $100 per year for a group insurance plan. In that case the Experiment paid the $100 premium to the employer or insurance company on an as-incurred basis and reimbursed the participant the additional $20.

The timing of the payment was also an issue. Paying it as a lump sum at the beginning of the year might give participants an incentive to leave the Experiment before the end of the final year. A problem would arise, for example, if the person had completed half of the final year with no spending and suddenly had a bill equal to the MDE that the preexisting policy would fully cover. Paying the lump sum at the end of the year would solve that problem but might make the original offer of enrollment not seem credible, thus increasing our refusal rate.[12] We therefore decided to pay a prorated share of the PI every four weeks.

For those with large expenditures late in the year, this arrangement still left a potential incentive to leave before the end of the final participation year. To eliminate this incentive we developed the Completion Bonus, a bonus paid for completing the Experiment, equivalent to the largest participation incentive payment in any year. We covered the cost of this bonus by reducing the annual PI payments accordingly.[13]

Detail on Quantitative Design Decisions

In this section we describe the rationale for the number of sites, the number of individuals enrolled, and the allocation of individuals to plans.

Number of Sites and Individuals Enrolled

As a result of initial power calculations (Newhouse 1974) we decided initially to enroll 2,000 fee-for-service families in four sites. These numbers were used by the federal government to determine a budget, within which there could be some flexibility.

If there had been no fixed costs per site, the best approach would have been to enroll a completely dispersed sample of 2,000 families. Fixed costs were, however, substantial, including those for a field office in each state. Accordingly we had to calculate a tradeoff between the total number of persons enrolled and the number of sites. As a result we estimated the optimal number of sites for a budget implied by a 2,000-family, four-site Experiment.

In choosing the number of sites and sizes of the samples at each, we sought to minimize the variance of estimated health care expenditure per person for this budget, taking into account the contribution of additional sites to reductions in *between-site variance* and the contribution of additional families within a site to reductions in *within-site variance*. The formula we used, derived by Carl Morris, is described in Archibald and Newhouse (1988). The estimates of within-site and between-site variance used to implement the formula came from the 1970 national survey by the Center for Health Administration Studies and the National Opinion Research Center (Andersen, Kravits, and Anderson 1975).[14]

For our budget (and our estimates of cost per site, cost per family, and between-site and within-site variances), the optimum number of sites was relatively insensitive between four and nine (with corresponding adjustments in the number of families sampled). We chose 2,000 families from four metropolitan sites and two nearby rural sites because the marginal cost of adding the latter was small: we needed only four field offices and contacts with four state officials. The budget and sample size calculations for the HMO samples are described below.

We decided to enroll all eligible individuals in a family not only because of the relationship between MDE and family income, but also because most people live in families and have family insurance coverage. In addition, for a given number of individuals in the sample, a family-based sample required far fewer PIs than did a sample based on individuals. As a result, however, we had to account for within-family correlations when calculating standard errors. Children or grandparents living with parents who were not economically dependent upon the parents were enrolled as their own family. Individuals living alone were enrolled as single-person "families." (Administrative issues pertaining to the definition of the family unit are discussed in Chapter 10.)

Number of Families per Plan

The fee-for-service plans. The formula used to determine the allocation of the 2,000 families among plans and among sites was the simple one that is optimal for analysis of variance methods. The number on each plan and in each site was proportional to the square root of $w(i)/c(i)$, where $w(i)$ was the weight or relative policy interest in plan *i,* and *c(i)* was its estimated marginal cost.

The task of estimating cost was relatively straightforward. In Dayton, demand elasticities from nonexperimental studies were used to estimate increased use in plans with less cost sharing and for costing out the implications of oversampling low-income families. In the other sites estimates of the relative cost by plan were made based on preliminary experimental data. Claim costs and PI payments, which varied by plan, were estimated at about one-third of the cost of adding a family to the free plan. The costs of enrolling a family, paying it to fill out questionnaires, and processing data on utilization and health status were approximately independent of plan. Therefore, we normalized the estimated claims and PI payments on the free-care plan to 100 and added 200 to all cost figures to account for costs that were independent of plan. Adding the constant, of course, sharply reduced the variation in estimated cost per plan. As a result, variation in the weights *w(i)* assigned to each plan drove the allocation by plan.

What determined the weights? Not only did the weights assigned to each plan change somewhat from site to site, but even the plans included in the Experiment changed as our objectives evolved. Table B.2 summarizes the distribution of plans by site.

Table B.2   Distribution of fee-for-service insurance plans, by site

Coinsurance rate (%)	MDE (as % of income)			Individual Deductible[a]
	0	5 or 10	15	
0	All sites	—	—	—
25	—	All sites	All sites	—
25/50[b]	—	All sites but Dayton	All sites but Dayton	—
50	—	Dayton only	All sites but Seattle	—
95[c]	—	All sites	All sites	All sites

a. Out-of-pocket limit of $150 per person or $450 per family; coinsurance applies to outpatient services only.

b. 50% coinsurance for dental and mental health services, 25% coinsurance for all other.

c. 100% in Dayton, year 1.

The idea of a plan with 25 percent coinsurance for all services except dental and mental health, which had a 50 percent coinsurance rate, had not occurred to us when the Dayton sample was enrolled. Hence the Dayton sample was allocated among the other plans. The weights used for this were 450 for the zero coinsurance rate plan and 50 for every other plan, where each combination of coinsurance rate and percentage-of-income MDE limit counted as a plan. The additional weight for the zero coinsurance rate plan in effect gave each coinsurance rate the same weight; the three percentage-of-income limits were given equal weight within each coinsurance rate in Dayton.[15]

The next site to become operational was Seattle; by that time both the plans and the weights for allocating the sample among the plans had changed. In Seattle we decided to drop the plans with 50 percent coinsurance for all services (in other words, to give them zero weight), for the following reasons: (1) We had originally included the 50 percent plan(s) to help us estimate how response varied with respect to coinsurance rates. There was relatively little policy interest in the 50 percent plan, however, and even less in higher rates, because they were uncommon in private policies. (2) Given that we wished to add a set of plans with a split coinsurance rate (25 percent for all but mental health and dental services), there was some value to reducing the absolute number of plans for those analysts (including ourselves ultimately) who did not wish to impose a functional form on the response, but wished simply to estimate plan means.

The allocation weights on the other plans changed because of advances both in our theoretical work on how deductibles affected demand and in our plans for measuring health status.

Our original design for deductibles was oriented heavily toward estimating demand along a "coinsurance" dimension, for two reasons: (1) There was a theory linking the coinsurance dimension to utilization, essentially the standard economic theory of the consumer, in which per-unit price is a constant (Phelps and Newhouse 1974). By contrast, there was no such theory for deductibles, which involve a nonlinear price schedule. (2) Estimates of how demand responded to a constant price varied so widely per unit that a reasonably precise estimate of this response would be a contribution. Because of the theory linking demand response to coinsurance variation, a design that focused on estimating the response of demand to this dimension of variation seemed less risky than one that focused on estimating the response to variation in deductibles.

By the time we began to enroll participants in Seattle, however, we had made theoretical advances relating demand to variation in a deductible (Keeler, Newhouse, and Phelps 1977). This newly developed theory, which was one of the methodological contributions of the Experiment, focused on episodes of treated illness and the timing of events within the year. More important, it had implications for estimation, as described in Chapter 4. Hence, by the time we began in Seattle the deductible dimension had some theoretical underpinning.

Moreover, estimating demand in response to variation in a deductible appeared important because deductibles had several attractive features: (1) if sufficiently high they did not importantly distort markets for nonhospital services, because most participants in the market would not satisfy the deductible; (2) administrative costs were lower because those who did not exceed the deductible did not need to file claims; and (3) there was maximum protection against risk for a given premium (Arrow 1963, 1973). In addition, by the mid-1970s more had been learned empirically about the response of demand to variation in coinsurance than when we were planning for the Dayton site (Scitovsky and Snyder 1972; Phelps and Newhouse 1974), but little if anything was known about the response of demand to variation in deductibles.

For all these reasons we decided to reorient the Experiment toward estimating demand response to variation in a deductible. This involved increasing the relative weight on the Family and Individual Deductible plans, especially the Individual Deductible plan, which in Dayton had only about one-third the number of families that the 0, 25, and Family Deductible plans had. The Family Deductible plans were useful because they provided for the largest cost sharing and hence offered the maximum chance of determining whether there was any effect of cost sharing on demand or health status. The Individual Deductible plan, however, well approximated the coverage provided by typical insurance plans, and by this time we knew that we would have no formal fee-for-service control group. The Individual Deductible plan could approximate a control group. Since we judged these two factors as roughly offsetting each other, we gave the Family Deductible and Individual Deductible plans equal weights of 100 for Seattle and subsequent sites. In the Family Deductible set of plans, we decided to give more weight to the 15 percent-of-income limit as an extreme point. Hence, 45 percent of the Family Deductible weight went to the 15 percent-of-income plan; 30 percent went to the 10 percent-of-income plan; and 25 percent went to the 5 percent-of-income plan.

The zero coinsurance (free-care) plan was given a weight of 150 for three reasons: (1) it was an extreme point, (2) in Seattle it would be used for comparison with the HMO group, and (3) there was considerable policy interest in it in 1975. The six remaining plans (straight 25 percent coinsurance or 25 percent coinsurance except for mental health and dental) together received a combined weight of 125.

All these considerations related to analyzing demand. By 1975 we had also made considerable progress in developing methods for measuring health status outcomes. The analysis plan for health status envisioned contrasting the free-care plan with each of the other coinsurance rates in turn (that is, aggregating plans with the same coinsurance rate and different percentage-of-income limits, though treating the Individual Deductible as a separate plan). This approach implied a greater allocation to the free-care plan than the demand analysis had indicated.[16] We were left with the issue of how to weight the demand and health status goals. The prospect of obtaining results about health status, about which virtually nothing was known led us to give the health status objectives equal weight with the demand estimation objectives in allocating the sample among plans.

By the time we began operation in Massachusetts (1976), we had reconsidered the importance of the 50 percent coinsurance, 15 percent-of-income MDE plan. The reasons were two. (1) Enough data had accumulated on the experience in Dayton to suggest that a substantial fraction of families on the 95 percent coinsurance plans would exceed their MDE (and indeed, as mentioned above, this fraction turned out to be 35 percent on the Family Deductible plans). This was a worrying development because one of the purposes of the 95 percent plan was to provide a rough estimate of what might happen if a service was not covered. If a large fraction of families exceeded the MDE, this objective would be compromised. Obviously, the 50 percent plan could not yield information directly on what would happen if a service was not covered. But as long as relatively few families on that plan exceeded the MDE, it would at least allow us to measure the effect of half coverage in contrast to the effect of full coverage. To ensure that enough families stayed within their MDE to make this possible, the 5 and 10 percent-of-income limits were not used in conjunction with the 50 percent coinsurance plan in Massachusetts and South Carolina. (2) Concern lingered that families on the 95 percent plan might substantially underfile because of the relatively modest pecuniary incentive to file claims, a result that would jeopardize the estimated demand elasticities. If the "extreme" 95 percent point became compromised because of underfiling, the 50 percent plan would become the extreme point, and thus more important to the analysis.

The reasoning behind dropping the 5 and 10 percent-of-income limits in Massachusetts applied, in principle, also to Dayton. Should the Dayton families on 50 percent coinsurance plans with 5 and 10 percent-of-income limits have that limit changed? Because changing the limit risked introducing transitory effects that would themselves threaten the analysis, we decided not to change these families' limits. Instead, we decided to account for the Dayton families allocated to the 50 percent coinsurance, 15 percent-of-income limit plan when determining the total to be allocated to that plan over all sites, and thus the total new families to be allocated to that plan in Massachusetts and South Carolina. The 50 percent coinsurance, 15 percent limit plan was given a weight of 50 on the demand analysis dimension and a weight of zero on the health status dimension in the Massachusetts and South Carolina sites.

Allocation of families between the pure 25 percent coinsurance rate plans and the plans with 25 percent coinsurance for everything but dental and (outpatient) mental health services raised a similar issue, because the latter was not used in Dayton. Had we accounted only for the distribution of the entire sample by plan, we would have given equal weight over the entire sample to these two plans, compensating for the Dayton allocation in the remaining sites; that is, we would have disproportionately allocated families in those sites to the 25/50 plans. In order to keep more balance in the plan allocation by site and to protect against a site-plan interaction, we elected to use equal weights in Seattle and we changed to weights that yielded only a 40–60 division (60 percent on the split plan) in the Massachusetts and South Carolina sites. This move left slightly more families on the straight 25 percent coinsurance plans than on the split plans.

The number of families we intended to enroll on each plan and the number we actually enrolled are shown in Table B.3. The intended values come from application of the square root $(w(i)/c(i))$ formula described above. The difference between the intended and the actual number reflects refusals. As far as is known, the refusals were random within plan (see below). We compensated for refusals in the first two sites in our allocations by plan for the last four sites, but for operational reasons we made no compensation for refusals in the last four sites. As described below, the refusal rate for the free-care plan was lower than for the other plans; hence the number enrolled in it was larger than intended.[17] Even so, the final allocation by plan is close to that of the original design.

These changes in our thinking during the Experiment led to some imbalances across sites in the allocation of sample by plan (see Table B.2) and placed a greater burden on the analysis. These imbalances were relatively minor, however, and we would probably make the choices in the same way today, given our initial sample allocation decisions. For the most part, the allocation by plan and by site served us well. The only major difficulty we encountered as a result of changing our minds about the importance of the 50 percent coinsurance plan and the late introduction of the split 25/50 percent coinsurance plan was in the analysis of outpatient mental health services. As explained in Chapter 3, the 50 percent plan yields some anomalous results in that analysis.

Table B.3   Intended and actual sample allocation, by plan

Plan[a]	Optimal % for demand analysis	Optimal % for health status analysis	Average of columns 2 and 3	Intended number of families[b]	Actual number of families
0/0	24.2	36.2	30.2	604	635
25/5 (25)	7.1	6.7	3.8	76	78
25/5 (50)			3.1	62	60
25/10 (25)	6.8	6.4	3.6	72	76
25/10 (50)			3.0	60	67
25/15 (25)	6.6	6.3	3.5	70	71
25/15 (50)			2.9	58	44
50/15[c]	13.1	0	6.5	131	131
95/5			6.4	129	127
95/10	20.3	21.3	6.6	131	118
95/15			7.8	156	142
Individual Deductible	21.9	23.1	22.5	450	456
Total fee-for-service families				2,000	2,006

a. The first value is the coinsurance rate; the second value is the percentage of income limit. The figure in parentheses for the 25% coinsurance rate plans is the coinsurance rate for dental and mental health.

b. Intended number of families equals column 4 × 2,000.

c. Includes 28 families in the 50/5 plan and 19 in the 50/10 plan in Dayton.

With the benefit of hindsight we might also have increased the number of families assigned to the 50 percent coinsurance plan. As explained in Chapter 3, we first estimated mean expenditure by coinsurance rate, and then estimated regression equations to explain expenditure. In those regressions we generally used dummy variables for each coinsurance rate rather than imposing a functional form on the response to variation in coinsurance. Proceeding in this fashion has at times caused a modest expositional problem. In part because of the small sample size on the 50 percent plan and in part because of one outlier person, mean expenditure on that plan has the largest standard error of any plan, and the raw mean expenditures show a small and statistically insignificant reversal for the 50 percent plan (that is, the mean expenditure rate for the 50 percent plan exceeds that of the 25 percent plan; see Chapter 3). This reversal is not found when more robust estimation techniques are used or when a simple adjustment for the site imbalance is made. For that reason the reversal has not much complicated the exposition of our results.

The HMO plans. The size of the experimental HMO sample, those to be randomly assigned to the HMO, was set to give a Type I error of 5 percent and Type II error of 10 percent in detecting a 20 percent reduction in admission rates at the HMO—on the assumptions (discussed below) that the HMO participants were equally divided between three- and five-year enrollments and that the fee-for-service participants were divided approximately 70–30 between three- and five-year enrollments. Our calculations took account of the correlation within an individual's expenditures over time as well as intra-family correlation. These calculations indicated a sample size of around 300 families. At the time these calculations were made, we anticipated participation of two HMOs in the Experiment; thus, 50 families were added to estimate HMO-specific effects. Finally, an attrition rate of 25 percent was assumed, implying an initial enrollment of 466 families in two HMOs. The fact that we ultimately included only one HMO reduced the required sample size to about 403. A total of 449 families were enrolled in the HMO experimental group.

A control group at the HMO was also enrolled, in part to measure selection effects by comparison with the experimental group. Theoretically we could have assessed selection effects by using HMO-wide administrative data, available at no cost to the Experiment. Such data, however, were problematic in two ways: (1) the populations were not strictly comparable because of potential eligibility restrictions on HMO experimentals (such as the absence of elderly enrollees); and (2) the HMO-wide data could not reflect any effects on use attributable to the Experiment's data collection instruments. As a result, we elected to enroll a control group, setting a target enrollment of 303 families; actual enrollment was 302 families.

Allocation of Sample by Site

When the Experiment began in Dayton the federal government had not approved expansion of the project beyond that site. Because the identities (or existence) of any additional sites had not been determined, we could not determine the optimal sample size for Dayton. One could, of course, assume that there would be six sites and that the policy interest in and cost of each site would be the same. In this case, 2,000 families would be equally divided among six sites, implying a sample of 333 families in Dayton. However, we increased this number to 400 in case expansion was not approved. In fact we enrolled 388 families in Dayton.

By the time we began enrollment in Seattle, we knew that we would have a six-site Experiment, and we even knew what the sites would be. Hence it was possible to take account of site characteristics in allocating the 2,000 families by site. The characteristics used were city size, region, and cost. For cost we used an index based on Medicare expenditure per enrollee by county, which took the following values: Dayton, 100; Seattle, 106; Charleston, 61; Georgetown County, 61; Fitchburg/Leominster, 138; Franklin County, 111.[18] As in the case of allocation by plan, however, the choice of weight for each site was not straightforward.

By design the sites differed by size and census region (see below). In allocating the sample to sites, we therefore decided to take account of the distribution of the U.S. population by size and region. We decided to give the marginal distributions of both city size and region equal weight.

We arbitrarily grouped cities as follows: the largest 20 Standard Metropolitan Statistical Areas (SMSAs) had 31 percent of the U.S. population; Seattle represented this class. The next 30 largest SMSAs had 14 percent of the population; Dayton represented this class. The next 50 largest SMSAs had 11 percent of the population; Charleston represented this class. All other SMSAs had 13 percent of the population; Fitchburg/Leominster represented this class. The groupings were chosen to make the three smaller categories approximately equal in size (that is, 14, 11, and 13 percent); because Seattle was only the seventeenth largest SMSA, we were compelled to give the largest city size group a substantially larger weight. Northern rural areas had 18 percent of the population; southern rural areas had 13 percent. Franklin and Georgetown counties, respectively, represented these two classes.

We also accounted for census region. In 1970 the distribution of U.S. population by census region was: Northeast, represented by Massachusetts, 24 percent; North Central, represented by Dayton, 28 percent; South, represented by South Carolina, 31 percent; and West, represented by Seattle, 17 percent.

At the time we made these allocations, 8 of the 388 families we had enrolled in Dayton had dropped out. We decided to make up for this attrition in the other five sites by endeavoring to enroll a sample of 1,620 new families (1,620 = 2,000 − [388 − 8]). The weights and estimated costs we used resulted in an allocation among the sites as shown in Table B.4.

Enrollment offers were made in each site on the basis of projected refusals. In Seattle and Fitchburg/Leominster the estimated number of refusals proved accurate, but we overestimated the refusal rate in Franklin County. Hence, by the time we began enrollment in South Carolina, we had more families than we wanted. We therefore reduced the Charleston and Georgetown targets accordingly. In the event, however, we underestimated the Charleston refusal rate and overestimated the Georgetown refusal rate, so that we had about 5 percent fewer Charleston families than we desired. Even so, the distribution of the sample across sites was close to what we intended.

The decision about the Dayton sample size, which was made in ignorance of the other sites, turned out fortuitously to be nearly optimal. The unconstrained optimal sample size to enroll in Dayton, given the weights by region and city size, and relative costs, would have been 415, compared with the intended 400 or the actual 388.

Table B.4   Intended and actual enrollment, by site (number of families)

Site	Intended enrollment based on weight and cost	Actual enrollment
Dayton	400	388
Seattle[a]	479	486
Fitchburg	247	248
Franklin County	294	316
Charleston	291	262
Georgetown County	309	306

a. Fee-for-service only.

Finally, as described below, the actual analysis of the HMO data compared the results from the Seattle HMO with the results from the Seattle fee-for-service system rather than with the results from all the sites. If this analytic method had been foreseen, we would have increased the weight of the Seattle site.

Matching Families to Insurance Plan: The Finite Selection Model

When the Experiment began, we faced several options for deciding which family would be assigned to which plan. The most straightforward method would have been simple random assignment. But it was clear that stratification by, say, age and income would be better than simple random assignment. The income maintenance experiments had used methods developed by Conlisk and Watts (1969) rather than either simple random or stratified random assignment. Their method developed an optimal allocation for estimating a specified regression equation(s).

In fact we used none of these methods, but rather one developed by Carl Morris (1979), the Finite Selection Model (FSM). The FSM can be regarded as a special case and a major extension of the Conlisk-Watts model (see Appendix D for a comparison). The FSM balances the characteristics of the groups assigned to the different plans better than would have occurred on average with random assignment; that is, families were assigned in such a way that the groups of people on the various plans were similar to one another with respect to important characteristics such as prior year's physician visits, self-perceived health status at enrollment, income, family size, education, and wage rate.

Simple random sampling can produce unbalanced designs, albeit with low probability (for example, a disproportionate number of sick individuals could be enrolled in one plan). Stratification (or blocking) provides some protection against such imbalances. The FSM is in some ways a generalization of stratification; the protection it offered us against imbalance translated into an expected 25 percent gain in efficiency relative to simple random assignment (Morris 1979). But the FSM has two advantages over stratification. (1) In order to keep stratification manageable, one can stratify on only a small number of variables, whereas the FSM can consider a large number of variables. (2) Also for reasons of manageability, stratification must treat certain continuous variables as discrete; for example, age groups might be broken into 0–17, 18–44, and 45 and over. The FSM, in contrast, can treat such variables continuously and thus can account for variation within the discrete group, such as the difference between a 46-year-old and a 60-year-old.

We used the FSM to balance the sample as much as possible not only across insurance plans but also across the subexperiments described in the next section. Thus, we constructed groups of families that resembled one another as much as possible along a number of dimensions. The dimensions and their importance (that is, the weight they received) are summarized in Table B.5. Variables with higher weights were dimensions along which the model "strove harder" to balance the sample.

We constructed a series of balanced groups (one for each plan plus a "throwaway" group) from the sample that completed a baseline interview. The groups were, in effect, randomly assigned to plan. The actual operation of the model had to take account of the unequal allocations by plan, as described in Morris (1979).

Rationale for Length of Enrollment

Several conflicting considerations bore on our decision to enroll some families for three years and others for five. On the one hand, for a given budget, observation of more families for a shorter period yields more precise estimates of use because of the intertemporal correlation of the same person's use; it also yields final results sooner. On the other hand, health status consequences of variation in use take time to manifest themselves. Furthermore, those enrolled in a plan for a longer period might have the confidence to engage in behaviors that they would not be willing to risk over a shorter period. For example, if the new insurance plan made them consider changing doctors, a longer period of enrollment might make them more willing actually to change, since it would give them more time over which to recover the costs of the search.

The need to identify any transitory effects dictated that we split the sample. At the beginning there might be transitory demand for services that produce benefits over time and are deferrable, such as dental services or eyeglasses. These effects might vary by plan. At the end there might be transitory effects for the same types of services, if the health insurance plan to which the participant was returning differed in generosity from the experimental plan. The possible existence of transitory effects argued for a longer period of enrollment because we wished to measure steady-state behavior, and any transitory effects would clearly reduce the time during which we could observe such behavior.

Table B.5   Variables and weights used in the Finite Selection Model

Variable	Specification	Number of variables	Weight
Annual physician visits			
Children (<18)	Average among family	1	100
Adults (18+)	members in age group	1	100
Self-perceived health status	Excellent, good, fair-poor	3	100
Income	Logarithmic, adjusted for family size, using two years of data[a]	1	100
Family size	Logarithmic	1	100
Age	Proportion of family members in each of four categories (0–5, 6–17, 18–44, 45+)	4	100
Education of male head	Scaled according to ability to predict income	1	100
Education of female head	Same as education of male head	1	100
Maximum wage rate	Maximum of hourly wages over all heads[b]	1	100
Pain	Proportion in family experiencing pain at least fairly often	1	80
Worry	Proportion in family with at least some health worry	1	80
Health insurance	Had health insurance at time experiment began	1	80
Number of heads		1	80
Race	White or other	1	80
Sex	Proportion of females in family	1	50
AFDC recipient		1	50
Employed head	Categorical variable, indicating at least one employed head	1	30
Nonwage, nontransfer income	Logarithmic	1	30
Location	Miles from a fixed point within site	2	30
Annual hospital admissions	Proportion in family with at least one	1	30
Constant term		1	10

a. Adjusted for family size using equivalence scale described in Chapter 6.

b. Salaried workers were imputed an hourly wage based on annual earnings and hours worked, as were individuals with other forms of compensation such as commissions and bonuses.

To identify transitory effects we elected to split the sample between three- and five-year periods of enrollment. In Dayton we split the sample 50–50 between these two periods. Subsequent data on the intertemporal correlation of utilization showed that the efficiency per dollar (for estimating utilization and ignoring transitory demand) of five-year families was about 70–75 percent that of three-year families. Hence, in all subsequent sites 75 percent of the sample was allocated to the three-year period and only 25 percent to the five-year period.

Different considerations prevailed at the HMO. The Seattle Model Cities project, which was being completed just as the Experiment began, had been undertaken at the same HMO used in the Experiment, the Group Health Cooperative of Puget Sound. Model Cities data, shown in Table B.6, showed a striking increase in hospital use at the Group Health Cooperative over time.

Since those enrolled at Group Health in the Model Cities project, like those in the Experiment, had not previously been enrolled at Group Health,[19] it seemed plausible that, as the Experiment enrollees familiarized themselves with Group Health, hospital use might increase. Moreover, the data suggested that such a trend might take longer than three years to manifest itself. In light of this possibility, we raised to 50 percent the proportion of the Group Health experimental group allocated to the five-year period of participation.

However, we enrolled the entire Group Health control sample for five years. Two reasons guided our choice. (1) Because we did not pay for the health care use of the controls, they were much less expensive than the experimental participants. (2) Unlike all the other groups, we could not expect many of the Group Health control group to stay in the sample to completion, because their presence in the control group depended on continued eligibility for benefits at Group Health. Such eligibility might be

Table B.6   Hospital days in fee-for-service and HMO systems, Model Cities Project

	Hospital days per 1,000			
	Year 1	Year 2	Year 3	Year 4
Fee-for-service	700+	700+	700+	689
Group Health	±350	±350	±480	657

Source: Unpublished data from project team.

lost, for example, with a change in employment. Enrolling everyone for five years could help compensate for the anticipated higher attrition rate.

Rationale for Site Choices

We decided not to locate the first site in the West or South. We did not want the first site to be in the West because the HMO site was most likely to be there, and we felt we might make a mistake in the first site that would reduce its comparability with the other sites. This would be particularly damaging if it affected the HMO site. We did not want the first site to be in the South, because it appeared that the southern site might be the largest site (in numbers enrolled), given the region's lower medical prices. Finally, we wanted to benefit from field work in a medium-sized city before tackling a large one.

We were particularly concerned that we had no experience with how state and local authorities would react to the Experiment. For example, there were legal uncertainties, such as whether state insurance laws would apply to the experimental insurance plans. Because of the high costs of searching across several states and localities, we decided to narrow our search to northeastern or north-central states with several medium-sized cities. Ohio fit this description well: Dayton, Akron, Columbus, Toledo, and Youngstown all had 1970 metropolitan populations of approximately the size we wanted, between 500,000 and 1,000,000. We chose Dayton because both state and local authorities were most favorable to our proceeding there.

We next picked a site with an HMO, the western site. We wanted a reasonably large, well-established HMO. We spoke with officials of the Kaiser-Permanente Health Plan, then located in California, Oregon, and Hawaii; and the Group Health Cooperative of Puget Sound, located in Seattle, Washington. The Kaiser-Permanente officials preferred that we work at the Portland, Oregon, plan. However, from our perspective Portland did not add nearly as much variation in city size or in waiting times as did Seattle. Its metropolitan population was about the same as Dayton's, whereas Seattle's population was about twice as large. Its waiting times to an appointment in the fee-for-service system were quite close to the national average, as were Dayton's (although we had not known any waiting times when we chose Dayton). Seattle, by contrast, had lower-than-average waiting times to appointments. For these reasons we chose Seattle.

If we were to have sites in each census region, our remaining metropolitan sites had to be in the South and the Northeast. Furthermore, in order to economize by having four rather than six field offices, we wanted rural sites near the southern site and near one of the three other sites. Given our objectives of variation along the dimensions described above, our preferred combination of remaining sites was the combination we actually used. We considered other urban sites in the Northwest and South and other rural sites, but they did not contrast as well with Dayton and Seattle and with each other; moreover, we encountered no state or local problems in any of these sites.

Details of the Enrollment Process

Once we had selected a site, we used cluster sampling to choose families. Typically we defined around 100 clusters of about four city blocks each and contacted every nth dwelling unit (usually n was six or eight) on those blocks.

We first approached subjects with a short screening interview to get information on the family units that lived at the dwelling unit and to determine which, if any, met the eligibility restrictions for the Experiment (such as being less than 62 years old). If the entire household failed the eligibility test, the process was terminated.[20]

In sites in which low-income households were oversampled, a proportion of non-low-income households was terminated at random at the screening interview. For example, in Massachusetts and South Carolina, where families whose incomes were below 150 percent of the poverty line had a one-third greater chance of being included, 25 percent of families whose incomes did not fall below 150 percent of the poverty line were terminated at random at this point.

To those families not terminated we administered a baseline interview. A principal purpose of this interview was to obtain a listing of all health insurance policies held by the family. If the family held group insurance—typically through the employer—the group was ascertained and then contacted for a description of the policy. A family with individual coverage was asked for the name of the insurance company and an identifying number for the policy; the details of the policy were then obtained from the insurance company. These details were necessary to compute the proper amount of the PI payments.

The baseline interview also collected detailed information about income, previous utilization of medical services, patient satisfaction with medical and dental care, a few measures of health status, and some demographic information, such as education. This information was used in the FSM to assign families to plans.

After the baseline interview, the FSM was used to form homogeneous groups for assignment to plan, including a "discard" group whose size was to equal the number by which the families who completed the baseline interview and whose insurance plans were verified exceeded the number we sought to enroll in each site. The order in which groups were assigned was randomized to preclude bias in the assignment of families to plans.

We then sought to enroll the families. We saw the enrollment task primarily as one of making the offer credible, because it might well appear "too good to be true." To this end we solicited endorsements from local officials and included in the enrollment brochures a list of local telephone numbers (such as the better business bureau and the local congressman's office) that the families could call to verify the project's legitimacy. As the families left the Experiment we administered a questionnaire about their reactions to our enrollment techniques. Results from this questionnaire are reported in Chapter 10.

Schedule of Benefits in the Family Health Protection Plan

This appendix outlines the main medical, dental, and mental health benefits provided by the experimental insurance plans, which were administered through the Family Health Protection Plan (FHPP). The FHPP was the insurance carrier established solely for the Experiment, for which the fiscal intermediary was Glen Slaughter and Associates, in Oakland, California.

"Prior authorization" refers to an action of the FHPP Administrator; "per year" refers to an accounting, not a calendar, year. More complete documentation of operational details can be found in Clasquin and Brown (1977).

Benefits

Inpatient Hospital Care

The following items were covered for an unlimited number of days for treatment of illness, injury, or pregnancy while the enrollee was an inpatient in a general, maternity, or mental hospital: (1) standard charges for other than a private room or for a private room, intensive care unit, or isolation room if certified as medically necessary or if no semiprivate room was available; and (2) standard charges for medically necessary or prescribed supplies and services, to include use of operating room, anesthetic supplies, surgical supplies, dressings, and cast materials, physical therapy, drugs, x-ray and laboratory services, and private duty nursing services if medically necessary.

Outpatient Hospital Care

Standard charges were covered for services performed and supplies provided in the emergency room or outpatient department in conjunction with diagnosis or treatment of any illness or injury.

Skilled Nursing Facility

The following were covered for an unlimited number of days while the enrollee was an inpatient in a skilled nursing facility upon recommendation of a physician that such occupancy was medically necessary: (1) standard charges for other than a private room or for a private room if medically necessary or when no semiprivate room was available; and (2) standard charges for medically necessary or prescribed supplies and services.

Physician Services

Reasonable or standard charges were covered for professional services provided by a physician on an inpatient or outpatient basis. (Acupuncture was covered only when performed by a physician.)

Surgical Benefits

Reasonable or standard charges for medically necessary surgical services in or out of a hospital were covered, including those provided by surgeons, assistant surgeons, anesthetists, and consultants during or after an operation.

Maternity Benefits

Reasonable or standard charges were covered for services related to maternity for the mother and child(ren) on either an inpatient or outpatient basis and including both hospital and physician services.

Psychiatric Services

Reasonable or standard charges were covered for psychiatric services rendered by psychiatrists, clinical psychologists, and mental health teams, up to a maximum of 52 visits per year.

Prescription Drugs

Reasonable or standard charges were covered for drugs requiring a prescription.

Reasonable or standard charges were covered for certain drugs that could be purchased without a prescription for selected conditions (including chronic allergic conditions, arthritis and rheumatism, chronic lower or upper gastrointestinal disease, pregnancy, chronic respiratory disease, and chronic skin conditions). A physician had to complete an insurance claim form certifying that the condition existed before payment was made, and purchases of nonprescription drugs so covered were limited to $100 per person for each condition per year.

Dental Services

The following were covered when provided by a dentist and staff: diagnostic procedures, preventive services, restorative services, oral surgery, endodontics, periodontics, preventive orthodontia, and prosthodontics (except any fixed bridge of seven or more units and replacement of any satisfactory denture or fixed bridge). Prior authorization was needed for any treatment plan exceeding $500 (except emergency care) and for replacement of crowns, bridges, or dentures.

Vision Care

Reasonable or standard charges were covered for services and supplies related to vision care, with the following limitations: (1) only one eye examination for refractions by an ophthalmologist or optometrist per year; (2) only one pair of corrective lenses per year; (3) additional costs for contact lenses or for light-sensitive, tinted, or shaded eyeglass lenses only when certified by an ophthalmologist or optometrist as medically necessary and given prior authorization; and (4) only one pair of eyeglass frames every two years, with a maximum payment based on the normal price of standard frames in the area.

Hearing Care

Reasonable or standard charges were covered for one hearing examination by a certified audiologist per year upon recommendation by a physician.

Reasonable or standard charges were covered for one hearing aid device prescribed by a certified audiologist every two years, with prior authorization and maximum payment based on the normal price of hearing aids in the area.

Care by Other Practitioners

Reasonable charges were covered for health care services provided by the following practitioners: (1) chiropractors; (2) podiatrists or chiropodists, when medically necessary; (3) physical, occupational, or speech therapists, when medically necessary and as part of a treatment plan given prior authorization; (4) private duty nurses (RN or LPN) when medically necessary (and with prior authorization if such services extended beyond 30 days in any one year); (5) Christian Science nurse, practitioner, or sanatorium.

Home Health Care

Reasonable or standard charges were covered for medically necessary services and supplies provided by a home health agency or others under a treatment plan established and periodically reviewed by a physician and provided on a visiting basis at home or at a hospital, skilled nursing facility, or rehabilitation center. Such services and supplies included: (1) part-time or intermittent nursing care; (2) physical, occupational, or speech therapy; (3) medical social services; (4) part-time or intermittent services of a home health aide; and (5) selected medically necessary equipment, appliances, and supplies (other than drugs) allowed by Title XVIII of the Social Security Amendments of 1965 (Medicare), subject to some limitations and prior authorization.

Other Health Services and Supplies

Reasonable or standard charges were covered for the following: (1) x-ray and laboratory tests authorized by a physician (including x-ray, radium, and radioactive isotope therapy); (2) ambulance services when medically necessary; (3) family planning services provided by an agency licensed by the state. Sterilization procedures for persons over 21 required prior authorization, and such procedures for persons under 21 or who were judicially declared mentally incompetent were not reimbursed at all. After 1977 abortion was not a covered service. (4) alcoholism treatment (from licensed or federally approved centers); (5) drug rehabilitation (from physician-directed or federally approved centers); (6) prosthetic devices, including braces, limbs, eyes, and replacements; (7) other medically necessary equipment, appliances, and medical supplies allowed by Medicare, subject to some limitations and prior authorization.

Exclusions

Apart from the few limitations noted above, the FHPP did not cover, or covered only with broad restrictions, the following types of services: (1) cosmetic surgery, except for repair of physical damage arising from accidental injury while the plan was in effect; (2) all orthodontics except those procedures considered interceptive or preventive (such as space maintainers and appliances needed to forestall later orthodontic treatment); (3) cosmetic dental services except for repair of physical damage arising from accidental injury while the plan was in effect; (4) supplies or services for injuries or conditions that were compensable under workers' compensation, employers' liability laws, or automobile accident insurance policies, until those resources had been exhausted; (5) any custodial, personal, or other care that was not medically necessary; and (6) any care rendered outside the United States that could have been deferred until the enrollee returned to the United States (that is, emergency medical care outside the country was covered).

Appendix D

Comparison of the Finite Selection and Conlisk-Watts Models of Sample Allocation

The output of the Conlisk-Watts (CW) model is the number of families with various characteristics that one should assign to each treatment in order to estimate optimally an equation the analyst specifies, given a fixed budget and a specified cost per family. If the equation to be estimated is an analysis of variance specification (in our case, average expenditure on each plan), the Conlisk-Watts model reduces to the formula given in Appendix B for allocation of families to plan — that is, the square root of $w(i)/c(i)$. In that sense our design is a special case of the CW model. Although the income maintenance experiments did not use this design, if they had, they would presumably have assigned families to treatments using simple or stratified random assignment, and the drawbacks of those methods described in Appendix B would apply.

The CW model as actually used in the income maintenance experiments, however, was quite different and led to an unbalanced design that we did not want to emulate.

The problem can be illustrated by assuming that the only explanatory variables in the regression equation to be estimated (such as in an equation explaining labor supply) are the experimental treatment and income. The advance believed to be embodied in the Conlisk-Watts model for estimating this equation was that it optimized the allocation of family characteristics for a given experimental budget by accounting for the cost of a family on alternative experimental treatments. In the context of the income maintenance experiments, high-income families were relatively cheaper on more generous plans. (Although they were less likely to receive payments

431

on all plans, the relative difference in plan payments was greater on the generous plans). As a result, in a model with a main effect for experimental treatment and income, the optimal allocation assigned the high income families to the more generous plans and the low income families to the less generous ones, thereby impairing the estimation of any interaction between treatment and income. Put another way, the model was attempting to exploit an assumption of no interaction between treatment and income because if there was truly no interaction, precision could be improved by disproportionate assignment. The result, however, greatly impaired one's ability to determine if there were such an interaction.

The problem could be mitigated by including an interaction term between treatment and income in the equation to be estimated, but the allocation would then reflect the assumed form of the interaction term and would not necessarily be a desirable design if the assumed form of the interaction were incorrect. Because theory provided little or no guidance on the magnitude of any interaction effect, the sensitivity of the result to the specification was undesirable.

In addition, the CW model, as implemented in the income maintenance experiments, failed to account for the costs of finding a family with given characteristics. In effect, it assumed that one sampled costlessly from an infinite population. In practice, however, if one wanted to consider a number of characteristics, it was possible that the optimal allocation would not only be unbalanced (because of a failure to specify a full set of interactions in the equation to be estimated) but also quite costly, because it would ask one to find families with a combination of characteristics that might be rare (for example, the model may specify a large number of well-to-do, poorly educated, sick families). For these reasons we preferred the FSM to the CW model.

Notes

1. Background

1. In addition, Newhouse and Archibald (1978) contains abstracts of the nonexperimental work undertaken as part of the Health Insurance Study.
2. This objective, though paramount in the Experiment, is listed second because it logically follows the first question, whether a service should be covered at all. The Experiment's design could only approximate an answer to the first question, the effect of covering a service. See Chapter 2 for further discussion.

2. The Design of the Experiment

1. A staff model HMO employs its physicians, who typically work full-time on salary.
2. In the first site, Dayton, Ohio, in the first year of the experiment, the highest coinsurance rate was 100 percent. The value was changed to 95 percent to encourage participants to file claims, although at that time there was no evidence of underfiling. Subsequent analysis showed that in the 95 percent plan there was a differential underfiling rate for physician office visits of perhaps 5 to 10 percent by comparison with the other plans. See Chapter 3.
3. Budget constraints led us to reduce the $1,000 maximum MDE to $750 for those on the 25 percent coinsurance plans and the 25/50 coinsurance plans (50 percent coinsurance for dental and mental health services, 25 percent for all other) for all site years other than the first two years in Dayton and the first year in Seattle. For those three site years the maximum MDE was $1,000 in all plans.
4. Prior authorization was required for any plan of dental treatment whose cost would exceed $500 and for any replacement of crowns, bridges, or dentures.
5. Control participants typically paid $8 to $10 per visit for psychotherapy visits in excess of 10 (the first 10 visits were free). There was also some cost sharing

for drug, vision, and hearing services. Inpatient mental health benefits were minimal. The overall amount of cost sharing was sufficiently small, however, that we treat the HMO control group as facing approximately no cost sharing.

6. The following conditions and drugs were covered (a physician had to complete a claim form indicating the presence of the condition for the Experiment to cover the drug): for chronic allergic (respiratory) conditions, decongestants and antihistamines; for arthritis/rheumatism, aspirin and similar aspirin-containing preparations; for diabetes, insulin and associated supplies; for family planning, contraceptives; for chronic lower gastrointestinal disease, stool softeners, bulk formers, and laxatives; for chronic upper gastrointestinal disease, antacids; for pregnancy, iron preparations, prenatal vitamins, stool softeners, bulk formers, and laxatives; for chronic respiratory disease: bronchial dilators, expectorants, and cough suppressants; for chronic skin conditions, anti-acne agents, antipsoriatic agents, and anti-eczema agents. Written materials describing this benefit to the participants gave examples of drugs in each category.

7. Additionally, those 60 or 61 years old at enrollment were assigned to a three-year enrollment period so that they would not become eligible for Medicare during their period of participation. The resulting minor imbalance between the three- and five-year plans is adjusted for in the analysis.

8. We adopted this method after the Dayton three-year group began its second year and hence did not apply it in that group.

9. In our written report to the designated physician we highlighted abnormal results and even telephoned if we thought there was an urgent problem.

10. Instead of an exit screening exam, those who withdrew from the Experiment early were given a followup self-administered questionnaire. Those who had moved out of the area during the Experiment but continued to participate were given a partial screening examination. The enrollment screening examination was given to a subsample of the South Carolina pre-enrollment group in 1976, contemporaneously with its administration to the South Carolina five-year group but two years before the three-year group was switched to experimental coverage. For reasons of cost, the three-year group in South Carolina did not receive a screening exam when experimental coverage began in 1978.

11. For budgetary reasons, at the end of July 1978 use of the Health Report was suspended for all except the Group Health Cooperative control group and the three-year South Carolina group (which had just enrolled); beginning in October 1979 the five-year families in Seattle, Massachusetts, and South Carolina again began to receive the form.

12. We sampled all of the 100 largest SMSAs, 51 of the remaining 143 SMSAs (1970 definition), and 63 rural clusters of counties.

13. This outcome remains to be reconciled with the literature on choice under uncertainty.

14. We did not conduct a similar analysis for children because so few died, were institutionalized, or became eligible for Medicare.
15. For those lost through attrition, data were recovered only on measures for which data were collected by self-report. All health status analyses, however, include the enrollment value of the health status measure as a covariate, which minimizes bias.
16. Chi-square (4) = 2.67, $p > .50$.
17. Group Health Cooperative stipulated as a condition of participation that Cooperative members would not be invited to enroll in the fee-for-service plans.
18. For more details on methods of measuring use by fee-for-service participants, see K. Marquis (1977).
19. The answer to this question appears to be no; lower cost sharing, if anything, stimulated telephone visits.
20. In analyses not reported here we tried to determine the relationship, if any, between the time and travel costs of using medical services and the rate of use. We were unable to detect a relationship.
21. For more details on methods of measuring use by HMO enrollees, see G.A. Goldberg (1983).

3. Total Annual Per-Person Expenditure

1. Individuals were suspended from the Experiment for joining the military, for example, as well as terminated for noncompliance with Experiment requirements. An accounting year begins on the anniversary of an enrollment date.
2. In technical terms they do not allow for convolution of observations.
3. The effective variation in the upper limit is much reduced by the $1,000 maximum.
4. The Dayton participants began in 1975, the South Carolina three-year group began in late 1978 (about a quarter participated for two months and another quarter for one month of that year), and the remainder of the sample enrolled in 1976 or early 1977. Most of those enrolled in the latter half of 1976. Hence, any joint effect of acute illness on income *and* medical expenditure will be weak. We used data from periods that slightly overlapped with the experimental portion of the Experiment because we believed that the greater reliability of the relatively recent data outweighed the danger of slight joint income and medical expenditure effects.
5. This equation includes *both* inpatient and outpatient medical expenses for any-inpatient users.
6. Moreover, when the normal assumption does hold, the smearing factor has high efficiency (90 percent or more) relative to the normal retransformation for a wide range of parameter values, including those in this analysis (see Duan 1983, sec. 5; and Mehran 1973).

7. That is, we have a vector of covariates for each person we enrolled. We used that vector plus an assumed plan assignment to obtain a predicted expenditure for each plan, which we then average. Thus, we do not use only the group we assigned to each plan to predict expenditure for that plan. This strategy controls for any small imbalance among plans (e.g., in proportion of children).

8. See also the analysis of episodes in Chapter 4.

9. Here and elsewhere in this book we use the word *(in)significant* to mean statistically (in)significant.

10. This is an example of a difference between the response to a marginal price or coinsurance and the response to plan.

11. For example, the ANOVA estimates of the response to cost sharing for total expenses (not adjusted for site) show a statistically insignificant reversal between the 50 percent and 25 percent plans ($831 versus $884; see Table 3.2). Although such a reversal is compatible with theory (because of the MDE), in this case the reversal is much more likely to reflect chance. One participant on the 50 percent plan had a very expensive hospitalization (total medical expenses of $194,000 in one year in 1991 dollars); that single observation, which was the most costly in the sample, adds $139 to the 50 percent plan mean, 16 percent of that plan's raw mean. An adjustment for site removes the reversal.

12. The reversal seen in Table 3.2 for the 50 percent coinsurance plan in total expenditure is not present in Table 3.3.

13. The values are calculated as follows. Each site's population is divided by thirds of the income distribution and then alternatively placed on different plans by successively turning on plan dummies in the four-equation model, similar to the results in Table 3.3. The division among income groups is site-specific because (1) the medical expenses are not corrected for cross-sectional differences in prices and (2) we did not want to confound income and site. See Manning et al. (1988), app. D, for the ANOVA estimates by income tertile.

14. Manning et al. (1988) give details on the probabilities of exceeding the upper limit by income group. See also Table 7.9.

15. Manning et al. (1988), app. A, tables 2–4 and 6, present the actual coefficients of income.

16. The test statistics for the null hypothesis that income has no effect are $\chi^2(7) = 94.21$ for any use of medical services, $\chi^2(5) = 10.41$ for the probability of any inpatient use given any medical use, $\chi^2(5) = 44.83$ for the (log) level of outpatient-only use, and $\chi^2(3) = 3.96$ for (log) level of medical expenditure if any inpatient use. These tests include plan-income interactions and missing value-replacement terms. The 94.21 and 44.83 values of the test statistic are significant at 0.001; the 10.41 value at 0.08.

17. $\chi^2(4) = 5.19$ using ANOVA estimates for the probability of any inpatient use, and $\chi^2(4) = 5.36$ for the admission rate. Another possible hypothesis is no dif-

ferential plan response for children relative to adults. We can reject this hypothesis; the test statistics are $\chi^2(4) = 16.49$ for the probability of any inpatient use and $\chi^2(4)=14.08$ for total admissions. Hence it appears that children and adults respond differently and that children do not respond to cost sharing for inpatient care.

18. $\chi^2(3) = 24.56$ for the probability of any inpatient use and 16.31 for the admission rate.

19. For expenditures $\chi^2(2) = 1.69$, for total admissions $\chi^2(2) = 0.73$, and for the probability of any inpatient use $\chi^2 = 1.39$ (see Manning et al. 1988, app. C, table 2, for the ANOVA estimates).

20. See Manning et al. (1988), app. D, for the ANOVA estimates.

21. $\chi^2(19) = 14.96$, ($p > .50$); see Manning et al. (1988), app. D, for the ANOVA estimates.

22. For further discussion of transitory effects, see Metcalf (1973); Arrow (1975).

23. For this test, the middle years of the study are year 2 for the group enrolled for three years, and years 2–4 for the group enrolled for five years.

24. $\chi^2(8) = 9.49$, $p > 0.30$, with similar results for the other measures of use of medical services; see Manning et al. (1988), app. D, for the ANOVA estimates.

25. Newhouse (1989) argues that the medical care component of the Consumer Price Index is inaccurate as a price index, but it seems more likely to overadjust than to underadjust for inflation, meaning that the true time trend may be even larger than shown in Table 3.7. Nor is aging within the cohort an explanation, because age is a covariate in the regression and only the characteristics at enrollment are used to predict.

26. We observed no such trend for median expense; see Manning et al. (1988), app. A, for the order statistics and other summaries by plan and year for total medical expenditures.

27. We used the first and second years of dental coverage.

28. We obtain the same inferences when we limit the sample to those present in both years.

29. This result is found by dividing the expense per enrollee by the proportion of users.

30. If we use the data from all plans, the contrast is significant ($t = -2.09, p = .04$). This result is based on using as a plan variable the logarithm [max(coinsurance rate, 1)] rather than plan dummies for the free, 25, 50, and 95 percent plans.

31. Although the results for the 25/50 plan are shown in Table 3.13, the statistical test reported in the text is based on the five plans with the same coinsurance rates for dental and other health services. We exclude the plan with a 25 percent coinsurance rate for medical care and a 50 percent coinsurance rate for dental and outpatient mental health care. The test requires that each individual

act as his own control. If we did not omit the 25/50 plan participants, we would be comparing the person's dental and other health services response without adjusting for the differential coverage of the two types of services. We do not feel that the omission of the 25/50 plan affects the conclusion, because the remaining contrasts are so consistent with a greater response in year 1 for dental services than for nondental services and less response in year 2.

32. Data in Tables 3.19–3.21 and 3.23 are from the subsample; data in Tables 3.22 and 3.24 are from the full sample.

33. See Tenney (1968); Berkanovic (1974); Roghmann (1974); Federspiel, Ray, and Schaffner (1976); Sharftstein, Towery, and Milowe (1980); Schwartz et al. (1980).

34. On our claim forms the provider described the procedures, diagnoses, and medications; the patient recorded the "reason for visit" information.

35. In other words, we believe that the rate of false-positive identification of visits with mental health content should be lowest for the procedure and diagnosis criteria, intermediate for the psychotropic medications, and highest for the reason-for-visit criterion.

36. Stimulants used as antidepressants are grouped with antidepressants.

37. The data come from the physician Medical Expense Report (claim form), where the physician indicated a drug was prescribed at the visit, rather than from the drug Medical Expense Report (which gives data on prescriptions filled).

38. The last category is included because sleep disturbance is commonly associated with mental and medical problems. When associated with a mental health diagnosis, the visit would be identified by the "higher" diagnosis criterion. When only a medical diagnosis is present, the visit cannot be justified as a mental health visit. However, we believe that a reported diagnosis of a sleep disorder with no accompanying medical diagnosis is likely to indicate a mental health visit.

39. Year 2 has a full combination of sites and plans and is also the most likely steady-state year of use.

40. The estimate from our most conservative definition (7.1 percent of enrollees) should be most comparable to other estimates based on insurance claims. By comparison, in 1975 4.6 percent of the population covered by Michigan Blue Cross/Blue Shield submitted any hospital or outpatient claims for mental disorder (Liptzin, Regier, and Goldberg 1980). Estimates from four organized health settings (Goldberg, Regier, and Burns 1980) vary from 4.7 to 12.3 percent.

41. For example, $163 = 134 + 29 = 128 + 35 = 123 + 40$.

42. To determine the appropriateness of this specification, we examined the records of all persons who had mental health services from both a nonformal and formal provider in all sites in year 1. Of the persons in this category, 78 percent appeared to have formal mental health visits only as an adjunct to

nonformal mental health care (for example, referrals to a formal provider or medical consultations for medications related to formal care). The remaining 22 percent seemed to use both formal and nonformal providers as independent sources of mental health care.

43. We do not analyze number of visits per user, because this ratio is very sensitive to individuals with high levels of use. For a more complete discussion of the choice of expenses for measuring level of use, see Wells et al. (1982).

44. For this proration, psychotropic medications and reasons for visit are counted as diagnoses.

45. For example, the basic visit charge is either prorated by the proportion of all diagnoses that are mental health for that visit (lower bound) or counted in its entirety as a mental health expense (upper bound).

46. The standard population that we use in the mental health analysis consists of all full-year participants from year 2. We first make a prediction for each full-year participant from year 2, including those not on the free plan, as if everyone were on the free plan. We then average these individual predictions. The average prediction is our standardized prediction for the free plan. We then do the same for the 25/25 plan and all other plans. This procedure is analogous to the usual age- and sex-adjusted (standardized) comparison, carried out on a more extensive scale; we standardize (adjust) for all included covariates other than the plan itself.

47. The inclusion of diagnosis raises the probability of any mental health use because it includes more visits to informal providers, but because that use is such a small component of spending, it has little effect on spending.

48. Site dummy variables are in the regression, but the sample is not well suited to determining whether the reversal is due to a differential response to cost sharing across sites (that is, interaction between site and plan).

49. If the 25/50 and 50/50 plans were combined, the spending rate of the combined group would be 57 percent of the free plan rate. If outpatient mental health expenditures were subtracted from ambulatory expenditures, the percentages would be nearly unchanged.

50. Before reaching a conclusion on this matter, one should analyze effects on outcomes (taken up in Chapter 6) as well as cross-price effects (on which the Experiment did not obtain much information).

51. Calculated from data in Tables 3.1, 3.2, and 3.22.

52. See Reed, Myers, and Scheidemandel (1972) for comparable findings using nonexperimental data.

53. The test statistic was a $\chi^2(3) = 3.21$, which is statistically insignificant at $p = 0.25$.

54. Psychiatrists per 100,000 population range from 3 and 5 for the two rural sites, to 7 for Dayton and Fitchburg, to 18 and 22 for Charleston and Seattle, respectively.

55. However, the fact that 35 percent of the participants in the 95 percent coinsurance plan exceeded the MDE, in contrast to only 21 percent in the 25 and 50 percent plan, mitigates the differential between plans; it also mitigates underfiling in the 95 percent plan. We return to this point in Chapter 11.

56. Rogers and Newhouse (1985) present details of this analysis and further analysis of underreporting. They find that although some of the overall underfiling was attributable to plan effects, some was due to personal disorganization; specifically, in addition to plan, underfiling was associated with low education and poor mental health.

57. This result is based on predicted values for the enrollment population, on the assumption that everyone had free medical care.

58. These results use an ANOVA specification of insurance plan.

59. Using ANOVA, the largest χ^2 statistic for the seven use measures was $\chi^2(4) =$ 3.40 for the probability of any medical use.

60. This result is based on predicted values for the enrollment population, on the assumption that everyone had free medical care, for all years of the study. This standardization was required because different sites had different treatments. The differences have t-statistics of 0.25 and -0.10, respectively. Dollars are 1991 dollars.

61. Using ANOVA, the largest χ^2 statistic for the seven use measures was $\chi^2(8) =$ 11.36 for inpatient dollars.

62. This result is based on predicted values for the enrollment population, on the assumption that everyone had free medical care, for the first three years of the study. We limit the comparison to the first three years to avoid confounding three- and five-year estimates with the upward drift in expenses mentioned in the text.

63. This result used ANOVA on data from the first three years of the study. The largest χ^2 statistic for the seven use measures was $\chi^2(4) = 2.43$ for total admissions.

64. Those with an entry examination had 2 percent more dental visits during the entry year ($t = 0.58$) and 2 percent more visits during the middle years of the study ($t = 0.48$) than those without an entry examination. Those enrolled for three years had 1 percent fewer visits during the entry year of the study ($t = -0.19$) and 3 percent more visits during the middle years of the study ($t = 0.67$) than those assigned to the five-year group. Those assigned to fill out weekly health diaries had 9 percent more visits in the entry year ($t = 0.83$) and 8 percent more in the middle years ($t = 0.77$) than those who filled out diaries biweekly. Those not assigned to fill out diaries had 6 percent more visits during the entry year ($t = 0.84$) and 11 percent more visits during the middle years of the study ($t = 1.37$).

4. Episodes of Treatment

1. The rule in the simple form stated in the text requires the additional assumptions of risk neutrality and separability of the utility function in health and wealth (income). Nonetheless, the intuition behind the rule is basically sound and will be exploited in this chapter. For expositions of the theory see Keeler, Newhouse, and Phelps (1977) and Ellis (1986).

2. The 100 percent coinsurance value is an extrapolation from the reduction of 55 percent at 95 percent coinsurance, described later in this section.

3. For results using other combinations of coinsurance and MDEs see Keeler et al. (1988), table 5.6.

4. Economists may note the analogy with rational expectation models.

5. See Lohr et al. (1986b) for a much simpler method of defining episodes.

6. With one exception, expenses connected with an episode that spanned two accounting years are split, with the second year's expenses beginning on the first day of the new year. The exception is a person who was an inpatient at the end of the first accounting year; in that case we allocated all expenses for the stay to the same episode. This reflects reality in that participants did not have to cost share in two different accounting years for an uninterrupted hospitalization, whereas they did for other types of episodes (such as two office visits for the same episode that straddled an accounting year).

7. These were the last three years in South Carolina and the first three years in other sites. Thus, the years in which only the five-year sample participated are excluded.

8. In analyses of medical expenditure the 25/50 percent plan is treated as 25 percent coinsurance, and in analyses of dental and mental health expenditure it is treated as 50 percent coinsurance (see Chapter 3).

9. Whereas the four-part model is appropriate for a continuous variable such as expenditure, the negative binomial is appropriate for discrete data such as episode counts.

10. See Keeler et al. (1988), app. A, for an analysis of the departures from lognormality.

11. There is a good economic reason for this. As noted in Chapter 3, more than one-third of the 95 percent plan participants had free care at the margin. Thus, in addition to the across-person variance, within the 95 percent plan sample there is an analogue to between-plan variance, because some people did not exceed their cap and faced 95 percent coinsurance whereas other people did exceed their cap and faced zero coinsurance.

12. Under the negative binomial method, which can be used for counts of discrete phenomena such as episodes but not for a continuous variable v such as

expenditure, zeroes need not be modeled separately; this method also readily aggregates data over time.

13. This is actually a weak assumption because we allow elements of β_1 and β_2 to be zero.

14. Because of this exploratory work to determine which variables were important, the significance levels associated with the t-statistics on other than the plan variables should not be taken too literally.

15. We show in the next chapter that if the variable measuring use is the likelihood of any use of specific kinds of services, poor-sick children exhibit the greatest response to cost sharing of any group.

16. Alpha is the shape parameter of the gamma mixing distribution of unmeasured propensities for episodes. This distribution has a coefficient of variation of $(\alpha\beta^2)^{1/2}/\alpha\beta = \alpha^{-1/2}$.

17. The marginal price is the amount the family pays if it buys an additional \$1 of medical services.

18. It is also important for long mental health episodes, as described later in the chapter and in Keeler, Wells, and Manning (1986).

19. The appropriate inflator for the \$400 figure would be a medical care price index, but we have refrained from using it because of problems in interpreting it (Newhouse 1989). From 1978 to 1991 the overall CPI rose by slightly more than a factor of 2, while the medical care component rose by just under a factor of 3. Unless indicated otherwise, in this book we use the all-items CPI to inflate dollars.

20. We could not estimate the effect of very large deductibles (say \$6,000 in 1991 dollars) on catastrophic hospitalizations from the experimental data because the Experiment did not contain such deductibles. An attempt to do so from premium data supplied by two insurance companies failed. Analysis of those data revealed that the companies' guessed premiums were not consistent with the economic assumption that larger deductibles should lead to reduced use of medical services.

21. For example, the first day has as many acute episodes as 22 ordinary days. We thus count the first day as 22 days and say that someone who exceeds the MDE on the third day has had $(22 + 2)/(22 + 364)$ of the year's experience in the pre-MDE stage.

22. Families occasionally have several episodes on the day the MDE is exceeded. We assume that all such episodes belong to the pre-MDE period. Alternative assumptions that put some of the multiple episodes into the post-MDE (free care) period have no discernible effect on pre-MDE price ratios and raise the free period price ratios by 0 to 5 percent, depending on plan and type. The problem of exceeding the MDE from multiple episodes is similar to the case of someone with only a little MDE remaining who has a very large episode.

Multiple episodes are discussed in more detail in Keeler et al. (1982), apps. D and E.

23. For reasons of cost we estimated δ_k using a least-squares regression of the square root of individual episode frequencies on individual characteristics in preference to the negative binomial regressions. The predicted frequency was then summed within family. It turns out that both models give substantially the same predictions. See Keeler et al. (1988), app. E.

24. Because the regression estimates d_k of rates based on demographic character-istics are unbiased (the sum of the d_k equals the sum of the n_k), the estimated mean of the Gamma distribution should be close to 1. The mean of a Gamma is given by $\alpha\beta$ (approximately 1) and the variance by $\alpha\beta^2$, where α is the shape parameter and β the scale parameter. Because $\alpha\beta$ is approximately 1, the variance approximately equals β; the higher β, the lower α because the product is a constant.

25. The standard errors shown assume that errors in estimating the effects on cost per episode and the number of episodes are independent, and that the true standard error of the reduction in number is 1.5 times the maximum-likeli-hood estimate (see Keeler et al. 1988 for an explanation of this correction in the estimates).

26. The fact that the maximum MDE was reduced to $750 for most site-years on the 25 percent coinsurance plan, whereas it was left at $1,000 in the 50 per-cent coinsurance plan, presumably accounts for the similar percentage exceeding the MDE in these two plans.

27. But not statistically significantly different from it.

28. We actually use an approximation to the negative binomial regression. This approximation uses ordinary least squares to estimate the square root of the number of episodes.

29. An alternative explanation, that sickly persons are more likely to be in the small MDE range, is not consistent with the test-of-methods findings in Table 4.16. If the alternative explanation were true, rates of hospital episodes during the small MDE period on the test-of-methods plan should substantially exceed those in the large MDE period.

30. Specifically it is $r/2$ times the variance, where r is Pratt's approximation to constant absolute risk aversion. It can be shown that this is the approximate premium that makes a person indifferent between facing $E(x)$ minus a risk premium with certainty or facing a gamble in out-of-pocket expenditures, pro-vided that expenditure is small relative to income. We use $r = .001$, so $r/2 = .0005$. If anything, this is a rather high value, but values of risk reduction over most of our range are small even with this value of r.

31. We have left the results in this section in 1983 dollars. Values in 1991 dollars, based on the all-items CPI, would be about 37 percent higher.

32. The values for no MDE should be almost the same on average as the effect of pure price on total medical expenditure as shown in Table 4.17. The only difference is that in the simulation, catastrophically large hospitalizations (over $11,000, 1986 dollars) are assumed to be price insensitive, whereas in Table 4.17 they are treated like any other hospitalization.

33. The region of low-cost hospitalization, or division between the large- and small-MDE period, is shown as $600 rather than $400 to account for inflation between approximately 1978 and 1983.

34. Use with no insurance is assumed to be valued at out-of-pocket cost. Additional use induced by insurance is assumed to be valued at out-of-pocket cost plus consumer surplus; a linear approximation is used to calculate consumer surplus.

35. The far left point on the 50 percent coinsurance line corresponds to no limit.

36. For these comparisons, we limited our analyses to four-person families in our original Current Population Survey subsample. This yielded 134 families, and we performed 20 replications within each comparison run.

37. Keeler, Relles, and Rolph (1977a, 1977b) showed the opposite—that equivalent family limits were generally superior to individual limits—but their analysis assumed that price had no effect on use. In this analysis we relax that assumption and reach a different conclusion.

38. The higher values in these ranges correspond to $300 initial deductibles rather than $100.

39. One of the principles of insurance is to insure less well those services that respond more to price. Thus, if one is allocating a fixed subsidy to encourage consumption, and if demand curves capture marginal social benefit, one is better off with differential coinsurance rates such that the service with the greater demand response is less well insured. On the other hand, if one is allocating a fixed total amount of spending (e.g., premium), one is better off insuring all services at the same rate. This follows from the argument that if the services are insured at different rates, it will pay to give up some units of the better-insured service for the less well-insured service. The argument is reinforced to the degree that there is fraud in labeling services, that is, collusion between the physician and patient against the insurer; for example, labeling something as treating a medical problem that was in fact well care, or treating a mental health problem in order to obtain the more generous insurance benefits.

40. This conclusion ignores the value of these services to others and assumes that price measures the value of forgone opportunities (i.e., social cost) and that the cost of the services is small relative to income. See Chapter 11 for further discussion.

41. Because of the varying propensity to seek care on the different plans, severity of illness may have varied; i.e., the additional people on the free care plan who sought care may have been less sick.

42. In exit interviews, however, 70 percent of patients said that their doctor knew or had been told of their insurance status; only 10 percent said they did not know whether the doctor knew their insurance status. (See Chapter 10.)

43. But see note 39 above.

44. These hospitalizations are included in the analysis of hospital episodes earlier in the chapter.

45. Wells, Keeler, and Manning (1990) show that there is great persistence in treatment of mental health problems, a finding that suggests that unmeasured characteristics are important. Those under treatment in the previous month have a 78.5 percent chance of being in treatment this month; those not under treatment have only a 0.3 percent chance. Those with some treatment during the Experiment but not in treatment the previous month have a 6.4 percent chance of initiating treatment.

46. The plan was the same as the "test-of-methods" plan for medical services. Two-thirds of the families were given an initial MDE of $1,000 and one-third an MDE of $300, with a coinsurance rate of 40 percent. The distribution of MDE remaining roughly models that on the pay plans throughout the year.

47. As discussed in Chapter 3, the sample is unbalanced by site and year for the mental health analysis. Thus, the lack of an effect in Table 4.23 could be attributable to a true effect's being obscured by site and year effects.

48. $0.18 = 1 - \exp(-0.2)$, where -0.2 comes from Keeler, Wells, and Manning (1986), table 9.10, col. 2.

49. The prediction sample was taken to be those on the free plan in year 2 of the study. (The free plan had fewer refusals and fewer dropouts than the other plans, so this population is the most representative of the sites; see Chapter 2.) These rates are estimated for the personal characteristics of each person in the sample with behavior adjusted to year 2 in Seattle. The hazard and cost ratios corresponding to the different coinsurance rates are used to derive predicted values for each person and the average taken over all persons.

50. Because hazard rates are in the logarithm of time and the cost estimates are in the logarithm of costs, both variance estimates are in logarithmic scale and can simply be added.

51. We derived these figures by inflating 1986 dollars by the 40 percent increase in the physician services component of the CPI over the period 1986–1991. To the degree that inflation in the prices of mental health providers differs from that of physicians as a whole, these estimates will be inaccurate.

5. Specific Types of Use

1. We also looked at whether the level of emergency room use differed between those who left the Experiment and those who stayed. We could not reject the hypothesis that people who left the Experiment early for reasons other than death made emergency department visits at the same rate as people with similar health and demographic characteristics who completed the study ($t < 0.29$). Although those who died did have a higher visit rate, their number is small enough that we make no adjustment for these differences.

2. The F-statistic testing the hypothesis of the same response of emergency room use and ambulatory care use was 1.36 with 4,3688 degrees of freedom, not significant at the 10 percent level.

3. Income was defined as the average household income for two years before enrollment, adjusted for family size. Details of the family-size adjustment are described in Chapter 6. Results using a continuous measure of income are not appreciably different.

4. The Bonferroni test calculates a corrected probability level by dividing the nominal p value of interest (e.g., 0.05) by the total number of comparisons (n). The modified test statistic calculates a corrected probability level for each t-statistic; the procedure is to rank order each t-statistic of interest (e.g., those > 1.96) from highest to lowest and divide the nominal p value for the first statistic by n, that for the second by $n - 1$, and so on, stopping when the next t-statistic fails to reach significance according to the calculated value. See Kolm (1979).

5. All these comparisons were also significant at $p < 0.05$ with no correction. Nonsignificant differences were seen for highly effective care for chronic conditions (both age groups), highly effective care for "acute or chronic" conditions (children), and rarely effective care (children).

6. Use of nonprescription drugs (including those covered by the Experiment) is summarized in Leibowitz (1989). Use of nonprescription (over-the-counter) as well as prescription drugs increased as cost sharing decreased. Better-educated consumers made greater use of over-the-counter drugs. Both insurance plan and education affected primarily a decision to use over-the-counter drugs rather than the amount used conditional on some use. Persons more dissatisfied with waiting times to an appointment were likely to spend a higher share of their drug dollar on over-the-counter drugs. For further details see Leibowitz (1989).

7. Income was adjusted for family size; see Chapter 6 for details of the adjustment.

8. This value differs from the 80 percent shown in Table 5.15 because the 85 percent value is a predicted value from the negative binomial model, whereas the values in Table 5.15 are raw values.

9. Why inappropriate admissions occur at all—and certainly at the rates described here—is not clear. The free plan leaves the issue of locus of care solely to nonpecuniary considerations; in some cases hospitalization may be more convenient for the patient, the physician, or both. One would expect, however, that cost sharing would reduce this category to near zero, because for much of the sample it cost $1,000 to be admitted, less whatever other medical expenses the family incurred during the year. (This would be around $2,000 in 1991 dollars, using the all-items CPI to inflate.) On the presumption that most clinically appropriate admissions would be considered economically appropriate as well, the effect of cost sharing would be limited to a small percentage of clinically appropriate admissions. Put another way, one would have expected cost sharing to have reduced inappropriate admissions markedly, with a much more modest reduction in clinically appropriate admissions.

One can make the observed pattern consistent with the theoretical prediction if the percentage reduction in economically inappropriate but clinically appropriate admissions caused by cost sharing is large relative to the reduction in clinically inappropriate admissions. Such an outcome cannot be ruled out but seems implausible; that is, it seems more plausible that the effect of cost sharing would be as great or greater on those admissions that are inappropriate by both criteria. If the response is as great, the statement in the text is correct.

10. Further details of this analysis are available in Lillard et al. (1986) and Lurie et al. (1987).

6. Adult Health Status and Patient Satisfaction

1. Extensive discussions of these measures, including their construction and properties, can be found in the following references: Brook et al. (1984); Davies et al. (1988); Davies and Ware (1981); Donald and Ware (1982); Donald et al. (1978); Foxman et al. (1982); Rogers, Williams, and Brook (1979); Stewart et al. (1978); Stewart, Ware, and Brook (1977, 1981, 1982a, 1982b); Veit and Ware (1983); Ware (1976, 1984); Ware, Davies-Avery, and Brook (1980); Ware, Davies-Avery, and Donald (1978); Ware, Johnston, and Davies-Avery (1979); Williams, Ware, and Donald (1981). In several of the references listed in this chapter the General Health Index is called the General Health Rating Index.

2. Although any individual can score only 0 or 100 on the RFI, the average of a group can obviously lie between these values.

3. The 38 MHI items are listed in abbreviated form in Veit and Ware (1983). For a complete listing see Brook et al. (1979), app. H; or Davies et al. (1988).

4. Scoring is described in Donald et al. (1978); Donald and Ware (1982); and Davies et al. (1988).

5. They are considered ratings as opposed to reports because they reflect individual differences in how people evaluate the information they have about their health.

6. Further details can be found in Beck et al. (1981a, 1981b); Berman et al. (1981); Brook et al. (1980a, 1980b, 1981a, 1981b, 1984); Brook, Lohr, and Goldberg (1982); Foxman et al. (1982); Keeler et al. (1987); Lohr et al. (1986a); Rosenthal et al. (1981); Rubenstein et al. (1982, 1983); Scott et al. (1980, 1981); Smith et al. (1978); Zielske et al. (1981, 1982).

7. The 9.52 intercept term is correct; the 4.92 value in Brook et al. (1984) is incorrect.

8. As noted in Chapter 2, during the first year of the Experiment in the first site (Dayton), we asked a random half of the sample to fill out the form weekly rather than biweekly in order to test for reporting effects. Also in 1978, budgetary reasons compelled us to stop administering the questionaires to all participants except the three-year group in South Carolina (which had just enrolled) and the Group Health Cooperative control group in Seattle (which collected a nontrivial share of participation benefits from filling out the biweekly forms).

9. The basis for this conclusion is summarized in Brook et al. (1984), app. C, and is described in detail in the various individual volumes relevant to these measures: Davies and Ware (1981); Donald et al. (1978); Stewart et al. (1978); Ware, Davies-Avery, and Brook (1980); Ware, Davies-Avery, and Donald (1978); Ware, Johnston, and Davies-Avery (1979).

10. A detailed discussion of the reliability of the specific measures is found in each of the tracer disease monographs: Beck et al. (1981a, 1981b); Berman et al. (1981); Brook et al. (1980a, 1980b, 1981a, 1981b); Brook, Lohr, and Goldberg (1982); Foxman et al. (1982); Lohr et al. (1986a); Rosenthal et al. (1981); Rubenstein et al. (1982, 1983); Scott et al. (1980, 1981); Zielske et al. (1981, 1982).

11. The deflator for family size is as follows: 0.37 + 0.18 (number of adults over 18) + 0.15 first child + 0.12 second child + 0.10 (number of third and subsequent children). Thus, a two-adult, two-child family has a value of 1.0: [0.37 + 2(0.18) + 0.15 + 0.12]; adding a third child increases the value to 1.10. Site cost-of-living indices are based on the annual budget of a four-person family at an intermediate standard of living in autumn 1973. The values for the Massachusetts sites are for Hartford, Connecticut; those for the South Carolina sites are an average of Atlanta, Georgia, and Durham, North Carolina. See Polich et al. (1986), pp. 62–66, for further details.

12. Brook et al. (1990) analyze a somewhat different set of indicators concerning pain, worry, and symptomatic relief. They find little difference overall between the free care and cost-sharing plans (their table 4), but a small differ-

ence favoring free care for the poor and cost sharing for the nonpoor (their table 5).

13. Within the free care group the estimated effect is 0.3 mm Hg. See Keeler et al. (1985), app. B.

14. The analysis in this section draws on Rogers et al. (1991).

15. Income was adjusted for family size as described in note 11 above.

16. An alternative but implausible inference is that the effect of cost sharing among the working population all occurs on weekends or other nonworking days.

17. Since per person per month use of antibiotics with free care was almost double that for the cost-sharing plan (see Chapter 5), adverse medication effects could have occurred more frequently on the free-care plan.

18. The values shown in the tables are predicted from regression equations that included as explanatory variables in addition to dummy variables for plan: enrollment value of measure, years of education if adult, years of education of female head if child, age, gender, income, family size, whether three- or five-year enrollee, data quality and examiner variables, and interactions between plans and both education and enrollment values. Further details on methods of analysis are available in Bailit et al. (1985); Spolsky et al. (1983) have further details on measurement methods.

19. Beck et al. (1981a, 1981b); Berman et al. (1981); Brook, Lohr, and Goldberg (1982); Brook et al. (1980a, 1980b, 1981a, 1981b); Foxman et al. (1982); Lohr et al. (1986a); Rosenthal et al. (1981); Rubenstein et al. (1982, 1983); Scott et al. (1980, 1981); Spolsky et al. (1983); Zielske et al. (1981, 1982).

20. Taking the initial examination had less effect on the free care plan.

21. This number differs from that described earlier because we included participants with a near- or far-vision impairment at entry or exit.

7. Pediatric Health Status

1. The other tested conditions were cancer, convulsions, dental conditions, bed-wetting, growth and development disorders, lead poisoning, and urinary tract infections. Dental health measures are discussed at the end of the chapter.

2. A more detailed discussion is found in Beck et al. (1983); Eisen et al. (1980); Foxman, Lohr, and Brook (1983); Foxman et al. (1986); Kamberg et al. (1983); Lohr et al. (1983); Rubenstein et al. (1985); and Valdez (1986), app. B.

3. Beck et al. (1983); Davies and Ware (1981); Eisen et al. (1980); Foxman, Lohr, and Brook (1983); Foxman et al. (1986); Kamberg et al. (1983); Lohr et al. (1983); Rubenstein et al. (1985); Smith et al. (1978); Ware, Johnston, and Davies-Avery (1979); Ware et al. (1984).

4. Data on the sensitivity, specificity, and predictive power of screening tests are discussed at length in Beck et al. (1983); Foxman, Lohr, and Brook (1983); Foxman et al. (1986); Kamberg et al. (1983); Lohr et al. (1983); Rubenstein et al. (1985).
5. The regression equations are available in Valdez (1986), app. D.
6. We excluded those in the third quarter of the income distribution from this comparison to sharpen the contrast and to increase our ability to detect a difference.
7. Again to sharpen the contrast we omitted the third quarter of the distribution.
8. The values in Table 7.8 are well below those of Table 7.6 because Table 7.8 includes all children in the income group, not just those at elevated risk.

8. Use of Services

1. A staff model HMO employs physicians, usually full-time on salary, to deliver care to their members.
2. In particular, if there were any unmeasured interaction effects that caused the effects by site to vary, our results would be biased.
3. Indeed, Cherkin, Grothaus, and Wagner (1989) find that a $5 copayment per visit at Group Health Cooperative reduced primary care visits 11 percent and specialty care visits 3 percent.
4. The GHC Control Group, of course, represents a self-selected population that is not strictly comparable to the other groups. The 2 percent figure given in Chapter 2 for the difference in refusal rate between the experimental and cost-sharing groups differs from the 19 − 16 figures given here because of rounding error.
5. Specifically, 4 comparisons out of 16 are nominally significant at the 5 percent level. Higher-income families were more likely to refuse the offer, especially the offer of the free-care plan and the Group Health experimental plan. The mean difference in income between those who accepted and those who refused on these plans is about $8,000 (1991 dollars). Similarly, older individuals were more likely to refuse the offer of those two plans. Those with group insurance were more likely to refuse the Group Health experimental plan than those without, but more likely to accept Group Health control status. Note that one can join Group Health Cooperative either through the place of employment or as an individual.
6. For those with complete data, we cannot reject the hypotheses that the GHC experimentals had the same characteristics as those on the fee-for-service plans. The test statistics are $F(18,19359) = 0.90$ for personal characteristics (for example, health status) and $F(8,4236) = 0.98$ for family characteristics (for example, income and family size). See also Morris (1985), tables 3.7 and 3.8.

7. For those with complete data, the test statistics are $F(4,4236) = 9.68$ for family characteristics and $F(9,19359) = 7.55$ for personal characteristics.

8. Precision is further reduced if data are included on individuals who completed only partial years. Making neither of these changes (that is, excluding covariates and including partial years) leaves the estimated expenditure largely unaffected, but sufficiently decreases precision to the point that one can reject the null hypothesis of no difference in expenditure between the experimental group and the free-care plan with a probability of only 0.08 (two-tail test).

9. The test statistic for a differential expenditure response to plan by early departure is $F(5,3083) = 0.81$. The test statistic for any difference (main effect or plan interaction) is $F(6,3083) = 0.78$. The average person who left early spent $59 (1991 dollars) more per person per year than those who stayed until the end of the study, with a standard error of $75. These tests are based on generalized least-squares estimates rather than four-part model estimates (see Manning et al. 1985). We also compared admission and visit rates and found no significant differences for admissions—$[\chi^2(5) = 2.90]$—but significant differences for visits—$[\chi^2(5) = 13.60]$—largely limited to the 95 percent plan. Both of these tests excluded people who died during the Experiment, who had much higher use rates but were few enough that our estimates are not sensitive to their inclusion. Correcting for sample loss changes none of the entries in Table 8.4 by more than 5 percent.

10. As was the case in Chapter 3, the model used to analyze expenditure requires equal periods for each observation, because it does not allow convolution of observations. Thus, people who participated for only part of a year could appear to be different even though their underlying behavior was the same. Although the part-year participants had more physical limitations and were more likely to be enrolled in less generous plans, we found no evidence that the part-year people, other than those who died, behaved differently. Decedents, who account for less than 1 percent on any plan (Table 8.3), are too few to estimate any plan effect. Our modeling of episodes using fee-for-service data (Chapter 4) does permit convolution of observations. We did not carry out such an analysis for the HMO sample because the main purpose of the episode expenditure analysis is to analyze within-year price effects, which are irrelevant for the HMO sample.

11. The GHC controls do have a 4.2 percentage point higher probability than the GHC experimentals of using any medical services ($p < .01$). Although part of this result is due to different characteristics (for example, age and gender), we found that a significant difference persists even when we control for such characteristics.

12. The GHC experimental and free fee-for-service plan face-to-face visit rates are not significantly different ($t = 0.22$). The rate for the GHC controls may be higher than that for the GHC experimentals ($t = 1.73$). The GHC controls have

an insignificantly higher visit rate than the free fee-for-service experimentals ($t= 1.46$).

13. Manning, Wells, and Benjamin (1986) provide greater detail on the analyses in this section.

14. Ignoring roundoff error, formal visits per user are visits per enrollee divided by users per enrollee, or $16.9 = 1.06/.0628$; $4.7 = .31/.065$; 1.06 and .31 come from the (rounded) figures in row 4 of Table 8.7, and .0628 and .065 come from row 2 (divided by 100) of Table 8.7.

15. Controls could visit mental health specialists free of charge only 10 times per year; thereafter they had to pay $8 to $10 per visit, with the number of such visits unlimited. The existence of the copayment may help explain why GHC control participants were more likely than fee-for-service participants to seek mental health care from general medical providers, but it cannot explain why GHC experimentals, who had no copayment, were more likely to do so.

16. Otherwise the percentage reduction in days would have been less than 40 percent.

17. Figures for 1977 and 1987 are calculated from National Center for Health Statistics (1978, table 16; 1988, table 74). Data for other years are presented in Table 11.2 of this volume.

9. Health and Satisfaction Outcomes

1. Further details on the analyses reported in this chapter are available in Davies et al. (1986); Ware et al. (1986, 1987); Sloss et al. (1987); Siu et al. (1988); Valdez (1989); and Valdez et al. (1989).

2. See also Wells, Manning, and Valdez (1989a), showing no effect on two subscales of the Mental Health Index, positive well-being and psychological distress.

3. The risk of dying is omitted because it is a function of three of the included variables. This test was run among the first set of health outcome variables that were analyzed. It was not repeated on subsequent variables. See Ware et al. (1987).

4. See, for example, the data on cancer survival rates, limitation of activity, disability days, and self-assessment of health in National Center for Health Statistics (1990).

5. See Valdez (1989) and Valdez et al. (1989) for additional details on the analysis reported in this section.

6. Figures for Seattle only are not available, but we believe the percentage who saw a specialist would, if anything, be higher there than in Dayton.

7. Persons who had had an eye examination in the two years before the Experiment were excluded from the samples being compared.

8. Further details are available in Siu et al. (1988).

9. Further details of this analysis are found in Davies et al. (1986).
10. GHC's market share at that time was around 15 percent, but we do not have data on the fraction of the Seattle market who could have enrolled at GHC at their place of employment.
11. From the point of view of economic theory, the marginal consumer should be indifferent, given that cost is a dimension included in the satisfaction scale. The empirical measure tests the equality of the average consumer in each group rather than the marginal consumer; however, if the marginal consumer has the same satisfaction, it is not surprising that the average consumer would not be measurably different in the two groups.
12. We did not appraise the degree to which GHC passed through cost savings, but in a consumer cooperative one might expect that at least some of the benefits would be passed through.

10. Administrative Lessons

1. The rationale for our decisions is detailed in Clasquin and Brown (1977).
2. Even in the Individual Deductible plan, there was not only a $150 per person per year limit on out-of-pocket expenditure, but also a $450 per year per family limit.
3. Chapter 2 presents our reasons for not assigning 60- and 61-year-olds to five-year plans and for not enrolling persons over 61.
4. If there were two or more individuals in a household who could have been defined as a "head" and such individuals did not claim each other as spouses, then each individual was designated as head of his or her own family unit, and other people in that household were assigned to one of the units according to the dependency and relationship criteria.
5. Despite the simple language of the Certificate of Benefits regarding the scope of covered services, we found the insurance policies difficult to administer. By the end of the Experiment we had made several hundred policy decisions or interpretations of the Certificate of Benefits regarding the scope of covered services.
6. Throughout this chapter the answers are of necessity from those who finished the Experiment. No attempt has been made to adjust for selection bias, although some bias is undoubtedly present for some of the questions. Any correction for selection bias would involve arbitrary (i.e., not theoretically based) assumptions; and in most cases the results are likely to be little affected, given an attrition over the entire Experiment of only 10 percent (see Chapter 2).
7. For example, at a probability of 27 percent for a favorable response, a decrease of 50 points in the Socially Desirable Response Set Scale, which ranges from 0 to 100, decreases the probability of a favorable response only to 19.5 percent.

8. This material is covered in greater detail in Archibald and Newhouse (1988) and Brown (1984).

9. Research and administrative considerations do not inevitably conflict. For example, one decision that we made for research reasons—to recognize family splits only on the anniversary of the accounting year—was also administratively advantageous.

10. For example, two very common problems occur in independent evaluations of demonstration projects that have been both proposed and implemented by advocates. Aside from the problem of whether the treatment will be replicable if carried out by someone else, decisions made inadvertently by the group implementing the demonstration may compromise the evaluation.

11. Although it is not likely that computerized networks and critical path algorithms such as those provided by PERT will prove cost-effective in most social experiments (the cost of input and update may well exceed the cost of more conventional methods), the basic principles underlying the use of these techniques will have to be applied in one form or another.

12. Not only may the budget from the primary sponsor be uncertain, but there may be possibilities for seeking funding from multiple sources.

13. One will certainly want to engage in some analysis during the experiment, if only because sponsors want earlier results. But the early analysis may in fact be sufficient for the purpose at hand. (One usually has an estimate of power at the beginning of an experiment, but this is only an estimate, and the data may yield more precise estimates than one anticipates.) Thus, the data collected later in the experiment may subsequently be deemed not worth analyzing.

11. Central Findings and Policy Implications

1. The standard economic argument assumes that subsidized or insured care will induce use that is valued lower than nonsubsidized care. In light of the non-specific effects of cost sharing (Chapter 5), reality appears more complex. Nonetheless, given the outcome effects described next, the conclusion of the economic argument appears largely sustained. The last part of this chapter discusses this issue at greater length.

2. The likelihood is that hospital services would be more responsive to price without the cap on out-of-pocket expenditure, but this is probably due to income effects from large expenditure; thus, the increased demand for hospital services with a cap cannot necessarily be interpreted in the usual fashion as indicating a welfare loss (De Meza 1983; Goddeeris 1984a, 1984b). The same logic may apply to mental health services.

3. Those who do not wish to reject a null hypothesis except at the 5 percent level of significance may not want to accept this statement, because the estimated main effect of plan (across the entire sample) is significant at the 5 percent

level, whereas the test of the interaction term (whether subgroups differ in their response) is not. Nonetheless, the effect sizes differ; for example, the estimated effect for poor hypertensives is 2.3mm Hg of diastolic blood pressure, whereas for high-income hypertensives it is −0.1mm Hg (i.e., approximately zero, but actually of the wrong sign). The p value for the t-statistic on the difference between free care and cost sharing for the poor hypertensive group is 0.08 (two-tail test; arguably a one-tail test is appropriate). The estimated functional far vision effect is over four times larger for the poor myopic group than for the high-income myopic group, and the estimated risk of dying effect is more than twice as high. The risk-of-dying effect is significant at the 5 percent level for the poor sick group, albeit with no corrections for multiple comparisons.

4. In particular, there is no measurable interaction between the response of total expenditure and plan across sites (chi-square with 19 d.f. = 14.96, $p > .50$).

5. This data series has subsequently been revised by the Health Care Financing Administration. The revised data show that the out-of-pocket share was 5.2 percent in both 1980 and 1985; estimates for intermediate years are not published (Office of National Cost Estimates 1990). These numbers, as well as the original numbers cited in the text, combine data on those over and under age 65; nonetheless, the latter account for about two-thirds of total expenditure, and one would have expected to see a larger effect of the initial cost sharing if there were not compensating changes for very large bills. Moreover, the over-65 are covered by Medicare. Little of increase in the Medicare hospital deductible in this period would appear as increased cost sharing in the numbers in the text, since for most Medicare beneficiaries it was covered by either a Medigap policy or Medicaid.

6. Medicaid pays for little hospitalization among people under 65 (e.g., under 10 percent in 1980; Gibson and Waldo 1981). Cost controls at the state level were not widespread in the period after 1983 and in any event often regulated per diem rather than per-stay rates.

7. See, e.g., Evans (1984) and Blumenthal et al. (1986). Theoretically one could conceive of lump-sum transfers to such individuals to offset this burden; in the real world, however, some additional burden seems inescapable if there is any cost sharing.

8. Other difficulties also arise. For example, administrative complexities in accounting for past cost sharing would occur if insurance were employment based and the individual changed employers.

9. In particular, under section 131 of the Tax Equity and Fiscal Responsibility Act (TEFRA) of 1982, states may impose a nominal deductible, coinsurance, copayment, or similar charge on the categorically needy or medically needy for any service offered, with the following exceptions: services furnished to

those under 18, pregnancy-related services, services to certain institutionalized individuals, emergency services, family planning services, and services to categorically needy HMO enrollees. No more than one type of charge may be imposed on any one service.

10. Medicaid, of course, covers both sick and healthy poor.

11. We do not discuss the seriousness of possible access problems for Medicaid beneficiaries caused by low provider payments, because visit rates among Medicaid beneficiaries do not appear to be affected by the present range of variation in physician reimbursement (Long, Settle, and Stuart 1986), although more of the care is delivered in emergency departments when payment is low.

12. Wagner and Bledsoe (1990) argue that outcomes most likely were similar at the HMO and in fee-for-service.

13. All these dimensions were rated less favorably by both HMO groups except access to specialists, which was rated less favorably only by the group randomly assigned to the HMO.

14. Additional reasons for the continuing low HMO share include partial or sometimes full subsidy of the premium difference between the HMO plan and other plans by the employer, as well as the tax treatment of employer-paid premiums.

15. These economists supported a mandatory rather than a voluntary program to prevent free riding. Others argued that subsidized care may offset the economic rent component of medical care prices (Crew 1969). Although there was and is little empirical evidence one way or the other on the magnitude of rents, an earlier study (Kessel 1958) suggested that physician supply had been restricted, with a corresponding monopoly rents to physicians. Because the number of physicians has increased in the past two decades, this argument has largely disappeared; however, there may well be rents for services whose price is heavily influenced by insurance company reimbursement policies. Rents would not by themselves justify free care, however, whereas externalities and consumer ignorance might.

16. In cases of very expensive services, such as kidney transplants, one also cannot presume overconsumption from the fact of insurance. In such cases the appropriate test is a consumer's willingness to pay the premium for an insurance policy; technically, income effects are important. We are, however, considering initial cost sharing versus free care, and income effects should not be important for most people.

17. As usually stated, however, it is a stronger argument than in the typical externalities argument in that it is independent of the initial income distribution. That is, the issue is not your willingness to pay for my medical care conditional on your income; rather, we are all entitled to efficacious medical services irrespective of the income distribution.

18. Correcting for our numerous comparisons would reduce the stated statistical significance of this result.

19. Given our sample size, it is unlikely that we would have been able to detect an effect of plan for a single uncommon condition, so this conclusion may have been inevitable. Physicians, however, may in fact be better at diagnosing a relatively common condition than a rare one.

20. One could (as the Experiment did) have frequency limits for refractions, new lenses, and frames (e.g., one per year) and dollar limits on these services (e.g., up to $70 for frames).

21. One might argue, as we do later for hypertension, that a specific benefit would not identify people with a vision problem, whereas a general benefit would. This argument, however, does not stand up well, for at least three reasons: (1) unlike hypertension, vision problems are reasonably self-evident; (2) there is substantial vision screening outside the medical care system, most notably for drivers' licenses; and (3) general physicians are more likely to screen for hypertension than for myopia.

22. See Chapter 3 for the estimated cost of dental services; we leave the cost of a vision benefit for future research, but rough estimates can be made from the data in Chapter 6.

23. Taxing Social Security benefits for upper-income groups is an example of a universal program with income-related benefits (through differential taxation).

24. See Stuart (1984); Ballard, Shoven, and Whalley (1985); Browning (1987); Fullerton (1991); and Ballard and Fullerton (1992) for estimates of the inefficiency. The amount of inefficiency depends critically on the degree to which the tax increase is on the last few dollars of income earned; the more that is the case, the greater the inefficiency.

25. Estimates by the Internal Revenue Service and others are that around 15 percent of individual income is not reported (Feinstein 1991). (The 15 percent figure is calculated from the values in Feinstein 1991 and uses individual income tax data from *Economic Report of the President* 1991, table B–77.)

26. Suppose a husband and wife each earns $20,000 and there is a limit on total expenditure of 5 percent of income, or $2,000 for the family of two. If each person is a "family unit," the limit is $1,000 per person. If one of the two has no expenses and the other has $2,000 of expenses, they are better off as separate family units.

27. We say "may" because the patient may simply file the bills in case the deductible is subsequently exceeded. Alternatively, the patient may follow a rule of sending all bills in to the insurer. The provider may also need additional transactions with collection agencies to recover the patient's payment.

28. There is also a potential issue of supplemental insurance to cover cost sharing, as is now the case with Medigap. If the cost sharing were only for

initial dollars (unlike Medicare, which leaves a beneficiary with unlimited liability), such insurance would have high administrative cost and thus might not attract many customers. (The high cost would reflect both marketing costs and the costs of processing small claims.) In any event, there will be no market for supplementary insurance if the main insurance policy insures only unreimbursed expenses, as is now the case for the medical expense deduction on the individual income tax. We comment further on this issue later in the text.

29. Although free medical care economizes on administrative costs in claims processing, it may impose another kind of administrative cost. Free care imposes a need to raise more money through taxes or premiums. These additional taxes may not only induce inefficiency but also themselves generate additional administrative cost—for example, more individuals may use tax preparers and more lobbyists may seek favorable tax treatment. Any such costs, of course, could offset the additional administrative cost of cost sharing.

30. Guaranteed renewability in a life insurance policy is somewhat analogous. One pays a higher premium initially to ensure that future premiums will be unaffected by changes in health status.

31. Brook (1991) argues that if guidelines could be developed to specify necessary care, such care should be provided without cost sharing.

32. See Baumgardner (1991) for an argument that managed care becomes more attractive than cost sharing as medical capabilities expand because it is better able to ration expensive but little-valued care.

33. We do not treat a deductible separately, because it is a special case of a coinsurance rate and MDE, namely 100 percent coinsurance up to an MDE (deductible).

34. This characterization abstracts from the uncertainty about what price one will face at the end of the year (i.e., which of the two "plans" one will be on), a topic discussed at length in Chapter 4. Chapter 4 also shows that if there had been no MDE, demand on the 95 percent coinsurance plan would have been a little over half as large as on the free care plan.

35. The average coinsurance rate is the aggregate amount paid out-of-pocket divided by the aggregate total expenditure.

36. As discussed in Chapter 4, there can be initial deductibles followed by positive coinsurance rates up to a limit (e.g., a $200 deductible followed by a 20 percent coinsurance rate with a $2,000 stop-loss feature or MDE). The same tradeoff will apply; the higher the initial cost sharing, whether deductible or coinsurance, the more people will exceed a given MDE.

37. One might also study the question of whether a higher deductible than that on the Individual Deductible plan would be even better. This is partly a question of how the poor would fare with a higher individual deductible.

38. There is also the variation from the $150 per person limit in the Individual Deductible plan as compared with the other plans, but this is confounded with the effect of varying the coinsurance rates between inpatient and outpatient care.

39. Exactly how late 1970s dollars should be inflated to the present is not clear, but the change in the all-items CPI from 1978 to 1991, a little more than a factor of two, would be a conservative figure. The $1,000 per family can be translated to an equivalent figure per individual of $500–600 (see Figure 4.6 and the discussion that follows here).

40. The loading fee is the percentage markup over payout by the insurer. Additional analysis based on the hypothetical supplementation questions shows that a coinsurance rate around 50 percent with no stop-loss provision was preferred (Manning and Marquis 1989). The analysts, however, are not confident about this inference, because their data are not well suited to estimating the necessary parameters.

41. M. S. Marquis (1992) finds that the sustainability of a supplementary insurance market depends upon the degree to which the premium is community rated. With modest adjustments to account for individual characteristics, the market does appear sustainable, but not with full community rating.

42. Although, as in the case of the Individual Deductible plan, there might also be some family limit to protect against many family members' incurring the full deductible.

43. Relative expenditure across plans was unaffected by this increase.

44. A deductible of some size would adversely affect those who need expensive maintenance drugs for a chronic disease year after year, although they would obviously be better off than if drugs were excluded altogether. To protect such individuals there may need to be a "circuit-breaker" provision—i.e., the deductible, if satisfied for a certain number of years in a row, would be waived. Provisions should be in place to prevent stocking up on quantities in the postdeductible or sale period. Alternatively, the cost sharing for certain chronic conditions whose treatment requires expensive continuing medication might be made condition specific.

45. Two departures are worth noting: Latinos are only 0.6 percent of the Experiment's sample but were 6.5 percent of the U.S. population in 1980 (and over 8 percent by 1990). Latino health insurance and health care use differ from the national average; see Estrada, Trevino, and Ray (1990) and Trevino et al. (1991). Also the very largest metropolitan areas (New York, Los Angeles, Chicago) are not represented.

46. The chi-square statistic on this interaction is 9.49 with 8 degrees of freedom, $p > .30$.

47. An alternative explanation for the increase in the right tail might appear to be that the real value of the MDE fell over time, since it was kept fixed at a nom-

inal $1,000 for most of the sample. This explanation, however, would generate a plan by year interaction, because the increase in the right tail would not be observed in the free care plan. Contrary to this hypothesis, however, we did observe an increase in the right tail in the free care plan.

48. Taube (1990) estimates that in 1980 spending on mental illness accounted for 8.4 percent of personal health care spending (including the institutionalized population); on the basis of work by Rice and others we estimate that the figure was 11.4 percent in 1985 (Waldo, Levit, and Lazenby 1986; Rice et al. 1990; Taube 1990). These figures do not count spending on treatment for substance abuse, which was probably growing as well.

49. The argument is part of a lengthy theoretical controversy among economists about the existence and magnitude of so-called supplier-induced demand. For a review of the recent literature, see Feldman and Sloan (1988). McGuire and Pauly (1991) show that a small-scale change in fees may not call forth observable inducement, whereas a large-scale change might.

50. To the degree that utilization review by insurers accounts for this fall, one can infer that there are instruments to check any physician-induced demand for hospital services.

51. The argument that supplier-induced demand should not apply to hospital services has some irony, since the origins of the supplier-induced demand hypothesis were specifically for hospital services (Roemer and Shain 1959).

52. How 63 percent of the firms in 1984 could have a deductible for hospital charges and 42 percent could pay for all of the first day's stay is not clear, but both numbers suggest that around 30 percent of these firms (not weighted by number of employees) introduced some sort of initial cost sharing for hospital services during this period.

53. The 3 percent figure comes from 30 percent of the people having their demand reduced 10 percent.

54. It is not difficult to find explanations of why the decrease in demand was greater than 3 percent. (1) There were other increases in cost sharing (e.g., firms that already had deductibles for hospital services increased them; Table 11.1); this decrease in demand would not have been counted in the free-individual deductible plan comparison described in the text. (2) With the increase in ambulatory surgery, the number of inpatient surgical procedures declined 4 percent from 1979 to 1983, whereas the number of ambulatory surgical procedures increased 77 percent (Shannon 1985). Some of this decline, of course, may have been induced by the changes in cost sharing, but some may simply represent an exogenous change in technology. (3) The introduction of the Prospective Payment System in 1983 was associated with a decrease in admission rates among the over-65. Whether there is a causal relationship between the PPS and admission rates among the under-65—or for that matter between

the increased initial cost sharing among the under-65 and admission rates among the over-65—is unknown.

55. Fahs (1992), in a seeming counterexample, finds a decrease in use among a group of coal miners using a single group practice who faced increased cost sharing, but a concomitant increase in use among a group of steelworkers using the same medical group practice whose coverage did not change, thus suggesting induced demand among the steelworkers to offset the decreases among the miners. For several reasons these findings are not convincing. The increase in use among the steelworkers is predominantly for hospitalization, where the effect is huge; hospital days go up 34 percent, all from a $7.50 office visit copayment among the miners, but it is precisely in hospital behavior that the national data on time trends are most convincing that physicians cannot keep demand up. It is likely that Fahs's result is attributable to a small sample of hospitalizations. Additionally, Fahs analyzes changes over a three-year period (1976–1979), but her expenditure data are put in real terms by using a regional medical price index that may or may not represent behavior in the specific locality where the group practice was located. If this index understates modestly the inflation rate in the local area, the true finding for ambulatory spending would be no effect among the steelworkers and a decrease among the miners. The plausibility of such a bias is increased by the virtual constancy of the visit rate and services per visit among the steelworkers.

56. That a large-scale decrease is the important issue is consistent with the Experiment's finding that the difference in use between no cost sharing and some cost sharing was notably greater than differences *within* the cost-sharing plans.

Appendix B. Further Explanation of Design Decisions

1. Testing this hypothesis with experimental data requires the assumption of negligible cross-price elasticities between dental services and both medical services and mental health services, because the coverage rate for dental and mental health services moved together in the 25/50 plans. This assumption seems plausible.

2. We had something that approximated a fee-for-service control group because the sample was split between those participating for three years and those participating for five (this split is described in more detail later in the text). In all sites except those in South Carolina, the two groups were enrolled simultaneously. We collected limited utilization data on the three-year group after their exit from the Experiment; these data could in principle have been compared with use among the five-year group, but we did not have the resources to do so. In South Carolina the two groups were enrolled sequentially, and utilization data on the three-year group were collected during the first two years

of enrollment of the five-year group when they were not eligible for the experimental insurance. (During this period the three-year group constituted the
pre-enrollment group, or PEG.) Budget constraints prevented us from comparing their health care use with that of the five-year group during this period.

3. The limit was increased to $27,800 for families interviewed in 1975 (1974 income) and to $30,900 for families interviewed in 1976 (1975 income).

4. The results presented in Chapter 3 show that interactions of plan with income are of little quantitative importance. Even if very high-income individuals were to have no response to price differences, an absurd extreme, our esti-mates of the elasticity in the population would be only 3 percent too high.

5. Duncan and Hill (1985) have since shown that the reliability of earnings data extended back two years is exceedingly low, at least among employees of the firm whose earnings data they examined.

6. The cutoff points for families interviewed in 1975 (1974 incomes) were: 1 person, less than $3,800; 2 people, less than $5,000; 3 or 4 persons, less than $6,700; 5 or more people, less than $10,000. The cutoff points for families interviewed in 1976 (1975 income) were: 1 person, less than $4,200; 2 people, less than $5,600; 3 or 4 persons, less than $7,400; 5 or more people, less than $11,200.

7. Because of the quantitatively modest interactions of plan with income (see Chapter 3), the estimated effect of plan is little affected by this decision.

8. In order to ensure that families did not use their previous plan, we had the families assign the benefits of that plan to the Experiment. We then reclaimed against that plan. This had several advantages: (1) it ensured that the families would not use their old plan in addition to the Experimental plan, thereby defeating the purpose of the Experiment; (2) it offset some of the Experi-ment's costs to the government; and (3) it ensured that individuals would not become uninsurable by participating in the Experiment. In accordance with this last goal, we purchased an individual policy for individuals not covered by an insurance plan at the beginning of the Experiment (or who lost eligi-bility for coverage during the Experiment). The benefits of this policy were assigned to the Experiment; at the end of the Experiment (or earlier if the indi-vidual chose to leave the Experiment early) the individual had the option of keeping this policy in force at his or her expense.

9. These rare individuals were those with preexisting coverage for the few ser-vices the Experiment did not cover, such as orthodontia with fixed appliances. When such a situation arose, the Experiment simply passed through to the individual any benefits paid by his or her insurance plan.

10. At $1,600 an individual would be out of pocket $400 under both plans, and at $4,600 an individual would be out of pocket $1,000 under both plans.

11. Employer-paid premiums were ignored in these calculations.

12. We would also have had to consider building in an interest rate to cover the delay in payment. As it was, we ignored the possibility that out-of-pocket outlays might have occurred early in the accounting period.

13. The discount factors were: for the three-year groups in Dayton and Seattle, 25 percent; for the three-year groups in Massachusetts and South Carolina, 33 percent; for the five-year groups in Dayton and Seattle, 15 percent; for the five-year group in Massachusetts, 25 percent; and for the five-year group in South Carolina, 20 percent.

14. We thank Ronald Andersen for providing us with the raw data.

15. The square root of 450/50 is 3, and there were 3 MDE limits per coinsurance rate. In other words, if cost were ignored there would be 3 times as many enrollees on the free plan as on each coinsurance rate–MDE combination (except the Individual Deductible plan, which received a weight of 50 in Dayton).

16. On the assumption of no cost differences among plans, the optimal design for the health status analysis was to allocate 37 percent of families to the free-care plan and 21 percent to each of the three other groupings (25 percent coinsurance, Family Deductible, and Individual Deductible). The principal difference between the two was that optimal demand estimation implied only about a 28 percent allocation rather than a 37 percent allocation to the free-care plan.

17. When proportional deviations are compared by plan (e.g., the 25/10(50) plan versus the free plan), there is greater random variation in the plans with fewer total families.

18. In the case of Franklin County the index value was for a neighboring county, which at that time was considered a more likely choice.

19. Unlike those in the Experiment, however, those enrolled in the two systems under Model Cities had been able to choose their preferred system.

20. In certain families, some family members might be eligible and others not. In general such families were enrolled, provided there was at least one adult head of the family who was eligible. Any ineligible members of the family were enrolled as "persons of interest" but were not eligible for health insurance benefits. All families living at a given address (i.e., sharing a household) were contacted about enrollment.

References

Achenbach, T. M. 1978. "The Child Behavior Profile: I. Boys Aged 6–11." *Journal of Consulting and Clinical Psychology* 46:478–488.

———— 1979. "The Child Behavior Profile: II. Boys Aged 12–16 and Girls Aged 6–11 and 12–16." *Journal of Consulting and Clinical Psychology* 47:223–233.

American Hospital Association. 1984. *Hospital Statistics.* Chicago.

———— 1985. "1984 Hospital Cost and Utilization Trends." *Economic Trends* 1.

American Medical Association. 1973. *AMA Drug Evaluations.* 2d ed. Acton, Mass.: Publishing Sciences Group.

Andersen, Ronald, Joanna Kravits, and Odin Anderson. 1975. *Two Decades of Health Services: Social Survey Trends in Use and Expenditure.* Cambridge, Mass.: Ballinger.

Archibald, Rae W., and Joseph P. Newhouse. 1988. "Social Experimentation: Some Why's and How's." In *Handbook of Systems Analysis: Craft Issues and Procedural Choices,* ed. Hugh J. Miser and Edward J. Quade, pp. 173–214. New York: North Holland.

Arrow, Kenneth J. 1963. "Uncertainty and the Welfare Economics of Medical Care." *American Economic Review* 53:941–973.

———— 1968. "The Economics of Moral Hazard: Further Comment." *American Economic Review* 58:537–539.

———— 1973. *Optimal Insurance and Generalized Deductibles.* Santa Monica: RAND Corporation (Pub. no. R-1108-OEO).

———— 1975. *Two Notes on Inferring Long-Run Behavior from Social Experiments.* Santa Monica: RAND Corporation (Pub. no. P-5546).

———— 1976. "Welfare Analysis of Changes in Health Coinsurance Rates." In *The Role of Health Insurance in the Health Services Sector,* ed. Richard N. Rosett. New York: National Bureau of Economic Research.

Bailit, Howard L., et al. 1984. "The Effect of Cost Sharing on the Quality of Dental Care." *Journal of Dental Education* 48:597–604.

———— 1985. "Does More Generous Dental Insurance Coverage Improve Oral Health? A Study of Patient Cost-Sharing." *Journal of the American Dental Association* 110:701–707.

———— 1986. "Dental Insurance and the Oral Health of Preschool Children." *Journal of the American Dental Association* 113:773–776.

Ballard, Charles L., and Don Fullerton. 1992. "Distortionary Taxes and the Provision of Public Goods." *Journal of Economic Perspectives* 6(3):117–131.

Ballard, Charles L., John B. Shoven, and John Whalley. 1985. "General Equilibrium Computations of the Marginal Welfare Costs of Taxes in the United States." *American Economic Review* 75:128–138.

Barer, Morris, Robert Evans, and Greg Stoddart. 1979. *Direct Charges to Patients: Snare or Delusion?* Toronto: Ontario Economic Council.

Baumgardner, James R. 1991. "The Interaction between Forms of Insurance Contract and Types of Technical Change in Medical Care." *RAND Journal of Economics* 22:36–53.

Baumol, William J., and David F. Bradford. 1970. "Optimal Departures from Marginal Cost Pricing." *American Economic Review* 60:265–283.

Beck, A. T. 1967. *Depression—Causes and Treatment.* Philadelphia: University of Pennsylvania Press.

Beck, Sjoerd, et al. 1981a. *Conceptualization and Measurement of Physiologic Health for Adults: Hay Fever.* Santa Monica: RAND Corporation (Pub. no. R-2262/13-HHS).

———— 1981b. *Conceptualization and Measurement of Physiologic Health for Adults: Hearing Loss.* Santa Monica: RAND Corporation (Pub. no. R-2262/14-HHS).

———— 1983. *Conceptualization and Measurement of Physiologic Health for Children: Allergic Conditions.* Santa Monica: RAND Corporation (Pub. no. R-2898/1-HHS).

Berkanovic, Emil. 1974. "An Appraisal of Medicaid Records as a Data Source." *Medical Care* 12:590–595.

Berki, Sylvester E., and Marie L. F. Ashcraft. 1980. "HMO Enrollment. Who Joins What and Why: A Review of the Literature." *Milbank Memorial Fund Quarterly* 58:588–632.

Berman, Daniel M., et al. 1981. *Conceptualization and Measurement of Physiologic Health for Adults: Angina Pectoris.* Santa Monica: RAND Corporation (Pub. no. R-2262/4-HHS).

Besley, Timothy J. 1988. "Optimal Reimbursement Health Insurance and the Theory of Ramsey Taxation." *Journal of Health Economics* 7:321–336.

Blumenthal, David, et al. 1986. "The Future of Medicare." *New England Journal of Medicine* 314:722–728.

Boruch, Robert F., and Henry W. Riecken, eds. 1975. *Experimental Testing of Public Policy: The Proceedings of the 1974 Social Science Research Council Conference on Social Experiments.* Boulder: Westview Press.

Brennan, Troyen A., et al. 1991. "Incidence of Adverse Events and Negligence in Hospitalized Patients: Findings from the Harvard Medical Practice Study I." *New England Journal of Medicine* 324:370–376.

Broder, I., et al. 1974. "Epidemiology of Asthma and Allergic Rhinitis in a Total Community, Tecumseh, Michigan, III. Second Survey of the Community." *Journal of Allergy and Clinical Immunology* 53:127–138.

Brook, Robert H. 1991. "Health, Health Insurance, and the Uninsured." *Journal of the American Medical Association* 265:2998–3002.

Brook, Robert H., Kathleen N. Lohr, and George A. Goldberg. 1982. *Conceptualization and Measurement of Physiologic Health for Adults: Thyroid Disease.* Santa Monica: RAND Corporation (Pub. no. R-2262/9-HHS).

Brook, Robert H., et al. 1979. *The Effect of Coinsurance on the Conceptualization and Measurement of Health for Adults in the Health Insurance Study: Overview.* Santa Monica: RAND Corporation (Pub. no. R-1987/8-HEW). Also published as "Overview of Adult Health Status Measures Fielded in RAND's Health Insurance Study," *Medical Care* 17 (suppl.).

—— 1980a. *Conceptualization and Measurement of Physiologic Health for Adults: Acne.* Santa Monica: RAND Corporation (Pub. no. R-2262/2-1-HHS).

—— 1980b. *Conceptualization and Measurement of Physiologic Health for Adults: Hypertension.* Santa Monica: RAND Corporation (Pub. no. R-2262/3-HHS).

—— 1981a. *Conceptualization and Measurement of Physiologic Health for Adults: Diabetes Mellitus.* Santa Monica: RAND Corporation (Pub. no. R-2262/7-HHS).

—— 1981b. *Conceptualization and Measurement of Physiologic Health for Adults: Hypercholesterolemia.* Santa Monica: RAND Corporation (Pub. no. R-2262/11-HHS).

—— 1984. *The Effect of Coinsurance on the Health of Adults: Results from the RAND Health Insurance Experiment.* Santa Monica: RAND Corporation (Pub. no. R-3055-HHS). An abridged version was published as "Does Free Care Improve Adults' Health? Results from a Randomized Controlled Trial," *New England Journal of Medicine* 309(1983):1426–34.

—— 1990. "Quality of Ambulatory Care: Epidemiology and Comparison by Insurance Status and Income." *Medical Care* 28: 392–433.

Brown, Marie E. 1984. *Lessons Learned from the Administration of the Rand Health Insurance Experiment.* Santa Monica: RAND Corporation (Pub. no. R-3095-HHS).

Browning, Edgar. 1987. "On the Marginal Welfare Cost of Taxation." *American Economic Review* 77:11–23.

California Medical Association, Committee on Relative Value Studies. 1975. *1974 Revision of the 1969 California Relative Value Studies.* San Francisco: Sutter Publications.

Chassin, Mark, et al. 1987. "Does Inappropriate Use Explain Geographic Variations in the Use of Health Care Services? A Study of Three Procedures." *Journal of the American Medical Association* 258:2533–37.

Chen, Martin. 1976. Letter to the editor. *Medical Care* 14:958.

Cherkin, Daniel C., Louis Grothaus, and Edward H. Wagner. 1989. "The Effect of Office Visit Copayments on Utilization in a Health Maintenance Organization." *Medical Care* 27:1036–45.

Clasquin, Lorraine A., and Marie E. Brown. 1977. *Rules of Operation for the RAND Health Insurance Study.* Santa Monica: RAND Corporation (Pub. no. R-1602-HEW).

Commission on Professional and Hospital Activities. 1973. *Hospital Adaptation of the ICDA (International Classification of Diseases Adapted for Use in the United States)*. 2d ed. Ann Arbor, Mich.

Comrey, A. L. 1970. *Comrey Personality Scales*. San Diego: Educational and Industrial Testing Services.

Conlisk, John, and Harold Watts. 1969. "A Model for Optimizing Experimental Designs for Estimating Response Surfaces." *Proceedings of the American Statistical Association, Social Statistics Section*, pp.150–155.

Costello, C. G., and A. L. Comrey. 1967. "Scales for Measuring Depression and Anxiety." *Journal of Psychology* 66:303–313.

Council on Dental Care Programs. 1972. "Code on Dental Procedures and Nomenclature." *Journal of the American Dental Association* 85:789–792.

Crew, Michael. 1969. "Coinsurance and the Welfare Economics of Medical Care." *American Economic Review* 89:906–908.

Cromwell, Jerry, and Janet B. Mitchell. 1986. "Physician-Induced Demand for Surgery." *Journal of Health Economics* 5:293–313.

Cronbach, L. J. 1951. "Coefficient Alpha and the Internal Structure of Tests." *Psychometrika* 16:297–334.

Culyer, Anthony J. 1971. "Medical Care and the Economics of Giving." *Economica* 151:295–303.

Dagenais, M. G. 1971. "Further Suggestions concerning the Utilization of Incomplete Observations in Regression Analysis." *Journal of the American Statistical Association* 66:93–98.

Davies, Allyson R., and John E. Ware, Jr. 1981. *Measuring Health Perceptions in the Health Insurance Experiment*. Santa Monica: RAND Corporation (Pub. no. R-2711-HHS).

——— 1988. "Involving Consumers in Quality of Care Assessments." *Health Affairs* 7(1):33–48.

Davies, Allyson R., et al. 1981. *Scoring Manual: Adult Health Status and Patient Satisfaction Measures Used in RAND's Health Insurance Experiment*. Santa Monica: RAND Corporation (Pub. no. N-2190-HHS).

——— 1986. "Consumer Acceptance of Prepaid and Fee-for-Service Medical Care: Results from a Controlled Trial." *Health Services Research* 21:429–452.

——— 1988. *Scoring Manual: Adult Health Status and Patient Satisfaction Measures Used in RAND's Health Insurance Experiment*. Santa Monica: RAND Corporation (Pub. no. N-2190-HHS).

Davis, Karen, and Cathy Schoen. 1978. *Health and the War on Poverty: A Ten-Year Appraisal*. Washington, D.C.: Brookings Institution.

De Meza, David. 1983. "Health Insurance and the Demand for Medical Care." *Journal of Health Economics* 2:47–54.

Dionne, Georges, Alain Langlois, and Nicole Lemire. 1987. "More on the Geographical Distribution of Physicians." *Journal of Health Economics* 6:365–374.

Dohrenwend, B. P., P. E. Shrout, G. Egri, and F. S. Mendelsohn. 1980. "Nonspecific Psychological Distress and Other Dimensions of Psychopathology." *Archives of General Psychiatry* 37:1229–36.

Dohrenwend, B. S., B. P. Dohrenwend, and D. Cook. 1973. "Ability and Disability in Role Functioning in Psychiatric Patient and Non-Patient Groups." In *Roots of Evaluation,* ed. J. D. Wing and H. Hafner. London: Oxford University Press.

Donald, Cathy A., and John E. Ware, Jr. 1982. *The Quantification of Social Contacts and Resources.* Santa Monica: RAND Corporation (Pub. no. R-2937-HHS).

—— 1984. "The Measurement of Social Support." In *Research in Community and Mental Health,* ed. J. F. Greenley. Greenwich, Conn.: JAI Press.

Donald, Cathy A., et al. 1978. *Conceptualization and Measurement of Health for Adults in the Health Insurance Study: Social Health.* Santa Monica: RAND Corporation (Pub. no. R-1987/4-HEW).

Duan, Naihua. 1982. "Models for Human Exposure to Air Pollution." Santa Monica: RAND Corporation (Pub. no. N-1884-HHS).

—— 1983. "Smearing Estimate: A Nonparametric Retransformation Method." *Journal of the American Statistical Association* 78:605–610.

Duan, Naihua, et al. 1982. *A Comparison of Alternative Models of the Demand for Medical Care.* Santa Monica: RAND Corporation (Pub. no. R-2754-HHS). Abridged version published in *Journal of Business and Economic Statistics* 1(1983):115–126.

—— 1984. "Choosing between the Sample-Selection Model and the Multi-Part Model." *Journal of Business and Economic Statistics* 2:283–289.

Duncan, Greg J., and Daniel H. Hill. 1985. "An Investigation of the Extent and Consequences of Measurement Error in Labor Economic Survey Data." *Journal of Labor Economics* 3:508–532.

Economic Report of the President. 1991. Washington, D.C.: U.S. Government Printing Office.

Eisen, Marvin B., et al. 1980. *Conceptualization and Measurement of Health for Children in the Health Insurance Study.* Santa Monica: RAND Corporation (Pub. no. R-2313-HEW).

Ellis, Randall P. 1986. "Rational Behavior in the Presence of Coverage Ceilings and Deductibles." *RAND Journal of Economics* 17:158–175.

Ellis, Randall P., and Thomas G. McGuire. 1984. "Cost Sharing and the Demand for Ambulatory Mental Health Services." *American Psychologist* 39:1195–99.

Enterline, Phillip, et al. 1973. "The Distribution of Medical Services before and after 'Free' Medical Care—The Quebec Experience." *New England Journal of Medicine* 289:1174–78.

Estrada, Antonio L., Fernando M. Trevino, and Laura A. Ray. 1990. "Health Care Utilization Barriers among Mexican Americans: Evidence from the HHANES 1982–84." *American Journal of Public Health* 80 (suppl.):27–31.

Evans, Robert G. 1984. *Strained Mercy: The Economics of Canadian Health Care.* Toronto: Butterworths.

Fahs, Marianne C. 1992. "Physician Response to the United Mine Workers' Cost Sharing Program: The Other Side of the Coin." *Health Services Research* 27:25–45.

Federspiel, C. F., Wayne A. Ray, and W. Schaffner. 1976. "Medicaid Records as a Valid Data Source: The Tennessee Experience." *Medical Care* 14:166–172.

Fein, Rashi. 1971. Testimony in Health Care Crisis in America, Hearings before the Subcommittee on Health of the Committee on Labor and Public Welfare, U.S. Senate, 22 and 23 February 1971, p. 146.

Feinstein, Jonathan S. 1991. "An Econometric Analysis of Income Tax Evasion and Its Detection." *RAND Journal of Economics* 22:14–35.

Feldman, Roger, and Frank Sloan. 1988. "Competition among Physicians, Revisited." *Journal of Health Politics, Policy, and Law* 13:239–261.

Feldstein, Martin S. 1971. "A New Approach to National Health Insurance." *Public Interest* 23:93–105.

———— 1973. "The Welfare Loss of Excess Health Insurance." *Journal of Political Economy* 81:251–280.

———— 1977. "The High Cost of Hospitals—and What to Do about It." *Public Interest* 48:40–54.

Ferreira, Joseph. 1974. "The Long-Term Effects of Merit Rating Plans on Individual Motorists." *Operations Research* 22:954–978.

Fishman, George S. 1973. *Concepts and Methods in Discrete Event Digital Simulation*. New York: John Wiley & Sons.

———— 1978. *Principles of Discrete Event Simulation*. New York: John Wiley & Sons.

Follette, W., and N. A. Cummings. 1967. "Psychiatric Services and Medical Utilization in a Prepaid Health Plan Setting." *Medical Care* 5:26–35.

———— 1968. "Psychiatric Services and Medical Utilization in a Prepaid Health Plan Setting, Part 2." *Medical Care* 6:31–41.

Foxman, Betsy K., Kathleen N. Lohr, and Robert H. Brook. 1983. *Measurement of Physiologic Health for Children: Anemia*. Santa Monica: RAND Corporation (Pub. no. R-2898/5-HHS).

Foxman, Betsy K., et al. 1982. *Conceptualization and Measurement of Physiologic Health for Adults: Chronic Obstructive Airway Disease*. Santa Monica: RAND Corporation (Pub. no. R-2262/8-1-HHS).

———— 1986. *Measurement of Physiologic Health of Children: Urinary Tract Infection*. Santa Monica: RAND Corporation (Pub. no. R-2898/6-HHS).

———— 1987. "The Effect of Free Care on the Use of Antibiotics: Results from a Population-Based Randomized Controlled Trial." *Journal of Chronic Diseases* 40:429–437.

Friedman, Bernard, and Mark Pauly. 1981. "Cost Functions for a Service Firm with Variable Quality and Stochastic Demand." *Review of Economics and Statistics* 63:610–624.

———— 1983. "A New Approach to Hospital Cost Functions and Some Issues in Revenue Regulation." *Health Care Financing Review* 4(3):105–114.

Fuchs, Victor R. 1978. "The Supply of Surgeons and the Demand for Operations." *Journal of Human Resources* 13 (suppl.):35–56.

Fullerton, Don. 1991. "Reconciling Recent Estimates of the Marginal Welfare Cost of Taxation." *American Economic Review* 81:302–308.

Gertman, Paul M., and Joseph D. Restuccia. 1981. "The Appropriateness Evaluation Protocol: A Technique for Assessing Unnecessary Days of Hospital Care." *Medical Care* 19:855–870.

Gibson, Robert M. 1979. "National Health Expenditures, 1978." *Health Care Financing Review* 1(1):1–36.

Gibson, Robert M., and Daniel R. Waldo. 1981. "National Health Expenditures, 1980." *Health Care Financing Review* 3(1):1–54.

Goddeeris, John H. 1984a. "Insurance and Incentives for Innovation in Medical Care." *Southern Economic Journal* 51:530–549.

——— 1984b. "Medical Insurance, Technological Change, and Welfare." *Economic Inquiry* 22:56–67.

Goldberg, George A. 1983. *The Health Insurance Experiment's Guidelines for Abstracting Health Services Rendered by Group Health Cooperative of Puget Sound*. Santa Monica: RAND Corporation (Pub. no. N-1948-HHS).

Goldberg, I. D., Daryl A. Regier, and Barbara J. Burns, eds. 1980. *Use of Health and Mental Health Outpatient Services in Four Organized Care Settings*. Washington, D.C.: U.S. Government Printing Office (Pub. no. ADM 380–859).

Goldsmith, Jeff. 1984. "Death of a Paradigm: The Challenge of Competition." *Health Affairs* 3(3):12.

Greenberg, David H., and Philip K. Robins. 1986. "The Changing Role of Social Experiments in Policy Analysis." *Journal of Policy Analysis and Management* 5:340–362.

Greenwood, M., and G. U. Yule. 1920. "An Enquiry into the Nature of Frequency Distributions Representative of Multiple Happenings, with Special Reference to Multiple Attacks of Disease or Repeated Accidents." *Journal of the Royal Statistical Society* 83:255–279.

Hausman, Jerry A., Bronwyn Hall, and Zvi Griliches. 1984. "Econometric Models for Count Data with an Application to the Patents–R & D Relationship." *Econometrica* 52:909–938.

Health Insurance Association of America. 1980 and 1986. *A Profile of Group Major Medical Expense Insurance in the United States*. Washington, D.C.

Helms, L. Jay, Joseph P. Newhouse, and Charles E. Phelps. 1978. "Copayments and Demand for Medical Care: The California Medicaid Experience." *Bell Journal of Economics* 9:192–208.

Hester, James, and Irving Leveson. 1974. "The Health Insurance Study: A Critical Appraisal." *Inquiry* 11:53–60.

Hill, Daniel B., and James E. Veney. 1970. "Kansas Blue Cross/Blue Shield Outpatient Benefits Experiment." *Medical Care* 8:143–158.

Hornbrook, Mark C., Arnold V. Hurtado, and Richard E. Johnson. 1985. "Health Care Episodes: Definition, Measurement, and Use." *Medical Care Review* 42:163–218.

Huber, Peter J. 1967. "The Behavior of Maximum Likelihood Estimates under Nonstandard Conditions." In *Fifth Berkeley Symposium on Mathematical Statistics and Probability*, pp. 221–233. Berkeley: University of California Press.

Hulka, Barbara S., and Jane C. Cassel. 1973. "The AAFP-UNC Study of the Organization, Utilization, and Assessment of Primary Medical Care." *American Journal of Public Health* 63:494–501.

Johnson, N. J., and S. Kotz. 1969. *Discrete Distributions.* Boston: Houghton Mifflin.

Kamberg, Caren J., et al. 1983. *Measurement of Physiologic Health for Children: Seizure Disorders.* Santa Monica: RAND Corporation (Pub. no. R-2898/3-HHS).

Keeler, Emmett B., Joseph P. Newhouse, and Charles E. Phelps. 1977. "Deductibles and Demand: A Theory of the Consumer Facing a Variable Price Schedule under Uncertainty." *Econometrica* 45:641–655.

Keeler, Emmett B., Daniel A. Relles, and John E. Rolph. 1977a. "An Empirical Study of the Differences between Family and Individual Deductibles in Health Insurance." *Inquiry* 14:269–277.

―――― 1977b. "The Choice between Family and Individual Deductibles in Health Insurance Policies." *Journal of Economic Theory* 16:220–227.

Keeler, Emmett B., and John E. Rolph. 1988. "The Demand for Episodes of Treatment in the Health Insurance Experiment." *Journal of Health Economics* 7:337–367.

Keeler, Emmett B., Kenneth B. Wells, and Willard G. Manning. 1986. *The Demand for Episodes of Mental Health Services.* Santa Monica: RAND Corporation (Pub. no. R-3432-NIMH).

Keeler, Emmett B., et al. 1982. *The Demand for Episodes of Medical Treatment: Interim Results from the Health Insurance Experiment.* Santa Monica: RAND Corporation (Pub. no. R-2829-HHS).

―――― 1985. *How Free Care Reduced Hypertension in the Health Insurance Experiment.* Santa Monica: RAND Corporation (Pub. no. R-3326-HHS). Abridged version published as "How Free Care Reduced Hypertension in the Health Insurance Experiment." *Journal of the American Medical Association* 254:1926–31.

―――― 1987. "Effects of Cost Sharing on Physiological Health, Health Practices, and Worry." *Health Services Research* 22:279–306.

―――― 1988. *The Demand for Episodes of Medical Treatment in the Health Insurance Experiment.* Santa Monica: RAND Corporation (Pub. no. R-3454-HHS).

Keesey, Joan, Emmett B. Keeler, and William Fowler. 1985. *The Episodes-of-Illness Processing System.* Santa Monica: RAND Corporation (Pub. no. N-1745-1-HHS).

Kendall, M. G., and Alan Stuart. 1963. *The Advanced Theory of Statistics.* Vol. 1: *Distribution Theory.* 2d ed. New York: Hafner Publishing.

Kessel, Reuben. 1958. "Price Discrimination in Medicine." *Journal of Law and Economics* 1:20–53.

Kilpatrick, S. J., Jr. 1977. "An Empirical Study of the Distribution of Episodes of Illness Recorded in the 1970–71 National Morbidity Survey." *Applied Statistics* 26:26–33.

Kolm, S. 1979. "A Simple Sequentially Rejective Multiple Test Procedure." *Scandinavian Journal of Statistics: Theory and Applications* 6:63.

Leibowitz, Arleen. 1989. "Substitution between Prescribed and Over-the-Counter Medications." *Medical Care* 27:85–94.

Leibowitz, Arleen, Willard G. Manning, and Joseph P. Newhouse. 1985. "The Demand for Prescription Drugs as a Function of Cost Sharing." *Social Science and Medicine* 21:1063–70.

Levit, Katherine R., et al. 1985. "National Health Expenditures: 1984." *Health Care Financing Review* 7(1):1–35.

———— 1991. "National Health Expenditures, 1990." *Health Care Financing Review* 13(1):9–54.

Lewis, Charles E., and Harold W. Keairnes. 1970. "Controlling Costs of Medical Care by Expanding Insurance Coverage." *New England Journal of Medicine* 282:1405–12.

Lillard, Lee A., et al. 1986. *Preventive Medical Care: Standards, Usage, and Efficacy.* Santa Monica: RAND Corporation (Pub. no. R-3266-HCFA).

Lindsey, Cotton M. 1969. "Medical Care and the Economics of Sharing." *Economica* 144:351–362.

Liptzin, B., Daryl Regier, and J. D. Goldberg. 1980. "Utilization of Health and Mental Health Services in a Large Insured Population." *American Journal of Psychiatry* 137:553–558.

Lohr, Kathleen N., et al. 1983. *Measurement of Physiologic Health for Children: Middle Ear Disease and Hearing Impairment.* Santa Monica: RAND Corporation (Pub. no. R-2898/2-HHS).

———— 1986a. *Conceptualization and Measurement of Physiologic Health for Adults: Overview of Chronic Disease in a General Adult Population.* Santa Monica: RAND Corporation (Pub. no. R-2262/1-HHS).

———— 1986b. "Use of Medical Care in the Rand Health Insurance Experiment: Diagnosis- and Service-Specific Analyses in a Randomized Controlled Trial." *Medical Care* 24 (suppl.):S1–87.

Long, Stephen H., Russell F. Settle, and Bruce C. Stuart. 1986. "Reimbursement and Access to Physicians' Services under Medicaid." *Journal of Health Economics* 5:235–251.

Luft, Harold S. 1978. "How Do Health Maintenance Organizations Achieve Their 'Savings'? Rhetoric and Evidence." *New England Journal of Medicine* 298:1336–53.

———— 1981. *Health Maintenance Organizations: Dimensions of Performance.* New York: John Wiley & Sons.

———— 1982. "Health Maintenance Organizations and the Rationing of Medical Care." *Health and Society* 60:268–306.

Luft, Harold S., and Ellen Morrison. 1991. "Alternative Delivery Systems." in *Health Services Research,* ed. Eli Ginzberg. Cambridge, Mass.: Harvard University Press.

Lurie, Nicole, et al. 1984. "Termination from Medi-Cal: Does It Affect Health?" *New England Journal of Medicine* 311:480–484.

———— 1986. "Termination of Medi-Cal Benefits—A Followup Study One Year Later." *New England Journal of Medicine* 314:1266–68.

———— 1987. "Preventive Care: Do We Practice What We Preach?" *American Journal of Public Health* 77:801–804.

———— 1989. "How Free Care Improved Vision in the Health Insurance Experiment." *American Journal of Public Health* 79:640–642.

Maddala, G. S. 1983. *Limited-Dependent and Qualitative Variables in Econometrics.* New York: Cambridge University Press.

Manning, Willard G. 1988. *Estimating Health Demand Functions with Health Insurance Data.* Santa Monica: RAND Corporation (Pub. no. N-2729-HHS).

Manning, Willard G., Naihua Duan, and Emmett B. Keeler. 1988. "Attrition Bias in a Randomized Trial of Health Insurance." Mimeo.

Manning, Willard G., Naihua Duan, and William H. Rogers. 1987. "Monte Carlo Evidence on the Choice between Sample Selection and Two-Part Models." *Journal of Econometrics* 35:59–82.

Manning, Willard G., and M. Susan Marquis. 1989. *Health Insurance: The Trade-off between Risk Pooling and Moral Hazard.* Santa Monica: RAND Corporation (Pub. no. R-3729-NCHSR).

Manning, Willard G., Jr., Joseph P. Newhouse, and John E. Ware, Jr. 1982. "The Status of Health in Demand Estimation: Beyond Excellent, Good, Fair, and Poor." In *Economic Aspects of Health,* ed. Victor R. Fuchs, pp. 143–184. Chicago: University of Chicago Press.

Manning, Willard G., Kenneth B. Wells, and Bernadette Benjamin. 1986. *Use of Outpatient Mental Health Care: Trial of a Prepaid Group Practice versus Fee-for-Service.* Santa Monica: RAND Corporation (Pub. no. R-3277-NIMH).

Manning, Willard G., et al. 1984. "Cost Sharing and the Use of Ambulatory Mental Health Services." *American Psychologist* 39:1077–89.

———— 1985. "A Controlled Trial of the Effect of a Prepaid Group Practice on the Utilization of Medical Services." Santa Monica: RAND Corporation (Pub. no. R-3029-HHS). Abridged version published in *New England Journal of Medicine* 310:1505–10.

———— 1986a. *The Demand for Dental Care—Evidence from a Randomized Trial in Health Insurance.* Santa Monica: RAND Corporation (Pub. no. R-3225-HHS). Abridged version published in *Journal of the American Dental Association* 110 (1985):895–902.

———— 1986b. "How Cost Sharing Affects the Use of Ambulatory Mental Health Services." *Journal of the American Medical Association* 256:1930–34.

———— 1987. "Health Insurance and the Demand for Medical Care: Evidence from a Randomized Experiment." *American Economic Review* 77:251–277.

———— 1988. *Health Insurance and the Demand for Medical Care: Results from a Randomized Experiment.* Santa Monica: RAND Corporation (Pub. no. R-3476-HHS).

———— 1989. *Effects of Mental Health Insurance: Evidence from the Health*

Insurance Experiment. Santa Monica: RAND Corporation (Pub. no. R-3815-NIMH/HCFA).

Marquis, Kent H. 1977. *The Methodology Used to Measure Health Care Consumption during the First Year of the Health Insurance Experiment.* Santa Monica: RAND Corporation (Pub. no. R-2126-HEW).

Marquis, M. Susan. 1981. *Consumers' Knowledge about their Health Insurance Coverage.* Santa Monica: RAND Corporation (Pub. no. R-2753-HHS).

——— 1983. "Consumers' Knowledge about Their Health Insurance Coverage." *Health Care Financing Review* 5(1):65–80.

——— 1985. "Cost-Sharing and Provider Choice." *Journal of Health Economics* 4:137–157.

——— 1992. "Adverse Selection with a Multiple Choice among Insurance Plans: A Simulation Analysis." *Journal of Health Economics* 11:129–151.

Marquis, M. Susan, Allyson R. Davies, and John E. Ware, Jr. 1983. "Patient Satisfaction and Change in Medical Care Provider: A Longitudinal Study." *Medical Care* 21:821–829.

Marquis, M. Susan, and Charles E. Phelps. 1985. *Demand for Supplementary Health Insurance.* Santa Monica: RAND Corporation (Pub. no. R-3285-HHS).

Mathematica Policy Research. 1976. "Report on the Physician Capacity Utilization Telephone Surveys." Vol. 1. Princeton.

McCarthy, Thomas R. 1985. "The Competitive Nature of the Primary Care Physician Services Market." *Journal of Health Economics* 4:93–117.

McCombs, Jeffrey S. 1984. "Physician Treatment Decisions in a Multiple Treatment Model: The Effects of Physician Supply." *Journal of Health Economics* 3:155–171.

McGee, D., and T. Gordon. 1976. "Section 31. The Results of the Framingham Study Applied to Four Other U.S.-Based Epidemiologic Studies of Cardiovascular Disease." In *The Framingham Study: An Investigation of Cardiovascular Disease,* ed. W. B. Kannel and T. Gordon. Bethesda: National Heart and Lung Institute, National Institutes of Health (DHEW Pub. no. NIH 76-1083).

McGuire, Thomas G., and Mark V. Pauly. 1991. " Physician Response to Fee Changes with Multiple Payers." *Journal of Health Economics* 10:385–410.

Mehran, F. 1973. "Variance of the MVUE for the Lognormal Mean." *Journal of the American Statistical Association* 68:726–727.

Metcalf, Charles E. 1973. "Making Inferences from Controlled Income Maintenance Experiments." *American Economic Review* 63:478–483.

Morris, Carl N. 1979. "A Finite Selection Model for Experimental Design of the Health Insurance Study." *Journal of Econometrics* 11:43–61.

——— 1980. *Nonresponse Issues in Public Policy Experiments, with Emphasis on the Health Insurance Study.* Santa Monica: RAND Corporation (Pub. no. N-1346). Also published in Committee on National Statistics, National Research Council, *Symposium on Incomplete Data: Preliminary Proceedings, Panel on Incomplete Data,* Washington, D.C.: National Research

Council, 1979; and in *Incomplete Data in Sample Surveys,* vol. 3, chap. 15, 313–325, New York: Academic Press, 1983.

—— 1985. *Sample Selection in the Health Insurance Experiment: Comparing the Enrolled and Nonenrolled Populations.* Santa Monica: RAND Corporation (Pub. no. N-2354-HHS).

Morris, Carl N., Joseph P. Newhouse, and Rae W. Archibald. 1979. "On the Theory and Practice of Obtaining Unbiased and Efficient Samples in Social Surveys and Experiments." In *Experimental Economics,* vol. 1, ed. Vernon Smith. Westport, Conn.: JAI Press. Reprinted in *Evaluation Studies Review Annual,* vol. 5, ed. Ernst Stromsdorfer and George Farkar, Beverly Hills: Sage, 1980.

Myers, Jerome K., et al. 1972. "Life Events and Mental Status: A Longitudinal Study." *Journal of Health and Social Behavior* 13:398–406.

National Center for Health Statistics. 1974. *Limitations of Activity and Mobility Due to Chronic Conditions: United States, 1972.* Rockville, Md.: National Center for Health Statistics (DHEW Pub. no. HRA 75-1523).

—— 1978. *Current Estimates from the Health Interview Survey, 1977.* Washington, D.C.: Government Printing Office (DHEW Pub. No. PHS-78-1554).

—— 1982. *Utilization of Short-Stay Hospitals: Annual Summary for the United States, 1980.* Washington, D.C.: Government Printing Office (DHHS Pub. no. PHS 82-1725).

—— 1988. *Current Estimates from the National Health Interview Survey, 1987.* Washington, D.C.: Government Printing Office (DHHS Pub. no. PHS 88-1594).

—— 1990. *Health, United States, 1989.* Washington, D.C.: Government Printing Office (Pub. no. 90-1232).

Nelsen, Mark, and Carol A. Edwards. 1986. *HIE References.* Vol. 1: *Codes Used in HIE Claims—Diagnoses, Symptoms, Procedures, Drugs, and Supplies.* Santa Monica: RAND Corporation (Pub. no. N-2349/1-HHS).

Newhouse, Joseph P. 1974. "A Design for a Health Insurance Experiment." *Inquiry* 11:5–27.

—— 1981. "The Erosion of the Medical Marketplace." In *Advances in Health Economics and Health Services Research,* vol. 2, ed. Richard Scheffler. Westport, Conn.: JAI Press.

—— 1987. "Health Economics and Econometrics." *American Economic Review* 77(2):269–274.

—— 1989. "Measuring Medical Prices and Understanding Their Effects." *Journal of Health Administration Education* 7:19–26.

—— 1991. "Controlled Experimentation as Research Policy." In *Health Services Research,* ed. Eli Ginzberg. Cambridge, Mass.: Harvard University Press.

—— 1992. "Medical Care Costs: How Much Welfare Loss?" *Journal of Economic Perspectives* 6(3):3–21.

Newhouse, Joseph P., and Rae W. Archibald. 1978. *Overview of Health Insurance Study Publications.* Santa Monica: RAND Corporation (Pub. no. P-6221).

Newhouse, Joseph P., Charles E. Phelps, and William B. Schwartz. 1974. "Policy Options and the Impact of National Health Insurance." *New England Journal of Medicine* 290:1345–59.

Newhouse, Joseph P., et al. 1979. "Design Improvements in the Second Generation of Social Experiments: The Health Insurance Study." *Journal of Econometrics* 11:117–129.

———— 1981. "Some Interim Results from a Controlled Trial of Cost Sharing in Health Insurance." *New England Journal of Medicine* 305:1501–07. The article, together with additional backup material, is available in a RAND monograph with the same authors and title, Santa Monica: RAND Corporation (Pub. no. R-2847-HHS), 1982.

———— 1982a. "Does the Geographical Distribution of Physicians Reflect Market Failure?" *Bell Journal of Economics* 13:493–505.

———— 1982b. "Where Have All the Doctors Gone?" *Journal of the American Medical Association* 247:2392–96.

———— 1987. "The Findings of the RAND Health Insurance Experiment—A Response to Welch et al." *Medical Care* 25:157–179.

Office of National Cost Estimates. 1990. "National Health Expenditures, 1988." *Health Care Financing Review* 11(4):1–41.

O'Grady, Kevin F., et al. 1985. "The Impact of Cost Sharing on Emergency Department Use." *New England Journal of Medicine* 313:484–490.

Ostrander, L. D., D. E. Lamphiear, and W. D. Block. 1976. "Diabetes among Men in a General Population: Prevalence and Associated Physiological Findings." *Archives of Internal Medicine* 136:415–420.

Patrick, Donald L., James W. Bush, and Martin M. Chen. 1973. "Toward an Operational Definition of Health." *Journal of Health and Social Behavior* 14:6–23.

Pauly, Mark V. 1968. "The Economics of Moral Hazard." *American Economic Review* 58:231–237.

Phelps, Charles E., and Joseph P. Newhouse. 1974. "Coinsurance, the Price of Time, and the Demand for Medical Services." *Review of Economics and Statistics* 56:334–342.

Polich, Suzanne M., et al. 1986. *Master Sample Series.* Vol. 2: *Codebook for Full Sample Demographic File.* Santa Monica: RAND Corporation (Pub. no. N-2264/2-HHS).

Raiffa, Howard. 1968. *Decision Analysis;* Reading Mass.: Addison-Wesley.

Ramsey, Frank. 1927. "A Contribution to the Theory of Taxation." *Economic Journal* 37:47–61.

Reed, Louis S. 1974. "Utilization of Care for Mental Disorders under the Blue Cross and Blue Shield Plan for Federal Employees, 1972." *American Journal of Psychiatry* 13:964–975.

Reed, Louis, Evelyn Myers, and P. Scheidemandel. 1972. *Health Insurance and Psychiatric Care: Utilization and Cost.* Washington, D.C.: The American Psychiatric Association.

Rice, Dorothy P., et al. 1990. *The Economic Costs of Alcohol and Drug Abuse and Mental Illness: 1985.* San Francisco: Institute for Health and Aging, University of California at San Francisco.

Riecken, Henry W., and Robert F. Baruch. 1974. *Social Experimentation: A Method for Planning and Evaluating Social Intervention*. New York: Academic Press.

Rivlin, Alice. 1974. "How Can Experiments Be More Useful?" *American Economic Review* 64:346–354.

Roemer, Milton I., and Max Shain. 1959. *Hospital Utilization under Insurance*. Chicago: American Hospital Association.

Roemer, Milton I., et al. 1975. "Copayments for Ambulatory Care: Penny-Wise and Pound-Foolish." *Medical Care* 13:457–466.

Rogers, David E., Robert J. Blendon, and Thomas Moloney. 1982. "Who Needs Medicaid?" *New England Journal of Medicine* 307:13–18.

Rogers, William H., and Joseph P. Newhouse. 1985. "Measuring Unfiled Claims in the Health Insurance Experiment." In *Collecting Evaluation Data: Problems and Solutions*, ed. Leigh Burstein, Howard E. Freeman, and Peter H. Rossi, pp. 121–133. Beverly Hills: Sage.

Rogers, William H., Kathleen N. Williams, and Robert H. Brook. 1979. *Conceptualization and Measurement of Health for Adults in the Health Insurance Study*. Vol. 7: *Power Analysis for Health Status Measures*. Santa Monica: RAND Corporation (Pub. no. R-1987/7-HEW).

Rogers, William H., et al. 1991. "Effects of Cost Sharing on Disability Days." *Health Policy* 18:131–139.

Roghmann, Klaus G. 1974. "Use of Medicaid Payment Files for Medical Care Research." *Medical Care* 12:131–137.

Rolph, John E., Jan Chaiken, and Robert Houchens. 1981. *Methods for Estimating Crime Rates of Individuals*. Santa Monica: RAND Corporation (Pub. no. R-2730-NIJ).

Rosenthal, Marc, et al. 1981. *Conceptualization and Measurement of Physiologic Health for Adults: Congestive Heart Failure*. Santa Monica: RAND Corporation (Pub. no. R-2262/5-HHS).

Rossiter, Louis, and Gail R. Wilensky. 1983. "A Re-examination of the Use of Physician Services: The Role of Physician-Initiated Demand." *Inquiry* 20:162–172.

Rubenstein, Randi S., et al. 1982. *Conceptualization and Measurement of Physiologic Health for Adults: Vision Impairments*. Santa Monica: RAND Corporation (Pub. no. R-2262/12-HHS).

——— 1983. *Conceptualization and Measurement of Physiologic Health for Adults: Surgical Conditions*. Santa Monica: RAND Corporation (Pub. no. R-2262/15-HHS).

——— 1985. *Measurement of Physiologic Health for Children: Vision Impairments*. Santa Monica: RAND Corporation (Pub. no. R-2898/4-HHS).

Russell, Louise B. *Is Prevention Better than Cure?* 1986. Washington, D.C.: Brookings Institution.

Schroeder, Steven A. 1992. "Physician Supply and the U.S. Medical Marketplace," *Health Affairs* 11(1):235–243.

Schwartz, A. H., et al. 1980. "Psychiatric Diagnoses as Reported to Medicaid and as Recorded in Patient Charts." *American Journal of Public Health* 70:406–408.

Scitovsky, Anne A., and Nelda M. Snyder. 1972. "Effect of Coinsurance on Use of Physician Services." *Social Security Bulletin* 35(6):3–19.

Scott, Bonnie, et al. 1980. *Conceptualization and Measurement of Physiologic Health for Adults: Anemia.* Santa Monica: RAND Corporation (Pub. no. R-2262/6-HEW).

———— 1981. *Conceptualization and Measurement of Physiologic Health for Adults: Joint Disorders.* Santa Monica: RAND Corporation (Pub. no. R-2262/10-HHS).

Searle, S. R. 1971. *Linear Models.* New York: John Wiley & Sons.

Shannon, K. 1985. "Outpatient Surgery Up 77 Percent," *Hospitals* 59:54.

Shapiro, Martin F., John E. Ware, Jr., and Cathy D. Sherbourne. 1986. "Effects of Cost Sharing on Seeking Care for Serious and Minor Symptoms: Results of a Randomized Controlled Trial." *Annals of Internal Medicine* 104:246–251.

Sharfstein, S. S., O. B. Towery, and I. D. Milowe. 1980. "Accuracy of Diagnostic Information Submitted to an Insurance Company." *American Journal of Psychiatry* 137: 70–73.

Siu, Albert L., Willard G. Manning, and Bernadette Benjamin. 1990. "Patient, Provider, and Hospital Characteristics Associated with Inappropriate Hospitalization." *American Journal of Public Health* 80:1353–56. Longer version available from Santa Monica: RAND Corporation (Pub. no. R-3741-NCHSR).

Siu, Albert L., et al. 1986. "Inappropriate Use of Hospitals in a Randomized Trial of Health Insurance Plans." *New England Journal of Medicine* 315:1259–66.

———— 1988. "Use of the Hospital in a Randomized Trial of Prepaid Care." *Journal of the American Medical Association* 259:1343–46.

Sloss, Elizabeth M., et al. 1987. "Effect of a Health Maintenance Organization on Physiologic Health: Results from a Randomized Trial." *Annals of Internal Medicine* 106:130–138.

Smith, Lisa H., et al. 1978. *The Health Insurance Study Screening Examination Procedures Manual.* Santa Monica: RAND Corporation (Pub. no. R-2101-HEW).

Somers, Herman M., and Anne R. Somers. 1961. *Doctors, Patients, and Health Insurance.* Washington, D.C.: Brookings Institution.

Spolsky, Vladimir, et al. 1983. *Measurement of Dental Health Status.* Santa Monica: RAND Corporation (Pub. no. R-2902-HHS).

Stano, Miron. 1985. "An Analysis of the Evidence on Competition in the Physician Services Markets." *Journal of Health Economics* 4:197–211.

Starr, Paul. 1982. *The Social Transformation of American Medicine.* New York: Basic Books.

Stewart, Anita L., Robert H. Brook, and Robert L. Kane. 1979. *Conceptualization and Measurement of Health Habits for Adults in the Health Insurance Study: Smoking.* Santa Monica: RAND Corporation (Pub. no. R-2374/1-HEW).

———— 1980. *Conceptualization and Measurement of Health Habits for Adults in the Health Insurance Study: Overweight.* Santa Monica: RAND Corporation

(Pub. no. R-2374/2-HEW). Abridged version published as "Effects of Being Overweight," *American Journal of Public Health* 7(1982):250–261.

Stewart, Anita, John E. Ware, Jr., and Robert H. Brook. 1977. "The Meaning of Health: Understanding Functional Limitations." *Medical Care* 15:939–952.

—— 1981. "Advances in the Measurement of Functional Status: Construction of Aggregate Indexes." *Medical Care* 19:473–488.

—— 1982a. *Construction and Scoring of Aggregate Functional Status Indexes.* Vol. I. Santa Monica: RAND Corporation (Pub. no. R-2551-1-HHS).

—— 1982b. *Construction and Scoring of Aggregate Functional Status Indexes.* Vol. II: *Appendixes.* Santa Monica: RAND Corporation (Pub. no. N-1706-1-HHS).

Stewart, Anita L., et al. 1978. *Conceptualization and Measurement of Health for Adults in the Health Insurance Study: Physical Health in Terms of Functioning.* Santa Monica: RAND Corporation (Pub. no. R-1987/2-HEW).

Stuart, Charles. 1984. "Welfare Costs per Dollar of Additional Tax Revenue in the United States." *American Economic Review* 74:352–362.

Taube, Carl A. 1990. "Funding and Expenditures for Mental Illness." In *Mental Health, United States, 1990,* ed. R. W. Manderscheid and M. A. Sonnenschein. Washington, D.C.: U.S. Government Printing Office (Pub. no. ADM 90-1708).

Tenney, J. B. 1968. "Diagnostic Precision for Insurance Records: A Physicians' Survey." *Inquiry* 4:14–19.

Tobin, James. 1958. "Estimation of Relationships for Limited Dependent Variables." *Econometrica* 26:24–36.

Trevino, Fernando M., et al. 1991. "Health Insurance Coverage and Utilization of Health Services by Mexican Americans, Puerto Ricans, and Cuban Americans." *Journal of the American Medical Association* 265:233–237.

U.S. Bureau of the Census. 1988. *Statistical Abstract, 1988.* Washington, D.C.: U.S. Government Printing Office.

—— 1991. *Statistical Abstract, 1991.* Washington, D.C.: U.S. Government Printing Office.

U.S. Public Health Service. 1972. *National Drug Code Directory.* Washington, D.C.: U.S. Government Printing Office.

Valdez, R. Burciaga. 1986. *The Effects of Cost Sharing on the Health of Children.* Santa Monica: RAND Corporation (Pub. no. R-3270-HHS).

—— 1989. *The Effect of a Prepaid Group Practice on Children's Medical Care Use and Health Outcomes Compared to Fee-for-Service Care.* Santa Monica: RAND Corporation (Pub. no. N-2618-HHS).

Valdez, R. Burciaga, et al. 1989. "Prepaid Group Practice Effects on the Utilization of Medical Services and Health Outcomes for Children: Results from a Controlled Trial." *Pediatrics* 83:168–180.

van de Ven, Wynand P. M. M., and Bernard M. S. van Praag. 1981. "Risk Aversion and Deductibles in Private Health Insurance: Application of an Adjusted Tobit Model to Family Health Care Expenditures." In *Health, Economics, and Health Economics,* ed. Jacques van der Gaag and Mark Perlman. Amsterdam: North Holland.

Veit, Clarice T., and John E. Ware, Jr. 1983. "The Structure of Psychological Distress and Well-Being in General Populations." *Journal of Consulting and Clinical Psychology* 51:730–742.

Veney, James E. 1974. "The Rand Health Insurance Study." *Inquiry* 11:3–4.

Wagner, Edward H., and Turner Bledsoe. 1990. "The RAND Health Insurance Experiment and HMOs." *Medical Care* 28:191–200.

Wagner, Judith L., Roger C. Hardman, and David W. Alberts. 1989. "Well Child Care: How Much Is Enough?" *Health Affairs* 8:147–157.

Waldo, Daniel R., Katherine R. Levit, and Helen Lazenby. 1986. "National Health Expenditures, 1985." *Health Care Financing Review* 8(1):1–45.

Waldo, Daniel R., et al. 1989. "Health Expenditures by Age Group, 1977 and 1987." *Health Care Financing Review* 10(4):111–120.

Ware, John E., Jr. 1976. "Scales for Measuring General Health Perceptions." *Health Services Research* 11:396–415.

—— 1984. "The General Health Rating Index." In *Assessment of Quality of Life in Clinical Trials of Cardiovascular Disease*, ed. N. K. Wenger, M. E. Mattson, C. D. Furberg, and Jack Elinson. New York: Le Jacq.

Ware, John E., Jr., and A. H. Karmos. 1976. *Development and Validation of Scales to Measure Perceived Health and Patient Role Propensity*. Vol. 2. Springfield, Va.: National Technical Information Service (NTIS Pub. no. PB 288-331).

Ware, John E., Jr., Allyson Davies-Avery, and Robert H. Brook. 1980. *Conceptualization and Measurement of Health for Adults in the Health Insurance Study*. Vol. 6: *Analysis of Relationships among Health Status Measures*. Santa Monica: RAND Corporation (Pub. no. R-1987/6-HEW).

Ware, John E., Jr., Allyson Davies-Avery, and Cathy A. Donald. 1978. *Conceptualization and Measurement of Health for Adults in the Health Insurance Study: General Health Perceptions*. Santa Monica: RAND Corporation (Pub. no. R-1987/5-HEW).

Ware, John E., Jr., Allyson Davies-Avery, and Anita L. Stewart. 1978. "The Measurement and Meaning of Patient Satisfaction." *Health and Medical Care Services Review* 1:1–15.

Ware, John E., Jr., Shawn A. Johnston, and Allyson Davies-Avery. 1979. *Conceptualization and Measurement of Health for Adults in the Health Insurance Study: Mental Health*. Santa Monica: RAND Corporation (Pub. no. R-1987/3-HEW).

Ware, John E., Jr., M. K. Snyder, and W. R. Wright. 1976. *Development and Validation of Scales to Measure Patient Satisfaction with Health Care Services*. Vol. 1, Part A: *Review of the Literature, Overview of Methods, and Results Regarding Construction of Scales;* Part B: *Results Regarding Scales Constructed from the Patient Satisfaction Questionnaire and Measures of Other Health Care Perceptions*. Springfield, Va: National Technical Information Service (Pub. no. PB 288-329).

Ware, John E., Jr., et al. 1983. "Defining and Measuring Patient Satisfaction with Medical Care." *Evaluation and Program Planning* 6:247–263.

—— 1984. "Health Status and the Use of Outpatient Mental Health Services." *American Psychologist* 39:1090–1100.

——— 1986. "Comparison of Health Outcomes at a Health Maintenance Organisation with Those of Fee-for-Service Care." *Lancet* 1:1017–22.

——— 1987. *Health Outcomes for Adults in Prepaid and Fee-for-Service Systems of Care.* Santa Monica: RAND Corporation (Pub. no. R-3459-HHS).

Weinstein, Milton C., and William B. Stason. 1976. *Hypertension: A Policy Perspective.* Cambridge, Mass.: Harvard University Press.

Wells, Kenneth B., Emmett B. Keeler, and Willard G. Manning. 1990. "Patterns of Outpatient Mental Health Care over Time: Some Implications for Estimates of Demand and for Benefit Design." *Health Services Research* 24:773–789.

Wells, Kenneth B., Willard G. Manning, and R. Burciaga Valdez. 1989a. *The Effects of a Prepaid Group Practice on Mental Health Outcomes of a General Population: Results from a Randomized Trial.* Santa Monica: RAND Corporation (Pub. no. R-3834-NIMH/HCFA). Abridged in *Health Services Research* 25(1990):615–625.

——— 1989b. *The Effects of Insurance Generosity on the Psychological Distress and Well-Being of a General Population: Results from a Randomized Trial of Insurance.* Santa Monica: RAND Corporation (Pub. no. R-3682-NIMH/HCFA). Abridged as "The Effect of Insurance Generosity on the Psychological Distress and Psychological Well-Being of a General Population," *Archives of General Psychiatry* 46:315–320.

Wells, Kenneth B., et al. 1982. *Cost Sharing and the Demand for Ambulatory Mental Health Services.* Santa Monica: RAND Corporation (Pub. no. R-2960-HHS).

Williams, Ann W., John E. Ware, Jr., and Cathy A. Donald. 1981. "A Model of Mental Health, Life Events, and Social Supports Applicable to General Populations." *Journal of Health and Social Behavior* 22:324–336.

Wooldridge, Judith. 1976. "Report on the Physician Capacity Utilization Telephone Surveys." Princeton: Mathematica Policy Research.

World Health Organization. 1948. "Constitution of the World Health Organization." In *Basic Documents.* Geneva.

The Wyatt Company. 1986. *1986 Group Benefits Survey.* Washington, D.C.

Zeckhauser, Richard J. 1970. "Medical Insurance: A Case Study of the Tradeoff between Risk Spreading and Appropriate Incentives." *Journal of Economic Theory* 2(1):10–26.

Zielske, John V., et al. 1981. *Conceptualization and Measurement of Physiologic Health for Adults: Urinary Tract Infection.* Santa Monica: RAND Corporation (Pub. no. R-2262/16-HHS).

——— 1982. *Conceptualization and Measurement of Physiologic Health for Adults: Stomach Pain and Peptic Ulcer Disease.* Santa Monica: RAND Corporation (Pub. no. R-2262/17-HHS).

Zung, W. K. 1965. "A Self-Rating Depression Scale." *Archives of General Psychiatry* 12:63–70.

Index

RAND books are available on a wide variety of topics.
To obtain information on other publications, write or call
Distribution Services, RAND,
1700 Main Street, P.O. Box 2138,
Santa Monica, California 90407-2138
(310) 393-0411